DATE DUE

			PRINTED IN U.S.A.

Children's
Literature
Review

Guide to Gale Literary Criticism Series

For criticism on	Consult these Gale series
Authors now living or who died after December 31, 1959	*CONTEMPORARY LITERARY CRITICISM (CLC)*
Authors who died between 1900 and 1959	*TWENTIETH-CENTURY LITERARY CRITICISM (TCLC)*
Authors who died between 1800 and 1899	*NINETEENTH-CENTURY LITERATURE CRITICISM (NCLC)*
Authors who died between 1400 and 1799	*LITERATURE CRITICISM FROM 1400 TO 1800 (LC)* *SHAKESPEAREAN CRITICISM (SC)*
Authors who died before 1400	*CLASSICAL AND MEDIEVAL LITERATURE CRITICISM (CMLC)*
Black writers of the past two hundred years	*BLACK LITERATURE CRITICISM (BLC)*
Authors of books for children and young adults	*CHILDREN'S LITERATURE REVIEW (CLR)*
Dramatists	*DRAMA CRITICISM (DC)*
Hispanic writers of the late nineteenth and twentieth centuries	*HISPANIC LITERATURE CRITICISM (HLC)*
Poets	*POETRY CRITICISM (PC)*
Short story writers	*SHORT STORY CRITICISM (SSC)*
Major authors from the Renaissance to the present	*WORLD LITERATURE CRITICISM, 1500 TO THE PRESENT (WLC)*

ISSN 0362-4145

R

volume 33

Children's Literature Review

Excerpts from Reviews,
Criticism, and Commentary
on Books for Children
and Young People

Gerard J. Senick
Editor

Sharon R. Gunton
Alan Hedblad
Associate Editors

 Gale Research Inc. • *DETROIT* • *WASHINGTON, D.C.* • *LONDON*

STAFF

Gerard J. Senick, *Editor*

Sharon R. Gunton, Alan Hedblad, *Associate Editors*

Deron Albright, Zoran Minderović, Anna J. Sheets, *Assistant Editors*

Jeanne A. Gough, *Permissions & Production Manager*
Linda M. Pugliese, *Production Supervisor*
Donna Craft, Paul Lewon, Maureen Puhl, Camille P. Robinson, Sheila Walencewicz, *Editorial Associates*

Sandra C. Davis, *Permissions Supervisor (Text)*
Maria L. Franklin, Josephine M. Keene, Michele M. Lonoconus, Shalice Shah, Kimberly F. Smilay,
Permissions Associates
Jennifer A. Arnold, Brandy C. Merritt, *Permissions Assistants*

Margaret A. Chamberlain, *Permissions Supervisor (Pictures)*
Pamela A. Hayes, Arlene Johnson, Keith Reed, Barbara A. Wallace, *Permissions Associates*
Susan Brohman, *Permissions Assistant*

Victoria B. Cariappa, *Research Manager*
Maureen Richards, *Research Supervisor*
Mary Beth McElmeel, Donna Melnychenko, Tamara C. Nott, Jaema Paradowski, *Editorial Associates*
Maria Bryson, Julie A. Kriebel, Stefanie Scarlett, *Editorial Assistants*

Mary Beth Trimper, *Production Director*
Catherine Kemp, *Production Assistant*

Cynthia Baldwin, *Art Director*
Barbara J. Yarrow, *Graphic Services Supervisor*
C. J. Jonik, *Desktop Publisher*
Willie Mathis, *Camera Operator*

Library of Congress Catalog Card Number 86-645085
ISBN 0-8103-8472-8
ISSN 0362-4145

Printed in the United States of America
Published simultaneously in the United Kingdom
by Gale Research International Limited
(An affiliated company of Gale Research Inc.)
10 9 8 7 6 5 4 3 2 1

The trademark **ITP** is used under license.

Contents

Preface   vii

Acknowledgments   xi

Preface

Literature for children and young adults has evolved into both a respected branch of creative writing and a successful industry. Currently, books for young readers are considered the most popular segment of publishing, while criticism of juvenile literature is instrumental in recording the literary or artistic development of the creators of children's books as well as the trends and controversies that result from changing values or attitudes about young people and their literature. Designed to provide a permanent, accessible record of this ongoing scholarship, *Children's Literature Review (CLR)* presents parents, teachers, and librarians—those responsible for bringing together children and books—with the opportunity to make informed choices when selecting reading materials for the young. In addition, *CLR* provides researchers of children's literature with easy access to a wide variety of critical information from English-language sources in the field. Users will find balanced overviews of the careers of the authors and illustrators of the books that children and young adults are reading; these entries, which contain excerpts from published criticism in books and periodicals, assist users by sparking ideas for papers and assignments and suggesting supplementary and classroom reading. Ann L. Kalkhoff, president and editor of *Children's Book Review Service Inc.,* writes that "*CLR* has filled a gap in the field of children's books, and it is one series that will never lose its validity or importance."

Scope of the Series

Each volume of *CLR* profiles the careers of a selection of authors and illustrators of books for children and young adults from preschool through high school. Author lists in each volume reflect these elements:

- an international scope.

- representation of authors of all eras.

- the variety of genres covered by children's and/or YA literature: picture books, fiction, nonfiction, poetry, folklore, and drama.

Although earlier volumes of *CLR* emphasized critical material published after 1960, successive volumes have expanded their coverage to encompass important criticism written before 1960. Since many of the authors included in *CLR* are living and continue to write, their entries are updated periodically. Future volumes will supplement the entries of selected authors covered in earlier volumes and will include criticism on the works of authors new to the series.

Organization of This Book

An author section consists of the following elements: author heading, author portrait, author introduction, excerpts of criticism (each followed by a bibliographical citation), and illustrations, when available.

- The **Author Heading** consists of the author's name followed by birth and death dates. The portion of the name outside the parentheses denotes the form under which the author is most frequently published. If the majority of the author's works for children were written under a pseudonym, the pseudonym will be listed in the author heading and the real name given on the first line of the author introduction. Also located at the beginning of the introduction are any other pseudonyms used by the author in writing for children and any name variations, including transliterated forms for authors whose languages use nonroman alphabets. Uncertainty as to a birth or death date is indicated by question marks.

- An **Author Portrait** is included when available.

- The **Author Introduction** contains information designed to introduce an author to *CLR* users by presenting an overview of the author's themes and styles, biographical facts that relate to the author's literary career or critical responses to the author's works, and information about major awards and prizes the author has received. The introduction begins by identifying the nationality of the author and by listing the genres in which s/he has written for children and young adults. Introductions also list a group of representative titles for which the author or illustrator being profiled is best known; this section, which begins with the words "major works include," follows the genre line of the introduction. For seminal figures, a section that begins with the words "major works about the author include" follows when appropriate; this section lists important biographies about the author or illustrator that are not excerpted in the entry. The centered heading "Introduction" follows the major works section and announces the body of the text. Where applicable, introductions conclude with references to additional entries in biographical and critical reference series published by Gale Research Inc. These sources include past volumes of *CLR* as well as *Authors & Artists for Young Adults, Classical and Medieval Literature Criticism, Contemporary Authors, Contemporary Authors Autobiography Series, Contemporary Authors Bibliographical Series, Contemporary Literary Criticism, Dictionary of Literary Biography, Drama Criticism, Nineteenth-Century Literature Criticism, Poetry Criticism, Short Story Criticism, Something about the Author, Something about the Author Autobiography Series, Twentieth-Century Literary Criticism,* and *Yesterday's Authors of Books for Children.*

- **Criticism** is located in three sections: **Author's Commentary** (when available), **General Commentary** (when available), and **Title Commentary** (in which commentary on specific titles appears). Centered headings introduce each section, in which criticism is arranged chronologically. Titles by authors being profiled are highlighted in boldface type within the text for easier access by readers.

- The **Author's Commentary** presents background material written by the author or by an interviewer. This commentary may cover a specific work or several works. Author's commentary on more than one work appears after the author introduction, while commentary on an individual book follows the title entry heading.

- The **General Commentary** consists of critical excerpts that consider more than one work by the author or illustrator being profiled. General commentary is preceded by the critic's name in boldface type or, in the case of unsigned criticism, by the title of the journal. *CLR* also features entries that emphasize general criticism on the oeuvre of an author or illustrator. When appropriate, a selection of reviews is included to supplement the general commentary.

- The **Title Commentary** begins with the title entry headings, which precede the criticism on a title and cite publication information on the work being reviewed. Title headings list the title of the work as it appeared in its first English-language edition. The first English-language publication date of each work is listed in parentheses following the title. Differing U. S. and British titles follow the publication date within the parentheses.

Entries in each title commentary section consist of critical excerpts on the author's individual works, arranged chronologically by publication date. The entries generally contain two to seven reviews per title, depending on the stature of the book and the amount of criticism it has generated. The editors select titles that reflect the entire scope of the author's literary contribution, covering each genre and subject. An effort is made to reprint criticism that represents the full range of each title's reception, from the year of its initial publication to current assessments. Thus, the reader is provided with a record of the author's critical history. Publication information (such as publisher names and book prices) and parenthetical numerical references (such as footnotes or page and line references to specific editions of works) have been deleted at the editor's discretion to provide smoother reading of the text.

■ Selected excerpts are preceded by **Explanatory Notes,** which provide information on the critic or work of criticism to enhance the reader's understanding of the excerpt.

■ A complete **Bibliographical Citation** designed to facilitate the location of the original book or article follows each piece of criticism.

■ Numerous **Illustrations** are featured in *CLR*. For entries on illustrators, an effort has been made to include illustrations that reflect the characteristics discussed in the criticism. Entries on authors who do not illustrate their own works may also include photographs and other illustrative material pertinent to their careers.

Special Features

Entries on authors who are also illustrators will occasionally feature commentary on selected works illustrated but not written by the author being profiled. These works are strongly associated with the illustrator and have received critical acclaim for their art. By including critical comment on works of this type, the editors wish to provide a more complete representation of the author's total career. Criticism on these works has been chosen to stress artistic, rather than literary, contributions. Title entry headings for works illustrated by the author being profiled are arranged chronologically within the entry by date of publication and include notes identifying the author of the illustrated work. In order to provide easier access for users, all titles illustrated by the subject of the entry are boldfaced.

CLR also includes entries on prominent illustrators who have contributed to the field of children's literature. These entries are designed to represent the development of the illustrator as an artist rather than as a literary stylist. The illustrator's section is organized like that of an author, with two exceptions: the introduction presents an overview of the illustrator's styles and techniques rather than outlining his or her literary background, and the commentary written by the illustrator on his or her works is called "illustrator's commentary" rather than "author's commentary." Title entry headings are followed by explanatory notes identifying the author of the illustrated work. All titles of books containing illustrations by the artist being profiled as well as individual illustrations from these books are highlighted in boldface type.

Other Features

■ The **Acknowledgments,** which immediately follow the preface, list the sources from which material has been reprinted in the volume. It does not, however, list every book or periodical consulted for the volume.

■ The **Cumulative Index to Authors** lists all of the authors who have appeared in *CLR* with cross-references to the various literary criticism series and the biographical and autobiographical series published by Gale Research Inc. A full listing of the series titles appears before the first page of the indexes of this volume.

■ The **Cumulative Nationality Index** lists authors alphabetically under their respective nationalities. Author names are followed by the volume number(s) in which they appear. Authors who have changed citizenship or whose current citizenship is not reflected in biographical sources appear under both their original nationality and that of their current residence.

- The **Cumulative Title Index** lists titles covered in *CLR* followed by the volume and page number where criticism begins.

A Note to the Reader

CLR is one of several critical references sources in the Literature Criticism Series published by Gale Research Inc. When writing papers, students who quote directly from any volume in the Literature Criticism Series may use the following general forms to footnote reprinted criticism. The first example pertains to material drawn from periodicals, the second to material reprinted from books.

[1]T. S. Eliot, "John Donne," *The Nation and the Athenaeum,* 33 (9 June 1923), 321-32; excerpted and reprinted in *Literature Criticism from 1400 to 1800,* Vol. 10, ed. James E. Person, Jr. (Detroit: Gale Research, 1989), pp. 28-9.

[1]Henry Brooke, *Leslie Brooke and Johnny Crow* (Frederick Warne, 1982); excerpted and reprinted in *Children's Literature Review,* Vol. 20, ed. Gerard J. Senick (Detroit: Galc Research, 1990), p. 47.

Suggestions Are Welcome

In response to various suggestions, several features have been added to *CLR* since the beginning of the series, including author entries on retellers of traditional literature as well as those who have been the first to record oral tales and other folklore; entries on prominent illustrators featuring commentary on their styles and techniques; entries on authors whose works are considered controversial; occasional entries devoted to criticism on a single work or a series of works; sections in author introductions that list major works by the author or illustrator being profiled; explanatory notes that provide information on the critic or work of criticism to enhance the usefulness of the excerpt; more extensive illustrative material, such as holographs of manuscript pages and photographs of people and places pertinent to the authors' careers; a cumulative nationality index for easy access to authors by nationality; and occasional guest essays written specifically for *CLR* by prominent critics on subjects of their choice.

Readers who wish to suggest authors to appear in future volumes, or who have other suggestions, are cordially invited to write the editor.

Acknowledgments

The editors wish to thank the copyright holders of the excerpted criticism included in this volume, the permissions managers of many book and magazine publishing companies for assisting us in securing reprint rights, and Anthony Bogucki for assistance with copyright research. We are also grateful to the staffs of the Detroit Public Library, the Library of Congress, the University of Detroit Mercy Library, Wayne State University Purdy/Kresge Library Complex, and the University of Michigan Libraries for making their resources available to us. Following is a list of the copyright holders who have granted us permission to reprint material in this volume of *CLR*. Every effort has been made to trace copyright, but if omissions have been made, please let us know.

COPYRIGHTED EXCERPTS IN *CLR,* VOLUME 33, WERE REPRINTED FROM THE FOLLOWING PERIODICALS:

The ALAN Review, v. 13, Spring, 1986. Reprinted by permission of the publisher.—*Appraisal: Children's Science Books,* v. 6, Spring, 1973; v. 7, Fall, 1974; v. 8, Fall, 1975; v. 13, Spring, 1980; v. 19, Fall, 1986; v. 20, Summer, 1987; v. 21, Winter, 1988; v. 23, Spring, 1990; v. 23, Summer, 1990; v. 24, Winter, 1991. Copyright © 1973, 1974, 1975, 1980, 1986, 1987, 1988, 1990, 1991 by the Children's Science Book Review Committee. All reprinted by permission of the publisher.—*The Atlantic Monthly,* v. 196, December, 1955. Copyright 1955, renewed 1983 by The Atlantic Monthly Company, Boston, MA.—*Best Sellers,* v. 40, September, 1980; v. 43, October, 1983; v. 46, April, 1986. Copyright © 1980, 1983, 1986 Helen Dwight Reid Educational Foundation. All reprinted by permission of the publisher.—*The Book Report,* v. 11, May-June, 1992. © copyright 1992 by Linworth Publishing, Inc., Worthington, Ohio. Reprinted with permission of the publisher.—*Book Week—New York Herald Tribune,* February 27, 1966. © 1966, New York Herald Tribune Inc. All rights reserved. Reprinted by permission of the publisher.—*Book World—The Washington Post,* November 7, 1971. © 1971 The Washington Post Writers Group. Reprinted with permission of the *Chicago Tribune* and *The Washington Post.*/ November 9, 1980; January 10, 1982. © 1980, 1982 The Washington Post Writers Group. Both reprinted with permission of the publisher.—*Booklist,* v. 73, March 15, 1977; v. 73, June 1, 1977; v. 74, December 15, 1977; v. 74, May 15, 1978; v. 75, December 1, 1978; v. 74, December 15, 1978; v. 75, January 1, 1979; v. 76, November 1, 1979; v. 76, May 15, 1980; v. 77, March 1, 1981; v. 77, July 15-August, 1981; v. 78, November 1, 1981; v. 78, March 15, 1982; v. 78, June 1, 1982; v. 78, August, 1982; v. 79, February 1, 1983; v. 79, March 1, 1983; v. 79, June 15, 1983; v. 80, January 15, 1984; v. 80, March 1, 1984; v. 80, April 15, 1984; v. 80, August, 1984; v. 81, November 15, 1984; v. 81, August, 1985; v. 83, January 1, 1987; v. 84, September 1, 1987; v. 84, January 15, 1988; v. 84, May 15, 1988; v. 85, January 15, 1989; v. 85, March 1, 1989; v. 85, June 1, 1989; v. 86, November 15, 1989; v. 86, January 15, 1990; v. 86, February 15, 1990; v. 87, September 1, 1990; v. 87, May 15, 1991; v. 87, June 1, 1991; v. 87, July, 1991; v. 88, December 15, 1991; v. 88, February 15, 1992; v. 88, April 15, 1992; v. 89, September 1, 1992. Copyright © 1977, 1978, 1979, 1980, 1981, 1982, 1983, 1984, 1985, 1987, 1988, 1989, 1990, 1991, 1992 by the American Library Association. All reprinted by permission of the publisher.—*The Booklist,* v. 71, June 1, 1975. Copyright © 1975 by the American Library Association. Reprinted by permission of the publisher.—*The Booklist and Subscription Books Bulletin,* v. 62, December 1, 1965. Copyright © 1965 by the American Library Association. Reprinted by permission of the publisher.—*Books for Keeps,* n. 63, July, 1990. © School Bookshop Association 1990. Reprinted by permission of the publisher.—*Bulletin of the Center for Children's Books,* v. XVIII, January, 1965; v. XVIII, May, 1965; v. 19, June, 1966; v. 20, September, 1966; v. 21, September, 1967; v. 21, February 6, 1968; v. 21, May, 1968; v. 22, January, 1969; v. 22, February, 1969; v. 23, July-August, 1970; v. 24, May, 1971; v. 25, October, 1971; v. 25, April, 1972; v. 27, October, 1973; v. 27, February, 1974; v. 27, July-August, 1974; v. 28, September, 1974; v. 28, November, 1974; v. 28, February, 1975; v. 28, May, 1975; v. 29, November, 1975; v. 30, December, 1976; v. 31, September, 1977; v. 31, September, 1977; v. 31, October, 1977; v. 31, December, 1977; v. 31, February, 1978; v. 32, February, 1979; v. 32, April, 1979; v. 33, January, 1980; v. 34, September, 1980; v. 34, January, 1981; v. 34, February, 1981; v. 35, February, 1982; v. 36, January, 1983; v. 36, April, 1983; v. 38, December, 1984; v. 39, November, 1985;

COPYRIGHTED EXCERPTS IN *CLR,* VOLUME 33, WERE REPRINTED FROM THE FOLLOWING BOOKS:

PERMISSION TO REPRODUCE ILLUSTRATIONS APPEARING IN *CLR*, VOLUME 33, WAS RECEIVED FROM THE FOLLOWING SOURCES:

Children's
Literature
Review

Judie Angell

1937-

(Also writes as Maggie Twohill and Fran Arrick) American author of fiction.

Major works include *Steffie Can't Come Out to Play* (as Fran Arrick, 1978), *Tunnel Vision* (as Fran Arrick, 1980), *What's Best for You* (1981), *Where'd You Get the Gun, Billy?* (as Fran Arrick, 1991), *What You Don't Know Can Kill You* (as Fran Arrick, 1992).

INTRODUCTION

The author of realistic fiction for middle graders, junior high school students, and young adults, Angell is a prolific and popular writer whose books address the challenges, hardships, and triumphs associated with maturing from childhood to adolescence and from adolescence to adulthood. She is often praised as an author whose works reflect both her literary craftsmanship and her understanding of young people and their concerns. In addition, she is recognized for her facility with characterization and dialogue as well as for the variety of her works, which range from fast-paced stories to moving and compelling explorations of contemporary social issues. Though the majority of her works are written for younger teens, Angell also writes for middle graders as Maggie Twohill and for young adults as Fran Arrick. In her books as Arrick, Angell combines serious issues such as divorce and the loss of one's parents with the anxieties surrounding new experiences such as first jobs and first crushes with humorous circumstances to create touching, realistic, and amusing stories about important transitions. Regarded as both magical and highly entertaining, her books as Maggie Twohill are significantly lighter in content, centering on such topics as discovering a good luck charm and getting along with siblings. These works also contain valuable messages; in *Jeeter, Mason and the Magic Headset* (1985), for example, Jeeter receives warnings and predictions through her headphones from Mason, her Cabbage Patch doll, and must decide what to do when her older sister wants to use Mason's magic for personal gain. In contrast to her works for younger audiences, Angell's books as Fran Arrick are substantially darker in tone and often address such controversial and thought-provoking social issues as suicide, teenage violence, prostitution, and AIDS. Despite their differences in subject matter, character ages, and reading levels, however, critics have found Angell's works similar in several respects. For example, her books tend to focus on how certain problems affect young people rather than centering on the problem itself; in *Tunnel Vision*, a book about a fifteen-year-old boy who commits suicide, Anthony's death occurs prior to the beginning of the story so that Angell may better develop her characters and their methods for overcoming the situation. Regarding this technique, Laura Geringer has asserted that "it's refreshing to find a realistic problem novel that doesn't read like a psychological case study." Angell's books are con-

sidered especially appealing to younger audiences because of their noble depictions of her protagonists, both boys and girls who are characteristically intelligent, self-reliant, and creative in their solutions to problems. Moreover, reviewers have noted that Angell's character development is not limited to young people; she often writes about the impact of a particular situation—such as divorce or antisemitism—on an entire family, peer group, or community at large, thus giving equal time to adults as well as children.

A former elementary school teacher, Angell draws the material for her fiction from her classroom experiences as well as from her own childhood memories. "I think growing up heads the list of The Hardest Things To Do In Life," Angell has asserted. "It's so hard that some of us never get there. But even if the world changes as rapidly as it does, the feelings that we have while we're coping with those changes don't. I take a lot of those feelings, hug them, wrap them carefully in some words, and present them in a book with an invisible card that says, maybe this'll help a little—make you laugh—make you feel you're not alone." Angell's first critically successful work published under her own name is *A Word from Our Spon-*

sor: *Or, My Friend Alfred* (1979), in which Alfred and two of his friends discover that a promotional cup being marketed by Alfred's father, an advertising executive, contains dangerous levels of lead. After conducting some experiments on the cup, the three boys reveal their findings to the public, thus halting further distribution of the item. Although some reviewers found the writing inconsistent and slow-paced, most critics lauded the novel, arguing that the work contains some genuinely funny moments while offering important messages about advertising, consumer protection, and individual responsibility. Another of Angell's most popular books, *What's Best for You*—a novel about a family undergoing the process of divorce—is acclaimed for its depth, credibility, and rich characterizations. Zena Sutherland attributes this success to Angell's ability to "[deal] perceptively with the intricate pain of separation and the subtle ways in which each member of the family group affects and is affected by the others."

In the late 1970s, Angell adopted the name of Fran Arrick and shortly thereafter assumed the pseudonym of Maggie Twohill. While Angell's books as Twohill are acknowledged for their humor, sensitivity, and positive messages, her books as Fran Arrick have proven extremely popular among young adults and critics alike. Regarded as her most important work, Angell's *What You Don't Know Can Kill You,* describes the impact on the family and community of eighteen-year-old Ellen, who contracts HIV from her boyfriend. The story openly discusses AIDS, its causes, effects, and the prejudices generally associated with the disease as well as the importance of friendship and familial support. While some reviewers found the book somewhat preachy, others have asserted that the novel contains some valuable messages, the most important of which is the fact that AIDS can happen to anyone. Other popular titles by Angell as Arrick include *Steffie Can't Come Out to Play,* in which fourteen-year-old Steffie runs away from home to become a model but becomes a prostitute instead, and *Where'd You Get the Gun, Billy?* where two of his classmates try to find out where Billy obtained the gun he used to murder his girlfriend. In addition to her contemporary realistic fiction, Angell has written such works as *One-Way to Ansonia* (1985), the reminiscences of a determined and independent Russian immigrant girl in turn-of-the-century New York that is based on the experiences of Angell's grandmother, and *Suds: A New Daytime Drama* (1983), a slapstick parody of soap operas. Angell has won several child-selected awards for her books.

(See also *Contemporary Literary Criticism,* Vol. 30, *Something about the Author,* Vol. 22, *Something about the Author Autobiography Series,* Vol. 22, *Contemporary Authors,* Vols. 77-80, and *Authors and Artists for Young Adults,* Vol. 11)

TITLE COMMENTARY

In Summertime It's Tuffy (1977)

Tuffy (Elizabeth is her rest-of-the-year name) proves her mettle and adolesces one summer at camp Ma-Sha-Na when her righteous indignation and a homemade voodoo doll teach the head counselor, Uncle Otto, a lesson or two in compassion and fairness. Unlike Terris' *Whirling Rainbows* (Doubleday, 1974) which is also a camp story, nothing much really happens here. This is just a light read for the pre-teeners who go to all the Ma-Sha-Nas and will see their own summers in the descriptions of bunkmates (one is fat, one compulsively neat, one boy-crazy, one arty, etc.), counselors, campfires, activities (to show off on visiting day), letters to and from home, etc. All the characters are too likable to be real, (except for exaggeratedly militaristic Uncle Otto) and this is obviously a nostalgic trip back for the author to the Ma-Sha-Na of her own youth. A dearth of camp novels will make this popular, but it really doesn't deserve it.

> *Marjorie Lewis, in a review of "In Summertime It's Tuffy," in* School Library Journal, *Vol. 23, No. 9, May, 1977, p. 58.*

[Effervescent] Tuffy loses no time in psyching out her cabin partners (from boy-crazy Natalie to quiet, sensitive Iris) and learning the lay of camp-land, all of which Angell relates through peppery, up-beat dialogue. Obviously familiar with camp life, the author spews out humorous episodes surrounding swimming tests, evening activities, clean-up medals, Parents' Weekend, and the camp musical, where Tuffy forces talented Iris out of her shell. Even their muddling in voodoo magic, to get even with the camp director, is handled with a light touch. Although a meandering, overly crowded plot line dulls the total effect, the author carries off humor well.

> *Barbara Elleman, in a review of "In Summertime It's Tuffy," in* Booklist, *Vol. 73, No. 19, June 1, 1977, p. 1492.*

There's an effervescent air to eleven-year-old Betsy's account of summer camp, where she prefers being called Tuffy. This isn't a story with much depth or substance, but it's believable and amusing as Tuffy describes the girls in her cabin, the usual pranks of the subteen culture, and the group's adjustment to the inevitable after they are angered by the dismissal of a favorite counselor.

> *Zena Sutherland, in a review of "In Summertime It's Tuffy," in* Bulletin of the Center for Children's Books, *Vol. 31, No. 2, October, 1977, p. 25.*

Ronnie and Rosey (1977)

Actually the twosome of the title starts out as a threesome: there's Rosey (short for Robert Rose), a good-natured klutz who's a whiz at the keyboards; Ronnie ("short for nothing") Rachman, new in Uniondale, Long Island, and jittery over her first week at Ben Franklin Junior High; and Rosey's oldest friend, Evelyn Racanelli, a chubby mother hen type who immediately takes Ronnie under her ample wing. At first you expect a classic triangle to develop with Evelyn odd man out as Rosey and Ronnie start to make "I like you as more than a friend" noises. But no. Wisecracking Evelyn adjusts with good enough grace and so for half the book you're wondering what exactly is the purpose of this rather coy romance. Then suddenly from out of left field—or left lane—a car comes plowing into Ronnie's father, killing him instantly. In short order Ronnie's dithery artist mother turns into a walking zombie who refuses to adjust and who does her level best to see that Ronnie doesn't either—until finally a sympathetic gym teacher makes Mrs. Rachman see that both she *and* Ronnie need to be independent. Inoffensive, inconsequential, and basically the kind of book another more famous Judy does better. (pp. 1096-97)

> *A review of "Ronnie and Rosey," in* Kirkus Reviews, *Vol. XLV, No. 20, October 15, 1977, pp. 1096-97.*

A fresh, tart first-person novel about 13-year-old Ronnie Rachman's first year in Uniondale, New York. There are good times with new friends, including a hilarious evening when the kids thwart the efforts of a more sophisticated older teenager to get Ronnie to himself. The story turns suddenly sober when Ronnie's father is killed in a car accident and her mother withdraws in grief, but Ronnie's growing affection for Robert Rose (the Rosey of the title) sustains her then, too. Wholesome contemporary fare, peopled with pleasant characters. (pp. 52-3)

> *Peggy Sullivan, in a review of "Ronnie & Rosey," in* School Library Journal, *Vol. 24, No. 4, December, 1977, pp. 52-3.*

The interest, even novelty, of [this] book derives from watching the friendship between Ronnie and Rosey develop. Although not physically intimate they share interests, humor, and fun and are able to realize that their individual weaknesses are only the obverse of their strengths—a particularly reassuring basis for love.

> *Charlotte W. Draper, in a review of "Ronnie and Rosey," in* The Horn Book Magazine, *Vol. LIV, No. 2, April, 1978, p. 161.*

Tina Gogo (1978)

Tina Gogo—actually Bettina Gogolavsky—first shows up in Sarajane's boring-summer life as the edgy and defensive babysitter for two neighbors, who keeps her distance ("I don't want anybody to get to know me better") but stays around long enough for both of them to grow wiser. It's a familiar ploy, schematically developed and tactfully handled, as Tina learns to trust again (after a painful succession of foster homes) and Sarajane finds a friend, briefly visits the big city, and sees her own stable family in a new light. Unifying the story is both girls' work in SJ's family's busy restaurant—Sarajane reluctantly, Tina willingly, and SJ's little sister quite skillfully—and the gradual recognition and resolution of Tina's predicament when her mother wants her back. Smooth and involving, but a bit deliberate.

> *A review of "Tina Gogo," in* Kirkus Reviews, *Vol. XLVI, No. 6, March 15, 1978, p. 310.*

When 11-year-old Bettina Gogolavsky (nicknamed Tina Gogo) descends upon peaceful Lake Meridian, Sarajane first tries to avoid her, then reluctantly succumbs to her friendly (if obstreperous) overtures and braces for a turbu-

lent summer. Raised by loving, hardworking parents who run their own restaurant, Sarajane finds dealing with the contradictions and deceptions that surround her strange new friend baffling. Tina is staying in a rented cottage with the kindly Harris couple while her mother, she claims, is traveling around the world writing her long letters on air-mail stationery. And then there are the sounds Sarajane hears when she spends the night at Tina's—two different voices both coming from Tina's mouth. In a well-paced plot that is never melodramatic, Angell gingerly peels away the layers of hurt and mistrust beneath which Tina, a foster child, has buried herself revealing a miraculously resilient and sturdy core. Bolstered by the Harris' patience and Sarajane's friendship, Tina opts to live with her natural mother when the opportunity arises—although conditions will be less than ideal. Relationships between the characters are skillfully drawn and this is, altogether, nicely done.

> *C. Nordhielm Wooldridge, in a review of "Tina Gogo," in* School Library Journal, *Vol. 24, No. 9, May, 1978, p. 73.*

Despite a few stray ends, Angell's story is well conceived. It's principally a character study, but the pace never flags as the episodic development proceeds. Supporting characters are refreshingly unstereotyped; Sarajane's busy restaurant-owning parents are warm and caring, Tina's social worker is neither saint nor villain, nor is her indigent mother the low-lifer one might expect. And in the end readers will thoughtfully contemplate the painful conflict in the Harrises' and Mrs. Gogolavsky's yearning for the same child. Most important though is Tina's new-found internal stability, which is the final measure of her psyche's rehabilitation and the story's impact.

> *Denise M. Wilms, in a review of "Tina Gogo," in* Booklist, *Vol. 74, No. 18, May 15, 1978, p. 1489.*

Lurking in the minds of many children is the fantasy that they are foundlings and that somewhere out in the world is the true and perfect mother waiting for the return of her true and perfect child.

In the case of foster children, as 11-year-old Tina Gogo so vividly expresses it, the fantasy of a fairy godmother takes on a sad, surreal quality, because there is a *real* mother in the wings; whatever the mother's reason for giving up her child, the child's ideal of a loving mother is not easily abandoned.

Yet, it is only after Tina puts aside her make-believe world and assumes more than a child's share of responsibility for a sickly mother resigned to a life of struggle that she really achieves a sense of belonging. In fiction as in life, there are no magic endings and certainly no perfect mothers.

If Judie Angell had allowed spunky Tina the chance to tell her story in her naturally tough language, instead of giving the job to her dull friend Sarajane, the author might have created a bond of understanding between middle-class and poor kids. She gives the impression that all a mixed-up foster kid from the city needs in order to straighten out is to live for a couple weeks in the country—where she can rub elbows with children who, even as young as 9, do all sorts of honest work.

Readers are treated to the simple-minded notion that if children are kept busy doing meaningful labor alongside busy adults they will not get into trouble and can adjust to life's hard knocks. And never mind about child-labor laws.

Too bad the author chose this path, for Tina is a child readers can identify with, and most would opt any day for her chancy life over the predictable one of Sarajane.

*Bryna J. Fireside, in a review of "Tina Gogo,"
in* The New York Times Book Review, *July
23, 1978, p. 21.*

Steffie Can't Come Out to Play (as Fran Arrick, 1978)

Both parents work, so 14-year-old Stephanie Rudd cooks, cleans, and looks after her younger brother as well as her querulous, pregnant older sister until she finally runs away from Clairton, Pennsylvania to pursue a modelling career in New York City. She can hardly believe it when the man of her dreams appears at the train station and slips a protective arm around her shoulder. "Favor" is young, handsome, rich, and one of the slickest pimps in the Big Apple. He gradually slips Stephanie out onto the street where she justifies the horrors she sees and takes part in by reminding herself that it's all for Favor—the man she loves. While for the most part resisting the temptation to sensationalize, Arrick unfortunately resorts to a super-man-type rescue for her protagonist: one of two cops (whose third-person account of the street scene is interspersed with Stephanie's first-person narrative) suddenly shakes off 19 years of remaining uninvolved and breaks Favor's leg in the process of convincing him to let Stephanie go. It works. Stephanie finds herself inexplicably shut out by her "daddy" and "sisters," turns to a shelter which takes in young girls in her situation, and finally goes home. Neither plot, characterization, nor writing style emerge as distinctive in any way and the message to young teens weighs a bit heavy. All told, this is a just-adequate foray into some scantily explored and decidedly rough subject territory.

C. Nordhielm Wooldridge, in a review of "Steffie Can't Come Out to Play," in School Library Journal, *Vol. 25, No. 3, November, 1978, p. 72.*

Steffie Can't Come Out to Play, is . . . [a] book that makes evil sound like fun, not by explicit sexual detail, but by its omission.

The book's subject is that classic cliché of the country girl seduced into prostitution. The story follows the stereotype point by point: Pretty Stephanie arrives at the big city bus station encumbered with dewy innocence and a large suitcase. A charming gentleman offers his assistance. Dressed in expensive clothes, he sweeps her off her feet with attention, gifts, and assurances of affection. By the end of the week she is working the streets for him. The other girls are mean to her; the customers are kooky; and in the end she returns home, wiser but embittered. There she is forgiven

by her family, who are too distracted by her sister's death to ask a lot of questions.

In avoiding the prurient pitfalls of last year's *Dawn,* the author has tried so hard for "good taste" that she has made prostitution seem like a pleasanter way to earn a living than bagging burgers at MacDonald's. There is not one description of a sexual encounter. The weirdest behavior Steffie has to cope with is from a man who asks her to stand in front of an open window, and from another who gets his jollies from slipping her a dose of LSD. Granted, Steffie's very first experience is embarrassing because she has to approach the man; but her discomfort seems no worse than the sufferings of less sophisticated teenagers at the senior prom. On the other hand, there is lots of explicit talk of exactly how much money Steffie earns (it beats MacDonald's $2.65 an hour) and loving descriptions of the pretty clothes—silver boots, French jeans—her pimp buys her. Here is a book that would have been less problematic if it had had more sordid detail.

Patty Campbell, in a review of "Steffie Can't Come Out to Play," in Wilson Library Bulletin, *Vol. 53, No. 4, December, 1978, p. 341.*

In this unsensationalized story of teenage prostitution, ingenuous, small-town Stephanie arrives in New York with modeling aspirations, slips inevitably into The Life, and returns home after several months, appropriately wised up and apprehensive about her future. Author Arrick has used restraint and judgment in treating such a knotty subject, but the book seems plotted by intent rather than by inspiration. Steffie goes through the paces, enjoying a glittery new wardrobe and A-one attention from her glamorous pimp Favor, but her movements seem curiously mechanical, her experiences too carefully orchestrated. The 14-year-old hears about rather than witnesses the most treacherous Times Square scenes (drugs, violence) but has her share of eye-openers, presented with a little literary tailoring: her sequential losses of innocence (first trick, kinky request, arrest, etc.) are intercut with dreamy memories of home and "realistic" patrol car conversations between two cops assigned to the "Pussy Posse." Also walking the street are some seedy Times Square regulars, including Favor's tough main lady and the rest of his stable—none of whom warms up to the talented newcomer. Ultimately Favor turns her out when one of the cops, interceding on Stephanie's behalf, breaks a few of the pimp's favorite bones: then, too quickly, Steffie is approached by the Greenhouse, a social agency which helps her off the street and onto a bus home. Youngsters who look beyond the provocative jacket—Steffie, in low-cut gown and fur, leaning against an adult book store—will find a skewed but unmoralizing story with a much manipulated central figure.

A review of "Steffie Can't Come Out to Play," in Kirkus Reviews, *Vol. XLVI, No. 24, December 15, 1978, p. 1361.*

A Word from Our Sponsor: Or, My Friend Alfred (1979)

Rudy, twelve, tells a story that, despite the yeasty style of writing and the humor of the dialogue, has a painlessly pithy message about harmful products, advertising, and consumer protection. Rudy and Gillian help a third friend, Alfred, get public attention focused on a drinking cup (a promotional giveaway) that they've tested and in which they've found a dangerous amount of lead; the fact that Alfred's father is responsible for the sponsor's advertising makes it difficult—but they are successful. There's a bit too much cuteness from a young brother, but it's easily outweighed by the tight structure, the believable achievement, the combination of light tone and serious purpose, and the solid friendship and cooperation among the three children.

> *Zena Sutherland, in a review of "A Word from Our Sponsor or, My Friend Alfred," in* Bulletin of the Center for Children's Books, *Vol. 32, No. 8, April, 1979, p. 129.*

Alfred is "tuned-in" to the misuse of television in this well-written story. His brother, a firm believer in TV commercials, becomes disenchanted with a new muscleman doll whose head falls off when he pushes the button to move his karate-chop arm. Alfred's mother, addicted to prepared foods commonly seen on the tube, serves Pepperidge Farm marble cake with her own special topping of Coolwhip and maraschino cherries for dessert. Ruby, a friend, likes old movie reruns so much that he skips school to catch the TV matinees and may be expelled. And Alfred's father, an advertising executive, has just completed a commercial for a product that could be dangerous to young children. While helping his friend stay in school, Alfred conducts experiments to prove the presence of lead in his dad's product—a "Sandlewood Sam" mug—and prevents it from going on the market. Through the process, everybody receives new-found wisdom, and even Mom tries to cook an organic meal of questionable quality which turns out "green, yellow, orange and purple." The story is slow paced with 140 pages devoted to a single issue, but it is enjoyable, easy reading, and presents some humorous encounters with the issue of integrity.

> *Judie Thoms, in a review of "A Word from Our Sponsor: Or, My Friend Alfred," in* School Library Journal, *Vol. 25, No. 8, April, 1979, p. 52.*

Secret Selves (1979)

Julie Novick is 13 and has a crush on Rusty Parmette, who underneath his facade of conceited jock, resents living in a household where the macho ethic is glorified. Encouraged by her best friend, Julie calls Rusty pretending to be someone else and he plays along. Via the telephone, their **Secret Selves** are allowed to emerge: Julie (as Barbara) is assertive and direct; Rusty (as Wendell) likes classical music and feels okay about asking for help in math. In public, however, their relationship is antagonistic. When the two face each other in a school debate (on whether or not the U.S. is ready for a woman president), they finally realize each other's identity, and, in a convenient ending, Julie's grandmother brings the two together. The author never explains why Julie and Rusty don't recognize each other's voice when they interact at school and the subplot

(involving Julie's grandmother, who is supposed to be crazy but is really wise) dangles loosely. Awkwardly written, the story is too forced and "phone-y" to do justice to the underlying themes of male and female roles and the games people play to maintain an image.

> *Cyrisse Jaffee, in a review of "Secret Selves," in* School Library Journal, *Vol. 26, No. 3, November, 1979, p. 73.*

Angell amplifies her deftly woven narrative with clever subplots and individualistic, amusing characters that meld smoothly into the story. The author, whose talent for successfully transporting contemporary young people onto the written page has been growing in books such as **A Word from Our Sponsor,** reaches a satisfying new level with this engrossing, funny tale.

> *Barbara Elleman, in a review of "Secret Selves," in* Booklist, *Vol. 76, No. 5, November 1, 1979, p. 442.*

Thirteen-year-old Julie has a crush on Rusty, and is egged on by her friend Ellen into telephoning him, pretending she's looking for a "Wendell Farnham." Rusty is so pleased by having a telephone call, just like his older brother, that he says he is Wendell. Julie says she's Barbara. And so begins a long series of calls in which both display their best traits, while at school Rusty ignores shy Julie and Julie finds Rusty overbearing. It's Julie's grandmother, who's been eavesdropping on an extension, who brings the two together to face their duplicity and to discover that the "pretense" of their other selves is not pretense at all, but simply the existence of interests and traits each had been too self-conscious to exhibit when they met. It's an original conception, nicely executed and perceptive in its insight into the difficulties of the boy-girl relationship in adolescence. The writing is weakened slightly by the shifting of viewpoint (not only Julie's and Rusty's viewpoint, but those of several minor characters) but the book holds up well nevertheless, and the writing is strengthened by the natural dialogue. (pp. 86-7)

> *Zena Sutherland, in a review of "Secret Selves," in* Bulletin of the Center for Children's Books, *Vol. 33, No. 5, January, 1980, pp. 86-7.*

Based on the premise that the image one presents for public scrutiny may differ from the personality behind it, the novel blends a variety of currently popular motifs—aging, feminism, and parental insensitivity to adolescent insecurity—with the familiar theme of the junior high-schooler's first romantic encounter. The result is a light concoction, ingeniously plotted, somewhat determinedly nonsexist, but nonetheless entertaining. . . . Cleverly constructed, the book indicates that the author has a sympathetic appreciation for adolescent gaucherie—as revealed in the dialogues between Julie and Rusty. (pp. 52-3)

> *Mary M. Burns, in a review of "Secret Selves," in* The Horn Book Magazine, *Vol. LVI, No. 1, February, 1980, pp. 52-3.*

Tunnel Vision (as Fran Arrick, 1980)

Anthony, a 15-year-old "A" student, star of his high school swim team, respected by his teachers, idolized by his friends, favored by his parents, and nicknamed Mr. Perfect by his more rebellious sister, hangs himself with his father's neckties, leaving no note. Shocked and guilty, his nearest and dearest condemn themselves for not sensing that the boy's terminal depression of several months duration was more than teenage angst. But readers will be at as much of a loss as to why this particular kid wanted to end it all. True, his father is on the road a great deal and rules the roost in absentia; his mother is ineffectual; his English teacher doesn't understand his essays at their deepest level; and his Czech girlfriend, an orphan and rape victim, will not let him kiss her; but are those reasons to die? A nice, neighborhood cop, commenting upon the statistical frequency of juvenile suicide attempts in the American small town he inhabits, attributes the phenomenon to *Tunnel Vision:* "It's like each of them was caught inside a tunnel and they couldn't see any end to it or anything at all outside." Not much of an explanation but it's refreshing to find a realistic problem novel that doesn't read like a psychological case study. The small, linked group of people who must come to terms with the tragedy described here are likable and ordinary. They are not particularly marked for disaster. It visits them almost casually. Arrick's spare, understated handling of their struggle to come to terms with the decision of a child they all loved to leave them and life behind rings true, and should prompt some heated discussions. (pp. 119-20)

> *Laura Geringer, in a review of "Tunnel Vision," in* School Library Journal, *Vol. 26, No. 8, April, 1980, pp. 119-20.*

It's all here—the shock, the bewilderment, the guilt, and the anger that are the classic symptoms of the aftermath of suicide. . . . While the motive for Anthony's death may be obvious to readers, Arrick leaves it credibly speculative for her characters and tackles the emotionally charged subject with intensity that approaches the sensational only once—in her handling of the tangential episode of Jana's rape. Noteworthy as well is Arrick's avoidance of a completely downbeat ending—she ensures that at least some of her characters emerge from the tragedy with broadened insight and newfound inner strength. Purposeful, but skillfully and successfully so. (pp. 1355-56)

> *A review of "Tunnel Vision," in* Booklist, *Vol. 76, No. 18, May 15, 1980, pp. 1355-56.*

There is not one superfluous word in this *tour de force* relating the effects of 15-year-old Anthony Hamil's suicide on those left behind. The guilt experienced by Anthony's friends, mother, girlfriend, and favorite teacher is depicted with sensitivity and insight. Only the father, whose neckties Anthony used to hang himself with, cannot look directly at the possibility that he might have had some part in the decision. Arrick does not make the mistake of trying to explain "why" Anthony killed himself, a wise decision since we never know truly why this choice is made.

The book will be popular with YAs, more and more of whom are being personally touched by teenage suicide. It deserves to be brought to the attention of parents and teachers as well.

> *Dorothy M. Broderick, in a review of "Tunnel Vision," in* Voice of Youth Advocates, *Vol. 3, No. 3, August, 1980, p. 29.*

An inoffensive but uninspired attempt to deal with teenage suicide via the reactions and memories of the parents, sister, cousins, friend, and sort-of girl-friend of a 15-year-old boy who has just hung himself. Until the last months Anthony had been a top jock and all-A student. Now friend and cousin blame themselves for not recognizing the seriousness of his depression. His mother blames herself for accepting her husband's reassurances and not getting the kid to a psychiatrist. The girl blames her physical distance. (A rape victim, she's in bad shape herself.) And his sister blames their father who is preoccupied with business. Despite all their flashbacks, we never do get close to Anthony, his motives, or his personality. His English-class essay about death as "Peace" shows that he had been drawn to suicide for a while but otherwise reveals only an unintended sleazy sensibility. Of the survivors, Arrick leaves the school-skipping, pot-smoking, burnout sister on the way to self-rehabilitation and the girlfriend able to touch the others in shared grief. None of this is lurid, but it isn't very affecting either.

> *A review of "Tunnel Vision," in* Kirkus Reviews, *Vol. XLVIII, No. 15, August 1, 1980, p. 983.*

Anthony Hamil, aged fifteen, hung himself with his father's neckties. The end of his life is the beginning of this story. Fran Arrick lets us in on the relentless horror, bewilderment, and grief suffered by members of his family and friends. The story is non-stop reading accompanied by an ache in the throat and misty eyes. (pp. 207-08)

From [the] point of complete despair the survivors are drawn together, and slowly and agonizingly share their anger and guilt along with their shock. Utterly vulnerable, they begin to see in each other and in themselves strengths and weaknesses they never looked for before.

Fran Arrick writes as if she knows her subject and characters well, and the subject matter is of particular interest these days, suicide being the second leading cause of death in American young people.

This book is recommended for parents of any age child. But for kids I worry that the ending could be construed as possibly encouraging or condoning suicide; also because the problem of guilt is dispensed with on the book jacket—"All felt to blame and none was." Blame is perhaps too harsh a word to use, but in every human relationship there are elements of imperfection that need examining and forgiveness. The universal guilt that accompanies suicide is perhaps the living out of the Biblical question, "Am I my brother's keeper"? (p. 208)

> *Gail Tansill Lambert, in a review of "Tunnel Vision," in* Best Sellers, *Vol. 40, No. 6, September, 1980, pp. 207-08.*

[The following excerpt is from an interview with George Nicholson by Roni Natov and Geraldine DeLuca. From

his experiences as editor-in-chief of the Books for Young Readers division of Dell Publishing Company, Nicholson discusses trends in children's book publishing. When asked about novels dealing with suicide, he compares Tunnel Vision *with Susan Beth Pfeffer's* About David.]

When **Tunnel Vision** opens, the boy is already dead. And what you find out, and why it's an impressive book from my point of view, is what both the adult and the young adult characters in the novel think about what has happened. There are very, very good adult characters in this novel, and all the characters have different and very confusing notions of what precisely has happened. There's jealousy and uncertainty among all of them, toward one another, as well as toward the boy, who is the classic case. I mean, he's a brilliant student who finished all his papers before he did himself in. Yet the book is in no sense a didactic novel, from my point of view. It shows some of the blinding mistakes that adults make with young people. For instance, the boy is a writer who is working on themes for his English teacher. His English teacher is deeply impressed and reads part of one of his papers to the class. But the boy is offended because he feels his confidence has been betrayed. The teacher, of course, thought he was praising him. It's a very simple scene, but it shows how two people can go right past each other. Also you suddenly begin to see that this boy was missing the boat terribly, that he was far more disturbed than anyone realized. I think it's a very good book. (pp. 102-03)

[*About David*] is a very different kind of story—more conventional but many people feel better because it doesn't appear to vaguely condone suicide as an alternative. I don't think Arrick does in her novel at all, but a number of other people appear to think she does. Certainly that was not her intention.

Neither [**Tunnel Vision** nor *About David*], are necessarily great works of art, but they are more than just sociological novels. There's a seriousness of purpose that I think kids recognize. (p. 103)

> *George Nicholson, in a review of "Tunnel Vision," in* The Lion and the Unicorn, *Vol. 5, 1981, pp. 102-03.*

Dear Lola: Or, How to Build Your Own Family   (1980)

However preposterous, this saga about some runaway children who triumph over the Department of Social Services will gladden the hearts of many young readers. Eighteen-year-old "Lola"—nicknamed for the advice column he writes—and five assorted youngsters escape from an orphanage on foot and try to settle down in the country to live unobtrusively as a family. But there's no anonymity in the country, and their cover is blown. Their case comes to court, they lose and miraculously escape again; they end up in California, happily picking fruit. Soul-wrenching stories about the children's past lives and touching scenes that point up the callous disregard for the rights and feelings of minors are balanced by the upbeat first-person narration and some pretty slap-stick humor.

This would be a good choice for slow readers in junior high and high school.

> *Marilyn R. Singer, in a review of "Dear Lola: Or, How to Build Your Own Family," in* School Library Journal, *Vol. 27, No. 5, Janaury, 1981, p. 56.*

A junior *Miss Lonelyhearts,* sentimental and cute and spurious. When orphan Arthur Beniker was little, he learned such "a whole lot about problems and feelings" from being unloved, that at 18 he's great at solving other people's problems. He's secretly "Dear Lola," author of a newspaper advice column. The column pays for him and five younger orphans—ten-year-old narrator Annie; Al-Willie, her twin; Ben, five; Edmund, nine; James, 13—to flee from St. Theresa's Home and School. They head west, on foot, spending rainy days in libraries, reading Poe, Twain, and Washington Irving. In the town of Sweet River they buy an old house. The toilet doesn't work, which gives Annie a chance to show that girls can fix plumbing. Other problems are as easily solved now that the orphans live together as they'd dreamed, as a family: Ben stops swallowing all small objects—barrettes, keys, Christmas-tree ornaments, etc.; Edmund stops throwing "real wild tantrums . . . twice a day"; and James stops being autistic. These were just responses to not getting enough love. All but Arthur, busy with the column, go to school. Everything is dandy till busybody townsfolk inquire, who has custody? Why, Grandfather, alias Arthur. But his masquerade fails when his moustache falls off. The case goes to court. Arthur has boned up on law to be the orphans' own lawyer, but it's no use; under oath, he must reveal that he's Dear Lola. The newspapers get hold of this. Since "people don't want . . . advice from an 18-year-old boy," he loses the job. Since there won't be any money, the judge refuses him custody of the others. This sets Edmund back: he throws a tantrum. His cat throws one also. This provides the diversion the orphans need to flee once again. They head farther west, in a van. "We've been moving around California, picking fruit, living on farms . . . and we all love it." Ah for the happy life of under-age fruitpickers. . . . This time Angell has applied her glibness to a serious subject, with disastrous results.

> *A review of "Dear Lola: Or, How to Build Your Own Family," in* Kirkus Reviews, *Vol. XLIX, No. 1, January 1, 1981, p. 5.*

Patient, loving, wise, and compassionate, Lola is one of the nicest father figures in fiction; if the story isn't wholly believable, it's still wholly beguiling: good style, good characters, a fresh plot, and the perennial appeal of a dream come true. (p. 106)

> *Zena Sutherland, in a review of "Dear Lola; Or, How to Build Your Own Family," in* Bulletin of the Center for Children's Books, *Vol. 34, No. 6, February, 1981, pp. 105-06.*

An orphan story with a contemporary flair, the saga of the six Benikers (only two of whom are actually blood kin) moves rapidly through a series of capers which begins with the great escape from St. Theresa's Home and School and ends in the sun-drenched fruit groves of California.

Narrated by ten-year-old Annie, the chronicle—like Dorothy Crayder's *She, The Adventuress*—depends upon the author's creating a plausible, if somewhat improbable, situation to ensure the reader's willing suspension of disbelief. An introductory sequence boldly outlines the salient features of each personality, from the surrogate father's secret career as the agony columnist Dear Lola to five-year-old Ben's bizarre penchant for eating small objects. The exploits of the characters transcend credibility as the Benikers move into the small community of Sweet River after three months spent searching for a house. Needless to say, the curiosity of the townspeople conflicts sharply with the Benikers' desire for privacy; the resulting confrontations become increasingly more hilarious as "Lola" tries to continue the education of his young charges and resolve the question of legal guardianship. Just the right note of poignancy tempers the high jinks; the children are as self-sufficient as Robinson Crusoe was, and they ultimately succeed in out-witting the denizens of bureaucracy—a highly successful variation of a tried-and-true formula.

> *Mary M. Burns, in a review of "Dear Lola, Or, How to Build Your Own Family," in* The Horn Book Magazine, *Vol. LVII, No. 1, February, 1981, p. 48.*

Chernowitz! (as Fran Arrick, 1981)

Arrick writes an effective, if not subtle, novel, designed to expose the mindlessness and insidiousness of prejudice. Bob's emotions and even his revenge against his tormentor are quite believable, though the novel's strength is not due to character depth but to the author's competent manipulation of plot. The narrative tension winds down too quickly, and Arrick's resolution is overworked; however, the story is involving and not totally pessimistic and may lend itself well to class discussion.

> *Stephanie Zvirin, in a review of "Chernowitz!" in* Booklist, *Vol. 77, Nos. 22-3, July 15-August, 1981, p. 1444.*

When at 10 p.m. you say, I'll just read a few pages to get started and next you look up and it's midnight, it is hard to be critical of a book, and even harder to explain how so engrossing a read leaves one annoyed, frustrated and stomping around the house. The plot of *Chernowitz* is the first person narration of Bobby Cherno's harassment by bully Emmett Sundback solely because Bobby is Jewish. There are name callings, a fiery cross (albeit it very small) tossed on the Cherno lawn, a swatiska painted on a family car, and isolation from the other boys in the class. All because this bunch of suburban boy sheep follow blindly the leadership of an adolescent victim of child abuse by his divorced, drinking father. When Sundback injures Bobby's cat by swiping him with his motorcycle, Bobby vows revenge and sets Sundback up as a thief. True to the adolescent code, Bobby shares none of his harassment with anyone until his sense of guilt forces him to confide in his parents. The antisemitism being experienced is a personal problem and he will cope with it.

And therein lies the problem and weakness of the book.

A book on such a serious problem must offer some insight into motivation, both of the victim and the victimizer. Antisemitism is not in the same category as harassment because one is too fat or too tall or too short. It is NOT a personal problem of the victim but a social problem and to treat it as less is to deny reality. Bobby is a reasonably okay kid: he plays soccer, skates, has a sailboat, is smart in school and has one reasonably good friend, although he is not a mad socializer. What escapes the reader is why Sundback singles Bobby out for harassment when in the community being portrayed there must be many Jews. As for bully Sundback, why does he choose antisemitism as his cause? Is being a battered child enough to make an antisemite? Why, being successful in his harassment does he not expand his harassment to other Jews?

A book that raises that many questions must be bought and discussed. It should be in the hands of history teachers and those dealing with values education and human relations. What the individual reader will gain from it is anyone's guess. It would be great disservice to both victims and survivors of the Holocaust for YAs to assume that bigots are simply victims themselves. Finally, it must be said that the real villains in *Chernowitz* and society as a whole are those Jewish parents who are failing to treat their Jewishness as nothing more than the basis for celebrating a couple of extra holidays each year. Had Bobby been made aware of his Jewish roots and what they mean, he might have understood that there are issues in life so large that the adolescent code of dealing with things oneself must fall by the wayside. Not only did he not have that insight at the beginning, he does not have it at the end even after viewing films on Auschwitz and Dachau concentration camps. Both Sundback and Bobby are exactly the same at the end and while I know in my gut there are people who learn absolutely nothing from experience, I resent books with that message, particularly when I suspect the message received was not the message the author thought she was sending.

> *Dorothy M. Broderick, in a review of "Chernowitz," in* Voice of Youth Advocates, *Vol. 4, No. 3, August, 1981, p. 23.*

This is an "issue" novel on the ramifications of anti-Semitism in contemporary society. One is never sure why Emmett acts the way he does nor why Bobby's friends so easily swallow Emmett's line. The story is filled with predictable stereotypes: Bobby's sympathetic, marginally Jewish parents; Emmett's fatness and failings; Bobby's sweet girlfriend; etc. And yet, because of the author's directness in raising important issues and her refusal to explain away the unrepentant Emmett as merely a product of a bad environment, the story has real merit. It's not often that one recommends a story for study use, but that's where this book belongs.

> *Jack Forman, in a review of "Chernowitz!" in* School Library Journal, *Vol. 28, No. 1, September, 1981, p. 132.*

A one-issue but lifelike and involving novel about what happens when a sadistic school bully launches a campaign against a Jewish classmate. . . . [Eventually] Sundback involves the other ninth-grade boys, so that Bobby is ostracized by all of them, and even Brian Denny greets him on the school bus with "Move over, Jew bastard, you take up too much room." This from a former best friend, and the fact that Bobby hasn't one defender, is a little hard to accept—it might be more believable if we knew something about Brian and had a glimpse of Sundback at work on the others. However, Brian's overall behavior—avoiding or taunting Bobby when with the gang, calling him as if nothing had happened when Sundback is out of town—is all too recognizable, and Arrick's general picture of mass adolescent cruelty expressed in anti-Semitism is similarly convincing. . . . Arrick doesn't provide much insight into the psychology or dynamics of anti-Semitic behavior, but she makes the occurrence seem appallingly possible, and she effectively fastens kids' identification on its victimized but not defeated target.

> *A review of "Chernowitz," in* Kirkus Reviews, *Vol. XLIX, No. 22, November 15, 1981, p. 1413.*

What's Best for You (1981)

Although divorce stories abound, Angell's novel is set apart by its penetrating characterizations. She incisively shows how each member of a family deals with this very personal trauma. The lives of the Currie children have been totally disrupted by their parents' divorce: the family house is being rented out, 12-year-old Allison and 7-year-old Joel are off to New York City to live with their mother, and 15-year-old Lee will spend the summer on Long Island with her father, her favored parent. Lee's parents have tried very hard to work out a reasonable life-style for their children and themselves, but as the summer progresses everyone has unexpected feelings. The younger children have problems adjusting, Lee does not want to rejoin her family in the city, and the senior Curries find single parenthood is not quite what they anticipated. The plot is linear—a summer in the life of the Currie family. But the complex and delicate relationships explored bring depth and fullness to this highly readable story, perhaps Angell's best. (pp. 383-84)

> *Ilene Cooper, in a review of "What's Best for You," in* Booklist, *Vol. 78, No. 5, November 1, 1981, pp. 383-84.*

The author is better at the dialogue and characterization of kids than of adults. Her adults talk like adolescents. They cannot handle crises and allow their children to lead them. Both Lenore's parents remain curiously celibate in contrast to her friends' divorced parents. (Her father does plan a post-denouement weekend with a female guest.) The story is touching in its sadness, but only mildly interesting. Two comparable novels also have shrewish mothers and affable fathers (and incidentally are also set in New York). *Taking Sides* by Norma Klein (Avon, 1974) has more color but less warmth. By far the most satisfying is the piquant *Leap Before You Look* by Mary Stolz (Harper, 1972)—even though her adolescents talk like adults.

> *Marsha Hartos, in a review of "What's Best for You," in* School Library Journal, *Vol. 28, No. 5, January, 1982, p. 72.*

Each child reacts to stress in a different way, but their problems are serious, and Angell deals perceptively with the intricate pain of separation and the subtle ways in which each member of a family group affects and is affected by the others. They all do adjust; the story ends on a positive note that has been realistically achieved, as new interests, new people, time and acceptance of change blur both Lee's open anger at her mother and Allison's carefully-buried resentment. There's no strong story line developed, but there is vigor and contrast in the development of the situation and the exploration of characters.

> *Zena Sutherland, in a review of "What's Best for You," in* Bulletin of the Center for Children's Books, *Vol. 35, No. 6, February, 1982, p. 102.*

The characterization of Lee is very good and teens will readily identify with her. The problems of her friends (whose parents are also divorced), her parents who have to adjust to their new lives, and her younger sister are also interesting. However, the sister's difficulties and the parents' problems leading to the divorce need more explanation. What is especially good is that the focus of the book is on the effects of the divorce, particularly on Lee, as well as the fact that their lives do continue despite the divorce as they each try to discover what is best for them.

> *Susan Levine, in a review of "What's Best for You," in* Voice of Youth Advocates, *Vol. 4, No. 6, February, 1982, p. 28.*

[*The following excerpt is from an essay which discusses how mothers are depicted in recent books for young readers. Critic Ann Donovan compares* What's Best for You *with Linda Weltner's* Beginning to Feel the Magic.]

An equally trendy family, one even more closely related to the superficial family of mass media, is found in Angell's **What's Best for You**. The novel, as the title implies, involves a morass of parental concern for the ninth grade heroine, Lee, who is a true pill. A strong note of adolescent whining is distracting and unpleasant. The reader is asked to empathize with Lee's desire to live with her hassle-free father instead of with her hard-pressed mother, who is trying to get restarted in a job in the city and who has legal custody of the three children. However, Lee's cozier relationship with her father is complicated by his new girlfriend. Aimed at the middle-school reader, this is a serious novel, but since the main character is so unappealing, the focus is confused. The story is further addled by an indecisive switching from adult to child point of view. Although clearly intended to gain the reader's sympathy for all and reveal conflicting needs and emotions, this actually fragments the story and results in a welter of stereotypes. Once again the temptation to write as if for an adult reader seems to have been irresistible.

Both of these last novels suffer from an excess of self-indulgence on the part of the characters. Readers are given an uninspiring variety of whiners with whom to sympathize. These facile stories are not salvaged by equally simplistic resolutions strongly reminiscent of soap operas. Even the dialogue in Angell's book echoes these interminable afternoon "human dramas." Do novels even, or especially, for the young really need to stoop to such overworked and expendable material? (p. 136)

Ann Donovan, "New Mothers in Current Children's Fiction," in Children's literature in education, *Vol. 14, No. 3, Autumn, 1983, pp. 131-41.*

The Buffalo Nickel Blues Band (1982)

Sixth-graders Eddie, Ivy, and Georgie form a band, but rather than play rock like everyone else, they focus on rhythm and blues. With the addition of Shelby's horn and Reese's bass guitar, their sound becomes even more fully developed. Shelby and Reese add some mystery to the band as well. With Reese it's his tough-guy posture and catch-as-catch-can life-style, while Shelby has the group wondering why he must sneak around to all his gigs (his parents insist that he become a classical musician). The band turns out to be a huge success, but Shelby's discovery by his father leads to the band's dissolution. Each member fondly recalls those halcyon days but must go on to other pursuits. While it's peopled with three-dimensional characters, the book nonetheless centers around 1960s music, with which kids' familiarity may be minimal. And while the strong characterizations do carry the plot, one off-note is Eddie's stereotypical parents, an overbearing (though good-hearted) Mrs. Portnoy type and a retiring father. Otherwise, this is smoothly written Angell fiction in which a group of integrated kids play well off each other.

Ilene Cooper, in a review of "The Buffalo Nickel Blues Band," in Booklist, *Vol. 78, No. 19, June 1, 1982, p. 1308.*

These children, sixth and seventh graders, are driven by an intense love for blues (rather than rock) music, and they are mature beyond their years. These factors, as well as the cheerfully helpful parents who come through when needed, are slightly unrealistic. But the story is engaging and readers are made to care for the players, so that this minor flaw can be overlooked.

Holly Sanhuber, in a review of "The Buffalo Nickel Blues Band," in School Library Journal, *Vol. 28, No. 10, August, 1982, p. 110.*

This is a funny yet sensitive story of friendship. The book's humor is strong but not overbearing with at least one chuckle per page. The story is true to life even though the band members are mature beyond their years and the parents are much more cooperative than most. Each character is presented and developed thoroughly through the eyes of Eddie, and changes as Eddie and the reader get to know the other band members better.

Margaret Smith, in a review of "The Buffalo Nickel Blues Band," in Catholic Library World, *Vol. 54, No. 9, March, 1983, p. 333.*

Suds: A New Daytime Drama (1983)

This is a romp from page one, and the author must have

had as much fun as her readers will, savoring the blatant spoof of soap operas. Sue Sudley's story begins when her parents, each flying solo (in different directions) collide in midair while Sue descends in her designer parachute. She leaves her mansion to live with an aunt and uncle in a small town and becomes involved in the pseudo-dramatic, nonsensical, and highly enjoyable complexities of life—including the boy next door, a football hero confined to a wheelchair because he can never walk, who regains the use of his legs when he impulsively propels himself onto the gridiron during a homecoming game. This has everything the soaps have: the trite situations, the cardboard characters, the contrived dialogue, all presented in bland style with tongue firmly in cheek.

Zena Sutherland, in a review of "Suds: A New Daytime Drama," in Bulletin of the Center for Children's Books, *Vol. 36, No. 8, April, 1983, p. 142.*

Written in the style of a soap opera, the story feels like a put on and that any moment the real story will begin. It's not so much the failure of technique, using dramatic events or fantastic coincidence (M. E. Kerr pulls this off royally), but the story just doesn't have much excitement and the characters are not well developed.

After the death of both her parents Sue Sudley goes off to live in a small town with her mother's sister's family. Despite her wealthy life style Sue always dreamed of being just like other kids. Almost immediately she's plunged into two romances, a small town secret, and gets a scoop for the school newspaper. She exposes the horror of video game addiction! The video game theme is one of the wittiest elements in the novel. Everything turns out well for all the characters but like the soaps it's unlikely the course of small town life will run smoothly and Angell may find this ripe for a sequel. . . .

The story is easy to read and moves quickly but *Suds* doesn't have the impact of a real soap.

Sari Feldman, in a review of "Suds: A New Daytime Drama," in Voice of Youth Advocates, *Vol. 6, No. 2, June 2, 1983, p. 95.*

In true soap opera tradition, the plots and subplots are connected by unbreakable static cling, characters are one dimensional, situations outrageously incredible. Even the dialogue is appropriately soppy. A spoof that children can enjoy, particularly those who race home to watch *General Hospital* et. al. It's good clean fun—and funny.

Trevelyn Jones, in a review of "Suds: A New Daytime Drama," in School Library Journal, *Vol. 29, No. 10, August, 1983, p. 72.*

The idea of this soap-opera spoof is irresistible. *Suds* opens with an amusing cast of characters and recaps the last episode: "As you remember," poor little rich girl Sue Sudley lost both parents in a midair collision—Daddy was in the Lear jet, Mummy in the Cessna—and Sue wafted down to the planes' wreckage in the designer parachute she'd just received for her 15th birthday. . . .

What follows is not a plot that twists and turns; this plot accumulates, like a snowball rolling down a hill. Sue, in her monogrammed ("S.O.S.") sweater, discovers Leon's Neon, a videogame parlor, and through school gossip discovers that Dinah, a games junkie, plays to forget that her cheating boyfriend Rick may be "behind the bleachers, breathing on Bonnie." Meanwhile, Rick and Roger pursue Sue, who prefers the comfortable boy next door, Storm, a former junior varsity football star who's now in a wheelchair.

After Sue saves Dinah from her computer habit, gossip reveals that an English teacher has written a juicy *roman à clef* for Tacky Press. Then, from the sidelines of the homecoming football game, Storm illegally pilots his wheelchair onto the field to help his former teammates win. When he regains consciousness, his toe is twitching. We didn't doubt for a moment that Storm would walk again, but getting there was half the fun.

Suds' farcical plot is amusing, but there is no satirical bite to the humor. The result is a mildly funny, squeaky-clean soap without a whit of seriousness.

> *Sally Holmes Holtze, in a review of "Suds: A New Daytime Drama," in* The New York Times Book Review, *August 28, 1983, p. 22.*

The premise of *Suds* is pretty wild. It's a spoof of soap operas for kids—sort of a juvenile *Mary Hartman, Mary Hartman,* complete with black humor, absurd coincidences, and scandal (nothing too shocking, however). Whether kids will get the joke is anybody's guess; the cover art makes the book look fairly serious and unless you read the quotes on the back (where the book is described as "a blatant spoof of soap operas"), you could feel rather baffled. As for the story itself, I found the beginning and end to be quite funny, but things bogged down in the middle. Recommended for the hip crowd.

> *Fran Lantz, in a review of "Suds: A New Daytime Drama," in* Kliatt Young Adult Paperback Book Guide, *Vol. XIX, No. 1, January, 1985, p. 4.*

God's Radar   (as Fran Arrick, 1983)

Moving from Syracuse to a small southern town is somewhat of a culture shock for the Cables—especially for 15-year-old Roxie—but it isn't long before their neighbors, the Pregers, make them feel welcome by introducing them to the Stafford Hill Baptist Church community. Affected by the Pregers' enthusiasm and devotion to the church, Roxie's parents (especially her mother) gravitate toward the insularity and family-centered fundamentalist philosophy of Stafford Hill and, fearing negative influences of Howertown's secular community on their daughter, join the church and enroll Roxie in parochial school. While her parents seem satisfied with Stafford Hill, Roxie isn't sure how she feels, and her struggle to sort out her confusion forms the crux of the story. Some readers will undoubtedly view the book as a judgment of fundamentalism, but the author does attempt to balance her portrait of the church. While she draws Stafford Hill members as unashamed proselytizers who lard everyday conversations with Bible verses (this includes young people as well as

adults), she also emphasizes their sincerity and good works. Individual characterizations are not so evenhanded. Most supporting characters have been deliberately fashioned to express specific points of view about the church. Yet despite this lack of subtlety, Arrick has put together a compelling story, and what comes across with particular force is the frightening vulnerability of teenagers and the effect peer pressure has on their intellectual freedom.

> *Stephanie Zvirin, in a review of "God's Radar," in* Booklist, *Vol. 79, No. 20, June 15, 1983, p. 1333.*

This is a scathing and highly oversimplified indictment of fundamentalist Christianity carried to a legalistic extreme. Since Arrick has already passed judgment on the issue (even at their nicest, the Baptists wear the black hats), the tension is only plot deep and fails to truly challenge readers on a moral level.

> *C. Nordhielm Wooldridge, in a review of "God's Radar," in* School Library Journal, *Vol. 29, No. 10, August, 1983, p. 72.*

God's Radar is a disturbing book. I hope it was meant to be. Roxie Cable is 15 years old. Her family has moved from Syracuse, New York, to a small town in Georgia, following her father's promotion. Glenna, her older sister, has graduated college, and is settling happily into the excitement of a job in New York City. Of course, Roxie misses home; her friends, her favorite shops, her school. Her story of overcoming loneliness and accepting change might be the daily drama we all live and seldom read about, were it not for the Stafford Hill Baptist Church. . . .

In Syracuse Roxie's judgment in friends and fun was respected and understood; now she is pressured into seeing only members of the Stafford Hill youth group, is chaperoned on dates, and is denied her favorite music, dancing and movies. Her actions are monitored by her own best friends, and discipline is imposed in the worst form of punishment, ostracism.

Roxie is a good kid. Respect for her parents and love of her family enable her to understand their need to belong. But her independence of spirit maintains an open attitude about the church and its teachings. In an inevitable crisis of trust, Roxie's own sense of right is overwhelmed by the very people who are trying so hard to protect her. Roxie's story ends abruptly, and we are left troubled, uncertain that she will survive 1984.

I recommend this book to young readers *only* as a challenge to their attitudes on conformity and self-discipline. (pp. 270-71)

> *Carolyn S. Lembeck, in a review of "God's Radar," in* Best Sellers, *Vol. 43, No. 7, October, 1983, pp. 270-71.*

The family's "takeover" is gradual and chillingly logical so the reader can understand much of the why behind moral majoritarians. An important topic as fairly treated as may be possible, the reader's biases will impact this book more than the author's. I suspect Jerry Falwell or Cal Thomas would find this a positive story rather than a potential ban. A definite candidate for Best Books though reviewers will be split on this one.

Susan B. Madden, in a review of "God's Radar," in Voice of Youth Advocates, *Vol. 6, No. 4, October, 1983, p. 196.*

In part, this novel explores the conflict between fundamentalism and humanism; however, the novel's outstanding achievement is its depiction of a teenager caught in the middle of a clash of beliefs. . . .

Fran Arrick has written another balanced portrayal of disparate influences on America's youth. If you liked her insightful portrayal of teenage prostitution in **Steffie Can't Come Out to Play,** of anti-Semitism in **Chernowitz!** and of teenage suicide in **Tunnel Vision,** you will like her equable treatment of fundamentalism in **God's Radar**. . . . Highly recommended.

Jane Yarbrough, in a review of "God's Radar," in The ALAN Review, *Vol. 13, No. 3, Spring, 1986, p. 41.*

First the Good News (1983)

First the Good News, is a satisfying ethnic Nancy Drew-type thriller set in contemporary New York.

A mystery it's not. There's no crime to solve—only a dilemma: How can a group of ninth-grade girls wangle an interview with the hottest TV idol and win the interschool journalism award?

These bright and independent girls have formed a group called the "Adam's Ribbers," to work for the "common good of mankind." While all too often it seems their time is taken up with arguing about the color of their club sweater, they manage to squeeze in such projects as working in a soup kitchen, singing Christmas carols at a home for the elderly, and writing columns on world affairs.

So where does stalking celebrity Hap Rhysbeck fit in this plan? Josephine says, "There's something he gives people. . . . It's more than just being funny. He speaks to kids. The way our parents and our teachers don't."

The teen's speech rings true—a difficult feat in the face of their constantly changing speech habits. The parent's dialogue, however, goes whole hog into ethnic stereotypes. It's not a major flaw; in fact, the ethnicity of the story is part of its charm.

How these five friends manage to cope with protective doormen and prying students, keeping their morale up (and their weight down), plus trying to figure out the identity of the suitor, makes for fast and entertaining reading.

Catherine Foster, "Ninth-Graders Search out the News," in The Christian Science Monitor, *October 7, 1983, p. B2.*

Five ninth-grade New York City girls try everything to interview Hap Rhysbeck, star of television's *Sound Stage 3* (alias *Saturday Night Live*), for the school paper. All of their efforts are in vain, until they attend an SS3 performance, where Annabelle's older sister is revealed to be Rhysbeck's fiancée. Five 15 year olds are a lot to characterize between two covers, and Angell succeeds marvelously with three: Annabelle, the restless mover and shaker; Helaine, whose mother's overbearing nature is the source of her resistance and determination and Josephine, rooted in a large and colorful family. What stands out is the lively and effective portrayal of ninth-grade social dynamics; the factual television background will also be of interest to young readers. The romantic revelation at the book's end is a bit hard to swallow, but clues planted in the story line prevent it from being unpalatable. Overall, the uncomplicated plot and silly goings-on combine with a satisfying un-fairy-tale-like ending to make a light, readable, city adventure.

Carolyn Noah, in a review of "First the Good News," in School Library Journal, *Vol. 30, No. 3, November, 1983, p. 72.*

Who Has the Lucky-Duck in Class 4-B? (as Maggie Twohill, 1984)

Victoria is devastated when she loses her secret Lucky-Duck charm, but for Tommy, who finds it, the key chain brings good luck on the baseball field. Then Ralph's lottery ticket wins just after Tommy gives him the charm, which motivates Melissa to steal it. She quickly becomes disillusioned with its powers and hands it over to Elfrida, who gives it to Carrie. The conclusion of this witty circular tale is inventive in itself—and thoroughly satisfying. As for the six fourth-graders, all of whom are fully portrayed, they have dabbled in a bit of magic and have each come away a bit wiser.

Barbara Elleman, in a review of "Who Has the Lucky-Duck in Class-4-B?" in Booklist, *Vol. 80, No. 16, April 15, 1984, p. 1195.*

Characterization is superficial, the conversational style is clichéd and gimmicky and extraneous details often interfere with the flow of the story. Although accessible to third graders in terms of reading level and format, this story will not hold their attention.

Lynne (E. F.) McKechnie, in a review of "Who Has the Lucky-Duck in Class 4-B?" in School Library Journal, *Vol. 30, No. 10, August, 1984, p. 78.*

A Home Is to Share . . . and Share . . . and Share . . . (1984)

The Muchmore children live up to their name—they feel the more animals they have as pets, the better. Not surprisingly, their parents think they have quite enough pets now and so are not pleased when Bucky, Jeanette, and Harry bring home a pregnant dog. They issue an ultimatum: Sparky can stay for one night, and then she must go to the town animal shelter. But when Mr. and Mrs. Muchmore call the shelter, they learn it is about to be shut down for lack of state funds. If homes cannot be found for the animals already living there, they will have to be put to sleep. With the help of the neighborhood children, the Muchmore kids decide to take on the job of preventing that from happening. The problem seems as though it might be easily solved by Uncle Leonard, also known as the Great Leonardo, a magician who uses a duck in his act. Leonardo gets a little carried away and takes a number of the unwanted animals, but after he spends a few hours with them, they are not wanted by *him* either; he doesn't even want his duck anymore. Instead of getting rid of Sparky, the Muchmore family winds up opening their home to a whole new host of pets. This situation can't go on, so the next day Bucky, Jeanette, and Harry set up shop at the mall, where they try to find homes for the pets and garner publicity for the failing animal shelter. They succeed admirably on both fronts, and the next day the shelter owner tells them that with the pledges of money and help he has received, he'll be able to carry on. As a thank you, he gives the Muchmores just what they need—a pair of rabbits. Slim characterizations keep the book's focus on situation. The problems of the kids and the animals tumble across the pages and then are neatly tied up at the end, making this a light, effortless read.

> *Ilene Cooper, in a review of "A Home Is to Share . . . and Share . . . and Share," in* Booklist, *Vol. 80, No. 22, August, 1984, p. 1622.*

Animal lovers will applaud the determination and ingenuity of the Muchmore children as they try to save an assortment of victims when the underfunded Nelkin Falls Animal Shelter must close. . . . Angell captures readers with a fast-paced plot, funny dialogue and warm-blooded characters. Subtle messages on family life are conveyed, particularly the special place of adopted children and the importance of caring and sharing.

> *Gerry Larson, in a review of "A Home Is to Share . . . and Share . . . and Share . . . ," in* School Library Journal, *Vol. 31, No. 1, September, 1984, p. 112.*

" 'We can't keep Sparky,' " Mr. Muchmore announces, thereby galvanizing his three children and their neighborhood gang into a series of funny adventures. Sparky is a stray dog—pregnant, of course—another in a long line of animals the children have rescued; their long-suffering parents are tired of playing host to the world's homeless. . . . The author's usual facility with dialogue and her appreciation of family relationships are evident, and the animal characters, as well as the human, impress their individual personalities on the action.

> *Charlotte W. Draper, in a review of "A Home Is to Share . . . and Share . . . and Share . . . ," in* The Horn Book Magazine, *Vol. LX, No. 5, September-October, 1984, p. 589.*

Nice Girl from Good Home (as Fran Arrick, 1984)

When Dory Hewitt's father is fired from his high-paying job as an advertising executive, the strain on the family is intense. Her mother, a compulsive spender after a child-

hood of poverty, tries to deny the change; she becomes increasingly depressed and eventually has a breakdown. Fifteen-year-old Dory, who has always been her father's princess, withdraws from friends and family, joins an anti-social crowd, and in her rage telephones a bomb threat to her school. Only her brother Jeremy is able to adjust to the change realistically, and he is finally able to help the others. Heavily over-written and overexplained, this has little of the dramatic concentration of Arrick's earlier novels. But Dory's slide into delinquency is convincing, and the family's division into isolated units is movingly depicted.

> *Hazel Rochman, in a review of "Nice Girl from Good Home," in* Booklist, *Vol. 81, No. 5, November 15, 1984, p. 435.*

As the story ends, all signs are encouraging; even Mom, in an institution where she is getting therapy, is slowly improving. Arrick's story is dark and starkly realistic; the characters are convincing and their problems (and solutions) believable; the one weakness of the book is that Dory's rebellion and her temporarily hostile attitude seem over-reactions. (pp. 59-60)

> *Zena Sutherland, in a review of "Nice Girl from Good Home," in* Bulletin of the Center for Children's Books, *Vol. 38, No. 4, December, 1984, pp. 59-60.*

The Hewitt family has always had everything: a large home, nice clothes, memberships in country clubs. But when Brady Hewitt suddenly loses his lucrative advertising job, his family is faced with a radical change in their lifestyle, one which none of them can accept. Brady finds solace in meaningless "job-hunting" treks to the city. His spoiled, child-like wife Deborah simply ignores their altered circumstances and continues to spend money and charge as if nothing had happened. A crisis arises when Brady orders his daughter Dory to return an expensive dress; Dory keeps it, wears it, and then, fearful of what she has done, discards it. Brady is furious, and Dory reacts to his fury by cutting school to hang out with the class lout. The two of them go so far as to plan a bomb threat, which Dory carries out to somehow get revenge on her father, a rather preposterous plot twist that is completely unbelievable, given Dory's somewhat pallid character. . . . Things begin to look up when Dory's older brother resolves to forgo college to start a house-painting business with his father—a highly unbelievable solution to the Hewitts' financial predicament. But it's all too late for Deborah, who is institutionalized. The novel lacks the power and believability of Arrick's ***Tunnel Vision*** because of a wildly unbelievable plot and flat characterization; Deborah may be typical of a lot of spoiled girls/wives/mothers, but her retreat into complete madness is simply not realistic, and Dory's reaction to her father's plight is also too fantastic to be believable. The book does, however, have something to say about money and status, and the tremendous value that many in our society place on them. Readers of Arrick's earlier books will probably want to read this one, but they may be more than a little disappointed in it.

> *Audrey B. Eaglen, in a review of "Nice Girl*

from Good Home," in School Library Journal, *Vol. 31, No. 4, December, 1984, p. 88.*

[*In the following excerpt, critic Mary K. Chelton refers to the rating system used by* Voice of Youth Advocates *magazine. "Q" is used to designate the quality of a book. A "4Q" rating signifies "better than most, marred only by occasional lapses;" a "5Q" rating signifies "hard to imagine it being better written."*]

With her usual skill and insight, Arrick covers a lot of territory, and all of it uniquely well—the father's despair at interviews with former colleagues who deem him "overqualified" without recognizing that he is desperate; the older brother's decision to postpone college and become a house painter to help out financially, even though it means giving up his dream of rooming with his best friend at school; Dory's inability to face the fact that she can no longer expect the luxuries her mother wants for her, and the divisiveness this decision causes between her parents; but the best characterization is of the mother. Deborah was a poor girl who married a wealthy man who promised to take care of her, and when he lost his job, she could not face returning to the poor 14-year-old inside herself and literally fell apart. The only reason that I gave it a 4 rather than 5Q is because of the unnecessary ending in which Dory visits her mother in a mental institution. It would have been a richer book if it had ended with the previous seven paragraphs depicting a tired commuter father returning from the city to greet a suburban wife and a little girl who calls out, "Hi Daddy, what did you bring me?" This entire story is about what happens when he can't bring her (wife and daughter) anything anymore. It is an important and vital story, well worth Best Books consideration, which should be widely discussed with and promoted to young adults. A possible secondary use would be the discussion of sex roles and the trauma wrought by buying into them and then, through circumstances beyond anyone's control, having the contract broken.

> *Mary K. Chelton, in a review of "Nice Girl from Good Home," in* Voice of Youth Advocates, *Vol. 7, No. 5, December, 1984, p. 261.*

Jeeter, Mason and the Magic Headset (as Maggie Twohill, 1985)

Author of the popular **Who Has the Lucky-Duck in Class 4-B?,** Twohill concocts another sprightly mix of magic and mirth, soaring off with Jeeter Huff's 10th birthday. Jeeter receives a Cabbage Patch doll she names Mason and a headset so she can listen to rock-and-roll horrors without blasting her parents and sister Carol-Ann out of the house. The little girl doesn't know that her secret wish for a fairy godmother has also been granted until a warning from the radio saves her from being run down by a 10-speed bike. Through the headset, Jeeter hears a boy called Mason giving her vital information each day. The phenomenon is greatly appreciated until Carol-Ann begins to lean on Jeeter, demanding that she get Mason to provide advice on attracting boys, on hairstyles and on passing school exams. This is the problem that Jeeter disposes of in the story's funny, surprising finale.

> *A review of "Jeeter, Mason and the Magic Headset," in* Publishers Weekly, *Vol. 227, No. 23, June 7, 1985, p. 81.*

The author has capitalized upon the current craze for Cabbage Patch dolls and integrated it into a clever, lively tale for pre-adolescents. Characters are believable, the dialogue and action on-target. It all makes you want to believe it could really happen. No problem novel here, just an entertaining story.

> *Margaret Gross, in a review of "Jeeter, Mason and the Magic Headset," in* School Library Journal, *Vol. 32, No. 1, September, 1985, p. 140.*

One-Way to Ansonia (1985)

The story of Rose, one of a large immigrant family, begins as she buys a ticket to Ansonia at Grand Central Station in 1899. Sixteen, she is taking her baby away from the squalor of tenement life, choosing her destination by what she can afford to spend for transportation. The story, told in separate episodes, then goes back to the arrival, six years earlier, of Rose and her siblings in New York; they were to be a surprise for their father's new wife, but they were all hastily put in separate but equally crowded homes and put to work. Rose was the rebel, willing to work hard but secretly going to night school—secretly because Papa wouldn't approve. Papa is a despicable character: selfish, deceitful, boastful. He is, however, more strongly drawn than anyone else. Characterization is good, but the book is weakened by the fact that it doesn't really have a story to tell (not usual in an Angell book) but seems to impose on a set of family reminiscences a picture of the living conditions and the beginnings of labor unrest in the factories and tenements of the Lower East Side.

> *Zena Sutherland, in a review of "One-Way to Ansonia," in* Bulletin of the Center for Children's Books, *Vol. 39, No. 3, November, 1985, p. 42.*

Once again Angell shows the struggle of a young girl trying to perserve her family, for by the time Rose reaches 16 she has worked for several years, married, and been a mother. Angell shows Rose's determination to be independent and to make a better life for herself despite the opposition of her father. The hardships the immigrants faced when they reached New York and their attempts to cling together are clearly shown.

> *Beverly B. Youree, in a review of "One-Way to Ansonia," in* Voice of Youth Advocates, *Vol. 8, No. 5, February, 1986, p. 382.*

Rose is different from her brother and sisters. She wants to learn English, to read and to write. She wants to pick out her own husband rather than one [her father] Moshe finds for her, even though she'd rather not marry at all. She is ambitious and in the course of this interesting story finds ways to achieve her ambitions.

For contemporary readers these ambitions don't seem too difficult. But for a young Russian immigrant in the late nineteenth century, they are revolutionary. Rose wants to fit into her new world, and does so, even though it causes consternation among her family. But despite Rose's revolutionary ideas, and her father's rather unusual method of parenting, the family stays close. This is the best lesson from this book—acceptance of change and honor of the parent. I recommend this book for the older adolescent.

> *Mary Perlick Finnegan, in a review of "One-Way to Ansonia," in* Best Sellers, *Vol. 46, No. 1, April, 1986, p. 38.*

Bigmouth   (as Maggie Twohill, 1986)

"Bunny was happiest when she was talking. And she was happy most of the time." The problem is that when Bunny Squill talks, she *can't* listen. She doesn't hear the skating-rink manager tell her that a party she's planning will have to be held on Friday; Bunny and her friends show up on Thursday. She's talking so fast when her father's boss calls that she mixes up the phone message—and accidentally sets the whole family packing up to move to England. When her mistake is discovered, Bunny shuts up for good. Family and friends, who are surprised to find that they miss her chatter, manage to coax Bunny out of her silence, in a funny, realistic ending. Readers, like Bunny's family, will put up with her endless monologues because she is so sweet and well-meaning—and because Twohill gives them a humorous closeup of a heroine rushing headlong toward disaster.

> *A review of "Bigmouth," in* Publishers Weekly, *Vol. 230, No. 18, October 31, 1986, p. 69.*

This fast-paced, often funny but gentle story ends on a satisfying note when Bunny learns to listen well enough to sing on key in the chorus for the annual community Christmas program at the local school. The story should appeal to young readers who may know someone (or themselves be) just like Bunny.

> *Virginia Golodetz, in a review of "Bigmouth," in* School Library Journal, *Vol. 33, No. 4, December, 1986, p. 110.*

The Weird Disappearance of Jordan Hall   (1987)

When 16-year-old Jordan Hall takes a job at a magic store, he has no idea what will develop. At first, Jordan is merely delighted to be working with his new girlfriend, Emma Major, whose father owns the shop. But when the store acquires a disappearing box once owned by the late, great magician, Louis Langhorn, Jordan's foray into the box renders him invisible. His state brings problems with Emma, of course. It's not much fun to date a "see through" boy, and there's the not-easily-solved puzzle of getting Jordan to materialize. This contains a few plot holes, including the exact method of Jordan's disappearance and the ramifications of it (hinted at in the story's conclusion), but on the plus side, this is brisk and breezy with plenty of appeal for those looking for a nondemanding read. Because Jordan and Emma are teenagers, this

story makes a good choice for libraries needing to beef up hi-lo shelves.

> *Ilene Cooper, in a review of "The Weird Disappearance of Jordan Hall," in* Booklist, *Vol. 84, No. 1, September 1, 1987, p. 57.*

Angell's premise is ripe with possibilities to amuse readers and keep them interested, but the novel fails in execution. While Jason is invisible, he does not have any of the lively experiences that readers might expect, thus limiting the appeal of the book. One inconsistency is the fact that although the objects that Jordan handles while he is invisible remain visible, his clothing does not, even when he changes clothes. The ending is a further let-down, as the secret of his invisibility is never revealed. This is a pleasant story, but there's no real magic here.

> *Laura Dixon, in a review of "The Weird Disappearance of Jordan Hall," in* School Library Journal, *Vol. 34, No. 3, November, 1987, p. 102.*

Judie Angell's mastery of her craft is attested to by the fact that she can make two such goody-goody characters as Emma Major and Jordan Hall so likable. Indeed, they are as amiable a pair of charmers as we've seen since Beaver Cleaver and big brother Wally grinned their way into American culture. . . . In a satiric style more subtly shaded than in **Suds,** Angell projects an image of two ideal teenagers as they cheerfully take exams, plan wisely for the future, and submit uncomplainingly to their parents' restrictions. The only dark cloud hovering over their otherwise golden days is the fact that they never get enough time to be alone together. Two nice young people obviously deserve whatever help they can get, and assistance of the supernatural sort isn't, apparently, too much to ask. The novel quickly takes on elements of fantasy as Jordan becomes invisible upon chasing a black cat into the tall "disappearing box." The inevitable problems arise, complicated by Jordan's conscientious concerns that he not miss an important math test or be marked absent in school when he is actually, though not visibly, there. Playing hooky is, of course, out of the question. Even the principal is enlisted as an ally by Jordan's earnestly possessive mother. One of the small wonders of the book is that Angell manages to make everything seem perfectly plausible without any apparent strain. A return trip to the box reunites boy and girl at the end, and although a somewhat weak plot is not quite a match for the sublimeness of the characters or the wit of the author, this crafty farce should find a wide audience.

> *Nancy Vasilakis, in a review of "The Weird Disappearance of Jordan Hall," in* The Horn Book Magazine, *Vol. LXIV, No. 1, January-February, 1988, p. 61.*

Leave the Cooking to Me   (1990)

Shirley Merton, 15, is lucky to have an attractive, talented mother who is single-handedly raising her two daughters while successfully running her late husband's law practice. Mrs. Merton has little time to cook, so Shirley has been at home in the kitchen for years when she impulsively accepts a job preparing a dinner party for a friend's mother, without her mother's knowledge or permission. With the first meal a resounding success, Shirley and her friends adopt the name "Vanessa" for their catering service and move on to other jobs, while the money rolls in. Problems arise when Shirley's mother finds a wad of cash, and worries that her daughter is into drug dealing. The climax comes when Mrs. Merton and her date are invited to a party catered by "Vanessa." Though shocked at seeing her daughter, Mrs. Merton's pride is soon evident, realizing that Shirley not only has a legitimate job, but that she's very good at it. The spirited third-person narrative is marked by lively dialogue, warm humor, and characters developed sufficiently to catch readers' interest, especially those who like to cook. So what if Shirley's cooking and organizational skills seem a bit unbelievable for a teen. Scenes like the one in which Shirley defeats an overconfident, handsome jock at tennis provide a light and amusing read.

> *Phyllis Graves, in a review of "Leave the Cooking to Me," in* School Library Journal, *Vol. 36, No. 1, January, 1990, p. 120.*

This book is a pleasant read, with a plot that moves along quickly, many comic moments, and light commentary on contemporary issues such as single parent households, sex roles, and teenagers' needs for independence and accomplishment.

> *Carleen Blake Ryan, in a review of "Leave the Cooking to Me," in* Voice of Youth Advocates, *Vol. 12, No. 6, February, 1990, p. 340.*

Don't Rent My Room! (1990)

Lucy Weber, 15, is upset that her parents have relinquished their respective careers in New York City to own and manage a Cape Cod inn. Her grandmother wants Lucy to stay in the city with her, but Mr. and Mrs. Weber insist that Lucy give the inn a try during summer vacation. Angell clearly depicts how the move, and running the hostelry, affect the family. Although this is supposedly Lucy's story, the emphasis intermittently shifts to her two younger brothers. As a central figure, Lucy is lamentably weak; she feigns interest in environmental issues to attract a new friend's brother, and feels immediately threatened when a week-long guest admires the fellow. The few elderly characters are portrayed in an unflattering light as well. The ending, however, manages to surprise, and the novel, despite its shortcomings, is a pleasant read.

> *A review of "Don't Rent My Room!" in* Publishers Weekly, *Vol. 237, No. 28, July 13, 1990, p. 56.*

Lucy and her brothers are surprised when their parents—a Wall Street broker and a university professor—quit their jobs to own and manage a Cape Cod inn. The transition from urban to rural living is a challenge to the entire family. While Mom and Dad struggle to keep the inn occupied and find a reliable waitress, 15 year old Lucy falls for a local boy and hopes to return to New York in the fall; Henry, 13, contemplates quitting school to become a commercial fisherman; and young Nathan discovers a ghost haunting the sleeping porch. A few other colorful characters complete the cast.

Despite a ghost, a hurricane, and a cute boy, this novel fails to generate much excitement. The story is told from various points of view which, rather than enhancing, distracts from the narrative. Younger readers may be interested in Lucy and her brothers; they will care less about the adult discussion of occupancy rates or aerobics class attendance. This is an adequate family story with a somewhat unexpected ending, which will appeal to Angell fans.

> *Judy Sasges, in a review of "Don't Rent My Room!" in* Voice of Youth Advocates, *Vol. 13, No. 3, August, 1990, p. 158.*

Though much of the story here is told from Lucy's point of view, the vantage point bounces from Weber to Weber; the writing and characterization are utilitarian, but the action does build and the denouement is both satisfying and believable. An entertaining page-turner by a veteran author of juveniles. (p. 1082)

> *A review of "Don't Rent My Room!" in* Kirkus Reviews, *Vol. LVIII, No. 15, August 1, 1990, pp. 1081-82.*

A lighthearted novel of family life. . . . [The] subplots are interesting enough, if predictable from the outset and occasionally preachy. The inn's guest list fills out the book's characters. Mr. Ainsley, an elderly year-round resident, helps Nathan Weber solve the mystery of the inn's ghost; and Cousin Joan, freshly dumped by her husband, ends up saving the day when a hurricane hits. The characterizations, save Lucy's parents, are adequate, and on the whole, they are an entertaining lot. Although the mood wanders as each of the various storylines comes up in its turn, it's a safe bet that ***Don't Rent My Room!*** will be enjoyed by young teens.

> *Joyce Adams Burner, in a review of "Don't Rent My Room!" in* School Library Journal, *Vol. 36, No. 9, September, 1990, p. 246.*

Lightweight entertainment in which sensible teenager Lucy has to decide whether to stay and help her family operate their newly acquired New England inn or return to New York for a school year with grandma. Characters are sunny and slight, as is the plot. . . . Then there's a silly subplot in which Lucy's youngest brother encounters and bests the inn's resident ghost. But the novel incorporates snatches of broad comedy—crotchety old Mr. Ainsley hears precisely what he wants to hear, and the chronic waitress shortage in the inn dining room becomes a hackneyed but pleasant joke. Those splashes of humor help push the book along and make it comfortable, undemanding reading.

> *Stephanie Zvirin, in a review of "Don't Rent My Room!" in* Booklist, *Vol. 87, No. 1, September 1, 1990, p. 44.*

Where'd You Get the Gun, Billy? (as Fran Arrick, 1991)

[*The following excerpt is from an advance review of* Where'd You Get the Gun, Billy?]

Classmates Liz and David can't believe that 16-year-old Billy shot and killed his girlfriend, but what they really cannot understand is how he got the gun in the first place. In this version of *The Story of a Penny*, the short and tragic history of a handgun is traced by a world-weary cop in a small upstate New York town. Cornered by Liz and David, Lieutenant Wisnewski explains about gun control and then constructs a hypothetical journey by which the gun gets to Billy. Strongly slanted toward handgun regulation, Arrick's novel sacrifices verisimilitude for tabloid-style sensationalism. The cardboard characters fit into shallow niches—preppies, battered wives, macho types—giving the novel a dated and didactic feel. The message is worthy, but the clunky approach will turn readers off.

> *A review of "Where'd You Get the Gun, Billy?" in* Publishers Weekly, *Vol. 237, No. 51, December 21, 1990, p. 57.*

While raising some of the key issues on gun control and violence, Arrick dilutes them with hypothetical convolutions, coincidences, eccentric occurrences, and twists of fate. If the intention is to demonstrate just how absurdly easy it is for teen-agers to get guns, the book fails: here it seems unrealistically difficult. The story's contrivances—cutting back and forth between scenes concerning the gun's journey and scenes with David, Liz, and the police officer—fail to obliterate the fact that it is a flawed moral lesson on a worthy cause, unworthily parading as fiction.

> *A review of "Where'd You Get the Gun, Billy?" in* Kirkus Reviews, *Vol. LIX, No. 1, January 1, 1991, p. 43.*

After Billy Federson kills his girlfriend, the victim's best friend and another boy in their school have one question. Where did he get the gun? A gruff-but-kindly policeman tells them—and us—a lengthy, contrived, and very silly tale of how Billy *might* have gotten the gun. Okay. *Maybe* a man bought it to protect his family but his wife freaked when she found the baby playing with it so she took it and maybe threw it into the woods where an old couple found it and took it home for make-believe target practice until maybe a thrill-seeking rich kid robbed them and took the gun to a party where maybe a girl intent on the thrill-seeker's attentions hid it in her purse to taunt him with later instead maybe lost it to a drug dealer while she was scoring some cocaine for her bored-debutante friend . . . if getting ahold of a gun were this complicated, gun control would be a dead issue. The vapid story is matched by the melodramatic style and characterization, and Arrick's paperback-romancing is shameless: "Her eyes glistened. 'You know what's awful, David? If it hadn't been for this, we probably wouldn't have even gotten to know each other. It took a tragedy for us to really meet.' 'Yeah,' he murmured." And why did Billy do it? A lack of self-esteem, of course.

> *Roger Sutton, in a review of "Where'd You Get the Gun, Billy?" in* Bulletin of the Center for Children's Books, *Vol. 44, No. 6, February, 1991, p. 136.*

As a teacher who has seen too many of her students die from handguns, I applaud this book, But will it affect the target audience? The title and the cover illustrations will make them check it out, but the story may lose them after the first chapter. The author starts with a fifteen-year-old being shot by her boyfriend. That part works fine, but then the author has a policeman telling two young people how the boy might have obtained the gun with hypothetical stories. That doesn't work well because the story becomes very dry. It should be in library collections simply because it might help someone.

> *Jennifer Brown, in a review of "Where'd You Get the Gun, Billy?" in* Children's Book Review Service, *Vol. 19, No. 8, March, 1991, p. 92.*

As in her other novels, Arrick skillfully personalizes a controversial social issue. Although readers meet the characters only briefly, their motivating experiences and psychology are authentic and representative of society's various reactions to a gun. As the weapon makes its way from owner to owner, the various ills of society that result in violence are visited. To her credit, Arrick portrays these ills as the real problem, and the availability of handguns as the catalyst that, mixed with emotional deprivation, anger, and fear, results in senseless deaths. The gun control issue is complex and deeply disturbing. This book offers no solutions, but with its straightforward style and episodic plot, it effectively examines the problem.

> *Ellen Ramsay, in a review of "Where'd You Get the Gun, Billy?" in* School Library Journal, *Vol. 37, No. 3, March, 1991, p. 211.*

Superbowl Upset (as Maggie Twohill, 1991)

Fifth-grade classmates Ginger Bidwell and Lucas Ridley, both avid sports fans, were rivals long before they became unwilling step-siblings four months ago—but their happy parents are unfailingly patient, even through most of the disasters. Mom wins a dream weekend for four—all expenses paid to the Super Bowl in New Orleans—during which *everything* goes wrong from the time the tickets don't arrive: the plane's late, obnoxious strangers "befriend" them, and then the replacement tickets never materialize, so that the family ends by watching the game on TV in their hotel room—in the company of several unwelcome extras. Predictably, Mom and Dad finally lose their cool, providing a negative example that nudges the kids toward beginning to mend their differences.

The situations here never get as comic as Twohill probably intended, perhaps because the family's difficulties are all too plausible; nor does she delve beneath the kids' bickering surface enough to make this more than another sitcom about learning to get along in a new family. Still, a moderately amusing, easily read example of its genre.

> *A review of "Superbowl Upset," in* Kirkus Reviews, *Vol. LIX, No. 5, March 1, 1991, p. 324.*

This novel's title is right on the mark for Twohill . . . fills her diverting plot with upsets aplenty—some of which will make middle-grade readers roar with laughter. . . . A feisty pet, an obnoxious, clinging family, irritating relatives who arrive unannounced and lost football tickets all add to the calamity—and hilarity. Twohill scores with this one.

> *A review of "Superbowl Upset," in* Publishers Weekly, *Vol. 238, No. 12, March 8, 1991, p. 74.*

This is competently written but plotted in almost-slapstick pattern, with a series of mishaps culminating in the family's watching the game on television, crowded into a motel room with obnoxious relatives on a surprise visit and with an even more obnoxious family who have pushed their way in. This is the sort of disaster humor that many children find hilarious; they'll tend to overlook the implausibility of the story.

> *Zena Sutherland, in a review of "Superbowl Upset," in* Bulletin of the Center for Children's Books, *Vol. 44, No. 9, May, 1991, p. 230.*

This could have been a hilarious story, but it falls short. . . . Confusion reigns at the beginning of the story as readers try to sort out the relationships, a situation caused by the children calling adults by their first names, including an aunt and uncle. The antagonists of the story, the aunt and uncle, and an obnoxious family at the airport are stereotyped to such a degree that they are one-dimensional. The parents are the best-developed characters as they grapple with the situations and two children who insist on not liking each other. The ending is much too pat; the characters suddenly seem to like each other and not mind the fact that everyone's trip is in tatters. Mediocre at best. (pp. 112-13)

> *Nancy P. Reeder, in a review of "Superbowl Upset," in* School Library Journal, *Vol. 37, No. 6, June, 1991, pp. 112-13.*

Valentine Frankenstein (as Maggie Twohill, 1991)

Amanda is Walter's only friend, and she can't understand why. He's nice, smart—so what if his laugh sounds more like a snort? That seems insufficient reason for the other fifth-graders to ridicule him. His low self-esteem and extreme shyness underscore the problem that, with Valentine's Day approaching, Amanda decides to rectify. She stuffs the class mailbox with valentines for Walter, all signed anonymously. The results are amazing: Walter's persona changes instantly and his classmates all start to like him. At first Amanda is thrilled, until her friend becomes too busy for her. Has she created some sort of Frankenstein? Twohill . . . explores the vagaries of popularity, the anguish of those wishing to achieve it and the wonders rendered by bolstering confidence. Though the premise is a bit farfetched (that Walter could go from laughingstock to junior BMOC in the course of a few days), Amanda cuts a spirited, thoroughly human figure. (pp. 72-3)

> *A review of "Valentine Frankenstein," in* Pub-

lishers Weekly, *Vol. 238, No. 50, November 15, 1991, pp. 72-3.*

Twohill has combined just the right amount of friendship and humor with a touch of boy/girl interest to create a readable, lighthearted story. Although the plot is predictable, the characters and situations are realistic and the result of Amanda's plan is hilarious. The ending is a bit too pat, but that won't matter to the young romantics who will enjoy this funny book.

> *Nancy P. Reeder, in a review of "Valentine Frankenstein," in* School Library Journal, *Vol. 38, No. 1, January, 1992, p. 117.*

Although the premise is overextended and the writing made occasionally bumpy by a shifting point of view, the story has a farcical tone that's a blessed breeze in the sometimes over-earnest world of middle-grade fiction. The resolution is fresh as well: Walter has changed, he's not going to follow Amanda around anymore, and she cuts her losses. A good follow-up to Barbara Cohen's *213 Valentines*.

> *Roger Sutton, in a review of "Valentine Frankenstein," in* Bulletin of the Center for Children's Books, *Vol. 45, No. 6, February, 1992, p. 171.*

At some point, a character remarks that she's seen this scenario before on television. The plot does seem like it fell right out of a sitcom, but kids won't mind that. The problems here are mostly structural: pointless passages, loose writing ("Most of the class tried hard to pay attention, but it was hard"), and characters who, except for Amanda and Walter, are almost indistinguishable. Still, a Valentine setting is always a winner, and Amanda and Walter are appealing. Title and dust jacket will sell the tale, but as much attention to detail should have been taken inside as out.

> *Ilene Cooper, in a review of "Valentine Frankenstein," in* Booklist, *Vol. 88, No. 12, February 15, 1992, p. 1107.*

What You Don't Know Can Kill You (as Fran Arrick, 1992)

[*The following two excerpts are from advance reviews of* What You Don't Know Can Kill You.]

Arrick's disturbing novel depicts the consequences of forgoing safe sex practices in these AIDS-stricken times. Ellen, 18, is smart, beautiful and has a bright future that is likely to include Jack, her longtime boyfriend. When her blood drive donation reflects the HIV virus, Ellen is sure it's a mistake—she and Jack have been monogamous—until he admits to a few sexual indiscretions while away at school. The story incorporates AIDS-related information, the need for friendship and familial support, the prejudices born of ignorance, and the psychological strains heaped on family members—Ellen's parents and Debra, her 13-year-old sister, are overwhelmed with grief. Although introductory portions of the narrative and some of the dialogue evince an unnatural tone, ensuing passages are filled with heartrending anguish and should dispel notions of "It can't happen to me" among careless, sexually active readers.

A review of "What You Don't Know Can Kill You," in Publishers Weekly, *Vol. 238, No. 53, December 6, 1991, p. 74.*

Despite the book's title, a rather mocking commentary on a harsh reality, Arrick deals with the issues surrounding AIDS with sensitivity. Unfortunately, she preaches at the expense of her narrative—facts pop up at random, often not very convincingly. Young adults may applaud Ellen's and Debra's strength and resolve, but the parents' inability or unwillingness to seek help, especially after so much time, is hard to believe. Not surprisingly, birth control, sexual activity, and safe-sex practices are addressed.

Karen Hutt, in a review of "What You Don't Know Can Kill You," in Booklist, *Vol. 88, No. 8, December 15, 1991, p. 758.*

While showing the broad, indiscriminate sweep of this national crisis is commendable, this novel is too short to delve into any aspect of it in more than a fleeting, superficial manner, and readers are bound to feel confused by the sheer number of the relationships of the many adults and teenagers involved. Plenty of solid information on AIDS is clumsily shoe-horned into the narrative; meanwhile, for those who believe themselves beyond the reach of this illness, Arrick does make a strong case regarding the possibilities for infection of the middle class mainstream.

A review of "What You Don't Know Can Kill You," in Kirkus Reviews, *Vol. LX, No. 1, January 1, 1992, p. 47.*

[Since] there's virtually no characterization, [this] book is really an endless series of sometimes confusing messages. Fact is occasionally subordinated to drama ("Ellen and Jack both had AIDS," states a paragraph, when they don't yet) but more often drama is subordinated to authorial infopreaching (Ellen's boyfriend, while proposing a suicide pact, raves "You have to get your T-4s checked every few months . . . !" to which Ellen responds "If you had a support system you wouldn't even consider this suicide talk"). A few sensible statements come from Debra ("She was stupid not to make him wear a condom"), but otherwise Ellen is portrayed as a shining martyr to romantic love, betrayed by an erring knight. We know even nice people can contract HIV and that they need help if they

do, and it's laudable to want to make this clear to those most in need of the information, but it takes more than a mission to make a good book. For a fictional look at teens and AIDS, skip this and try Doris Humphreys' *Until Whatever;* to bring home the reality of the people who suffer from it, look at Susan Kuklin's *Fighting Back.* (pp. 147-48)

Deborah Stevenson, in a review of "What You Don't Know Can Kill You," in Bulletin of the Center for Children's Books, *Vol. 45, No. 6, February, 1992, pp. 147-48.*

Set in yuppie east coast suburbia, this story provides a vehicle for lessons on AIDS, safe sex, and facile comments about a serious social problem. What romance exists in the plot is quickly erased by the concerns of family and community under assault. The novel deals with contemporary issues, but it's full of heavy-handed didacticism. The AIDS dilemma demands strength of character and logical behavior instead of panic-driven, knee-jerk reactions. A book that offers little except the warning to practice safe sex, or to abstain.

Gail Richmond, in a review of "What You Don't Know Can Kill You," in School Library Journal, *Vol. 38, No. 2, February, 1992, p. 107.*

This treatment of sexually active teenagers and AIDS is both delicate and urgent. . . . The horror and denial of AIDS is poignantly portrayed through the reactions of Ellen, Jack and the members of Ellen's family. Furthermore, they all face hostility from the community. There is no indication that sex for Ellen and Jack is promiscuous, although it is premarital. Taking responsibility for the consequences of sex is demonstrated when, earlier in the story, Ellen gets birth control pills. Readers can see that this is no protection against AIDS. The book contains very little profanity and no detailed accounts of sex. The title itself will draw students to the book, and the way the subject is handled will make an impact on the reader. Highly Recommended.

Pam Whitehead, in a review of "What You Don't Know Can Kill You," in The Book Report, *Vol. 11, No. 1, May-June, 1992, p. 41.*

Guy (René) Billout
1941-

French-born American author and illustrator of nonfiction and picture books.

Major works include *Number 24* (1973), *Stone and Steel: A Look at Engineering* (1980), *Thunderbolt and Rainbow: A Look at Greek Mythology* (1981), *Squid and Spider: A Look at the Animal Kingdom* (1982).

INTRODUCTION

Billout is the creator of informational books that take an uncustomary approach to conventional subjects and challenge readers of all ages to view the familiar with new insight. Typically, his works discuss educational subjects through factual texts that are enhanced by his comic paintings. As he states in a postscript to *Stone and Steel,* "Even though the technical details are as exact as I could make them, this book is not a reference book; my main purpose was to convey a poetic mood." Billout's first book was the wordless, fanciful *Number 24,* in which a commuter stoically waits for his bus while numerous vehicles—including a tank, plane, rowboat, and steamshovel—pile up in a massive accident at his bus stop; Selma Lanes calls this work "as mysterious as a roomful of René Magritte paintings and equally Gallic in flavor." While his later books feature a variety of subjects, Billout's approach to his work has been consistent. Although critics have sometimes questioned whether Billout's texts are too difficult or dry for young readers, his illustrations are praised for their exceptional execution and unique vision. His stark, poster-like watercolor paintings, with large expanses of space, bold color, and precise linear perspective, are distinguished by such whimsical touches as a man chasing his hat in front of the Boone windmill and a snake encountering its own tail while winding through a topiary maze.

After studying at a school for applied arts in Paris, Billout worked as a designer in that city for six years. Following the publication of *Number 24,* he wrote and illustrated *By Camel or by Car: A Look at Transportation* (1979). In this work, Billout examines fifteen types of transportation, including the camel, bus, balloon, plane, and spaceship. For each, he writes a paragraph of historical and technical information and a paragraph of personal experiences or reminiscences. When explaining travel by boat, for example, he relates that as a child observing ships at sea he "could not figure out how huge steel ships could stay afloat when the tiniest stone would sink right down to the bottom." Coupled with the text, Billout presents pictures which show colorful, exact representations of each mode of transportation. Each illustration also contains Billout's trademark: a surreal twist which helps the reader contemplate the subject in a new, often humorous way. Considered by many the most notable example of Billout's style, *Thunderbolt and Rainbow: A Look at Greek Mythology* envisions a visit to Manhattan by Greek gods. While the text

gives information about the gods and attempts to explain natural phenomena through a series of thought-provoking comparisons, the illustrations offer young urban dwellers a novel view of city sights. For example, readers find Zeus poised on top of the World Trade Center, ready to hurl his lightning bolts until he notices a "Throwing Objects Is Forbidden" sign; steam escaping through a grate in the sidewalk is accompanied by an explanation of Hephaestus, the god of fire and smiths; and Hades is depicted as an unlit subway tunnel. In two additional books, *Stone and Steel* and *Squid and Spider,* Billout explains the function of several worldwide architectural structures and examines animal behavior while placing each animal in an unconventional urban setting that according to Ilene Cooper "will get observant readers giggling, thinking, or both." Billout was presented with two gold medals from the Society of Illustrators in 1974, and his works have appeared on several best-illustrated lists.

(See also *Something about the Author,* Vol. 10 and *Contemporary Authors,* Vols. 85-88.)

TITLE COMMENTARY

Number 24 (1973)

A surreal work, as mysterious as a roomful of René Magritte paintings and equally Gallic in flavor, it tells wordlessly of an anonymous little man, briefcase in hand, who patiently awaits the arrival of a No. 24 bus. Though car, tank, plane, rowboat and steamshovel appear inexplicably over the horizon, they are summarily (and with deadly logic) dispatched. At last, the long-expected bus arrives, picks up the hero and rides off. There has probably never been a book that so perfectly captures the feel of waiting for something to happen—that odd admixture of suspense, frustration, anger and emptiness. The children in my family loved it.

> *Selma Lanes, "In Paperbacks, Picturebacks and More," in* The New York Times Book Review, *November 4, 1973, p. 30.*

Using no text, Billout employs surreal, futuristic drawings to tell of an exceedingly patient, briefcase-carrying commuter who waits at Bus Stop #24 while a series of vehicles travel by him, each colliding with the preceding one. Only after this bizarre parade, which includes a locomotive, a tank, a rowboat, an ocean liner, airplanes, and a troop of knights in armor, does he eventually board Bus #24. Children might respond to the visual humor on a surface level but will be confused by the man's unresponsive presence; symbolic meaning—that no disaster deflects programmed modern man from his routine—is strictly for adults.

> *Judith Shor Kronick, in a review of "Number 24," in* School Library Journal, *Vol. 20, No. 6, February 15, 1974, p. 59.*

[*Number 24*] is a nonsensical, uninteresting book with airbrush drawings of a man waiting at a sign with 24 on it, with each vehicle that approaches him—an auto, a biplane, a rowboat, being smashed by a larger vehicle until the bus number 24 approaches, with the front cover showing that the bus also will be smashed. Not funny even in terms of slapstick.

> *William Anderson, in a review of "Number 24," in* Children's Literature: Annual of the Modern Language Association Seminar on Children's Literature and The Children's Literature Association, *Vol. 3, 1974, p. 217.*

By Camel or by Car: A Look at Transportation (1979)

Whether one travels by haughty camel, the inefficient auto or any of the other 14 modes of locomotion described here, Guy Billout is a superb companion and guide. Throughout the text and in his spectacular illustrations he always has reins, wheel or stick firmly in hand.

For each conveyance he devotes a succinct paragraph of description—history, weight, speed, fuel consumption and life expectancy—followed by another paragraph of personal recollections or observations. Of the spaceship he notes that "When using their space suits astronauts wear diapers." Playfully he recalls his childhood awe of ocean vessels with "I could not figure out how huge steel ships could stay afloat when the tiniest stone would sink right down to the bottom."

It is in his stunning poster illustrations that Mr. Billout sets new records for creativity on land, sea and in the air. Bold, colorful and precise, his illustrations are dominated by a stark linear perspective and are tinged with a slightly mordant wit. There is a sizable gap in the elevated ocean highway the motorcyclist has just passed over; a bicyclist stands alone with his machine on a snow-covered Alpine peak; two trucks seem headed for a collision on a ribbon of road hugging a canyon wall; subway riders awaiting the A train are a rat, rabbit and fox attired as human commuters.

With French-born Guy Billout you can get from here to there in grand style—in fact, first class all the way.

> *George A. Woods, in a review of "By Camel or by Car," in* The New York Times Book Review, *October 14, 1979, p. 40.*

The illustrations in Guy Billout's picture book on transportation are wonderful: clear, simple nearly to the point of austere yet meticulous in detail, with a bold use of color, and a linear perspective that is long and expansive. (The sole disappointment lies in his one use of smiling, clothed animals waiting for a train.) Opposite each drawing is a page with a short factual paragraph on the particular mode of transportation, followed by a paragraph of personal memories or sentiments, sometimes relating to his coming to the United States from France or to his experiences in the war. While the personal touch is interesting and vivid, it may not easily be understood by the very young and is not written in a vocabulary they readily could comprehend. But this matters not, as the illustrations redeem all and even young children will enjoy them. Other picture books on transportation tend to focus on one mode; although Swallow's *Cars, Trucks and Trains* (Grosset, 1974) is miniencyclopedic and geared to a similar age group, it is less contemporary than futuristic, with unaltered Anglicisms, and without Billout's art work. (pp. 71-2)

> *Connie Tyrrell, in a review of "By Camel or by Car," in* School Library Journal, *Vol. 26, No. 4, December, 1979, pp. 71-2.*

Excellent, colorful illustrations are featured in this offbeat introduction to different modes of transportation. After a brief description of each transportation system, with notes on its historical development, the author enlivens his text with personal anecdotes and observations. The statistical data, although accurate in detail, seems a little much for the author's young readers. Certainly such statements as "The four turbofan engines deliver a total of 175,000 pounds of thrust . . ." calls for an adult's interpretation and explanation.

> *Douglas B. Sands, in a review of "By Camel or by Car: A Look at Transportation," in* Appraisal: Children's Science Books, *Vol. 13, No. 2, Spring, 1980, p. 15.*

From By Camel or by Car: A Look at Transportation. *Written and illustrated by Guy Billout.*

Stone and Steel: A Look at Engineering (1980)

Stone and Steel: A Look at Engineering is similar [to Alan Lewis's *Super Structures*], but tries to be more poetic—the illustrations by Guy Billout have a certain cartoon-like quality, like frames from an animated film. They are pleasing, but the text is more like a set of captions than anything else, and tells little. The focus is more on how things work than on how they are made, and the amiable quality of this book is just not quite enough to make up for the lack of information on how these works of engineering are actually constructed, which may frustrate even younger children.

> *Paul Goldberger, in a review of "Stone & Steel: A Look at Engineering," in* The New York Times Book Review, *November 9, 1980, p. 67.*

Pittsburgh's Cathedral of Learning, India's Towers of Silence, the Hoover Dam, and others are each twice-seen on large, facing pages: in diagrammatic outline with a scattering of factual text and in accurately rendered, full-color, poster-like paintings. Billout's colors are individual, evocative rather than true-to-nature, suavely "arty": reality seen through a special lens. As in fairy tales, the real and magical worlds seamlessly blend in the paintings, as when a sea serpent matter-of-factly pokes its head out of the waters off Boston Bay, taking the measure of the Minots

Ledge Lighthouse, which Billout, keeping a straight face, reports "took 5 years to build . . . was completed in 1860 . . . is built of 1,079 stones." Readers anxious for "the facts" will find their curiosities whetted if perhaps not satisfied; daydreamers will be well in their element.

> *Leonard S. Marcus, "Down with The Empire State Building," in* Book World—The Washington Post, *November 9, 1980, p. 12.*

Billout presents engineering marvels in a readable style with historical development of the ideas. The illustrations are drawings made from photographs by the author with imaginative embellishments that will delight children of all ages. His choice of stone and steel structures in Europe, Asia and America gives the reader an appreciation for the contribution engineering makes to all world cultures. Although the author's intent "was to convey a poetic mood," the facts are there and the presentation is delightful. Billout recognizes the renowned architects of the buildings but, alas, the engineers remain anonymous. The author's postscript should be read first since it explains the art form of the presentation, which might be useful for art classes. Parents and teachers will find the material useful for reading to groups of children from kindergarten through the fifth grade.

> *S. W. Dobyns, in a review of "Stone & Steel: A Look at Engineering," in* Science Books & Films, *Vol. 17, No. 1, September-October, 1981, p. 34.*

Thunderbolt and Rainbow: A Look at Greek Mythology (1981)

Guy Billout was born and raised in France, and he has the great French gift of style and discretion. His earlier books for children—***Number 24, By Camel or by Car*** and ***Stone & Steel***—revealed him as wonderfully, blessedly, mercifully sparing—both in word and image. There was no excess in those bracing volumes.

In ***Thunderbolt & Rainbow*** he starts from a daring premise and proceeds with brilliance and economy. What if the Greek gods no longer inhabit Mount Olympus? What if they have moved to Manhattan?

It was a very good notion. Manhattan is all the world, to those who live in it and like it. Myth and legend are of its very nature. Going about our daily business, we see symbol and portent on every hand. Sometimes the myths in question are Wagnerian, with Valhalla somewhere up in the smog and Nibelheim, that place of dread and oppression, way down below. But on those clear dazzling days with which Manhattan is so often blessed it is of the Greek gods and their disorderly offspring that we think first.

Guy Billout begins at the beginning, with Zeus on top of the World Trade Center. Zeus has his thunderbolts at the ready, only to be halted by a sign that says "Throwing Objects Is Forbidden." Should we sit back and congratulate ourselves on the triumph of civic good sense? Not yet: Mr. Billout reminds us that lightning and thunderbolt between them may still zigzag down inside one of the tall buildings that we throw up in such profusion.

This is primarily a picture book, and it shows us a great city purified, simplified and depopulated: a Precisionist Manhattan, the art historians might say. But on every facing page there is a short text that keys us in. Roosevelt Island in Mr. Billout's hands turns into the distant fastness in the Tyrrhenian Sea, the home of the winds. When steam rises through a downtown grating, Mr. Billout identifies it as the work of Hephaestus, god of fire and of smiths. Our familiar yellow taxi, at large in the deserted street, turns into Helius's golden chariot. Looking along 51st Street from west to east at dawn, we see at the end of it a pinkish glow; and thanks to Guy Billout we recognize that inconsolable Eos has just passed by on her way to shed "the tears that appear each morning in the form of dewdrops sparkling on flowers, grass, and trees."

In this way, imaginations are stretched and familiar sights made new. *Thunderbolt & Rainbow* convinces us that the Greek gods and goddesses have indeed taken up residence in Manhattan, and that like so many other immigrants they feel perfectly at home. And what a pretty book this is! Brief, in this case, is beautiful.

> *John Russell, in a review of "Thunderbolt & Rainbow," in* The New York Times Book Review, *November 29, 1981, p. 42.*

Winner of awards for *Stone & Steel* and other impressive nonfiction, Billout presents a witty collection of Greek myths as well as an epitaph to the modern American myth, King Kong. (All the yearning ape needed, the author notes, were Zeus's thunderbolts to conquer his foes and rule forever on top of the Empire State Building.) The writing is swift and unfailingly interesting in paragraphs about the foibles, fads, rivalries and tragedies caused by Uranus, Poseidon, Eos, Selene, et al. But the genius effects are found in the big, full-color paintings that suggest *art-nouveau* influences. Each scene is a familiar part of New York City, territory of a particular god. The most fitting is the domain of Hades: a dark subway tunnel.

> *A review of "Thunderbolt & Rainbow: A Look at Greek Mythology," in* Publishers Weekly, *Vol. 220, No. 23, December 4, 1981, p. 50.*

The old myths get a little ribbing in this book, but Billout's poster-like illustrations, . . . have a classical simplicity and austerity. Billout, a talented French graphic artist, and the author most recently of *Stone & Steel,* here juxtaposes brief summaries of the Greek myths with illustrations of eerily unpopulated cityscapes of New York. . . . There is a subtle humor in these juxtapositions, and an occasional incongruity (such as a tugboat pulling a bridge in a spread on the river gods) that should delight the observant child, but Billout's text is awfully flat and he does not always seem to have a sure sense of what he is up to—why, for instance, does King Kong make an appearance in the last spread? Was there ever so hairy an Olympian?

> *Brigitte Weeks and Robert Wilson, in a review of "Thunderbolt & Rainbow: A Look at Greek Mythology," in* Book World—The Washington Post, *January 10, 1982, p. 10.*

This op-pop-mythology picture book makes an important cultural statement. The undistinguished text is, literally speaking, your basic Encyclopedia Mundane, as tedious as only a synoptic retelling of Greek myths, peppered with dead deities' names, can be. The illustrations are stunning, striking, original. Featuring great, flat masses of urban structures cubistically bisected by shadow and a sickly light, they bespeak the void the deadness of the gods. Of the seven faceless human beings in the book, each is either fleeing or looking into an emptiness, as does Zeus on the cover. Geometries, surfaces, wedges of flat color juxtaposed against the bland, dry text, make their own statement. Zeus is a thin thread of lightning just barely able still to touch a skyscraper wedged between other buildings; Eos (Dawn) a white sun rising weakly in a flesh-colored urban sky; and Helius (Sun) merely a short-lived reflection on concrete surface. The typeface on the cover suggests a machine manual. Billout's earlier *Number 24,* stylistically similar, had a warm whimsy. None of that here. *Thunderbolt & Rainbow,* by its very chill, is a significant reflection of the age in which all myth is dead.

> *Peter Neumeyer, in a review of "Thunderbolt & Rainbow: A Look at Greek Mythology," in* School Library Journal, *Vol. 28, No. 6, February, 1982, p. 64.*

This experimental book does not always succeed, but when it does the artistic interpretations are stunning. Billout takes natural phenomenon such as the stars and fire, explains them simply in terms of Greek myth, and then sets them visually in the steel and concrete splendor of New York City. Thus, the sun's travels are depicted here as a yellow taxi cruising at dawn. Making use of cool, clear colors and intriguing shadows, he provides art almost deco in its simplicity. The pictures can be admired on their own but are sometimes obscure in relation to specific details of the text, while the last vignette, which portrays a modern mythical figure, King Kong, is humorously incongruous with the general tone. A clever teacher, parent, or librarian could make much of this, and most children will need that kind of guidance to catch the book's subtleties.

> *Ilene Cooper, in a review of "Thunderbolt & Rainbow: A Look at Greek Mythology," in* Booklist, *Vol. 78, No. 14, March 15, 1982, p. 955.*

Squid and Spider: A Look at the Animal Kingdom   (1982)

"Handsome is as handsome does," a persnickety grade school teacher of mine used to say. And by this unbending standard, Guy Billout's latest illustrated book warrants less than unqualified praise. As always, the artist's pictures are handsome indeed, as well as arresting and eloquently expressive of their creator's antic outlook on the world.

Mr. Billout's animals no longer roam in the wild; instead they seem entirely acclimated to man's increasingly cultivated domain. A septet of elephants ambles across a suspension bridge; a snake meets up with its own tail while traversing a topiary maze; an ostrich struts on a well-manicured golf course (presumably it can bury its head in a sand trap if the going gets rough). But the mostly factual text accompanying each flight of graphic fancy is curiously random and often trivial.

The wittiest of the illustrations are somehow diminished by the adjoining words, and the reader's ultimate reward is only the merest smattering of information about each creature under scrutiny. Mr. Billout's jacket illustration and final page, which suggest a puzzling latter-day Noah's Ark framework for the intervening art and text, add yet another confusing element. In all, it is an oddly disjointed and uneven work.

> *Selma G. Lanes, in a review of "Squid & Spider," in* The New York Times Book Review, *December 19, 1982, p. 26.*

Billout, who last brought his quirky perspectives to Greek mythology in **Thunderbolt and Rainbow,** now sets his sights on the animal kingdom. Tigers, wolves, and snakes are among the 13 animals treated in short paragraphs containing miscellaneous facts and in startlingly attractive full-color pictures. As before, Billout places his subjects in unusual situations or habitats that will get observant readers giggling, thinking, or both. In some pictures, the irony is obvious; for instance, there is one depicting a buffalo crossing the tracks in front of a derailed locomotive. Less clear to readers might be the picture of the elephant who looks as if he's about to jump off a bridge (the text discusses elephant death practices, though bridge jumping is not one of them). Few artists can match Billout's stark, cool-colored pictures for sheer style, but adults may need to show young readers how to get below the art's topmost layer. Excellent for use with gifted children.

> *Ilene Cooper, in a review of "Squid & Spider: A Look at the Animal Kingdom," in* Booklist, *Vol. 79, No. 13, March 1, 1983, p. 902.*

Crocodiles cannot survive in sewers, nor do ostriches hide their heads in sand, nor elephants seek to die in secret graveyards. Taking thirteen familiar animals, the author deftly dispenses with a few myths, offers some interesting and unusual information, and skillfully whets the appetite of the curious reader. The brief text is lighthearted, accurate as far as it goes, and has nothing whatsoever to do with an encyclopedic discussion of animal habitat or life

cycles. For most readers it will be the illustrations which dazzle and capture the imagination. Vanishing points plunge to distant horizons; bright colors glow in clearly delineated landscapes where space and mass are carefully balanced. Some of the pictures, however, are puzzling; for instance, why is the giraffe eyeing two sculptured horses in a fountain? A few of the pictures perhaps require some knowledge: Does the young eagle view the olive branch and the clutch of arrows by his nest as portents of a future likeness on a dollar bill, and is that King Kong amid the skyscrapers? No matter. With their sly wit and eye-catching brilliance the illustrations are striking and memorable.

> *Ethel R. Twichell, in a review of "Squid & Spider: A Look at the Animal Kingdom," in* The Horn Book Magazine, *Vol. LIX, No. 2, April, 1983, p. 181.*

"Do elephants, like humans, ponder about the finality of death?" Thirteen one-page essays—often difficult in vocabulary, syntax and ideas—present miscellaneous bits of information on selected animal species. The text appears to have been contrived as an accompaniment for a collection of striking paintings and includes odd bits on myth, behavior and human attitudes and misconceptions towards the particular animal. The bold, flat pictures are surreal, sardonic and comic at times, ranging from a string of elephants crossing a high steel and concrete bridge to Santa Claus throwing out gifts to appease a pursuing wolf pack as a single reindeer pulls his sleigh across the snow. The final page depicts pairs of animals aboard a modern steamship with only the top of the Chrysler Building above water; opposite is a passenger list of animal classes and the number of species in each. Larger collections and libraries having a readership for sophisticated picture books will find that this extends the range of material in this format.

> *Margaret Bush, in a review of "Squid & Spider: A Look at the Animal Kingdom," in* School Library Journal, *Vol. 29, No. 8, April, 1983, p. 120.*

Francesca Lia Block

1962-

American author of fiction.

Major works include *Weetzie Bat* (1989), *Witch Baby* (1991), *Cherokee Bat and the Goat Guys* (1992).

INTRODUCTION

A writer for young adults whose originality and inventiveness has prompted both controversy and comparisons to such distinguished authors as Paul Zindel and M. E. Kerr, Block examines serious themes concerning love, identity, and the meaning of life in works that integrate contemporary Los Angeles popular culture with elements of fantasy and folklore. Written in a prose style described by Roger Sutton as "post-modern poetry" and Patrick Jones as "slam-slam-bang, punk-inspired, pop-culture-driven, sentimental-tone prose poetry," her works revolve around the character Weetzie Bat, a young Hollywood punk with a blond flattop who yearns for security and affection. The daughter of divorced substance abusers, Weetzie befriends Dirk, a boy from her high school with similar longings. Weetzie and Dirk, who is gay, find love respectively with My Secret Agent Lover Man and Duck, a blond surfer. The four cohabit, raising two children, Cherokee Bat, daughter of Weetzie, Dirk, and Duck, and Witch Baby, My Secret Agent Lover Man's child from a previous relationship. Block chronicles the exploits of her characters, who appear to have limitless talent and money as they pursue a basically adult-free lifestyle punctuated by exotic dishes, patio parties, and cruises in expensive cars, with an abundance of detail that reflects glamorous particulars, fairy tale touches, and hip cultural references. Underneath this bright and quirky surface, Block addresses the struggle to retain idealism despite the harsh realities of modern living. Through their surrogate family, the characters develop a bond that sustains them as they face cynicism, cruelty, and other experiences that threaten their love and loyalty. Underscoring Block's themes is her portrait of Los Angeles and its alternative subculture, which she defines with such images as harlequin sunglasses, slam dance clubs, and houses decorated, as Weetzie's is, with "beads and feathers, and white Christmas lights, and dried roses." Reviewers generally agree that Block's style is highly distinctive, a reflection of her characters and setting that ranges from whimsical to dark in tone. As Patrick Jones has written: "All of these stories are told with wildly imaginative prose and dialogue loaded with L.A. 'slanguage,' making Block, operating alone in her genre of fantastic realism, a unique voice in young-adult literature."

A native Angeleno, Block grew up in an artistic family: her poet mother and painter father, who inspired Block's love of myth through his drawings and bedtime stories of Greek legends, encouraged her early interest in writing. While still in high school, Block saw a teenage hitchhiker in a 1950s prom dress and cowboy boots. Picturing her as epitomizing the essence of Los Angeles, Block later no-

ticed a similar girl in pink sunglasses, driving a pink car with license plates reading "Weetzie," and thus christened her fictional character. Weetzie was to become the subject of cartoons and short pieces of fiction Block wrote while in high school; later she assembled the stories into a book-length manuscript which was published without revision as *Weetzie Bat.* This first book chronicles Weetzie's search for love and stability, aided by a genie who grants her three wishes. Weetzie's requests—partners for her and Dirk and a home for them all—reflect predominantly orthodox concerns. Although there are fairy tale elements in the work, they are coupled with such real-life traumas as infidelity and death. Significantly, the book ends with Weetzie's assertion: "I don't know about happily ever after . . . but I know about happily." *Witch Baby* is a sequel which explores the emotional turmoil of its title character, now a teenager who uses drumming and photography as a means of catharsis. Distressed by feelings of isolation within her extended family, she leaves home to find her birth mother and an answer to her query, "Where do I belong?" *Witch Baby* concludes with the family reunited, after the characters affirm their love and learn to accept one another unconditionally. In *Cherokee Bat and the Goat Guys,* Cherokee, now also a teenager, and Witch

Baby are left in the care of the Native American holy man Coyote, a family friend. Along with their associates Raphael Chong Jah-Love and Angel Juan Perez, Cherokee and Witch Baby form a rock band, The Goat Guys. Coyote presents each member with a magical totem that represents parts of a Pan-like mythical goat. The potency of the gifts, which evoke hedonistic behavior, overwhelms the group and leads to decadence and self-abuse. Much more grim than Block's earlier books, *Cherokee Bat and the Goat Guys* takes its characters into the depth of excess, but ends with their rite of passage leading to both remorse and wisdom.

Block's books, especially popular with young adults on the West Coast, have been given a mixed reception by adults. Although they stress the importance of the family and other traditional values, the works have been reproached for their seeming approval of teenage sexual relations and a bohemian lifestyle. Although Block does not depict sexual scenes, drug abuse, or unconventional behavior in graphic detail, her casual approach to sexuality and her characters' autonomy from parental supervision has raised objections from some commentators as well as the public and school librarians who have refused to carry her books. Others, however, have praised Block for her authentic depiction of a particular locale and an unusual and intriguing way of life. As Patty Campbell has written: "Trying to analyze these delicate contemporary fairy tales is dangerous, like pulling off a butterfly's wings to find the flutter. But it is important to understand that the setting is not fantasy—Ms. Block writes about the real Los Angeles better than anybody since Raymond Chandler. . . . [She] is a brilliant addition to the canon of respected young-adult authors."

GENERAL COMMENTARY

Patrick Jones

"Love is a dangerous angel," writes Francesca Lia Block—author of the young-adult novels *Weetzie Bat, Witch Baby,* and *Cherokee Bat and the Goat Guys*—and so is she. She's not dangerous to her readers, but she scares those who evaluate and buy young-adult materials. Not that her reviews have been negative; she's received glowing reviews. Yet almost every one conjured up the twin specters of "unconventional" and "controversial." That is strange, because in many ways Block's books are conventional young-adult literature, just much better than most. The controversy centers not so much around the usual suspects—sex, violence, or foul language—but rather the alternative lifestyles of Block's characters. The passion and division which Block creates in the YA world is not new: in fact, it is as old as contemporary young-adult literature itself.

S. E. Hinton helped create that literature with *The Outsiders, That Was Then, This Is Now,* and *Rumble Fish.* Although all are now considered classics, there was a certain amount of controversy over them when they first came out. Librarians were concerned about the tone, the matter-of-fact violence, the lack of adult role models, and the

starkness of the message about trying to grow up good in bad times. (p. 697)

Block's books have provoked controversy for many of the same reasons that Hinton's did: tone and language; matter-of-fact attitude (in Block's case, about sex rather than violence); the lack of adults and conventional families; and the overriding concern about becoming a good person in a world filled with death and disaster. Idealism in the face of realism is the common theme: Hinton's Pony Boy talks about "staying gold" just like Weetzie Bat says, " 'I don't know about happily ever after . . . but I know about happily.' "

To summarize the Bat "almost-family" saga, begun in *Weetzie Bat:* in Los Angeles, a.k.a. Shangri-L.A., a.k.a. Hell-A, Weetzie bonds with Dirk in high school because he's the only one who understands. They find a magic lamp and then love, Weetzie with My Secret Agent Lover Man and Dirk with Duck. The four of them have a baby, Cherokee Bat, together; another child, Witch Baby, is left on their doorstep, a reminder of My Secret's past. They form an extended family, adding friends and pets, while spending their time listening to punk music, eating a lot of great food, and living an L.A., materialistic life. They find independence through this new family. In the second book, Witch Baby rejects her extended family, seeking out love and her own place in the world. *Cherokee Bat and the Goat Guys* finds Cherokee seeking excitement when her family is away. Using music as her method, Cherokee forms a band and strives for success. All of these stories are told with wildly imaginative prose and dialogue loaded with L.A. "slanguage," making Block, operating alone in her genre of fantastic realism, a unique voice in young-adult literature.

Characters in literature and real people do not—except perhaps in Los Angeles—have names like My Secret Agent Lover Man. Right from the beginning readers are alerted that something is strange here, as the line between fiction and fairy tale is blurred. *Weetzie Bat* is based on the story of the genie and three wishes; *Witch Baby* on "once upon a time"; while *Cherokee Bat* is a replay of *The Wizard of Oz,* as each character acquires something to make him or her whole. With characters with wild names, magical transformations, and spaced-out dialogue, it is not possible to read Block as one would the straight narratives of S. E. Hinton. Hinton's language was Tulsa tough; Block's world is that of punk/pop culture L.A. Terms like *slinkster* and *clutch pig* come not just from the mouths of characters but from the voice of the author. Block also draws upon L.A. pop culture for numerous references. At times her books seem less novel and more travelogue for those wanting to find the hip and well-read—and well-fed, for there are many references to food. As Hinton did with her working-class neighborhoods, Block draws the reader into her settings with her eye for detail and catalogue of cool. For the hour it takes to read one of Block's books, one can't help but be pulled into Weetzie's world.

And a wild world it is. Hinton's world was one of violence and desperation; Block's is one of love and extravagance. Hinton's characters are poor without many prospects, while Block's crew are artists with seemingly unlimited potential, talent, and cash reserves. Pony Boy's desperation breeds violent reaction, but Weetzie only wants love of all kinds, including sexual. Just as Hinton approaches violence in a matter-of-fact way, Block writes similarly about the sexual habits of her characters. In ***Cherokee Bat,*** the sexuality is more pronounced than in the other books—the sexual drives of the characters are much stronger, and so is the description.

It's not that the sex is explicit; it is not. It is just that Block's characters *have* sex lives. Young-adult books are only about sex to the extent that it is the "problem." Not so in Block: there is no hand-wringing, no stock scenes of visits to birth-control clinics, and no anguished decision-making. Block's not saying teen sex is right, but she's not saying it is wrong, either. In the age of AIDS—whose ugly shadow appears—anything less than a "safe sex or no sex" stance is bound to be controversial. The most controversial aspect of the books, according to most reviews, is the homosexual relationship between Duck and Dirk. Duck, Dirk, and Weetzie make a baby together, and it is valued as a good thing. This situation is hard for many adults to handle. Again, there is matter-of-fact feeling to the description of an alternative lifestyle—it is just not a big deal in their lives or in their family.

The whole concept of the Bat extended family is perhaps the strongest element in Block's books. There are some minor older adult characters, but for the most part, in all these books, adults are absent. As a family saga, however, we do get to see Weetzie and the others as adults after ***Weetzie Bat,*** but they are adults with such a different perspective from any other in young-adult literature that they might as well be adolescents. In the first book Weetzie gets along just fine without adult supervision. In ***Cherokee Bat,*** the rest of the Weetzie clan is away making a movie, so Cherokee and the band are left on their own. The group of friends/lovers/band members then becomes the surrogate family, just as the gang does in Hinton's novels. Thus, to steal a phrase from the 1992 political landscape, the controversy over Block comes down to a question about "family values."

Could there be a more loving family than that of Weetzie Bat and her clique? Like Hinton, these characters are not the product of happy two-parent households, yet somehow they turn out all right—thanks in part to the love of their surrogate families. The characters don't live in a conventional world: they live in one that was handed them and that they have shaped by making the best choices they can. The Bat family is probably the closest and warmest to appear in young-adult literature in a long time. Even though it is an alternative arrangement, it is one that readers will be able to relate to and might even wish they were part of.

As in most great literature, Block doesn't create pretty pictures; she presents mirrors in which readers may find reflections of their own emotional lives. The basics of adolescent developmental tasks are explored: the search for independence (***Weetzie Bat***), acceptance and identity (***Witch Baby***), and excitement (***Cherokee Bat***). Block's slam-slang-bang, punk-inspired, pop-culture-driven, fable-laden, sentimental-tone prose poetry both under-

lines and distracts from her basic themes. *Underlines* because the unique language backs up the uniqueness of the characters; *distracts* in the same way the language of Tom Robbins or John Irving does—with rampant cleverness overload.

Because of the style or the fiction/fairy tale mix, or maybe even because of the strange, dreamlike L.A. setting, the truth is that many adolescents and many more librarians just don't understand the books. They can't get past the weirdness to meet the characters. Circulation of Block's books, in my experience, is limited. I've given them to The Cure rock band fan-club kids, and they've loved them, but unlike Hinton, who reaches most adolescents, Block hasn't broken through in the same way. Hinton also appeals to a larger age range, while Block seems appreciated mostly by older adolescents. There's an audience for her books, but it is probably small and made even smaller by the lack of access many might have to her work. Despite the rave reviews, fears about the alternative lifestyles in Block's books have kept them out of many school and public libraries.

Yet, considering how concerned librarians are about finding multicultural literature, why are we not concerned with *sub*cultural literature? Although punk has perhaps peaked on the coasts, in the rest of the country libraries see their share of mohawks, skateboards, and "Sid Lives!" T-shirts. Except for *Crosses* by Shelley Stoehr . . . there are few other books with punk characters. Like Hinton's greasers, these are characters who aren't normal and who delight in it.

Weetzie Bat and its sequels are books that remind us why we need separate young-adult collections. I can't imagine having these titles in a juvenile section; I can't imagine a young-adult collection that wouldn't want them. They divide the YA world along institutional lines: many public librarians love them; many school librarians hate them. Block demonstrates what S. E. Hinton did twenty-five years ago—that there are still lines to cross in young-adult literature and that the journey is well worth it. (pp. 697-701)

Patrick Jones, "People Are Talking about . . . Francesca Lia Block," in The Horn Book Magazine, *Vol. LXVIII, No. 6, November-December, 1992, pp. 697-701.*

Patricia J. Campbell

Driving north on Fairfax in my old VW van, I pass the Farmer's Market, where I sold melons and figs when I was in college, and where Weetzie Bat bought plastic palm tree wallets and tomahawks. Up the street is the silent movie house, with pictures of Charlie Chaplin looking like My Secret Agent Lover Man, and Canter's, where I adore the hot pastrami but Weetzie prefers the potato knishes. A little farther on, the street is lined with Jewish bakeries, falafel restaurants, and strange dark shops like the place where Witch Baby found the globe lamp. I turn a corner, find the address I am looking for, and park under the row of double pink oleanders that line the curb. Across the street is a witch's house with a roof like spilled silly sand.

This is Francesca Lia Block's Los Angeles—and mine. A

native Angeleno, I fled my hometown three years ago, driven out by the darkness that is the flip side of Shangri-L.A. But now I am back for a day, seeing it all through Weetzie's pink Harlequin sunglasses, and it looks good. I've come to meet the author of *Weetzie Bat, Witch Baby,* and *Cherokee Bat and the Goat Guys* and to satisfy my curiosity about the person whom Michael Cart of the Los Angeles *Times* called "one of the most original writers in the last ten years." And to gather material to offer another perspective on her work from that of Patrick Jones, who in his article in the November/December 1992 issue of the *Horn Book* referred to Block's world as "strange" and "dreamlike."

It is a striking literary irony that Block's work is perceived as fantasy. Although there are magical elements in her books and the tone is pure fairy-tale, I know of no other writer who has written so accurately about the reality of life in Los Angeles—or one of many realities that make up this complex multicultural city. I know because I've been there. I grew up in the Hollywood Hills, just one canyon over from the neighborhood where Vixanne Wigg presided over the Jayne Mansfield coven. When I was a child I could see the Hollywood sign from my bed at night, and I know what a feat it was for Weetzie and My Secret Agent Lover Man to climb up there with real wine glasses in their backpack, because I've done it. I used to live at Venice Beach, where Duck and Dirk and my surfer son occasionally slept on the picnic tables. Three of my children were born at the Kaiser on Sunset, where Brandy Lynn gave birth to Weetzie and where Weetzie gave birth to Cherokee. As Charlie Bat did, I took my children to Kiddieland when they were little, and my parents took me to the Tick Tock Tea Room when I was little. As a child I roamed the wild hills and canyons that are in the midst of the city and occasionally saw a holy man like Coyote living in a shack on a mountaintop. Like Weetzie's family, I've hosted parties in the back yard under twinkling trees where the table was decorated with Guatemalan fabric and roses in juice jars, and the food was a reasonable facsimile of Vegetable Love-Rice and Jamaican plantain pie, depending on the ethnic propensities of the guests. Weetzie and Brandy Lynn and Duck and Dirk and Darlene are all, with a change of names, people I've known.

Will I recognize Francesca Lia Block, too, I wonder, as I ring the bell? The door is opened by a tall, slim young woman with long dark hair, who welcomes me in. At first glance I think the house is unoccupied because it is so bare; then I recognize the simplicity as art. A few pieces of furniture hold single pieces of fine pottery or sculpture, and one high cabinet is topped with a pair of antlers. A far cry from Weetzie's house strewn with "beads and feathers, and white Christmas lights, and dried roses." We sit on a pale pink sofa, and she offers me iced pink peppermint tea in a handblown Mexican glass.

Francesca Lia Block is definitely not Weetzie Bat, I decide—a conviction that is only a little shaken when she explains that this house belongs to her brother, an actor. Perhaps Witch Baby? True, she has long tilty eyes and is wearing black cowboy boots, but her smooth, dark brown hair has no tangles, and her manner is serene and elegant. (pp. 57-8)

She grew up in Los Angeles, of course, in this very neighborhood, and then just over the hills in the San Fernando Valley in her teen years, where she went to North Hollywood High. Her father, a renowned painter, and her mother, a poet, nurtured her talents from the beginning. "I always did write, as far back as I have memories," she says. Her parents read to her a lot—"there were always books"—and encouraged her work. In school she was in gifted programs and developed a circle of close likeminded friends, with whom she played imaginative games in which they made up magic lands. She remembers her childhood as "very peaceful," although in adolescence she had "a couple of really bad years."

In high school she and her friends were enchanted with Hollywood. In a recent article in the Los Angeles *Times Book Review* she describes how they used to drive through Laurel Canyon in a vintage blue Mustang convertible. On one of these trips they passed "a punk princess with spiky bleached hair, a very pink '50s prom dress, and cowboy boots" with her thumb in the air. The image stayed in Block's mind as the spirit of Los Angeles, and later, when she spotted another blonde pixie wearing big pink Harlequin glasses in a pink Pinto on the freeway, the license plate "WEETZIE" gave the image a name.

Block went on to study English literature at the University of California at Berkeley. There a poetry workshop led by Ron Loewinsohn and a class in the modernist poets taught by Jayne Walker solidified what Block was trying to do with "concrete imagery, yet very spare." She wrote a number of minimalist short stories under the guidance of Loewinsohn, and did her thesis on Emily Dickinson and Hilda Doolittle. During this time of very intense reading and growth, she became nostalgic for Los Angeles, and for her own consolation put together a little book about the punk princess, who had already been the subject of some stories and cartoons that Block had done in high school. "I didn't take it very seriously at the time," she remembers. "It felt so personal to me, and not like my more serious work."

But shortly after she graduated, a family friend sent a copy of the manuscript to Charlotte Zolotow of HarperCollins, who immediately recognized its quality and offered to publish it as a young-adult novel. Block was thrilled at the prospect of working with the famous editor whose books had been an important part of her childhood. "*Mr. Rabbit and the Lovely Present* is like one of my top ten books ever," she enthuses. *Weetzie Bat* was published just as she wrote it; *Witch Baby* needed more editorial work. Like the character, "it was tangly." Since the publication of *Cherokee Bat and the Goat Guys,* she has been at work on a fourth book about Weetzie's family, *In Search of Angel Juan.* An adult book, *Ecstasia,* is forthcoming in May from New American Library. Although the story, like *Cherokee Bat,* is about a group of young people who form a band, it is, as Block explains, "very, very different. The first part is based on Orpheus, the second part on Persephone, and it has a lot to do with the idea of aging and how the world responds to that."

Thinking of Patrick Jones's rueful report that many librarians are put off by what they perceive as the strangeness of Block's ambiance, I ask, "Why do you think people who haven't lived in Los Angeles see it as so unreal, not just your books, but the whole L.A. experience?" "Well," she muses, "I haven't had experience with a lot of other places, so in a way I take it for granted, but I think that what is reality for us here may just be very foreign to them."

But why should that be? Many novels are set in New York, and while readers in other parts of the country notice that it is not their reality, they are willing to accept it as a valid or even enviable way to live. No one thinks those books are strange or labels them as depicting "an alternative lifestyle" because the characters ride to work on the subway or shop at Bloomingdale's or live in apartments with doormen. Why should the second largest city in the United States be perceived so differently?

It is doubly puzzling considering that America sees mostly Los Angeles every night on television. But the downtown of "L.A. Law" is a very different place from the Los Angeles that Francesca Lia Block celebrates. The secret neighborhoods of L.A. and the people who really live there are invisible to television and to most visitors to the city. Weetzie's L.A. is made up of Hollywood and the Beverly-Fairfax district; the canyons, especially Laurel and Beachwood; Venice Beach; and Silverlake—areas that are geographically widely separated but culturally contiguous. Block is documenting a very particular time and place, and she has got it exactly right. Far from being subcultural, this setting is upper middle-class—a fact that Block admits but finds uncomfortable. As Jones noted, Weetzie and her family have unlimited time and money for their happy pursuits and pretty toys—although they would most certainly reject his adjective *materialistic* as descriptive of their attitude toward them.

Block's strong sense of style pins down "the time that we're upon." Images are very important to her—a fact that she feels stems from the influence of her artist father—and she uses not only pictures but smells and textures and tastes to evoke mood, place, and character with great economy. As a minimalist, she is a master of the single telling detail—Brandy Lynn's gold mules with clusters of fake fruit over the toes, for instance. Her bent for poetry suffuses her style, as in the tender scene of My Secret Agent Lover Man's return, where the sweetness of the couple's loving forgiveness is symbolized by the morning light on the flowers heaped on Weetzie's bed.

More fallout from Block's background in poetry is her sure feel for rhythm, as in phrases like "the singing trees and the early traffic," or "what time are we upon and where do I belong?" So I was not surprised to hear her talk about her lifelong love of dance. She is currently taking classes in ballet and in modern and Brazilian dance and has studied African dance. The three books have several cathartic celebrations where the whole company, even the puppies, get up and "toss their heads, stamp their feet, shake their hips, and begin to dance."

An element in Block's work that is often overlooked is the

humor stemming from the collision of the fairy tale and the real world. Perhaps the best example is Weetzie's attempt to cure My Secret Agent Lover Man of the effects of the witch's curse by giving him megadoses of vitamin C and putting on videos of cartoons. The incongruities resulting from the ethnic and racial mix of L.A. are also amusing—Valentine and Ping's lunch of noodles and coconut milk shakes, for instance.

Block's satirical ear for voices is keen. She is too good a writer to fall into the easy trap of producing a gloss of currency with popular slang. Nothing dates a book faster, as any young-adult specialist is well aware. Phrases like *clutch pig* and *lanky lizards* are not real "L.A. slanguage," as Jones assumes, but words coined by Block and her friends and used as tags for characters. But she does capture the way particular kinds of people talk, and the type of things they say—the punk, the aging starlet, the beach ex-hippie, the surfer. Duck, after all, never refers to anything as *gnarly*, but his voice is no less authentic for that.

Under this dazzling stylistic surface are stories that wrestle with the hard facts of pain and evil. As everyone who watched the riots knows, terrible things can happen in the city where it's never winter and the jacaranda always blooms. Block is keenly aware of the paradox of L.A., "where it was hot and cool, glam and slam, rich and trashy, devils and angels." This duality extends to her characters. The darkness of Witch Baby, who tapes newspaper clippings of dreadful happenings to her wall, and her father, My Secret Agent Lover Man, who agonizes in the night over such things, is contrasted with the lightness of blonde Weetzie's loving optimism and Cherokee's potential as "White Dawn."

Block's most intriguing creation is Witch Baby—"who is not one of them." With snarls on her face and in her hair she rollerskates through a nightmare of loneliness, carrying the world's pain on her small shoulders. In her angry self-alienation she represents the powerful but unacceptable part of every teenager that skulks and watches and cares for nobody while caring for everybody. I ask Block about the meaning of Witch Baby's puzzling behavior at the beginning of *Cherokee Bat and the Goat Guys,* where she burrows into the mud as a seed. "In the sense of the earth and nature . . . Witch Baby is always kind of curling up—her toes curl and everything. At the same time she's going to blossom in a way; she's going to grow and change out of that. She's going to get wings, you know, so she's going to ascend."

Witch Baby is a raven; Cherokee is a deer; and Raphael is a dreaming obsidian elk. The atavistic animal elements in *Cherokee Bat* form a metaphor that resonates to the dawn of mythology. The head with antlers is one of the oldest human symbols. The horned and goat-legged god Pan, in his total detachment from any social or moral value, is the most ancient god in the Greek pantheon. Dionysus and his accompanying goat-satyrs pursued the wild Bacchantes or Maenads, who gave themselves up to ecstatic states. More soberly, the Blackfoot Indians and other Native Americans revered the principle of acquiring power through identifying with the energies of certain animals.

"I've always had a thing about fauns and satyrs," says Block. "That human/animal split really fascinates me. My Dad would draw a lot of them, and talk about them. He told me Greek myths for bedtime stories. The animal thing of this book, the idea of them coming into their sexuality and the wildness of it . . ." The theme appears in the chapter titles: Wings, Haunches, Horns, Hooves, Home. These are the totems that Cherokee begs from Coyote as costumes for the rock band that she, Witch Baby, Raphael, and Angel Juan have formed. Patrick Jones compares them to the gifts of the Wizard of Oz that bring wholeness to the characters, but this is a misunderstanding. In fact, these gifts bring power beyond the control of the recipients, power that almost destroys them. The hooves, horns, and feathers are given for a price paid by both giver and receiver, and in the end the gifts must be returned, sacrificed for redemption.

Cherokee's initiation into the great adult secret of sex and the fever of sensuality that consumes the two pairs of young lovers ought to be the most uncomfortable aspect of Block's work to date for those who are made nervous by such things. Although there are no explicit descriptions of sex, Block has made the wildness of uncontrolled ecstasy very vivid—but also the nastiness and the perils. As Patrick Jones observed, these are books about love and family. But love is a dangerous angel in the nineties, whose wings cast a dark shadow over all three books—and over all young people's lives. Block is acutely aware of "the AIDS thing. It's something so huge—I just get overwhelmed. I mean, it's hard enough to be my age dealing with it, but I try to imagine what it would be like to be a teenager now—to be thirteen or fourteen, and to not only be afraid of all the normal things, but AIDS, too." She feels that this sense of encroaching darkness pervades her work. "People need help in thinking about it," she says, and hopes that her books have provided at least "one little tiny touch on that."

Francesca Lia Block's works have been referred to as "Mozartean." There is a deliciousness of detail, a deceptive smallness and lightness, a distilling of the style of a particular time and place, and a serious contemplation of life and death under the sparkling surface. Block is a brilliant addition to the canon of respected young-adult authors. Block's readership may be small in Patrick Jones's part of the country, but it is certainly large on the West Coast. I do, however, agree heartily with Jones that "there are still lines to cross in young-adult literature and that the journey is well worth it"—and that it would be a great shame if the extraordinary books of Francesca Lia Block were kept from young people by even one librarian's fear of the unfamiliar. (pp. 59-63)

Patricia J. Campbell, "People Are Talking about. . . Francesca Lia Block," in The Horn Book Magazine, *Vol. LXIX, No. 1, January-February, 1993, pp. 57-63.*

TITLE COMMENTARY

Weetzie Bat (1989)

Only in Los Angeles. Like much of the new-wave culture it celebrates, there's no doubt that this is the kind of book that's mostly style: " 'You are my Marilyn. You are my lake full of fishes. . . . my pink Cadillac, my highway, my martini, the stage for my heart to rock and roll on, the screen where my movies light up,' he said." That's My Secret Agent Lover Man comforting Weetzie Bat after the death of her father. Weetzie met My Secret Agent Lover Man when a genie gave her three wishes. My Secret Agent Lover Man was one, a beautiful house was another, and "a Duck for Dirk" the third. Dirk is Weetzie's best friend, a Duck is a cute guy, and with the genie's help, Dirk meets the perfect Duck named Duck and everybody moves into a beautiful house (left to Dirk by his just-dead Grandma Fifi), where they all have a baby, Cherokee Love. Oh, and don't forget Cherokee's evil twin, Witch Baby: "As soon as she could talk, she would go around chanting, 'beasts, beasts, beasts,' over and over again." Stranger than any of this is the fact that the author makes it all work. Her theme is friendship, her tone affectionate, her imagery sentimental but true to type. The prose alternates rhapsodies-in-neon with I-can-read conversations: " 'I feel weird,' Weetzie said. 'Me too,' Dirk said. Duck scratched his head." You will too, but despite its startling subject matter, this is one innocent—*sweet*—book.

Roger Sutton, in a review of "Weetzie Bat," in Bulletin of the Center for Children's Books, *Vol. 42, No. 6, February, 1989, p. 142.*

A brief, off-beat tale that has great charm, poignancy, and touches of fantasy. Weetzie, now 23, is a child of Hollywood who hated high school but loves the memories of Marilyn Monroe and Charlie Chaplin, plastic palm-tree wallets, and the rollerskating waitresses at Tiny Naylor's. She wears a bleached-blond flattop and Harlequin sunglasses, covers her '50s taffeta dresses in glittery poetry, and sews fringe down the sides of her minis in sympathy with the plight of the Indian. Nobody understands her, least of all her divorced bicoastal parents, until she meets Dirk, who takes her slamdancing at the hot clubs in L.A. in his red '55 Pontiac. When he tells her he's gay, they decide to go "duck-hunting" together. He meets his ideal blond surfer, and Weetzie finds her Secret Agent Lover Man. They all move in together, make movies that become underground successes, and have a baby. This recreates the ambiance of Hollywood with no cynicism, from the viewpoint of denizens who treasure its unique qualities. Weetzie and her friends live like the lillies of the field, yet their responsibility to each other and their love for the baby show a sweet grasp of the realities that matter. As in Rosemary Wells' *None of the Above* (Dial, 1974), these kids spend no time considering college or career. Their only priority is finding love and keeping it once they find it. " 'I don't know about happily ever after . . . but I know about happily,' Weetzie Bat thought." (pp. 116-17)

Anne Osborn, in a review of "Weetzie Bat," in School Library Journal, *Vol. 35, No. 8, April, 1989, pp. 116-17.*

The most satisfying thing about Robinson Crusoe is the way he creates a home out of nothing, which is what many children in our society must do to survive, and what the children in these two novels do. Eleven-year-old David, in

[Dean Hughes's] *Family Pose,* is an orphaned runaway who finds shelter in a Seattle hotel, where the night-shift staff becomes a makeshift family. . . .

[*Weetzie Bat*] is a punk, young adult fairy tale, an ingeniously lyrical narrative of two friends, Weetzie and Dirk, who weave a nest of Hollywood illusions and hardcore loyalty. . . . Although each of the four main characters is shaken by a terrible loss, the group survives through the knowledge that they are all each one has. "Love is a dangerous angel" and can bring pain, but the bond is primitively strong. "I heard that rats shrivel up and die if they aren't, like, able to hang out with other rats," Duck says.

While the characters reach adulthood and assume responsibility for their lives, they evince the innocence and effervescence of a fancied childhood. The book is full of magic, from the genie who grants Weetzie's wishes to the malevolent witch Vixanne, who visits the family three times. There are beauties and beasts and roses, castles and Cinderella transformations. What *Family Pose* develops with traditional realism, *Weetzie Bat* achieves through vivid imagery. Ms. Block's far-ranging free association has been controlled and shaped into a story with sensual characters. The language is inventive Californian hip, but the patterns are compactly folkloristic and the theme is transcendent. "I don't know about happily ever after . . . but I know about happily," Weetzie Bat thinks at the end.

These books are both entertaining. Credibly, even indelibly, they tell children that every adult results from a child, outgrown or not, who needed family. They both tell us that we can take our families where we find them or, lacking the luck to find them, make new ones. This is a poignant message and one desperately needed in an era of broken bonds. Beyond the immediate impact of both stories is another implication: the power of human imagination is such that even books can become family.

> *Betsy Hearne, "Pretty in Punk," in* The New York Times Book Review, *May 21, 1989, p. 47.*

This is a slice of hip L.A. life with a cast of characters thus: Weetzie Bat, My Secret Agent Lover Man, Duck, Dirk, Cherokee, Witch Baby—a collection of caricatures or occult figures? It's difficult to decide.

The book is an acquired taste and the reaction of the reader is likely to be strong. I feel that cult status is sought here, but the cynical reader might accuse Block of parody. I'm very curious to see what my 4th and 5th year pupils will make of this book—88 pages of confusion or amusement?

> *Val Randall, in a review of "Weetzie Bat," in* Books for Keeps, *No. 63, July, 1990, p. 16.*

Wow! I haven't read a YA novel like this since the '70s when people like M. E. Kerr, Kin Platt, and Paul Zindel were shaking up the field. Block writes in a candy-colored fairy tale style that perfectly captures the flavor of contemporary L.A. *Weetzie Bat* is funny, entertaining, and poignant. Highly recommended. (p. 5)

> *Fran Lantz, in a review of "Weetzie Bat," in*

> Kliatt Young Adult Paperback Book Guide, *Vol. XXV, No. 6, September, 1991, pp. 4-5.*

Witch Baby (1991)

This sequel to the extraordinary *Weetzie Bat* revisits L.A.'s frenetic pop world, again using exquisitely crafted language to tell a story whose glitzy surface veils thoughtful consideration of profound contemporary themes.

Witch Baby—child of Weetzie Bat's lover (My Secret Agent Lover Man) and taloned Jayne Mansfield-groupie Vixanne Wigg—is at odds with all her complicated family (which still includes gay lovers Dirk and Duck). She's jealous of Weetzie's daughter Cherokee, beloved of Raphael, biracial son of other characters in book #1; she's a drummer whose music echoes her inner turmoil and a photographer whose disturbing shots reflect her distress at the world's horror—a glowering personality whose excesses trouble both herself and others. Still, like Weetzie Bat's, Witch Baby's quest for meaning ends on an up beat: though her first love is deported to Mexico, there's hope of finding him again; meanwhile, her honesty results in a reconciliation between Duck and his mom; Witch Baby also learns who her "real" parents are and returns to the fold after meeting the many-masked Vixanne.

Like her adoptive mother, Witch Baby is painfully aware of many kinds of cruelty—to the homeless, to the environment, to people who are "different"; but, again, generosity and love triumph in a far-from-perfect world. Block's deft wordplay, connections, and allusions continue to delight in this satisfying extension, which will be most easily enjoyed by those familiar with the earlier book.

> *A review of "Witch Baby," in* Kirkus Reviews, *Vol. LIX, No. 15, August 1, 1991, p. 1007.*

This sequel to *Weetzie Bat* lights up readers' smiles and touches the heart just as its predecessor did. Block takes Witch Baby through her search for the answer to the question, "What time are we upon and where do I belong?" Witch Baby feels separate from the other members of her extended family. They love her, but she thinks she doesn't belong. She acts out her isolation through her photographs of the family, which all exclude her; through her collection of newspaper articles of various disasters; and through acts of hostility such as pulling apart her semisister Cherokee's kachina Barbies. She ultimately finds her birth mother (who escapes life's pain in the Jayne Mansfield Fan Club), realizes her place in the family, and teaches them all some lessons in understanding. Block's writing features charming imagery, gently surreal characters and events, and the recurring theme of tolerance through love. In *Witch Baby* she also explores the danger of denying life's pain. Only by facing ugliness can one begin to change it and to appreciate its accompanying happiness. Block has a limited but devoted audience—she may be just a tad too southern California sophisticated for broad appeal. Nevertheless, she's a superior writer and has created a superior cast of characters.

> *Ellen Ramsay, in a review of "Witch Baby,"*

in School Library Journal, *Vol. 37, No. 9, September, 1991, p. 277.*

The reviewer's best friend is the easy comparison. "Leon Garfield is a 20th-Century Dickens." "Charles Dickens is a 19th-Century Leon Garfield." And so on. Imagine the reviewers' discomfort, then, when Francesca Block's first young-adult novel *Weetzie Bat* was published, and readers discovered one of the most original books of the last 10 years. The best we critics could do was to describe it as a punk fairy tale. If that meant that the eponymous heroine Weetzie and her film-maker husband, My Secret Agent Lover Man, lived happily ever after, what of the other members of their nontraditional family, Dirk and his lover Duck of the perfect blond flat top, and what of the two little girls, Cherokee and Witch Baby, whose respective parentage is . . . problematical? What became of them? In Block's wonderful new book, *Witch Baby,* we find out. The answers are as unpredictable as those that concluded the first book. If "once upon a time" is the setting of this sweetly satisfying sequel, then—its heroine Witch Baby wonders—"What time are we upon and where do I belong?" How Witch Baby undertakes to discover these answers is the substance of this extraordinary encore story.

Michael Cart, in a review of "Witch Baby," in Los Angeles Times Book Review, *October 27, 1991, p. 7.*

Cherokee Bat and the Goat Guys   (1992)

Block's third visit to the pop L.A. world focuses on Weetzie Bat's teenage daughter and her lifelong friends Raphael, Witch Baby, and Angel Juan, who start a rock band (the "Goat Guys") while their parents are in South America making a film, leaving the kids in care of Native-American friend Coyote. In outline, *Cherokee* is simpler than the earlier books: four chapters ("Wings," "Haunches," "Horns," "Hooves") portray the young musicians' rite of passage into adulthood as each receives, as an apparently liberating gift, an object representing part of a mythical goat. Their empowerment is Faustian: the joy of creating the music and of sexual awakening are both lost in the demands of success and the seductions of the drug culture. Fortunately, this is a fable; in the last chapter ("Home"), Coyote awakes from his "Dreaming of past sorrows and the injured earth" to help his young friends recall themselves to a more wholesome being as their parents return.

More predictable than *Weetzie Bat* or *Witch Baby*, but Block continues to illuminate serious contemporary themes with fresh, tellingly allusive imagery and a wonderfully lyrical and original style. Not to be missed.

A review of "Cherokee Bat and the Goat Guys," in Kirkus Reviews, *Vol. LX, No. 13, July 1, 1992, p. 846.*

While Coyote is a tiresomely sentimentalized Noble Native American, and the author's rhapsodic segues occasionally verge on self-parody, this is a stronger book than its vague predecessor *Witch Baby,* with both the language

and the action controlled by the folkloric patterning that made *Weetzie Bat* so convincing. Block can effectively turn from swooning romance to scary cocaine sequences; the darker scenes, in fact, reveal a power in her writing that's been untested by the charming whimsy for which she has been celebrated.

Roger Sutton, in a review of "Cherokee Bat and the Goat Guys," in Bulletin of the Center for Children's Books, *Vol. 46, No. 1, September, 1992, p. 6.*

Three years ago *Weetzie Bat* burst on the young adult book scene like a rainbow bubble showering clouds of roses, feathers, tiny shells and a rubber chicken. Hardened critics, who thought they had seen all the possible variants of the coming-of-age novel, were astonished by the freshness of Francesca Lia Block's voice.

Since then there have been two sequels of increasing depth and beauty of imagery. Trying to analyze these delicate contemporary fairy tales is dangerous, like pulling off a butterfly's wings to find the flutter. But it is important to understand that the setting is not fantasy—Ms. Block writes about the real Los Angeles better than anybody since Raymond Chandler. The sensuous details sprinkled like sugar on a cookie—the streets, restaurants, flowers, costumes, food—ground the stories in reality, although such L.A. waking dreams seem the stuff of illusion to New Yorkers like Weetzie's father, Charlie Bat. This is not the style of Beverly Hills, nor the West L.A. of transplanted Easterners, but of the secret Angeleno neighborhoods of Silverlake and Melrose-Fairfax and Laurel Canyon where, like Weetzie's bizarre family, people really do have parties among the purple jacaranda and poison pink oleanders in backyards strung with twinkling lights. . . .

[With] her *Cherokee Bat and the Goat Guys,* Ms. Block's distinctive style has taken on breadth and sureness in a story that resonates with arcane animal symbolism and explores the dark power of unleashed sexuality. Weetzie and the rest of the family have gone off to South America to make a movie, leaving Cherokee and Witch Baby, now teenagers, in the somewhat casual custody of their Native American friend Coyote. No sooner are they gone than Witch Baby, still dysfunctional, burrows into the mud in the garden shed, pretending to be a seed, and refuses to come out. To save her, Cherokee goes to Coyote at his mountaintop retreat and is given feathers by the wind, which she makes into wings for her "almost-sister." Together with her lifelong friend, Raphael Chong Jah-Love, whose parents have also gone off with the film crew, Cherokee plans a party to entice Witch Baby out of the shed. The long-lost Angel Juan Perez, Witch Baby's childhood love, arrives, and she emerges to play her drums for him and receive her magical wings.

The four of them form a rock band that they call the Goat Guys, but their first attempt to play in a nightclub is a failure, and Raphael grows remote and despondent. Cherokee again appeals to Coyote. Goats come out of the hills to him to be shorn, and Cherokee makes pants like goat-haunches with the fur. Wearing them, Raphael emanates lust and power. He and Cherokee burn with lovemaking, and onstage the group becomes a wild success. But Angel

Juan is jealous of Raphael's popularity, so Cherokee begs Coyote for his sacred goat horns as a performance costume for Angel. Coyote refuses to give her the powerful totem antlers, but Witch Baby steals them, and soon she and Angel Juan are also swept away. A mysterious package arrives for Cherokee; in it are a pair of boots like goat hooves that torture her feet but make her dancing a Dionysian frenzy.

The group descends into the bacchanalian hell of the nightclub scene with its tequila and cocaine, skull lamps and lingerie-clad groupies drenched in cow's blood. When Angel Juan slashes himself onstage, Cherokee knows it is time to quit, to give back the horns and fur. But the others protest that they need their costumes for a party they are giving the next night for the record companies. At the height of the wild destructive festivities, Coyote arrives at last to save them.

In a quiet final scene of repentance and redemption, they each reluctantly renounce the power of their totems and give back the wings, haunches, horns and hooves to the natural world, to be cleansed of the pain and guilt. But not before they have cleaned up the house.

> *Patty Campbell, in a review of "Cherokee Bat and the Goat Guys," in* The New York Times Book Review, *September 20, 1992, p. 18.*

Matt Christopher

1917-

(Also writes as Fredric Martin) American author of fiction.

Major works include *The Lucky Baseball Bat* (1954), *The Catcher with the Glass Arm* (1964), *The Year Mom Won the Pennant* (1968), *No Arm in Left Field* (1974), and *The Spy on Third Base* (1988).

INTRODUCTION

Christopher is a popular and prolific writer of fiction for primary and middle graders who is best known for creating sports stories that are praised for their action and insight. Called by *Kirkus Reviews* a "steady winner who counts with kids," he is commended for his vivid and accurate play-by-play descriptions of a variety of sports ranging from baseball to skateboarding as well as for addressing such issues as prejudice and sexism. Characterized by simple plots and language, his stories emphasize sportsmanship and team effort by demonstrating how their young protagonists, including minority and disabled characters, learn to overcome personal fears through discipline and self-acceptance. In all of his books, Christopher features subjects that he believes will appeal to his audience; several of the works combine fantasy and reality, while others blend mystery, romance, and adventure. Acknowledged for their lack of condescension, his books are written in an easy-to-read style that has a special appeal to reluctant readers. At the same time, however, Christopher has received a mixed reception: he is criticized for presenting only a superficial exploration of the problems he identifies, and is faulted for patterned and predictable storylines which are often viewed as trite and clichéd. Nevertheless, Christopher continues to maintain widespread popular appeal, especially among boys. *Kirkus Reviews* has identified in his writing "a quality authentic in its boyishness," and Fellis L. Jordan has noted that "although the author may never win an award for his writing style, he repeatedly demonstrates the ability to write a story for the reader, especially boys, who are looking for that stepping-stone to a more sophisticated, involved story."

Christopher grew up near Ithaca, New York. The two principal interests of his younger life were sports (primarily baseball) and writing. He began writing seriously at fourteen, working primarily on mystery stories which he would complete within a week. At fifteen, he began to play semi-professional baseball. Although he never attended college, he played professional baseball briefly with a New York Yankees farm club until a knee injury forced him out of the game. During this time Christopher continued to hone his literary craft; at eighteen, he received a *Writer's Digest* award which, according to Christopher, "was an inspiration for me to continue writing." Over the next two decades he published in various magazines a number of short works of mystery and science fiction, as well as one-

act plays, humorous verse, and teenage fiction, and composed his first novel, the adult mystery *Look for the Body*. In 1953, dissatisfied in his search for a suitable baseball book for young readers, Christopher determined to create his own sports stories and met with immediate success, publishing *The Lucky Baseball Bat* the following year. In this work, young protagonist Marvin realizes that he, and not a bat that he has been given, is responsible for his skill as a little league ballplayer. *The Lucky Baseball Bat* and subsequent stories are unified, according to *School Library Journal,* by the "usual elements of underdeveloped talent, impatient teammates, and a solution obtained through diligence and sportsmanship—all set against the introduction of an unusual character." For example, in *No Arm in Left Field* and *The Basket Counts,* minority players overcome the hostility of their teammates; and in *Glue Fingers* and *Long Shot for Paul,* Christopher introduces athletes with disabilities (stuttering and slight mental retardation, respectively) who eventually become part of the team. In addition to his longer works, Christopher is the author of *Lucky Seven: Sports Stories* (1970), a collection of short stories that originally appeared in periodicals and reflect the subjects and styles of his other sports-oriented works. Christopher, who participates in many of the sports he describes in order to write about them authoritatively, receives letters daily from his young fans, and especially delights in those from readers who identify with the characters in a given story. Reflecting on his work, Christopher has written, "I was—and still am, thank God—able to put down on paper what I had enjoyed doing in real life, and enlarge upon it using my imagination to the fullest." Christopher received the Milner Award in 1993.

(See also *Something About the Author,* Vols. 2, 47; *Something About the Author Autobiography Series,* Vol. 9; *Major Authors and Illustrators for Children and Young Adults; Contemporary Authors,* Vols. 1-4; and *Contemporary Authors New Revision Series,* Vols. 5, 36.)

AUTHOR'S COMMENTARY

[*The following excerpt is from an interview by Lee Bennett Hopkins.*]

Children in the middle grades, especially sports-minded boys and girls, take to Matt Christopher's books as they take to the annual World Series. Baseball has always been Mr. Christopher's prime interest next to writing. At one time he seriously considered baseball as a career and was offered an athletic scholarship to Cornell University. However, he lacked credit for a required course in mathematics, and since he was the oldest of nine children (seven boys and two girls), he decided to take a job to help bolster the family income.

Mr. Christopher was born in Bath, Pennsylvania, on August 6, 1917, and grew up in Portland Point, New York, near Ithaca. "My mother came from Hungary, my father from Italy," he told me. "I can remember building miniature electric poles, roads, and steam shovels out of wooden boxes when I was still of preschool age. Later, after moving from Bath to Portland Point, my interests became more sophisticated. I built model airplanes and model ships. My father worked at a cement plant, drawing wages barely sufficient to keep our large family in food and clothing. For a time we weren't able to afford a car. We had to ask neighbors to cart us to the doctor, about a ten-mile drive, whenever one of us became so ill that it worried our parents. We raised pigs and chickens, which helped supplement our meat supply, and in summers we had a garden, the pride and joy of my parents and grandfather, who lived with us. We played the usual games kids did at that time—Annie-over, lost turkey, duck-on-the-rock, and, of course, baseball, which we played with a tennis ball and broom handle."

At the age of fourteen, Mr. Christopher began writing poems and short stories. "I wrote airplane and detective stories just for the fun of it during study periods in high school," he recalled.

In 1937 he entered a national short story writing contest and won a prize. "This proved to be the fatal bite of the bug!" he exclaimed. At fifteen he began to play semi-professional baseball. This was followed by professional playing in the Canadian-American League. He also played in an exhibition game against the New York Giants; on another occasion he was selected the Freeville-Dryden baseball team's most valuable player of the year and was honored by a Matt Christopher Day.

He continued writing and selling humorous verse, one-act plays, teen-age stories, and serials. In 1952 an adult mystery, *Look for the Body,* was published by Phoenix Press. After writing a total of about eighty pieces, he considered writing a baseball book for young people. "Frankly, I couldn't find one I really liked, or thought young people in the fourth or fifth grades would really like, so I tried doing one," he explained.

This was *The Lucky Baseball Bat* (1954). Other titles about baseball, basketball, and football followed. In all his books the author not only gives a clear account of the game about which he is writing but in each develops a main character and a problem theme. Remembering his first book for children, Mr. Christopher remarked: "In his wish to play baseball, Marvin, the hero, thinks that the bat given to him by a friend is the only bat with which he can hit a baseball. He is unaware of the fact that he is naturally athletic and that baseball is a game that came to him much easier than it has to other boys. When something happens to the bat, his hopes sink, because he thinks the bat was responsible for his good playing, not believing it was himself.

"Having played baseball many years myself, I have seen boys react very much the same way as Marvin did toward their bats. The book has plenty of baseball in it. Marvin's sister, his mother, and dad, are drawn into the story too, which makes me believe, at least hope, that girls would like the book also.

"I tried to accomplish a few things in the book: Marvin's courage in striving on to play the game he loves best in spite of obstacles, his obedience to his family, and his learning that one cannot always succeed at the first try. I wanted to show too, that at his age, he was still susceptible to tears when everything seemed to have gone against him—even as it does sometimes with adults. I wanted this to be not only a baseball story, but also a story of Marvin, a boy to be remembered. I hope I succeeded."

Mr. Christopher then talked about his work habits and how his story ideas are developed: "First, I decide what kind of story I plan to write—baseball, football, or some other sport. Then I decide on a nucleus, the main character's problem. The next step is to devise scenes applicable to the story, select names of my characters, write a plot outline, and then compose from it on my typewriter. After the first draft is written, I got over it about three to four times, polishing it, tightening it, making the story as suspenseful as I can, as plausible as I can. I am the main character in that story. I suffer and laugh with him. I have witnessed incidences in baseball that I have used in my novels. The boy getting hit on the head by a pitched ball, for example, in *The Catcher with a Glass Arm* was based on an incident that had happened to my nephew." (pp. 78-82)

He is an active man. He has taken flying lessons so that he could write airplane stories authentically and has sailed and boated for the same reason. . . . Having played baseball, football, and basketball, he naturally still has an avid interest in these sports, "Although I can only *watch* now!" he conceded.

I asked Mr. Christopher if he had a favorite amongst his books. "My favorite," he replied, "is usually the last one. But this time I'm quite certain about it, for it's the first time I can recall laughing with tears in my eyes while reading the galleys for *The Kid Who Only Hit Homers.* It's my thirty-eighth book!" (pp. 82-3)

> *Lee Bennett Hopkins, "Matt Christopher," in his* More Books by More People, *Citation Press, 1974, pp. 78-83.*

GENERAL COMMENTARY

Zena Sutherland and May Hill Arbuthnot

If there is one fault common to most sports stories, it is the formula plot; for example, the beginner, from school playground to professional team, who can't get along with another member of the team or the whole team or the coach because he or she is cocky or wants things his or her own way, eventually rising to heights of glory and acceptance all by saving the final game in the final minute of play. Although game description is the most appealing element to some readers, another fault common to such stories is the thin plot wrapped around long and often tedious game sequences, some of which have unrealistic series of plays. Perhaps more than any other kind of realistic fiction, the sports story needs good characterization and good style to give it depth, especially since there is usually little variation in setting and often little opportunity for a meaningful theme. . . .

The popularity of each individual sport is echoed proportionately in children's books, with baseball and football stories far outnumbering all others. One of the most dependable writers for the nine-to-eleven group is Matt Christopher, whose productivity is impressive. *Johnny Long Legs* and *The Great Quarterback Switch* are examples of his style: simple, undistinguished plots; good game descriptions; and an emphasis on sportsmanship and team effort.

> *Zena Sutherland and May Hill Arbuthnot, "Sports Stories," in their* Children and Books, *seventh edition, Scott, Foresman and Company, 1986, p. 373.*

Joan McGrath

Two junior sports stories for boys, *Catch that pass!* and *Face off,* bear more than a family resemblance. Both easy-to-reads deal with the fears that may assail promising young team players. Scott Harrison of *Face off* is a terrific speed skater but crippled as a team member of the Golden Bears by his fear of being hit by the puck; and there's no worse epithet for a hockey player than "puck shy"! Jim Nardi of *Catch that pass!* would be his team's greatest asset if he could get over his paralyzing fear of being tackled. These two stories, while slight and predictable, do adopt a sympathetic and encouraging attitude that may be of real help to youngsters whose confidence in themselves

is undermined by fears that time and practice can and will conquer.

> *Joan McGrath, in a review of "Catch that Pass!" and "Face Off," in* Emergency Librarian, *Vol. 17, No. 5, May-June, 1990, p. 58.*

TITLE COMMENTARY

The Lucky Baseball Bat   (1954)

Young Marvin has just moved to a new town where he wants to play baseball but is too unsure of himself to make much of an impression on the local sand lot team. A friendly high school boy gives him a bat which is supposed to be lucky and with it Marvin earns for himself a place on the team. In time, of course, he comes to realize that the bat is not lucky but that it is his own ability that is responsible for his good batting and fielding average. A very thin story, and few boys will appreciate Marvin's constant reliance on his younger sister Jeannie for help in solving all of his problems. (pp. 27-8)

> *A review of "The Lucky Baseball Bat," in* Bulletin of the Children's Book Center, *Vol. VIII, No. 4, December, 1954, pp. 27-8.*

[*The following reviews consider the 1991 revised edition of* The Lucky Baseball Bat. *The protagonist's name has been changed from Marvin to Martin.*]

First published in 1954, this short chapter book has been revised, re-illustrated, and released anew as part of the Springboard Book series. Martin wants to play baseball, but he begins to play well only after an older boy gives him a special bat. When the bat breaks, Martin loses confidence. He learns in the end that skill, not luck, was what really enabled him to succeed. While the basic plot is the same as in the original book, the text has been shortened considerably. Some of the play-by-play action has been left out, and the plot is not as well developed, making the less credible elements of the story more noticeable than ever. [Dee] DeRosa's gray pencil drawings, which replace the original illustrations [by Robert Henneberger], add contemporary visual appeal. Recommended for libraries with a heavy demand for baseball fiction at this reading level.

> *Carolyn Phelan, in a review of "The Lucky Baseball Bat," in* Booklist, *Vol. 87, No. 19, June 1, 1991, p. 1883.*

Martin is new to the neighborhood and wants to play little league. When an older boy gives him his old mitt and bat, Martin finds he can both hit and catch, and attributes these skills to the equipment, not to himself. When he can't find his bat, he accuses a teammate of stealing it. In an unbelievable sequence, he jumps in front of an approaching car to pull a younger boy to safety; coincidentally, the boy happens to be the one who took the bat. In the end, Martin hits a home run and wins the championship game for his team. The plot is as evenly paced as that in *The Hit-Away Kid,* with a controlled vocabulary and short chapters intended to help children make the leap to chapter books. The moral is also as conspicuous.

> *Denise Krell, in a review of "The Lucky Base-*

ball Bat," in School Library Journal, *Vol. 37, No. 7, July, 1991, p. 72.*

Baseball Pals (1956)

Good baseball and character development are emphasized in this sports story that will be welcomed by the youngest baseball fans. While writing is somewhat uneven, the many sports terms should add interest. Print is good and illustrations [by Robert Henneberger] are adequate, but libraries should buy prebound. Recommended particularly for boys of 8-10 and for easy reading for older pupils.

> *Helen E. Walker, in a review of "Baseball Pals," in* Library Journal, *Vol. 2, No. 7, March, 1956, p. 30.*

Just as the season was beginning for the Grasshopper League, Jimmie, the Captain of the Planets, and Paul, his best friend, were both determined to be pitcher. Moreover, Paul was a much better pitcher than Jimmie. This led to trouble. The team suffered and so did their friendship. Even Jimmie's kid brother was upset. Boys of nine or ten will certainly read this easy baseball story with interest, wondering if Jimmie will be stubborn to the end and lose the crucial first game to the Red Rockets. It is a good extra

Christopher at age twelve.

story for this age. The lesson is not too obvious, the boys quite natural, the print clear, and the illustrations of Robert Henneberger pleasantly boyish.

> *Margaret Sherwood Libby, in a review of "Baseball Pals," in* New York Herald Tribune Book Review, *May 6, 1956, p. 9.*

Jimmie felt that as captain of his baseball team he had the right to chose the position he would play, and he wanted to be pitcher. Even though it cost the team the services of his friend Paul, who had been the pitcher the previous year, and even when Jimmie proved himself unable to handle the position, he continued in his stubbornness. Finally he realized what he was doing to the team, persuaded Paul to return, and went back to his position in the infield. The moral is made as obvious as Jimmie's lack of pitching ability, detracting from what otherwise might have made a good addition to baseball stories for young readers. (pp. 109-10)

> *A review of "Baseball Pals," in* Bulletin of the Children's Book Center, *Vol. IX, No. 10, June, 1956, pp. 109-10.*

Basketball Sparkplug (1957)

After two baseball stories, Matt Christopher has written a book about basketball which is good bait for the slow reader. Very easy reading, it uses a limited vocabulary, is easy to follow and is set in fairly large type with content matter of high interest to boys in elementary grades. Kim O'Connor's teammates on the Arrows basketball team can't resist the chance to tease him about his singing lessons in Mrs. Kelsey's choir. Often his two interests conflict. Though Kim would rather participate in basketball practise, for his mother's sake he attends choir rehearsals. Kim's persistence in both fields is rewarded when the Arrows win the Small Fry Championship from their rival, the Comets, with surprise help from Mrs. Kelsey and the choir.

> *A review of "Basketball Sparkplug," in* Virginia Kirkus' Service, *Vol. XXV, No. 12, June 15, 1957, p. 412.*

Two Strikes on Johnny (1958)

Johnny's Doane's brother Michael thought Johnny was a top notch ball player. Actually Johnny was a poor hitter, who deceived Michael into believing that pleasant fiction. And the Cardinals, his teammates, helped to support the illusion. Finally Johnny confesses the truth to Michael—then resolves to stop playing. But Michael overcomes his disillusionment and remains as staunch a rooter as ever for his brother. All very unmotivated and a little maudlin.

> *A review of "Two Strikes on Johnny," in* Virginia Kirkus' Service, *Vol. XXVI, No. 2, January 15, 1958, p. 34.*

Little Lefty (1959)

[*Little Lefty*] never actually mentions Little League or Little League competition by name, but it is concerned with boys of that age and the emotional pressures—good or bad—that go into serious competition for small fry. This one has added plot, but its center is baseball and how it is played, told in big league fashion but in language understandable to its prospective audience.

> Irving T. Marsh, "Spring Sport Books to Tempt the Fans," in New York Herald Tribune Book Review, *May 10, 1959, p. 31.*

Bill's desire to pitch in the Little League is in conflict with his friendly relationship toward Larry, who is not baseball-minded. A near drowning and a chipped elbow convert Larry, while strengthening Bill's determination to pitch for the Blackhawks. Chief appeal lies in Bill's success in spite of his small size and the typical interests of 8-9-year-old boys. Average Christopher story for Little League fans in grades 3-4. Recommended where needed.

> Olive Mumford, in a review of "Little Lefty," in Library Journal, *Vol. 84, No. 13, July, 1959, p. 2222.*

Touchdown for Tommy (1959)

Tommy, an orphan, is bewildered by his insecure role as a foster child. Living in a rough neighborhood, he joins in the midget football games in the only spirit he has ever known—kill or be killed. His gradual understanding that there are more sportsmanlike ways to play runs parallel with his increasing desire to be an adopted rather than a foster child. A somewhat uninspired integration of the orphan problem with the question of gamesmanship.

> A review of "Touchdown for Tommy," in Virginia Kirkus' Service, *Vol. XXVII, No. 14, July 15, 1959, p. 491.*

Shadow over the Back Court (1959)

High school student, Jeff Dooley, was as ardent in his love of basketball as was his scientist father in his love of aviational research. Opposed to his son's preoccupation with the game, which he believes keeps him from devoting himself to interests more closely related to his own, he forbids Jeff to participate in the school team. How father and son reconcile their differences is the core of this story which includes a rich basketball background and many play by play descriptions which will excite any enthusiast of the game.

> A review of "Shadow over the Back Court," in Virginia Kirkus' Service, *Vol. XXVII, No. 16, August 15, 1959, p. 603.*

Long Stretch at First Base (1960)

Young Bobby Jamison is determined that his older brother, Kirby, be chosen for the Grasshopper League All-Star team. So blinded is he by sibling loyalty that he refuses to acknowledge the fact that his brother's rival is better equipped for the post. Kirby and Bobby learn a good deal about baseball, but more, still, about integrity in this simply written but engrossing story of a game and its ardent young fans. A wholesome depiction of a healthy family, their problems, and their development, light but consistently sensible.

> A review of "Long Stretch at First Base," in Virginia Kirkus' Service, *Vol. XXVIII, No. 4, February 15, 1960, p. 146.*

Bobby's noble desire to have older brother Kirby selected as first baseman of the Grasshopper League's All Star Team almost makes a thief of him. Otherwise, his endless good humor, the high ideals of each member of his family, the long series of baseball games, make this dull reading even for the fans. Not recommended.

> Olive Mumford, in a review of "Long Stretch at First Base," in Junior Libraries, *Vol. 6, No. 7, March, 1960, p. 137.*

Break for the Basket (1960)

A story in which art and basketball merge, this is an account of Emmett, an athletic star in his own backyard. When Emmett is asked to join a team, his playing becomes somewhat inhibited until a friendly artist intervenes and teaches him that fear is ninety-nine percent ignorance. Emmett repays his debt by helping the gentle painter achieve recognition. A departure from the straight sport yarn, the introduction of a secondary theme gives dimension to this "best of all possible worlds" story which should appeal, primarily, to aspiring grade school athletes. And the dual lesson it teaches—that art and manliness are not incompatible, and that lack of confidence has a cure—are well worth learning at the age for which this book is directed.

> A review of "Break for the Basket," in Virginia Kirkus' Service, *Vol. XXVIII, No. 13, July 1, 1960, p. 498.*

Wing T Fullback (1960)

Bernie Morello's football gave off sparks, not only of his fine athletic prowess but of a fierce and hostile need to win. A boy from the wrong side of the tracks, Bernie is unable to be a really fine player because of his antagonism toward his team which he feels rejects him. Caught in a paradox of playing to prove his worth and playing as a path of aggression toward his own team, Bernie suffers intensely. But a wise coach and reassuring experiences release him from his dilemma and he emerges as a better fullback and healthier person. Football and psychology once more make a compatible marriage in this story for boys.

> A review of "Wing T Fullback," in Virginia Kirkus' Service, *Vol. XXVIII, No. 15, August 1, 1960, p. 631.*

Tall Man in the Pivot (1961)

The *Condors* made a great team, both on and off the basketball court. Their coordination, team spirit and cooperation resulted in some striking victories. How disheartening for Chuck when he finds that his precious marble bag has been raided by a locker room thief. It was certainly good to know Steve was innocent but shocking and disappointing when the evidence points to his closest pal Mickey. How could a fellow trust anyone if such a thing could happen! What a sweeping relief then to welcome Mickey's vindication and his reinstatement as a "pal", a super-special designation outdoing the mundane "friend". Play by play descriptions of on-the-court action combine with a sensitive glance at the values and ideals of typical youngsters and convey a quality authentic in its boyishness. This is sure to find an appreciative audience among the lower echelons of this age group.

> *A review of "Tall Man in the Pivot," in* Virginia Kirkus' Service, *Vol. XXIX, No. 12, June 15, 1961, p. 500.*

Challenge at Second Base (1962)

With brother Phil's professional status as a ballplayer always looming over him, young Stan can't help regarding even his minor errors on his Little League team as indications of his general failure. Aside from cushioning himself with outside interests in space-age science, Stan is also helped along by a series of mysterious notes of encouragement from an anonymous source. Stan's efforts to improve his game are crowned by a final congratulatory note from the same sender whose identity he finally discovers. Unexceptional but acceptable action for the younger fan who will identify with this miniature hero's predicaments.

> *A review of "Challenge at Second Base," in* Virginia Kirkus' Service, *Vol. XXX, No. 4, February 15, 1962, p. 177.*

Crackerjack Halfback (1962)

Matt Christopher exchanges the baseball diamond for the gridiron as his young hero Freddie grows from fearful backfielder to crackerjack halfback. As a member of the Sandpipers, Freddie makes long runs, scores touchdowns but freezes on the tackle. Hero worshipping Jimmie, half Freddie's size, demonstrates the ease with which taller boys can be tackled. Slowly Freddie takes courage. A few off-the-field experiences, in which bravery is called into play, help too. In the end Freddie tackles with the best of them vindicating Coach Sears' faith in him and spurring his team on to defeat the Bluejays and the more formidable Cardinals. There is a natural boyish quality to this simple story of growth and good sportsmanship—lots of play by play description too.

> *A review of "Crackerjack Halfback," in* Virginia Kirkus' Service, *Vol. XXX, No. 8, April 15, 1962, p. 386.*

Baseball Flyhawk (1963)

Once again (as in *Challenge at Second Base* and others), Matt Christopher has demonstrated his ability to describe a baseball game play by play, in this simple story about a Puerto Rican boy who is hypersensitive to the criticism of his teammates. String, the favorite player for the Royals, pointedly insults Chico each time he makes an error. The little outfielder gains the respect of String and the other players when he reveals his courage away from the ball park, and then proves himself to be a good athlete. The character studies are oversimplified and the plot is somewhat trite, but the book will nonetheless appeal to the younger sport fans in this age group.

> *A review of "Baseball Flyhawk," in* Virginia Kirkus' Service, *Vol. XXXI, No. 2, January 15, 1963, p. 57.*

Chico seemed to make one mistake after another during the Grasshopper League games; he was sure nobody liked him and he felt that as a newcomer and a Puerto Rican his mistakes were watched for. One day he rescued a member of the team who was in danger of drowning; shortly thereafter his fielding of a long drive held the opposing team scoreless and won the approbation of all. The book has some good baseball, and it may encourage the reader to appreciate the sensitivity of the outsider. There are several weaknesses in the story, however, the most important being the hostile behavior of most of Chico's team-mates. Small details of the story are often unconvincing: Chico, who lived in New York before moving to town, remembers a day with flags but doesn't know it is the Fourth of July, which seems improbable in view of the normal excitement generated by the occasion.

> *Zena Sutherland, in a review of "Baseball Flyhawk," in* Bulletin of the Center for Children's Books, *Vol. XVI, No. 10, June, 1963, p. 156.*

Sink It, Rusty (1963)

Rusty called fouls from the sideline as he watched the other boys run easily, jump and shoot for baskets. Rusty had been slowed down for two years now by the effects of polio; his feet always ended up in a tangle and he grew tired quickly. Hypersensitive to the ribbing of his classmates, he practised basketball and relentlessly—but always by himself. The appearance of twenty-five year old Alec Dawes on the scene caused Rusty to change his attitude. A story which veers from the center of realism as Rusty rapidly becomes quite the star, is nonetheless a fast-paced one which focuses directly on basketball and play-by-play-descriptions—and it is certain to be a winner among young boys.

> *A review of "Sink It, Rusty," in* Virginia Kirkus' Service, *Vol. XXXI, No. 12, June 15, 1963, p. 557.*

Catcher with a Glass Arm (1964)

This title is a compelling one, and the troubles of the hero,

Jody, have appeal; he can't throw and he can't hit. Forgetting himself in his concern for his pet cat, Jody demonstrates his bravery. When he discovers that an adult, too, can be afraid, he overcomes his fear and hits the ball. The author's crisp reporting of the sports action combined with his simple, briefly treated story line make his book the perfect length for a Little Leaguer and for slow or reluctant readers in 7th and 8th grades.

> *Marybeth Martin, in a review of "Catcher with a Glass Arm," in* School Library Journal, *Vol. 10, No. 8, April, 1964, p. 60.*

Jody Sinclair was afraid of a pitched ball *and* he couldn't throw, a tough situation for the catcher of a team going toward the playoffs. A glass arm, taunted some of the fans in the bleachers. Lots of practice and the interest of a friend's father help Jody overcome his difficulties in this fast-moving story. Breezily written in slangy baseballese with play-by-play descriptions of exciting games, this book catches the mood of Little League for 7-11's.

> *Marian Sorenson, "—Baseball, That Is," in* The Christian Science Monitor, *May 7, 1964, p. 4b.*

Catcher With a Glass Arm offers a couple of interesting cases in adult pathology: a father who flies into a rage because his son doesn't throw hard enough and a wistful chap who worries himself to a shadow about boys who are timid at the plate. Such infantile fixations on the part of grown men (and their scary effects on the young) must be one of the more interesting features of little league. Alas, the author treats them as the adult norm, and does so in a style aimed at children much too young to know about baseball.

> *Wilfrid Sheed, "Diamond Kinks and Kicks," in* The New York Times Book Review, *May 10, 1964, p. 6.*

Jody was a good catcher, but he didn't throw well and he knew that some of the boys on his team felt that he was responsible for lost games. When he was hit by a pitched ball and thereafter backed away from the pitch, Jody had double trouble. With practice, and with help from the father of one of his team-mates, Jody improved—in fact, he helped win the league championship game. Routine as a baseball story, but better balanced than the strictly-baseball books; Jody's family and his friends do play a part in his life.

> *Zena Sutherland, in a review of "Catcher with a Glass Arm," in* Bulletin of the Center for Children's Books, *Vol. XVII, No. 11, July-August, 1964, p. 167.*

Wingman on Ice   (1964)

Young Tod of the Bantam Hockey League is a poor stick-handler and, blaming his equipment, he hopes for a new stick for Christmas. When he gets it, however, he realizes that he doesn't deserve it, and he puts it away in his closet until he does. With lots of speed, Tod has the potential of a good wingman, and through self-discipline and applica-

tion he improves his rink performance to win the admiration of the coach, his father, and his teammates . . . Score? perhaps not as much of a sporting chance as Christopher's baseball, basketball, and football books since ice hockey doesn't have as strong a spectator or participant interest at this age level. The story itself is serviceable for its moral values and rules of play. . . .

> *A review of "Wingman on Ice," in* Virginia Kirkus' Service, *Vol. XXXII, No. 13, July 1, 1964, p. 595.*

The Counterfeit Tackle   (1965)

The author has once again coined the genuine article in terms of realistic, on the field performance by the smallest size gridmen. Corky was right tackle for the Otters, and an enthusiastic player. He wanted to take the opportunity to go with his father to watch a pro game but was afraid he would be removed from the team if he didn't show up for play. His twin brother Buzz's sport was chess, but Buzz offered to fill in for Corky and discovered that without his glasses, he looked exactly like his brother. During the course of the game, Buzz manages to pick up some important pointers to improve his play, and afterwards comes to understand why Corky has so many more friends than he does. Easy to read and to emulate.

> *A review of "The Counterfeit Tackle," in* Virginia Kirkus' Service, *Vol. XXIII, No. 15, August 1, 1965, p. 752.*

Buzz and Corky are identical twins, alike in looks only. To give his brother a chance to see a pro football game, Buzz substitutes for him at tackle. He soon discovers he enjoys playing football and being part of the gang, but he is accepted only when the others think he is Corky. Christopher handles this situation deftly, without sentimentality.

> *Jeraline N. Nerney, in a review of "The Counterfeit Tackle," in* School Library Journal, *Vol. 12, No. 2, October, 1965, p. 251.*

[**The Counterfeit Tackle**] is a more conventional sub-teen football yarn about identical twins [than Beman Lord's *The Perfect Pitch*]: Corky, a promising tackle, and Buzz a chess wizard. I found it not very original, less so even than the Baseball Joe epics of my own distant youth; but fans of Mr. Christopher's 16 other junior sports stories are entitled to, and probably will, disagree. (pp. 54-5)

> *Al Hine, in a review of "The Counterfeit Tackle," in* The New York Times Book Review, *November 7, 1965, pp. 54-5.*

The Mystery on Crabapple Hill   (as Fredric Martin, 1965)

It's about as innocuous as a mystery can be. A painter moves into a house on top of Crabapple Hill, and Billy Boniff and his best friend immediately become suspicious of him on the basis of some totally mundane, unstartling evidence. Eventually a crime turns up—paltry petty thievery—and a surprise ending, in case anyone's still paying attention.

> *A review of "The Mystery on Crabapple Hill,"* in Virginia Kirkus' Service, *Vol. XXXIII, No. 15, August 1, 1965, p. 752.*

Billy Boniff and his chum, Phil, are suspicious of the man who has just put up a prefabricated house on the top of a nearby hill. Mr. Curtis says he is an artist, and that he is living on the hill because of the view, but the boys feel sure that Mr. Curtis is a petty thief. The culprit turns out to be the pleasant woman who has been acting as house-keeper while Billy's mother is ill, her thefts of food, cloth-ing, and toys having been perpetrated on behalf of a poor family with nine children. The plot seems quite contrived, all of the suspicious behavior of Mr. Curtis being due to the fact that he was secretly helping a friend who was a police detective.

> *Zena Sutherland, in a review of "The Mystery on Crabapple Hill,"* in Bulletin of the Center for Children's Books, *Vol. 20, No. 1, September, 1966, p. 15.*

Too Hot to Handle   (1965)

The Kroft name was well-known among local athletic en-thusiasts; David's father, his uncles, even his older brother Don were skillful baseball players. David, despite his ear-nest desire to maintain the family tradition, was no better than mediocre, and his errors were costly for his team. When a broken leg put Don out of commission for the sea-son, David felt particularly responsible for carrying on the Kroft reputation, even though his family applied no pres-sure. With conscientious practice his game steadily im-proved, and by the end of the summer he realized that he would probably never be an outstanding player but was satisfied to have done his best. The author has written nu-merous sport stories for this age group and has captured the tension of a little league game. Sturdy and standard.

> *A review of "Too Hot to Handle,"* in Virginia Kirkus' Service, *Vol. XXXIII, No. 2, January 15, 1965, p. 58.*

Not unusual, but a good baseball story for middle-grades boys; the illustrations [by Foster Caddell] are fairly pedes-trian. David Kroft feels that he ought to be better than he is at third base; he's good enough to play in the Grasshop-per League, but he isn't good enough to keep up the family tradition. David's father and his two older brothers have been excellent players, but David is shorter than the oth-ers. This is the theme, and the solution of David's problem is his sensible and realistic acceptance of his own limita-tions. Although there are a few threads of sub-plot (a neighbor who likes David comes to a game and learns to enjoy baseball) most of the text consists of descriptions of games.

> *Zena Sutherland, in a review of "Too Hot to Handle,"* in Bulletin of the Center for Chil-dren's Books, *Vol. 19, No. 10, June, 1966, p. 161.*

Christopher writes that this 1938 photo shows him "wearing the baseball uniform and jacket presented to me by the Freeville-Dryden team for being Most Valuable Player." The team was lo-cated in Ithaca, New York.

Long Shot for Paul   (1966)

This book, like this usually capable sportwriter's recent **The Reluctant Pitcher,** suffers from a myopic view of a problem which should receive careful scrutiny. Paul is a thirteen year old mentally retarded boy, but his special problems are only scantily introduced. His brother Glenn, assisted by their sister Judy, decided to teach him basket-ball, a sport which was not included on Paul's curriculum. After only a couple of weeks of practice, Glenn brought Paul along to his school team, the Sabers. Although the Sabers were part of a league and presumably somewhat competitive about membership, the coach barely hesitates to agree to let Paul work out with them and to play in their games. Some of boys demurred though. Their gradual un-derstanding of Paul's personality does not lead to their ac-ceptance of him, but his final, successful performance on the court does win them over and a prejudiced parent as well. The story is not realistically, nor even admirably de-veloped, and the fact that one of the characters is named Sticky Keester will just help to keep readers from taking it seriously.

A review of "Long Shot for Paul," in Virginia Kirkus' Service, Vol. XXXIV, No. 12, June 15, 1966, pp. 575-76.

Retarded Paul Marlette is helped by his brother to become a member of the league basketball team in Matt Christopher's **Long Shot for Paul.** Helping the retarded is the major point and overrides the basketball background enough to suggest that this is really to be judged less as a sports book than as bibliotherapy.

A review of "Long Shot for Paul," in School Library Journal, Vol. 13, No. 9, May, 1967, p. 76.

The Mystery at Monkey Run   (as Fredric Martin, 1966)

It's another rickety little mystery by the author of **The Mystery on Crabapple Hill** and again it features junior detectives who run into mystery as easily as most boys skin knees. Bunker and George find their suspect before they find out the crime—he's Mr. Hale, a neighbor at their summer lake resort, and he makes a project of studying the bats in a local cave. Some vague clues encourage the boys to go skindiving for a little black case which eventually turns out to contain part of a valuable coin collection. And they just barely miss giving away the whole show when they turn the goods over to the bogus game warden who is the real criminal. It's all genuine cliché.

A review of "The Mystery at Monkey Run," in Virginia Kirkus' Service, Vol. XXXIV, No. 12, June 15, 1966, p. 576.

A mystery that can count two boys, a summer beach, and the webbed footprints of a skin diver on the sand among its features, would make you figure it's a good mystery to take to young beachcombers. And when you know it is written by the same author as the one who wrote, **The Mystery of Crabapple Hill,** you can be sure. (Eight to 12 makes no sense for its proper age group—7-10 is more like it.)

A review of "The Mystery at Monkey Run," in Publishers Weekly, Vol. 190, No. 6, August 8, 1966, p. 60.

The Reluctant Pitcher   (1966)

This popular sportswriter for the youngest readers has, as usual, the knack for describing junior ball in terms that are both easy and enjoyable to read and never patronizing. This baseball story is not one of his better ones, probably because he has failed to follow through on the surprise plays he tossed in here. Wally liked to play right field, but Coach Hutter kept encouraging him to pitch. Cab Lacey, a newcomer and an ex-pro, agreed that Wally should be fielding and not pitching. But Wally felt a personal obligation to the Coach who had saved his life in an accident. Hutter's son had been killed in that same accident, and Wally knew that the Coach wanted him to take the dead boy's place. The problem of how to decide between two adults who offer variant advice is a pressing one and is illustrated here quite naturally, as is the difficulty of decid-

ing the degree of precedence to give to gratitude and pity. Unfortunately, however, the solution, which is removed from Wally's hands, is a little too glib. At the same time the very short story becomes garbled by too many side issues—Lacey's daughter is discovered to be a deaf-mute; Wally barely rescues her and Hutter's daughter from being blown up in a quarry; Wally and a friend are locked up in a milk cooler. Fair ball, but with too much stretching between the innings.

A review of "The Reluctant Pitcher," in Virginia Kirkus' Service, Vol. XXXIV, No. 2, January 15, 1966, p. 57.

Miracle at the Plate   (1967)

In **Miracle at the Plate** . . . Skeeter Miracle bats crosshanded and hits 700 but is a dud as a fielder. Large type, lots of action, but insipid plot. Might possibly be useful for unwilling readers at a higher grade level.

A review of "Miracle at the Plate," in School Library Journal, Vol. 13, No. 9, May, 1967, p. 76.

Another pro in the baseball story league (of stories for young readers) has chosen the Rival for *his* theme—too young to fight over a girl, the two protagonists square off over a pet. A side trip to Idaho and the thrills of skateboarding interrupt the rivalry but the battle is joined on the baseball diamond, and the young hero wins his self-confidence, the team wins its game, and everybody goes home happy as a bird.

A review of "Miracle at the Plate," in Publishers Weekly, Vol. 191, No. 23, June 5, 1967, p. 175.

The Team That Couldn't Lose   (1967)

The worst team in the twelve-year-olds' league hits a winning streak when an anonymous fan sends the coach a new play every week. The strategy of these plays dates from the high school team of forty years ago, and the benefactor turns out to be the skinny, bright, piano-playing team manager. The shy coach gets the girl and the team goes undefeated, playing the last game without a gimmick and winning through skill. It's not much of a mystery and the story is pretty obvious, but Christopher readers will respond.

A review of "The Team That Couldn't Lose," in Kirkus Service, Vol. XXXV, No. 12, June 15, 1967, p. 694.

When quarterback Chip Chase and the other Cayugans of the Midget Football League learn that their new coach knows very little about football, they become discouraged and anticipate a poor season. But a new play strategy sent each week by a mysterious benefactor brings new life and victory to the team. Author Matt Christopher's football action is good. The mystery and the message of a team finding faith in itself are added points in the book's favor.

The Team That Couldn't Lose is a good purchase for young readers.

> A review of "The Team That Couldn't Lose," in School Library Journal, *Vol. 14, No. 4, December, 1967, p. 90.*

The Mystery under Fugitive House (as Fredric Martin, 1968)

Newcomer and telescope-gazer Bantam Berns sleuths around the boarding house, traces the mean crook and his loot to the underground cave once used by fugitive slaves. Suspense is slight as the clues fall like ripe plums and rescue seems comfortably probable; characterization is also nil. It's another case of piquant title, pablum plot.

> A review of "The Mystery under the Fugitive House," in Kirkus Service, *Vol. XXXV, No. 12, June 15, 1967, p. 694.*

The Year Mom Won the Pennant (1968)

The Flat Rock Thunderballs need a coach but nobody's father has the time. Nick Vassey's dad thinks his four years without a pennant show they need new blood. Gale Matson's dad, the only Negro on the police force, sometimes has to work nights, and Wayne Snow's father is almost always away on business. Mrs. Vassey volunteers, and the team admits that a female coach is better than none. Nick is embarrassed at first, especially when Coach Stevens of the Tornadoes grins and their other opponents snicker from the dugout. But Mom has her moments, and she manages to win Nick's support and enough games to take the flag. A sub-plot about Wayne as poor-little-rich-boy seems like an afterthought and Mom's recipe is an unclear combination of luck and strategy; this reads better than most, and better than some recent Christophers.

> A review of "The Year Mom Won the Pennant," in Kirkus Service, *Vol. XXXVI, No. 5, March 1, 1968, p. 260.*

The members of the team, faced with the choice of Nick's mother as coach-or no coach and no season—chose Mom. The title tells the story; as usual, Mr. Christopher writes competently about baseball games and tosses in a bit of humor, a bit of brotherhood, and a bit of sub-plot—this time the neglected rich boy whose parents wake up to a realization of the problem. Pleasant, realistic and low-keyed.

> Zena Sutherland, in a review of "The Year Mom Won the Pennant," in Bulletin of the Center for Children's Books, *Vol. 21, No. 9, May, 1968, p. 139.*

Mr. Christopher's fans are sure to acquire some female followers, thanks to the original twist which he gives this timely baseball story. The humor as well as the action adds spice to the twist.

> Rose H. Agree, in a review of "The Year Mom Won the Pennant," in Instructor, *Vol. LXXVII, No. 9, May, 1968, p. 128.*

The Basket Counts (1968)

Score another for a steady winner who counts with kids. Mel Jensen and friend Cotton (both Negroes) don't get their share of passes from basketball teammate Caskie Bennett who obviously resents an integrated court. Coach Thorpe counsels the team to work together, and Mel explains it to his father ("It isn't all the whites, Dad. It's just a few") but Caskie remains remote. Even Mel's civil return of the Bennett's strayed kitten doesn't break the ice; a coach-to-mother conversation, however, and bench-warming (after the two boys come to blows) do start a thaw. Mr. Jensen had said "They'll get used to us and we'll get used to them" and here is a sober unfolding of possibility. The source of Caskie's change of heart is vague—which may be the most realistic solution; furthermore, Mel is no Simple character either, which may well enlarge his potential audience. Best of all, it has its own rhythm.

> A review of "The Basket Counts," in Kirkus Service, *Vol. XXXVI, No. 13, July 1, 1968, p. 690.*

Both Mel Jensen and his pal had joined the basketball team when they transferred to Hillcrest. Knowing that they might encounter prejudice there as well as in their new community, the boys were determined to combat it by being pleasant. "It isn't all the whites, Dad. It's just a few," Mel said, but when one of the few is a team member who won't pass the ball to you, it isn't easy to get a basket. The situation is handled with restrained realism, since the thaw is gradual and the easing of tension is due in large part to Mel's good sense and patience. Characterization is competent but not deep, the dialogue is natural, and the story has a good balance of home and school episodes, with plenty of action in the court sequences. (pp. 36-7)

> Zena Sutherland, in a review of "The Basket Counts," in The Saturday Review, *New York, Vol. LI, No. 42, October 19, 1968, p. 36.*

This is both a story about junior high school basketball and about Negro-white relationships, with the former the predominant emphasis. Mel Jensen and Cotton Brady are Negro, both fairly new to the school and both having trouble because some of the boys on the team taunt them. Mel's father, during family discussions, is calm about prejudice. "Don't worry, they'll get used to us and we'll get used to them." Although both the basketball sequences and the gradual improvement of relationships are predictable, they are realistic; there is one incident in which Mel helps rescue a boy who has fallen through the ice while skating, but it is not a melodramatic life-saving operation.

> Zena Sutherland, in a review of "The Basket Counts," in Bulletin of the Center for Children's Books, *Vol. 22, No. 5, January, 1969, p. 75.*

Hard Drive to Short (1969)

You might think a good teammate would tell the others that he has to leave early to babysit for his sisters. But Sandy is ashamed, and afraid that his friends will razz him. They, in turn, assume he's off with Rod Temple, an older boy equipped with a cool scooter and a hot temper. Sandy *is* pleased by Rod's attention, but he sees through his ploys (forgetting his wallet) and genuinely misses his friends. All's well in the end—he bids Rod goodbye and works at regaining his teammates' good will. The several strands come together effectively with the play-by-play, although his reluctance to tell may seem suspect to some readers.

> *A review of "Hard Drive to Short," in* Kirkus Reviews, *Vol. XXXVII, No. 4, February 15, 1969, p. 178.*

This entertaining, but not exceptional story of baseball is about a young boy who must learn the value of friendship. His teammates, whom he has ignored for some time, win out in the end, but readers will be more interested in the play-by-play descriptions of the games.

> *A review of "Hard Drive to Short," in* Publishers Weekly, *Vol. 195, No. 16, April 21, 1969, p. 66.*

Because of his personal stubbornness, Sandy Varga nearly loses both his baseball ability and his friends. But popular author Matt Christopher resolves all problems satisfactorily in *Hard Drive to Short,* a story divided equally between baseball action and the everyday personal life of the characters. The paucity of sports stories for the age group [grades 3-5] should make this competent addition welcome.

> *A review of "Hard Drive to Short," in* School Library Journal, *Vol. 15, No. 9, May, 1969, p. 111.*

Catch That Pass! (1969)

Linebacker Jim Nardi's an intrepid tackler but he's terrified of being tackled himself and, after several dropped passes, everybody knows it. "You'll play until you get the feeling knocked out of you, one way or another," swears big brother Doug, team coach, former high school star and—Jim learns from old clippings—a one-time fumbler himself. After a week's respite due to a burned arm and with his crippled-from-polio (today?) friend Chuckie's pluck to stiffen him, Jim braces himself and hangs on. Almost continuous play but not really much fun, and the guidelines are full of holes.

> *A review of "Catch That Pass!" in* Kirkus Reviews, *Vol. XXXVII, No. 15, August 1, 1969, p. 775.*

Jim Nardi's struggle to overcome his fear of being tackled is adequately presented . . . in *Catch That Pass!* The plot is encumbered by some irrelevant episodes; however, the paucity of sports material for this young age group insures a good reception for the story.

> *A review of "Catch That Pass!" in* School Library Journal, *Vol. 16, No. 4, December, 1969, p. 65.*

Shortstop from Tokyo (1970)

Stogie is bugged by newcomer Sam Suzuki's "I always play shortstop" but the chief problem here is winning each game. And Sam's *good*—off the field too. Stogie'd like to hate him, does leave his prized glove on the ground overnight . . . but he didn't destroy it, no matter what Sam thinks. Meanwhile Coach Dirkus puts Sam in at short and would shift Stogie to second but Stogie balks and finds himself warming the bench. He comes around—Sam hasn't squealed, sometimes "he misses 'em too," covering second isn't child's play either; and when he's able to pin the mangled glove on a porcupine, everything falls into position. Sam may seem like an all-American Japanese (not altogether unreasonably) and the illustrations [by Harvey Kidder] may make him look like a chiseled Caucasian (they do), but the beauties of playing shortstop come across—a kid can appreciate what Stogie's up against.

> *A review of "Shortstop from Tokyo," in* Kirkus Reviews, *Vol. XXXVIII, No. 8, April 15, 1970, p. 451.*

Matt Christopher's *Shortstop from Tokyo* is adequate for boys with a baseball interest and reading problems. Stogie Crane wants to like Sam Suzuki, his new teammate from Japan, even though Sam replaces him at shortstop. The loss of Sam's favorite glove, an outburst of temper, and a porcupine complicate things for Stogie until the dénouement. The use of a Japanese ball player in the story is incidental, serving only to introduce the fact that baseball is played widely in Japan.

> *A review of "Shortstop from Tokyo," in* School Library Journal, *Vol. 16, No. 9, May, 1970, p. 93.*

[A] book for younger boys is Matt Christopher's *Shortstop from Tokyo* in which Stogie resents it when his position is challenged by a Japanese boy visiting the States for a year. Heavy on game descriptions, the story has a limp subplot and a trite good-fellowship ending.

> *Zena Sutherland, "Hits and Errors," in* The Saturday Review, *New York, Vol. LIII, No. 26, June 27, 1970, p. 38.*

Stogie would certainly have been shortstop in the starting lineup if it hadn't been for Sam Suzuki, in town for only one year and popular after the first day. Stogie knew Sam was really a fine player, but it was hard to like someone who usurped your place. The only ancillary bit of plot is Sam's suspicion that Stogie had damaged his favorite mitt, and the discovery by Stogie that a wandering porcupine was almost certainly the culprit. Otherwise, the book is just a compilation of baseball sequences, very patterned.

> *Zena Sutherland, in a review of "Shortstop from Tokyo," in* Bulletin of the Center for Children's Books, *Vol. 23, No. 11, July-August, 1970, p. 173.*

Johnny Long Legs (1970)

The feelings evoked in Christopher's *Johnny Long*

Legs . . . are intensity and commitment, both on and off the basketball court. Longlegged Johnny Reese persistently practices his jumping and pivoting skills with Toby, his new stepbrother, while at the same time attempting to befriend and reform Jim Sain, a classroom antagonist and basketball rival. Johnny's off-court behavior in this regard almost smacks of interference and contrived rehabilitation, but Christopher manages to control the situation by ascribing to Johnny a fairly believable set of values. Game descriptions are highly detailed with a considerable emphasis given to scores and league standings.

> *A review of "Johnny Long Legs," in* School Library Journal, *Vol. 17, No. 4, December, 1970, p. 77.*

Lucky Seven: Sports Stories   (1970)

Matt Christopher, best known for his books, has also written widely in various magazines. *Lucky Seven,* for grades 4-6, includes six short stories which originally appeared in periodicals—about baseball, football, and hockey and one new mini-novel about slot-car racing. Christopher's familiar, simple story lines and uncomplicated style are very much in evidence in this collection.

> *A review of "Lucky Seven," in* School Library Journal, *Vol. 17, No. 4, December, 1970, p. 79.*

Look Who's Playing First Base   (1971)

It's Yuri Dontzel, *the boy from Russia.* Once past the inevitable epithet and proper reply—"I am not a communist. I never was . . . we came to the United States to get away from communism"—the problem is Yuri's ineptitude as the Checkmates' newest recruit. He has claimed no particular skill and he fails at batting and fielding alike; but the team fails at sportsmanship—even when Yuri gets into the habit of hitting home runs, catcher Dan (jealous?) ribs him unmercifully, threatens that he'll quit himself (and absolutely nobody else can catch). Yuri improves but stubborn pride conquers Dan and he does quit; and then he comes back truly sorry. And that's that except for the play-by-play game after game after game: din in search of a story. (pp. 50-1)

> *A review of "Look Who's Playing First Base," in* Kirkus Reviews, *Vol. XXXIX, No. 2, January 15, 1971, pp. 50-1.*

Look Who's Playing First Base, for grades 3 to 6, features the usual elements of undeveloped talent, impatient teammates, and a solution obtained through diligence and sportsmanship—all set against the introduction of an unusual character. Yuri Dotzen's family has defected to the U.S. on their Russian travel permit, and now he wants to play Little League baseball as part of his new American way of life. He learns to bat well, but his inept fielding causes team dissension. There's lots of the standard, tedious, detailed play action but only the barest of political explanations, as well as a simplistic resolution of Yuri's fear of being hit by the baseball.

> *A review of "Look Who's Playing First Base,"*

in School Library Journal, *Vol. 17, No. 9, May 15, 1971, p. 85.*

Yuri Dotzen, whose family had come from Russia the year before, has had no baseball experience, but Mike is sure he can fill in at first base. Yuri's play is full of errors, but he develops fast as a hitter; not fast enough to keep Don, the catcher, from taunting him and threatening to quit. Don calls Yuri a communist and Yuri explains that his parents had decided to leave Russia to get away from communism. Don quits, then returns to apologize and take his old position. Yuri wins a game with a home run on the last page, in a patterned ending to a formula story. Adequately written, the book has little substance save for the detailed baseball sequences.

> *Zena Sutherland, in a review of "Look Who's Playing First Base," in* Bulletin of the Center for Children's Books, *Vol. 24, No. 9, May, 1971, p. 133.*

Tough to Tackle   (1971)

Boots Raymond wants to be quarterback but he weighs in too heavy at 139; it takes pep talks from as far away as

Christopher calls this 1941 photograph "My first story sale: a fifty-dollar check from Fiction House."

CHILDREN'S LITERATURE REVIEW, Vol. 33

Vietnam where his brother is fighting "Charlie" to change him from a colossally bad sport into a determined tackle. Between the play and the petulance there's no room for anything as prosaic as characterization or coherent plotting, and in the breach on and off the field Boots comes across as an oversized eight-year-old—humorless, has-been, and hollow.

> *A review of "Tough to Tackle," in* Kirkus Reviews, *Vol. XXXIX, No. 13, July 1, 1971, p. 675.*

Matt Christopher's **Tough To Tackle** is worth noting only because defensive linemen as fictional heroes don't exactly abound (they've no stardust). Hero Boots, the feisty kid in a lackluster position, is likeable enough, but the dingy prose and shopworn situations rough the reader.

> *A review of "Tough to Tackle," in* School Library Journal, *Vol. 18, No. 4, December, 1971, p. 75.*

Boots Raymond had hoped to be a quarterback, but the limit for backfield players was 125 pounds, and he was 139. Disappointed, Boots did less than his best until a letter from his brother in Vietnam helped him to change his attitude, and his improved playing helped his team to a championship. The story has football game sequences that should appeal to readers, but the story line is patterned, and the book has neither depth nor characterization to support the plot. The writing is capable, although it is sprinkled with such flat statements as, "It's a good contact sport and should prepare him in many ways for the future."

> *Zena Sutherland, in a review of "Tough to Tackle," in* Bulletin of the Center for Children's Books, *Vol. 25, No. 8, April, 1972, p. 119.*

The Kid Who Only Hit Homers (1972)

The Kid Who Only Hit Homers by Matt Christopher is average fare about supernatural aid for a young homer hitter. Sylvester Coddmyer III has a mysterious supporter who is always there in the stands when he hits a home run. Sylvester's record—he hits a home run every time at bat—eventually attracts national attention to Hooper Junior High School games. He has just turned down a magazine biography contract when his strange friend, who wears a baseball cap saying "N.Y." and who is invisible to everyone else, announces that he must leave. The mystery man's name is George Baruth, which sounds suspiciously like George Herman "Babe" Ruth. Presumably Sylvester's ability to hit homers will leave him after Mr. Baruth's departure, but this easy-to-read book will still make a hit with fans.

> *A review of "The Kid Who Only Hit Homers," in* School Library Journal, *Vol. 18, No. 9, May, 1972, p. 93.*

Face-Off (1972)

Scott is no chicken; he proves that to our satisfaction when he chases a puck so recklessly that he goes over the treacherous falls. But after Del invites him to join the Golden Bears hockey team and he impresses them all with his fast skating and hard playing, Scott discovers that he is puck shy. His good plays and a few brilliant goals don't compensate for all those times that he closes his eyes and covers his face when he should be in there fighting, and Del becomes more and more scornful until Scott finally faces up to the puck and wins the team's respect. Christopher keeps the outcome in doubt right up to the finish and provides plenty of ice action along the way, but this is surely one of his standard plays.

> *A review of "Face-Off," in* Kirkus Reviews, *Vol. XL, No. 18, September 15, 1972, p. 1097.*

Geared for young readers, Matt Christopher's sports fiction is often their introduction to the genre. Unfortunately, **Face-Off** is a mediocre first encounter. Scott Harrison's fast skating attracts Del Stockton and Skinny McCay, who invite him to join the Golden Bears. Scott's problem—he's puck shy—is exacerbated by Del's disgust and nasty remarks which add to Scott's insecurity. The characters are uninteresting, and the story never manages to take off.

> *A review of "Face-Off," in* School Library Journal, *Vol. 19, No. 4, December, 1972, p. 78.*

Mystery Coach (1973)

Though it may only be Little League, Chris and his gang field the dugout slang with ease—which will give young readers something to turn over on their tongues, if not in their minds—as the mystery coach who relays instructions via anonymous telephone calls very soon reveals himself to be none other than smart-aleck Steve Herrick's wheelchair-bound father. Mr. Herrick's appearance in the flesh magically enables the feuding Blazers to go the route, but this mystery man seems like little more than a spin-off from the more enigmatic George Baruth, coach of **The Kid Who Only Hit Homers.** (pp. 382-83)

> *A review of "Mystery Coach," in* Kirkus Reviews, *Vol. XLI, No. 7, April 1, 1973, pp. 382-83.*

The Blazers, with an ailing coach, are falling apart on the baseball diamond until players begin receiving calls from a mysterious coach who supplies game winning advice. The clues to the coach's identity will not be overly obvious to middle graders. Christopher keeps his story simple and easy to read, but many characters—team members, parents, the ailing coach, and the mystery coach—are sketchy prototypes. The leadership struggle between players Chris Richards and Steve Herrick is not fully developed. However, swift game action speeds up the predictable plot which will appeal to youngsters hooked on baseball and looking forward to Christopher's latest.

> *Donna Hummel, in a review of "Mystery*

Coach," in School Library Journal, *Vol. 20, No. 5, January, 1974, p. 46.*

Ice Magic   (1973)

Fly League hockey player Pie Pennelli has two problems, teammate Terry the Terrible Mason's unexplained hostility and a pair of over-sized hand-me-down skates that trip him up during crucial plays. But just when this begins to read like a replay, Christopher introduces the little Byrd twins next door, whose 1896 toy hockey game has the apparent power to predict the course and outcome of upcoming games. Just as a pregame trial on the Byrds' toy has foretold, Pie loses the last game and is put out of action by a broken blade, but the final outcome is friendship with Terry and a new pair of skates. Thus when Terry's cat Tipper at last breaks the antique game's magic it has already accomplished its purpose—not only for Pie but also as supernatural assist to a formula sports story.

A review of "Ice Magic," in Kirkus Reviews, *Vol. XLI, No. 18, September 15, 1973, p. 1035.*

An old hockey game found to have powers of prediction is the fanciful element flirted with in Matt Christopher's **Ice Magic.** Christopher seems more concerned with the conflict between the protagonist and a real-life antagonist, but this aspect of the story actually strains believability more than the fantasy. The plot is poorly knit, characterization is shallow, and the ice action is dreary. A half-dozen substandard illustrations [by Byron Goto] finish off any hopes for this book.

Raymond J. Marafino, in a review of "Ice Magic," in School Library Journal, *Vol. 20, No. 4, December, 1973, p. 65.*

Pie had two problems as a member of the Fly League hockey team, the Penguins: one was the fact that he was using his brother's skates and they slowed his game because they were too big; the other was that one of his teammates, Terry, ragged him constantly. Then Pie discovered that an old hockey game belonging to his neighbors would always magically predict the events of any game if it were used the day before the game. At the close of the story, Pie is to get new skates because his old ones have broken, he and Terry have become friendly, and the magic game has lost its power. The fantasy (never explained) and the realism never quite mesh, and the ending of the story is anticlimactic; although the magic game and real game sequences have little relationship beyond the oddity of coincidence, there is a sure appeal to hockey fans in the action of the team's game sequences. (pp. 91-2)

Zena Sutherland, in a review of "Ice Magic," in Bulletin of the Center for Children's Books, *Vol. 27, No. 6, February, 1974, pp. 91-2.*

Desperate Search   (1973)

Two old enemies, Ginger the dog and Whitey the cat, become fast friends when they're locked in the back of a delivery truck together and have to make their way back home through strange territory full of threatening dogs.

Meanwhile Tommy and Jamie set out on Tommy's pony Buck in search of their missing pets only to get lost themselves in a late December blizzard. Boys, dog, cat and pony all make it back home in time for Christmas turkey—winding up a real holiday tail thumper for Christopher's easy reading following.

A review of "Desperate Search," in Kirkus Reviews, *Vol. XLI, No. 22, November 15, 1973, p. 1264.*

The author of a string of sports books has here switched to a swiftly paced animal story having the subtheme of racial separation. Two days before Christmas in upstate New York, Whitey, a dignified Persian cat, and Ginger, a big brown-and-white dog, get trapped in a delivery van miles away from home. Their owners, Tommy and Jamie, set out on Tommy's horse, Buck, to find their pets before a blizzard hits. Tommy is white and Jamie black, but this fact, which had previously separated them, is now ignored. Although the animals' points of view are regrettably anthropomorphized, the intensity of the perils facing the foursome is effectively heightened in the taut story and in Leslie Morrill's pen-and-ink illustrations.

Susan L. Pickles, in a review of "Desperate Search," in School Library Journal, *Vol. 20, No. 6, February, 1974, p. 60.*

No Arm in Left Field   (1974)

Another sports book by this prolific and popular writer concerns black player, Terry Delaney, who can hit and catch well but suffers from a poor throwing arm, and his white baseball teammates, but particularly his relationship with Tony Casterline. Swift game action, teamwork, plenty of baseball jargon, and a satisfying conclusion. This one's a good one. A guy can get awfully tense when his man almost strikes out! Less able readers in junior high will also read this work with enthusiasm.

Geneva Van Horne, in a review of "No Arm in Left Field," in Instructor, *Vol. LXXXIII, No. 9, May, 1974, p. 95.*

Matt Christopher hangs everything on an overused and underdeveloped racial theme. Influenced by bigoted parents, Tony, a white shortstop, refuses to run into the outfield and help Terry, a black player with a weak throwing arm, relay the ball to the infield. When Tony finally gets it into his thick skull to help out (and thus save the last game), he instantly becomes friendly toward Terry. A sloppy plot contrivance—Terry is taken for a dune buggy ride by Tony's brother (who just pops up), the car tips over, and when they go to clean up Tony's parents see what a good guy Terry is—along with shallow characterization and Byron Goto's useless illustrations all fail here, just as they did in **Ice Magic.**

A review of "No Arm in Left Field," in School Library Journal, *Vol. 20, No. 9, May 15, 1974, p. 71.*

Baseball stories in which the newcomer or the player who is a member of a minority group encounters hostility are a dime a dozen, and baseball stories in which a newcomer gets over a weakness in his style are just as easily found. Yet this story, which has both elements in the plot, is written with such candor and directness that it has a firm unity. Terry is black and a newcomer and has a weak throwing arm—but no miracles happen. Tony, who has openly shown his prejudice, becomes less hostile, not because of Terry's efforts and his understanding; Tony's hostility is explained to Terry by his (Tony's) older brother and discussed frankly by other members of the team. The book has plenty of game sequences for the baseball fan, and there's more of a lesson about sportsmanship to be gained from Terry's behavior than any preaching the author might have done—but wisely didn't.

> *Zena Sutherland, in a review of "No Arm in Left Field," in* Bulletin of the Center for Children's Books, *Vol. 27, No. 11, July-August, 1974, p. 172.*

Jinx Glove (1974)

Christopher touches on the ball player's nemesis—superstition. Hankering for a new glove, Little Leaguer Chip tosses his old one—a relic from his dad—into a lake. The new glove, however, is jinxed—riddled with holes. Unable to retrieve the old mitt, Chip is ready to bench himself rather than risk the big game, but just in the knick of time, the glove is returned and Chip helps his team to victory. A totally predictable offering for youngest fans somewhat pepped up by Chartier's humorous color drawings.

> *Donna Hummel, in a review of "Jinx Glove," in* School Library Journal, *Vol. 21, No. 3, October, 1974, p. 103.*

Chip was a good fielder, but when he threw away the old glove he'd been using, one that his father had used, and bought a new one, he couldn't seem to catch anything. He asked a small boy whose big brother had retrieved the old glove from the lake where Chip had thrown it if he could have the old glove back. The boy refused, but he later showed up at the diamond and gave Chip the old glove. Chip gave him the jinx glove, happy that he was fielding well again. A very slight plot, but young baseball fans will probably enjoy the game sequences and the sustaining of the superstition of lucky objects. Large print, simple writing style, and illustrations that are not outstanding but that lend a bit of humor to the story.

> *Zena Sutherland, in a review of "Jinx Glove," in* Bulletin of the Center for Children's Books, *Vol. 28, No. 3, November, 1974, p. 39.*

Front Court Hex (1974)

How could last year's basketball star play three games straight without scoring a point? Witchcraft, that's how, but it takes the better part of the season before Jerry is convinced that little Danny Weatherspoon really is a warlock (*and* a distant relation) who is hexing his shots so that Jerry will learn to "live decently, not to steal, and to show

his love for his parents" by doing his chores. With belief in Danny comes remorse, with reform comes success on the court, and in the end even Jerry's bitter enemy Freddy is shouting "Good play, Jerry. You're really cookin' with gas." Of course as served up by Christopher it's a lot like warmed over *Ice Magic.* (pp. 1059-60)

> *A review of "Front Court Hex," in* Kirkus Reviews, *Vol. XLII, No. 19, October 1, 1974, pp. 1059-60.*

In *Front Court Hex,* Matt Christopher again unsuccessfully attempts to mix fanciful and realistic elements. Jerry Steele, last year's basketball star, cannot sink a single basket. The slump is due to a hex put on Jerry by a warlock relative who makes mysterious appearances warning him to give up petty stealing, cheating in school, and being lazy at home. The resolution is unsatisfying: Jerry's reformation comes about solely because he's losing points on the court and not because he's gained insight into his behavior.

> *A review of "Front Court Hex," in* School Library Journal, *Vol. 21, No. 4, December, 1974, p. 53.*

Stranded (1974)

Matt Christopher is well out of his sporting element here, with this heartstring-shredding entertainment in which young, blind Andy and his setter Max are marooned on a desert island after a sailing accident and more than a few "moments of unbelievable terror." The island has the usual quota of quicksand, steep cliffs, fighting iguanas and unsavory visitors (two men who steal both Max and the food left in the wreckage). Fortunately, Max can understand English ("Okay, Max, take me to a small tree. I want to hang these up to dry") and none of the crises is allowed to last more than several pages. The style is strictly wet behind the ears.

> *A review of "Stranded," in* Kirkus Reviews, *Vol. XLII, No. 21, November 1, 1974, p. 1150.*

Blind 12-year-old Andy and his dog Max are stranded on a Caribbean island after a tropical storm has washed his parents overboard. Andy, who has food from the beached sloop but no radio to contact rescuers, explores the island with his pet and saves a seagull with a broken wing. Although a good story about blindness, this is marred by Christopher's anthropomorphizing of the animals.

> *Susan L. Pickles, in a review of "Stranded," in* School Library Journal, *Vol. 21, No. 5, January, 1975, p. 43.*

Caught in a tropical storm, the Crossett family's boat is trapped on a reef after Andy's parents have been washed overboard. Andy and his dog Max manage to survive on the island because Andy can get at the food in the sailboat and because Max is so well-trained. Andy is blind. The dog is taken off the island by two young men who don't see Andy or the boat; Andy is later rescued and, just in time, the dog (who has swum back from the neighboring island) is picked up too. The story closes with a happy reunion of all (including Max) at the hospital. The story boils down to very little, although the situation of ship-wreck-and-blindness-and uninhabited island is dramatic: boy loses dog, boy finds dog. There are elements of coincidence that weaken the story; for example, the two men who take the dog find the boat and deplete the larder but don't look for a human survivor (Andy's sound asleep). And there are too many instances of the dog's comprehension that stretch credibility, as when Andy takes off his wet clothes and says, "Okay, Max, take me to a small tree. I want to hang these up to dry," and Max looks about, sees a tree with low-hanging branches, and leads Andy to it.

*Zena Sutherland, in a review of "Stranded,"
in* Bulletin of the Center for Children's Books,
Vol. 28, No. 6, February, 1975, p. 91.

Glue Fingers   (1975)

"I would give anything to play football on a team! But I can't! The guys would laugh me off the field!" And so at first Billy Joe, who stutters, turns down Mr. Davis' offer even though he's a whiz playing with his brothers around the farm. But realizing that night that "he wouldn't have to talk while he played," Billy Joe changes his mind, and though he doesn't start out all that well in his first game, he ends up winning both the game and his teammates' cheers by catching two different passes for touchdowns. Even easier, shorter and less dressed up than Christopher's usual recreation therapy, with awkwardly executed football-suited figures in black and white [by Jim Venable], all smeared hit or miss with yellow and a thick cherry red. A fumble.

A review of "Glue Fingers," in Kirkus Reviews, *Vol. XLII, No. 11, June 1, 1975, p. 602.*

Should a handicap make a child feel he can't join a team sport? Not when stuttering is the handicap. A coach had seen Billy Joe playing football with his brothers, and asked him to join the team. Billy Joe refused, changed his mind although he was worried about being teased, came into his first game to make two of the three winning touchdowns. Although stuttering is a serious problem to the child who does it, it seems to be a contrived one here because it never really comes up as an issue, i.e. neither before nor during the football game does anyone tease Billy Joe; it serves only as a prelude to a game account. There is no explanation of why the coach is at Billy Joe's home, he just appears saying, "Hi, Billy Joe, you have a nice big farm here." There is a brief establishment of good family rapport, but the slight plot and the formula treatment weaken the book.

Zena Sutherland, in a review of "Glue Fingers," in Bulletin of the Center for Children's Books, *Vol. 29, No. 3, November, 1975, p. 40.*

Billy Joe nearly lets his stuttering keep him from enjoying his favorite sport of football. Afraid the other boys will laugh at his speech problem Billy Joe refuses to join the team but, unable to sleep one night, he finally decides to take a chance and calls the coach the next morning with his decision. (Unrealistically, the coach arrives with the membership papers, a physician gives him a physical, and he gets his uniform before the evening is over.) The illustrations [by Jim Venable] are action-packed and well integrated with the overall acceptable story which presents with understanding and insight the anxieties of a young boy who stutters.

Donna Hummel, in a review of "Glue Fingers," in School Library Journal, *Vol. 22, No. 3, November, 1975, p. 44.*

Billy Joe, youngest of four brothers, stutters. Despite his skill as a "glue fingers" football player, he refuses to join the football team for fear the other boys will make fun of him. Finally deciding to play, but vowing never to speak a word, Billy Joe discovers that silence is impractical and begins to speak—stutter and all. No one makes fun of him, mainly because he also wins the game for his team with some spectacular plays.

Moral? Perhaps the author means to say that a handicap is okay so long as one is a super-something. But what if one does not happen to be a super-something? In that case, one must look for a better book.

Books which purport to deal with a problem but violate their subject by fudging on the salient issues are, at best, a rip-off. They also do a disservice to the many people who have one sort of handicap or another. They are an insult to the intelligence of all children. (pp. 40-1)

*"Pre-School and Early Years: 'Glue Fingers',"
in* Human—and Anti-Human—Values in Children's Books: A Content Rating Instrument for Educators and Concerned Parents, *edited by the Council on Interracial Books for Children, Inc., Racism and Sexism Resources Center for Educators, 1976, pp. 40-1.*

The Pigeon with the Tennis Elbow   (1975)

Baseball players have their guardian angels; all Kevin has is a curmudgeonly pigeon, the avatar of a great-great uncle with Wimbledon ambitions, to whisper encouragement in his ear as he works his way toward a tournament final with rival Roger Murphy. Kevin's ambivalence about competition makes psychological sense, but this Matt Christopher formula has had more incarnations than Buddha's big toe.

*A review of "The Pigeon with Tennis Elbow,"
in* Kirkus Reviews, *Vol. XLIII, No. 21, November 1, 1975, p. 1227.*

Kevin O'Toole has designs on the town tennis tournament championship but he has three matches to go, the big game being the final against nasty Roger Murphy. Kevin's confidence in his game has flown away but is replaced by a talking pigeon who is Kevin's reincarnated great-great Uncle Rickard. The uncle, who for no reason insists on being called Charlie, was a near Wimbledon champ who lost out because of tennis elbow. The pigeon restores Kevin's confidence, and guess who wins the championship! Incredibly, that's all there is to the story. Even more incredible, the kids seemingly get a court anytime they want one! Christopher, with more than 40 stories to his credit (mostly football and baseball), has his first tennis novel here and it's a double fault all the way.

Robert Unsworth, in a review of "The Pigeon with the Tennis Elbow," in School Library Journal, *Vol. 22, No. 5, January, 1976, p. 44.*

Earthquake **(1975)**

Jeff's decision to run away from camp and cover the thirty-odd miles across the Adirondack wilderness to his home with his horse Red may have been foolhardy. But one really can't blame him for not anticipating being caught in an earthquake—6.5 on the Richter scale, the epicenter smack in his path. The quake is as gratuitous as Jeff's conflict with his camp director is predictable. However Christopher makes something of Jeff's passing encounters—with a buck, a beaver colony, a family of campers, and his flashy editing, quick-cutting from Jeff's close calls to his distraught parents and back again, might sustain the short attention spans of the unsophisticated audience he aims for.

A review of "Earthquake," in Kirkus Reviews,
Vol. XLIII, No. 23, December 1, 1975, p. 1335.

Jeff Belno runs away from a summer camp with his horse and attempts to cross the Adirondacks to reach home. The trail is rough and while trying to ford a fast moving stream, he loses his map, compass, and knapsack. A friendly family of campers helps him and he continues on his way following a stream which he knows will eventually pass his town. An earthquake occurs in which he and his horse narrowly escape injury. Finally Jeff reconsiders his camp experience; decides he had overreacted; and determines to return and finish the season, (he signals a rescue helicopter which sends help). Although Jeff is described as a slow learner, he has flawless command of the language and when using a compass, he compensates for the difference between true and magnetic north—hardly convincing behavior for a slow learner. Unfortunately, *Earthquake* is a strangely flat and lethargic story for Christopher whose books are generally full of action, crisis, and confrontation. The message is delivered with the usual lack of subtlety, but the compensatory excitement is missing.

Karen H. Harris, in a review of "Earthquake," in School Library Journal, *Vol. 22, No. 6, February, 1976, p. 44.*

Christopher presenting a copy of his first children's book, the Lucky Baseball Bat, *to librarian Florence Kramer, 1954.*

The Team That Stopped Moving (1975)

A red-haired warlock, Jack Wanda, stops time, action, and the Tigers baseball team to give three players advice. Attempts at characterization are concentrated on one player singled out for coaching from the sports wizard—first baseman and team organizer Dick Farrar who is unrealistically philosophical about the benefits of playing ball and team cooperation. As seen in the insipid black-and-white line drawings [by Byron Goto], the Tigers' roster is all white and all male; there is a single episode where Dick's sister hits pop flies and grounders to allow the boys to practice their fielding. Sexism, racism, and tokenism aside, the game descriptions teeter on the brink of tedium.

> *Michele Woggon, in a review of "The Team That Stopped Moving," in* School Library Journal, *Vol. 22, No. 6, February, 1976, p. 37.*

The Submarine Pitch (1976)

Whereas the **Pigeon With Tennis Elbow** gave us coaching from beyond the grave, Bernie learns his game-winning submarine pitch from Dave who won't be able to throw it himself because he's dying of a liver disease. Death or no, attention is focused on the baseball diamond, and you'll recognize the delivery . . . though the aim is low and outside even for Christopher.

> *A review of "The Submarine Pitch," in* Kirkus Reviews, *Vol. XLIV, No. 8, April 15, 1976, p. 468.*

Yet another sports offering by the prolific Matt Christopher. Young Bernie Shantz learns to master a difficult and little-known pitch. Bernie perseveres on the mound in order to please his friend Dave Grant who is suffering from a mysterious disease. Most of the off-the-field action is concerned with the genuine concern and sensitivity the two boys show toward one another. Unfortunately, the dialogue is stilted and sounds artificial; the game descriptions are extremely slow-moving and, in some cases, difficult to follow; and the ending, in which Bernie and a long-time adversary become friends in their mutual grief over Dave's hospitalization, is maudlin. A strike out.

> *Richard Luzer, in a review of "The Submarine Pitch," in* School Library Journal, *Vol. 23, No. 5, January, 1977, p. 88.*

Power Play (1976)

Rabbit's faith in the efficacy of a candy bar called Choco-Power transforms him from the basketball team's worst player into its high-scoring star and leaves him so swell-headed that even his big brother, Bones, is turned off. But later Rabbit's cockiness lures him into an uneven race against a speeding locomotive on a narrow railroad bridge. That close call prompts Rabbit to throw away the Choco-Power he finds mysteriously soon after, and you won't be surprised to see his swagger disappear along with his lucky charm though, oddly, his new self-esteem seems to linger on. Compared to the botched up **Glue Fingers**, this has some staying power and [illustrator] Ray Burns at least

makes the kids look bright and wholesome . . . though their Doublemint smiles have a purely commercial appeal. (pp. 682-83)

> *A review of "Power Play," in* Kirkus Reviews, *Vol. XLIV, No. 12, June 15, 1976, pp. 682-83.*

Although he makes his share of baskets, Rabbit wants to be a better basketball player, especially to be better than his brother Bones. He finds a candy bar that advertises itself as a source of power, eats it and plays brilliantly, and becomes so conceited that Bones and the other boys are irritated. Then, crossing a dangerous railroad bridge, he has a narrow escape; seeing another bar of "Choco-Power Plus," he throws it in the river, deciding that the first one had made him a "bragging, self-centered kid." Next game, he plays as a team member rather than a star and finds the others friendly again. The plot is thin, since Rabbit's credulity about the power of the candy is not made convincing; everything happens a bit too quickly. However, the sports background and the scenes of team play will appeal to readers, and the writing style is adequate. (pp. 54-5)

> *Zena Sutherland, in a review of "Power Play," in* Bulletin of the Center for Children's Books, *Vol. 30, No. 4, December, 1976, pp. 54-5.*

A young boy eats a "magic" candy bar and turns into an outstanding player but obnoxious ball hog in Matt Christopher's **Power Play.** Eventually he returns to normal, hopefully having gained from his experience. The trouble is that by then readers really don't care.

> *A review of "Power Play," in* School Library Journal, *Vol. 23, No. 4, December, 1976, p. 71.*

Football Fugitive (1976)

Formula sports-action-cum-personal-problem fare. Protagonist Larry Shope, who plays center on a midget football team, is troubled by his busy lawyer father's failure to attend his games and by the disappearance of his hero, pro footballer Yancey Foote, following an arrest in a barroom brawl. Yancey shows up at Larry's games because he wants Larry's father to represent him (in payment for Larry's go-between services, Yancey slips him a few key plays which naturally turn the team's fortunes around). Mr. Shope wins the case, and on literally the last page, promises to be a better father (presumably because Larry pushed a little business his way). There is also a totally unrelated subplot concerning Larry's best friend who is almost deaf but does not appear to have impaired verbal skills—he must be the most loquacious deaf ten-year-old on record. Forgettable on every score.

> *Richard Luzer, in a review of "Football Fugitive," in* School Library Journal, *Vol. 23, No. 6, February, 1977, p. 62.*

Devil Pony (1977)

A crafty combination of high-interest lures—ghosts and horses—doesn't sustain this humdrum story of bumps and whinnys in the night. With clues like Wilbur's shifty eyes and dark looks (or is it shifty looks and dark eyes?), readers will be more disappointed than surprised to learn he's the poltergeist—pulling strings and wires—who's been trying to prevent Cousin Stu from taking a favorite Morgan pony back seat. Hammering hearts, "burning desires," and overlaid remarriage/stepson tensions notwithstanding, it's far from exciting, though easily digestible.

> *A review of "Devil Pony," in* Kirkus Reviews, *Vol. XLV, No. 5, March 1, 1977, p. 223.*

Wilbur is attached to Midnight, a year-old Morgan horse (which Christopher mistakenly calls a pony), that he has raised from a colt, but the horse has been promised to his cousin Stu. To convince Stu that Midnight is dangerous, Wilbur creates a series of poltergeist incidents—burrs under saddles, smashed crockery—that keep Stu—if not readers—puzzled. (What's going on won't be any mystery to most fourth-graders who will peg Wilbur as the culprit right away.) The real mystery is why Christopher didn't take the trouble to find out that horses are *not* full-grown at one-year-old, and that no responsible owner would ride a horse that young. A similar carelessness attends the plot and characterizations. Artificially inserted incidents such as an encounter with a mountain lion (difficult to find these days outside a zoo) fail to liven things up, and Wilbur's natural feelings about losing his treasured horse are explored only superficially.

> *Whitney Rogge, in a review of "Devil Pony," in* School Library Journal, *Vol. 23, No. 9, May, 1977, p. 60.*

The Diamond Champs (1977)

Kim had played football and run track, but he'd never been a baseball player and he couldn't understand why Coach Stag insisted he play. Why had the other boys and two girls each been called and urged to join the Steelheads team? Why did Stag's assistant never do anything? Kim made some effort to solve the mystery, but most of the time he was busy practicing or playing in a game—and the oddly assorted team enjoyed their own improvement as much as the coach did. As is clear from the title, the Steelheads win the Bantam League title; the coach proves to be a man who had been told he couldn't play as a boy because of poor eyesight and who had asked the sons and daughters of the team members of his boyhood so that he could prove he knew baseball. There's a bit of contrivance occasionally, and some variation in the quality of the dialogue, but the plot is fresh, at least in re the coach if not in the come-from-behind victory. For baseball buffs, the game sequences will, as always, be appealing. (pp. 9-10)

> *Zena Sutherland, in a review of "The Diamond Champs," in* Bulletin of the Center for Children's Books, *Vol. 31, No. 1, September, 1977, pp. 9-10.*

Johnny No Hit (1977)

Johnny Webb's self-respect is at stake when the local bully, a pitcher on another baseball team, threatens him if he hits the bully's balls in the next game. Johnny struggles briefly, complies up to the last pitch, then hits a home run. His last-minute solution: he decides to call the bully's bluff. Though this may not work in real life, the message of courage and honesty holds true. Readers will enjoy the conflict and resolution, the game action, and the informal writing style.

> *Judith Goldberger, in a review of "Johnny No Hit," in* Booklist, *Vol. 74, No. 8, December 15, 1977, p. 687.*

Johnny Webb, a good hitter, is threatened by a player on a competing baseball team. Afraid of being beaten up, Johnny strikes out intentionally his first two times at bat against his rival. Then Johnny suddenly decides the other boy is bluffing and hits a home run. There is a never-ending demand for sports stories on the third and fourth grade level, and this short, large-print offering with adequate red, green, and white illustrations on every page [by Ray Burns] does fill a need in spite of a contrived plot and insufficient motivation for Johnny's about-face.

> *Martha Barnes, in a review of "Johnny No Hit," in* School Library Journal, *Vol. 24, No. 5, January, 1978, p. 87.*

Afraid of bullying Roy Burke, Johnny Webb, playing in a baseball game, remembers that Roy had threatened Johnny would "get it" if he touched one of Roy's pitches. After two strikes, Johnny decides he won't let Roy bluff him; he swings and gets a home run. He'd remembered that Roy, watching a game as participant, had yelled that the batter was a big bluff. "Who's a big bluff now?" he jeers at Roy, as he walks happily off the field. The writing is passable, the story has enough description of baseball plays to satisfy young fans, and the message is a sensible one; however, the theme of resisting a bully is only superficially developed, and the story as a whole is woefully slight. (pp. 90-1)

> *Zena Sutherland, in a review of "Johnny No Hit," in* Bulletin of the Center for Children's Books, *Vol. 31, No. 6, February, 1978, pp. 90-1.*

The Fox Steals Home (1978)

It's hard to keep your mind on baseball when your parents are splitting up—but, in the nick, twelve-year-old Bobby Canfield, "the not-so-famous third baseman for the not-so-famous Sunbirds," discovers that he has a talent for stealing bases. His slightly scatty mother is involved in her own affairs, his more compatible, outdoorsy father is dating the mother of a rival ballplayer, truculent Walter Wilson. But, thinks Bobby, *"Both of us have only a mother living with us. . . . Maybe he's going through the same kind of strain I am."* And, when Walter's lit cigarette blows up the Canfield boat—and, worse, he lies about it—Bobby defends him. Meanwhile, coaching by both Dad and (maternal) Grandpa Alex has improved Bobby's base-stealing and set him up to handle his biggest crisis, Dad's impending departure for that round-the-world trip he's always wanted to take. A canny balance of action and introspection, with only the last-minute suggestion that Bobby's parents may get together again to mar the honest handling of an all-too-common problem. (pp. 1246-47)

> *A review of "The Fox Steals Home," in* Kirkus Reviews, *Vol. XLVI, No. 22, November 15, 1978, pp. 1246-47.*

A light, untaxing story that blends baseball with a boy's efforts to deal with his parents' recent divorce. Pace is unflagging, thanks to plentiful dialogue and moderate doses of play-by-play action. Characterizations are interesting but not fully developed: protagonist Bobby Canfield's mother cares little about baseball and never materializes beyond a shallow background figure; his father, a somewhat stronger presence, ultimately disappoints Bobby with his decision to absent himself for a year to work on a round-the-world freighter. Bobby himself adjusts reasonably, reluctantly accepting his father's restlessness and taking pride in his own developing athletic abilities that have spawned the nickname "Fox" from baseball buddies. A good prospect for reluctant but not substandard readers who won't be bothered by the book's sometimes mechanically toned exposition. (pp. 748-49)

> *Denise M. Wilms, in a review of "The Fox Steals Home," in* Booklist, *Vol. 75, No. 9, January 1, 1979, pp. 748-49.*

Bobby acquires the nickname of "Fox" because, coached by his father and grandfather, he has become so quick as a base stealer. Although there is a slight overlap, most of the story falls into distinct segments: game sequences, which are given play by play (possibly tedious for all but the most devoted baseball buffs), and Bobby's problems in adjusting to the fact that his recently divorced parents are in conflict, that they are dating other people, and finally that his father decides to go away for a year. Adequately written, but rather patterned, the story has only the slightest of characterizations and the two aspects of the story never fully mesh, but the audience for sports fiction will undoubtedly enjoy the book nevertheless.

> *Zena Sutherland, in a review of "The Fox Steals Home," in* Bulletin of the Center for Children's Books, *Vol. 32, No. 6, February, 1979, p. 96.*

Jackrabbit Goalie (1978)

In Matt Christopher's **Jackrabbit Goalie,** the actions of the main character (he tells a lie which works out to his advantage) might be considered morally ambiguous if the plot were substantial enough to sustain serious interest. Further hampered by inappropriate cartoon illustrations [by Ed Parker] which lend a comic tone that is absent from the text, this is an ill-conceived and shoddily executed book.

> *A review of "Jackrabbit Goalie," in* School Library Journal, *Vol. 25, No. 4, December, 1978, p. 70.*

In one of Christopher's more perfunctory formula numbers, Pepper, who's not very tall, moves to a new town and lies about having been a soccer goalie back home so he can join the new kids' team and make friends. But after doing well at one game he fakes a sprained ankle to get out of playing in another where the opponents are reputed to be very big. It's a fish that changes Pepper's mind—yes, a spirited eight-pounder that Pepper fears will be too big for him to land. But catch the fish he does—"that fish is big too. And I pulled it in. I licked it!"—and so, natch, he's off to beat the Giants. For new readers, it's hardly worth the struggle.

> *A review of "Jackrabbit Goalie," in* Kirkus Reviews, *Vol. XLVI, No. 24, December 15, 1978, p. 1356.*

Dirt Bike Racer (1979)

The basics of minibike ownership-and-racing with some sappy melodramatics on the side. Ron Baker, 12, and his buddy Tony Franco go scuba diving and find a dirt bike, of all things, 50 feet under. (The whole story doesn't bear much scrutiny.) And since the folks who lost it from a houseboat two years back collected insurance, Ron can keep it—with his sportsman father's carefully qualified okay and no opposition from his ideal mom. But he must earn the money to replace its damaged parts, and that's where he has his luckiest strike—the one answer to his ad for lawn-mowing, hedge-trimming jobs comes from elderly, blind Mr. Randolph Perkins, "the richest guy in Ordell County," who just happens to be a one-time bike racer too. Lonely old Mr. Perkins naturally takes a shine to eager, gentlemanly Ron. His spoiled, snotty nephew warns Ron off (why, he can't imagine)—and even, in full daylight, pays a competitor to give Ron trouble on the track. But at least there's no big confrontation-and-exposure scene: Ron just gets good enough, with practice, to hold his own. For kids heavily into minibikes and good at skimming.

> *A review of "Dirt Bike Racer," in* Kirkus Reviews, *Vol. XLVII, No. 11, June 1, 1979, p. 636.*

When young Ron Baker salvages and restores a dirt bike he finds in a lake near his home, his enthusiasm for his new sport is tempered by the responsibility of finding a job to raise money to finance repairs and entry fees for local competitions. Complicating the formula plot are some seemingly menacing bikers, sabotage attempts on his bike, and the jealousy and vindictiveness of the nephew of Ron's kindly old employer who happens to have been a cycle enthusiast in his younger days. The accurate description of the jolts of a motocross competition, and Ron's unfailing honesty and good sportsmanship make this a fast moving, entertaining entry on Christopher's roster of sports titles for this age group [grades 3-5].

> *Barbara C. Campbell, in a review of "Dirt Bike Racer," in* School Library Journal, *Vol. 26, No. 1, September, 1979, p. 132.*

The Twenty-one Mile Swim (1979)

Matt Christopher's latest is weakly developed and predictably executed. Built around Joey Vass' "runt" complex, the story is his on again off again quest to cross the lake— *The Twenty-one Mile Swim.* By the time he finishes, three pages from the end, we've fought a bond issue and been thoroughly steeped in his Hungarian background. Because of the unrelated detours his accomplishment is at best an anti-climax.

> *A review of "The Twenty-one Mile Swim," in* School Library Journal, *Vol.26, No. 4, December, 1979, p. 100.*

The Dog That Stole Football Plays (1980)

When Mike communicates by telepathy with a dog (Harry) in the pet shop, he convinces his parents to buy him. Harry's unusual ability allows him to help Mike's football team by overhearing the opposition's plays and relaying them to Mike. When Harry is sick during the big game, Mike learns a lesson about achieving a victory through an unfair advantage. An amusing story that incorporates sports, pets, and psychic phenomena, *The Dog That Stole Football Plays* should hold Matt Christopher's readers.

> *A review of "The Dog That Stole Football Plays," in* School Library Journal, *Vol. 26, No. 9, May, 1980, p. 87.*

"Hi, Harry." "Well, hi, kid! It's about time." That the dog in the pet shop window answers Mike's greeting is all the more incongruous as [illustrator Bill] Ogden pictures the animal as a blocky, cartoony stuffed toy. But despite this suggestion of drollery, the story is pure dotted-line Christopher (and much shorter than the ones he used to write). At football games, Harry eavesdrops on the opponents' coach's instructions, then relays them to Mike. As a result, Mike's team chalks up four straight wins. Then one Saturday Harry gets sick, and the opponents are big and tough and lead 21-0 at the half. But guess what? Mike's Dad gives him a peptalk, Mike passes it on to the team, and the game ends in a 21-21 tie without Harry's help. Zippy enough for reading practice, but no front runner.

> *A review of "The Dog That Stole Football Plays," in* Kirkus Reviews, *Vol. XLVIII, No. 14, July 15, 1980, p. 909.*

Run, Billy, Run (1980)

Fourteen-year-old Billy signs up for the track team, but has to overcome several obstacles: teammates who jeer because he comes in last in a race, fatigue because he has to help his father saw and chop wood for fuel, and the discomforting candor of a brother who thinks Billy will never make it. In the last sports sequence of the story, Billy rises to the occasion, winning two events, placing second in another, and leading the school team to victory. The fact that Christopher has tried to give the story balance by including family matters, Billy's first friendship with a girl, and some classroom sequences compensates somewhat for the patterned story line, but it remains basically a formula plot: beginner copes with tough coach and jeering team-

mates but saves the day in a big competition. The characters have little depth; the writing style is adequate but no more than adequate.

> *Zena Sutherland, in a review of "Run, Billy, Run," in* Bulletin of the Center for Children's Books, *Vol. 34, No. 1, September, 1980, p. 4.*

This is one of those books that gives the strong impression of having been padded. The basic story line, while trite, is solid and generally well handled. Billy Chekko, a high school freshman, achieves success as a distance runner after many disappointments and frustrations and, in the process, wins back the girl he thought he had lost forever. The sections having to do with running are quite good, conveying a real feel for the tension and excitement of the competition. The author also displays considerable insight and sensitivity in his treatment of the awkwardness, anguish, and exhilaration of first love. Unfortunately, we have to wade through a confusing jumble of unrelated incidents to get to the heart of the story. Rocks falling on the house, a sister's illness, a troublemaking younger brother, Billy's mysterious dizzy spell, and a car accident are all thrown in with no coherent pattern.

> *Richard Luzer, in a review of "Run, Billy, Run," in* School Library Journal, *Vol. 27, No. 2, October, 1980, p. 153.*

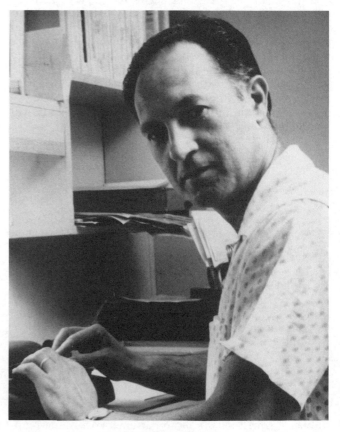

Christopher at his desk.

Wild Pitch (1980)

Since the time that his father was passed over for a promotion which went to a woman, Eddie Rhoades has been resentful of women intruding "where they weren't welcome." That is why he is not impressed with Phyl (short for Phyllis) Monahan, who plays first base for the Surfs. But when Eddie throws a *Wild Pitch* which injures Phyl, his perspective shifts, and he develops a new relationship with Phyl that changes his ideas about the male/female situation. Matt Christopher is more introspective than usual, and the portrayal of Eddie's guilt and recovery is admirable, but the circumstances of his original phobia are just a bit too clichéd.

> *A review of "Wild Pitch," in* School Library Journal, *Vol. 27, No. 4, December, 1980, p. 74.*

Eddie is upset when he finds that the first base player on another league team is a girl, Phyl; when they meet in a game, he is more than upset because she's knocked out by his wild pitch. Phyl is hospitalized, and Eddie tries twice to see her before he is admitted; he can see that her mother is angry at him and he already knows that her older cousin is vengeful. Contrite, Eddie urges Phyl to reconsider when she says she won't play again; he helps her with batting practice after she's out of the hospital, but he doesn't really feel relaxed until after they have again met in competition and he has pitched as adequately as she has faced him and batted. The two threads of the plot (Eddie's prejudice against girl players and his guilt about having hit an opponent) are adequately meshed, but the book has a stretched story line, shallow characterization, and detailed game sequences that do not further the story line although they may add to the book's appeal for baseball buffs.

> *Zena Sutherland, in a review of "Wild Pitch," in* Bulletin of the Center for Children's Books, *Vol. 34, No. 5, January, 1981, p. 89.*

Eddie Rhoades suddenly has more to worry about than his occasional wild pitches when he learns an opposing team has a girl as a celebrity member. Unsure just why this rankles him, Eddie tries to find out more about Phyl Monahan and ends up knocking her and her groceries off her bike by accident. His life becomes even more entangled with her after a wild pitch puts Phyl in the hospital. Eddie withstands threats from Phyl's cousin and tries to make amends by visiting Phyl and convincing her to return to baseball after her traumatic accident. As their relationship turns warm, Eddie learns more about his own feelings. The final game in the novel proves a satisfying resolution as the returning girl star makes good against Eddie's slightly matured pitches. Chrisopher treats both the sex-role issue and suggestions of romance with a light touch and makes strong ethical points, all in a framework set with fast baseball action. Fans won't be disappointed.

> *Judith Goldberger, in a review of "Wild Pitch," in* Booklist, *Vol. 77, No. 13, March 1, 1981, p. 926.*

Tight End (1981)

Reading the latest Matt Christopher novel is like sitting down to an evening of TV. The opening moments grab you: just after his father is released from prison where he has been serving time for embezzlement, Jim Cort receives the first of several anonymous phone calls telling him to quit the football team, because "nobody will want to play with an ex-convict's son." Jim becomes determined to uncover the identity of his tormentor. In keeping with Christopher tradition, most of the action centers on the football field; Jim goes through an array of suspects while trying to maintain the starting berth he has earned on the Port Lee High team. When his shrewd detective work finally unmasks the true culprit, Jim shows no bitterness, leaving everyone with a warm feeling. A very ordinary, predictable story, to be sure, but similar enough to programs that achieve high Nielsen ratings to command an audience.

> *Chris Hatten, in a review of "Tight End," in* School Library Journal, *Vol. 28, No. 1, September, 1981, p. 134.*

The Return of the Headless Horseman (1982)

The plot idea here, the reappearance of a local headless horseback rider, is more exciting in premise than in its execution. Two young boys, Steve and Jim, see the phenomenon on a night fishing trip and are anxious to deliver the scoop to Steve's father's failing newspaper, but no one believes them. They then decide, Jim reluctantly, to chase the headless horseman when he reappears and find out the truth about him. There are a few exciting moments, but the almost nonexistent characterizations and the contrived ending greatly hamper. Because this does fill a need for a third- or fourth-grader craving a fast-paced mystery/adventure story, it is recommended.

> *Ilene Cooper, in a review of "The Return of the Headless Horseman," in* Booklist, *Vol. 78, No. 22, August, 1982, p. 1521.*

A thin storyline, weak characterization, and a predictable conclusion are all in evidence in this latest Christopher novel. Like so many of his novels, this one does have enough suspense and action to keep a reader interested. Although the author may never win an award for his writing style, he repeatedly demonstrates the ability to write a story for the reader, especially boys, who are looking for that steppingstone to a more sophisticated, involved story.

> *Fellis L. Jordan, in a review of "The Return of the Headless Horseman," in* Children's Book Review Service, *Vol. 10, No. 14, August, 1982, p. 135.*

This is a mundane offering by a prolific author. Bland and prosaically written, the story reads more like magazine fiction than a novel. Two boys in rural Florida see a Headless Horseman. After unsuccessfully trying to convince Steve's poor, sick dad to run the story as a scoop for his floundering newspaper, they research a local horse thief who was hung. Then they have a midnight chase on horseback to discover Grandpa was the culprit. Honest reporting leads to business revival for the paper. For quality, stay with Farley and Hall for horse stories; go to Fisk's *Monster Maker* (Macmillan, 1980) or Levy's *Frankenstein Moved*

in on the Fourth Floor (Harper, 1981) for compelling scari-
ness.

Leslie Chamberlin, in a review of "The Return
of the Headless Horseman," in School Library
Journal, *Vol. 28, No. 10, August, 1982, p. 112.*

Drag-Strip Racer   (1982)

Sixteen-year-old Ken Oberlin is thrilled to receive the
drag-racing Chevy, "Li'l Red," bequeathed to him when
his uncle dies of a heart attack. Ken's older brother Dana,
a highschool dropout with a loud motorcycle and a pool-
hall job, is jealous of Ken's good fortune. Younger sister Janet idolizes Ken and encourages his racing efforts,
which are disapproved of by their father. Brake failure in
Ken's first competition causes a crash that breaks his left
ankle and jeopardizes his racing future. Then Scott "Rat"
Taggart, town bully, gets, from Dusty Hill's Automotive
Parts store, the financial backing that Ken had hoped to
garner. "Rat" also hints to drag-strip officials that Ken
was drunk when he crashed, thereby getting Ken banned
from future competition. With much help from Dana,
however, all works out in the end with good triumphing
over bad. Although supposedly contemporary, this story
could have taken place just as easily in the 1950s or 1960s.
Such two-dimensional characters and predictable plots
with just a smattering of sports action are timeless.

Ann G. Brouse, in a review of "Drag-Strip
Racer," in School Library Journal, *Vol. 29,
No. 1, September, 1982, p. 117.*

The Dog That Called the Signals   (1982)

Mike is put in as substitute quarterback by his coach;
when the coach leaves the field because of an injury (tripping and falling) Mike is left on his own. He wins the game
for his team because his dog Harry, with whom he has
telepathic communication, beams the coach's directions.
The coach (watching the game through field glasses) is
calling plays, and Harry is with him, so Mike makes the
right plays. Lightly told but not convincing, this is a poor
blend of realism and fantasy and has the game sequences
as its only appeal.

Zena Sutherland, in a review of "The Dog
That Called the Signals," in Bulletin of the
Center for Children's Books, *Vol. 36, No. 5,
January, 1983, p. 84.*

A very slight story that may be used as a step-up from
easy-to-reads, especially with boys. Mike and his dog,
Harry, can read each other's minds. When Mike must suddenly take over as quarterback for his football team, he's
worried. He does all right during the game as long as the
coach keeps sending someone in with the signals. But then
the coach turns his ankle and must leave the field. Fortunately, Harry follows and the telepathic dog is able to
relay the coach's instructions, helping the team win the
game. Undeniably a soft story, and the line illustrations
[by Bill Ogden] are just adequate, but for a hard-to-suit
audience, this is worth consideration.

Ilene Cooper, in a review of "The Dog That
Called the Signals," in Booklist, *Vol. 79, No.
11, February 1, 1983, p. 723.*

When Mike substitutes for the regular quarterback, he
is apprehensive. His dog, uniquely endowed with ESP,
comes to his aid in the last quarter of the game by trans-
mitting the disabled coach's suggestions. Like many sports
stories, the plot dominates and is contrived. The opening
paragraphs seem especially so, as they are a condensed introduction to the three themes in a complicated plot. The
confusion is extended by such terms as "razzle-dazzle"
and "stiff-arm" which are not only unfamiliar to most
children, but are also inappropriate for children's football.

Audrey K. Conant, in a review of "The Dog
That Called the Signals," in School Library
Journal, *Vol. 29, No. 8, April, 1983, p. 111.*

Dirt Bike Runaway   (1983)

Sixteen-year-old Peter Lewinski, orphaned at the age of
two, has run away from a home where his foster brother
turned alcoholic and abusive, but his real problems begin
when he meets up with Dexter Pasini's gang. Perceiving
Peter's mechanical ability, Dex loans Peter a motorcycle
so he can join them in a motocross competition, a sport
Peter learned to love at the home for orphaned children.
It's not until later that Peter fully understands his part of
the deal, and he firmly refuses to help Dex and the others
pirate car parts. The timely appearance of Giff MacKenzie, another bike racer, saves Peter from an ugly beating, and Peter goes to stay with Giff and his attractive
sister, D.C., also a champion rider. Blow-by-blow action
sequences, which evidence Christopher's thorough knowledge of the rugged sport, are interwoven with a sensitive
portrayal of Peter's plight as his story is revealed in flashbacks. Tough bad guys and tense rivalries, together with
an emphasis on good sportsmanship, combine in a novel
that should have tangible appeal for motocross fans as well
as older reluctant readers. (pp. 746-47)

Karen Stang Hanley, in a review of "Dirt Bike
Runaway," in Booklist, *Vol. 80, No. 10, January 15, 1984, pp. 746-47.*

Dirt Bike Runaway opens with a fight between foster
home runaway Peter Lewinski and Dex Pasini. Dex then
invites Peter to stay with him if he will consent to some
shady dealings. Peter refuses and is taken in by good guy
Giff MacKenzie, his beautiful sister D. C. and their parents. The condition this time is one with which Peter is
both comfortable and happy: to keep Giff's and his sister's
dirt bikes in good racing condition. An added attraction
is that he will be able to fix up and ride one of Giff's old
bikes. Sounds wonderful—except for the recurring dark
cloud of Dex Pasini and his gang as well as the specter of
his former foster family. Aficionados of dirt bike racing
will relate best to this sports story but no inside knowledge
is needed. The morals are obvious but not overbearing and
the relationship between Peter and D. C. is believable. Although clichéd, **Dirt Bike Runaway** is entertaining and informative, and the color jacket photograph of dirt bike
racers in action should attract readers.

L. Michael Espinosa, in a review of "Dirt Bike Runaway," in School Library Journal, Vol. 30, No. 7, March, 1984, p. 156.

Favor for a Ghost (1983)

The ghost of Billy Marble, a school bully while alive, appears to Lennie Burnside and asks him to dig up his dog (he's buried in a pet cemetery "among a bunch of strangers") and bury it next to him. The obstacle is Billy's cousin Ralph, an unpleasant character who was given the dog when Billy died. His refusal to allow Lennie to dig up the dog causes Lennie first to attempt to move the dog at night; when he is caught, he then challenges Ralph to a race. Lennie wins, Ralph accepts defeat and allows the body to be moved and Billy's wish is fulfilled. Although characterization is minimal and there's no emotional involvement, children may enjoy the fast-paced (though far-fetched) adventure.

James G. Hicks, in a review of "Favor for a Ghost," in School Library Journal, Vol. 30, No. 6, February, 1984, p. 67.

There's undemanding, fast-paced reading in this light ghost story about a boy's involvement with a spirit in need of aid from the real world. Twelve-year-old Lennie Burnside doesn't know what to make of the ghost of one-time bully Billy marble, who has been dead for more than a year. Lennie is scared, of course, and doesn't quite know how he'll arrange Billy's last earthly, eerie request: that his dog, Jeepers, be removed from the pet cemetery and reinterred beside Billy's own grave. Simple sentences that stop short of being choppy and just enough character development to give the story dimension make this a strong candidate for reluctant readers. Boys, in particular, may find the story's dog/ghost elements appealing.

Denise M. Wilms, in a review of "Favor for a Ghost," in Booklist, Vol. 80, No. 13, March 1, 1984, p. 966.

The Great Quarterback Switch (1984)

A traditional sports story gets an ESP veneer. Tom and Michael are twins, but they are easy to tell apart: Michael is the one in the wheelchair. Ever since his accident two years ago, Michael has had to sit on the sidelines watching his brother excel at sports. Michael remains cheerful in spite of his adversity, yet he continues to wish that one day he'll have the chance to be out on the field again. Then, because of some extrasensory experiments the brothers have been performing, it looks as though Mike might have his chance. The boys have been trying out thought transference—Michael thinks of football plays from his wheelchair, and Tom, the quarterback, responds by calling the play. Now they are ready to go one step further. A neighbor, old Mr. Ollie Pruitt, has told the twins about TEC, Thought-Energy Control, a process whereby the boys may be able to change places. The twins concentrate, wish, strain, and then, in the middle of a game, Mike finds himself out on the field running with the ball. The story then settles into a series of problems the boys have keeping their

secret and ends with TEC helping them win an important game. Unfortunately, the implications of this extraordinary phenomenon are never really explored, and the book's abrupt ending will have readers wondering what the boys intend to do with this talent in the future. Even though Christopher does not use the story's unique aspect to its best advantage, the ESP angle puts this a notch above regulation football fare. (pp. 1623-24)

Ilene Cooper, in a review of "The Great Quarterback Switch," in Booklist, Vol. 80, No. 22, August, 1984, pp. 1623-24.

In a predictable story which combines paralysis, football and ESP, a handicapped 12-year-old is given a break (and a football team an illegal advantage). Michael Curtis, confined to a wheelchair, and his twin brother Tom, ace quarterback for the Eagles, have been experimenting with ESP and are now ready for Thought-Energy Control, the physical exchange of bodies. Guess what—it works! Michael becomes Tom for several key plays in several key games, the Eagles either win or tie, and the boys get the girls. It's wonderful to see a plucky kid up and having a well-deserved good time, but the book falls down in the willing suspension of disbelief. The boys change identities as easily as frowning, and Michael, now Tom, has no trouble with his new freedom. Christopher's football action and play diagrams are entertaining, but fail to overcome dull off-the-field dialogue and awkward description. Any football story will sell to young fans, but it would be a shame to push this one. (pp. 114-15)

Amy G. Gavalis, in a review of "The Great Quarterback Switch," in School Library Journal, Vol. 30, No. 1, September, 1984, pp. 114-15.

Supercharged Infield (1985)

Christopher adds another title to his collection of sports fiction, this time focusing on Penny Farrell's bafflement when one by one, the girls on her softball team begin to play with robotlike strength and accuracy. Credibility is stretched, however, as Penny seeks the source of what has improved their skills: Jonny Keech's computer experiments have stimulated the girls' muscles but sapped their personalities, leaving them cold and emotionless. Although the plot premise is thin, Penny's efforts to solve the mystery and her concern for her teammates contrast well with the other characters whose desire to win blinds them to the girls' endangered health. Christopher raises some important issues within a well-paced and readable text, and his new title should have broad appeal despite its flaws.

Linda Callaghan, in a review of "Supercharged Infield," in Booklist, Vol. 81, No. 22, August, 1985, p. 1662.

Supercharged Infield never quite jells as a mystery, sports story or romance. It is certainly not as well-done as the old *Not Bad for a Girl* by Isabella Taves or Mel Cebulash's "Ruth Marini" series for older girls. Penny Farrell, captain of her all-girl baseball team, investigates the mysterious change that turns four of her teammates into super athletes. Eventually, she fixes the blame on the team scorekeeper Harold and a teammate's brother, Jonny. Penny, 12, has a crush on Jonny and is horrified to discover that he has developed a computer program that can direct a pattern of electrical vibrations that strengthen the muscles of his subjects but deaden their emotions. Only at Penny's insistence does Jonny admit that the experiment has gotten out of hand and must be reversed. Christopher's latest effort lacks both the on-the-field action and the sturdy character development found in his earlier titles.

> *Kathleen L. Birtciel, in a review of "Super-charged Infield," in* School Library Journal, *Vol. 32, No. 1, September, 1985, p. 130.*

The Hockey Machine   (1986)

Save for the several game sequences that are always appealing to fans of a particular sport, this hockey story has less substance and credibility than most of the prolific Matt Christopher output. A fine skater and hockey player, young teenager Steve is kidnapped by a thirteen-year-old multimillionaire entrepreneur (Kenneth) who is a college graduate and who has a captive hockey team complete with guards and an isolation room to punish anyone who tries to get away. Although caught, Steve does manage to get away long enough to telephone the police, and his parents show up with police and FBI to rescue Steve and the other boys and break up the operation. During his captivity, Steve has continued to take part in games. Not a believable story, and the plot weakness is not compensated for by any depth of characterization, alleviated by humor, or distinguished by the writing style, which includes a lapse like: "Steve had never seen a look in the young co-owner's eyes as he was seeing now."

> *Zena Sutherland, in a review of "The Hockey Machine," in* Bulletin of the Center for Children's Books, *Vol. 40, No. 4, December, 1986, p. 63.*

A typical Matt Christopher sports adventure. Thirteen-year-old Steve Crandall, an excellent young hockey player, is kidnapped by a teenage genius to play on his professional junior hockey team. Hockey plays are presented in an accurate manner with correct terminology along with a suspenseful, but predictable, plot. Steve's survival is based on a winning record and his own ingenuity. The mixture of dialogue and description lend reality to a story that seems a little far-fetched, but the story should capture young hockey enthusiasts and readers of sports adventures. The black-and-white sketches of events from the story help to lend credibility.

> *Janice C. Hayes, in a review of "The Hockey Machine," in* School Library Journal, *Vol. 33, No. 5, January, 1987, p. 72.*

Thirteen-year-old Steve Crandall senses no danger when a boy his age, Kenneth Agard, lures him to a junior pro-hockey training camp under the pretense that Steve's parents have consented to his joining the team. Flown to a secluded camp and held incommunicado, Steve soon real-

izes he has been kidnapped for his sports skills. Who would have believed that Kenneth is a preteen business genius capable of forging Mr. Crandall's signature? Christopher's loyal readers will not be daunted by such a leap of faith; the brisk, exciting hockey action as well as the adventure of Steve engineering his escape will satisfy. The generous typeface and compact appearance will appeal to those attempting chapter books for the first time. (pp. 706-07)

> *Linda Callaghan, in a review of "The Hockey Machine," in* Booklist, *Vol. 83, No. 9, January 1, 1987, pp. 706-07.*

Red Hot Hightops   (1987)

Kelly is a real pro when she's playing basketball at home, not in a school game. But when the team is counting on her, she freezes up. Then a mysterious pair of red hightop sneakers shows up in her locker. When Kelly puts them on she plays better than she ever has—she's aggressive to a fault. But she agonizes over where the shoes came from, and finds out only after she decides to destroy them, because they work a little too well. She learns that they were magic, a plot device that doesn't jibe well with the realistic sportsplay. Some of the writing is simplistic, glossing over a situation or issue that would have been better depicted in a scene ("Kelly and her siblings never minded doing tasks their mother asked them to do"). All sorts of people pay more attention to Kelly's shoes than is reasonable to expect, and the answer to the mystery of her benefactor is too easy. But the book is packed with brisk, authentic action scenes on the court for which Christopher is well known, with appeal for middle reader sports lovers. (pp. 110-11)

> *A review of "Red-Hot Hightops," in* Publishers Weekly, *Vol. 232, No. 14, September 25, 1987, pp. 110-11.*

Kelly is a great basketball player, so long as she doesn't have to perform in front of a crowd. But after finding a pair of red hightop sneakers in her locker, she suddenly becomes a confident, aggressive, and slightly wild player. Everyone attributes the change to the new sneakers. Are they hexed? Kelly thinks so, and she begins to doubt her ability to play without them, even though they cause trouble with teammates and opponents. Christopher throws in clues to implicate many of Kelly's friends and the coach as the anonymous sneaker doner, but many of them are dead ends contrived to make this slight plot into a sports story with a mystery angle. There's little suspense in either category. The sports action is full of shot-jab-foul-shot, but even in the close games the tension isn't there to make it exciting. There's an unfortunate reference to not being an "Indian giver." Once the unbelievable secret of the sneakers is revealed—best friend Ester had them chemically treated to improve Kelly's game—the story comes quickly to a close. It's hard to believe the sudden interest everyone has in the power of Kelly's sneakers in this far-fetched story that is taken oh-so-seriously.

> *Susan Schuller, in a review of "Red-Hot High-*

Christopher in front of the statue "Casey at the Bat" in Rock Hill, South Carolina.

tops," in School Library Journal, Vol. 34, No. 4, December, 1987, p. 84.

Kelly is a capable basketball player when going one-on-one with her friend Ester, but when she's in the public eye during games she freezes and loses her confidence. Her shyness also prevents her from speaking to Anthony, a boy in whom she's interested. After a pair of red sneakers mysteriously appears in her locker, Kelly's performance begins to improve, causing her to think her assured, aggressive playing is the result of the magical hightops. While one expects her new confidence to come from inside Kelly, Christopher instead provides a solution about the sneakers' power that is a bit contrived. Despite this element, the lively pace and natural dialogue will keep readers speculating on the mystery as Christopher again provides a story filled with plenty of game action for middle-grade sports fans.

> *Linda Ward Callaghan, in a review of "Red-Hot Hightops," in* Booklist, *Vol. 84, No. 10, January 15, 1988, p. 861.*

The Dog That Pitched a No-Hitter   (1988)

In this addition to Christopher's *The Dog That . . .* series,

young Mike is scheduled to pitch against the toughest team in the league, but he's pitching wild. Mike once again calls on his dog Harry, who happens to be gifted with ESP. Harry can telepathically communicate information on each batter's weaknesses and strengths to his master. This works early on, but by the game's important climax, Mike has gained confidence and is guided by his own instincts. He pitches a no-hitter. Although this is a sports fantasy directed at the early chapter-book audience, it strains credulity and is so predictable and preachy that all but the most diligent fans of the series will lose interest early on.

> *A review of "The Dog That Pitched a No-Hitter," in* Publishers Weekly, *Vol. 233, No. 14, April 8, 1988, p. 94.*

In a sequel to **The Dog That Stole Football Plays,** Christopher again entertains readers with a new tale of Mike and his dog Harry, whose powers of ESP have aided the boy in two prior stories. When Mike can't control his pitches in a tough game against the Peach Street Mudders, Harry not only uses his powers to coach Mike on the batters' weaknesses but also resorts to distracting them to help Mike win the game. This sports fantasy features Christopher's well-known blend of action and humor and places familiar situations at a reading level accessible to independent readers. As spring turns thoughts to the ballpark, children will find satisfaction in this lighthearted tale . . . . (pp. 1606-07)

> *Linda Ward Callaghan, in a review of "The Dog That Pitched a No-Hitter," in* Booklist, *Vol. 84, No. 18, May 15, 1988, pp. 1606-07.*

Mike and his telepathic dog, Harry, return for their third adventure following **The Dog That Stole Football Plays** and **The Dog That Called the Signals.** Mike, the less-than-stellar pitcher for the Grand Avenue Giants, gets special help from Harry, who can spot each batter's weakness and advise Mike on the best pitches to throw. Unfortunately, Mike's arm isn't always up to Harry's coaching, and when the Giants face the Peach Street Mudders, Harry decides a new tactic is in order. Enlivened by plentiful pen-and-ink sketches [by Daniel Vasconcellos], this is basically just one incident which has been stretched into a short book, and therefore there is very little plot to develop. There is, however, plenty of humor, and Christopher's fans will greet his latest offering with enthusiasm.

> *Kathleen Brachmann, in a review of "The Dog That Pitched a No-Hitter," in* School Library Journal, *Vol. 34, No. 11, August, 1988, p. 79.*

The Hit-Away Kid   (1988)

[This] is calculated to tide kids over the quantum leap from easy reading materials to fiction. There's lots of game play here as the main character realizes, through two baseball games, that cheating doesn't pay and honesty does. In the first game, he drops a ball, getting credit for catching it but losing his sister's respect; in the second, he misses a base and acknowledges it, forfeiting a wager but gaining stature—and getting back his little brother's prize possession, taken by a rival player. This is predictable in theme if not in plot (Barry's team loses), but kids will get the reading practice they need on a subject that's palatable and popular. (pp. 174-75)

> *Betsy Hearne, in a review of "The Hit-Away Kid," in* Bulletin of the Center for Children's Books, *Vol. 41, No. 9, May, 1988, pp. 174-75.*

Descriptions of strategies, both offensive and defensive, abound in Christopher's latest sports story, and an understanding of baseball terms and plays would be helpful for enjoying the action that is described. Barry McGee, a left fielder and hit-away batter, learns an important lesson in fair play after his sister sees him cheat. Character development has been sacrificed for action and description, but younger readers should enjoy this for the excitement of the game and the typical dialogue of young players. The book can also serve older readers who need high-interest material with easy vocabulary and sentence structure.

> *Janice C. Hayes, in a review of "The Hit-Away Kid," in* School Library Journal, *Vol. 35, No. 8, May, 1988, p. 96.*

The Spy on Third Base (1988)

T. V. Adams is not a real spy—he's simply a very close observer of the playing styles of his teammates and opponents. Because he is often able to predict how a ball will be pitched and batted, others misinterpret his skill as psychic ability and resent him. Heavy on blow-by-blow descriptions of baseball games and strategy, light on characterization and plot, this slim novel will just barely maintain the reader's attention. T. V.'s dilemma would have been more compelling if his character had been more developed. For fans of this prolific sportswriter, the undistinguished plot may be offset by the emphasis on sportsmanship and the sheer abundance of baseball lingo.

> *A review of "The Spy on Third Base," in* Publishers Weekly, *Vol. 234, No. 22, November 25, 1988, p. 67.*

Standard Christopher fare, with a minor mystery, a little misdirection, a happy wrap-up, and plenty of baseball action.

T. V. Adams, third-baseman for the Peach Street Mudders, is proud of his ability to tell what batters are about to do; but hecklers, teammates who don't like being ordered around, and especially a series of threatening anonymous phone calls leave him with troubled dreams and persuade him to keep his predictions to himself. But after a miserable loss to a rival team, as well as reassuring, confidence-building talks from his father and a doctor, he changes his mind—whick leads to a thrilling, last-minute victory for the Mudders; the unmasking of the (repentant) caller; and some new friends.

Easy reading, easy lesson.

> *A review of "The Spy on Third Base," in* Kirkus Reviews, *Vol. LVI, No. 23, December 1, 1988, p. 1737.*

By carefully studying the way opposing players stand at the plate and the way they swing the bat, T. V. Adams is able to predict where they are likely to hit the ball. He puts his skill to use in his team's games with mixed results. Some teammates seem to resent his well-intentioned directions on how to play the hitters, a newspaper reporter mentions T. V.'s talent in a column, and an anonymous caller tells him not to use his "psychic" ability in the next game "or else." The lengthy descriptions of the game action leave little room for developing any of the problems, however, and the solutions come too quickly and simply. Children making the transition from beginning readers to "real" novels may find a use for this otherwise forgettable effort.

> *Elaine Fort Weischedel, in a review of "The Spy on Third Base," in* School Library Journal, *Vol. 35, No. 5, January, 1989, p. 62.*

In this sequel to **The Hit-Away Kid** third baseman T. V. Adams displays his seemingly uncanny ability to figure out what the opposing team is going to do next. Nothing magic about it; T. V. simply has learned to observe and remember the styles and skills of the other players. But a newspaper picks up on the "psychic" angle, and T. V. has to endure the jealous taunts of his teammates as well as threatening phone calls that warn him to keep quiet. Like the first book, this has a lot of detailed baseball action that will appeal to fans, but it lacks a strong narrative. The phone calls seem pitched in only to mark time between games, and the revelation of their source is out in left field. Still, an easy walk. (pp. 144-45)

> *Roger Sutton, in a review of "The Spy on Third Base," in* Bulletin of the Center for Children's Books, *Vol. 42, No. 6, February, 1989, pp. 144-45.*

Tackle without a Team (1989)

After someone plants marijuana in his duffel bag, a young lineman is thrown off his team.

Scott knows he's been framed, but how can he prove it? Even his parents doubt his innocence. He has some suspects—a girl with whom he recently broke up; an unfriendly former teammate—but the coach needs hard evidence before Scott can be reinstated. Meanwhile, he joins a newly formed team that plays more roughly than he likes—an opportunity for the author to comment on good and poor sportsmanship.

Christopher can always be counted on for plenty of tense sports-action plus a plot twist or two, but here the denouement is rather artificial, with Scott contriving to extract a confession on the playing field via a mini-recorder hidden in his gear. On the other hand, the anti-drug message here is convincing—in part because it is not heavyhanded. A glib, easy story to draw reluctant readers.

> *A review of "Tackle without a Team," in* Kirkus Reviews, *Vol. LVII, No. 1, January 1, 1989, p. 46.*

Scott Kramer, the right tackle for the Greyhawks, finds

himself kicked off the team when marijuana cigarettes are found in his duffel bag. The plot begins to spiral when Scott joins another team and his problems continue. The story then begins to unfold as Scott's girlfriend, his mother, and his own ingenuity help to discover the person trying to discredit him. Dialogue and descriptions of various football plays are used throughout the story. An understanding of football is helpful, but not necessary for enjoyment. Five black-and-white drawings [by Margaret Sanfitippo] provide visuals of the characters who display human qualities, but are often stereotyped. The small page size and the large print may discourage middle-school students from reading the book; however, because sports, jealousies, and drugs are part of the school milieu, students should find this sports adventure appealing.

> *Janice C. Hayes, in a review of "Tackle without a Team," in* School Library Journal, *Vol. 35, No. 7, March, 1989, p. 177.*

The Greyhawks' right tackle, Scott Kramer, is determined to find the person who framed him after marijuana is found in his duffel bag and he's kicked off the team. Christopher adds punch to his story with in-the-huddle flavor as tensions and rivalries build prior to finding the incriminating stash. Scott has no quarrel with his coach's straight-arrow ethics but is determined to exonerate himself. Eager to play again, he quickly seizes the opportunity to join a nonleague team where rough-and-dirty play is the norm. As Scott zeros in on several suspects, a second frame-up happens (his best friend's wallet is stolen), straining credibility rather than adding zest to the intrigue. The author does devise an effective mechanism for his hero to trap the culprit, and Scott rejoins the Greyhawks—with a renewed appreciation for their clean, hard style of play. Christopher's message—that smoking cigarettes or pot is a bummer—comes through loud and clear. Lots of action and enough suspense hold the plot together.

> *Phillis Wilson, in a review of "Tackle without a Team," in* Booklist, *Vol. 85, No. 13, March 1, 1989, p. 1188.*

Takedown (1990)

Sean Bailor has never known his father, who took off when he was a baby. His stepbrother, Carl, is two years younger, but is a couple of inches taller than Sean. To top it off, Sean is always getting into fights at school. His escape is wrestling, believing that if he can do well at that, it won't matter that he's small, that he can't stand his stepbrother, and that his mother and stepfather ignore him. The book centers around a rivalry that develops between Sean and a bigger, better wrestler from a nearby school. The details about the sport are accurate and abundant, but the ending, in which Sean beats the rival wrestler, thus gaining the attention and respect of his mother, stepbrother, and stepfather, is a bit contrived. However, those interested in the sport will overlook this flaw and enjoy the story.

> *Deirdre R. Murray, in a review of "Takedown," in* School Library Journal, *Vol. 36, No. 1, January, 1990, p. 103.*

A hot-tempered teen-ager wins a crucial wrestling match and has some of the edge taken off his loneliness in this problem-cum-sports novel.

After his mother tells him that the father he never knew was a wrestler, scrappy Sean goes out for the sport. Sean is angry all the time; he feels that his stepfather ignores him; his younger (but larger) stepbrother puts him down at every opportunity; and he's being harassed on the street by Max "The Octopus" Rundel, a tough wrestler from a rival junior high. When assistant referee Clint Wagner shows interest in him, teaches him some holds, and even takes him fishing, Sean entertains—and clings to—the idea that Wagner is actually his father. In the end, everything works out: Sean gets to face Max on the mat; his stepfather and stepbrother prove their affection for him; and Wagner leaves town for another job.

Carefully described sports action punctuates the story without dominating it; occasional line drawings [by Margaret Sanfilippo] add bits of character and detail, but won't be much help to readers who aren't familiar with wrestling's subtle shifts of weight and grip.

> *A review of "Takedown," in* Kirkus Reviews, *Vol. LVIII, No. 1, January 1, 1990, p. 45.*

Sean Bailor's sport—wrestling—is an apt metaphor for his life. Burdened by a tangle of troubles both at home and at school, he finds himself frequently at odds with the world. Sean is deeply curious about the father he never knew (an alcoholic whom his mother divorced), and has managed to convince himself that his stepfather favors his natural son. Then there's "the Octopus," a local bully who keeps challenging him to fights and winning. When an assistant referee takes an interest in Sean and begins coaching him on the side, Sean's gratitude soon turns to hero-worship and he begins to wonder if the man could possibly be his real father (he isn't). Although the story isn't a particularly deep one, and the ending is pat, this is offset by the book's potential to lure sports fans into the world of books. Christopher is well-versed in the sports story genre and he details wrestling with accuracy and color.

> *A review of "Takedown," in* Publishers Weekly, *Vol. 237, No. 1, January 12, 1990, p. 61.*

Wrestling provides the backdrop for this story of 14-year-old Sean, who has a quick temper and is often in trouble for fighting. The story's central conflict involves Sean's troubles with a local bully, whom he finally bests on the wrestling mat. Almost as important are Sean's problems with his family: he and his stepbrother don't get along, his stepfather shows little interest in him, and his mother is quick to condemn him for any troubles he encounters. For awhile, Sean draws emotional support from Clint Wagner, a referee who befriends him, but when Clint takes an out-of-town job, Sean is left to sort out his troubles independently. Christopher's story isn't seamless, but it moves easily and may appeal particularly to boys. The question of whether or not to fight a bully isn't really resolved, though Christopher does imply alternatives for at least some circumstances. Engaging sports fiction.

Denise Wilms, in a review of "Takedown," in Booklist, *Vol. 86, No. 10, January 15, 1990, p. 999.*

Because of its high interest and easy readability, younger adolescent readers and lower-ability junior-high readers will find **Takedown** a beneficial reading adventure. They won't have to spend a lot of time with the story because, like the dozens of other sports stories by Matt Christopher, the content is exciting, moves quickly, and provides a feeling of accomplishment and triumph in the end for the protagonist.

David M. LaMar, in a review of "Takedown," in English Journal, *Vol. 80, No. 7, November, 1991, p. 89.*

Skateboard Tough   (1991)

When a builder digs up a skateboard with the name "Lizard" on it, Brett is thrilled, since he's an avid skateboarder and Lizard is so much better than his old board. This is a three-ply plot: there's a competitive enmity between Brett and another skater; there's the question (not very convincingly presented) of whether Lizard has magical powers that make Brett skate better; there's the range of adult acceptance, from Brett's mother's apparent disapproval to the elderly neighbor next door who spends her own money to build a rink on her property. Ardent skateboarders will probably enjoy reading about their sport, but the book is crammed with descriptions or definitions of stunts to an extent that slows the story, which is not up to Christopher's usual standard structurally or stylistically. (pp. 212-13)

Zena Sutherland, in a review of "Skateboard Tough," in Bulletin of the Center for Children's Books, *Vol. 44, No. 9, May, 1991, pp. 212-13.*

When excavators unearth a box in Brett's yard, he's delighted by the treasure inside—the Lizard, a blue-and-white skateboard with a double-kick tail. When he rides it, Brett uncannily performs difficult tricks he's never done before. What's more, he discovers that the board once belonged to Crackerjack Hawker, a national skateboard champion who was killed by a car while riding the Lizard. Then a series of life-threatening accidents leads Brett and his friends to wonder whether the glory's worth the risk. While this sounds like a variation on the "lucky bat" motif, there's a difference. Here, Christopher implies that the board is indeed hexed and that Brett's only reasonable course is to get rid of it. Despite the "skateboard from hell" theme, the book's tone owes more to "Leave It to Beaver" than to "The Twilight Zone." Characterization is thin, but that won't stop Christopher's fans from reading one of the few skateboard novels around. (p. 1798)

Carolyn Phelan, in a review of "Skateboard Tough," in Booklist, *Vol. 87, No. 18, May 15, 1991, pp. 1797-98.*

A Stephen King-style mystery for the younger set. "Doesn't it make you wonder?" Brett is asked after he unearths a skateboard and claims it as his own. The plot builds suspensefully, yet readers never learn who buried the object, or why Brett can do difficult tricks he never dreamed of attempting before. Eventually he figures out the age-old adage "to thine own self be true," returning to his old skateboard and relying on his own abilities. Followers of Christopher's other novels and *Thrasher,* a skateboard magazine, will enjoy this. Although some savvy readers will be annoyed by the use of the term "rink" when referring to a skateboarding area, they will appreciate Christopher's descriptions of tricks.

Blair Christolon, in a review of "Skateboard Tough," in School Library Journal, *Vol. 37, No. 6, June, 1991, p. 74.*

Brett Thyson finds a skateboard buried in his new yard and suddenly can perform tricks with it that he's never even seen, much less tried. He learns that it belonged to Lance Hawker, a nationally known skateboarder who died in an accident. A friend warns Brett against riding it, but how can he stop before he's proved that he's a better skater than sneering neighbor Kyle Robinson?

Christopher fluidly works his usual themes of sharp rivalry defused and personal problems handled, tied together here with an ambiguous fantasy element plus plenty of sports action and information.

A review of "Skateboard Tough," in Kirkus Reviews, *Vol. LIX, No. 11, June 1, 1991, p. 728.*

Centerfield Ballhawk   (1992)

Christopher continues the saga of the Peach Street Mudders baseball team in his latest Springboard chapter book. José Mendez is a great center fielder, but his batting average is nowhere near the .375 that his father hit in the minor leagues. To make things worse, José's 11-year-old sister is hitting extremely well for her softball team. Afraid he's disappointing his dad when his hitting fails to improve, José is surprised when his father praises his fielding and promises to be more sensitive to his feelings. The play-by-play action is less dominant in this story than in previous books, but game descriptions will appeal to readers anyway, as will the familiar characters. Christopher also avoids the miraculous, delivering instead a believable and satisfying conclusion.

Karen Hutt, in a review of "Centerfield Ballhawk," in Booklist, *Vol. 88, No. 16, April 15, 1992, p. 1527.*

Worrying about how he can't match his father's .375 minor-league batting average, José (9) barely notices the spectacular plays he himself makes on defense for the Peach Street Mudders. Despite evidence to the contrary, he's convinced that he's a disappointment to team and father both, but finally his father sets him straight. Christopher has come up with stronger plots, but the episodic structure and minor cliffhangers here might appeal to less able readers. Eight full-page b&w illustrations [by Ellen Beier] capture the high spots of this "Springboard Book," though José makes one of his miraculous outfield plays with what looks like a catcher's mitt, and many figures are awkwardly posed. Rudimentary dynamics in José's motherless Hispanic family add a social dimension to the sports action.

> *A review of "Centerfield Ballhawk," in* Kirkus Reviews, *Vol. LX, No. 11, June 1, 1992, p. 717.*

José Mendez feels he has disappointed his father, a former minor league player, because he doesn't hit a baseball as well as he thinks he should. The boy fails to realize until the final chapters that he is a good outfielder and that is where the team needs him the most. Christopher's characters are well developed and support positive values of caring and self-worth. José's mother has died, and his father is raising his son and daughter. The child tries to do the right thing, but to his dismay, accidents do happen. The format in this easy-to-read chapter book is open and unintimidating full-page, black-and-white drawings add to the appeal.

> *Blair Christolon, in a review of "Centerfield Ballhawk," in* School Library Journal, *Vol. 38, No. 6, June, 1992, p. 90.*

Return of the Home Run Kid (1992)

Coaching by the mysterious Mr. Baruth made Sylvester Coddmeyer III the Redbirds' home-run king in *The Kid Who Only Hit Homers.* The sequel opens at the start of the new season with Sylvester, dejected that he can't seem to hit or field, questioning his own abilities. This time, a man calling himself "Cheeko" encourages Sylvester to be more aggressive and confident. While Sylvester's aggressive play pays off on the field, his friends criticize his new style, and he's troubled when he finds old baseball cards whose portraits bear an uncanny resemblance to Mr. Baruth (Babe Ruth) and Cheeko (Eddie Cicotte, the 1919 White Sox pitcher). Christopher reprises the plot gambit that served him well in the first novel, and despite the hiatus, Sylvester remains an appealing character, learning to play his best despite pressure and self-doubt. Fans will welcome his return, delivered with Christopher's reliable pace, style, and action-packed text.

> *Linda Callaghan, in a review of "Return of the Home Run Kid," in* Booklist, *Vol. 88, No. 16, April 15, 1992, p. 1527.*

After starring as a power-hitting outfielder the year before, Sylvester Coddmyer finds himself relegated to the bench at the start of the new season because of a prolonged slump. He misses the coaching he received the previous season from the mysterious Mr. Baruth. Soon the boy is approached by the equally mysterious Cheeko, who offers to pick up where Mr. Baruth left off, and soon Sylvester is clobbering homers again. However, Cheeko also encourages him to play—some would say—an aggressive, dirty game. Sylvester's tricks and lack of team spirit eventually alienate him from everyone, including the reappearing Mr. Baruth, and these threads are not resolved in the conclusion. Also left ambiguous are the true identities of the coaches: Mr. Baruth is perhaps none other than the ghost of Babe Ruth, while Cheeko is probably the ghost of a pitcher discredited in the Black Sox scandal. All of this may be leading to a sequel that's reminiscent of the movie, *Field of Dreams.* This book, however, leaves everything hanging.

> *Todd Morning, in a review of "Return of the Home Run Kid," in* School Library Journal, *Vol. 38, No. 5, May, 1992, p. 112.*

The prolific Christopher has written yet another action-packed sports story, this one a sequel to *The Kid Who Only Hit Homers.* A new baseball season has started, but Sylvester Coddmyer III is not hitting home runs like last year. In fact, he is hardly hitting the ball at all, until mysterious Cheeko appears and teaches Syl about aggression on the field. Though the boy begins to play well, he cannot help but question Cheeko's advice and is even more confused when his evasive coach from last season appears and advises him differently. Ultimately Syl must make his own decisions about how to play the game. This tale aptly explores the intangible aspects of baseball: attitude, confidence, camaraderie and respect. The author successfully balances sizzling play-by-play accounts of games with brief, general descriptions, thus creating a quick-paced story that vividly captures the sport's sights, sounds and spirit. With many facets of his life addressed, Syl becomes a believable and likable protagonist.

> *A review of "Return of the Home Run Kid," in* Publishers Weekly, *Vol. 239, No. 25, June 1, 1992, p. 63.*

Marie Hall Ets

1893-1984

American author and illustrator of picture books, fiction, and nonfiction.

Major works include *The Story of a Baby* (1939), *In the Forest* (1944), *Play with Me* (1955), *Mister Penny's Race Horse* (1956), *Nine Days to Christmas* (with Aurora Labastida, 1959).

INTRODUCTION

A celebrated author/illustrator of books for preschoolers and primary graders, Ets is considered an especially original and sensitive contributor to the field of children's literature. Lauded as a genius for creating deceptively simple books that reflect both her artistry and understanding of young children, she has been described by Ruth Irvine as "an author-artist of remarkable talent" and "a born story-teller in tune with the interests and feelings of the very young." Her works, often presented as first-person narratives, have been praised for capturing the lively interaction between imagination and reality in the mind of a child, and are commended for depicting situations and characters that appeal to children. Featuring boys, girls, and animals as protagonists in picture books and longer stories that are either realistic or blend realism with fantasy, Ets characteristically addresses the child's search for identity and need for both friendship and solitude. Written in a rhythmic, poetic prose that often includes gentle humor, her texts mimic the repetitious chanting with which children so frequently entertain themselves when playing alone. Many commentators have noted that her stories are characterized by uncomplicated plots which help young people relate to the text without confusion or frustration. At the same time, however, these works combine action, humor, and even pathos in a manner that engages and enlightens the young reader. Ets's illustrations have also been praised for their simplicity, while her depictions of the moods, expressions, and gestures of a child are admired by many. She characteristically worked in black line, a medium in which she is considered a master, and soft pastel wash; in addition, several of her works feature a paper-batik process in which gum arabic projects figures and other highlighted features while ink applications provide dark, contrasting backgrounds. Praised for the expressiveness and what Barbara Bader has described as the "happy spontaneity" of her art as well as for her design sense, Ets is commended by Bader for creating drawings that "have the merit—and the appeal to children—of being at once filled to the frame, uncluttered and distinct."

Born in Wisconsin, Ets demonstrated an early talent for art and as a first grader was invited to attend an adult drawing class taught by an instructor who admired her work. On summers away from school she enjoyed vacationing with her family in the North Woods of rural Wisconsin, where she developed the love of animals that informs the majority of her stories. After studying at the

New York School of Fine and Applied Arts, she began working as an interior decorator in San Francisco. Following the death of her first husband in World War I, she returned to the Midwest and resumed her education, receiving her Ph.B from the University of Chicago in 1924. Ets was trained as a social worker during these years, working especially with children; she married a physician and moved to New York in 1929 or 1930. While studying the responses of children to art at Columbia University several years later, Ets crafted her first published picture book, *Mister Penny* (1935). The first of three works featuring the Doctor Dolittle-like title character, *Mister Penny* introduces a comical group of farm animals who learn such lessons as the rewards of industry and the value of teamwork through a series of misadventures. Ets considered her second book, *The Story of a Baby,* her most important contribution to children's literature. Sketching from an exhibition of human embryos that her husband helped prepare for the 1933 Chicago World's Fair, Ets determined to prepare a factual book for children that would help them understand the miracle of birth. She interviewed mothers as well as medical experts and visited hospitals to ensure the accuracy of her material. The text accompanying her illustrations relates the growth of a fetus with comparisons which observers note are easily understood by children, giving them an appreciation, for instance, of the chorionic sac as "a house with no windows or doors—a house smaller than a grain of salt from the shaker."

While *The Story of a Baby* gained acclaim as a first-of-its-kind effort, Ets's first-person stories of the natural world as perceived by a small child have been her most successful. *In the Forest* and its sequel *Another Day* (1953), as well as *Play with Me* and *Just Me* (1965), relate what Ruth Irvine has described as "the child's happily egocentric, anthropomorphic world." Animal figures are prominent in these works, which have been lauded for convincingly capturing a typical afternoon's play in the life of a child. Similarly, *Nine Days to Christmas,* Ets's realistic depiction of a Mexican child celebrating the holiday season in her familiar urban environs, was praised as sensitive and sympathetic; created to dispel cultural stereotypes, *Nine Days* was awarded the Caldecott Medal in 1960. Two other of Ets's books relate directly to her experience as a social worker: *My Dog Rinty* (1946), a story on which she collaborated with children's author Ellen Tarry, was inspired by Ets's recognition of the need for realistic books about black inner-city life and is considered a unique and influential work; *Good Boy, Bad Boy* (1967) describes the process through which Spanish-speaking Roberto adjusts to the American society against which, out of frustration with the language and customs, he had earlier rebelled. In addition to her picture books and fiction for children, Ets is the author of a book of verse for young readers and a biography for adults about an Italian emigrant to America. Along with her Caldecott Medal, she has received several further awards: *In the Forest, Mr. T. W. Anthony Woo* (1951), *Play with Me, Mister Penny's Race Horse,* and *Just Me* were Caldecott honor books for their respective years of publication, while *Play with Me* was also named to the Honour List of the International Board on Books for Young People (IBBY). Several of her other titles have received awards and honors from the *New York Times* and the *New York Herald Tribune.* In 1975, Ets was presented with the Kerlan Award from the University of Minnesota for her body of work.

(See also *Something about the Author,* Vol. 2; *Major Authors and Illustrators for Children and Young Adults; Contemporary Authors,* Vols. 1-4; *Contemporary Authors New Revision Series,* Vol. 4; and *Dictionary of Literary Biography,* Vol. 22.)

GENERAL COMMENTARY

Ruth R. Irvine

Marie Hall Ets' books are the reflection of a many-faceted life. She was born in Wisconsin, one of six children of a doctor who later became a minister. Her childhood love for animals, wild and tame, finds continued expression in the skill and feeling with which she depicts all kinds of animals in text and drawing. Art student, interior decorator, social worker (always with, or for children), the wife of a doctor—from this potpourri emerges an author-artist of remarkable talent, who for the past twenty years has been

enriching the field of books for young children. She is a "born storyteller" in tune with the interests and feelings of the very young. She is a delightful artist and knows how to use illustration to complement and enhance her stories. That she has only produced ten books in twenty years is suggestive of the care and thought which have gone into her work.

In any one of her storybooks the reader will find a simple but absorbing plot which is developed to a logical and satisfying conclusion, involving a situation and characters with natural appeal to children. A happy blend of rhythmic prose, action, humor, pathos, charm, and fantasy is characteristic of her work.

Her illustrations are distinguished by their artistry, composition, pleasant informality, and appropriateness to each story. She captures the subtility of emotional reaction as well as direct action in her drawings. She is meticulous (but never dull) in the reproduction of detail in the text. She is a master of the medium of black and white and uses it with such strength, richness, and variety that one never wishes for a more colorful palette.

Mr. Penny has a timeless appeal which belies its early publication date. It is the story of a poor, kindly old man and his large family of mischievous animals. The animals are the familiar farm animals dear to the hearts of children. They are conceived with humor and affection. Their frailities and vanities are human and yet related to their species. The family consists of an old horse named Limpy "who used to limp on his right foreleg because he liked to have it rubbed with liniment and tied up in a bandage like a racehorse," Mooloo the cow "who had beautiful eyes, but who never chewed her cud as other cows do because she was too lazy," Splop the goat, Pugwug a pig, Mimkin the lamb, Chukluk a fat hen, and Doody a rooster, "who arched his tail and strutted when he walked."

Mr. Penny is a good father to his family, up before dawn, cleaning the shed and preparing food for them. When he leaves for his daily work in the factory of the Friend-in-Need Safety Pins in the town of Wuddle, he says goodbye to each animal and tells them to be good while he is gone. He asks Doody "to try to be good!" How like any parent leaving his brood for the day! And just as any group of seven children left to their own devices would get into mischief, the animals led on by Doody have a field day in the neighbor's garden. Retribution comes swiftly. The animals are chased away ignominiously by the angry farmer and his bulldog, Doody loses his beautiful tail to the dog, the animals are sick from overeating, and disaster threatens when the irate farmer delivers his ultimatum, that Mr. Penny must either pay for the damage, repair it, or lose his animals. The animals come to the rescue and, working secretly at night, restore the garden and plow the fields. Mooloo chews her cud and gives quarts of milk. Chukluk eats the nasty hen's tonic-and-grit and lays beautiful eggs. Doody follows the plow pulled by Limpy and weighted down by Pugwug, and picks up worms for Mr. Penny to sell. Mimkim clips the grass, and Splop clears the fields of stones. The animals learn that it is more fun to work than to be lazy. With their help Mr. Penny soon has the most beautiful garden in Wuddle, he is able to retire from his hated job in the factory, and they all live happily and prosperously together.

The illustrations in **Mr. Penny** are vigorous, humorous, expressive, and faithful to the action and mood of the story. In **Mr. Penny** the author demonstrates her gift for devising singularly appropriate and original names for her characters. The names are as distinctive as portraits.

The Story of a Baby is an extraordinary piece of work and in a class quite by itself. In a large size picture storybook the growth of a baby is described from its beginning as "a life too small to be seen at all," through the many stages of embryonic development, to birth and the baby's first smile. It is a book for parents and children to enjoy together, and it is a particularly beautiful way in which to satisfy a child's curiosity about the origin of babies. Text and illustration are sensitive and scientifically accurate, yet rendered in a manner meaningful to a young child. The changing size of the embryo is given reality to the child by continual comparisons with things the child knows—from the size of a tail of a comma (,), to a kernel of rice, to a pussywillow bud, to a grandmother's thimble. The chorionic sac is first described as "a house with no windows or doors—a house smaller than a grain of salt from the shaker, or a grain of sand from the beach. But this was a house that could grow, and a house that was going to have roots." In similar vein and with stately cadence the story of a new life unfolds in all its wonder.

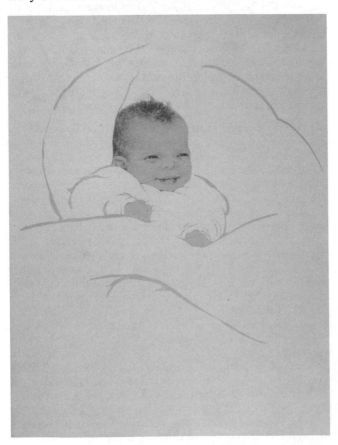

From The Story of a Baby. *Written and illustrated by Marie Hall Ets.*

This book has to be seen and read to be fully appreciated. Its enthusiastic endorsement by the *Journal of the American Medical Association* is a tribute to its quality.

A happy return to fiction is effected with **In The Forest.** This is a story of more subtle fantasy than **Mr. Penny.** Here the author shows great skill in capturing the blend of fancy and matter-of-factness which is found in children's imaginative play. A little boy with a paper hat and a new horn goes for a walk in the forest. There he meets, by ones and twos, wild animals which children all know from storybooks, hearsay, and visits to the zoo. This is the child's happily egocentric, anthropomorphic world. The animals stop whatever they are doing and go along with the boy, but first, each in his way has to get ready, just as a child would for a trip. The lion must comb his hair; the baby elephants stop their bath, dry themselves, and get partially dressed as a very young child would do; the bears stop counting their peanuts and eating jam; the monkeys get "their best suits from a hole in a tree"; the mother and father kangaroos interrupt the lesson in hopping they were giving their baby; the stork says nothing, but comes too; and the timid rabbit joins the parade on the child's invitation.

Each encounter with a new animal is beautifully developed, with three full-page illustrations and a line or two of text on each page, and tied into the theme of the story by the repetition of the phrase "when I went for a walk in the forest." The animals are good old friends by the time they are seen in a double-page illustration of all eleven of them and the child on their walk. A picnic, with ice cream and cake, and games, is perfectly natural in this make-believe story. The transition back to reality is delightfully handled. Children will appreciate the father who respects his child's fantasy, but takes him safely home to the real world.

My Dog Rinty was written in collaboration with Ellen Tarry. The story takes place in Harlem and is one of the few better children's books dealing with a minority group. Young readers will enjoy the mischievous dog, Rinty. They will sympathize with the anguish of his young master, David, when the boy's father insists that the dog be sold because of the trouble he causes—following David to school, chewing holes in carpets, and causing inadvertant damage in shops. Children will share David's joy when a reformed Rinty is returned to him and when they learn that Rinty's mischief was really due to his being a born mouser. A warmly satisfying conclusion is reached when David and Rinty win fame and fortune as the Pied Pipers of Harlem.

What could have been a sprightly, entertaining story is weighted down with a brief plea for slum clearance, a subject of little interest to young children. The book is illustrated with unimaginative photographs in an unsuccessful attempt to add reality to the story. There is much emphasis in the text on the poverty of David's family; yet in each picture the family appear well dressed and groomed, and they seem to be living in quite comfortable quarters. Even street scenes in Harlem do not convey the reality of poverty. They are just dull and drab, and could be any city anywhere. There is not one photograph in this book which suggests poverty as well as Marie Hall Ets' drawings do in *Mr. Penny.*

My Dog Rinty doubtless reflects Mrs. Ets' interest in social work, but one cannot help feeling that it would have been more successful had she done it independently and with her own art work. In all probability the social work flavor would then have evaporated and an engaging story would have resulted.

It is a pleasure to find Marie Hall Ets her own true self again in the delightful story, *Oley, The Sea Monster.* This is the saga of an appealing seal pup who loses his mother and has many adventures before he finds her again. Children will respond to Oley's grief and longing for his mother and the harbor by the sea where he was born. The sadness of this separation is relieved by Oley's success as the chief attraction at the museum in the big city far from the sea, and by the humor of the confusion and turmoil he creates when he is mistaken for a terrifying sea monster after he is set free in Lake Michigan. His safe return after a long trip through the Great Lakes, down the St. Lawrence River, and along the coast of Maine to his own harbor by the sea and to his mother brings the story to a satisfying conclusion.

This book is animated with one hundred and forty drawings, one for each line of text, a feature which will delight children. Variety in the size of the illustrations adds to their appeal. Each simple drawing is filled with action and feeling. Only a very skillful artist could produce on this scale and maintain such a high level of performance throughout. The double-page picture map of Oley's long trip home adds reality to his journey, and incidentally is an irresistible lesson in geography!

Little Old Automobile is the tale of a naughty little car whose response to every request is "No, I don't want to! I don't want to and I won't!" Children will recognize some of their own negativism in the auto's reactions and for a while may wish they could get away with as much as the car does. They will enjoy his run down the hilly road and the discomfort he causes everyone in his way,—a frog, two rabbits, a duck and two hens, a gentle cow, and a farmer's wife with a pig and basket of eggs in her arms. But children know instinctively that such irresponsible behavior cannot continue unchecked without calamity. It is almost a relief when Little Old Automobile meets his comeuppance in a crash with the big, black train. Little Old Automobile goes up in the air, just the way his own victims did earlier in the story, "but Little Old Automobile never came down again. Just pieces came down." There is a quality of poetic justice in the tranquil peace with which his former victims enjoy the salvaged parts of Little Old Automobile.

The illustrations are particularly noteworthy. They successfully define in simple black and white lines the characters, the action, mood, and setting of the tale. Every one of them speaks affectionately of the bucolic charm of rolling, hilly farm country.

Mr. T. W. Anthony Woo is well qualified to become one of the classics of young children's books. This is the story of a cat, a dog, and a mouse who live with a kind old man,

the Cobbler of Shooska. The cat and dog fight continually, all but demolish the cobbler's shop in the course of their battles, and terrify the little mouse, Mr. T. W. Anthony Woo. An intolerable situation arises when the cobbler's sister, who hates animals, moves in to keep house for him. However, because of Miss Dora's fear of mice, timid little Mr. Woo becomes the reluctant hero of the tale and frightens her away. The dog and cat learn that fighting does not pay, and thereafter the three animals and the cobbler live together in harmony and peace.

Mr. T. W. Anthony Woo is reminiscent of *Mr. Penny,* involving as the earlier book does a kind old man with a family of mischievous animals. However, *Mr. T. W. Anthony Woo* is an even more convincing and satisfying story because the cat, dog, and mouse are more realistically conceived than the farm animals and because the plot development is more soundly based on the facts of animal life. Children also will particularly enjoy a laugh at adult's expense when they laugh at Miss Dora's terror of Mr. Woo.

The illustrations are distinguished by their humor, action, and expression. They clarify the folksy quality of the story and add reality to the details of the text. Mrs. Ets' unfailing skill as an artist is a continual pleasure.

Beasts and Nonsense is a venture in nonsense verse, for the most part zoo-inspired. Each verse is accompanied by one of Marie Hall Ets' inimitable drawings. The humor of the verses, however, is rather sophisticated and adult, and of doubtful appeal to young children. Youngsters find zoo animals completely fascinating as they are and will not, I think, particularly enjoy the fun Mrs. Ets pokes at them.

Another Day is a sequel to *In The Forest.* Here we meet the same boy, with his paper hat and horn, again in the forest where he joins a confab of the animals. "Each one will show what he can do. Then we'll decide which thing is the best," Old Elephant explains to the child. Each animal performs and shows off one of his natural talents. The child stands on his head and laughs as he tries to pick up peanuts with his nose the way Young Elephant did. His laugh is declared to be the best thing of all. Again, the fantasy ends with Dad calling the child.

This is a charming story, and children will enjoy the sociable animals and their stunts. The illustrations are delightful, full of humor, expression, and action and up to Marie Hall Ets' high standards of draftsmanship and composition. However, the story does not seem as successful as *In The Forest.* In *Another Day* the animals are introduced as a group. The reader never gets to know them as well as the ones in the earlier story. Also, featuring the child's laugh as the most wonderful thing in the world is surely an adult concept and does not reflect a child's feeling. A young child is no more conscious of the beauty of his laugh than he is of his appearance or the sound of his voice.

Play with Me is happy proof that Marie Hall Ets continues to grow as an author-artist. This story of a little girl's experience in making friends with meadow and woodland animals is related with a disarming simplicity of great subtlety. There is deep understanding here of a child's yearning to play with all creatures, the frustration which comes when the feeling is not reciprocated, and the exquisite joy felt when a wild creature loses its fear and responds, no matter how tentatively, to the child. This is the most real of all of Mrs. Ets' stories. The animals do not talk, think, or act as people do. They remain unchanged throughout. It is the child who changes, profiting from past experience, so that the animals lose their natural fear of her and "play" with her in their own quiet way.

The pastel illustrations (Mrs. Ets' first use of color in her drawings) are exquisite. The more they are studied, the more one appreciates their subtlety, superb drawing, expression, and appropriateness to a gentle tale. A surprising amount of variety is achieved with a minimum of change in scene and situation. Each gesture of the child is meaningful, even the direction of her eyes. Slight changes in the position of the animals reflect the development of the story. The very restrained use of color somehow manages to illuminate each drawing. Most admirable of all is the way each picture captures a bit of the essence of beauty found in young children and wild creatures.

It is to be hoped that Marie Hall Ets will continue to bring her many talents to the field of literature for young children. First and foremost she is a born storyteller. Her plots are simple and straightforward, involving characters and situations of interest to youngsters. There are no extraneous details, subplots, or incidental characters to confuse young readers. Each character and incident is important to the development of the story, just as each word is essential in the text. A poetic quality in her prose adds to its charm and appeal. Fantasy is never abused with exaggeration. The imagination and humor characteristic of her work have their roots in reality.

The high qualities and skills which Marie Hall Ets brings to storytelling are equally matched by the artistry, good taste, simplicity, directness, and sensitivity of her illustrations. This fortuitous combination of talents makes her one of the outstanding figures in the field of children's picture storybooks. That adults, as well as children, can enjoy her books is an added tribute to her work. (pp. 259-65)

> *Ruth R. Irvine, "Marie Hall Ets: Her Picture Storybooks," in* Elementary English, *Vol. XXXIII, No. 5, May, 1956, pp. 259-65.*

Frances Lander Spain

[A] book by Mrs. Ets is always a signal for rejoicing, for she has the rare gift to create a book not only perfect in itself, but, because of her understanding of small children, also perfect for them.

> *Frances Lander Spain, in a review of "Cow's Party," in* The Saturday Review, *New York, Vol. XLI, No. 19, May 10, 1958, p. 40.*

[*The following two excerpts are from essays written by May Massee, Ets's editor at Viking Press.*]

May Massee

Look for the background of any artist who has a genius for making books for little children and you probably will find a child whose love of fields and woods and all earth's beauties was fostered even before he was conscious of it. Marie Hall Ets is living proof of this.

"The happiest memories of my childhood," she says,

> are of summers in the North Woods of Wisconsin. I loved to run off by myself into the woods and watch for the deer with their fawns, and for porcupines and badgers and turtles and frogs and huge pine snakes and sometimes a bear or a copperhead or a skunk. Later, when old enough to be trusted alone in a flat-bottomed boat, I loved to explore the lakeshore under low-hanging trees, or the channels between the lakes.

There were the beginnings of the animal stories: *Mister Penny, Mister Penny's Race Horse, Mr. T. W. Anthony Woo, Cow's Party, Play with Me. In the Forest* and *Another Day* just naturally included elephants, kangaroos, and other later acquaintances. *Oley: The Sea Monster* has cartoon drawings of Chicago so real that anyone who has ever known Chicago feels right at home when he looks at them, even though each drawing is only about four inches square. And in *Little Old Automobile* the drawings are just specially made for a small boy who loves smashes and clashes.

There are the animals, but whence came the ability to draw anything she wanted to put on paper, the use of a strong, slow-moving line in some of the animal drawings, the strong contrasts of black and white in *Mister Penny* and others, the use of soft gray wash in *The Story of a Baby*? The combination of a soft gray background with just a bit of yellow and flesh color to picture an adorable little girl discovering her world and her place in it with the other animals—that's *Play with Me,* and that's just pure genius, which we recognize and love but don't know what makes it.

All this comes from a lifetime of drawing, which began when Marie was a very little girl. The art teacher in her first grade of school took her into a special class of adults, and she's been working ever since in art schools in San Francisco, New York, Chicago, and Europe, and always in her own studio. Marie once heard her mother tell a friend that she had never known a child as sensitive as Marie—she hardly dared to correct her at all—and then she added, "or one as stubborn either." We can bless that stubbornness because it has made her try various techniques and stop at nothing in the way of work to get what she wanted in her pictures.

But where did she get her lovely sense of play, her feeling for words, and her stories that seem so simple—but aren't? They too came from that touch of genius that a few people have.

And now comes *Nine Days to Christmas,* a new experiment in color work. The story was written in collaboration with a Mexican friend, Aurora Labastida. They wanted to make it a story of a little Mexican girl who lived in the city, because Senorita Labastida said Mexicans resent the fact that all of our books about Mexican children made them villagers wearing ponchos and following burros, when 70 per cent of all Mexicans live in cities. Mrs. Ets explains, "To avoid possible criticism of bias and unfairness in picturing the Mexican people, I used actual characters throughout, except for the little girl (the real Ceci was too large and too blonde). So in the end the child I had come to picture in my mind as most typical was the child I used. The difficult job was giving my characters the actions I wanted and putting them in the places where I wanted them after I got home, without a model. Anyway, the Mexicans' reaction has been one of delight in recognizing themselves in the book, even though some of them are in unfamiliar places and doing things with people they never saw before."

Mrs. Ets spent two long winters in Mexico. The first year Senorita Labastida took her around to see her friends and to visit Mexican homes which ordinary visitors never see. She took her to the parks and markets where the children love to go—in short, she showed her the way children live in Mexico City. When Mrs. Ets went back to Mexico to make the pictures for her book she knew what she wanted to see, where she wanted to go, and she spent the whole time making hundreds of drawings. The story called for day scenes and night scenes, and because of the budget she couldn't use too many colors. She needed two reds, which are the most dominant colors used in Mexico, so she sacrificed blue and instead used a soft light gray for the background of the day scenes and a darker gray for the background of the night scenes. And the brilliance of the colors is made with the red, the yellow, and the black, that take you right to Mexico City.

The story tells of the day-to-day adventures of a little girl who goes to kindergarten and plays with her doll Gabina. It ends with her first Christmas party—her *posada*—and the beautiful star *piñata*. When the *piñata* was smashed by the children and the toys and sweetmeats scattered, then came the touch of magic that comforted Ceci, for her star flew up to the sky.

> *No one can ever break it now!* she thought. *And it will always be mine, mine and Gabina's.* Suddenly Ceci disappeared around the corner of the house. A minute later she was back, with Gabina in her arms.
>
> 'Look, Gabina!' she said. 'They couldn't break it because it was *real!* They only broke the pot inside. And *we—we* have given the world a new star for Christmas. *Our* star, Gabina! Can you see how it's blinking just at us?'

And Gabina looked and she nodded her head three times.

And so we are all happy that Marie Hall Ets, most talented and versatile artist, is to be given the Caldecott Medal for *Nine Days to Christmas.* (pp. 114-16)

May Massee, "Marie Hall Ets Wins Caldecott Award," in Junior Libraries, *Vol. 85, No. 6, March 15, 1960, pp. 114-16.*

May Massee

Glimpses of the child that was can often show the character and talents of the woman that is. So we tried to make Marie Ets remember. She was the fourth of six children, three boys and three girls, all spread four or five years apart. When she was little there were her own sisters and brothers. "I'll never forget the first time I was allowed to rock my baby brother to sleep. We were shut off in a room by ourselves, and I hardly dared breathe as I sat at the head of the cradle and rocked. And I was happy for days remembering how he had gone off to sleep the same as he did for the grown-ups."

When she was older there were the children of her older sisters and brothers. There are always children around her though she has none of her own; she has never been without intimate contact with them. She has never forgotten what it is to be a child.

There were plenty of outdoor games, boisterous play, Pom Pom Pullaway, Andy Andy Over. "That was my favorite group game. I loved the suspense which came from not knowing whether the group on the other side of the barn had caught the ball or not. If there was absolute silence you could guess they *had* caught it and were sneaking around the barn to catch *you.*"

Another picture: pigtails flying straight back, Marie is running for a path that leads into the woods near their summer home. She is running to get away from her older brother, an inveterate tease—about freckles, about being a girl, about not taking dares—he gave her no peace. But she has found her refuge. Out of sight in the woods she slows down and walks quietly not to disturb her friends, the animals and birds that live there. She loves to climb a favorite tree and stretch out on a branch growing over a deer trail. There the young artist can watch "for the deer with their fawns, for porcupines and badgers, and turtles

From In the Forest. *Written and illustrated by Marie Hall Ets.*

and frogs and skunks and huge pine snakes and sometimes a copperhead." Then she will run home and draw what she has seen and thought about.

She knew the woods and the creatures that live there, and she knew the farms round about and the characters who made friends of their animals. And with a vivid imagination and maturer years it is not surprising to meet Mister Penny and find his animals reciprocating his friendship when he needed their help. And the cobbler in *Mr. T. W. Anthony Woo* is right out of an old-fashioned cobbler's shop in a Wisconsin village. Mrs. Ets says she thought that story gave the children the chance to laugh at a grown-up and that was good for them.

Marie made pictures from the time she could hold a pencil or a brush. Her drawings were so good that when she was in the first grade the art supervisor asked for the "privilege" of having Marie in her class for adults. Thus began Marie's formal instruction in art and from that time on she was always drawing or painting in her spare time, much to the disgust of the older brother who was thus deprived of a victim—and doubtless of a much-loved companion. Ever since then Marie has worked at her drawing and painting in various art schools in San Francisco, Chicago, New York, and Europe.

Marie hip-hopped through the grades and high school—into high school from the seventh grade and through it in three years. Then to Lawrence College where, Marie writes, "I had my first bout with what I thought Social Injustice. I was rushed by several sororities, especially by the one to which my sisters had belonged. But a newly made friend, a drab girl from the country who had to earn her way, was entirely ignored. The idea of sororities seemed cruel and unjust and I would have nothing to do with them, in spite of my outraged sisters. (And I still think I was right.)" Marie's mother was once heard to say that she never had known a child as sensitive as Marie and then added, "or one as stubborn." The child was to need both these traits when she grew up.

After a year at Lawrence Marie decided she was wasting time—she wanted to be an artist and she should be going to an art school. She finally persuaded her parents and arrived at the art school in New York to find that no one under eighteen was allowed in life classes. So she enrolled in Interior Architecture and Decorating. At the end of a year she had a two-year diploma and a job in San Francisco, where she made sketches for three decorators who couldn't make their own. Two happy years in San Francisco and one in Los Angeles, and then tragedy ended that phase of her life. She was engaged to a young engineer, Milton Rodig, while they were both volunteer English teachers in Little Italy in San Francisco. It was during World War I, and Mr. Rodig was given a furlough from camp before going overseas. They were married and had two weeks together in a little cabin on a cliff overlooking the ocean at La Jolla. Then he went back to camp, to measles and pneumonia and death before Marie reached him. Some of the camp personnel, in an effort to help her through her sorrow, suggested that she volunteer for war work. She was sent to do protective work for girls at the Great Lakes Naval Training Station with headquarters in Waukegan. During the year that she worked there her superiors discovered that she had a gift for social work. They arranged for her to live at the Chicago Commons, a justly famous social settlement where she did volunteer work while she took her degrees at the University of Chicago, and at the School of Civics and Philanthropy. But she never lost sight of children. She writes, "Of all my volunteer work at the settlement house I think I liked best my classes in toy-making and street games with little children." That's probably where she excelled, because it used her understanding of the child's world and her inventive genius—perhaps inherited from her grandfather who was author, doctor, minister, and inventor of the first automobile, made in 1873.

After work in various sections of this country Marie was sent to Czechoslovakia to help establish child-health clinics. "But this year in Europe ended my social work, since the experimental shots given to protect me from all the possible diseases I might encounter—one set given twice by mistake—ended my health. So when I returned to Chicago I went back to studying art."

"When or where the idea of doing children's books came to me, I don't know. Perhaps from my sister's five children. It was while playing with a little nephew who loved 'smashups' that I decided a little story with pictures might save his toys, so I made him a cloth book. It was *Little Old Automobile.* He wore it threadbare, but it never occurred to me to try to do it for publication until years after I had started doing picture books. Summers, at the cottage, the children spent all their time with the animals at a nearby farm, and I used to go up and draw. The farmer and his children and his animals were all our good friends, but the young bull grew too fast. One day when I had my back to him, sketching pigs, he made a running leap and butted me into the brook."

Marie had known Doctor Harold Ets when she was living at the Chicago Commons. He too was a volunteer worker there while he was teaching at Loyola University Medical School. When she came back from Czechoslovakia they were married and lived in a charming house in Ravinia which was then in the woods on the North Shore beyond Chicago. Marie's health grew worse, and she spent the next few years back and forth between the Mayo Clinic in Rochester, Minnesota, and Chicago, trying to do children's books at the same time. During one spell of treatment she says she "needed some comic relief and got it by the story of *Oley the Sea Monster.*"

Loyola University had made for the Century of Progress Fair in Chicago an exhibit of the human embryo from "a life too small to be seen at all" through the months of growth to the baby's birth. Doctor Ets helped make the exhibit, and Mrs. Ets worked on it as a volunteer attendant. She said that it never failed, groups would come in talking and laughing but as soon as they looked around them they would quiet down and by the time they left they would go almost on tiptoe—so under the spell of the wonder and the beauty revealed to them. So Mrs. Ets made exquisite, accurate drawings and simple text for a picture book from "a life too small to be seen at all to a baby's first smile." And thousands of children who could never see the exhibit have pored over the book and have been shown with reverence and truth how a baby grows within its mother's body.

Anyone as ill as Marie might easily make a career of it, but there is never a hint of it in her children's books.

Doctor Ets enjoyed them with her. He used to love to tell people that he was her model for the pig caught under the fence in *Mister Penny.* But Doctor Ets was taken ill while they lived in Ravinia. By this time Marie was well enough to care for him while she was making *In the Forest.* Two years later, when the doctor died, Marie brought her memories to New York and has lived there ever since except for periods in Rochester, New York, the backwoods of Alabama, in Mexico—and last summer following the circuses in Wisconsin.

I think my favorite of all her books is *Play with Me.* That is a perfect little girls' book and a nice thing about it is that little boys like it just as much as little girls, because it is a universal experience—the child first becoming aware of the world outside of home—always supposing that she lives where she can have "the green grass growing all around." The joy in the face of that little girl when she realizes that if she stays perfectly still all the little animals will come to her is one of the most delightful moments in the picture-book world. The fact that it is vicarious experience for thousands of children who love it just means that, thank goodness, we're still born with an instinctive love of Nature and the desire to know that we belong.

Marie Hall Ets is a brave and delightful woman with a wonderful sense of humor and play, great talent as artist and writer, and just plain genius, the greatest and most demanding gift of all. (pp. 278-82)

May Massee, "Marie Hall Ets," in The Horn Book Magazine, *Vol. XXXVI, No. 4, August, 1960, pp. 278-82.*

Barbara Bader

Marie Ets was trained as an artist and schooled as a social worker; her work with children and—after further study in child psychology—her interest in their response to drawings led to the making of her first book.

Mister Penny is, in effect, Doctor Dolittle as a poor old man. His jacket closed with a giant safety pin, his home "a tumbledown shed on a stony field by a path to the village of Wuddle," he is the willing victim of kindness to animals—to an old horse, Limpy, who feigns injury because a bandaged foreleg makes him feel like a race horse; Mooloo, a cow too lazy to chew her cud; Splop, an inquisitive goat; a lamb and a pig and a fat hen and, most trouble of all, Doody the cocky rooster.

When Mister Penny is off earning money to feed them, they raid the cranky neighbor's garden; and bring down upon Mister Penny the demand that in recompense he plow and weed and mow for the neighbor—stay home and lose his job—or, alternatively, give over the animals: "I suppose the hog would do for bacon, and the lamb for stew." Limpy overhears, and in the dark of the night—a solid black picture—the animals bestir themselves and do

the work. Work, they discover, has its rewards, and when last seen Mister Penny and his ménage have the sprucest, most comfortable home in Wuddle as well as the happiest.

Droll, loose-limbed, a little ragged at the edges, the illustrations set the tone. As pictures they have the merit—and the appeal to children—of being at once filled to the frame, uncluttered and distinct. The forceful blend of positive and negative images is achieved by a batik process whereby, as Marie Ets describes it, the original drawing is transferred to linen paper and the white parts are painted out with gum arabic. "When the gum has hardened, but before it begins to crack, I brush the whole drawing with ink." Then, "When the ink has dried—usually overnight—the solid black drawing goes under a shower of warm water," washing away the gum arabic and, "as if by magic," revealing the picture. It is a method that admits of surprises and unexpected effects, and gives to the results a happy spontaneity; one whereby, furthermore, forms stand out against a contrasting ground with few details and almost no shading—except in the night scenes which, almost totally in black, achieve a striking chiaroscuro.

Other stories about Mister Penny appeared after a long interval, *Mister Penny's Race Horse*—who but Limpy?—in 1956 and *Mister Penny's Circus* in 1961, while the separate *Mr. T. W. Anthony Woo* is very much in the same spirit. But far from exploiting the success of *Mister Penny,* Marie Ets came forth in 1939 with an entirely different kind of book, the sensitive and realistic—thoroughly real—*Story of a Baby.*

The previous year *Life* magazine had published photographs of the birth of a baby. Anticipating some objections from subscribers, the editors alerted them in advance; parents who didn't want their children to see the pictures could remove them (and mine did). Nonetheless that particular issue was banned in parts of the United States and in all of Canada, and newsdealers excised the offending section in other places.

In this climate of opinion, Marie Ets's description and drawings of embryo and fetus from fertilization of the egg to birth of the baby appeared and, so delicate was the handling, met no opposition. It is an instructive and, equally, a dramatic book. Large originally, then small, now large again, it starts with a speck in a shadowed uterus—"a house with no windows or doors—a house smaller than a grain of salt from the shaker, or a grain of sand from the beach. But this was a house that could grow, and a house that was going to have roots."

In a uniform frame, the house grows—Ets retains the image without forgoing the scientific terms—and the baby-to-be grows faster, so fast that at three months he has to fold his legs beneath him, "like a Buddha in a shrine"; at six months "curl up like a monkey when it sleeps, and move here and there to find room for his head." Hair appears on his body, "as if he were going to have down like a baby bird or beast. But he was not going to be a baby bird or beast, and the hair would stop growing and fall off . . . before he was ready to be born." (Earlier, parallel pictures suggest the first stages of phylogenetic recapitulation.) "And the eighth month passed. And the ninth," until "he was so squeezed that he scarcely could move."

With the tenth month, "the time had come, and the walls in the mother started pushing. . . . It was the middle of the night. But she told the baby's father it was time for him to take her to the hospital near by, where everything was waiting for a baby to be born." And at last "there he was—a baby newborn—a baby with all of his fingers and all of his toes, with two ears, and two eyes, and a mouth, and a nose. The nurse quickly covered him with warm towels—all but his face—for he was wet and must not get cold. Then she looked at the clock, for most people want to know what time their baby came. But the doctor was watching the baby. It was time for him to breathe. Why didn't he breathe?

"We can't wait for him much longer, thought the doctor. We must try to *make* him breathe. And he slapped the newborn baby on the bottoms of his feet."

The baby's first cry is not the end of the book; there is much about his care those early weeks that is, like the rest, informative and reassuring. The book was conceived for young children and it is addressed to them; there is firmness in its delicacy and, in both pictures and text, the sweet quick beauty of confrontation with new life.

What came next, in 1944, was *In the Forest,* timeless, placeless, a child's own dream of dominion as if he were speaking it:

> I had a new horn and a paper hat
> And I went for a walk in the forest

A "big wild lion," hearing the horn, wakes up, combs his hair, and comes too; two elephant babies stop their splashing and put on sweaters and shoes, two big brown bears bring their peanuts and jam; and one by one or two by two, the animals forsake ponds and trees and fall in line . . . "When I went for a walk in the forest." He is the piper, the host at the party; they are themselves and children, animal children. The lion is unmistakably king of the beasts, he wears his crown; but the rabbit too shy to speak leads the parade with the little boy.

The dream ends in a game of hide-and-seek; the little boy, eyes closed, is *It,* the animals vanish, and his father appears in their stead. "*He* was hunting for *me.*" Riding piggyback, he is borne homeward, dependent again and secure; he'll hunt for his animals another day "when I come for a walk in the forest." (Later, in 1953, there was to be *Another Day.*)

The simple rhythmic telling with its refrain has the ring of a child's chanting, the pattern and cumulation represent a folktale-type ordering of what children practice naturally, with or without logic. The speech is to-the-point, sensory, first-hand, sharing with *In My Mother's House* the first-person mode of address but less reflective, more immediate—a cultural difference, perhaps. It is not, however, the flat assertion that attention to children's utterances and, more particularly, the wish to make the story *theirs,* were just then bringing into use; not a communication—"I take Daddy's hand and we go" (*Saturday Walk,* 1941)—

but a reverie, self-communion. (And often discomfiting to adults reading aloud, who take refuge in declamation.)

The pictures, for their part, approximate a mime drama, with movement and character conveyed chiefly by the silhouetted figures. Yet there is a visual richness in the semblance of texture and tone achieved by the use of a grainy paper that corresponds to the richness of the story and sets the book apart from a surface narrative like *Mister Penny.* "Complete integrity of conception and execution" was Marcia Brown's summation.

During the furor over comic books, Ets produced, in *Oley the Sea Monster,* one of the few books in strip form to stand up independently, and the only one in true strip form—several frames to a page—that has endured. A baby seal had turned up on the Chicago waterfront, to the consternation of the populace, and Ets mocks the wholesale panic (and the benefit to businessmen of a new tourist attraction) at the same time that she engages our sympathy with poor friendly, friendless Oley.

The book that explodes, though, demolishing conventional virtue and flouting safety first, is *Little Old Automobile.* He's a willful demon on wheels (otherwise an average four-year-old) as he barrels down the country road, throwing over animals and people, scorning pleas that he stop, chanting, "I don't want to! I don't want to AND I WON'T!" His comeuppance is equally drastic: totally demolished when he challenges an oncoming train, his parts are divided among his victims, human and animal, the front seat falling to the farmer, odd parts to the rabbits "for their hide-and-seek." A fine bit of bluster it is, drawn on handkerchief linen for a right, raggedy look; and a reminder of what we've always known from "The Gingerbread Boy," that nothing is as satisfying as a complete catharsis.

Play with Me is as serene and tentative as *Little Old Automobile* is violent and definite. Unlike *In the Forest,* its solitary child finds the animals she encounters to be diffident, wary, and it is not until she sits quietly, not trying to touch them or catch them, just watching "a bug making trails in the water," waiting "without making a sound," that they return and gather round her. She tells it in her own words but there is this difference too, that it is an experience she relates, a could-be-true revelation, and what makes it a child's is her way of seeing—the bug "making trails," the snake "sneaking . . . zigzagging and sliding," or the need to be still "So they wouldn't get scared and run away." One could cast it into the third person, substitute 'she' for the occasional 'I,' with little loss of feeling; but then one would have to give her a name or ostentatiously *not* name her, use the awkward and remote 'the little girl.' If an experience is to be universal, better that it not be Susan's or Mark's; and if it's to be anybody's, better that it be somebody's. So we have, handy, the first person; but it is the child's perception of the experience that validates it, not the choice of pronoun.

Tending to reinforce the universality is the sketchy, scattered drawing. The child is neither an individual nor a type, she embodies eager, clumsy, unpretty little-girlness. It was Marie Ets's first book in color—in nominal color, that is, for in her earlier books she achieves what has been

From Mr. T. W. Anthony Woo: The Story of a Cat and a Dog and a Mouse. *Written and illustrated by Marie Hall Ets.*

called "that curious richness of color which seems possible only in black and white." Nor is this color for the sake of being colorful, of giving form to objects or atmosphere to the scene. The dominant color, in fact, is once again white, the white of the paper, now chastened by the faun background as earlier, in *Mister Penny,* it was emboldened by the black. And because the sun and its rays are white too, the little girl's golden cap of hair comes to be the cynosure, the true sun.

The whole outdoors and no green. How paradoxical, then, that Marie Ets won the Caldecott for her one book done in local color, the Mexican story *Nine Days to Christmas.* But the use is such that the artist's term 'local color,' meaning correspondence with objects, becomes also the writer's term, projection of the setting; and that, specifically, is what the color is for.

Corollary to the picture stories is *Beasts and Nonsense,* a collection of rhymes with pictures—or pictures with rhymes—that is equally about the peccadilloes of people and the peculiarities of animals, and often about both. Which comes off better (or worse) is a moot question; what is certain is that, man and beast, we're all in this together—in a word, absurd. It's Belloc without the uppish-

ness, Thurber devoid of gloom—with a special dispensation for children, who also suffer indignities at the hands of adults.

In one way or another the commonality of man and animal, raised to communion in *In the Forest* and *Play with Me,* runs through the best of Marie Ets's books without exception; it appears as faithfulness among friends in *Mister Penny* and as jointly bearing the blows, jointly sharing the spoils in *Little Old Automobile.* Visually, too, all things are one: a sort of stylization that holds down details and dispenses with descriptive color, concentrating on contour, on expressive form, has the effect of conveying life as a continuum and, it might be added, making of the real and the unreal a single realm. (pp. 167-74)

> *Barbara Bader, "Two Masters, Marie Hall Ets and William Pène Du Bois," in her* American Picturebooks from Noah's Ark to the Beast Within, *Macmillan Publishing Co., Inc., 1976, pp. 167-229.*

Jon C. Stott

While she was a student of social work, Ets became interested in how children interpreted drawings, and when she began illustrating she "tried to keep my eye and mind on the child—not the art critics." Her language is simple yet sensitive, expressing observations as a child would. Generally her pictures are presented with soft-edged oval borders suggestive of the perceiving eye of a child. Although Ets seldom uses four colors, when she does they are muted. Her pastels delicately suggest the living world of which her characters are gradually becoming aware. (p. 103)

Jon C. Stott, "Marie Hall Ets," in his Children's Literature from A to Z: A Guide for Parents and Teachers, *McGraw-Hill Book Company, 1984, pp. 102-03.*

Zena Sutherland

Marie Hall Ets' sensitive and perceptive watercolors for *Play with Me,* about a little girl learning to be quiet with shy woodland creatures, are quite the loveliest she has ever produced. *Nine Days to Christmas* won the Caldecott Medal but is, in spite of full, bright colors, less interesting than some of her other books. *Gilberto and the Wind* and *Talking Without Words* are among her most effective books. (p. 143)

[*In the Forest* is an] enjoyable story . . . simple enough so that young children can dramatize it. There are twelve animal characters in addition to a boy and his father, so it is possible to involve quite a large group. Response to the story will surely be at the emotional level as children interact with the joyousness of the walk. Some children will show involvement with the characters through good pantomime.

Because the pictures are not large, you may want to gather children closely around you for the reading. Following that, let them think over the characters to decide which they enjoyed most. A second look at the pictures may aid them in remembering the cast of characters. As a story character is identified, you might want to let children imitate the character, encouraging them to use bodily motion and good facial expressions to develop the pantomime. When all characters have been identified and mimed, let children choose their parts and find places in the room. Read the story, pausing so children can play out the character roles, adding appropriate noises when they can. (p. 605)

Zena Sutherland and May Hill Arbuthnot, "The Twentieth Century," in their Children and Books, *seventh edition, Scott, Foresman and Company, 1986, pp. 142-57.*

TITLE COMMENTARY

Mister Penny (1935)

This tale of Mr. Penny and his animals should be greeted with jubilation and no doubt it will be, for it is one of the most delightful and entirely convincing bits of nonsense that has appeared in many a day and is a book that adults will find as entertaining as the 6 and 7 year olds to whom they may read it. Nine and 10 year olds as well and even their older brothers and sisters, will not want to miss these

deliciously absurd drawings that have not only the quality of real humor but, in addition, an exaggeration that satisfies children's love for the grotesque without ever descending to vulgarity. If we had more books like this we should find fewer children depending entirely on the comic strip for their amusement.

The very names have a touch of genius. Of course, kindly, jolly little Mr. Penny lived in the village of Wuddle, and what more inevitable than that his horse, sow, goat, pig, lamb, hen and rooster should be called Limpy, Mooloo, Splop, Pugwug, Mimkin, Chuklik and Doody! How these lazy animals justified their kind old friend's faithful affection by turning over a new leaf, how working at night, they surprised him with the most beautiful garden in Wuddle, so that he no longer needed to work in the factory but had money enough to build a long pink house, with seven doors in a row, is a tale that boys and girls will chuckle over delightedly. There, in the last picture, we leave them, the animals looking placidly out of the seven doors, Mr. Penny rocking on the doorstep, while the villagers gaze admiringly at the happy scene across flowerbeds and rose bushes.

Anne T. Eaton, in a review of "Mister Penny," in The New York Times Book Review, *August 25, 1935, p. 11.*

Looking back over *Mister Penny,* I find it has a definite moral tendency, even a moral lesson. I did not notice it at the time: I was too well amused. This book is amusing first and moral in the meantime. Mister Penny works in a factory to support a large family of animals with unlovely names: Splop the goat, Limpy the horse, Mooloo the cow, Pugwug the pig, and so on. When he goes to work he tells them, with tenderness but without much confidence, to be good till he gets back. With Doody the rooster he goes no further than "You can try to be good, can't you?" None of the animals makes much effort along these lines, yet Mr. Penny obstinately loves them all. When they wreck a neighbor's garden, he is not relieved by the man's offer to take all the animals permanently away: he is all but heartbroken at the thought of losing them. But how can he restore the garden and pay the man milk and otherwise ransom the creatures before the next new moon, and yet have time for his job at the factory?

The animals now have a change of heart. They work on the garden at night. Mooloo, who has been too lazy to chew her cud, lets down quantities of milk. Even Doody gets to work. Before the day the debt is paid by the "worthless animals." They are much happier than they were when they spent their days in mischief and ingratitude. This is the moral to which I referred. It is not a bad idea, especially when not hurled at you.

The pictures are grotesque full-page linoleum cuts in which much goes on at once.

A review of "Mister Penny," in New York Herald Tribune Books, *October 20, 1935, p. 10.*

Mister Penny is [a] frolicking picture-story book with fun and humour in every word and every picture. . . . The story flows with the ease of good story-telling and knits together well with the illustrations. A pity that children don't seem to find the appeal in pictures in black-and-white that they do in colour.

A review of "Mister Penny," in The School Librarian and School Library Review, *Vol. 8, No. 6, December, 1957, pp. 460-61.*

The Story of a Baby   (1939)

This important book tells for the first time for young children the story of a baby before it is born and until its first smile. It is the story of every human being; it is what every child longs to hear. Especially is it an intimate home book for mothers to read to their children. Without sentimentality and without evasion, Mrs. Ets traces the development of the embryo month by month. Here is nothing about seeds and flowers, nothing about baby rabbits, no reference to sex, only the fascinating record of the beginning of life told in simple language and beautifully illustrated. Even parents who hesitate to tell their children how the baby came will find nothing to object to in this telling. Many others who would gladly tell if they knew how will read eagerly this delicate yet scientific unfolding of the mystery of human embryology. Need for such a book is only too evident. It has been in preparation ever since Mrs. Ets saw the great interest aroused by the exhibit of embryos arranged by the Loyola School of Medicine at the Century of Progress, Chicago, 1933. Of picture-book size, with an arresting drawing on every page showing different stages of growth, we can think of no other fact book so likely to hold the affection of a young family. Doubtless there are many grown-ups as well to whom this information will be new and wonderful. (pp. 304-05)

Alice M. Jordan, in a review of "The Story of a Baby," in The Horn Book Magazine, *Vol. XV, No. 5, September-October, 1939, pp. 304-05.*

Mrs. Ets was inspired to write this book because of the genuine interest which visitors at the Century of Progress Exposition in Chicago evinced in the Loyola University School of Medicine's exhibit of normal human embryos. It is a lovely and conscientious piece of work which tells for children, in text and pictures, the life story. Every library will want the book in its mothers' room. Whether or not it is put in the children's room is a question on which each library must make its own decision. For the very young child the book would seem to give almost too much detailed and scientific information and illustration about the week to week development of the embryo. In using it with older children, one may find that questions in which they are vitally interested are left unanswered. The introduction seems a bit vague. The last portion which tells of the baby's birth, his care in the hospital, his homecoming and finally of his family's joy in his first smile is superbly done. An outstanding book in its field and one which deserves consideration by all libraries.

Eunice G. Mullan, in a review of "Story of a Baby," in The Library Journal, *Vol. 64, No. 17, October 1, 1939, p. 762.*

A Mrs. Ets has been troubled for some years with a problem (not by any means a *new* problem). When sissy or buddy is confronted with the fact of a new life coming into the family, how do you answer sissy's or buddy's questions? Does baby come from under a cabbage leaf? Is he brought by a fairy? The dear Middle Ages probably had no difficulties about all this. Baby was born of mother. Somehow I can't quite conceive that the Renaissance had many difficulties on this score either. But came dear Queen Victoria, and the trouble began—not that it was her fault. It was just that machines were doing everything else, so why be biological? Alas, the Victorian compromise, like all compromises, is at best a temporary solution. Sissy's and buddy's question remains. Mrs. Ets (sage lady) decided that "very small children were not interested in, or ready for, sex." But she also decided that "when they asked about babies they did not want to be told about the sex life of flowers. . . ." What inspired her to a solution of the matter was seeing the Loyola School of Medicine exhibit of human embryos at the Chicago world's fair in 1933-34. She decided that a carefully accurate story of how babies develop from "a life too small to be seen at all" to the pink object of terror delivered to the house after mother had been absent for two weeks was one solution of the problem. So she set to work and produced *The Story of a Baby.* It is a book which has already produced much controversy. In fact it is *the* innovation of the year. The cabbage-patch school has waxed indignant. They just don't want to have any truck with it. The materialist, secularist, naturalist (anti-God) school have equally rejoiced. The Catholics have been caught between the upper and the nether mill-stone. There is no reason for that. The silly advertising of the publishers ("a first book for any child") remains silly. But for parents with some sense who really want to give a rational answer to sissy's and buddy's question, the book can be a godsend . . . if they use their brains. . . .

A review of "The Story of a Baby," in The Commonweal, *Vol. XXXI, No. 6, December 1, 1939, pp. 132-33.*

In the Forest   (1944)

What could be simpler than this picture book with its tiny story in large type, a sentence to a page? A very little child will love and treasure it. What is there beneath and through its sweetness that strikes into the deeper emotions of an older reader and makes his throat unaccountably choke? Here is a tiny little boy with a new horn and a paper hat, who goes for a walk in the forest: first he meets a big wild lion who had fallen asleep in the midst of combing his hair, and who comes along, comb and all, "when I went for a walk in the forest," walking of course on his hind legs. Then they gather up two elephant babies, two brown bears, a pair of kangaroos teaching their baby how to hop—each of these is doing something scarcely according to natural history but completely natural to the very young. Before the procession is complete it has monkeys in it, a stork and one rabbit, who being timid walks in front under the little boy's protection. They have a picnic, play London Bridge and scatter for hide-and-seek. When the little boy opens his eyes, there is Dad. "Whom were you talking to?" says he. "To my animals. They are hiding, you see." So, from high on Dad's shoulder, he calls to them as he rides away. "Don't go away! I'll hunt for you another day, when I come for a walk in the forest."

At this point in the pictures the choke comes in the throat of a grown-up. Perhaps he has seen that "American primitive" called "The Peaceable Kingdom" in which a lamb-faced lion and a little child in pantalets lie down together in the midst of an outdoor zoo. Perhaps he thinks about the bit in the Bible that it illustrates. Perhaps he remembers when he too was very, very little and went for a walk in his own enchanted forest.

> *May Lamberton Becker, in a review of "In the Forest," in* New York Herald Tribune Weekly Book Review, *October 29, 1944, p. 5.*

The creator of Mister Penny gives us a book this year that all good booklovers should present to the youngest child in the family. Like *And To Think That I Saw It on Mulberry St.* and *Magic Michael* it is exactly the sort of adventure that a child would imagine with no effort at all and with that rare and precious humor that so seldom survives childhood. (p. 28)

It is a long, slender book printed on ivory paper. Think of getting such a book for only one round silver dollar! (p. 29)

> *Mary Gould Davis, in a review of "In the Forest," in* The Saturday Review of Literature, *Vol. XXVII, No. 46, November 11, 1944, pp. 28-9.*

Marie Hall Ets has given us that rare thing, a book of shared delight for adults and children. As effortless and

unselfconscious as a child's own make-believe, it takes the reader of any age along with the little boy as, with his new horn and a paper hat, he goes for a walk in the forest. . . . The text has rhythm and lovely cadence; there is real gaiety in the drawings.

> *Anne T. Eaton, in a review of "In the Forest," in* The New York Times Book Review, *November 12, 1942, p. 10.*

This 1945 Honor Book, by Marie Hall Ets, is filled with black and white illustrations depicting the story of a young boy's walk in the forest. As his walk progresses, the boy gathers a parade of animals strutting behind him, all of which disappear when the boy's father arrives upon the scene. The white figures of the small boy and the animals—a napping lion, baby elephants, brown bears, hopping kangaroos, an old stork, little monkeys, a silent rabbit—are a definite contrast to the dark backgrounds of the forest.

The effect of the drawings, which often take on the appearance of being done with the side of a piece of charcoal, is to draw the viewer's attention to the clean white figures, while the background remains fuzzy and indefinite. Because of the technique, the only sharp lines are those that define the outlines of the animals. This is achieved by surrounding the figures with solid areas of black, creating the greatest contrast between the figure and its immediate surroundings. Because of the technique, the figures are drawn with minimal detail, only including those lines which define the distinguishing characteristic of each species.

The cumulation of each of the types of animals through the text, which contains no obvious rhymes but flows with a definite beat, leads the entourage to a picnic area where a meal of peanuts, jam, ice cream, and cake is consumed

From Play With Me. *Written and illustrated by Marie Hall Ets.*

before the games commence. As the congenial group find their secret places for Hide-and-Seek, Dad appears and animals disappear, ending the tale of a little boy's fantastic walk in the forest.

There is evidence in the illustrations to indicate the fictitious presentation of the walk, the events and the behavior of the characters in the story, but the transition from reality to fantasy is not made clear in the beginning and may cause some confusion for a young audience. The surprise ending does help clarify the imaginative journey, but it is handled so abruptly that the effect may not be as it was intended. There is no need for the move from reality to fantasy to be explicitly spelled out, but the "crossing over" requires a delicate balance and careful selection of text to make it effective and understandable to the audience for which it was intended. (pp. 260-61)

> *Linda Kauffman Peterson, "The Caldecott Medal and Honor Books, 1938-1981: 'In the Forest'," in* Newbery and Caldecott Medal and Honor Books: An Annotated Bibliography *by Linda Kauffman Peterson and Marilyn Leathers Solt, G. K. Hall & Co., 1982, pp. 260-61.*

My Dog Rinty (with Ellen Tarry, 1946)

The photographers whose skill and sympathy so beautifully presented last year the Springfield plan [Alexander and Alexandra Alland] now collaborate with the authors of this distinctive dog book so successfully that Harlem goes on record as well. For David, whose dog Rinty just would not behave, lived there and went to school. Rinty behaved worse than Mary's lamb: he not only followed to school, but would go in. When David scolded, he hung his head, but he was wagging behind. When tied up at home he chewed his rope in two, ate three shoes and a hat and chewed a hole in the rug. Indeed, he kept on digging holes, or trying to. He was the most energetic, loving and determined of dogs, and wherever he went he damaged things. It kept David busy trying to pay up. At last Rinty really had to go and a nice lady bought him. She even hired David to exercise him, so the two were not altogether separated. But as the dog chewed up Mrs. Moseley's beautiful apartment, she sent him once a week to dog school, and with David's help he learned to "mind and behave."

But he still dug holes, or tried to. The trainer said they mustn't even try to change that. Rinty was a "born ratter and mouser." So when the lady's landlord said all pets must go and she gave him back to David for keeps, something wonderful came of it. The newspaper put in a notice that Rinty could be hired to clear out mice. Never before had the mice been so nobly kept at bay. Besides, people began to realize that old tenements in Harlem have too many mice, and something important was done about that.

In these large photographs Harlem life moves before the spectator: Joe Louis's house, the shops on 125th Street, vegetable stands, story-telling at the library, the local newspaper office, home and school life, the nuns, the hos-

pital. Through it all, mutual devotion of dog and boy maintains a glow.

> *A review of "My Dog Rinty," in* New York Herald Tribune Weekly Book Review, *May 19, 1946, p. 12.*

A very welcome and original dog and boy story of Rinty, who chewed rugs and behaved like a troublesome dog and kept his small master in constant trouble. This is the story of how Rinty became a socially desirable, extremely useful ratcatcher and precipitated his young owner, David, into Pied Piper fame. Substantial, well-written text—the Harlem background is treated as a matter-of-course—and every boy who has struggled to keep a dog against family and neighbor opposition will read this story with interest and sympathy.

> *A review of "My Dog Rinty," in* Virginia Kirkus' Bookshop Service, *Vol. XIV, No. 11, June 1, 1946, p. 252.*

This tale of a boy and his dog is compounded of old elements, but it has absolutely new magic, nor is this based entirely on the circumstances that Rinty and David live in Harlem, where wonders almost never cease.

A more important fact is Rinty himself, underrated and misunderstood and bandied about like a stepchild indeed, but finally discovered and appreciated for his special talents and true worth. . . .

The story of Rinty and David is told with great warmth and charm and illustrated by [Alexander and Alexandra Alland] with photographs that bring a vivid and recognizable Harlem to Life.

> *Arna Bontemps, in a review of "My Dog Rinty," in* The New York Times Book Review, *June 16, 1946, p. 33.*

[*The following excerpt is from Ellen Tarry's autobiography* The Third Door, *originally published in 1955.*]

May Massee of Viking Press wrote and asked me to meet with Marie Hall Ets, an author-illustrator who had suggested a juvenile which would depict the everyday lives of Negro boys and girls in an urban setting like Harlem. Marie and I met at the Viking offices on the same day New York was lashed by the August, 1944, hurricane and we made our first plans for the juvenile story which became *My Dog Rinty.* . . . (p. 250)

The story was written, but we had to find a "typical" family and get permission to take pictures. Though it was hard finding a family to fit our needs, getting permission to take pictures in homes, places of business, public service centers, and churches in Harlem was an enormous task. My people's understandable suspicion of the white man and anything connected with the white man's world created situations which would have defeated the purpose of the book if I had not presumed upon many friendships. By the time Alexander and Alexandra Alland had taken the last picture for the book, I was immune to insult. (pp. 252-53)

In the juvenile field, when I started my teaching career, there were almost no books for young readers which showed the Negro as other than Uncle Remus or Little

Black Sambo. Though Uncle Remus must be reckoned as an outstanding contribution to the folklore of the world and Sambo is universal, as a steady, exclusive reading diet such books would have given children a stereotyped idea of the Negro. Today, there are many beautifully illustrated juvenile books on library shelves which show Negroes in all walks of life. To have had a small part in adding to this list has been a privilege. Of such intangibles are the riches of an eventful life. (pp. 302-03)

> *Ellen Tarry, in her* The Third Door: The Autobiography of an American Negro Woman, 1955. *Reprint by Negro Universities Press, 1971, 304 p.*

[Stella Gentry Sharpe's] *Tobe* can be considered a catalog, [Jane Dabney Shackelford's] *My Happy Days* a catechism, but *My Dog Rinty* is a book—a piece of professional entertainment that has outlasted its purpose. Working with community groups on the South Side of Chicago, Marie Ets noticed the paucity of books about the black city child, and suggested the project; Ellen Tarry, an alumnus of the Bank Street Writers' Laboratory ("They wanted Claude McKay"—ET) and the author of two picturebooks, *Janie Belle* and *Hezekiah Horton,* was May Massee's natural choice as collaborator. A contest had been held in Harlem to choose the artist for *Hezekiah Horton* but this time ("Thank goodness") there was no need: Alexander Alland had just taken the photographs for *The Springfield Plan,* the record of a communitywide attack on racial and religious intolerance; he and his wife Alexandra were obviously qualified. . . .

Like many photographic books of the time, *The Springfield Plan* was conceived and constructed very like a documentary film—in this case knowingly: how wonderful it would be, says the jacket, if, inspired by one or another film, "we could take the pictures back with us, to study whenever we felt the need." ("Well, just that has been made possible in this book. . . .") Pare Lorentz's lyrical essays, the high-keyed March of Time reports, wartime evocations of bravery and sacrifice had all made their mark, and the semidocumentary—authenticity substantiating fiction—was in the offing. . . .

It is not too much to call *My Dog Rinty,* similarly shot 'on location,' a semidocumentary. Rinty is, yes, a bad dog who makes good and the story is wholly fabricated but it involves real places, public and private, and real people in their real-life roles—including the man reading picturebooks at the library (Spencer Shaw) and the 'story-lady' upstairs (Augusta Baker).

The realities of life in Harlem are broached too. Forever getting away and causing damage, Rinty is sent to obedience school and cured of every bad habit except making holes in people's carpets and trying to tear up their floors. He's a born ratter and mouser, the trainer explains, "worth a fortune." Fame instead comes to David and Rinty: "They were wanted at the hotel where dogs are not allowed. They were wanted at the hospital. They were wanted at the ten-cent store. They were wanted at the flower shop." Their picture is in the papers, they're the "Pied Pipers of Harlem." "But best of all, the owner of a block of old buildings where the poor people live in Har-

lem said: 'David and Rinty have shown me that my old buildings are full of holes. I'm going to tear them down and build new ones.'" There will be a big yard in the center and a welcome for well-behaved children and dogs—David and Rinty first.

Showing the social range in a community, any community, from hardship to decency to comfort to luxury (in Harlem from tenements to David's walk-up to a project, River House, to Sugar Hill "where Joe Louis lives when he's in town"); indicating that the poor in old buildings live poorly; suggesting a concrete solution, that the buildings be replaced: all this was novel in a picturebook in 1946. Documenting life in a black community, intending that Harlem be seen like other places, the authors and photographers made it possible for other places to be seen like Harlem.

Of course, *My Dog Rinty* lives for children for different reasons. A dog relinquished, then regained, everywhere shunned, then welcomed (the reiteration of "They were wanted . . . ") is not to be denied. But without the brick-and-mortar development, authenticated by the photographs, one wouldn't hold to the thought that, honestly, there must be something to it, some boy and dog who caught rats and got their picture in the paper. See, they're right here, on the last page. (pp. 377-78)

> *Barbara Bader, "Negro Identification, Black Identification: 'My Dog Rinty',"in her* American Picturebooks from Noah's Ark to the Beast Within, *Macmillan Publishing Co., Inc., 1976, pp. 377-78.*

Oley, the Sea Monster   (1947)

Any one who knows what a property in the home a book may be if it can be used over and over to entertain a very small child will not only recognize at once that this is just what this book can do but will in all probability enjoy it all by himself, right there in the bookshop. It is the story of a baby seal who lost his mother (temporarily) and had great adventures in trying to find her. The story is told in neat short sentences, each of which is the caption of a drawing: as there are no fewer than 140 of these, six to a page—the pages are large—the lure of the comic is felt from the first, but if the comics were as good as this we'd have no quarrel with them. Oley is an ingratiating baby; he wants to play with folks on a Chicago bathing beach, but as they take him for a sea monster he lacks cooperation. Three pictures, all different, one for each newspaper, show what its reporter thought he saw. Oley is a sensation. But when they identify him he slips away and swims across the waterways of a big map and along its shore till an old seal hears him calling. "Like a flash she raced to him. She lifted her head and looked into his face and knew it was her pup."

> *"Oley the Sea Monster," in* New York Herald Tribune Weekly Book Review, *March 16, 1947, p. 7.*

The story of Oley, a baby seal, is told in a succession of small black-and-white drawings placed five or six to a page, comic book fashion. Because of their smallness and closeness the tendency at first is to hurry from one picture to the next, right to the end of the book. Not until the reader has become accustomed to this type of picture arrangement and stops to see the details in each drawing is the story fully appreciated. Drawings which, at first glance, seem only to advance the action, show on second and third examination real humor and fun.

The elongated inkspot which is Oley becomes on closer acquaintance a lovable puppy seal, happy when he is with his mother, forlorn when he gets lost, amazed when he plays among swimmers and fishermen who think he is a sea monster. Interpretations of the caretaker at the aquarium, where Oley lives for a while, and of the people who come to admire Oley's swimming are very human and true to life. There is just the right amount of text with each of the pictures to add to the story told by the drawings. The 5-to-10 year olds will like Oley and so will the grown-ups in the house.

> *Lois Palmer, in a review of "Oley, the Sea Monster," in* The New York Times Book Review, *April 13, 1947, p. 40.*

The author and artist of **In the Forest** tells this story in a series of black and white cartoons and a cryptic, amusing text. Oley, who is a baby seal, is picked up on a beach by a sailor and sold to a collector, then sold by the collector to a museum in Chicago. From this point on Oley and his keeper in the museum vie with one another for our attention and affection. Oley, being homesick for his mother, brings tears to our eyes, and the keeper playing tunes for him on his trumpet is even more appealing. Finally the authorities in the museum decide that Oley must be quietly put to death, but the keeper carries him to the shore of Lake Michigan and lets him go. His adventures bring headlines to the Chicago papers about a "sea monster." He finally gets back to his mother—the geography of his trip beautifully shown in a "double-page spread." The story is bound in bright rose and black and is a joy in every possible way. Children will love it and their parents will read it from cover to cover.

> *A review of "Oley: The Sea Monster," in* The Saturday Review of Literature, *Vol. XXX, No. 16, April 19, 1947, p. 36.*

Little Old Automobile   (1948)

"Once there was a Little Old Automobile"—so begins the picture-story book which Marie Ets, author of the beloved picture book **In the Forest,** has written and illustrated. **Little Old Automobile** is no sooner introduced than he starts on his willful, disobedient way, down hill, with consideration for no one—from the frog playing "leap with some stones in the road" to the "big black engine going so fast he couldn't stop."

This is an engaging, modern little story with all the qualities of a folk tale or fable. Miss Ets has illustrated it with simple, ink brush drawings painted on cloth, from which they have been reproduced for the printed book.

> *A review of "Little Old Automobile," in* New

York Herald Tribune Weekly Book Review, *October 3, 1948, p. 8.*

The author of **In the Forest** and **Oley, the Sea Monster** tells the story of a forlorn, little old automobile that ran away and had various adventures with farm animals along a country road. . . . The drawings, beautifully printed in black and white on a large page, are a delight. Each one is worthy of long study for its fascinating details. Each one has a story to tell. The final one of the farmer and his wife sitting restfully on the little automobile's seat beside the pond, while the hen swings in one of the tires attached to a tree and the duck floats around happily on an inner tube is completely satisfactory. What the moral is, we are not quite sure; but we are sure that little children will love the story of the little old automobile.

> *A review of "Little Old Automobile," in* The Saturday Review of Literature, *Vol. XXX, No. 46, November 13, 1948, p. 22.*

Little Old Automobile, who defies all the rules of courtesy and conduct, says "I won't" once too often and receives his comeuppance, much to the satisfaction of the four- to seven-year-olds who read the book or hear it read to them. Miss Ets accomplishes humor and clarity with a few fine strokes in the black-and-white illustrations on every page set off by heavy black borders. Boards. Recommended.

> *Florence W. Butler, in a review of "Little Old Automobile," in* Library Journal, *Vol. 73, December 1, 1948, p. 1745.*

Mr. T. W. Anthony Woo: The Story of a Cat, a Dog, and a Mouse   (1951)

The cobbler of Shooshko believed in peace. Not so his

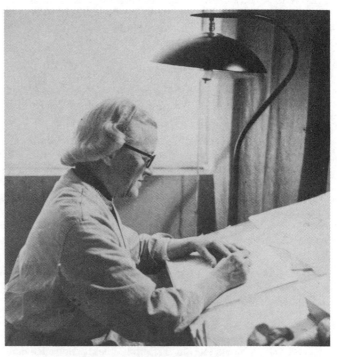

Ets at her desk.

cat and his dog, who waged a continuous war when they weren't both making life miserable for Mr. T. W. Anthony Woo, the cobbler's pet mouse. However, when trouble—in the shape of the cobbler's tidy sister and her noisy parrot—came to stay it was Mr. Woo to whom they turned for help. And so, once his tactics had proved successful, "they all lived together in peace."

This original story has the heartiness and the coziness of a folktale. It is good fun at any time, but it will be handy to have around when the children begin to bicker. Its special qualities are emphasized by Mrs. Ets' noteworthy illustrations—robust black and white drawings on paper batik.

Ellen Lewis Buell, "The Peaceable Kingdom," in The New York Times Book Review, *April 1, 1951, p. 36.*

The end papers alone are more than worth the price of this irresistible picture book. Like **Mr. Penny** and **In the Forest,** it has the quality that gives it enduring value. The children of today will claim it, and it will lose nothing with the passing of time. Mr. Woo was a mouse who lived with the admirable cobbler of Shooshko and his cat Meola and dog Rodigo. Although there were occasionally rather violent squabbles between Meola and Rodigo, the four of them lived happily together until Miss Dora, the cobbler's sister, and her parrot appeared on the scene. Instantly all was chaos. It was Mr. Woo, ably instructed by Meola and Rodigo, who solved the problem of getting rid of Miss Dora and the parrot. It is an immense relief when peace reigns again in the little house.

Never has Mrs. Ets created more appealing characters than Meola, Rodigo, and Mr. Woo. We look with great affection at the portrait of the tiny mouse, at Rodigo's sad eyes when Miss Dora shuts him out in the rain, at the peace of the final scene when the cobbler sits in a rocking chair and reads aloud. This is a book for children to own and to keep for their children.

Mary Gould Davis, in a review of "Mr. T. W. Anthony Woo: The Story of a Cat, a Dog and a Mouse," in The Saturday Review of Literature, *Vol. XXXIV, No. 16, April 21, 1951, p. 40.*

The kind of fun created in **Little Old Automobile** and **Oley, the Sea Monster,** is at its best in this "Story of a Cat and a Dog and a Mouse." The text is full of the sort of riotous action that small children love, and the many pictures are truly comical, full of humorous detail. Mrs. Ets has a magical touch with her unusual, black batik style, boldly decorative, every figure so simple yet so weighty with life. Everything is understandable on the four to eight age level.

We wish Mr. Woo and his cobbler a long, merry life. We urge children to observe the last, peaceful picture of the cobbler reading this book aloud to his pets, and to do likewise.

A review of "Mr. T. W. Anthony Woo," in New York Herald Tribune Weekly Book Review, *May 13, 1951, p. 7.*

It is a very small mouse whose imposing name appears as the title of one of Mrs. Ets' most delightful books. He lived with the Cobbler of Shooshko and his cat Meola and his dog Rodigo. The cobbler loved Mr. T. W. Anthony Woo dearly but it took a common enemy in the person of Miss Dora, who came to straighten out the house, to make Meola and Rodigo appreciate him. The story is full of fun and the pictures in black and white are wonderful. I have seldom seen such convincing proof that color is not essential for a perfect picture book if it has life, good drawing and fine bookmaking.

Jennie D. Linquist and Siri M. Andrews, in a review of "Mr. T. W. Anthony Woo," in The Horn Book Magazine, *Vol. XXVII, No. 3, May-June, 1951, p. 177.*

Exactly a quarter of a century ago—when writers and artists approached children's books less self-consciously than they do now and fashionable pressure groups were not hovering over typewriters and drawing boards—Marie Hall Ets' most spontaneous book was published. With its vigorous story and unfettered humor, the book was designed for the pure pleasure of children. . . . Abundant illustrations, sharply executed in black and white, reflect the action and the flavor of the story; more importantly, they stand as tangible proof that a picture book can succeed beautifully without a trace of color.

Ethel L. Hens, "A Second Look: 'Mr. T. W. Anthony Woo',' in The Horn Book Magazine, *Vol. LII, No. 1, February, 1976, p. 75.*

In a style that occasionally recalls the indistinct illustrations of **In the Forest** . . . , Ets employs black and white illustrations, encased within rounded, rectangular shapes, to interpret the tale visually. The strong patterns of light and dark, of black and white, offer a bold presentation of this tale, which has a humorous twist that would undoubtedly amuse children who are lovers of pets of all kinds. At times, however, due to the length of the text, the illustrations are tiresome to look at and become hard and heavy, when sensitivity and levity seem more in demand. (p. 290)

Linda Kauffman Peterson, "The Caldecott Medal and Honor Books, 1938-1981: 'In the Forest', 'Mr. T. W. Anthony Woo',' in Newbery and Caldecott Medal and Honor Books: An Annotated Bibliography, *by Linda Kauffman Peterson and Marilyn Leathers Solt, G. K. Hall & Co., 1982, pp. 289-90.*

Beasts and Nonsense (1952)

There is always a deceptive air of naiveté about Mrs. Ets' books, but beneath the apparent simplicity of her drawings there lies a cunning knowledge of line and form. **Beasts and Nonsense,** is no exception. This collection of verses, each accompanied by one or two pencil drawings, is chiefly concerned with beasts—in the zoo, in natural settings and, quite improbably, in the home and the school. The happy foolishness of a wart hog in a dentist's chair and an elephant in the living room will get a quick response from any small child. The author also takes some effective sideswipes at certain foibles of the human race, as the obstreperousness of a spoiled boy and the excessive fastidiousness of the female relatives who washed *Poor Bill* quite away. There are, to be sure, some limping lines, but the quick twists of absurdity, the unexpected rhymes more than redeem these.

> *Ellen L. Buell, "Happy Foolishness," in* The New York Times Book Review, *October 26, 1952, p. 32.*

All of Marie Ets's picture books bring satisfaction to a reviewer and infinite pleasure to the children. In this one she gives us a series of nonsense rhymes illustrated with black-and-white drawings that are very funny and very original. We particularly like the one of the alligator:

> Sophie Simmond's mother
> Once kept an alligator
> But the alligator ate 'er
> So she never kept another.

We like, too, the one of the two good little hippopotami, sitting in school with their paws crossed on their stomachs while the teacher writes on the blackboard:

> At home it's "It's me."
> At school it's "It is I."
> And hippopotamuses
> Are hippopotami.

The end-papers, with all the animals riding on the back of a whale, is as choice a picture as Marie Ets has ever drawn. We can only hope that . . . many little boys and girls will find this book under their Christmas tree.

> *A review of "Beasts and Nonsense," in* The Saturday Review of Literature, *Vol. XXXV, No. 46, November 15, 1952, p. 46.*

For older children, probably for the whole family, Mrs. Ets has collected a merry lot of wonderfully funny sketches of zoo animals, and a few others, such as the mouse who caused a lady to bathe with her clothes on. The text varies from limericks to long, informal rhymes. There are remarks like this: "Some birds are perpendicular like men, and some are horizontal like the hen," and a three-page prose story of the animals' march on City Hall. Each time you pick it up, you will find a new favorite. Mine, at the moment, is on the last page: "When Silas Stokes's troubles seem more than he can bear he goes out and whispers jokes to an old gray mare." An elegant book! We expect it to appeal even more widely than Mr. Belloc's nonsense books which are so much more neatly polished. Children will love the two-line story on the end-papers: grown-ups will appreciate such pages as the one where you are told to ask the old turtle, "Has it been any fun to live to be one-hundred-and-sixty or sixty-one?"

> *"Gay Nonsense by Favorite Artists," in* New York Herald Tribune Book Review, *November 16, 1952, p. 6.*

Another Day (1953)

Since its publication nine years ago, Mrs. Ets' *In the Forest* has established itself firmly in the affections of the pic-

ture book audience. *Another Day* is a companion story—a new tale about the same little boy in the same fantastic forest. This time the little boy strolls into a kind of impromptu circus act, where all his old animal friends are performing their best tricks. It is the little boy who wins the contest with his laughter, a gift denied to all animals except humans. Even so, the animals in these excellently drawn pictures are obviously enjoying themselves. So will small children who watch them cavorting in a gravely comic fashion, much as any youngster might picture them in his imagination.

> *Ellen L. Buell, "Animal Act," in* The New York Times Book Review, *September 13, 1953, p. 30.*

A happy sequel to *In the Forest,* with the same kind of paper-batik illustration. The little boy has gone back to the forest to meet his animal friends and finds Old Elephant and all the others "having a confab"—determining that "Each will show what he can do. Then we'll decide which thing is best." The show begins and there comes a delightful surprise at the end when the little boy takes his turn to perform. Children will appreciate his fun and enjoy the humor in each creature's expression.

> *Virginia Haviland, in a review of "Another Day," in* The Horn Book Magazine, *Vol. XXIX, No. 5, October, 1953, p. 347.*

Dozens, hundreds, probably thousands of children when they see this cover jacket will realize happily that they are to go again *Into the Forest* with Marie Ets's little boy. . . . All the charm and humor of Marie Ets's first picture book is in these drawings. They are done in paper batik instead of crayon, which gives them lightness and great delicacy.

> *A review of "Another Day," in* The Saturday Review, *New York, Vol. XXXVI, No. 46, November 14, 1953, p. 60.*

This sequel to *In the Forest* is better than the original book; it still does not quite come off. Miss Ets is an interesting artist, but she works with flimsy material. In *Another Day* her little boy goes into the forest to take part in a contest of talent between the animals. He wins because he alone can laugh. It is all rather thin, one of those books which begins as a private joke and never really communicates itself to a larger audience. Miss Ets' animals are delightful, particularly the elephants and the hippo. They deserve a better story.

> *A review of "Another Day," in* The Junior Bookshelf, *Vol. 20, No. 5, November, 1956, p. 265.*

Play with Me (1955)

Not in a long time has there been a picture book about a little child so entirely satisfactory as this one. Delicate drawings in gray, beige, yellow, and brown, and simple, rhythmic text tell the story of a very real little girl who wanted to play with the animals she found early one morning in a dew-drenched meadow. In her eagerness she frightened them away, and it was not until she sat quietly still that they came back to her.

The artless curiosity of the small girl, her wonderfully expressive little face, and the naturalness of the animals make *Play With Me* a delight to read with little children. Mrs. Ets, whose *In the Forest* and *Another Day* have already become children's classics, again shows that she has complete understanding of a child's excitement over small things. A rare and lovely picture book.

> *Frances Lander Spain, in a review of "Play with Me," in* The Saturday Review, *New York, Vol. XXXVIII, No. 38, September 17, 1955, p. 46.*

With the same sensitivity which distinguished her *In the Forest* and *Another Day,* Mrs. Ets tells of another child's country excursion. This time it is a little girl who wanders into a meadow, eager for a playmate. She tries to catch a grasshopper but it leaps away. So do the frog, the chipmunk and all the wild creatures for which she reaches so impetuously. Discouraged and lonesome she sits quietly by the brook, just watching and then, one by one, the animals reappear, ready for friendship with a child who has learned not to grab.

There's no need to point up the parable. The book is wholly delightful, with its candid, seemingly effortless prose and the pictures, done in muted tones of brown, gray and yellow, which accurately reflect the little girl's rapidly changing moods of eagerness, bafflement, disappointment and final happiness.

> *Ellen L. Buell, "In the Meadow," in* The New York Times Book Review, *October 16, 1955, p. 34.*

Mrs. Ets' first book in color, soft browns and yellows and grays, is one of the loveliest picture books of the year. It tells of a little girl who goes to the meadow one morning. "Will you play with me?" she asks all the creatures she sees, from the grasshopper on the leaf of a weed to a baby fawn hiding in the bushes. Mrs. Ets has caught perfectly the childlike way the little girl approaches and speaks to each one; her surprise and disappointment as each hurries away from her; the stillness in the meadow when she finally sits down, oh so quietly, on a little rock; and the happy outcome. It is a beautiful morning in the meadow; one can feel the freshness and the sunlight. A perfect choice for Christmas for the two- to four-year-olds.

> *Jennie D. Lindquist, in a review of "Play with Me," in* The Horn Book Magazine, *Vol. XXXI, No. 6, December, 1955, p. 447.*

Play with Me is, to my mind, one of the loveliest picture books of today, both for its illustrations and for its text. The story is charming and original, and as all proper picture-book stories should, it ends in a deeply satisfying manner.

Picture books for the very young should be easy to listen to and easy to look at. In *Play With Me* Marie Hall Ets has met both these requirements completely. Without leaving anything unsaid, she has managed to write her story in as simple a manner as possible. . . . (p. 210)

The delightful color illustrations for *Play With Me,* as simple and direct as the story itself, are drawn in black outline, and there is one picture on every page (some being double-spreads), with just two lines of text beneath. The color in these drawings is delicate and harmonious. There are notes of clear yellow, flesh, white and occasionally of brown, against an oyster-grey background. In every drawing the sun is shining down upon the little girl and upon the various creatures beside her, and the clarity and freshness of morning are apparent.

It is truly difficult to draw the look and gestures of a little child, no matter how good an artist's pens or pencils may be, but in her illustrations for *Play With Me* Marie Hall Ets has succeeded beautifully in doing so. The little yellow-haired girl with her white hair ribbon and her white pinafore fastened down the back by bows of tape is a very real and engaging child, alive in her every pose, movement and gesture, and in her various expressions of eagerness, disappointment, sadness and joy. Throughout the entire book she moves exactly as a little girl of that age would.

My favorite drawing in *Play With Me* is a double-spread toward the end of the book, in which a baby fawn who has been hiding in the bushes licks the little girl's cheek, nearly toppling her over. . . .

I am sure little children will delight in *Play With Me.* They will want to listen to the story and to look at the enchanting pictures over and over again. (p. 211)

> *Pamela Bianco, in a review of "Play with Me," in* The Horn Book Magazine, *Vol. XXXII, No. 3, June, 1956, pp. 210-11.*

[Every picture-story] deals with special characters, a special background, and its action develops with its own special emotions—excitement, sympathy, loneliness, surprise and so on. It is the responsibility of the artist to sense the basic mood of the story and so control the various elements of the book's physical form that, from the first impact of the jacket on through to the last drawing on the last page, the subtleties of page design, composition of pictorial units, the emotional effect of color, all reinforce the mood of the narrative.

Narrative moods, like the child's relation to the world about him, have the greatest range, and include moments both of rampaging excitement and of quiet wonder. With bright colors and pell-mell action on the part of the story's chief characters, excitement is the easier mood to establish. The quality of the quiet times is harder to achieve. Anyone who wants to see how a sympathetic representation of child and animal forms, combined with controlled pictorial composition and a subtle choice of color, can bring about this wonderful magic in mood will find it in a picture story of only a few years back, Marie Hall Ets' *Play With Me.* (pp. 19-21)

> *Lynd Ward, "The Book Artist: Ideas and Techniques," in* Illustrators of Children's Books, 1946-1956, *Ruth Hill Viguers, Marcia Dalphin, and Bertha Mahony Miller, eds., The Horn Book, 1958, pp. 14-35.*

Play With Me, a quietly illustrated, deceptively simple

From Mister Penny's Race Horse. *Written and Illustrated by Marie Hall Ets.*

story, . . . has survived the reigns of other more flamboyant books to become an enduring favourite. In it a little girl . . . invites successive small animals to play with her. All seem unenthusiastic, but one after the other they come back to join her, just as despair sets in.

Each full-page picture shows the same scene with minor but significant changes in grouping. The "action" is almost discernible from the pictures alone, so carefully and perceptively is each change in gesture or movement portrayed.

Marie Hall Ets, in all her books, demonstrates a sensitive awareness of the concerns of young childhood which is regrettably absent from the work of many modern authors. She encapsulates the small child's limited vision and sees the world from child height: the grasshopper on the leaf, the frog on the ground. She knows, and believes in, the importance of making friends. *Play With Me* was published in 1955 and has been constantly in print in an American edition ever since. Most New Zealand children do not know it, to their great loss. (pp. 14-15)

> *Dorothy Butler, "Cushla and Her Books: 'Play With Me',"* in Signal, *No. 22, January, 1977, pp. 14-15.*

The putty-colored backgrounds for the illustrations . . . allow the artist to make use of white as a color, as well as

offer a means to highlight and draw attention to the focal point—the little girl. In her simple white dress, the child's figure contrasts sharply with the neutral background; the addition of two other colors—yellow and a flesh tone—helps add interest and direct attention around the page, with light sketchlike lines of black completing the compositions.

Although the white rays of the sun extend into the foregrounds of illustrations, enveloping and containing the compositions, the white-clad figure remains the center of attraction on each page. The airiness of these compositions contrasts with the bold, heavy black and white compositions of two earlier Ets Honor Books, *In the Forest* and *Mr. T. W. Anthony Woo.* The diversification of style in these Caldecott works attests to her skill as an artist and author of children's books, but in *Play With Me* she is most successful in meshing word and picture. The appropriateness of the style to the mood and character of the text is highly important, but the style, in turn, does much to shape the reception of the words. Ets touches upon a subject of wide appeal and develops a visual interpretation which is just as pleasing. (pp. 305-06)

> *Linda Kauffman Peterson, "The Caldecott Medal and Honor Books, 1938-1981: 'Play with Me',"* in Newbery and Caldecott Medal and Honor Books: An Annotated Bibliogra-

phy, *by Linda Kauffman Peterson and Marilyn Leathers Solt, G. K. Hall & Co., 1982, pp. 305-06.*

Mister Penny's Race Horse (1956)

In literary chronology Marie Hall Ets' **Mr. Penny** has come of age. It is almost exactly twenty-one years since that title character made his first appearance, with a whole barnyardful of animals—but, despite the years, he is still that same gentle old man and, in his nice way, just a bit of a screwball. It is quite natural then that, in this new story, he should decide to show his animals at the fair—except Limpy, the knobby old plow horse—and to promise them all a ride on the Ferris wheel if they win enough prize money.

The excursion starts out demurely enough but soon develops into bedlam and near-disaster. Of course it is Limpy, with his secret ambition to be a racer, who pounds down the track to unconventional stardom and makes the trip a complete success. Skillfully mixing slapstick with honest sentiment, Mrs. Ets concocts a diverting extravaganza and dramatizes it with her own distinctive, high-spirited illustrations.

> *Ellen Lewis Buell, "Off to the Fair," in* The New York Times Book Review, *September 2, 1956, p. 16.*

Mister Penny, who made his first appearance more than twenty years ago, is back now in a second book getting his animals ready for the fair. . . . The illustrations in Mrs. Ets' "paperbatik" technique are so full of detail that they tell the hilarious story of the fair and Limpy's final triumph as graphically as the text does. The rust-colored cover has an amusing design, with the hero looking, if not quite like a race horse, at least very gay indeed with his bandaged leg held high. Children will like everything about the book. (pp. 345-46)

> *Jennie D. Lindquist, in a review of "Mister Penny's Race Horse," in* The Horn Book Magazine, *Vol. XXXII, No. 5, October, 1956, pp. 345-46.*

Mister Penny was published some twenty-one years ago and is well on the way to becoming a modern picture-book classic. The drama, humor, and childlike appeal of its story and black-and-white illustrations are all to be found in this second adventure of the gentle farmer and his family of animals. The adventure takes the animals to the Fair, where all are to be shown except Limpy, the knobby old horse. Yet it is Limpy who brings fame to the Penny ménage. "His impatience stirred up" by the false starts of the trotting races, he takes matters in his own hoofs, plunges on to the track, and runs a spectacularly comical race all by himself. A story of considerable substance and a worthy companion to its predecessor in text and picture.

> *Eulalie Steinmetz Ross, in a review of "Mister Penny's Race Horse," in* The Saturday Review, *New York, Vol. XXXIX, No. 46, November 17, 1956, p. 48.*

Limpy may have been "old and knobby" but he had a bandage on his leg just like race horses and like them he was harnessed to a cart with two wheels. "Well switch my tail," he said " . . . I'd rather be a race horse than a farm horse any day." Perhaps he could win a coveted ride on a Ferris wheel for all Mr. Penny's animal friends. Limpy had his wish in an hilarious fashion. That and the mischief of the other animals will please children under nine as did the nonsense of the first book about "Mister Penny."

Distinguished as is all of Marie Ets' work the composition of the brown batik pictures is remarkably effective. There is a most amusing contrast between the matter of fact doings at the fair and the ludicrous actions and expressions on Mr. Penny's cockeyed animals.

> *A review of "Mister Penny's Race Horse," in* New York Herald Tribune Book Review, *November 18, 1956, p. 4.*

We have not had to wait so long for this sequel to **Mr. Penny** (published in the States in 1956) as we did for the charming original book. To say that this has the weakness of most sequels is a small criticism. It has the same qualities of humour and sweetness. (p. 68)

This delightful book, written with simplicity and characteristic style, depends mainly on its pictures. Some people do not like Mrs. Ets' heavy style with its rather ragged black lines. Others react sharply to her keen observation and her ripe humour, and notice how sure her touch is, and with what skill she designs each picture. She is markedly successful, too, in planning the distribution of type and illustration on the page, so that the two march in step. A model, in fact, of picture-book design. I hope children will be given their opportunity to show their approval of its fun and its integrity. (p. 69)

> *A review of "Mister Penny's Race-horse," in* The Junior Bookshelf, *Vol. 23, No. 2, March, 1959, pp. 68-9.*

In black and white illustrations, Ets recreates the events of the story within the rectangular borders which are characteristic of her style. The black on white and white on black illustrations create some variation within the format, as do the full- and single-page spreads, but the length of the text and the monotony of the lights and darks in the illustrations both contribute to the overall impression of weightiness and lifelessness.

The compositions, in and of themselves, are interesting in terms of their balance of lights and darks and the patterns created, but they are not lively enough to compensate for the lengthy text and short attention spans of young audiences. The artist's style, so similar to those of previous Honor Books, **In the Forest,** and **Mr. T. W. Anthony Woo,** loses the creative and original impact of earlier works and seems a mere reproduction of pictures accompanying a new text. (p. 308)

> *Linda Kauffman Peterson, "The Caldecott Medal and Honor Books, 1938-1981: 'Mister Penny's Race Horse'," in* Newbery and Caldecott Medal and Honor Books: An Annotated Bibliography, *by Linda Kauffman Peterson*

and Marilyn Leathers Solt, G. K. Hall & Co., 1982, pp. 307-08.

Cow's Party (1958)

A barnyard birthday tale tells of the cow's party. Bluejay issued the invitations to the party. But he didn't tell horse, pig, goat, lamb, mouse, duck and hen that only grass would be served. Bluejay secretly thought all the guests would leave after the games. But he was wrong, for far into the night lamb and goat and horse munched grass in the pasture with cow. Pastoral sketches in pastel colors celebrate the cow's happy birthday party. Because birthday parties are such events to children we think they will take to this whimsical treatment which combines two familiar and cherished phenomena—birthdays and animals. It is also a good complement to farm study in primary grade.

> *A review of "Cow's Party," in* Virginia Kirkus' Service, *Vol. XXVI, No. 4, February 15, 1958, p. 132.*

A happy companion to **Play with Me,** simple, humorous, and with something of that book's charm for the youngest. Cow, who enjoys her pasture grass—" . . . so-o good. And pretty too-oo, with the buttercups in it"—decides, on Bluejay's suggestion, to give a party down in the pasture. A procession arrives of all the barn and barnyard occupants, including Mouse who was not invited. But would they stay—with only *grass* to eat? Pictures with pink and yellow wash and soft crayon lines reveal the sunniness of the party scene, the gaiety of the guests, and their changing feelings. Little lessons about contentment and about rash boasting slip in easily; the total effect is one of fun.

> *Virginia Haviland, in a review of "Cow's Party," in* The Horn Book Magazine, *Vol. XXXIV, No. 2, April, 1958, p. 104.*

When Cow has a party, all is well until she offers grass to her guests to eat. As Bluejay predicted, all leave. The party is a success, after all, however, because a few of the animals like grass and stay all summer. The ingredients of a good story: humor, pathos, joy, and suspense, are woven into the few lines under each picture. Pink background of the delightful illustrations add a party flavor to this lovely picture book.

> *Julie Coste Voss, in a review of "Cow's Party," in* Junior Libraries, *Vol. 4, May, 1958, p. 34.*

Will any child under five fail to enjoy the party Blue Jay planned for Cow? He told the robins to make a wreath for her head, "the way you make nests," he said, "only make it with flowers." All her friends were invited, Horse and Goat and Pig and Lamb and Dog and Cat and Goose and Hen and Cock. Of course they all came, "and Mouse (though Mouse had not been asked)." Such music, such games and " 'Happy Birthday to You' sung once for every one there, though it wasn't any one's birthday!" As the mischievous Jay had hoped, there was trouble about the food, trouble which provided a wonderful surprise. Can all this fun be reserved for the youngest alone? Look at Cow on the cover, happily munching buttercups and longing to share her joy with others, Cow on the jacket, soft-eyed and as gayly bedecked as a fairy queen, and look at the lovely pages, washed in palest pink with all the cavorting animals penciled in that childlike way that has the simplicity of genius! Tender, funny and exquisite, this has the perfection of Miss Ets' **Play With Me.**

> *A review of "Cow's Party," in* New York Herald Tribune Book Review, *May 11, 1958, p. 27.*

What a very pink book! It is quite a relief when night falls at last and only the yellow stars break the darkness.

This is a weakness, for which printing costs must be blamed, from which many Faber books suffer. *Cow's Party,* however, has many compensations, notably an exquisitely glamorous heroine and a pervading atmosphere of charming innocence. Even Bluejay, who tries to make Cow's party miscarry, is only mildly malicious. Mrs. Ets' humour is always gentle and kindly, and she draws animals with deceptive ease. How true every one of these figures is to his own nature! Not the best of this artist's work, but a welcome book nevertheless.

> *A review of "Cow's Party," in* The Junior Bookshelf, *Vol. 24, No. 1, January, 1960, p. 26.*

Nine Days to Christmas (with Aurora Labastida, 1959)

AUTHOR'S COMMENTARY

[The following excerpt is from Ets's Caldecott Award acceptance speech, which she delivered on June 21, 1960.]

Nine Days to Christmas is a book many people helped to make. Mexicans, as I learned after living in their country for some time, have long resented our children's books on Mexico. The beautiful May McNeer-Lynd Ward book, *The Mexican Story* (Ariel), outlining their history, is an exception. The Mexicans say that since almost half of their people live in cities, it isn't fair that we always show them as poor village Indians.

I tried to explain to Aurora Labastida, children's librarian in the Benjamin Franklin Library in Mexico City, who first told me of this, that we do more or less the same thing with all countries. We like to point out the picturesque and exotic, to emphasize the differences in costume and customs of children everywhere, but at the same time to show that they are all very much alike in their joys and their sorrows, in love of their families, their friends, their pets, in their goodness and their naughtiness. And it may be that we choose the poor because our sympathy is with them and we can more easily gain the sympathy of our readers.

I had not gone to Mexico to do a children's book and I did not want to do a book on the Mexican city child, showing that he uses bathtubs and gas stoves like ours. So when Aurora Labastida suggested it, I said that this was the story *she* should write. She said she'd like to, but how was she to start? How should she go about it? Where could she get an idea? I told her that if she wanted ideas to come, she would have to start thinking. And to think first of a good ending.

Some weeks later she came to me in great excitement. She had had an inspiration: a star *piñata* could become a real star. I thought this a fine idea and told her to write the story leading up to it. But that proved a more difficult task.

When I returned to New York, I brought our problem to May Massee at the Viking Press. And somehow, with Aurora Labastida's consent, I found myself writing this story of the little city child in Mexico, using her idea of the star *piñata* as the climax. This was not too difficult, but when Miss Massee read it she said, "Fine, if you will go back to Mexico to do the pictures."

I had many reasons for not wanting to go back at this time. But I have learned in the last twenty-five years that when it comes to children's books, May Massee knows what is necessary and right. So I went.

Some years earlier, in doing **My Dog Rinty,** whose purpose was to show a normal family life in Harlem, May Massee had decided that photographs were safer than drawings. With photographs we could not be criticized for bias and distortion. Remembering this, I decided that my drawings of Mexicans must be so photographically realistic that the people could recognize themselves and each other.

I started *first* to search for a little girl who was to be our main character. (The real Ceci was too large, and she was too blond to be typical.) I never could find the right child. But as I searched, the child I was looking for became so real in my mind that I finally used my mind's child. Everyone accepted her as real, though they couldn't quite place her. All other characters *are* real and they have been delighted to recognize themselves and each other in the pictures. They are only amused to see themselves in places where they have never been and with people they do not know. (What I didn't foresee was that the children *not* in the book would feel slighted and hurt.)

Drawing in public in Mexico was a bit difficult. Sunday afternoon in Chapultepec Park I sat on the ground next to a tree near the lake where I thought no one would notice what I was doing. But I hadn't been there many minutes when people started crowding around, watching and asking questions. Trying to understand their Spanish and answer in the few words I knew while still drawing was bad enough. But then all the boats I was sketching came crowding up to shore to learn what was going on.

The public market was still worse. Though I stood with my back to a blank wall, as much out of the way as possible, a small crowd soon gathered to watch and ask questions. I was just drawing the fountain when an unsuspecting old woman and little boy came and sat down on the edge of it. Quickly I sketched them in, too. The laughter and delight of my audience at this joke on the old woman attracted so much attention that in minutes I had a mob around me. Soon two policemen came pushing their way through to find out what was happening. I expected to be chased away as a public nuisance, but the words, "Just a picture for a children's book," in my painful Spanish, seemed to work magic. Instead of chasing *me* away, the police cleared away the mob in front of me so I could see. One of my arms was cramping and both hands were asleep

From Nine Days to Christmas. *Written and illustrated by Marie Hall Ets.*

from drawing so long with no rest, but with the police beside me holding back the people, I had to keep on drawing at full speed. One must go through a great deal, I thought, for a children's book.

Those words, *children's book,* seemed to work magic everywhere. When the owner of the little home factory for *piñatas* hesitated about letting me draw it, I had only to say, "Just a picture for a children's book," to get his consent. I know he wondered why I went out to the middle of the street to draw it, but I didn't have enough Spanish to explain. I wanted to show the aerials on the roofs beyond so that children in the States could see for themselves that Mexicans, too, have television.

And now my reward for all the torture and embarrassment of drawing in public—the Caldecott Award—which should help more than anything else to accomplish the purpose of the book. For this I am most grateful. My thanks to Mr. Melcher and to Miss Elizabeth Burr, Chairman, Newbery-Caldecott Awards Committee, to her committee and to all the children's librarians, not only for myself and my editor and designer but also for Aurora Labastida and all the friends in Mexico who did so much to help. Thank you very much. (pp. 275-77)

Marie Hall Ets, "Caldecott Award Acceptance," in The Horn Book Magazine, *Vol. XXXVI, No. 4, August, 1960, pp. 275-77.*

A charming picture book about a small girl who has a lovely Christmas experience. Ceci has her own piñata for the first time, and she loves it so that she doesn't want the other children to break it, although that's what it is for . . . and Ceci, feeling sad, looks up to see a bright star. The star-shaped piñata is gone, but the real star will always be there; the child is comforted. Enchanting illustrations enhance the warmth of the text, but the great charm of the book is that it shows, not the stereotype of a Mexican peasant, but an urban middle-class Mexican family and their holiday customs. The book is somewhat lengthy for kindergarten use but is nevertheless an appealing Christmas story.

A review of "Nine Days to Christmas," in Bulletin of the Center for Children's Books, *Vol. XIII, No. 3, November, 1959, p. 45.*

Anyone who has been to Mexico will want to own *Nine Days to Christmas.* And those who haven't will want to go there at once after seeing this beautiful picture book, the joint effort of Aurora Labastida, a children's librarian in Mexico City, and Marie Hall Ets. Small Ceci excitedly looks forward to her first *posada*—that special party given each night for nine nights before Christmas. She selects her *pinata* (a fanciful paper disguise for a clay pot filled with fruit and candy). But when the time comes she cannot bear to watch her blindfolded guests break and destroy the lovely golden star. Small children will share Ceci's wonderment at the miracle that takes place and delight in Miss Ets' glowing pictures which catch most eloquently the flavor and customs of Mexico and the gentle charm of its people.

Polly Goodwin, in a review of "Nine Days to Christmas," in Chicago Sunday Tribune Magazine of Books, *November 29, 1959, p. 30.*

The creator of *Play with Me* and her co-author, who has worked with children at the Benjamin Franklin Library in Mexico City, have together produced a charming Christmas picture book. The significance of the Mexican *posada* and *piñata* is demonstrated through the feelings of Ceci who now, at five, is allowed to stay up for one of the special holiday parties. . . . Ceci goes to the market place to select her *piñata;* her cousin Manuel leads the singing procession of the *posada;* the excited scrambling for the contents of the *piñata* climaxes the evening—all pictured with truth to small details of scene and costume, in brilliant touches of Mexican colors on a soft gray background for striking and original effects.

Virginia Haviland, in a review of "Nine Days to Christmas," in The Horn Book Magazine, *Vol. XXXV, No. 6, December, 1959, p. 469.*

As free of self-conscious intercultural commentary as if it had been written for Mexican children and then translat-

ed, this book about a South American Christmas has much to offer. It is all the more to be regretted, therefore, that at times the author abdicates to her heroine and allows matters of a five-year-old's fantasy and faith to be described as if they were actual occurrences.

A review of "Nine Days to Christmas," in The Saturday Review, *New York, Vol. XLII, No. 51, December 19, 1959, p. 43.*

Nine Days to Christmas is a story of urban Mexico showing the strong contrasts of new and old to be found in many old cities today. Pencil drawings on a gray wash background show Dairy Queens and supermarkets near old-style outdoor markets where a fantastic array of colorful articles awaits shoppers. Ceci and her mother are in search of a *piñata.* Swinging on strings in the wind, the *piñatas* come to life for Ceci and urge her to choose. This scene is one of the gayest in the book with bright yellow, fuchsia pink, and orange highlighting the figures of penguins, zebras, ducks and clowns, owls and parrots, whose eyes turn appealingly toward Ceci. She chooses for her *piñata* a big shining gold star.

When the *piñata* has been filled with good things to eat and hung in the garden, Ceci leads the Christmas procession after sunset. Now the gray backgrounds deepen as night draws in and the bright glow of candles and a spotlight shine on the garden. White calla lilies and red roses emerge from the dusk with a special beauty.

Because the artist is allowed a limited number of colors, she has chosen them well for the exotic scenes at her disposal. She obviously knows and loves Mexico, yet the book gives the impression of insufficient planning. The gray backgrounds do heighten the intensity of the colors, but they have not been used consistently as a stage where the reader looks for the action. On certain pages, instead of cutting into the illustration, the text might have been printed on the gray or placed by itself on the opposite page. Not all of the drawings are well integrated with the text which is storybook length.

The first doublespread shows a most detailed street scene and the factory where the *piñatas* are made. The assembly line view of their *papier-mâché* figures and the skillful composition of the scene make it one of the best in the book. However, Marie Hall Ets's *Play with Me* and *In the Forest* more nearly fulfill the requirements for a Caldecott Medal. (pp. 274-75)

Norma R. Fryatt, "Picture Books Today: 'Nine Days to Christmas'," in Newbery and Caldecott Medal Books: 1956-1965, *edited by Lee Kingman, The Horn Book, Inc., 1965, pp. 275-76.*

The very young will explore again and again these pictures where solid children are busy enjoying daily activities. The more they look, the more there is to find in this gentle story drawn in festive colors. Marie Hall Ets has that homespun touch of Wanda Gág, and presents her little heroine from a child's viewpoint.

Diana Klemin, in a review of "Nine Days to Christmas," in her The Art of Art for Children's Books: A Contemporary Survey, *1966. Reprinted by The Murton Press, 1982, p. 8.*

Old and new, traditional and modern are juxtaposed in this story of the celebration of Christmas. Bright yellow, magenta, and orange are placed on gray backgrounds, lending the colors added vibrancy. The neutral background allows white to be effectively utilized as if it were a color, a technique Ets employs in **Play With Me**. . . .

Though the text contains some lengthy portions not directly integral to the story, these segments help paint the culture from which the story rises. Ets fills her compositions, as well, with indicators of the story's culture, and her pencil backgrounds create a backdrop of markets, gardens, and parks that help convey an understanding of and appreciation for the culture and its traditions. (p. 317)

> *Linda Kauffman Peterson, "The Caldecott Medal and Honor Books, 1938-1981: 'Nine Days to Christmas',"* in Newbery and Caldecott Medal and Honor Books: An Annotated Bibliography, *by Linda Kauffman Peterson and Marilyn Leathers Solt, G. K. Hall & Co., 1982, pp. 316-17.*

The 1960 winner, **Nine Days to Christmas,** is the most realistic of all the [Caldecott Medal winners]. Little Ceci's first Christmas posada and piñata are illustrated by Marie Hall Ets, who wrote the text with Mexico City children's librarian Aurora Labastida. Determined to dispel Americans' stereotypical image of their Mexican neighbors as poor village Indians, Ets employed a natural system of proportion sensitively and sympathetically in quick recordings of arrested moments. Real people and events were observed on bustling city streets and in visits to Chapultepec Park, the public market, a kindergarten, a piñata factory, and homes. Almost like candid photography, contrasts in the illustrations revealed the old and new existing side by side in urban Mexico: a Dairy Queen next to a tortilleria, a late-model Detroit car next to a barefoot flower vendor. With a very informal arrangement of text across single- and double-page spreads, Ceci's story is illustrated in pencil on a gray field of action; warm touches of flat reds and yellows call attention to characters, toys, flowers, and, most of all, a star-shaped, treasured piñata. (p. 174)

> *Lyn Ellen Lacy, "Shape: 'The Big Snow, White Snow Bright Snow,' and 'The Snowy Day',"* in her Art and Design in Children's Picture Books: An Analysis of Caldecott Award-Winning Illustrations, *American Library Association, 1986, pp. 144-77.*

Mister Penny's Circus   (1961)

Apparently Mr. Penny's menagerie had become so famous that two circus fugitives, Olaf the bear, and Suzie the chimpanzee, found their way to it one cold winter's night. In an attempt to add these two newcomers to his "home", Mr. Penny takes the whole gang to the circus where they watch trained animal acts, join a few, and wait for the news that Olaf and Suzie could at least spend the winter

with Mr. Penny. Back home again, the two "professionals" instruct everyone in the art of circus cut-ups and all display their talent in "Mr. Penny's 2 Penny Circus", the highlight of the county fair. Their bang up success results in a permanent place for Olaf and Suzie among the happy members of Mr. Penny's "family". Miss Ets elicits a warm response to her animals in her gentle black and white drawings though her plot never builds to one satisfying climax, a flaw which weakens the total effect.

> *A review of "Mister Penny's Circus," in* Virginia Kirkus' Service, *Vol. XXIX, No. 16, August 15, 1961, p. 728.*

A new book about Mister Penny and his animals—Splop the goat, Limpy the horse, and the rest—is a happy event, especially when it shows the same loving care, the same delicious absurdities as two earlier stories. . . .

A summer's research at museums in the old Ringling circus grounds at Baraboo, Wis., and at Madison, have produced wonderfully detailed pictures of a county circus under tents. They should keep small children happy for hours on end.

> *Polly Goodwin, in a review of "Mr. Penny's Circus," in* Chicago Sunday Tribune Magazine of Books, *November 12, 1961, p. 10.*

Mr. Penny's heart is as big as ever and his sympathy reaches out for Susie the monkey and Olaf the bear, who prefer living with him to being caged when they are not performing. . . . The good-humored nonsense runs along with continuous activity in the pictures so that children will want to spend time on each spread. The soft blacks and white on pale gray background are effective.

> *Virginia Haviland, in a review of "Mr. Penny's Circus," in* The Horn Book Magazine, *Vol. XXXVII, No. 6, December, 1961, p. 547.*

Gilberto and the Wind   (1963)

In a suitable companion to **Play with Me,** which is one of the most satisfactory books ever made for the youngest children, Gilberto, a little Mexican boy, tells the story of how he plays with wind. The pictures are in skilfully employed black, brown, and gray—and white is also used as a color by allowing the white paper to show through. There is just enough of a little boy's natural tendency to personify to make the story seem precisely right. The jacket of the book is in bright, springtime green. Children may like to know that Gilberto was a real little boy in California.

> *A review of "Gilberto and the Wind," in* The Saturday Review, *New York, Vol. XLVI, No. 19, May 11, 1963, p. 46.*

A read-aloud picture book with a text in first person: a small boy (Gilberto's name is used only in the title) describes his experiences with the wind. "When the big boys on the hill have kites to fly Wind helps them out. Wind carries their kites way up to the sky and all around. But when *I* have a kite Wind won't fly it at all. He just drops it." The book's appeal lies in the familiarity of the child's activities and in the variations of posture and of facial expression in the illustrations. On grey paper, the only color is in the mobile small brown face; in each drawing a touch of white is remarkably effective—a white kite, sheets on a line, a balloon soaring off, or the white sail of a toy boat.

> *Zena Sutherland, in a review of "Gilberto and the Wind," in* Bulletin of the Center for Children's Books, *Vol. XVI, No. 10, June, 1963, p. 159.*

A charming, imaginative picture-story, reminiscent in spirit and illustrations of *Play With Me.* Here, a little Mexican boy thinks aloud about all the things his playmate the wind does with him, for him, and against him. The wind calls him to play, floats his balloon, refuses to fly his kite, blows his soap bubbles into the air, races with him, and rests with him under a tree. An unusually fine picture book.

> *Laura E. Cathon, in a review of "Gilberto and the Wind," in* School Library Journal, *Vol. 10, No. 1, September, 1963, p. 2772.*

Just Me (1965)

For a very young child this book is just right. A little boy, walking around a farm and the outlying woods, explains on each page his imitation of a different animal. Of course he can't fly like a bird, but he can walk like a cat or a rooster, take a bath- and- nap like a pig, hop like a rabbit, wriggle like a snake, and so on, and in the end he can just be himself going for a ride in his father's motor boat. There is just enough variation in the boy's reactions to the different animals to alleviate the repetition. The woodblock prints have a nice, simple rustic quality, and are very explicit on how each animal can be imitated (as they undoubtedly will be).

> *A review of "Just Me," in* Virginia Kirkus' Service, *Vol. XXXIII, No. 6, March 15, 1965, p. 308.*

In [*Play with Me*] a little girl's relationship with animals is shown, and now, in equally artful words and pictures, we have *Just Me,* in which a small boy tries to imitate what animals do. As Ursula Nordstrom, head of the children's book department of Harper & Row, said in a recent talk, you can't evaluate children's books such as those of Marie Hall Ets in terms of the number of words in them. I am particularly glad to have *Just Me* with its few well-chosen words, because three- and four-year-olds will not only listen to the story, they will play it.

> *Alice Dalgliesh, "An April Shower to Share," in* The Saturday Review, *New York, Vol. XLVIII, No. 17, April 24, 1965, p. 44.*

A very small boy describes his imaginative imitating of farmyard animals as he plays alone. The theme is slight and seems overextended; the illustrations are attractive but they, too, are repetitive. The book escapes being dull because the text has an unpretentious simplicity of style, but it is a read-aloud story perhaps more valuable as a po-

tential stimulus for imaginative play than for any pace or story line.

> *Zena Sutherland, in a review of "Just Me," in* Bulletin of the Center for Children's Books, *Vol. XVIII, No. 9, May, 1965, p. 128.*

A little boy plays a game commonly enjoyed by small children for its imaginative as well as muscular demands. He goes from one animal to another, mimicking its ambulation, moving "just like" it. When there is a chance to take a boat ride with Dad, the game ends abruptly, and another kind of imitation begins—emulation of father. Art and prose arc in the same repetitive style that characterized *In the Forest* and *Another Day,* giving expression to a tiny child's solitary play. The theme is less imaginative, but the experience is more universal. Similarity of pictures and text will seem comfortably familiar, and the animals—most of them domesticated—are obligingly co-operative. (pp. 382-83)

> *Priscilla L. Moulton, in a review of "Just Me," in* The Horn Book Magazine, *Vol. XLI, No. 4, August, 1965, pp. 382-83.*

Marie Hall Ets is a professional. Everything she does has the quality which comes from something more than competence. In *Just Me* she has a characteristic theme, of the little boy who imitates all the animals of the farmyard and the wood, but who remains happy in being "just me." She has always been most successful in her text, which is spare and carefully designed but never lacking in natural rhythm. The black-and-white drawings are a little stiff, as always, but beautifully composed. They give just enough variety to avoid monotony in a story which leans towards this danger.

> *A review of "Just Me," in* The Junior Bookshelf, *Vol. 30, No. 4, August, 1966, p. 242.*

[In *Just Me,* Marie Hall Ets] illustrates rather than verbalizes the experience of the child who, having imitated the movements of all the familiar animals around him, recognizes his own place among them and with his family. It would be easy to make profound remarks about the child's search for his own identity, but it is simpler to say that this book rings true, largely because of the delightful, loving pictures.

> *A review of "Just Me," in* The Times Literary Supplement, *No. 3378, November 24, 1966, p. 1082.*

The black and white illustrations for [*Just Me*] are contained within oblong formats and are very similar in style to *In the Forest.* . . . The figures on the pages are defined by the black backgrounds which outline the shapes in the pictures; the works almost take on the appearance of woodcuts.

Rust-colored type adds a variation to the book's format not seen in other Ets Caldecott books, but the contrasts produced by white against a darker background remain characteristically Ets. The artist captures the distinguishing traits of the animals of the story and mimics the movements of the imaginative child in a story that is not far

From Just Me. *Written and illustrated by Marie Hall Ets.*

from the truth in the creative imaginings and play of young children.

Linda Kauffman Peterson, "The Caldecott Medal and Honor Books, 1938-1981: 'Just Me'," in Newbery and Caldecott Medal and Honor Books: An Annotated Bibliography, *by Linda Kauffman Peterson and Marilyn Leathers Solt, G. K. Hall & Co., 1982, p. 333.*

Bad Boy, Good Boy (1967)

Roberto is younger than most of the children who'll hear about him/read about him, and for once this seems a good thing—the serious difficulties of a small child and his response to them are sure to arouse sympathy (and perhaps encourage older children who have similar problems). The middle child in a large Mexican family in California, Roberto hasn't learned English yet but he knows that everybody except his sweet mother thinks he's a bad boy; after his father drives her from the house (she can't cook, doesn't manage very well) and she disappears, he doesn't care how bad he is. But the law does, and Roberto's father is warned to take him to a Children's Center every day. At first Roberto is rebellious, but he warms to praise—"good" is his first English word—and gradually he learns not only to get along but also to write well enough to ask his mother (she's been in touch) to come home. Her absence is handled with matter-of-fact practicality, her return is effected without pathos—an unusually forthright treatment of a very real situation, the text solid but not difficult, the pictures purely functional.

A review of "Bad Boy, Good Boy," in Kirkus Service, *Vol. XXXV, No. 18, September 15, 1967, p. 1130.*

[*Bad Boy, Good Boy*] tells of a Mexican-American boy, Roberto, whose curiosity and lack of English gets him into frequent trouble. Also his mother leaves home after a quarrel. Yet the story isn't depressing: it ends happily, an excellent example of how to combine a frank description of a minority-group family with a good narrative.

Jerome Beatty, Jr., in a review of "Bad Boy, Good Boy," in The New York Times Book Review, *November 5, 1967, p. 63.*

Any child has some obstacles to overcome in learning socially acceptable behavior patterns, but Roberto's were enough to make him seem obdurate. He spoke only Spanish, and the neighbors and shopkeepers scolded him often when his behavior was based on lack of comprehension. His parents quarreled. He was too old for the babies and not old enough for school. Bored, fractious, bewildered, worried, the small boy was taken to a Children's Center when his mother left (temporarily) after an argument. As he learned skills and acquired confidence, Roberto's behavior changed. The story is told with too much candor and simplicity to be grim, but it is bluntly realistic. Five children sleep in one room—a teacher does lose her temper sometimes—parents do quarrel, and some people do, like Roberto's mother, find it hard to discipline or be disciplined.

Zena Sutherland, in a review of "Bad Boy, Good Boy," in Bulletin of the Center for Children's Books, *Vol. 21, No. 6, February 6, 1968, p. 93.*

Marie Hall Ets' **Bad Boy, Good Boy** is even more demeaning to Chicanos [than Elizabeth Morrow's *Painted Pig*]. It promotes the notion that a "bad" boy becomes a "good" boy when he learns English. Racism and sexism join hands in the spotlight when the hero's father, who had put his wife—a poor cook—out of the house, takes her back after a nice Anglo lady tutors her in English (and cooking). In addition, references to Roberto's dishonesty and the harsh treatment given him by his father leave the reader with a bad feeling about Chicano people. The story's aura of negativism is reinforced by unattractive and offensive illustrations, and the "perfect" unreal ending redeems nothing.

José Taylor, in a review of "Bad Boy, Good Boy," in Interracial Books for Children Bulletin, *Vol. 5, Nos. 7-8, 1975, p. 11.*

Talking Without Words (1968)

Your reviewer has no way of knowing how Marie Hall Ets feels about the UN, but it takes only one look at one of her books to know that she has a universal point of view. Any of her distinguished books could be translated into any language and be at home. **Talking Without Words,** in which she illustrated the many ways of conveying an idea, or a mood without words, is happily for small children, no exception. Its universality? No Margaret Mead, 2, but surely small Portuguese girls put their hands over their ears when they want to convey the idea, "I don't want to hear." And small Sengolese boys throw their arms around their mothers when they want to say "I love you."

A review of "Talking without Words," in Publishers Weekly, *Vol. 194, No. 6, August 5, 1968, p. 56.*

" 'I won't take it!' says Little Brother when Mother brings his medicine. But he doesn't use words. He just covers his mouth." A former winner of the Caldecott Award suggests some of the many ways in which one can communicate without speaking or writing. In a series of black-and-white illustrations she shows the cautionary finger-to-lips that means "Don't wake the baby," or the elbow-hugging shiver that says, as plainly as words, that one is cold. Children should find the idea intriguing and some of the examples very funny.

Zena Sutherland, in a review of "Talking without Words," in The Saturday Review, *New York, Vol. LI, No. 45, November 9, 1968, p. 46.*

Children should enjoy the familiarity of the gestures in the illustrations, those means of interpersonal communications which we take so much for granted we are almost unconscious of them. The simple text points out that "When Big Brother and I want a fight we don't say so with words.

We can say so better with our fists—like this." And there are two boys, squaring off. Some of the captions stand alone, some (like the example just quoted) are completed by the picture, and some may need adult interpretation. A book that should amuse the very young child and may prompt discussion of other means of silent communication. (pp. 91-2)

Zena Sutherland, in a review of "Talking without Words," in Bulletin of the Center for Children's Books, *Vol. 22, No. 6, February, 1969, pp. 91-2.*

Elephant in a Well (1972)

An initial absurdist situation ("One day Young Elephant was wandering about with a clothesline wound around her trunk and fell into a well") yields to gradual solution as page-by-page a horse, cow, goat, pig, lamb and dog pitch in to pull Young Elephant out—until the arrival of a mouse adds the final increment of strength. The mounting list of participants strung along the bottoms of the pages and the rope stretching across the black and white "batik" backgrounds are verbal and visual complements in this well-designed gesture of Good Samaritanship.

A review of "Elephant in a Well," in Kirkus Reviews, *Vol. XL, No. 3, February 1, 1972, p. 130.*

Simplicity is . . . the hallmark of **Elephant in a Well** by Marie Hall Ets. "Elephants" tend to be favorite characters, not far behind teddies and Winnie the Pooh. And this one "has some friends, see." The friends come one by one into the black and white batik illustrations (more like woodcuts—or potato cuts, they're that shape and texture) to help Young Elephant out of the well. . . . Yes, direct in theme and design . . . and read and recalled with pleasure by the smalls.

David Anable, "The Hippopotamus Wore Pink," in The Christian Science Monitor, *May 4, 1972, p. 82.*

Like Hewett's *Tale of the Turnip* (McGraw, 1961) in which the mouse's help gets the turnip pulled up, this suggests that even small creatures can be useful. The black-and-white drawings have the typical charm that mark Marie Ets' work, and the simplicity and cumulative repetition of the story will appeal to very young listeners and beginning readers.

Eleanor Glaser and Marion Delaney, in a review of "Elephant in a Well," in School Library Journal, *Vol. 19, No. 1, September, 1972, p. 116.*

Jay Bird (1974)

The text here is so simple as to be practically mindless: "A moo cow tinkling her bell. Tinkling, tinkling, tinkling. A mother humming to her child. Humming, humming, humming." Similar phrases relate to pictures of an airplane buzzing in triplicate, a jay bird scolding, a tomcat yowling, and so forth. The message is neither rhyme nor reason and the book isn't saved by the pictures, which are only adequate scenes of a small boy as he experiences various sounds throughout the day.

> *A review of "Jay Bird," in* Publishers Weekly, *Vol. 205, No. 18, May 6, 1974, p. 69.*

Slight in concept but with the appeals of rhythmic, patterned text and of pictures that echo its simplicity, this is almost a lullaby in print. It begins, "A JAY BIRD scolding in a tree. Scolding, scolding, scolding. A HOPTOAD croaking in the swamp. Croaking, croaking, croaking," and continues the catalog until a small boy says "Goodnight, JAY BIRD, scolding in the tree," and ends his farewell sleepily rubbing his eyes and saying goodnight to EVERYBODY. Lots of animals, lots of sounds to imitate, lots of familiar objects.

> *Zena Sutherland, in a review of "Jay Bird," in* Bulletin of the Center for Children's Books, *Vol. 28, No. 1, September, 1974, p. 6.*

An unnecessary bedtime story, each double-page shows a different creature or object and the sounds it makes. . . . Simple dark blue watercolor portraits are not outstanding but serve to reinforce the quiet mood of this slight story.

> *Eleanor Glaser and Marion Delaney, in a review of "Jay Bird," in* School Library Journal, *Vol. 21, No. 1, December, 1974, p. 58.*

Angela Johnson

1961-

African-American author of picture books.

Major works include *Tell Me a Story, Mama* (1989), *One of Three* (1991), *The Leaving Morning* (1992).

INTRODUCTION

As the author of books for preschool and early primary graders, Johnson depicts experiences common to young children in a manner that stresses the joys of daily life and personal relationships. Her stories, which feature black protagonists usually in the same age group as her readership, explore both sibling and intergenerational kinship, highlighting the value of close and affectionate family ties. Johnson is lauded for celebrating the uniqueness of African-American families while addressing themes that are not limited to any ethnic group—for example, aging, death, separation, loyalty, and love. Reviewers praise her engaging, first-person narration and simple texts while commending the emotional depth and sensitivity of her stories.

Johnson's first work, *Tell Me a Story, Mama,* relates a conversation between a young girl and her mother as the child prepares for bed. After begging, "Tell me a story, Mama, about when you were little," the girl proceeds to recount the familiar incidents herself. As the tales are related, Johnson offers the reader a portrait of a family whose members support one another through difficult times such as deaths and separations and share the joys of more happy occasions. *Kirkus Reviews* writes of this work that "love and a strong sense of continuity shine through partings and reunions, suggesting that the qualities that make a family strong are passed from one generation to the next through such a rehearsal as this." In her subsequent works Johnson continues to feature characters whose lives are enriched by familial affection and reassurance: *Do Like Kyla* (1990), described by Ilene Cooper as a "warm depiction of sisterly solidarity," depicts a young girl who adoringly imitates her older sister; *One of Three,* the story of a preschooler who recognizes her own worth in relation to her two sisters and her parents, relates what *Publishers Weekly* describes as "the feelings of any child, who has felt excluded by older siblings"; while *The Leaving Morning,* told in the words of its young narrator, describes the bittersweet partings of a family as they prepare to relocate. *Tell Me a Story, Mama* received the Ezra Jack Keats Bookwriting Award in 1991.

GENERAL COMMENTARY

Rudine Sims Bishop

As of this writing, Angela Johnson has had four picture books published since 1989, all except one illustrated by David Soman. . . . Her impressive debut, *Tell Me a Story, Mama,* is a charming dialogue between a mother

and daughter in which the child asks for a story about " 'when you were little.' " The story is so familiar that the daughter becomes the primary teller, while the mother simply fills in comments as needed.

Do Like Kyla, with paintings by James Ransome, depicts the relationship between a little girl and her big sister. All day long, the younger child imitates everything her big sister does. In the evening, however, just at bedtime, the tables are turned. In *When I Am Old with You* a young boy, wearing his hair in dreadlocks, imagines the things he will do with his grandfather when they are old together. In the meantime, they are actually doing all the things he dreams of. In *One of Three* a girl relates her experiences as the youngest of three sisters who do almost everything together. But sometimes the big sisters go off on their own, and so, with her parents, the narrator becomes one of a different three.

Angela Johnson's books, all of which have been well received by reviewers, center on loving family relationships, within and across generations. All of them feature charming first-person narrators and spare texts that make for good reading aloud. The characters are distinct individuals, but their emotions are ones shared across cultures.

The colorful and realistic paintings are lively and clearly reflect both the expressiveness of the characters and the affection the family members so obviously feel for one another. (p. 620)

Rudine Sims Bishop, "Books from Parallel Cultures: New African-American Voices," in The Horn Book Magazine, Vol. LXVIII, No. 5, September-October, 1992, p. 620.

TITLE COMMENTARY

Tell Me a Story, Mama (1989)

Together, a new author and a new illustrator [David Soman] make an outstanding debut.

In a bedtime dialogue between a six- or eight-year-old girl and her mother, memorable incidents in their family history are reviewed. The eager, well-loved child asks her mother to recount favorite events, but they are so familiar that she really tells them herself with only occasional comments from Mama: the time Mama got even with a mean neighbor and Grandmama made her apologize—but also gave her an extra sweet-roll; the time Mama and Aunt Jessie went to stay with Great-aunt Rosetta for a few months because their parents had to work; the time Grandmama cried at the airport when Mama moved away. Love and a strong sense of continuity shine through partings and reunions, suggesting that the qualities that make a family strong are passed from one generation to the next through such a rehearsal as this. (p. 49)

A wonderful book for sharing. (p. 50)

A review of "Tell Me a Story, Mama," in Kirkus Reviews, Vol. LVII, No. 1, January 1, 1989, pp. 49-50.

In this touching picture book, a mother and preschool-aged daughter talk together as the child is being prepared for bed. "Tell me a story, Mama, about when you were little," begs the child, and proceeds to tell all the stories herself, her headlong narrative punctuated by maternal commentary—sometimes expansion on the events related; sometimes reassuring answers to the questions that the stories inspire. Mama's childhood memories, as related by her daughter, are warm slices of life from a previous generation: a triumph over a mean neighbor, punished but understood by Grandmama; finding a puppy and being allowed to keep it; journeys away from home. The text consists solely of the dialogue between mother and daughter, which allows the stories and their reassuring lessons to flow naturally into one another while preserving their essence: not their specific incidents, but the love and caring that the memories convey, feelings which lend strength when difficult times and separations occur. Soman's vivid, lively watercolors capture the essence of the mood and message as they deftly portray the quotidian portraits of two generations of a black family. Both language and art are full of subtle wit and rich emotion, resulting in a beautifully realized evocation of treasured childhood and family moments. (pp. 163-64)

Christine Behrmann, in a review of "Tell Me a Story, Mama," in School Library Journal, Vol. 35, No. 7, March, 1989, pp. 163-64.

Asking children what sort of books they wish writers would write is always enlightening. Last year in Las Cruces, N.M., a group of schoolchildren pressured me for what they called "hand-me-down tales"—stories from a parent's or grandparent's own childhood. Modern children, with a full plate of MTV and Stephen King (their current favorite author, they said), actually requesting slices of history? Amazing.

Two new books for younger children [The Chalk Doll by Charlotte Pomerantz and Tell Me a Story, Mama] serve this need—and in remarkably similar ways. Both storybooks star little girls in bed, with loving mothers responding to the age-old plea, "Tell me a story." . . .

The nameless black heroine of Tell Me a Story, Mama . . . has a mother in jewelry and swirling dress, eager to share personal history from less affluent days. . . . This mother's loosely knit stories touch upon the reasons for tears, the meaning of hugs, the connections between generations, death and separation, and some other elementary facts of life.

Angela Johnson, in her first book, spins her tales solely in exuberant dialogue. Like [Charlotte] Pomerantz's Rose [in The Chalk Doll], Ms. Johnson's heroine is no mere passive recipient of the past. She knows these stories so well that she tells them herself, with Mama getting in well-chosen words edgewise.

Both of these books capture what is easy to lose at a time when many children are being raised in divorced families, or by two busy parents working full time, or by adults simply unaware of children's yearning to know about the past. Each book is a special treat in itself, with broader implications for the value of "hand-me-down tales": the importance and sweetness of sharing one's past with one's children.

Kathleen Krull, in a review of "Tell Me a Story, Mama," in The New York Times Book Review, June 18, 1989, p. 35.

Do Like Kyla (1990)

All day long, the young narrator imitates her older sister, Kyla. Whether it's standing at the window, tapping at the birds, or kissing the dog's head, she says, "I do like Kyla." But at the day's end, Kyla comments, "Birds must be asleep"; little sister taps at the window, and declares "Kyla does like me." The intentional repetitiveness of the text goes on a bit long, but otherwise, this warm depiction of sisterly solidarity is a joy. [Illustrator James E.] Ransome's solid oil paintings feature two lively black girls firmly placed in a loving home, with both father and mother, and a neighborhood that pulses with realism. The dust jacket, showing an exhilarated Kyla and her sister making snow angels, is indicative of the rest of the art, which features uncommon perspectives and bold shapings that capture the unbridled motion of childhood. Sweet in the best sense of the word.

Ilene Cooper, in a review of "Do Like Kyla," in Booklist, *Vol. 86, No. 12, February 15, 1990, p. 1165.*

This simply told story highlights such everyday events as eating oatmeal and walking to the store, aptly capturing a small child's sense of pleasure in imitating an older sibling. There is a nice twist on the last page; before going to bed, the younger sister taps on the window, and Kyla follows suit. The illustrations, done in richly colored oils, often add excitement by use of interesting perspectives. For example, readers see the children from above as they march home, stepping in their own snowy footprints. Unfortunately, in the pictures of Kyla, her expression is sometimes awkward and difficult to read. She looks angry, although there is no indication in the text that she ever loses patience with her sister. Despite this incongruity, the story will certainly strike a chord with many young listeners. A universal story that features a warm and loving black family.

Karen James, in a review of "Do Like Kyla," in School Library Journal, *Vol. 36, No. 4, April, 1990, p. 92.*

When I Am Old with You (1990)

"When I am old with you, Grandaddy," says a small black child, "I will sit in a big rocking chair beside you and talk about everything." And he does, rushing and tripping through all the activities they share—walking on the beach, riding the tractor, visiting friends. As in Johnson and Soman's *Tell Me a Story, Mama,* the success of this serene book depends on its portrayal of the relationship between a child and an adult. Although the repeated line "when I am old with you" is unnecessarily coy, and the plotless text is somewhat static, the joy the two characters have in each other's company is richly evoked by Soman's vivid, burnished watercolors. Yellow halos of light surround the fireflies, a summer wind blows embroidered curtains through a farmhouse window, morning sun reflects on the water—but most beguiling are the faces of the child and his grandfather, which shine with warmth and love.

A review of "When I Am Old with You," in Publishers Weekly, *Vol. 237, No. 30, July 27, 1990, p. 232.*

The bond between grandparent and grandchild transcends time, and sometimes transcends an adult's sense of logic, reaching a deeper level of truth. In this story, a small child imagines a future when he will be old with his Grandaddy and will sit beside him in a rocking chair and talk about everything. They will go fishing, drink cool water from a jug, and play cards "till the lightning bugs shine in the trees." The poignant reality that time will never allow these two to coexist at the same age is softened by the fact that they do not have to be the same age in order to share happy times. What the boy dreams of doing with his Grandaddy someday are the same things that they are doing now. This tender story is complemented by Soman's beautifully executed watercolors, which vibrate with life and love. The African-American child and grandfather are distinct individuals, yet also universal figures, recog-nizable to anyone who has ever shared the bond of family love across generations.

Anna DeWind, in a review of "When I Am Old with You," in School Library Journal, *Vol. 36, No. 9, September, 1990, p. 205.*

One of Three (1991)

An irresistible celebration of the joys of being a sister. "Since I can remember I've been one of three. Eva, Nikki, and me. . . . One of three sisters that walk to school together. Down the street together. One of three in the sun and the rain." Softly realistic watercolors [by David Soman] show a warm African American family, as the youngest child speaks of good times with her older sisters. They play hopscotch together, ride the subway, visit the bakery, and squeeze into the taxi on snowy days with Mama and Aunt Sara. Now and then, though, it's hard being the youngest: "Sometimes Eva and Nikki say I'm not invited to go with them. . . . I'm left behind. Not one of three, just one." That's when Mama and Daddy step in to make up a new group of three, one that's different but just as fine. Johnson's charming text is well served by Soman's appealing artwork. These paintings keep a strong focus on the sisters' reactions and ably convey the pleasure they take in each other's company and in their daily lives.

Leone McDermott, in a review of "One of Three," in Booklist, *Vol. 87, No. 21, July, 1991, p. 2049.*

Johnson and Soman (*When I Am Old with You; Tell Me a Story, Mama*) have never been better than in this wise and gentle book for preschoolers. That the setting is urban and the family black is incidental to the story's focus—the feelings of any child who has felt excluded by older siblings. [When] her sisters choose to leave her at home, the girl's parents let her know that "when it's just Mama, Daddy, and me, it's a different kind of three, and that's fine too." Soman's sunny watercolors of the "stairstep" sisters carrying daisies or riding the subway are as irresistible as Johnson's perceptive and understated text.

A review of "One of Three," in Publishers Weekly, *Vol. 238, No. 36, August 9, 1991, p. 56.*

Narrated by the youngest child in a black family, this brief book focuses on the joy of being one of three sisters. The simple text is extended by the skillful watercolor illustrations that give each sister a unique look and personality, but also emphasize the feeling of togetherness as the girls laugh, hold hands, or march down the street "like stair steps." Of course, the older sisters don't always want the youngest along, but then she gets to be one of a different kind of three with her mother and father. As in *When I Am Old With You,* Johnson and Soman work well together to capture, on a child's level and without sentimentality, the underlying love and strength of positive family relationships.

Karen James, in a review of "One of Three," in School Library Journal, *Vol. 37, No. 10, October, 1991, p. 98.*

All my unmarried life I wanted a sister. An only child, I thought I'd never be lonely if I had one. I was drawn to families and friends blessed with these female connections; I never tired of searching their faces for shared points of beauty, or marveling at their loyalty to one another. Three daughters have tempered my simplistic views. The mysterious, charged intimacy among sisters is a mixed bag. Still, I wish I had one.

In *One of Three,* Angela Johnson—who has written other storybooks about family relationships, including *Tell Me a Story, Mama*—explores the relationship among three sisters from the viewpoint of the youngest. . . .

One of Three evokes little of the passion sisterhood can engender. The language, tone and action in the sparsely written text pale against the fireworks and intrigues of my own family. Yet a quiet book can work its own magic. In its low-key way, a book like *One of Three* can encourage a preschool reader to explore her own feelings about such important issues as sibling bonds and rivalry, belonging and exclusion, and being one's own special self without having to keep up.

It is refreshing, too, that the family in this book happens to be black. David Soman's illustrations, inviting watercolors complementing the roominess of the text, also carry valuable, subtle messages. Facial expressions—ranging from joy, contentment and love to anger, concern and sadness—are real. These parents and children hold, touch and look directly at one another. The most powerful message of *One of Three* is unstated but clear: This is a family whose members communicate.

> *Frances Wells Burck, in a review of "One of Three," in* The New York Times Book Review, *November 17, 1991, p. 27.*

The Leaving Morning (1992)

As in *Tell Me a Story, Mama* and other books [Johnson and illustrator David Soman have] created, the importance of family gets thematic pride of place here. Preparing to move from an urban apartment, a black family spends more time saying good-bye to friends, neighbors, and relatives ("We said good-bye to the cousins all day long") than packing. In Soman's large, golden-brown wa-

tercolors, readers can follow the play of emotions in the faces of parents and children as they hug, kiss, shake hands, or just speak quietly to one another, until the narrator and his father, pregnant mother, and older sister sit smiling together in a room the movers have emptied, then wave one last good-bye from the street. A gently reassuring view of a common, and often traumatic, experience.

> *A review of "The Leaving Morning," in* Kirkus Reviews, *Vol. LX, No. 13, July 1, 1992, p. 849.*

The text allows the children to feel all the moments of leave-taking, without brushing off the sadness with some vista of a perfect house somewhere or instant friends in a new neighborhood. Nor is the apartment the children leave portrayed as "bad" in order for the move to be justified. David Soman's watercolors honor the diversity of faces and races, and are attuned to reflections in windows and the look of lived-with walls.

> *Mary Harris Veeder, in a review of "The Leaving Morning," in* Chicago Tribune—Books, *August 16, 1992, p. 4.*

"The leaving happened on a soupy, misty morning, when you could hear the street sweeper. Sssshhhshsh. . . . We pressed our faces against the hall window and left cold lips on the pane." This eloquent beginning sets the stage for a heartfelt story about a family as its members pack up their belongings and say good-bye to friends, neighbors, and cousins. Moving is often a bittersweet experience, with mixed emotions of sadness, uncertainty, anticipation, and hope. Seldom have the feelings of this event been so tenderly painted as they are in the rich full-page watercolors here. Soman's brush has a wide stroke as well as a fine point as it captures the essence of a home in bright hues—children's artwork taped to the walls, family photos on the tables, the view from atop the climbing bars where farewells are said, and the touching goodbyes. Related in the voice of a young boy, this story ends as it begins, with lip marks on the windows of a place sure to remain in the hearts and memories of the family members.

> *Deborah Abbott, in a review of "The Leaving Morning," in* Booklist, *Vol. 89, No. 1, September 1, 1992, p. 66.*

Jane Langton

1922-

American author of fiction, reteller, and illustrator.

Major works include *The Majesty of Grace* (1961; also published as *Her Majesty, Grace Jones*), *The Diamond in the Window* (1962), *The Boyhood of Grace Jones* (1972), *The Fledgling* (1980), *The Fragile Flag* (1984).

INTRODUCTION

The creator of fantasies and realistic stories for the middle and upper grades that often feature boys and girls whose sense of self is influenced by their contact with the past, Langton is praised as an especially original and inventive writer whose works reflect her profound appreciation for her New England roots. Celebrated for her understanding of children, her skill with characterization and narrative, and her elegant prose style, she is an author considered equally competent in the realistic and fantastic modes, one who masterfully incorporates realistic episodes into essentially fantastic discourses. Langton consistently addresses such themes as coming of age, moral and spiritual development, and the struggle between good and evil in her books, which blend messages about self-knowledge and environmental consciousness with exciting stories and comic, often ironic, humor. An important feature of Langton's works is her fascination with place: lauded for her use of setting, she weaves references to the rich history of Concord, Massachusetts, especially the intellectual movement of American Transcendentalism represented by such figures as Ralph Waldo Emerson and Henry David Thoreau, into her stories. David Rees remarks, "Jane Langton's novels have a strong sense of being the product of a New England influence; the writing, the material, the view of life, the moral values, the children at the center of the stories give the reader the feeling that the author is aware of, and in tune with, a particular and special place."

Born in Boston and currently residing near Concord, Langton studied astronomy and the history of art before withdrawing from academic life to raise a family. As a parent, she rekindled her childhood interest in juvenile literature and, after a course in book design, began writing and illustrating handmade children's books. One of these, *The Majesty of Grace*, became her first published work. A semiautobiographical story that is as yet the only one of Langton's juvenile books for which she has provided both text and pictures, *Majesty* describes a vibrant, imaginative young girl in 1930s Cleveland who seeks to flee the bleakness of her Depression-era childhood by maintaining that she is Princess Elizabeth's lost older sister and therefore the rightful heir to the English throne. A sequel, *The Boyhood of Grace Jones*, presents Grace's transformation from a tomboy to a young woman aware of both her own femininity and the power of poetry. *The Saturday Review* calls Grace "one of the most delightful characters in juvenile literature," and Ruth Hill Viguers notes that Grace is "a very special personality." In Langton's only young adult

novel, *Paper Chains,* she describes the frenzy of a first college semester in a lighthearted fashion. Set in the 1950s, *Paper Chains* revolves around narrator Evelyn, a six-foot tall redhead with a wry sense of humor whose character was inspired by Evelyn Underhill, the eminent English author of books on mysticism and religion. Langton, who uses a lively style featuring several capitalized words and exclamation points to describe Evelyn's relationships with a variety of fellow students, is praised for the insight, energy, and humor of her story.

Langton is perhaps best known for her five-volume fantasy series that begins with her second novel, *The Diamond in the Window* and also includes *The Swing in the Summerhouse, The Astonishing Spectroscope, The Fledgling,* and *The Fragile Flag.* The chronicle of a family of modern-day Transcendentalists, the Halls, the stories bear the mark of the ideas and world views of Thoreau and Emerson as they describe the breathtaking forays of the young protagonists—the brother and sister Eddy and Eleanor and their stepsister Georgie—into supernatural realms and various time periods. Prompted by, as Langton notes, "things that Thoreau had said, recited by a funny madman, their uncle Freddy," a professor at the Concord College of Transcendental Knowledge, and by Prince Krishna, the mysterious and almost mythical husband of the children's aunt, these revelatory magical adventures take the protagonists to such places as the scene of a primitive human sacrifice, the Last Supper, and colonial Concord before returning them home with increased awareness of the world both within and outside of themselves. In *The Fledgling,* a novel that is often regarded as her greatest achievement, Langton tells how Georgie not only learns to fly—with the help of a talking Canadian goose—but embarks on a great spiritual journey which leads her to commit to becoming a caretaker of the earth. Barbara Elleman writes that Langton's "superbly told story reaches beyond the confines of its finely tempered plot and leaves an echo that is at once touching and challenging." *The Fragile Flag,* which centers on a children's march to Washington led by Georgie against nuclear arms, reflects Langton's long involvement in a variety of grass-roots political actions, including protests against the war in Vietnam. Nicholas Lemann notes, "The portrayals of the children themselves are so effortless and true that it seems momentarily impossible that other writers could find it difficult to endow characters with distinctive personalities." In addition to her fantasies and realistic fiction, Langton is the reteller of international folktales and the author of popular mysteries for adults, several of which she has illustrated. *The Diamond in the Window* was the runner-up for the Edgar Allan Poe Award in 1963, and *The Fledgling* was a Newbery honor book in 1981 as well as a nominee for the American Book Award in 1992.

(See also *Something about the Author,* Vols. 3, 68; *Major Authors and Illustrators for Children and Young Adults; Something about the Author Autobiography Series,* Vol. 5; *Contemporary Authors New Revision Series,* Vols. 1, 18, 40; and *Contemporary Authors,* Vols. 1-4, revised edition.)

AUTHOR'S COMMENTARY

Children say to you, "Where do you get your ideas for books?" In other words, how do you know what you're going to write about, how do you know what to say, where does it come from? All I can do is shrug my shoulders and say I don't know, that it's a strange and mysterious thing.

In Joyce Cary's novel about the painter Gulley Jimson, the real subject is the creative process. The title of the book, *The Horse's Mouth,* is a mocking answer to the children's question. Where did Jimson get the visions he transformed into paintings? He had a straight tip, like a man betting at the racetrack, right from the horse's mouth. Which is no better than saying that they came to him by inspiration from God, by divine revelation. If the writer is inspired by God, then there is nothing more to be said on the subject. (Perhaps some writers are.) But if he is not, he has only two dependable oracles: The first is his memory of all the books he has read in the past; the second is real life.

Of course, he couldn't do the job at all without some dim recollection of the books he had read before, without some muddled mishmash which supplies him with a kind of unconscious mental pattern or set. Without an inherited literary pattern, a writer could not even begin to write. But

if the memory of other books is his only source, his rehash will remain hash. In other words, if he doesn't use his own life experience in some way, if he makes no reference to reality as he has encountered it, his book will be inert, an exercise, a formula. Live truth, reality, the life in which he is wading every day—it is into this well that the writer must dip his pail. It is inexhaustible, a clear fresh spring, never to be used up. And that is only one good thing about it. The other good thing is its power. "All truth is profound," said Herman Melville. The simplest reality when translated into words can deeply affect the reader. It sounds simple enough. The writer merely looks at the world around him and puts together what he has gathered from his experience in a new way. He merely tells the truth as he sees it.

But there are levels of truth-telling. There is a telling of the truth as it appears on the surface; and there is a telling of the truth a little farther in—and in contrast to this second kind of truth, the first level may seem obtuse and clumsy, if not actually false. Finally, there is a telling of the truth even farther toward the center, and this third truth may deny the other two. There is a many-leveled reality, and each level is true on its own plane. A writer of fiction chooses consciously or unconsciously to write at one or more of these levels.

Here is an example of the first level of truth-telling, a description of reality at the surface, a reporting of action, speech, appearance, of what is apparent only to the senses. In the work of a craftsman, this kind of surface description can be profound—in Melville's sense that all truth is profound. In William Mayne's *Pig in the Middle* (Dutton) when the boy Michael needs to know something about navigation, he asks his father:

> Dad said he did not know anything about navigation. Mum said navigate to bed, your Dad wants to watch the boxing. Michael went to bed.

Nothing is said about Michael's inner response. But, nonetheless, the reader twinges, winces, at this revelation of Michael's family life. The accuracy of the description of life at the surface plunges down through all levels of reality. It is as though the writer plucked one string inside the open case of a piano, and a number of other strings vibrated in resonance.

So much for the description of truth at the surface. It is truth-telling at the next level, a deeper level, that I want to examine at length. If you peel a sunburn, it feels good— unless you pull a little too far and expose raw skin. One name for this raw skin is the *quick.* It is the layer where feeling is most intense, where it is most sensitive, where it hurts. And, of course, another meaning of the word *quick* is *alive.* "The quick and the dead" means "the living and the dead." To write at this level of truth-telling, the level directly under the surface, is to wring both meanings from the word: The writer exposes this layer of intense sensitivity; and, at the same time, he brings his story vividly to life.

He brings it to life. In talking about writing everyone uses that phrase. And yet, we are talking about something impossible. The writer can't bring anything to life. He has nothing to work with but a piece of white paper. It is an inanimate object. It is a white marble slab with a corpse lying on it. His book is a dead body into which he must breathe some semblance of life. He is not God, after all. He is not creating Adam. That sheet of white paper is all that he has, and when he has finished, his readers will have nothing in their hands but a sheaf of white paper. It is an artificial process. The very best that any writer can do is to give the reader a momentary illusion of life.

Writing at this second level of truth, this down-to-the-quick layer of reality, is a powerful way of creating the illusion. It is a matter of peeling back the skin of surface appearances and laying bare the quick, sensitive flesh that lies below. Laying bare—in writing I often find myself thinking of edge tools. The words *pierce, rasp, scrape, hone, cleave, saw, razor, knife* spring to mind—sometimes even the word *axe,* as if I had to decapitate my book to get down to the quick, to make the live blood flow. It takes a sharp blade to lay bare this kind of truth. *We are so used to it, we don't know that it is there.* In his book *Twelve Great American Novels* Arthur Mizener explains why:

> It is difficult to know this truth, to clear away all secondhand opinions and habits of feeling and to expose to one's own understanding what one

Langton at age five, Belmont, Massachusetts, 1928.

does feel. It is even more difficult to say what that is after one has unearthed it, since words are always cluttered with the blurred, commonplace feelings of a society's routine assumptions about the meaning of experience.

Here is an example of what I mean by "laying bare," a commonplace event dissected. Imagine that you are meeting someone for the first time, shaking hands, saying hello. Each of you is getting an immediate impression of the other. Each of you is being known. There you are, the two of you, being perceived all at once as the mixtures of shape and color, light, shadow, and sound that are your physical selves. Now, I think we all care more than we commonly admit how we are being perceived. We wonder what kind of knowledge the other person is getting of us. We wonder whether or not he thinks what we would like him to think.

This ordinary encounter can, of course, be described at the surface level: how the two people look and what they say. But if one attempts to peel back the surface and reveal the next layer down, this simple event becomes endlessly intricate and interesting. Whenever I shake hands with a stranger there is, directly under the surface, *a flash of windows.*

> I am rushing through a city in an elevated train, flying past blocks of flats, of apartment houses; I have momentary glimpses of rooms, of homes, of people caught in mid-gesture. A score of windows flash by, a hundred, a thousand. And behind them, I know, are blocks and blocks of apartment houses; there is a city full of them, and across the country there are innumerable villages and cities. There are so many people in the world. And I am only one. How can I show this stranger that I am different from the rest?

This desire to be known as one person rather than as part of an endless horde is just beneath the surface, I think, in any meeting with someone we haven't met before. At any rate, it is part of my own unconscious but ever-present thought as I meet someone—this flash of windows. That it may be true of others, I know from my first meeting with a woman who responded to an invitation by saying, "Oh, no, I can't come on that day because I have to go to New York—to accept an award." To accept an award! With signals and signs and hints like this we reveal what lies below the surface. I recognized it immediately, that flash of windows on her consciousness, that need to be known, to be someone, to be a person who deserves an award.

What is it about yourself that you hope will become manifest as you meet someone you haven't known before? If you were eight years old, you could say it right out—you could get the fact across without delay—that you had won the spelling bee. You can't do that now. Yet there is this thing yearning to be expressed, without which this stranger cannot possibly know who you are. How can he be made to understand that you have won spelling bees in your day, that you have to go to New York to receive an award? One wishes for a friend at one's elbow, someone who could say, "I'd like you to meet so-and-so; she has just won the grand international interplanetary spelling bee."

And that's not all. While all of these thoughts are urging themselves forward during this same tedious encounter with this same tiresome person, there is something more going on. Side by side with our wish to be known as a person of worth, of accomplishment, is our uneasy awareness that, alas, all pride is vain, that one is thrusting forward the wrong triumphs, that they are dust and ashes, that if we want to be known for what is truly most important about ourselves it would not be for our little successes, it would be for our virtue. In the eyes of God this is what counts. Before the great bar of eternal justice, it is not the award we were given in New York that will be weighed in the balance, but our purity of heart. Therefore, it must somehow become evident that we are also good in some way.

And in distinction to that flash of windows, which is for me a symbol for the need to be somebody rather special, there is another image which stands for this wish to be known for one's goodness: a bonfire of vanities in Savonarola's Florence, a burning of mirrors and false hair and powder and paint and lutes and music books, a putting to the torch of all those material things that distract the soul from the contemplation of God.

So there we are, saying hello with all this going on underneath, this clash of psyche and soul, this flash of windows before the mind's eye, this wrinkling of the mind's nose at the smell of burning hair. For me all of these revelations are more or less unconscious, but they are real. They are down to the quick. They are absurd, but they are true. All that I am saying, of course, is that ordinary reality can be enormously complex, that this discovery of commonplace feeling can be endlessly interesting, that it comes to us trailing after it any number of images and pictures and allusions.

It is easy enough to say all this, but hard to put this understanding to use. Only rarely do I manage to get below the surface in my own books. My pen is a dull tool. Only once in a while do I feel satisfied that I have been working with a sharp instrument, as in this paragraph about my young heroine Eleanor in *The Astonishing Stereoscope.* She is about to attend a Catholic mass for the first time, without any preparation or understanding:

> She found a veil. It was exactly right, a long piece of black lace. Eleanor laid it carefully over her head with the edge framing her face and her long red hair hanging down evenly all around. Then she took off her glasses, leaned forward to study her reflection in the mirror, and smiled a faint, sad, secret smile. When she did that she looked exactly like pictures of the Virgin Mary. Anybody would see the resemblance. She must be careful not to show the braces on her teeth. "Ave Maria," said Eleanor to herself, feeling very holy, a proper Catholic already, smiling her faint sad smile.

Virginia Hamilton writes at this level with keenness and subtlety. There is an extraordinary combination of surface description and under-the-surface revelation in this passage from *The Planet of Junior Brown* [Macmillan]. (Junior's father had not come home when he had been expected.)

> Slowly Junior started eating the cereal his mother had wanted him to have. He ate it all while staring at her and willing her to sit down. She did come and sit down right next to him at the table. She gathered her skirt in around her. She crossed her legs under the table. She folded her hands in front of her and cast her eyes down to one side. . . .
>
> Junior could hear movement, televisions, in other apartments, so still were he and his mother. He could hear the street; and beyond their street, other streets. The city out there was loud and bright. All of it revolved around Junior like a wheel, like a system in an immense spiral. Junior knew he was the center and the point of it all.

How alive that is, how hollowly it resounds in us, how deep it goes. The bleakness of the moment as it is described on the surface level, and at a deeper level the image of the city revolving around Junior like a wheel—they strike chords, we have a sense of recognition.

And that is what is so important about getting down to the quick, down to this barely hidden level of daily reality. Whether he is a child or an adult, the reader recognizes it, he says, "Yes that's right; that's the way it is. I couldn't have said it that beautifully, but it's true." And then he feels a kind of relief at being found out, at being discovered. Bleak places in his own life are shown to be commonplace. His identical feelings are laid bare. Perhaps this is what universality means—the arousing of this sense of recognition, of relief. "If the boy in the story feels that way, then he is as alive as I; and what's more, I am as alive as he. I now notice for the first time that I often feel like that. I never was aware of it before."

So much, at last, for this second level of truth-telling. We still haven't explored the third level, where perhaps the profoundest springs of action and emotion exist, the deepest plungings of mind and heart, the core of the intellectual, spiritual, sexual self. As a writer I stop short. I steer clear. I don't think myself able. And I know many other writers steer clear, too, and rely on the plucked-string effect I referred to before, hoping to arouse chords and resonances by setting up a vibration in only one string. If they are deft enough at describing the surface, sharp enough at laying bare the level just under the surface, they will uncover gulfs and chasms along the way. Strip mining, in this case, is sound practice. In my opinion, for example, Mollie Hunter's *A Sound of Chariots* (Harper), which has deservedly received high praise, would have been even more powerful if the author had not attempted to plumb the depths of her young heroine's soul on every page.

So much, then, for all three levels of truth-telling. As I read over what I have said, I am struck by how grandiose it all sounds compared with the poor shriveled things my own books suddenly seem to be. I wonder if other writers feel this way. We work so hard making these pathetic little pieces of fiction, and they are such feeble things, compared to the vivid life that flows around us every day, so full of color and noise and motion and feeling. Unless we can charge our pieces of white paper with vitality, they will become nothing more than bundles of white paper in the hands of our readers. The dead body on the slab will not come to life.

There is a legend about the Spanish hero, the Cid, that when he was killed in war his generals dragged his body away before the enemy could learn that he was dead. Then they strapped the body into the saddle, tied it upright, slapped the horse's rump, and sent their leader back into the battle—an apparition, a fierce warrior with open staring eyes.

That, after all, is what we have to do. We must pick up the body on the slab, drag it upright, and send it galloping away in the hope that it will deceive you, the reader, into believing that it is alive, that it is quick and not dead. And that is no easy task. (pp. 24-30)

> *Jane Langton, "Down to the Quick: The Use of Daily Reality in Writing Fiction," in* The Horn Book Magazine, *Vol. XLIX, No. 1, February, 1973, pp. 24-30*

GENERAL COMMENTARY

Ruth Hill Viguers

In a realistic story *The Majesty of Grace* Jane Langton demonstrated quick wit, understanding of children, and ability to create memorable personalities. In *The Diamond in the Window* and *The Swing in the Summerhouse* she ventured into time without barriers and introduced some endearing, often funny, characters into stories that have romance, excitement, symbolism, and comedy. Both books are laid in a uniquely American town, Concord, Massachusetts, a perfect setting for imaginative tales in which past and present mingle. (p. 479)

> *Ruth Hill Viguers, "Worlds without Boundaries," in* A Critical History of Children's Literature *by Cornelia Meigs and others, edited by Cornelia Meigs, revised edition, Macmillan Publishing Company, 1969, pp. 467-82.*

Marcus Crouch

Jane Langton hides her essential seriousness behind a featherweight gaiety. In two books—*The Diamond in the Window* and *The Swing in the Summerhouse*—she explores the personalities of her principals through the medium of funny, witty, wise and exciting adventure stories. The books invite comparison with those of the greatest writers of comic fantasy, E. Nesbit and Mary Norton, not because they are in any way derivative but because they have a comparable vitality and inventiveness.

Like E. Nesbit's, Jane Langton's stories are deeply concerned with places. The Hall family—Aunt Lily, Uncle Freddy who is 'not altogether sound in his mind', Eleanor and Edward P. Hall, alias Trebor Nosnibor (he habitually talks backwards), the future President of the United States—live in Concord, Massachusetts, a town haunted by Thoreau, Emerson and the Alcotts. Among all those neat white board houses theirs—'a little like the Taj Mahal'—looks 'like an exotic tropical plant in a field of New England daisies'. It is a house made to breed wonders, and marvellous and very dangerous adventures come

in the course of the children's quest for treasure, which turns out to be a search for self-knowledge and wisdom.

The Diamond in the Window is a singularly perfect book, with an entirely satisfying conclusion. It took great courage to embark on a sequel, yet *The Swing in the Summerhouse* is as good as the original book. Again, this is a moral tale embodying precepts which would have been acceptable in a Victorian children's book but the interpretation is individual and there is a fine balance between humour and high seriousness. Above all, both books are about people, brilliantly sketched caricatures like Mr Preek and his secretary Miss Prawn, proud citizens of Concord—the glorious heritage of the Prawns is the memory that her 'own dear grandfather put Henry Thoreau in jail'; jolly surface portraits like the impossible Oliver Winslow who has caused trouble 'ever since he had discovered as a baby that everything he touched came apart in his hands', and loving portraits in depth. These include not only the Halls but Georgie, the little girl from next door who will be five 'pretty soon' and whose tragedy is that she cannot read yet or tell what's two and two. Georgie wants to know 'everything there is in the whole world', and Uncle Freddy helps her towards her heart's desire by unveiling the mystery of two and two and teaching the dictionary from either end, one word each night beginning with *abacus* and *zygolic*. (pp. 122-23)

> *Marcus Crouch, "Magic Casements," in his* The Nesbit Tradition: The Children's Novel in England 1945-1970, *Ernest Benn Limited, 1972, pp. 112-41.*

Diana Waggoner

[In *The Diamond in the Window*] Eleanor and Eddy follow their long-lost aunt and uncle, Nora and Ned, through a magic treasure hunt which was invented by Prince Krishna, their Aunt Lily's fiancé, who disappeared at the same time as Ned and Nora. Not only do they find all three, breaking the evil power of the Prince's wicked uncle, but they restore their philosopher-uncle Freddy to sanity and prevent the stuffy bank president from foreclosing the mortgage on their house. The fantasy is an extremely vivid and surprisingly believable blending of Indian magic and Transcendentalist philosophy, set in Concord, Massachusetts, and has a strong moral bent, although it is not didactically moralistic. Followed by [*The Swing in the Summerhouse* and *The Astonishing Stereoscope*].

Two more sets of adventures for Eleanor and Eddy, closely resembling those in *The Diamond in the Window*, in which Prince Krishna arranges for them to experience magic adventures with a moral purpose. Swinging on the summerhouse swing carries them into one set; looking through the old stereoscope enables them to enter the others. Characters, plot, and invention are as good as in the first book, but the moralistic tone is much more pronounced, which detracts from the fantasy.

> *Diana Waggoner, "A Bibliographic Guide to Fantasy: Jane Langton 1922-," in her* The Hills of Faraway: A Guide to Fantasy, *Atheneum, 1978, p. 215.*

Marshall B. Tymn, Kenneth J. Zahorski, and Robert H. Boyer

In *The Diamond in the Window,* Jane Langton shows that one can write a successful work of high fantasy using a specifically American heritage as basis. Her setting, which plays an important part in the book, is Concord, Massachusetts, some time in the first half of the twentieth century. Two children, Edward and Eleanor Hall, live with their Aunt Lily and her slightly crazed brother Fred in an old and rambling Victorian house on Walden Street. One day they discover an attic room, furnished for two children about their own age, with a large, stained-glass, keyhole-shaped window with an enormous diamond set in the middle. Their aunt, who had hoped they would never find this room, tells them that their other aunt and uncle, Ned and Nell, after whom they are named, had lived in the attic room until they suddenly disappeared some years before. Prince Krishna, who was visiting from India to study transcendentalism with Uncle Fred before he became crazed by Ned and Nell's disappearance, also vanished. Edward and Eleanor discover a series of riddles in a poem scratched into one of the facets of the keyhole-shaped window. The poem includes clues to nine treasures. The children move into the attic room, which, when light comes through the key-window at the proper angle, acts as a portal to various secondary worlds. The children enter these worlds as though in dreams, but they aren't dreams because one can get trapped in them, especially if one cannot solve the riddles; for each dream presents the children with one of the nine riddles from the poem. Here is where Langton is at her best. With unusual ingenuity and imagination, she employs quotations and events from the two great Concord transcendentalists, Emerson and Thoreau, and from another Concord writer, Louisa May Alcott, in several of the clues and treasures hinted at in the riddle-game verses. The rich creativity and fine style which Langton employs in these scenes make it difficult to describe them in synopsis form. These scenes, and the book as a whole, operate on various literary, historical, and philosophical levels, and this is what makes *The Diamond in the Window* a unique and highly successful all-ages fantasy. Jane Langton has written two other books involving Edward and Eleanor and the magical games of Prince Krishna: *The Swing in the Summerhouse* and *The Astonishing Stereoscope.* Both are fine books of all-ages fantasy, but though they contain some scenes of magic as good as any in the first book, they do not sustain the high level of literary excellence and ingenuity that *The Diamond in the Window* does.

> *Marshall B. Tymn, Kenneth J. Zahorski, and Robert H. Boyer, "Core Collection," in their* Fantasy Literature: A Core collection and Reference Guide, *R. R. Bowker Company, 1979, pp. 39-198.*

David Rees

Americans sometimes say—perhaps forgetting Ursula Le Guin—that fantasy in children's books is a peculiarly British product. It is probably indisputable that the British have written more fantasy than the Americans, and more of a higher quality: the work of Philippa Pearce,

Langton (right) with the telescope on the roof of the Franklin Institute, Philadelphia, 1942.

Alan Garner, and Penelope Lively, for example, is not matched by many American authors. It may well be because the British writer so often lives surrounded by the visible signs of history, and fantasy increasingly is a way in which the British children's author brings the past alive. Penelope Lively's *The Wild Hunt of the Ghost Hounds* was inspired by her living near Exmoor with its ancient legends of the ghostly hunt; Alan Garner's *Red Shift* by the Roman and seventeenth-century relics near his home in Cheshire. Indeed, the traditional historical novel, if not dead, is decidedly out of fashion, positively discouraged by publishers. "Children don't read that sort of thing any more," is a frequent cry. It isn't that America has no history, but that in many parts of the United States the past is less obvious or sometimes too recent for people to think it worthy of resurrection in a children's story.

One American author well-known as a writer of fantasy springing from history is Jane Langton. (Well-known at least in the United States; none of her books is currently in print in England, which is a great pity—her writing has an appeal that is much more than the merely local.) She lives in Massachusetts, a state of the Union with a past longer and more evident than most; her books are nearly all set there, and in her fantasies she often explores various facets of local history. She returns in her novels again and again to Concord, famous for its associations with Louisa May Alcott and with the Transcendentalists, Thoreau and Emerson; it was also an early Puritan settlement and, in 1775, "from behind each fence and farm-yard wall," the scene of the first shots to be fired in the War of Independence. Here, obviously, is a place with a great deal of interesting, visible history, and, like many British authors in similar surroundings, she has elected to write about that past, not in the medium of the standard historical novel, but through fantasy. Her feeling for the past is well summed up in this passage from *The Astonishing Stereoscope*:

> Looking at the familiar houses Eleanor thought again, as she did so often, that they were sitting on their own past. Here in Concord, Massachusetts, it was hard to forget that *now* was not only *now* but also *then*. She was putting her feet down, *tramp, tramp,* in the footsteps of Ralph Waldo Emerson, or Henry Thoreau, or Louisa May Alcott, or some minuteman who had fired a shot at the North Bridge. And even when she breathed the air she couldn't help remembering what Uncle Freddy always said about it, that it was the air of freedom. On this October day the air of Concord was cool and brisk, smelling slightly of skunk.

Yet it is sometimes forgotten that Jane Langton is also a creator of realistic stories. Three of her seven novels for children contain no element of the fantastic, except for what goes on inside the head of the central character of *The Majesty of Grace* and *The Boyhood of Grace Jones;* but that is fantasy in a different sense of the word. These books show a marked contrast to the mass of the most recent American realistic children's fiction. They have a distinctly old-fashioned air about them, and they are none the worse for that. Jane Langton's novels have a strong sense of being the products of a New England influence; the writing, the material, the view of life, the moral values, the children at the center of the stories give the reader the feeling that the author is aware of, and in tune with, a particular and special place. This cannot be said about every writer; S. E. Hinton's books, for example, are obviously set in a city in the United States, but where? It doesn't seem to matter.

The Majesty of Grace is Jane Langton's first novel. Its main theme is original and entertaining; Grace Jones thinks she is the long-lost elder sister of the princesses Elizabeth and Margaret (the events take place in the nineteen thirties) and that one day she will be the Queen of England. Some of the best writing in the book revolves around this idea:

> Grace tried to throw herself off the bike, but it was going so fast that now she couldn't lose her balance even though she wanted to. She gave herself up for lost. But even in her last moments she found time to imagine a wistful scene. She, Grace, was lying in a velvet-lined coffin in Westminster Abbey while the whole population of the British Isles filed reverently by, gazing with sorrow at the beautiful young princess who was never to take her rightful place upon the throne.

Unfortunately, this central theme is lost in a welter of other events—the problems with the neighbors, Dad losing his job because of the Depression, and so on; the result is that the structure of the book is a bit too loose. However, these secondary ideas are always interesting and well-handled, often with an engaging sense of humor. The scene in which Sophie, Grace's younger sister, tries to talk on the telephone with her father's ex-boss, Mr. Post, is delightful comedy; a little overdone maybe, but very funny nevertheless. It doesn't advance the narrative—indeed it's

a complete episode in itself; but it's so well-done that the loss of the story line here does not seem to matter.

The ending of the book is somewhat contrived. Pop gets his job back; the family acquire a new car; all their treasured possessions are taken out of pawn; Will makes his radio set work; Grace finds the missing piece of the jigsaw puzzle: it's all too much of an unreal happily-ever-after conclusion. However, *The Majesty of Grace* is a first novel by a writer of considerable talent; its weaknesses come from a lack of experience rather than poor invention or dull characterization. Particularly memorable is Jane Langton's rendering of sounds: the telephone, "Brrinngg!"; car horns, "Ah-OOGA, Ah-OOGA!"; a record of Sir Harry Lauder singing "Roamin' in the Gloamin' " on a wind-up gramophone that hasn't been sufficiently wound up, "my-Y-y-Y-y-Y-y La-a-A-a-A-a-SSIE-ie-IE-ie-IE-ie." Few writers even attempt such onomatopoeia, let alone bring it off successfully.

In *The Boyhood of Grace Jones* the central character is now starting junior high school, but she is just as wrapped up in a fantasy world as she was in the previous book. The preoccupations of her friends, Dot and Teenie Moon, with boys, fashion, and make-up, seem quite contemptible to her; much more important are the heroes and heroines of her reading—"Tom of *The Flying Cloud,* Trueblue Tom, that swashbuckling daring young sailor," and Captain Nancy Blackett of Arthur Ransome's *Swallows and Amazons.* Grace wishes she was a boy; she dresses like one, cuts her hair short, and cares absolutely nothing about what other people think of her. "What an odd child!"—her teacher says—"why doesn't she behave like a normal girl? There must be something basically, psychologically wrong with her, deep down inside." Yet by the end of the story this archetypal tomboy has been transformed into a "real" girl, in love with her music teacher and experimenting with Dot Moon's lipsticks. The idea is not particularly original, and the resolution of the story seems to suggest unfortunately that the stereotypical norm—what girls are *supposed* to be—is more to be desired than exploring the consequences of being unconventional. *The Boyhood of Grace Jones,* I imagine, would make a militant feminist seethe with rage, and I don't myself feel comfortable with Grace's conversion to "Whispering and giggling in high spirits, and comparing the pictures of movie stars on the lids of their Dixie cups," even though it is perhaps right for the period of the book. An opposite view of this is put forward in Gene Kemp's *The Turbulent Term of Tyke Tiler:* a contemporary story in which the boyishness of the heroine is something to be rejoiced in. Gene Kemp's novel won the Carnegie Medal in 1977, which suggests that the children's book establishment is at last taking note of what feminists have long been preaching: that belief in some male and female "norm" of manners, behavior, and family role is in part responsible for the inferior position of women in society.

That said, there are many pleasures en route in *The Boyhood of Grace Jones.* Characterization is excellent—a crowd of well-observed kids, with hard-faced Teenie being particularly convincing—and there is a great deal of entertaining incident and witty dialogue. The writing constantly sparkles with good humor and original, unusual language:

> "The flutes here at the beginning are just a pretty little babbling brook," said Mr. Chester, leaning over the twin girls who were the orchestra's flute section, Dolores and Dorothy Murphy, his less-than-an-eighth-of-an-inch of fat less than eight inches away from their twin faces. "Tiddily-tiddily, tiddily-tiddily, tiddily-tiddily-tiddle. Do you see, flutes?"

> Nearly fainting with rapture, the Murphy twins lifted their flutes and blew into them. "Whiff-puffety-whiff," they huffed, their lips pursed, their eyes crossed because Mr. Chester was standing so close. "Whiff-whiffety-whiff."

Grace's enthusiastic discovery of poetry is also seen as both admirable and amusing. She washes up dishes chanting *The Ancient Mariner,* and at the end of the book when she's written some of her own, she's bold enough to cry, "Move over, Samuel Taylor Coleridge!" The ambitions and limitations of the young adolescent are, in this novel, extremely well expressed.

Paper Chains is the most recent of Jane Langton's realistic stories, and I think the most successful. It is her only book that belongs to the young adult category; it portrays the life of eighteen-year-old Evelyn Underhill in her first semester at college—a similar theme to Rodie Sudbery's *Ducks and Drakes,* a less successful novel. The plot derives from a well-worn theme of second-rate romantic fiction: the plain, ordinary heroine—she's too tall and her teeth are as big as tombstones—falls in love with her classics professor who remains quite unaware of her infatuation, but nice young George, who appears first as a pretzel seller but is in fact a fellow student, wins her heart in the end. It sounds ordinary, but the remarkable thing about *Paper Chains* is how well Jane Langton handles such conventional material. Her achievement lies in the characterization of Evelyn and her friends, the realistic details of the start of university life—room-sharing, parties, work assignments, nights out at the movies—and, above all, the sense of humor, sometimes ironic, sometimes farcical, that is present on nearly every page. Kayo, Evelyn's roommate, arty, eccentric, and ultimately a drop-out; Frankie, naïve but attractive, who can't say no to the boys; "pompous prudish putrid Prue;" Archie, the Marxist, constantly in trouble because of his dog rather than his political opinions; Red Fred, lunatic and irresponsible; Evelyn herself, always undervaluing her own worth as a person and as an academic: they make a fine gallery of rounded portraits of real people.

The zany humor of much of the book is well illustrated by the six "unsendable letters" Evelyn writes to her classics professor; they are indeed never mailed to him, but are useful as an outlet, helping her get her feelings under control:

> Maybe you are Jesus Christ come back to earth as a humble professor of classics! And nobody knows but me! Except of course for Lady Godiva, that other girl who sits in the front row, the one with the long golden hair pouring over her

shoulders, back, front, knees, feet and toes. (No, no, forget Lady Godiva. I'm sorry I brought her up.)

> I noticed in class today that you were wearing a dirty shirt. I hope this is a clue to the mysterious life you lead outside of class. I think it must mean you are a bachelor.

The only fault in this novel is the paper chains of the title—Christmas decorations—which are a symbol of the unknown years stretching ahead as well as the years of growth Evelyn has left behind. In the last chapter, attention is drawn rather clumsily to their symbolic function: it is as if the author didn't quite know how to end the book, and felt, wrongly, that the beginning of Evelyn's relationship with George was not a significant enough way to bring matters to a conclusion. The last three pages sound as if they belong to a story in another genre. However, it is a small fault. It is refreshing to read a young adult novel in which problems do not loom large on every page, in which the reader is allowed for once to take pleasure in the mental and emotional development of the central character.

The fantasies, *The Diamond in the Window, The Swing in the Summerhouse, The Astonishing Stereoscope,* and *The Fledgling* are all concerned with the adventures of the same family—Eddy and Eleanor Hall; Georgie Dorian who becomes their cousin when Uncle Fred Hall marries her mother, Alex. Rather dotty Aunt Alex and Uncle Fred try to earn a living by turning their bizarre Victorian house into a school, the Concord College of Transcendentalist Knowledge. The characterization is as sharp, the humor as amusing, as in the other novels, and although the use of ideas and language borrowed from Emerson and Thoreau is subtle, it is never at a level that stretches beyond the grasp of the child reader. Fred Hall, in fact, is a parody of Emerson and Thoreau, and, mainly through him, the author's attitudes—complex and contradictory—to the Transcendentalists are revealed. Much about them she admires: their feelings for nature; their views, influenced by Wordsworth and Rousseau, of childhood; their unquenchable optimism. But they, she implies, like Uncle Fred, were often ridiculous and impractical, and their use of language could be inept or derivative. Some of Fred's ultra-enthusiastic pronouncements are an effective parody of the language, the bounding optimism, and the failure, at times, of the Transcendentalists to make real communication with ordinary people. When Eleanor asks him, in *The Astonishing Stereoscope,* what is the Unforgivable Sin, does Hell exist, and why are there so many different religions, his answer is so far above her comprehension that her mind wanders; she examines her face in the mirror to see if her looks are improving:

> "The religious impulse," he cried, striding back and forth. "One, the basic, primitive, mystic sense of awe. Two! The worship of a martyred hero. Three! The eternal that makes for righteousness. Four! The divine in nature. Five! The divine in man. Has the primordial religious impulse awakened in you at last, my pet?"

> "Well," said Eleanor doubtfully, "I don't . . . "

But Uncle Freddy didn't stop to listen. He went right on. And on and on and on. Eleanor discovered that she could just see herself in the mirror over the mantelpiece behind the parlor table.

In *The Swing in the Summerhouse* she quite rightly gets annoyed with her uncle's lack of worldly talents. His inability to make any money she sees as leading her and Eddy not to missing the basic necessities of life but to being deprived of some of its pleasures. Jane Langton is here thinking of the impracticality of the Transcendentalist utopia, maybe in particular of the selfish philosopher, Bronson Alcott. In *The Diamond in the Window,* when Fred tries to throw the bathers out of Walden Pond and is arrested by the police—an amusing and at the same time rather sad episode—the Transcendentalists' genuine creativity is shown as coming close to becoming mere eccentricity.

The fantasy sections of the first three of these books are a weakness: Each section is a self-contained scene, not part of a chapter with a continuous narrative, and this leaves the whole story with a disjointed feeling; throughout *The Diamond in the Window* and in parts of *The Swing in the Summerhouse* these scenes don't make much comment on or have direct relevance to the realistic tale of the Hall family's everyday life that is running parallel to the fantasy. In *The Diamond in the Window,* in particular, the language is inadequate in suggesting the full experience the children undergo:

> Prince Krishna's face was flaming. He dropped his book, and they both bent to pick it up, bumping their heads together. Aunt Lily stood up, laughing. But Prince Krishna's face when he stood up had an expression so serious and loving that she stopped laughing and bent her head. He took her hand, with a beautiful gentle gesture, and spoke to her softly. Aunt Lily looked down at the snow, then gave him her other hand. Then she looked up at him and smiled, and turned quickly and hurried away. Her long skirts passed near Eleanor, and looking up at her, Eleanor could see that her face glowed with happiness. Prince Krishna just stood where he was, his face, too, radiant with love, as he watched her go.

There are too many vague adjectives; nothing is observed with precision. "Expression so serious and loving," "a beautiful gentle gesture," "glowed with happiness," "radiant with love" are the threadbare clichés of romantic magazines. Linguistically, *The Diamond in the Window* is the least satisfactory of all Jane Langton's books; the adult reader becomes bored quite early on in what is, by the usual standards of children's fiction, a rather long novel.

The Swing in the Summerhouse, though still very episodic, is an improvement. The introduction of Georgie, the girl next door, as a major character, is an excellent idea; her amusing eccentricities make a neat contrast to down-to-earth Eddy and emotional Eleanor. Some, though not all, of the fantasy scenes comment directly on the realistic action. The chapter "What Are You Worth?" provides Eleanor with some of the answers to her questions about the family's financial problems; not everything, she discovers,

can be measured in terms of money. In the fantasy sequence she unwittingly sells her baby cousin for 876,542 dollars, and can only get him back by returning all the cash to the bank till:

> The machine wanted more. Five hundred thousand dollars wasn't enough. What a nasty bargain this was turning out to be! Eleanor felt soiled and grubby. She reached a trembling hand into her skirt once more and counted out another hundred thousand dollars. "Here's some more," she said, her voice quavering. "All this is for you." Then she transferred her skirt to her wounded right hand so that she could hit the CASH button with her left. Bang! "Oh, oh!" Eleanor flapped her hand up and down to see if the drawer was opening. It wasn't.

"Soiled and grubby" and that terse "it wasn't" are a much more individual use of English than "a beautiful gentle gesture."

The action in *The Astonishing Stereoscope* hinges on one crucial scene early in the book. John Green, a pupil of Uncle Fred's, climbs on to the roof of the house to hammer in a support for a loudspeaker—it's part of a Hallowe'en trick. He falls off and is taken to the hospital, where he remains in a coma for almost the rest of the story. When he falls he is trying to help Eddy, who has disobediently joined him on the ridge of the attic gable; at the same moment, Eleanor, indoors, is pretending to be a witch and chanting, "I have put a curse on this house! I have made a pact with the Devil himself! A curse! A curse! A curse upon this house!" *Both* children, therefore, feel responsible for the accident, and, until John Green regains consciousness, they experience an appalling sense of guilt which they attempt to expiate by turning to religion, Eleanor wholeheartedly and Eddy somewhat reluctantly. Not many contemporary children's writers attempt to portray a child's religious experiences (Peter Dickinson is an interesting exception.) *The Astonishing Stereoscope* is not only unusual in doing so, but Jane Langton views even this with her customary ironic humor. Eddy and Eleanor sample the different brands on offer in Concord—the Roman

Langton at the Freedom School stay-out, Boston, 1964.

Catholic Church, the First Parish Church—and in the fantasy episodes (again, unfortunately, only some of them are properly linked to the main theme) they visit a medieval cathedral, a human sacrifice at Stonehenge, and the Puritan chapel in seventeenth-century Concord. The children don't make any choices; in fact they find something repellent about every single one of these experiences. "How can you drink blood? That's just terrible," Eleanor says to the bewildered young Catholic priest; and the Puritans' catechism class they find insufferably boring. Miss Brisket, the gushing and hopelessly inefficient Sunday School teacher at the First Parish Church, is one of the book's delights, though one can scarcely believe the author's note that "Miss Brisket is myself." It's a very accurate observation of the wrong person doing the wrong job:

> "Arthur Downs," cried the teacher, "you sit down right here next to Cecily. George Pitman, you just get right off of Jimmy and sit over here beside me. Well, what's this we have here? A new student? Why, what a nice surprise. What is your name, dear? My, isn't that a pretty name! Isn't that a pretty dress! Now, class, first we'll have the lesson, and then we'll do our project for the day." Miss Brisket rushed to the blackboard, snatched up a piece of chalk, stared horror-struck at a huge drawing of a monster eating a horse, erased it swiftly, and began writing the lesson.

None of this makes the reader uncomfortable; religion itself isn't mocked, nor is a child's interest in why there are so many versions of Christianity being laughed at. "God," Uncle Freddy tells Eleanor, "is truth and righteousness and justice and beauty and love and joy." There is nothing ironic in that statement.

The Fledgling, however, is the most satisfying of these four books, because fantasy and realism are firmly woven together, and the language has at times a poetry, austere and controlled, that is missing from the other three. It's fall; the wild geese are flying south, and an old goose lets Georgie ride on his back, then teaches her how to fly. (Penelope Farmer's first novel, *The Summer Birds,* is concerned with a similar theme, but it is not as well written as *The Fledgling.*)

> She was filled with delight. The wind blew her hair streaming away from her face, it rippled the hems of her pajamas, and it breathed cool on her bare feet as she lay like a feather between the churning wings, looking down at the houses rushing away below her.

It is as if Jane Langton's linguistic ability were transformed from the serviceable and adequate into the perfect instrument for her purposes. There is in *The Fledgling* a use of rhythm and cadence, a care over choice of words and an attention to sound as well as meaning, that is absent from the previous novels:

> And nothing woke her until morning, not even the racket in the sky just after she fell asleep, as a last tardy flock of wild geese flew over the house, cleaving the air in a battering plunge, heading for Walden Pond, eager to break the fragile ice with the fury of their clamorous de-

scent. Low over the peaked roof and domed tower of Georgie's house they were shouting at each other, *Go* DOWN! *go* DOWN! *follow* ME! *follow* WHERE? *right* THERE? *over* THERE? *no,* HERE! *come* HERE! *come* HERE! HERE! HERE! *right* HERE! *come* DOWN! *right* HERE!

Mr. Preek's metamorphosis from a bumbling nuisance into a real villain may not be psychologically convincing, but Miss Prawn's development from an irritating busybody into an almost insane old woman does seem right. Planting her front garden with plastic roses that spell out the words "Welcome to Concord" is not only excruciatingly bad taste, but the opposite of all that is finest in Thoreau and Emerson; the reader is delighted when Georgie towards the end of the book removes most of these monstrosities. Mr. Preek and Miss Prawn are an effective contrast to Georgie and the goose: evil is pitted against good, and, as in real life, it nearly prevails. The goose is shot dead. Evil, as personified in Mr. Preek, cannot take pleasure in the mysterious, the beautiful, the unquantifiable elements in the universe—here a girl flying on a goose's back—and, because he is frightened by what he cannot understand, he has to destroy it to restore sense and propriety to his own narrow selfish existence. Georgie survives to mourn, but also to rejoice, because the goose has left her a present, a ball that in the dark becomes a magical globe showing the whole world:

> The blue surface of the ball was streaked with clouds, and below the clouds Georgie could catch glimpses of great land masses, of dark continents and snow-covered ice caps and deep jungles and blue oceans and lofty mountain ranges—the Andes, the Alps, the Himalayas.

> "Oh," breathed Georgie. "It's the world. It's the whole world."

The Fledgling is an achievement of a high order. The material, realistic and fantastic, is absolutely in balance and the prose is poetic, sensitive, and original; Jane Langton has here gone well beyond the limits of local history and Transcendentalist references. It has taken her a long time to knit together satisfactorily the various elements of her fantasies. Should she write another story about the Hall family, or a fantasy of a quite different nature, one would expect a fine book: she's arrived at a creative maturity.

> *David Rees, "Real and Transcendental: Jane Langton," in his* Painted Desert, Green Shade: Essays on Contemporary Writers of Fiction for Children and Young Adults, *The Horn Book Inc., 1984, pp. 75-88.*

TITLE COMMENTARY

The Majesty of Grace   (1961; also published as *Her Majesty, Grace Jones*)

A deep understanding of the function of fantasy in a child's life is the basis for this sound story, both touching and instructive, laced through with remarkably funny dialogue. "Ordinary" Grace Jones day dreams from her resemblance to Princess Elizabeth that she is the true heir to the British throne. Living in Cleveland during the difficult Depression years, Grace, her family and friends actually spend most of their time devising ingenious ways of having fun cheaply. When a wealthy but unfriendly neighbor is arrested for embezzlement, Grace's illusions explode. Her family has *faced* the hard times. The realization that she is not ordinary at all, that her virtues make her the one and only Grace Jones, replaces her dependence on a fantasy life. There is profound truth in the lesson of this story, charmingly told, richly humorous, realistic to the core.

> *A review of "The Majesty of Grace," in* Virginia Kirkus' Service, *Vol. XXIV, No. 1, January 1, 1961, p. 10.*

"Do you have any suggestions, your Royal Highness?" Thus Grace Jones ended her letter to George VI in "Buckingham Palace, London, England, British Empire" after she had told the King how her father had lost his job in the depression and the Jones family had had to sell their good car, Petunia. Grace had written to the King because she had secretly become convinced that that she was the elder sister of Princess Elizabeth and Margaret Rose, hidden in America as foster daughter of Mr. and Mrs. Jones because there was a threat against her life. Telling the facts of the Jones troubles and asking that final question seemed to her more tactful than a direct plea for help to her "real father," the King. This appeal was Plan A, undertaken by Grace, to aid her "foster" family during the hard times, and the "future Queen of England" could hardly bear it when she received no immediate answer. Plan B had then to be put into operation, one which will seem to readers as impractical as Plan A, but which had surprisingly successful results.

Grace is a girl to delight ten- and eleven-year-olds. They will laugh at her romantic notions and at the funny situations she manages to get into. Moreover the author can sketch her as well as describe her in words so that we come to know her intense and endearing character. A few incidents drag a little, and the members of the neighbor's family, who act as foils to the affectionate warm-hearted Joneses, are sterotyped, unnatural and overdrawn, but there is much fun, and Grace, her inventive brother Will and persistent and maddening small sister Sophie are characters to enjoy.

> *Margaret Sherwood Libby, in a review of "The Majesty of Grace," in* Books, New York, *March 12, 1961, p. 35.*

When Grace Jones, ordered to go back and wash her hands more effectively, stalks out saying, "I'll have you know you're talking to the future Queen of England," the presence of one of the most delightful characters in juvenile literature is established. Warmth and real laugh-aloud humor are present in equal and generous parts in this book, which should win the hearts of most girls and any boys sensible enough to look past the title page to find brother Will and look with him, astonished, at Grace's antics.

> *A review of "The Majesty of Grace," in* The Saturday Review, New York, *Vol. XLIV, No. 12, March 25, 1961, p. 29.*

The story moves briskly and is written with a great deal of humor, but there is unusual understanding of childhood also. Grace's parents, brother Will, and little sister Sophie are convincing; but effervescent, imaginative Grace emerges as a very special personality.

> *Ruth Hill Viguers, in a review of "The Majesty of Grace," in* The Horn Book Magazine, *Vol. XXXVII, No. 2, April, 1961, p. 160.*

Set in the Depression years, Jane Langton's story of childhood dreams of glory stars a little girl who cherishes the illusion that she is really the eldest of King George VI's *three* daughters (and therefore the future Queen of England) and not just plain, grouchy, clumsy Grace Jones with "six whole faults," whose father is out of work.

Although the story introduces words and phenomena archaic to today's children, establishes Cleveland, Ohio, as a swampy stop on the B & O, and rather too neatly tidies up all endings, the Virtue List, as with Grace, much outweighs those faults. The Jones' family life is realistically hilarious. Grace's grandiose disclaimer of her "ordinary" parentage is an almost universal escape for children when their self-depreciation hits the depths and many a girl will feel a kinship with her. Grace finds her way onto solid ground—the valuable and not-so-ordinary virtues of the Joneses, especially of Grace J. And for a bonus, a high measure of good fun.

> *Miriam James, "One of the Joneses," in* The New York Times Book Review, *April 9, 1961, p. 34.*

She liked to think she was no longer plain old Grace Jones, who was messy and clumsy, couldn't spell, bit her fingernails, was mean to her little sister, and cried. For now she had reason to believe she really was a royal princess and the future queen of England. Obviously, Grace was quite a girl, and to her gift of imagination she could add other virtues, which more than offset her "six faults." She and her family, hard hit by the depression of the '30s when Pop lost his job, are wonderfully real and lovable. Their story, a succession of hilarious incidents, should delight both children and their elders, who remember the model A Ford, Harry Lauder and the wind-up Victrola, noisy Fourths of July, and hungry tramps who came to the back door for handouts.

When, at story's end, Grace's dreams of glory are shattered forever, they are replaced by a reality so joyous its warm glow extends far beyond the printed page.

> *Polly Goodwin, in a review of "The Majesty of Grace," in* Chicago Sunday Tribune, *April 23, 1961, p. 10.*

The Diamond in the Window   (1962)

In her first book, **The Majesty of Grace,** Jane Langton revealed remarkable insight into the inner life of a very normal, very charming little girl—a child the reader could identify with. Grace's struggle to achieve a compromise between fantasy and reality held an important lesson as well as a profound truth for her young audience. This second book reflects a vast departure in theme and style. Reminiscent in structure of *Alice In Wonderland,* it gives full vent to fantasy in following the escapades of Eddy and Eleanor in a world of dreams and nightmares. An old New England house about to be usurped by creditors, is the setting. Tracing valuable treasure to save it,—the problem. The solid citizens of Concord have threatened Aunt Lily with eviction unless she can scrape up the back taxes on her house. Determined to help, Eddy and Eleanor begin rummaging through the attic and discover a hidden room where two children lived years ago. According to Aunt Lily, Ned and Nora disappeared from their beds along with her fiance, Prince Krishna. As Eddy and Eleanor settle down in the mysterious beds, they are thrown headlong into a series of dual dreams—exciting and colorful—each inspired by Uncle Freddy's quotations from Thoreau and Emerson or by a possible clue to the hidden treasure. The bubble dream climaxes a long odyssey. Eddy vanquishes the villain imprisoning the missing trio and Prince Krishna presents Aunt Lily with the Star of India, a precious jewel heretofore considered worthless. The fantasy, however rich in detail, is unaccented and too cumbersome to sustain attention, though there is much to be said in praise of Miss Langton's imagery. The attempt to weave New England history into the main fabric—to incorporate Thoreau's and Emerson's ideas, is fascinating but may be ineffectual for this age group. (pp. 522-23)

> *A review of "The Diamond in the Window," in* Virginia Kirkus' Service, *Vol. XXX, No. 12, June 15, 1962, pp. 522-23.*

The story has romance (a handsome prince from India), excitement (the dream adventures inevitably leave scars or treasure behind), and symbolism. It also has touches of slapstick humor, but children ready for the imaginative demands made by such a book as this bring a ready sense of humor and fun to their reading as well as lively imagination. Good writing, a lightness of touch, and understanding of the child's world characterize this fantasy as they did this author's more realistic story, ***The Majesty of Grace.***

> *Ruth Hill Viguers, in a review of "The Diamond in the Window," in* The Horn Book Magazine, *Vol. XXXVIII, No. 5, October, 1962, p. 481.*

To the bank representatives, the turreted, gabled and tax-ridden old Concord house seems a monstrosity that ought to be burned down. But to the two children, Eleanor and Eddy Hall, who live there with their spinster Aunt Lily and Uncle Freddy, the place "looked a little like the Taj Mahal." The bank people also view Uncle Freddy as touched in the head; but his niece and nephew recognize (as will any young reader) that things like his friendliness with the plaster busts of Emerson and Thoreau make as much sense as their own games.

Exploring, Eleanor and Eddy discover the secret attic playroom from which two earlier Halls, Nora and Ned, vanished one night. Guided by clues which a certain Prince Krishna has left behind, they seek the lost children and eventually set everything right.

The author's skill at creating character, atmosphere (New England style), and suspense, at balancing terror with humor, completely wins the reader. Where an older observer is aware of inconsistencies and unanswered questions, the untroubled child reader races along in shivery delight, oblivious to satire or symbolism. Nothing more serious than illustrator Erik Blegvad's vagaries bothers him—the black kitten who appears in the illustrations but never in the text and the "woman in a white dress," who is shown as a woman in a fur-trimmed dark suit. Mrs. Langton's ***Diamond in the Window*** is a real gem.

> *Sarah Chokla Gross, in a review of "The Diamond in the Window," in* The New York Times Book Review, *November 11, 1962, p. 48.*

"Nacirema Saznagavartxe", as Edward Hall, future President of the United States, would say. One of Eddy's many talents is fluency in Backwards English. "Sumatopoppih" he calls the awful and overweight Mr. Preek, and "Kcitsmoorb" is the only possible name for that repulsive banker's secretary Miss Prawn.

The Diamond in the Window is that rarest and most precious of books, a comic fantasy which, while wholly American, speaks an international language. The scene is Concord, Mass., home of Thoreau, Emerson and Louisa May Alcott. These great ones, being long dead, yet live in the hearts of those who live in the house on Walden Street,

Langton's home on Concord Road (now Baker Farm Road), Lincoln, Massachusetts, 1972; several of her works were written here.

so much that Eleanor arranges a wedding between Louisa and Henry Thoreau—or at least their busts. "Eleanor decided that they had been deeply in love for the best part of a century and ought to be married without further delay." Alas, just as Emerson is about to join the happy pair Uncle Freddy arrives and forbids the union.

The household, it would appear, is a little crazy. The fourth in the improbable quartet is Aunt Lily who struggles to keep the ramshackle home together by teaching unwilling children the piano. She is fairly sane despite a tragic love-affair long ago. The house, too, is appropriately strange, "like an exotic tropical plant in a field of New England daisies", with towers and domes and, high among the eaves, a little tower with a window like a keyhole. This was the room of Ned and Nora, who disappeared long ago at the same time as the beautiful and enigmatic Prince Krishna, a room full of wonders and with one horror.

In their exploration of these wonders and their search for the missing children, Eddy and Eleanor have marvellous and terrible dream-adventures by night and hilarious daytime escapades. Some of the episodes have a Nesbit-like intensity of imagination, but, despite the excellence of the invention, this is not a situation-comedy but a romantic comedy based on character. There are admirable thumbnail sketches, like Benjamin Parks whom Eleanor worships from afar, but it is in characterization in depth that Jane Langton excels. She lovingly adds layer after layer to the portraits of her principals until they acquire a three-dimensional quality. The story is tied up satisfactorily in a happy ending; but Eleanor and Eddy go on living and having adventures, for they have developed a life independent of the book. Inevitably there will be a sequel.

Oh, by the way, Louisa May married her Henry at the end, Waldo officiating, and Uncle Fred gave the bride away. A most satisfactory conclusion to what Eleanor called her "monumental romance."

The Diamond in the Window, illustrated definitively by Erik Blegvad, marks the English debut of a writer of outstanding quality.

"American Extravaganzas," in The Times Literary Supplement, *No. 3536, December 4, 1969, p. 1388.*

An original fantasy . . . set in the town of Concord with its literary associations with Emerson, Thoreau and the Alcott family. Eleanor and Edward live in the old house from which two other children and Prince Krishna disappeared mysteriously years ago. Not only Aunt Lucy lives there with crazy Uncle Freddy who lost his reason when the children disappeared. Eleanor and Eddy follow the same clues as did the lost children, sharing the same dreams. It is in these strange dreams—beautiful, exciting, funny and dangerous—that they draw nearer and nearer to the lost children until they are able to release them from their evil enemy. At the same moment Prince Krishna and the lost children, now grown up, come home again.

It is all very puzzling and leaves many questions unanswered but the story holds the reader's interest. Eleanor and Eddy are delightful creations and they are involved in some very funny incidents indeed. This is perhaps a book much of which children will skip judiciously but which they will want to finish for the interest and suspense of the story. The adult will be sceptical but the child will accept the improbabilities and the confused mixture of fantasy and reality.

A review of "The Diamond in the Window," in The Junior Bookshelf, *Vol. 34, No. 1, February, 1970, p. 39.*

The Diamond in the Window is fantasy-adventure, with a story of Arabian Nights diemension and a background in Concord, Mass., where the spirit of Thoreau, Emerson and Louisa Alcott seem to brood over the present day—especially over the Gothico-Byzantine house where Aunt Lily lives, lonely after the disappearance of her lover. . . . The awkwardness of a physical disappearance with a supernatural cause is not entirely avoided but most of the time the author disarms inconvenient reason by the ingenuity of her narrative, as the young namesakes follow clues which prove to be solvable in two worlds at once. This is a very picturesque tale, full of literary allusion, sharp descriptive points and analogies with toys, fairies, magicians. Erik Blegvad's oddball drawings, full of humour and the enjoyment of absurdity, help us to believe in the blurring of frontiers in their own way.

Margery Fisher, in a review of "The Diamond in the Window," in Growing Point, *Vol. 8, No. 8, March, 1970, p. 1484.*

Here is one of the most delightful fantasies of recent times. Set in Concord, home of Emerson, Thoreau and Louisa M. Alcott, this clever piece of writing should make a special appeal to girls, particularly in its visit to the Alcott home. The fantasy concerns Edward and Eleanor, who live in a strange house, with a hidden room in the attic. From here, once, two other children, Ned and Nora, had vanished mysteriously after searching for jewels, gifts from an Indian, Prince Krishna. Edward and Eleanor search for them and follow clues in a strange treasure hunt, which takes place partly in dreams, partly in reality, and is full of adventure.

The characters are very real, particularly Edward, whose great love is to talk backwards, and his practical sister. Amusing, sad, exciting, tranquil, this book can be read by children and enjoyed by their elders. I found the illustrations fitted the text admirably. (pp. 81-2)

R. Bradbury, in a review of "The Diamond in the Window," in The School Librarian, *Vol. 18, No. 1, March, 1970, pp. 81-2.*

The Swing in the Summerhouse (1967)

Three characters in search of themselves, with a swing to transport them and Mrs. Truth to light the last stretch: an allegorical fantasy in shifting dimensions. Eleanor and Eddy discover that by swinging through each of the archways of the summerhouse they will reach a different destination: first Eddy finds himself in THE MAN-CASTLE evoked by Uncle Freddy ("Your body is your castle, isn't it?") as the metaphor for human potential; then Eleanor investigates WHAT ARE YOU WORTH?, discovers the value of each person to be "beyond price"; MAKE NEW WORLDS takes her to the world that she has made with paper dolls and tinsel dreams, and she finds it tiresome; and so on to the forbidden portal, GROW UP NOW. There the children turn to marble and Mrs. Truth explains to Uncle Freddy who has never grown up: "one way to grow up is to stiffen and harden into one kind of person who is just the same forever." "But how can they help it? That's what growing up means." By keeping "the freshness and wonder of childhood all your life, even though you grow up in other ways." Because he has, he can release them; its time run out, the summerhouse, scene of their separate longings, explodes, but the rainbow—"a sign of the miracles that surround us every day"—remains. This is an independent sequel to *The Diamond in the Window,* and it is both less diffuse and more diverse; less diffuse because the pattern is obvious, more diverse because each episode reveals a different aspect of self-discovery and each transforms reality appropriately, immediately and inventively. Children will remember the giant cash register (WHAT ARE YOU WORTH) and the paper doll party (MAKE NEW WORLDS) and grave little Georgie, the aspiring reader (*and* the tingling illustrations [by Erik Blegvad]) much longer than the all-too-obtrusive MESSAGE. (pp. 561-62)

> *A review of "The Swing in the Summerhouse,"* in Kirkus Service, *Vol. XXXV, No. 9, May 1, 1967, pp. 561-62.*

If there is any fault in this book, it is that its virtues are excessive. Philosophy, fantasy and realism grow here as in a tangled garden. One longs to do some weeding of the too numerous themes: a magic summerhouse built by an Indian prince in Concord, Mass.; a swing inside the summerhouse which transports the rider to fantasy worlds; two children in the painful process of growing up; and their Uncle Freddy, a Transcendentalist scholar.

True, the children's swing journeys are exciting and their adventures revelatory. Each journey provides them with self-knowledge, and if this knowledge echoes Emerson and Thoreau, one must remember that the youngsters are the wards of Uncle Freddy. All of the book's characters are delightful, and none more so than Georgie Dorian: a 4-year-old next-door neighbor whose besetting sorrow is her inability to read. Georgie is haunted by indecipherable messages—in stores, on buildings, on the backs of forks—and the reader is terribly relieved when she wins a spelling-bee during one of the swing journeys. Which brings us full circle, for here is a truly sensitive book, marred only by the profusion of riches.

> *Barbara Wersba, in a review of "The Swing in the Summerhouse,"* in The New York Times Book Review, *August 20, 1967, p. 24.*

Charming illustrations [by Erik Blegvad] echo the graceful fantasy of the writing in a sequel to *The Diamond in the Window.* Here too there is a successful blending of the real and the fanciful, natural dialogue that is often humorous, and a spectrum of pleasant family relationships. The summerhouse has six sides, and swinging out through each one the children are transported to magical adventures, each of which has some relevance to the children's real life. Written with a light, sure touch.

> *Zena Sutherland, in a review of "The Swing in the Summerhouse,"* in Bulletin of the Center for Children's Books, *Vol. 21, No. 1, September, 1967, p. 12.*

A swing in a six-sided summer house transports Edward and Eleanor, first encountered in *A Diamond in the Window,* into a series of fantastic worlds. . . . The imagery employed by the author is vivid and the tone of the story provocative. Six swing rides may seem more than necessary and fantasy obviously used to illustrate a moral might have been a dismally patronizing device, but this is quite effective, a finished and original story to satisfy your above-average readership.

> *Elinor Cullen, in a review of "The Swing in the Summer House,"* in School Library Journal, *Vol. 14, No. 3, November, 1967, p. 68.*

How often a book of the highest merit and originality evokes comparison with E. Nesbit. She is the yardstick which no changes of fashion, none of the corrosions of time, can shrink or warp.

Last year a jewel of a book came out of America, shining out from among its contemporaries as splendidly as the Halls' house—which looked rather like the Taj Mahal—shone among the demure clapboards of Concord, Mass. *The Diamond in the Window* was a comic fantasy with philosophical undertones. *The Swing in the Summerhouse* is of the same kind, a little less funny, not quite so terrifying, at least as wise and humane. Jane Langton's second story of the Halls, which is also a further account of her love affair with the town of Concord, home of Emerson and Thoreau and birthplace of Transcendentalism, is a book in a thousand, a book which demands of the reader total surrender.

Time has passed since the idyllic conclusion of *The Diamond in the Window.* Eleanor has grown, alarmingly; even taller than her beau Benjamin Parks. For all her glasses and the braces on her teeth she aspires to elegant living. Edward has abandoned his earlier ambition to be President of the United States and has now dedicated his life to Junk. "He dreamed of discovering someday one perfect piece of junk, some marvellous object that would transform his life and make it a thing of poetry and joy." With Prince Krishna and Aunt Lily away—there is political trouble back in India—only Uncle Freddy is left to be the stabilizer, the apostle of transcendentalism and eternal youth.

Krishna has left the children a new plaything, a summerhouse. It is appropriately in the oriental manner, with a dome in whose apex a clock ticks unseen, and with six openings, each with a golden message above the arch. Edward discovers the screw eye in the roof and hangs from it a swing; from its seat the children, and not the children alone, hurtle into adventure.

The pattern of the book resembles that of its predecessor. The texture is enriched by some new characters, notably Mrs. Dorian, a witch who comes to live next door, and her daughter Georgie. Georgie, who will be five "pretty soon", is a most enchanting creation, a little girl oppressed almost beyond bearing by the magnitude of her own ignorance. She wants "to know *everything* there is in the whole world". In the kitchen Georgie looks at the cookery books.

> There was flour on one of the books and some sticky crumbs on another. Georgie sniffed the flour and then she stuck out her tongue and licked the crumbs. She could smell books with her nose and taste them with her mouth and feel them with her fingers, but what good was that if she couldn't read them with her eyes?

Uncle Freddy undertakes her education, with the aid of Webster's Unabridged Dictionary, and she has soon mastered *aardvark* and *zyzzogeton* and is all set to "squeeze this old dictionary from both ends like an accordion".

It is Georgie's passion for learning which precipitates the final crisis. On the first day of term, when Eleanor and Edward go back to school, she follows, imaginary lunchbox in hand, invisible notebook pressed against her chest until she can fill it with words and numbers. The humiliation that follows drives her to tears, to exhausted sleep, and finally, on the swing in the summerhouse, through the forbidden archway which says GROW UP NOW. One by one the others follow, to discover what it is like to be sensible, purposeful and dull and eventually to turn to stone. All, that is, but Uncle Freddy who, like Emerson and Thoreau, has kept intact the wonder and the joy of childhood. Uncle Freddy hauls them back from their frozen whiteness into the Concord of real children and adults, just as Prince Krishna's fabulous clock runs down and the summerhouse disappears into dust. An appropriately apocalyptic resolution of a story in which fun, drama and terror have been measured out into the most potent mixture by a master chemist.

It is as much as anything this mixture of realism and fantasy, this calculated use of incongruity to produce not only a laugh but also an increase in tension, which points the comparison with E. Nesbit. Not that Jane Langton is derivative. She and E. Nesbit draw on a common pool of experience and achieve comparable results because they are of the same kind and that the rarest. Both are Makers, and both perform the miracle of creation with disparate elements like bath-tubs and rainbows, and with cash-registers, rulers and compasses draw fundamental lessons of life.

When the summerhouse explodes there is still one arch through which the children have not swung. Over it is the legend YOUR HEART'S DESIRE. Your heart's desire always comes last, "like no dessert until you've eaten your spinach", as Georgie says. But each actor in this memorable drama achieves his desire in a most satisfying conclusion. Georgie adds two and two, Georgie's mother and Uncle Freddy find transcendental happiness together, Edward learns to reconcile ambition and enjoyment, and Eleanor has a party of Concord's Best People, "those celebrated Halls, those distinguished Dorians". A joyous, deeply satisfying book.

"To Heaven in a Swing," in The Times Literary Supplement, *No. 3555, April 16, 1970, p. 421.*

The Swing in the Summerhouse entertains a very practical magic; one might call it educational magic, and not only because Uncle Freddy and his Transcendental philosophy are once more in the forefront. Here are Edward and Eleanor again, left in their uncle's charge while their guardian aunt and her princely husband have flown to settle troubles in his eastern kingdom. As in **The Diamond in the Window,** the fantasy lies in very rapid transitions from the Boston they know to an adumbration of it. The transition is by means of a swing prepared for them by the Prince but with its fail-safe apparatus not quite ready for use. Each of the involuntary disappearances of the children teaches them something. Eleanor learns that love is worth more than money after a terrifying sojourn in a gigantic bank where the baby she is minding is trapped in an adding machine, and Edward's explorations of a huge head teaches him the value of the senses. Every one of the strange journeys starts through association with something said or done, yet these are not dreams so much as directed explorations, from which the boy and girl emerge a little more aware of the world around and inside them. In a sense this book does not belong with the bulk of 1960 fantasy but more with the Victorian Eyes-and-no-eyes type of didactic fact-fiction, and it has the same serene and kindly air of confidence. (pp. 1572-73)

> *Margery Fisher, in a review of "The Swing in the Summerhouse," in* Growing Point, *Vol. 9, No. 3, September, 1970, pp. 1572-73.*

The Astonishing Stereoscope (1971)

There is light, fast-paced fantasy in **The Astonishing Stereoscope.** This is Jane Langton's fourth contemporary story set in Concord, Mass., and it is again rich in entertaining elements and easily integrated allusions to the colonial, transcendental, and literary past. Giddy transport into the long ago is accomplished by magical new cards for Eddy's stereoscope which brings primitive Stonehenge, a medieval cathedral, and colonial Concord into a more than merely visual three dimensions. Mrs. Langton's powers of invention are equal to the task and her children are likably real.

> *Virginia Haviland, "A Magical Tour," in* Book World—The Washington Post, *November 7, 1971, p. 4.*

Reared in the intellectual atmosphere of Concord, Massachusetts by two parents seeped in the abstractions of transcendentalism, it's no wonder that Eleanor turns to the sepia-tinted fantasy world of the stereoscope (a present from her Hindu uncle Prince Krishna) for answers to her questions about guilt, redemption and the nature of the hereafter. Her stereoscopic journeys are historically eclectic, taking her to a primitive human sacrifice (unconsummated), a Gothic cathedral and a visit with a puritan ancestor, but the message is theologically specific with the trail of religious evolution leading right back home to Uncle Freddy's Yankee morality. Though skeptics will remain unconvinced by the final bit of family faith healing which absolves Eleanor's guilt over having caused injury to a friend, it's a mind-bending experience to follow her through the fast-paced revelations of her magic lantern catechism. (pp. 1212-13)

> *A review of "The Astonishing Stereoscope," in* Kirkus Reviews, *Vol. XXXIX, No. 22, November 15, 1971, pp. 1212-13.*

The Astonishing Stereoscope . . . tells of a brother and sister who enter the three-dimensional world of a magical stereoscope and gain new insight into the life around them in Concord, Massachusetts, home of the transcendentalists, and an understanding, too, of truth and guilt, and the oneness of all religions. Atmosphere, adventure and wit distinguish this literate story.

> *Elizabeth Minot Graves, in a review of "The Astonishing Stereoscope," in* Commonweal, *Vol. XCV, No. 8, November 19, 1971, p. 181.*

Following **The Diamond in the Window** and **The Swing in the Summerhouse,** a third story, set in Concord, in the big gabled, turreted house that was considered a blot on the landscape of the tidy, white-clapboard town. Busts of Thoreau, Emerson, and Louisa May Alcott still dominate the front hall; the life-sized bronze figure of a woman still stands like the Statue of Liberty on the newel-post with "Truth" emblazoned across her bosom; and Uncle Freddy

Langton at her typewriter, 1983.

and Aunt Alex still run their impoverished Concord College of Transcendental Knowledge. Eleanor, a little older, has been wrestling with grandiose philosophical questions of her own, worrying about newly-discovered problems of evil, pain, religion, and sin. Edward still plans to be President of the United States one day; and their little cousin Georgie is now an enthusiastic first-grader. Their remarkable uncle-by-marriage, Prince Krishna, sends Edward a set of cards for his antique stereoscope—five old, faded photographs which lead Edward and Eleanor into fantastic adventures involving primitive human sacrifice; a talking gargoyle on a medieval cathedral; a Sunday visit with their Puritan ancestors; a dizzying balloon journey into the infinite reaches of inner and outer space; and finally an intense "super-three-dimensional" experience in their own house. As in the previous books—great favorites of children—the writing is laced with overtones of idealistic wisdom. In all three stories, the fantastic sequences are Surrealistic extensions of the everyday happenings; all three are unified, successful, literate books.

> *Ethel L. Heins, in a review of "The Astonishing Stereoscope," in* The Horn Book Magazine, *Vol. XLVII, No. 6, December, 1971, p. 613.*

An amazing stereoscope from their Uncle Krishna, the Indian Prince who was also responsible for the time trips in **The Diamond in the Window** and **The Swing in the Summer House,** takes Eleanor and Eddy Hall on a religious investigation to determine whether or not there is a Hell. When they pull the tasseled rope hanging down in the middle of the view inside the stereoscope, the youngsters enter the worlds of the brown-tone viewcards, where they experience pagan rites, the Last Supper, Puritan services and meet their great-great-great-etc. ancestors. Ultimately, their Uncle Freddy, the founder of and lone professor at the Concord College of Transcendentalist Knowledge, joins them on a guided tour of infinity in a balloon. Upon returning home, he convinces them to put the stereoscope away, since " 'The world is magic already.' " Good plot development and believable characterizations sustain interest in this thought-provoking fantasy/adventure.

> *Anne Canarie, in a review of "The Astonishing Stereoscope," in* School Library Journal, *Vol. 18, No. 4, December, 1971, p. 59.*

Only a handful of writers produce stories of supernatural events, spiced with humor and experienced by believable, appealing persons. Langton is in that honored company, and this gripping novel is a prime example of why her books never lose their flavor. Young Eleanor, enamored of her Uncle Freddy's favorite student, John Green, pretends to curse the family's Concord home, adding a fillip to Halloween, and feels she has caused John's serious accident. Eleanor's brother Eddy also thinks he's guilty, since John has hurt himself trying to protect Eddy. The brother and sister seek for distractions in the new set of stereoscope cards sent by another uncle, an East Indian prince, and are transported inside the scenes where dicey adventures await, to teach the explorers vital truths. [Erik] Blegvad's drawings are ideal illustrations.

> *A review of "The Astonishing Stereoscope," in*

Publishers Weekly, *Vol. 223, No. 16, April 22, 1983, p. 104.*

The Boyhood of Grace Jones   (1972)

Her Majesty, Grace Jones has grown up a bit and transferred to the Winslow S. DeForest Junior High School, but she's still her old exuberant self—outwardly a tomboy in her father's old blue serge middy, inwardly Trueblue Tom straight out of her beloved *Swallows and Amazons.* Grace's hero worship of Chatty Peak, president of the Girls' Leader Corps and Captain Nancy incarnate, and her pursuit of the gold ring awarded to the best all-round girl both end in disillusionment. However, she has her full share of moments of glory. Poetry strikes her like a thunderbolt and she declaims *Kubla Khan* and the *Rime of the Ancient Mariner* with infectious gusto, while arguing a gut-level defense of free will with her heredity-environment conscious English teacher Miss Humminger. Trueblue Tom suffers an ignominious demise, beginning when Grace's first bout of real sailing ends in seasickness and sealed by her burgeoning puppy love for the music teacher Mr. Chester, and in the end Grace is a wiser, if—sadly—more feminized girl. The late '30's ambience is played to the hilt, though some of the attitudes—like Mr. Chester's distinction between Grace's hoydenish "divine discontent" and Chatty's unseemly masculinity—don't seem exactly right on today. The nostalgia, however, takes second place to Grace's spirited, sometimes giddy, enthusiasm for life which is guaranteed to bowl you over.

A review of "The Boyhood of Grace Jones," in Kirkus Reviews, *Vol. XL, No. 22, November 15, 1972, p. 1306.*

The author's first book—written before her three stories about the diamond-in-the-window house in Concord—was *The Majesty of Grace,* a story of the depression years. Now, after several years in the heroine's life have elapsed, the reader finds Grace in her last year of junior high school. The period atmosphere is unmistakable: The Great Depression has petered out; World War II has been rumbling fitfully across the Atlantic, but America as yet is uninvolved. Grace, still given to rapturous enthusiasms and a tendency to over-dramatize things, has turned into a tomboy. Her current love is the sea and sailing; and with her hair worn short and straight, she swaggers about wearing her father's old blueserge Navy middy over her school dresses. Often Grace is horrified by her closest friend, the girl next door, whose ruffled, flouncy bedroom is filled with perfume bottles, eyelash curlers, and photographs of movie stars. But when an English assignment introduces her to *Kubla Khan* and *The Rime of the Ancient Mariner,* she becomes "[d]izzy with incantation, intoxicated with rhythm." Full of contradictions, Grace still plays with families of paper dolls; desperately tries to qualify for the super-athletic Girls Leader Corps; hurtles around town on her brother's bike, shouting Coleridge at the top of her lungs; and, before the end of the year, succumbs (like all the other girls) to a full-blown crush on the debonair man who teaches music. The author has done more than skim the surface of early adolescence; she has plumbed the wellsprings of memory, has created individual, three-dimensional human beings, and written a wise and wonderfully entertaining book.

Ethel L. Heins, in a review of "The Boyhood of Grace Jones," in The Horn Book Magazine, *Vol. XLIX, No. 1, February, 1973, p. 49.*

A sequel to *Her Majesty, Grace Jones,* this has all the ebullience of the earlier story. Grace is now in Junior High School, yearning to be a boy so that she can have the adventurous life she doesn't expect as a girl (the time is post-Depression Era) and smitten by a forceful, athletic older girl. She achieves her goal of being chosen Best All-around Girl but becomes disenchanted with her heroine's envy and transfers her affection to the orchestra conductor (he calls her "Captain Bligh"); she becomes a poetry-lover and writer, and she does everything with zest and imagination. The characters and dialogue are sturdy, the writing style breezy, the period details colorful.

Zena Sutherland, in a review of "The Boyhood of Grace Jones," in Bulletin of the Center for Children's Books, *Vol. 27, No. 2, October, 1973, p. 30.*

The imaginative heroine asserts her real identity as Trueblue Tom, mate on the trusty ship Flying Cloud, but this most stalwart of tomboys is finally vanquished by the romance of Coleridge's "Kubla Khan." The author has a fine sense of the ridiculous, and her tale of this indomitable young girl of the '30's is marvelously told.

Jennifer Farley Smith, in a review of "The Boyhood of Grace Jones," in The Christian Science Monitor, *December, 1977, p. 812.*

[*Previous to the beginning of the following excerpt, critics Myra Pollack Sadker and David Miller Sadker addressed four books written for the middle and upper grades*—Veronica Ganz *by Marilyn Sachs,* A Girl Called Al *by Constance C. Greene,* Caddie Woodlawn *by Carol Ryrie Brink, and* The Witch of Blackbird Pond *by Elizabeth George Speare—that include what the critics call "stereotyped behaviors and comments and character portrayals that express contempt for the experience of being a girl or woman."*]

These four books are very well written. . . . Another book, not as well written as these and far more disturbing in its character portrayal, is *The Boyhood of Grace Jones* by Jane Langton. This story takes place during the late 1930s and chronicles Grace Jones's first year at Winslow S. DeForest Junior High School. Grace has a unique style of her own: she has short brown hair, wears her father's blue serge navy middy, strides rather than walks, and on her first day of school manages to beat one of the strongest boys in school in a wrestling match. Grace practices push-ups in her spare time and dreams of becoming a sailor. Another aspect of Grace's unique style is her contempt for girls; she merges all girls into a detestable mass of incompetence. . . . (p. 240)

The last quarter of the book documents the transformation of Grace Jones. For her birthday Grace's father fulfills his daughter's dream by taking her sailing. Grace's stomach and the water do not agree, and she is thoroughly sick. After her sailing fiasco, Grace begins to curl her hair and to wear an angora sweater and a gold locket. As the book closes, Grace is busily at work on a movie star scrap book. Grace stereotypes males and females and feels contempt for girls. Gradually she sheds her "tomboyish" behavior and, retaining nothing of her former spunk, conforms totally to the image she has previously despised.

This brief story is a devastating comment on sex roles. It is obviously an expression of male contempt for girls' doll play. It also illustrates a code of behavior that denies boys a full range of activities and emotions. (pp. 240-41)

> *Myra Pollack Sadker and David Miller Sadker, "Breaking out of the Pumpkin Shell: The Image of Women in Children's Literature," in their* Now Upon a Time: A Contemporary View of Children's Literature, *Harper & Row, Publishers, 1977, pp. 231-66.*

Paper Chains (1977)

Langton captures the uncertainties often experienced by young adults during their first semester at college in a lighthearted story narrated by Evelyn Jane Underhill, a six-foot-tall redhead with an exquisite sense of humor and a crush on her short, solemn philosophy professor. The tale is full of appealing individualistic characters—Evelyn's roommate Kayo, who's Jewish, a genius, and a world traveler; their next door neighbors, a blond bombshell and a "prune face"; Kayo's cousin Archie and his pet What Dog; and a mysterious stringbean of a fellow who keeps popping up in odd places. By the end Evelyn has survived the vicissitudes of the first semester, gotten over her crush, and become interested in a fellow student.

> *A review of "Paper Chains," in* Booklist, *Vol. 73, No. 14, March 15, 1977, p. 1082.*

Here, in separate short scenes and flashes, are the extracurricular highlights of Evelyn Underhill's first few months at college: the "unsendable" letters she writes to her philosophy professor; the madcap escapades (Langton wouldn't use the phrase but the spirit is the same) such as ringing the bell in the school's boarded-up tower; the conspiracy to keep a dog on campus; and the heady moments of cartwheeling with her friends across the square because the sign says "Don't walk." ("It felt marvelous to be stared at.") As for the friends, they're deftly sketched, familiar types: roommate Kayo, the universal genius who doesn't have to study or attend classes and who drops out just before finals; plumpish, tearful Frankie, another exam week dropout, who comes from a Catholic school and always seems to end up in a closet with a boy; and striving "Pruneface" Prue, whose clichéd agreement with Evelyn's groping speculation is worse than other people's arguments. Aside from an uncertain sense of era—fifties (or earlier) atmosphere, but more contemporary dorm arrangements, the main problem is that Langton's viewpoint seems limited to that of the glamor-struck participants—even Evelyn's visions of God, who keeps appearing to her as in Michelangelo's "Creation of Adam" ("though I honestly didn't believe in him at all"), are not seen as signs of any alarming emotional strain but are experienced rather as a sort of late-adolescent intellectual thrill. Yet Langton

does recapture the surface allure; and the paper-chain image—which expresses both Evelyn's predilection for school and her expectation of continuity—is felicitous.

> *A review of "Paper Chains," in* Kirkus Reviews, *Vol. XLV, No. 8, April 15, 1977, p. 436.*

Remember those college movies of the 50's with letter sweaters, frosh hops, dorm pranks, darling dialogue? **Paper Chains** is that kind of novel, and except for the fact that the dorms are now coed, nothing much seems to have changed since the Golden Age of Eisenhower.

Here is Evelyn (too tall, too big a mouth) and her Jewish roommate ("a universal genius"); here is cousin Archie and his contraband dog (called What Dog—as in "What Dog? I don't see any dog"); here is the overprotected girl from a convent school who finds Philosophy 101 and men too hot to handle (she drops out before exams to live with a male dancer); and here is "Pruneface" whose unctious, studious demeanor masks a heart as big as all outdoors.

Making his familiar cameo appearance is Professor Halverknap, to whom Evelyn writes UNSENDABLE LETTERS of passion ("Maybe you are Jesus Christ come back to earth as a humble professor of classics!"), while slightly to the left of center stage, irrepressible Red Fred conducts his merry prankster Band. Over at the Student Union, slopping spaghetti at the steam table, is working-his-way-through-college George, who looks appropriately like Honest Abe.

There's no sex to speak of, but there's plenty of off-limits mirth: ringing the bell in Founder's Tower, hiding What Dog in the dorm, stashing cheese and crackers in a pair of socks, drinking beer at a Halloween party. It's all so innocent, so bursting with pinkcheeked energy, so filled to the brim with snippets of Socrates and Michelangelo that one almost expects Connie Francis to grab up a beach blanket and belt out "Where the Boys Are" in bobby socks and halter top.

Paper Chains is meant for "ages 12 and up"—up to about 15 I'd say. The sheer enthusiasm of the author's style (lots of words capitalized, heavy on the exclamation points) develops enough good-humored momentum to carry young readers to the finish, but I'm afraid more jaded readers will cut out for a smoke.

> *Alix Nelson, "Just Like the Fifties," in* The New York Times Book Review, *May 1, 1977, p. 40.*

Evelyn Underhill, who tells her story in a cheerfully desperate fashion that is as engaging as it is credible, prattles on about a frenetic college semester. There is her roommate Kayo, who is a genius and knows it; there is cuddly little Frankie, who finds college a revelation; there is Pruneface, detested by all of them. There are males on the scene and one very large dog (illegally kept in Kayo's cousin's residence hall), but what fills Evelyn's horizon is Professor Halverknap, whom she adores from afar, to whom she writes never-to-be-mailed letters, past whose house she cycles, and who proves to be married. Evelyn recovers rapidly from this blow; she realizes that the paper chains (linked stages of her life) have not come to an end. Langton starts with verve and ends with a touching but not cloying scene in which Evelyn is teaching small children how to make paper chains. The writing has insight and humor, the mood is ebullient.

> *Zena Sutherland, in a review of "Paper Chains," in* Bulletin of the Center for Children's Books, *Vol. 31, No. 1, September, 1977, p. 19.*

The Fledgling (1980)

Little Georgie's pre-dawn flights on the back of a friendly goose (she calls him her swan prince) are not burdened by the allegorical content that characterized the mind trips of older step-cousins Eleanor and Eddy in three previous Langton novels. Rather, intense Georgie is the innocent child in love with sweet nature (but not preciously so). She longs to fly, and the goose teaches her how—at Walden Pond, no less. But insensitive adults must interfere: banker Ralph Preek buys a gun and launches a personal vendetta against the "giant duck"; and his secretary Miss Prawn, Georgie's next-door neighbor, becomes concerned that Georgie is either a saint or a changeling, and the goose, accordingly, an angel or a fairy about to steal her away. (As for Transcendental College proprietor Uncle Freddie, whose flat-footed literary welcome had earlier scared the bird away, he comes to believe that Georgie's goose is Henry Thoreau himself, reincarnated.) With Mr. Preek stalking clumsily throughout, the inevitable tragedy occurs. Georgie recovers from the goose's death, as children will, but only after she has located its parting "present": a rubber ball that becomes, in the dark, a glowing image of the planet Earth. Except for an opening false-note prematurely espousing the goose's viewpoint, Langton makes Georgie's story a successful blend of humor, charm, pathos, family feeling, and that hint of something transcendent that lights up all her fantasies.

> *A review of "The Fledgling," in* Kirkus Reviews, *Vol. XLVIII, No. 8, April 15, 1980, p. 513.*

Quiet, introspective Georgie, young cousin of Eleanor and Eddy (protagonists of the author's *Diamond in the Window* and other titles), yearns to fly. An encounter with a large, old Canadian goose, which stops at Walden Pond on its migratory journey south, brings her that chance. On moonlit nights when it taps on her bedroom window, she skims across the trees with her Goose Prince and, using his back as a springboard, swoops and glides in exhilarating circles. Then neighboring Mr. Preek, who tries to save Georgie from what he thinks is an attacking predator, and Miss Prawn, who sees the girl's feat as a saintly sign, interfere, causing Eleanor and Eddy to form the Georgie Protection Society. In the end, Mr. Preek seemingly wins as he brings the goose down with a blast from his gun, but Georgie still has the Goose Prince's present (a rubber ball that is magically transformed before her eyes into an image of the earth), his final words ("Take good care of it"), and memories to cherish forever. Langton's superbly told story reaches beyond the confines of its finely tempered plot and leaves an echo that is at once touching and

Langton calls this photo "The house on Walden Street in which five of my books take place." Alexandra Green, a young reader, was photographed in front of the house in Concord, Massachusetts, in 1984.

challenging. Fantasy and reality mesh well, the result of well-carved characters who are warm and believable. (pp. 1365-66)

> *Barbara Elleman, in a review of "The Fledgling," in* Booklist, *Vol. 76, No. 18, May 15, 1980, pp. 1365-66.*

The most amazing thing about eight-year-old Georgie Dorian is that she can "*flyyyyyyyyyyy*"—first, on the back of a goose, "her thin arms gently around his chest," and then with the goose at her side. Night after night they glide and soar in the crisp September air and land gracefully on Walden Pond in Concord, Massachusetts. The goose is the largest of his flock; Georgie is the smallest of hers. He is seasoned; she is a fledgling. He is "mighty in wingspread"; she is a "wisp of thistledown." Both are singular and majestic—spiritual descendants of Henry Thoreau; and they both stand in opposition to two synthetic and misguided citizens of the community: Madeline Prawn, who isn't sure whether Georgie is a saint or a fairy, and Ralph Alonzo Preek, who is bent on killing the goose to keep him from attacking little children. The precision with which style and meaning coalesce is as amazing as the flight itself. The writing is alternately solemn and funny, elevated and colloquial. It is mythic, almost sacred, in passages involving Georgie and the goose; it is satiric, almost irreverent, when it relates to Mr. Preek and Miss Prawn. The book is a modern legend with strong roots in transcendental New England. Its song is played by a flute made from a blade of grass, and the refrain is Henry Thoreau's: "In Wildness is the preservation of the World."

Barbara Harrison, in a review of "The Fledgling," in The Horn Book Magazine, *Vol. LVI, No. 4, August, 1980, p. 408.*

An evocative fantasy incorporating a mystical "present," an aged giant Canada goose, a young girl, her family, two villains, and Thoreau and his Walden Pond. Thistledown Georgie, eight, cannot forget the rapture of a dream of flying, and bruises and bumps attest to her desperate waking attempts to recapture the ecstasy. Her family worries about her fragility, her mental state, her intense communication with nature. Despite their unwitting interference and the motivated machinations of Mr. Preek (who *thinks* he likes children) and Mrs. Prawn (who dislikes them openly) the Canada goose and Georgie meet. In lyrical nocturnal sequences, Georgie learns to fly, to skydive from from the goose's back, twisting earthward in slow, diminishing spirals on the warm thermals over Walden Pond, caught by her "Goose Prince" before the final shock of landing. Her mother, aware of Georgie's nocturnal ventures, almost overwhelmed by anxiety, keeps silent to give Georgie her magic. Mr. Preek and Miss Prawn are also aware, with Mr. P. determined to kill the "attacker" goose, and Miss P. to profit from this "saintly" levitation. In a touching scene, the Goose Prince comes to bid farewell to a Georgie suddenly too tall for flying, bearing a parting gift. Mr. P., lying in ambush, shoots the bird. In the confusion, the gift is lost until spring, and when found, Georgie discovers her Goose Prince has given her the world. Langton has writen another carefully constructed and layered fantasy: a beautiful tale of girl and bird, giving neither more nor less than their due. While Mr. P. and Miss P. are one-dimensional, their hard edges contrast perfectly with Georgie's thistledown quality and the sleek softness of the great goose.

Patricia Manning, in a review of "The Fledgling," in School Library Journal, *Vol. 27, No. 1, September, 1980, p. 73.*

"And, after all, why should we not have been born with wings?" asks Uncle Freddy Hall, founder of The Concord College of Transcendental Knowledge (place: "the big house at No. 40 Walden Street" student body: 15). His 8-year-old niece Georgie wants to fly, "*Wanting* has turned into *believing*," says Aunt Alex. Tutored by a wild goose ("the Goose Prince"), Georgie succeeds. The descriptions of their flights, with their blend of the familiar and the fantastic are the most memorable sections of the book, "Glide, glide, float and glide, lift and soar! Oh, how far she could see! All the way to Boston! There it was . . . a cluster of dark towers against the sunrise."

But Madeline Prawn, who plants plastic flowers in her yard and does not like children ("Everybody has their own personal tastes. Some people don't like olives.") decides that Georgie is either a saint or a fairy worthy of "worship on the one hand and outrage on the other." And Ralph Preek, president of the bank, who loves children ("Well-behaved children. Polite, well-brought-up children.") goes after the Goose Prince with a gun and kills him. Unfortunately both characters are little more than symbols of the way people feel about those who march to a different drummer.

The Goose Prince leaves Georgie a rubber ball, "an image of the earth itself, shining and turning." "Take good care of it," he tells her. Thoreau would have approved. Indeed, a passage from his journals could stand as a comment on Georgie's story: "Our most glorious experiences are a kind of regret. Our regret is so sublime that we may mistake it for triumph." (pp. 33-4)

Nancy Willard, in a review of "The Fledgling," in The New York Times Book Review, *September 28, 1980, pp. 33-4.*

Langton's lovely fantasy soars like her dear child heroine, Georgie, and the Goose Prince who carries her off to help her fulfill her dream of flying. The little girl is blessed with devoted kin, her mother and stepfather who run a school near Walden Pond, and teenaged stepcousins Eddy and Eleanor. Georgie and the Goose Prince, a Canadian goose who lags behind his flock to teach the human fledgling, revel in their nocturnal flights and friendship. But officious neighbors come perilously close to changing an idyll into tragedy. Langton has been honored for this haunting, funny and unforgettable story with perfectly individualized characters, and no whiff of unearned emotion to mar its beauty.

A review of "The Fledgling," in Publishers Weekly, *Vol. 219, No. 17, April 24, 1981, p. 76.*

Fragile Flag (1984)

Was it only four years ago that we all laughed at the President of the United States for soberly reporting in a debate that his young daughter has told him she considered "the control of nuclear arms" to be "the most important issue" in America? Today the stance of an innocent child's horror over the blow-upability of the world is considered anything but cloying—it has become utterly respectable as a starting point for discussions of foreign affairs, and good liberals yearn for a President who would discuss the nuclear freeze in the terms that got Jimmy Carter tagged with a "gaffe" in 1980.

Jane Langton's **The Fragile Flag** is a child's novel in tune with the *Zeitgeist*. A group of children from Concord, Mass., led by a Gandhi-like 10-year-old girl named Georgie, walks all the way to Washington to ask President James R. Toby to cancel his new Peace Missile, which is sort of a combination of the MX (the name is similar; MX is officially "the Peacekeeper"), the Pershing II (the missile European students demonstrate against) and the Strategic Defense Initiative (it will be based in space). The President's grown-up arguments for the missile seem pathetic next to the children's simple ones against it.

The way in which most political novels fail is artistic, not political—issues are intelligently debated, but by cardboard figures. Here the opposite is true. The political questions the story raises are, for those not already converts, left utterly unresolved. Why are the children able to rest so easy with the Peace Missile out of the way, given that all the thousands of ICBM's, SLBM's and so on remain? Why do President Toby's pre-conversion statements about the necessity of nuclear deterrence to insure freedom fail to sound as absurd as they are meant to sound? These aren't matters *The Fragile Flag* addresses at all; on the other hand, it is a completely charming book.

Its milieu, the fiercely genteel and liberal western suburbs of Boston, is fondly drawn. The portrayals of the children themselves are so effortless and true that it seems momentarily impossible that other writers could find it difficult to endow characters that young with distinctive personalities. Georgie is a waif with a soul of granite; her half-sister Eleanor is sensible but losing that quality fast to adolescence; the President's grandson Robert is moony without being flaky. There is a clear foreshadowing of what kind of adults they'll be without their being at all just adults in miniature. Their long march along U.S. 1 is fantastic but just barely so, and paced just right—slow at the beginning and headlong at the end. Even the villains, a scheming Presidential assistant and a publicity-mad teen-age celebrity, are lovable.

Practically the only moment in which Mrs. Langton writes without empathy comes when the President falls into a reverie about America, with the following climax: "The new missile, nearly ready to be transported to the air base in Nevada, soon to be aloft in the starry sky, circling to earth, looking down at the enemies of America, ready to spot preparations for war, ready to attack, to annihilate, to win." This is a tiny but unmistakable lapse in the tone of a gentle book, a glimpse of something evil and nasty in people rather than in weapons. But if the President had been given a better reason to want his missile, *The Fragile Flag* would have had to be a very different book—deeper, perhaps, but no longer such a lovely confection.

> *Nicholas Lemann, "Children's Crusade," in* The New York Times Book Review, *November 11, 1984, p. 61.*

Georgie Hall, the wispy little girl who literally flies to fame in *The Fledgling,* reappears as the moving force in another of the author's astonishing stories. While the President of the United States is embroiled in controversy over his proposed "Peace Missile," he announces a letter-writing contest for schoolchildren on "What the Flag Means to Me." After Uncle Freddy hauls out of the attic a faded, motheaten flag, Georgie has a clairvoyant vision of the hideous possibilities of the new weapon. Imbued with her family's idealistic resolve, she determines to walk from Concord, Massachusetts, to Washington, carrying the ancient flag fastened to a mop handle, and deliver her letter to the President. Eddy and Eleanor, her step-cousins, agree to accompany her; so does a schoolmate—who happens to be the President's grandson. Laden with back-packs, the children begin the four-hundred-fifty-mile trek, walking along the littered edge of the road, passing endless stretches of fast-food places, gas stations, and garish shopping plazas. Then another girl joins them, pushing her enchanting baby brother in his stroller. At night, they all camp near the noisy, smelly road; but eventually they attract the attention of newspaper and TV reporters and acquire the protection of the state police. Before long, church groups await them, dispensing food, shelter, and encouragement. More children join the procession as it winds its way

through blazing heat and chilly rain; and when thousands of them converging from all parts of the country attach themselves to the innocent, unwashed, jostling, and often cranky marchers in the bedraggled cavalcade, it suddenly turns into a children's crusade that plods on to a heroic climax. The author's humor and humanity are never overshadowed by her passionate purpose, and her story is made irresistible by its symbols: a diminutive determined child and a threadbare flag with a magical will of its own—sometimes pale and limp, sometimes billowing bravely with clear, fresh colors. (pp. 758-59)

> *Ethel L. Heins, in a review of "The Fragile Flag," in* The Horn Book Magazine, *Vol. LX, No. 6, November-December, 1984, pp. 758-59.*

In Jane Langton's *Fragile Flag,* nine-year-old Georgie Hall does think for herself. To deflect attention from deployment of his unpopular Peace Missile, President Toby calls on American children to write him about "What the Flag of My Country Means to Me." After envisioning a horrific nuclear Armageddon in the stars and stripes of her Uncle Freddy's frayed flag, Georgie knows what to say: "The flag means the American people being friends with all the other people. . . ." Carrying the old flag at the end of a mop pole, Georgie walks 450 miles to hand-deliver her letter. By the time she reaches Washington, she is leading a children's crusade 16,000-strong.

There are a few credibility problems here. That parents would allow children to go on an unplanned, unprotected trek is just unbelievable. So is the cheerful participation of 14-month-old Carrington Updike. But then, this is a fantasy of sorts. There are a few happy coincidences as well. How convenient that the President's grandson is among the marchers and that Georgie's family lives in Concord, Mass. The march is born in the cradle of the American Revolution, in the heart of Thoreau country, and thus Georgie is inexorably linked with a brave tradition.

Like Maine's Samantha Smith before her, Georgie determines to make a difference with a letter. Langton creates a powerful image—the small, determined girl; the fragile, enduring flag; the innocent, idealistic plea. This image says something about a child's America in 1984, about a child's fears and faith.

> *Susan Faust, "Four Novels That Deal in Danger," in* The Christian Science Monitor, *February 1, 1985, p. B5.*

This exceptional novel tells of Children's Crusade to Washington, which becomes 16,000 strong, to protest the launching of the "Peace Missile" into space. A timely and much-needed fable, this book tells all children and the "children" within all adults that they can make a difference!

> *Ruth Anderson, in a review of "The Fragile Flag," in* Social Education, *Vol. 49, No. 4, April, 1985, p. 328.*

Here is a fantasy/allegory/realistic novel set solidly in the present. U.S. President James Toby is preparing to launch the Peace Missile, a Star Wars-type nuclear superweapon. He is *also* sponsoring a national essay contest for school children on "What the U.S. Flag Means to Me." Each state winner will be flown to Washington to spend a week at the White House carrying the President's ceremonial flag.

Georgie Hall is a shy, intense eight-year-old girl living in Concord, Massachusetts. Her essay begins, "The flag means American people being friends with all other people" and goes on to say that the Peace Missile must be stopped. When she misses the post office deadline, the story really begins: Georgie vows to walk the 450 miles to Washington to deliver her essay to the president himself. She is joined by other children, and the Children's Crusade for Peace begins.

This is both a compelling story and an accessible allegory, and the children I know have responded to it enthusiastically. The author combines fantasy and real life in a way that gives us reading pleasure and provides a tool for understanding the uses and abuses of power, and how groups of people—even children, the most powerless of all—can unite and organize to bring about change.

Since this *is* an allegory, many characters are one-dimensional representations of various forces or positions. We meet five children who have won the flag contest and they too are flat characters. A child from Louisiana, DuBose Boudreau, had written his essay about the Mississippi River and "Huckleberry Finn, who tried to free his friend Jim from slavery by drifting down the river on a raft." There is no reference to his color, but if DuBose is Black it is unlikely (to say the least) that he would proudly refer to *Huck Finn.* And if DuBose is not Black, then there are no explicitly Black characters in the book. The norm here is white, middle-class and Protestant, and this is the book's major flaw, especially because it deals with such universals as peace, brother/sisterhood and justice.

On the plus side, the female main characters are provided with a variety of roles. There's Georgie, of course—determined and resourceful. There is also Georgie's friend Frieda, who becomes the march's organizational leader, and Weezie, the trouble-maker. The boys are not ignored, but it is the girls who are most memorable.

The Fragile Flag, the most realistic of Jane Langton's fantasy series that began with *The Diamond in the Window,* is the sequel to *The Fledgling,* a 1980 Newbery Honor Book. A novel for both children and adults, this book is for anyone who wants to understand and/or explain the power of grassroots organizing and nonviolent resistance. It provides a good story, interesting characters and that little push we often need to Get Involved. Just imagine . . . 12,000 children marching on Washington.

> *Christine Jenkins, in a review of "The Fragile Flag," in* Interracial Books for Children Bulletin, *Vol. 16, No. 8, 1985, p. 20.*

The Hedgehog Boy: A Latvian Folktale (1985)

Soft and bright, paintings in the European folk tradition, romantic pictures with geometric borders, illustrate a tale that combines two familiar motifs: the animal-mate, and the child that is magically given to a childless couple. Here the child proves to be prickly-skinned (not depicted in the illustrations) and he demands the king's youngest daughter as payment for showing the monarch the way home. On their wedding night the princess sees that her groom has taken off a prickly coat of fur, burns it, and nurses back to health the husband who is now a handsome young man. Langton tells the story with a sense of drama, a sense of humor, and a fine narrative flow.

> *A review of "The Hedgehog Boy: A Latvian Folktale," in* Bulletin of the Center for Children's Books, *Vol. 39, No. 3, November, 1985, p. 51.*

Familiar folktale elements combine in an unfamiliar tale of Latvian origin. A farm couple yearns for a child; they are rewarded by the Forest Mother with an infant in a basket who is "covered with prickles, like a hedgehog." Years later, when the king is lost in the woods, the hedgehog boy trades directions home for his daughter's hand in marriage. On their wedding night, the princess burns the hedgehog coat. Her husband becomes sick and almost dies, but with the princess' loving care he heals and becomes a handsome normal man. The character of the bumbling, inept king particularly comes to life, and the entire story is deftly, clearly told with humorous, flowing prose. It may be too long for a read-aloud, however. Plume incorporates traditional Latvian colors and design in her illustrations, which are aglow with yellows, reds, blues and greens. Bordered full-page, lavish artwork alternates with smaller rectangular and circular illustrations. The overall design of the book is pleasing although there are a few questionable blank spaces. A quibble: though the story may be true to Langton's sources, the transformation from hedgehog boy to real boy is confusing. Children may want to know what exactly takes place. Does he take his coat off every night? Is there some kind of enchantment at work here? Is it love that saves him? Is it fair that the princess is essentially rewarded for her impulsive act of burning the coat? In spite of this lack of clarity, the book is still a charming and welcome addition to folktale collections. The score to a Latvian song, a daina, is included. (pp. 73-4)

> *Leda Schubert, in a review of "The Hedgehog Boy: A Latvian Folktale," in* School Library Journal, *Vol. 32, No. 35 November, 1985, pp. 73-4.*

In a time "when pretzels still fell from the sky," anything seems possible. Given this opening line, the reader becomes a charmed participant in the adventures of the sharp-witted peasant lad, covered with ugly hedgehoglike prickles, who is released from his enchanted state through marriage to a remorseful princess and is transformed into a fine, handsome bridegroom. The story of the hedgehog boy, or "hedgehurst" as he is known in some cultures, has a number of variants, but this particular retelling from the Latvian tradition is one of the most appealing for its flowing, rhythmic text, for its touches of humor drawn from common-sense responses to down-to-earth situations, and, of course, for its thoroughly satisfying romantic conclusion. The accompanying illustrations [by Ilse Plume], executed in the forthright yet never garish tones of true folk art, are particularly intriguing not only for the integration of Latvian designs and costumes into the overall composition, but also for the interpretation of the central character. Portrayed as a human being with some aspects of the creature for which he is named, he is more believable, perhaps, as an architect of his own destiny than he would be if the animal characteristics of his dual nature were emphasized. This choice is also a sensitive response to the text, which records a much more loving relationship between the enchanted child and the baffled parents than do other versions. Together, text and pictures demonstrate an exemplary blend of two distinct talents into one unified entity, notable for the way in which each complements and extends the other.

> *Mary M. Burns, in a review of "The Hedgehog Boy: A Latvian Folktale," in* The Horn Book Magazine, *Vol. LXII, No. 1, January-February, 1986, p. 50.*

Salt: A Russian Folktale (1992)

Everyone thinks Ivan the Fool, the youngest of a wealthy merchant's three sons, is too preoccupied with such questions as whether the world is round or flat to be trusted with a sailing expedition of his own. But Ivan protests and is given a boat with the least risky cargo imaginable: wooden spoons. He quickly finds a more lucrative replacement when he chances on an island with a mountain of salt. Sure enough, his newly acquired barrels of salt bring him good fortune: he wins the love of a princess wasting away from gustatory boredom when he secretly flavors her soup, and he wrangles a ride home from a giant by sprinkling salt on his wounded thumb until the giant promises him anything he desires. Despite interference from his brothers, who go so far as to dump him overboard after he has rescued them from their own failed expeditions, Ivan returns home victorious. Caldecott Honor recipient [Ilse] Plume's richly patterned illustrations are filled with Russian folklore motifs and framed in decorative golden borders, as is the text, a formal effect nicely balanced by the soft, glowing palette. The result: a dignified simplicity well-matched by Newbery Honoree Langton's fairytale vocabulary and graceful prose.

> *A review of "Salt: A Russian Folktale," in* Publishers Weekly, *Vol. 239, No. 42, September 21, 1992, p. 94.*

Following the time-honored motif of the youngest of three brothers triumphing over incredible odds, Langton retells a Russian tale that mixes derring-do with humor. Ivan outwits his brothers to discover a true treasure, an island with a mountain of salt, and gains the favor of his merchant father and the hand in marriage of a lovely tsarevna. Plume's illustrations reflect the Russian style, and are different shapes embedded in a gilded border. Students might be amazed to discover the value of salt, a commodity they take for granted.

> *M. Jean Greenlaw, in a review of "Salt," in* The New Advocate, *Vol. 6, No. 3, Summer, 1993, p. 215.*

Else Holmelund Minarik

1920-

Danish-born American author of fiction; poet; and translator.

Major works include *Little Bear* (1957), *Father Bear Comes Home* (1959), *Little Bear's Friend* (1960), *What If?* (1987), *Am I Beautiful?* (1992).

INTRODUCTION

An esteemed writer of works for preschoolers and primary graders, Minarik is praised for creating substantive narratives and characterizations for beginning readers that reflect her understanding of children and their world. Her "Little Bear" books, five tales about an anthropomorphic bruin for which she is best known, initiated publisher Harper and Row's "I Can Read" series. In a manner considered highly innovative because it deviated from the staccato-like, repetitive wording of existing easy-to-read books, Minarik composed texts of brief sentences and simple vocabulary which gracefully express a sophisticated, subtle humor and emotion while capturing thoughts and events drawn directly from the experiences of a small child. Her first book, *Little Bear,* introduces the reader to its title character, an endearing young cub with an abundance of imagination, curiosity, and energy, and also to affectionate, attentive Mother Bear, who offers him maternal consolation and approval. In the four succeeding stories, all of which are noted for their warmth, gentleness, and poignancy, Little Bear engages in inventive play and quests for independence while learning that he is surrounded by loving relatives and friends who take pleasure in his revelry and offer solace and support when he is discouraged or unhappy. Although Little Bear's world progressively expands, his widening circle of acquaintances and broader range of experiences merely reinforce the security of his existence; in this manner, Minarik appeals to the child's natural desire for safety and reassurance. Series illustrator Maurice Sendak wrote of *Little Bear:* "I felt the text was the ideal dream of an ideal childhood, for Little Bear's life seemed completely surrounded by love." Sendak chose to depict the characters in a Victorian milieu; Mother Bear wears voluminous skirts and comforts Little Bear in their folds while he rests in her massive lap. Critics have noted the appropriateness of Sendak's drawings, observing that the refined, quaint setting and costumes are a perfect counterpart to Minarik's soothing stories.

Born in Denmark, Minarik emigrated to the United States with her parents at the age of four. She was helped to overcome her initial difficulties with the English language by her father, who took her to western movies, and her mother, who taught her to communicate with other children on frequent trips to a neighborhood playground. Minarik later earned degrees in psychology and education; her experience as a teacher prompted her to begin writing books for children, as she found a dearth of material with which to encourage her students' fascination with reading. After

she submitted her manuscript for *Little Bear* to Harper and Row, she was lauded as the creator of the perfect vehicle for early independent reading. In five brief stories, Minarik relates vignettes full of whimsy and innocence. In a tale from the first title, Little Bear tries to fly to the moon by constructing a space helmet out of a box and leaping off a hill, carefully choosing a small one in case his experiment fails. Throughout, the tone is comforting and the book is permeated with the presence of devoted Mother Bear, who affectionately teases her cub while she patiently allows him to learn his own lessons. In the ensuing "Little Bear" books, Father Bear comes home from the sea and joins his son in imaginative play; Little Bear meets a human girl and, dismayed when she leaves for school, is assured by his mother that he will soon learn to write so they can correspond; the cub visits his grandparents, who coddle him and tell him stories; and Grandmother Bear sends a kiss to Little Bear by having it passed along from one animal to another. Minarik's enduring message of reassurance has kept her books timely; as Margery Fisher wrote in 1983: "The passing of two decades has done nothing to diminish the quiet charm and humor of the Little Bear books." Minarik has also written a book of poetry and several other works for young readers in which fantasy and innocent playfulness are prominent. In her recent *Am I Beautiful?*, Minarik returns to her theme of unconditional parental love; here a young hippopotamus is given evasive answers when he asks several animals to comment on his appearance, until his mother responds to his query by declaring that he is very beautiful to her. *Little Bear's Visit* was named a Caldecott honor book in 1962 for its illustrations.

(See also *Something about the Author,* Vol. 15 and *Contemporary Authors,* Vols. 73-76.)

GENERAL COMMENTARY

May Hill Arbuthnot

These epoch-making, easy-to-read books [the "Little Bear" books,] are just as popular today as they were when they were first published. Stories and [Maurice Sendak's] illustrations are equally beguiling. Despite their shortness and primerlike quality, the sentences sound natural and have a pleasant flow. The first book, perhaps, is the warmest and the funniest. When Little Bear thinks no one remembers his birthday, Mother Bear appears with a glorious cake complete with candles. When Little Bear returns after taking off for the moon, Mother Bear asks who he is, but this pretending soon goes too far for comfort. Finally, Little Bear says, "Mother Bear, stop fooling, / You are my Mother Bear / and I am your Little Bear, / and we are on Earth and you know it. / Now may I eat my lunch?" Maurice Sendak's drawings are exactly right and enhance the humor and the loving reassurance of the stories.

> *May Hill Arbuthnot, "Reading Begins, 6-7-8: 'Little Bear',"* in her Children's Reading in the Home, *Scott, Foresman and Company, 1969, p. 85.*

Barbara Bader

[Illustrations are important] as an attractant in readers. In primers, in easy readers, they have the further function of making the meaning plain. Ideally, everything in the pictures is implicit in the text, and the child, understanding what's happening, can anticipate the words. The premium is on simplicity, economy, clarity, and on expressiveness—attitudes and feelings made manifest. In Sendak's illustrations, the suppression of detail and background is apparent in *Little Bear* and continues generally through *Little Bear's Friend.* Nor was it usually his way to call into play the roll of the eye, the lift of the head, the motion of the arms—to *project* personality and attitude, that is, to the extent that he does here. In that sense, and in the sense that Little Bear is a character, he is not unlike the early winsome Mickey Mouse. But in his absolute bliss thinking of his new friend Emily, he is altogether human, as Mickey Mouse, confined to action and reaction—and denied reflection—cannot be.

No Fighting, No Biting followed, a book that—through the stories cousin Joan tells to ructious Willy and Rosa—did much to make bad behavior an acceptable, approach-

able topic; and then, imperatively, *Father Bear Comes Home.* He is not to be seen in *Little Bear* and we soon learn, as if in explanation as well as anticipation, that "He is fishing on the ocean." Then he is expected and, says Little Bear, Maybe he saw a mermaid, "And maybe she could come home with him." First Hen, then Duck, then Cat fall in, Henny-Penny fashion, but Father Bear, waiting at the door, has no mermaid. *No little mermaid!?!!* "But I said maybe," says Little Bear, "I did say maybe."

As much as Mother Bear is the embodiment of sustaining motherhood, Father Bear is the exemplar of bluff, shrewd fatherhood. It is written in and depicted. Little Bear has the hiccups and not Owl's wisdom, not Duck and Hen's surprise appearance cure him; but, without any notice being taken, Father Bear does. In *Little Bear's Visit* the focus is on Grandmother and Grandfather and what they mean to Little Bear: Grandmother Bear's good cooking and Grandfather Bear's stories—postponed when Grandfather Bear ("I am never tired!") falls asleep and Grandmother Bear tells him, instead, a story of Mother Bear when she was little. Then Grandfather Bear wakes up; and they both laugh. It is a sneaky, spooky, scary goblin story he tells, but nothing beats the look between them, or Little Bear's skip, Grandfather's glow, when it's over.

Father and Mother Bear come to retrieve Little Bear at the close (only to find him, they think, fast asleep—listening) and then one can see distinctly how each is both bear and prototype: in truth, mother, father, grandmother, grandfather and little *bear.* Most difficult and most striking is Mother Bear as a girl; not a little girl but a young pensive girl, the heroine as a young bear.

Perhaps, however, one should reserve the palm for the hazardous undertaking that *Little Bear's Friend* represents, the injection of a human character. Climbing down from a tree—from which he saw not only his own home but something of the world (a town, a shepherd on the road)—Little Bear meets a little girl, Emily, who is just enough bigger to be little-girl size next to a little bear, and not too big to be not only Little Bear's friend but tacitly, delicately, Little Bear's girl-friend. Though the separate episodes have not quite the snap of their predecessors, the book comes off beautifully—and beautifully is the word, for there is a new romantic, poetic aura about the proceedings. Effectually and emotionally, Little Bear looking out from among the branches sets the scene for what is to follow. (pp. 501-02)

> *Barbara Bader, "Maurice Sendak," in her* American Picturebooks from Noah's Ark to the Beast Within, *Macmillan Publishing Co., Inc., 1976, pp. 495-524.*

Myra Pollack Sadker and David Miller Sadker

Some humorous animal books express the day-to-day situations, the fears, the troubles, the pleasures that characterize the young child's world. The books about *Little Bear* . . . feature a realistic bear; that is, very real from the point of view of children. As he interacts with friends and relatives, plays "let's pretend," and feels the need for the warmth of a hug or of a reassuring comment, he is clearly one of their own. In *Little Bear's Visit* . . . Little

Bear enjoys visiting Grandmother and Grandfather Bear and hearing stories of his mother when she was a little bear. Little Bear also enjoys pretending to be asleep, so that he can overhear the grown-ups talking, a trick not unfamiliar to human children. (pp. 333-34)

> *Myra Pollack Sadker and David Miller Sadker, "Save Our Planet—Save Ourselves," in their* Now Upon a Time: A Contemporary View of Children's Literature, *Harper & Row, Publishers, 1977, pp. 267-359.*

Margery Fisher

The passing of two decades has done nothing to diminish the quiet charm and humour of the Little Bear books, arranged for beginner-readers. With clear, large print and simple sentences, the stories reflect family affection as they describe situations familiar to the young like birthdays, picnics, the onset of hiccups, a fishing expedition. Sendak's serene, enchanting chalk and line pictures have a gentle, uncomplicated appeal which still holds its own against his later, more complex work.

> *Margery Fisher, in a review of "Little Bear" and "Father Bear Comes Home," in* Growing Point, *Vol. 22, No. 2, July, 1983, p. 4110.*

TITLE COMMENTARY

Little Bear (1957)

A primer with a soothing quality, the story of Mother Bear and Little Bear is told with repetition of simple words for fledgling first-grade readers. The gently teasing way in which Mother Bear cajoles Little Bear, and Little Bear's methods of winning Mother Bear's attention and approval make a tender little tale just right for eager but inexperienced readers. Maurice Sendak's illustrations of Mother Bear's matronly dignity in coping with her little bear as he decides what to wear, as he makes vegetable birthday soup for fear she'll forget to bake him a cake, and as he makes a brief excursion to the moon, are pleasantly old-fashioned in brown, black and blue. A cuddly story which could be also be a boon to baby sitters at bedtime.

> *A review of "Little Bear," in* Virginia Kirkus' Service, *Vol. XXV, No. 12, June 15, 1957, p. 410.*

It is difficult to be practical about something charming—one wants only to be charmed. Yet this is a book that must be considered on two counts: its joyousness and its usefulness. It passes on both counts. One look at the illustrations and children will grab for it. A second look at the short, easy sentences, the repetition of words and the beautiful type spacing, and children will know they can read it themselves.

The four brief stories about Little Bear and his mother (who understands perfectly how little bears feel) have the right characteristics of tales for the young: a childlike imagination; a concern with things of the child's own world; and surprising, completely satisfying endings. Simple as they are, the stories have a poignance—particularly "Birthday Soup," in which Little Bear is afraid his mother has forgotten the birthday cake. When she brings it in and says, "I never did forget your birthday and never will," even an adult reader is moved and feels with Little Bear that mothers can be depended upon.

> *Phyllis Fenner, "Mother Didn't Forget," in* The New York Times, *September 8, 1957, p. 8.*

Maurice Sendak's best pictures, so far, illustrate stories that are tender and utterly charming, told simply enough for a six-year-old to read himself.

The four little stories, none more then seventy or so short lines, are as simple as a first-grade text, but they manage to create two unforgettable, endearing characters; busy, eager, hasty Little Bear and his affectionate, solicitous and patient mother. The delectable pictures, suggesting those in some old readers, show in gestures and on the furry faces every change of emotion. Indeed 1957 is the year for the beginning readers with two books to prove that a limited vocabulary need not result in dull stories; the jolly imaginative rhymes of Dr. Seuss in *The Cat in the Hat* and this lovely tale of a small bear's birthday party, his trip to the moon and his delightfully unreasonable wishes. Both are surely destined to be read and reread.

> *"Beguiling Animals in Handsome Pictures," in* New York Herald Tribune Book Review, *November 17, 1957, p. 4.*

[*Little Bear*] is a tender and eloquent book, and represents a genuine collaboration between author and artist. It is made up of four stories, the first three reappearing in the last in such a way as to induce Little Bear (and Little Reader) to give up and go to sleep. Mother Bear, moving about with heavy grace in the cumbersome skirts of 1903, is an endearing character. Her maternal patience, forbearance, amusement, and dignified pride in her little bear are apparent in spite of herself. Her jokes with him are in a very low key, sometimes nothing more than tiny variations in the repetitions of a question. What makes this book different from all the other children's books in which animals wear clothes and live in houses is that instead of being a tale told to amuse children it all seems to be happening within a child's head. Also, the fact that it is so full of love.

> *Emily Maxwell, "Christmas for First and Second Readers," in* The New Yorker, *Vol. XXXIII, No. 39, November 23, 1957, pp. 232-39.*

[*The following excerpt is from an interview with Maurice Sendak by Ursula Nordstrom.*]

When we first saw [Maurice Sendak's] pictures for Else Minarik's *Little Bear,* we asked him how he had been able to imagine such a warm and wonderful world. He replied at some length.

"I felt the text was the ideal dream of an ideal childhood," he said, "for Little Bear's life seemed completely surrounded by love. There was a sense of stability in the story, the kind of stability that comes from an unshakable love; I found it awe-inspiring. I wondered how I could add anything to what Else Minarik had done already.

"Of course I wanted Mother Bear to be an image of warmth and strength—nothing less than motherhood itself. So I dressed her in Victorian costume because those voluminous skirts, the voluminous sleeves and her voluminous figure all made for the strong and comforting tenderness I wanted her to exude. And when Little Bear sits in her lap, I had her envelop him. The folds of her skirt would surround him; her arms would surround him. There couldn't be a safer place in all the world than in Mother Bear's lap." (pp. 92-3)

Ursula Nordstrom, "Maurice Sendak," in Library Journal, *Vol. 89, March 15, 1964, pp. 92-4.*

Characterizations of creative children or their fictional representatives abound in children's literature. By allowing their protagonists to act out fantasies—either in dreams or waking—many works encourage children to believe in their own creativity and in the safety of expressing it. However, there are also children's books which, while appearing to offer such encouragement, actually foster the idea that the child's creative capacities should be selectively restrained. Two picture books that illustrate these contrasting attitudes are Edward Fenton's *Fierce John* and Else Minarik's **Little Bear.**

Fenton's story ostensibly encourages the child to act out his fantasies, but its hero John is, in fact, subtly thwarted for his creative role-playing in a way which is very discomforting to him. (p. 40)

Instead of a story in which a child's imagination is being encouraged, we are taken through an experience in which a child is tricked into believing that his imagination evokes unhappiness and even tears from those around him. They cause him to regret that he has tried to play the role of a lion, and when he attempts to give up the role, they confuse him by insisting that his play is reality and sadden him by denying him the ability to convince them it is not real. And so I find myself at the end with the following sense of what John has learned about his imagination: that it brings unhappiness to his family and himself, that he is unable to control its effects upon others, even when it becomes emotionally hurtful, and that if he will give it up, he will make everyone happy and be treated to ice cream. It's not an experience I would wish a small child to have.

Contrast Else Minarik's **Little Bear.** In an episode entitled "Little Bear Goes to the Moon," Little Bear, wearing a hat that looks like a cereal box with two springs coming out of it, announces to his mother than he has a new space helmet and is going to the moon.

> "How?" asked Mother Bear.
>
> "I'm going to fly to the moon," said Little Bear.
>
> "Fly!" said mother Bear. "You can't fly."
>
> "Birds fly," said Little Bear.
>
> "Oh, yes," said Mother Bear. "Birds fly, but they don't fly to the moon. And you are not a bird."
>
> "Maybe some birds fly to the moon, I don't

know. And maybe I can fly like a bird," said Little Bear.

> "And maybe," said Mother Bear, "you are a little fat bear cub with no wings and no feathers. Maybe if you jump you will come down very fast, with a big plop."
>
> "Maybe," said Little Bear. "But I'm going now. Just look for me up in the sky."
>
> "Be back for lunch," said Mother Bear.

John's family initially rejected John's wish to be a lion. Is Mother Bear's response here any different from theirs? Notice that her remarks arise, not from her being distracted from her own concerns, but from a desire to clarify the extent to which Little Bear can be imaginative without fear of harming himself. She is saying, in effect, that if he tries to be a bird, he had better not do so from too great a height. And so Little Bear, having understood her, goes "to the top of a little hill" and climbs "to the top of a little tree, a very little tree." He jumps with his eyes shut and comes down "with a big plop," as his mother had cautioned him. Little Bear then stands up and plays at being on the moon, noting how things on the moon look "just like the earth," the trees, the birds, a house that looks just like his. The story concludes:

> "I'll go in and see what kind of bears live here. Look at that," said Little Bear. "Something to eat is on the table. It looks like a good lunch for a little bear."
>
> Mother Bear came in and said, "But who is this? Are you a bear from Earth?"
>
> "Oh, yes, I am," said Little Bear. "I climbed a little hill, and jumped from a little tree, and flew here, just like the birds."
>
> "Well," said Mother Bear. "My little bear did the same thing. He put on his space helmet and flew to Earth. So I guess you can have his lunch."
>
> Little Bear puts his arms around Mother Bear. He said, "Mother Bear, stop fooling. You are my Mother Bear and I am your Little Bear, and we are on Earth, and you know it. Now may I have my lunch?"
>
> "Yes," said Mother Bear, "and then you will have your nap. For you are my little bear, and I know it."

What may be learned by sharing this experience with Little Bear? That, within safe limits, our imaginative play can give us enjoyment. That we do have control over its effects upon others, and those effects can be enjoyable to others. That we know what is imagined and what is real, and can return whenever we choose to the real. Little Bear is not threatened with any loss of the comfort and security of his home and his mother. He is cautioned about his imagination, but then encouraged to extend it, to explore the pleasures it can lead to. It is an experience I would wish a small child to have. (pp. 43-6)

William Glasser, "Creative Children: Charac-

terized and Criticized," in The Lion and the Unicorn, *Vol. 1, No. 2, Fall, 1977, pp. 40-6.*

No Fighting, No Biting! (1958)

Joan, a quite proper Victorian young lady, wants to read a book, but little Rosa and Will will not give her a moment's peace. They push, they squeeze, and oh, the questions they ask. And so Rosa has no recourse but to tell them an instructive and entertaining story about two baby alligators who behaved much like the two children. The story has it's effect for a while, but then the fighting recommences. This time a few sage words quiet the cousins and Joan goes demurely back to her book. Else Holmelund Minarik whose *Little Bear* indicated a uniquely charming talent has outdone herself here and Maurice Sendak's illustrations reaffirm the impression that he is one of the most gifted illustrators of contemporary children's books.

> *A review of "No Fighting, No Biting," in* Virginia Kirkus' Service, *Vol. XXVI, No. 14, July 15, 1958, p. 499.*

Mrs. Minarik has wisely not tried to repeat the tender mood of her first book—that was probably inimitable, even by its own author. This new one may not touch the emotions so sensitively and may not be so durable, but children should find very realistic the sketches of two youngsters engaged in one of those timeless routines of pinching, squeezing and general teasing. It's just like home today, even if the youngsters and Cousin Joan, the peacemaker, wear, for some inscrutable reason of illustrator Maurice Sendak's own, costumes reminiscent of the Eighteen Eighties. And there is real suspense, junior grade, and humor in the stories of two young alligators, also inclined to bicker, who never know exactly the intentions of a great hungry alligator. Mr. Sendak does handsomely by these cheery-looking reptiles.

> *Ellen Lewis Buell, in a review of "No Fighting, No Biting!," in* The New York Times, *October 5, 1958, p. 36.*

The "I Can Read" series made such a magnificent start with *Little Bear* last year that it is not quite fair to expect the next two volumes to equal that little masterpiece. *No Fighting, No Biting!* by the same author is delightful indeed in its way, although it has not the tender perfection of her first book. It is about Rosa and Willy who are a great nuisance to Cousin Joan, squeezing and pinching each other on the sofa beside her while she is trying to read. In desperation she calls them little alligators and they promptly insist on an alligator story, which Cousin Joan manages to turn into a light-hearted comment on what happens to squabbly children. Rosa and Willy like the story but do not let the moral affect their conduct, for they plunge into another quarrel about a lost tooth before they finally settle down to read. This story offers six-year-olds the pleasurable opportunity of watching other children both crocodile and human misbehaving. While to an adult the episode of the tooth seems an anticlimax, the subject is of considerable importance at six, especially when presents are to be had for placing the tooth under a pillow. Maurice Sendak has drawn charming turn-of-

the-century settings for the human squabbling scenes and a fine green world for the crocodiles both of which give this book the pleasant look of a real "grownup" book in contrast to the overbright cheeriness of school "readers."

> *"Humour to Start Six-Year-Olds on a Lifetime of Reading Fun," in* New York Herald Tribune Book Review, *November 2, 1958, p. 8.*

Father Bear Comes Home (1959)

Four episodes in the life of Little Bear, each abounding in that tender and gracious humor which distinguishes Else Minarik's hero from the usual run of teddy bears:—Little Bear embarks on a fishing trip, Little Bear gets and loses the hiccups, Little Bear welcomes Father Bear home from sea, and finally, Little Bear has an encounter with a mermaid. Maurice Sendak's mannered Victorian illustrations add a dimension of charm to the menage of animals which include a particularly beguiling owl, a cat, a duck, and of course, mama and papa bear. A simple but elegant vocabulary and a reassuring atmosphere of family tenderness make this an ideal selection for the apprentice reader.

> *A review of "Father Bear Comes Home," in* Virginia Kirkus' Service, *Vol. XXVII, No. 12, June 15, 1959, p. 400.*

Little Bear has endeared himself as a character with irresistible, childlike charm. He will be greeted warmly by "I Can Read" beginners who met him in *Little Bear* and by a new group able now to enjoy both books. Mr. Bear, a most fatherly parent who has been away fishing "on the ocean," comes home to the serene Victorian household presided over by motherly Mrs. Bear. Four stories again are centered in Little Bear's imaginative playing and thinking—from vanquishing hiccups to dreaming up a mermaid (which, he said, *maybe* his father might bring home). The drawings do much to establish the personality of each figure, including Little Bear's friends, Duck, Hen, Cat, and Owl, who follow him in every adventure. A book as worthy of admiration as its predecessor.

> *Virginia Haviland, in a review of "Father Bear Comes Home," in* The Horn Book Magazine, *Vol. XXXV, No. 5, October, 1959, p. 380.*

When Else Minarik's *Little Bear* was published two years ago it immediately charmed children and still does. Indeed, it promises to be a classic not only for readers who are just finding their way among the mysteries of type but also for their younger brothers and sisters. It would, perhaps, be too much to ask that a sequel would have the same tenderness and the same seemingly unforced feeling for the imaginative life of childhood and this one doesn't—it is a little contrived and not so easy-flowing. Yet since children love to know more about their favorite characters, they will very likely be glad to learn that Little Bear has a father (he was away fishing, before) and that he is much like a human father, understanding, a little quizzical but quite ready to join in Little Bear's flights of fancy.

> *Ellen Lewis Buell, "Reunited Family," in* The

New York Times Book Review, *October 18, 1959, p. 46.*

Little Bear's Friend (1960)

Once again the little bear of Else Minarik and Maurice Sendak (illustrator) proves himself to be as wistful and tender a little creature as exists in the child's library. In this episode, little bear makes friends with a child named Emily. With their friends, a duck, a cat, an owl, and a hen, they play all through the happy summer. Even when Emily's doll breaks an arm the pleasure the group finds in each other's company is not diminished. Only the departure of Emily brings tears to Little Bear who is consoled by his mother with his thought that, at least, he can write to her. Pathetic fallacies abound here, but somehow in the hands of this author-illustrator team, they merely compound the charm of the story.

A review of "Little Bear's Friend," in Virginia Kirkus' Service, *Vol. XXVIII, No. 13, July 1, 1960, p. 495.*

The author makes use of the restricted vocabulary to create an agreeable effect of exactness and decorum. The illustrations have an elaborate humor. Little Bear's mother is an ample Victorian with a brooch under her chin. Father Bear, genial though he is, certainly has it in him to be the heavy father. Emily carries a parasol, holds a sun-bonneted wooden doll, and wears a pinafore, but in spite of the nostalgia that hangs about her person she is a very lifelike small girl. The real creation, however, is Little Bear, and what makes him so appealing in this book, as in the two other books that have preceded it, is that he lives in, and is continually giving off, an atmosphere of love. (p. 228)

Emily Maxwell, "Scottish Fairies, the Chair Wind, and How to Talk to a Firefly," in The New Yorker, *Vol. XXXVI, No. 40, November 19, 1960, pp. 223-48.*

Cat and Dog (1960)

[*Cat and Dog* is] an animal farce very different from her much-loved Little Bear stories. In this one a dachshund chases a teasing, mischievous calico cat through a series of domestic near-catastrophes. Mrs. Minarik uses a minimum of words as captions for Fritz Siebel's pictures and although the latter are less than beautiful they are so full of action and comedy that children will go back to look and read again.

Ellen Lewis Buell, in a review of "Cat and Dog," in The New York Times Book Review, *January 29, 1961, p. 38.*

Little Bear's Visit (1961)

Another delightful book about Little Bear, again illustrated by [Maurice Sendak with] drawings that have a gentle humor. Divided into four sections: Little Bear visits his grandparents, he hears a story told by his grandmother,

he is told another story by grandfather, and there is a family gathering at the close of the day. The relationships are warmly described; the writing style is pleasantly ingenuous; the variety and the brevity of the stories are nicely gauged for the beginning reader.

Zena Sutherland, in a review of "Little Bear's Visit," in Bulletin of the Center for Children's Books, *Vol. XV, No. 1, September, 1961, p. 32.*

One of the many charms of the four books about Little Bear is that their author has never been persuaded or pushed into using the very short sentence. It is quite possible that they can be read only by "top" first-grade readers, and by those who have triumphantly reached second grade, but it also makes it possible for adults to read them to younger children with real enjoyment.

Among other delights of these stories are the relationships between Little Bear and his family, and the gentle, understanding humor that seems to come so naturally both to author and artist.

This time Little Bear visits his grandparents, and each of them tells him a story. Incidentally, this book is also a primer on how to be a good grandparent.

Alice Dalgliesh, in a review of "Little Bear's Visit," in The Saturday Review, *New York, Vol. XLIV, No. 38, September 23, 1961, p. 47.*

This is a charming account of one small bear's visit to his grandparents' house where he is treated to such delights as storytelling and the chance to clown around with his grandfather's hat and cane. The concise text of this book for early readers, along with Sendak's illustrations, creates a cozy, love-filled world that capture the special relationship that exists between children and grandparents—even when they're bears.

"What's New in Paperback?" in The Christian Science Monitor, *October 15, 1979, p. B5.*

Since 1961, Minarik's little books about Little Bear have been popular I Can Read fare for beginners, no small part of their appeal being, of course, the incomparable artistry of Sendak's masterful color pictures. Here, Little Bear spends a quiet but blissful day in the woodland home of Grandmother and Grandfather Bear. Seldom are the ordinary joys of childhood presented so effectively or with such understanding of the way children appreciate simple treats like trying on Grandfather's big hat, looking at pictures, Grandmother's flowers, listening to stories, etc. The sweetness and gentle quality of the book are enhanced by the old-fashioned setting, a stately Victorian house and gardens.

A review of "Little Bear's Visit," in Publishers Weekly, *Vol. 216, No. 22, November 26, 1979, p. 53.*

The Little Giant Girl and the Elf Boy (1963)

A brief encounter between a little giant girl and an elf boy, both sent to gather flowers by their respective mothers, ends with a sigh and the uninspired words "we can't all be the same size". Full color pictures [by Garth Williams] on every other page have an old fashioned flavor; they are flat and set, lacking in spark. All sugar and a little water; a let-down from Minarik.

> *A review of "The Little Giant Girl and the Elf Boy," in* Virginia Kirkus' Service, *Vol. XXXI, No. 17, September 1, 1963, p. 859.*

A small book with an appealing but slight story and with charming illustrations. A small giant girl was asked by her mother to pick a bush of flowers for the table, and on the bush she picked was a tiny elf boy who had been sent by his mother to pick a bud and a leaf for the table. The girl's mother smiled and said, "My goodness. A little elf! You must take him back where you found him." The giant girl wished that they could be of a size and be friends, but she consoled herself with the realization that there were advantages to her size. Although the plot is only a fragment, the theme has a wistful tenderness and the writing has a simple grace that makes the book a satisfying one to read aloud.

> *Zena Sutherland, in a review of "The Little Giant Girl and the Elf Boy," in* Bulletin of the Center for Children's Books, *Vol. XVII, No. 4, December, 1963, p. 62.*

The Winds That Come from Far Away, and Other Poems (1964)

A small collection of soft, comfortable, drowsy, prettily (if modestly) poetic lyrics about a rabbit, a pussycat, flowers and birds, Halloween and Thanksgiving, and even a mosquito. All of them are very gentle in their message and should serve primarily as a bedtime *envoi.*

> *A review of "The Winds That Come from Far Away and Other Poems," in* Virginia Kirkus' Service, *Vol. XXXII, No. 18, September 15, 1964, p. 951.*

Here is a world where "insects diligently reap / the pleasures / of their kind"; and where the poet can ask, in all seriousness, "Are you so poor / you've never hugged an apple tree?" If life were really this candy-sweet, we all should be the happier. However, despite their Victorianism, the poems have pleasant rhythms. . . .

> *Barbara Wersba, in a review of "The Winds That Come from Far Away," in* The New York Times Book Review, *December 13, 1964, p. 21.*

A small book of poems, most of them quite short and written in a direct approach on the child's level. Some of the selections are lightly humorous, some are lightly romantic; while the book has an occasional lyric phrase or novel idea, most of the contents are undistinguished but perfectly pleasant.

> *Zena Sutherland, in a review of "The Winds That Come from Far Away and Other Poems," in* Bulletin of the Center for Children's Books, *Vol. XVIII, No. 5, January, 1965, p. 77.*

A Kiss for Little Bear   (1968)

How delicious it must be to be established! Not a member of the Establishment, but established in the hearts of the best people in the world—the children. So that all they need to hear is that there is a new Little Bear story to bring them running. Delicious Little Bear is back, sending a picture to his grandmother who sends a kiss back to him, relayed to him by an animal pony express by a hen, a cat, a frog, and a skunk. Children will want to meet all of them. All of them will join the exclusive circle of characters that children love—delicious characters that they love.

> *A review of "A Kiss for Little Bear," in* Publishers Weekly, *Vol. 194, No. 9, August 26, 1968, p. 271.*

A *little* Little Bear book with very little of Little Bear and with illustrations [by Maurice Sendak] shadowed by the ominous overtones of *Higglety Pigglety Pop.* The story is a single brief episode: Grandmother asks Hen to take a kiss to Little Bear in thanks for the (monster) picture he has sent; Hen, distracted, passes the kiss on to Frog, who passes it on to Cat, who passes it on to Little Skunk, who gives it to a pretty girl skunk, who gives it back . . . starting an exchange of kisses that has nothing to do with Little Bear but which he watches fixedly from behind a fence. Then Hen puts a stop to "too much kissing," retrieves the kiss, delivers it to Little Bear, and refuses to take one in return. The skunks decide to get married; everyone comes; Little Bear, as best man, kisses the bride (while the groom scowls). Well. While ruminating, we scanned the quotes re earlier books on the back flap: "reassuring . . . family tenderness . . . atmosphere of love . . . charming childlikeness of Little Bear's delights." Hardly, albeit a droll vignette; have a look.

> *A review of "A Kiss for Little Bear," in* Kirkus Service, *Vol. XXXVI, No. 18, September 15, 1968, p. 1046.*

The publication of a Little Bear book after seven years is an occasion. It is only to be expected that the author and the artist—and, of course, Little Bear himself—will have changed. The story of Little Bear's kiss, which is sent to him by grandmother and passed from Hen to Frog to Cat to Skunk before it reaches him, is slight and almost incidental to the pictures. As in all the Little Bear books the artist's imagination complements and greatly extends the text. The illustrations, in muted greenish-yellow and brown, seem filled with an end-of-summer melancholy that is heightened by the expressions of alarm and watchfulness in many of the animals' eyes. There is, however, humor in each animal's reaction as he or she receives the kiss. The illustrations have many splendid touches, such as the mouse serving as an attendant to the pretty skunk bride; and Little Bear's kiss at the end shows that he is acquiring savoir-faire. (pp. 557-58)

> *Sidney D. Long, in a review of "A Kiss for Little Bear," in* The Horn Book Magazine, *Vol. XLIV, No. 5, October, 1968, pp. 557-58.*

What If ? (1987)

Minarik (*Little Bear*) and [illustrator Margaret Bloy] Graham (*Harry the Dog*), absent too long from children's books, return with the wintry tale of two striped kittens, Pit and Pat, thrown out into the cold by their owners for trying to climb the Christmas tree. The two begin a series of wishful "what ifs," imagining their own tree reaching the sky, decorated with ice mice and icicles, and a gigantic slide down to earth and snow from the highest branches. Then they ask, "What if we scratch on the door?" They do, and their one true wish is realized. This is very much a primer for readers on the art of wishing, and they soon will discover that the sky is, indeed, the limit, especially around Christmas. Graham's kittens are nicely dolled up for this holiday story; loosely dispersed snow dots and close-at-hand night stars bring the wish world nearer.

A review of "What If ?" in Publishers Weekly, *Vol. 231, No. 25, June 26, 1987, p. 70.*

In the late 50's and the 60's, Minarik performed an enormous service to children's literature by writing the *Little Bear* books, masterpieces that demonstrated that books for beginning readers could have charm, wit, insight into human nature, and poetic cadence that gracefully represented real speech. Now, after a long silence, she presents a very brief story about two kittens tossed out into the snow because they *will not* stop climbing the Christmas tree. . . .

There's a nice kernel of truth in this simple fantasy, enlivened by Graham's ebullient watercolors, which recall her illustrations for the perennially popular *Harry, the Dirty Dog*. Not important, but it should provide some chuckles when shared with the youngest.

A review of "What If ?" in Kirkus Reviews, *Vol. LV, No. 13, July 1, 1987, p. 996.*

It's Spring! (1989)

This is a sweet and simple collaboration by two long-time practitioners of the picture book art [Minarik and illustrator Margaret Bloy Graham]. Two fluffy cats cavort and play in a delighted welcome to a favorite season. Pit, orange-striped and green-eyed, exclaims, "It's Spring!" And Pat, gray-striped and yellow-eyed, echoes, "Spring, spring, spring." They imaginatively engage each other in a spirited rivalry, telling each other that they are so happy they could jump over a tulip, bush, tree, house, island, mountain, the moon and the sun. Finally they agree to simply take turns jumping over each other, "all through the tulips and the daffodils and the pretty little violets." This is ideal for preschoolers, who often celebrate each season with unbridled joy.

A review of "It's Spring!," in Publishers Weekly, *Vol. 235, No. 12, March 24, 1989, p. 68.*

Percy and the Five Houses (1989)

Ferd the fox would seem to be a predictable conniver as he persuades young Percy, a beaver, to part with his newly found lump of gold. Not so. In return for the gold, Ferd enrolls Percy in the House of the Month Club, entitling him to " 'an August house, a September house, an October house, a November house, and a December house.' " Else Minarik still makes as felicitous a text as one could imagine from strings of short simple sentences. James Stevenson's small sketches softly washed with watercolor are likewise in modest proportions. The words and illustrations work harmoniously, the text supplying the essential actions of the plot and dialogue, while the pictures accompany and interpret the printed segments on each page. One might expect that gullible Percy has been duped, but his houses are all delivered on schedule. Unfortunately each does not last long, but all are enjoyed. First there is a cardboard house and then "a real cardboard castle," "a beautiful Indian teepee all made of crepe paper," and in November "a dear little camper." When the December selection turns out to be an igloo, the mother beaver has had enough. She reminds Percy of the advantages of his own house and summons him and his companionable grandpa home for the winter. Ferd the fox cheerfully loads the igloo in his truck to head for a North Pole vacation, and Percy is last seen in the family circle of the beaver lodge, " 'the best house for beavers.' " The ritual of Percy's membership card, the monthly arrival of his houses, and the homey moral make a very satisfying package for preschoolers as both bedtime reading and story hour fare.

Margaret A. Bush, in a review of "Percy and the Five Houses," in The Horn Book Magazine, *Vol. LXV, No. 3, May-June, 1989, p. 361.*

There is charm in the variety of the houses: a paper Victorian cottage, complete with tabs for folding and assembling; a cardboard castle; a crepe paper teepee; a frozen igloo; a tiny trailer, just the size for mice; and dearest of all, the cozy beaver dam. However, the story itself is somewhat flat. Readers accustomed to the quirky humor of Stevenson's watercolors may be disappointed with Minarik's subdued text. The book, written for beginning readers, has straightforward, declarative sentences; large print; and a simple-to-follow story line. While not suited to children who are just learning to read, it may serve as an alternative to the standard easy reader choices for first and second graders.

Gail C. Ross, in a review of "Percy and the Five Houses," in School Library Journal, *Vol. 35, No. 11, July, 1989, p. 73.*

As a child, I grew up on Else Holmelund Minarik's classic "Little Bear" books for beginning readers. As a teacher, I have shared all her books with my young students. Her direct yet gentle language can inject interest into even the most ordinary of Little Bear's adventures, which were illustrated by Maurice Sendak over 30 years ago. I was pleased to find some of these qualities in *Percy and the Five Houses.*

Also satisfying are the cheery and welcoming drawings by the children's book illustrator and New Yorker artist James Stevenson. All his scenes, even December's snow and ice, give off a small warmth. His illustrations are light and delicate, befitting the flimsy structure of some of the houses. Children might well fear that these structures will fall down if they accidentally blow too hard upon the page. And Mr. Stevenson's Percy and Grandpa—one in husky-sized purple swim trunks and the other in striped tank top, hat and spectacles—make a cozy and heartwarming pair.

Yet the book disappoints. The opening scene is engaging. Is this fox up to no good? What's going to happen to Percy? The drama is ready to unfold. But the story does not gain much dramatic steam. From tepees to castles, the array of houses is tantalizing, but they appear and disappear without generating much reaction from Percy.

How well does Percy learn the time-honored lesson that there's no place like home? Ferd delivers the goods, and on time, yet all prove unsuitable. But if Ferd were more clearly either a conniving fox or an honest salesman, or if Percy had a strong case of wanderlust, the moral would pack more of a punch. To really absorb the lesson, children must be allowed to stumble and fall and learn right along with Percy that home is where the heart is.

> *Daniel Meier, in a review of "Percy and the Five Houses," in* The New York Times Book Review, *March 25, 1990, p. 29.*

The Little Girl and the Dragon　(1991)

[*The Little Girl and the Dragon*] is a very simple story for very young readers. In it, a dragon escapes from his book and proceeds to swallow all the little girl's precious objects: her minicomputer, her best game, her cash register and her stuffed dog. But the little girl demands her possessions back, and when the dragon asks her what will happen if he doesn't return them, she says she will sit on his book, and he will never be allowed back in. Frightened, the dragon capitulates. "And then the little girl let him back in the book—where he belonged."

I should point out here that this description is almost as long as the book itself, and I am, of course, safely beyond my first childhood, but I think I would have been unhappy with a book that packed a dragon back *where he belonged.* It is as if the author is saying the imagination is very nice, but it can be, like the dragon, unruly and dangerous, so let's not let it loose for too long a time. Among the many uses of enchantment, one of them is probably *not* the reinforcement of reality testing—at least not in the text itself.

> *Susan Fromberg Schaeffer, "There's No Escaping Them," in* The New York Times Book Review, *November 10, 1991, p. 53.*

Shimmering colored-pencil illustrations [by Martine Gourbault] amusingly depict a large greedy, green dragon

and a strong-willed blond child, but the slight story has little in the way of plot development or resolution. Simple as it is, there's something empowering about the child's stubbornness in standing up for her rights, and young readers will appreciate her independent triumph over the bullying monster.

> *Anna DeWind, in a review of "The Little Girl and the Dragon," in* School Library Journal, *Vol. 37, No. 12, December, 1991, p. 97.*

Am I Beautiful?　(1992)

The author of **Little Bear** here introduces another endearing character: a young hippo who decides to "have a nice little walkabout" while his mother wallows in the mud one hot day. He encounters a mother lion nuzzling her cubs; a father heron teaching his fledglings to dance; and a human mother playing with her baby. Since the parents tell their wee ones how beautiful they are, the hippo does his best to imitate each group of offspring in turn, asking if he, too, is beautiful. Of course no one can answer the question—until his own mother assures him that he is "the most beautiful of all, since you are mine!" [Yossi] Abolafia's (*Fox Tale; A Fish for Mrs. Gardenia*) sprightly watercolors deftly portray the affectionate relationships between these creatures and their young, reinforcing Minarik's effective variation on a theme no child can hear often enough: unconditional parental love.

> *A review of "Am I Beautiful?" in* Publishers Weekly, *Vol. 239, Nos. 32-3, July 20-1, 1992, p. 247.*

Though the lessons are obvious, they're gently made in this well-honed, repetitive tale. Abolafia's cheerfully ingenuous characters, deftly drawn in a cartoony style and colored, more subtly, in watercolor, make a perfect accompaniment. An engaging variant on a familiar theme; just right for sharing. . . .

> *A review of "Am I Beautiful?" in* Kirkus Reviews, *Vol. LX, No. 15, August 1, 1992, p. 992.*

Although there's nothing extraordinary about the story, it is pleasantly told, and the watercolor pen drawings have a sprightly air that enlivens the text. Young children will certainly identify with the hippo's need for reassurance, and this gives the book some added depth.

> *Ilene Cooper, in a review of "Am I Beautiful?" in* Booklist, *Vol. 89, No. 1, September 1, 1992, p. 68.*

Alan E(dward) Nourse

1928-1992

American author of nonfiction, fiction, and short stories.

Major works include *Star Surgeon* (1960), *Rx for Tomorrow: Tales of Science Fiction* (1971). *The Giant Planets* (1974), *Birth Control* (1986), *Sexually Transmitted Diseases* (1992).

INTRODUCTION

Best known for creating accessible informational books on astronomy and medical subjects for readers in the middle grades through high school, Nourse is also a respected author of science fiction for young adults that reflects his fascination with both medicine and the stars. A physician by training, he is praised for writing his nonfiction with the authority of a scientist and is considered among the most distinguished writers for young people on astronomy. Several of Nourse's books have been called unique for the distinctiveness of their coverage: both his fiction and nonfiction are commended for their concentration on relevant issues, authentic handling of medical details, and clear writing style. Nourse began his literary career by creating science fiction that typically features the adventures of young male protagonists who bravely encounter danger, alien beings, and futuristic technology while facing human obstacles such as prejudice. In his fiction, Nourse incorporates data as well as futuristic extrapolations based on current scientific knowledge into what are considered compelling, suspenseful, and imaginative narratives that offer fascinating visions of medicine and science in the world of the future. Characterized by humor and fast-moving plots, the stories also address such themes as the effects of eternal youth, the restrictions placed on personal freedom by society, and, especially, the future role of medicine. Nourse's pointed observations are noted for reflecting his deep concern for his subjects and cause his work to be considered thought-provoking for young people. Don D'Amassa writes that Nourse "remains one of the most noted names in the field of science fiction," while Sara Oswald adds that his "accurate and often imaginative use of medical details distinguishes his work from much other science fiction for adolescents." Nourse's more recent works, consisting mainly of career books and concept books generally in the areas of science and medicine, are praised as lucid, informative, and socially relevant. While his career books offer both historical and practical information for teenagers who are thinking about a future profession, Nourse's nonfiction addresses such sensitive—and crucial—issues as birth control, sexuality, disease, and emotional life. Nourse is often commended for the balanced and nonjudgmental approach of his books and for using comprehensible language to explain scientific principles and terms.

Born in Des Moines, Iowa, Nourse interrupted his studies as a premedical student to serve in World War II. His first science fiction stories began to appear in periodicals in

1951, the year that he received his B.S. Nourse published his first books while in medical school at the University of Pennsylvania. After interning, an experience that became the subject of his adult autobiography *Intern* (1955), he moved to Washington and devoted two years to writing before becoming a general practitioner. In 1964, Nourse left active medical practice to become a full-time writer. One of his most acclaimed early works is the young adult novel *Star Surgeon,* which describes the struggle of a young alien physician—the first nonhuman to be employed with Hospital Earth, the clinic of the galaxy—to gain the approval of his prejudiced human colleagues. Dal, who tells the story, surmounts discrimination when he diagnoses a virus that threatens a little-known planet. Acknowledged for addressing a controversial topic for its time, *Star Surgeon,* according to H. H. Holmes, "combines the attractions of the medical career novel, the exciting adventure tale, and the genuine article in scientific extrapolation, with a fascinating picture of the future of organized medicine and the puzzles of planet-hopping General Practice." Also dealing with otherness and alienation is *The Universe Between* (1965), a novel that explores the psychological conflicts and tensions of the future. The story describes the world of 2017, a time in which Earth is faced with the problem of limited natural resources.

When a transmitter machine is found to be taking material from a parallel four-dimensional universe, seventeen-year-old Robert Benedict becomes the liaison between Earth and the Thresholders; Alan Madsen comments, "Nourse does a commendable job of delineating the emotional turmoil of a boy facing a psychological crisis." In 1974, Nourse began to concentrate exclusively on his informational books. Focusing on topics he feels are most important to contemporary young adults, he often collaborates with specialists in their respective fields. Nourse is the author of books on professions such as doctor, scientist, and engineer as well as on such subjects as asteroids and the planets, but he is perhaps best known for his books about sexuality and the human body. His approach to such topics as birth control and sexually transmitted diseases is considered unique: for example, he presents a medical view of AIDS and shows how a blood bank screens for the virus, discusses the rhythm method and how to determine the time of ovulation, and, acknowledging that teenagers are sexual people, describes the correct use of the condom. Nourse is also the creator of guides to birth control, safe sex, AIDS and teen survival, works for younger teenagers written to provide information about their bodies and to outline the range of choices available to them; utilizing much of Nourse's material from his books for young adults, the works also feature a number of photos and diagrams. In addition to his works for young people, Nourse is a celebrated author of science fiction and nonfiction for adults that reflects his first-hand experience in the world of medicine; he also contributed award-winning articles to medical journals and essays to popular periodicals. A past president of Science Writers of America, Nourse has won child-selected awards as well as the Washington State Governor's Award in 1966 and 1974.

(See also *Something about the Author,* Vol. 48; *Contemporary Authors New Revision Series,* Vols. 3, 21; *Contemporary Authors,* Vols. 1-4, rev. ed.; and *Dictionary of Literary Biography,* Vol. 8.)

TITLE COMMENTARY

Trouble on Titan (1954)

Trouble on Titan, the first book-length story from a usually reliable magazine writer, seems to reflect some unnecessary writing down to the juvenile audience; surely Nourse would never employ such crudely overdrawn characterization in his adult stories—and writers like Longstreth, Keir Cross and Heinlein have shown that young readers enjoy a certain amount of recognizable complexity in people. But Nourse has a good story to tell, of the conflict between a bureaucratic Earth and the freedom-loving colonists on one of Saturn's moons and of how two likable boys one from Earth and one from the colony, made their stubborn elders reach a rational compromise. As a yarn, it's not bad—though the solution is awfully hard to believe.

> *Louis S. Bechtel, in a review of "Trouble on Titan," in* New York Herald Tribune Book Review, *May 23, 1954, p. 8.*

Tuck Benedict and his father become involved in an armed revolt on Titan while investigating disappearing supplies. Tuck befriends David Torm, son of Titan's leader, and between them they manage to capture the leader of the revolt. A common weakness in S-F youth titles is here, namely, that the teen-ager is too aware and the older people blind to what is going on. However, this is better than others and has good father-son relationships.

> *Learned T. Bulman, in a review of "Trouble on Titan," in* Library Journal, *Vol. 79, No. 11, June 1, 1954, p. 1065.*

Best of the three [books reviewed: *Rockets to Nowhere* by Philip St. John, *The Secret of Saturn's Rings* by Donald A. Wollheim, and **Trouble on Titan**] is Alan E. Nourse's tale of the relationship between a Terran boy and a youngster on Titan, one of Saturn's moons. . . . Mr. Nourse likes his characters. They possess an enviable warmth and vitality. It is a technique which the other writers in this series could well emulate.

> *Villiers Gerson, "In Outer Space," in* The New York Times Book Review, *August 8, 1954, p. 16.*

Junior Intern (1955)

How true it is to medicine I do not know; but since the author is currently interning in Seattle, I assume that it is factual in theory. These facts are telescoped, perhaps, into a shorter period of time than would make them the average experience of the average intern. Thus the book is crammed with every kind of excitement that several young medical students might conceivably run into, whether on hospital rounds, in the laboratory, or in a disaster field station. It's a spellbinder with a vocational message that is compelling.

> *Margaret Ford Kieran, in a review of "Junior Intern," in* The Atlantic Monthly, *Vol. 196, No. 6, December, 1955, p. 102.*

Ted loses a girl and finds a career during his summer as a junior intern in a city hospital, where he has taken a job to test his decision to become a doctor. Written by an intern, the book shows hospital practice, from bed-making to laboratory research, from delicate operations to the work at field stations during a devastating fire. Informational and interesting, it is a good addition to the career shelf. (pp. 39-40)

> *Ruth M. McEvoy, in a review of "Junior Intern," in* Junior Libraries, *Vol. 2, No. 5, January, 1956, pp. 39-40.*

Rocket to Limbo (1957)

Ad astra again—this time aboard the *SS Ganymede* with Lars Heldrigssen. Lars lives in the year 2008. Iceland was home to Lars, with flourishing wheat fields long since established by Lars' grandfather. His first star-run should only have lasted two months, for at embarkation the *Ganymede*'s goal was Vega III for a final check on a new colony site for men from over-crowded earth. But Lars had barely gotten his "spacelegs" when he began to suspect that Peter Brigham's presence on board presaged an entirely different destination—one that would involve Lars in attempted mutiny. This is no ordinary star-jump: author Nourse has conceived a really credible plot with three dimensional characters motivated by plausible reasoning. Furthermore, he has a most uncanny ability to visualize the strange sensations and settings of the world of the future. The season's best juvenile science fiction fabrication to date.

> *A review of "Rocket to Limbo," in* Virginia Kirkus' Service, *Vol. XXV, No. 16, August 15, 1957, p. 588.*

Smoothly written and excitingly told science fiction concerning the first space voyage of two new graduates of the Colonial Service Academy who find, first, mutiny and, finally, the long surmised alien intelligence existing through extra-sensory perception on an unknown planet. Plot and characterization develop according to a routine pattern well known to science fiction readers, but the story has pace, suspense, and conviction.

> *Dorothy Garey, in a review of "Rocket to Limbo," in* Junior Libraries, *Vol. 4, No. 4, December, 1957, p. 33.*

As in **Star Surgeon,** Alan Nourse leaps forward to the 24th century for this book, and tells an exciting story of the exploration of outer space. One of the problems of imaginative writing of any kind, whether it be of crime, detection, the West or space, is to find authors who can also rise to a reasonable literary standard. The word "literary" is used for all kinds of purpose today, but the fact is that Mr. Nourse can write and convincingly carries his reader along with him. It would be quite unfair to divulge any part of the plot, but reference must be made to the advanced state of E. S. P. (extra-sensory perception) which helps to make this such a fascinating story.

> *A review of "Rocket to Limbo," in* The Junior Bookshelf, *Vol. 28, No. 2, March, 1964, p. 94.*

[*The following excerpt is from a review of the edition published in 1986.*]

At the time of first publication in 1957, this novel probably offered something fresh and original for the young readers to whom it was aimed. Unfortunately **Rocket to Limbo** does not stand the test of time. The story is set in the year 2358 but (except for the high powered system called the Koenig drive, which blasts starships through time and space), the technology comes straight from the 1950's. Members of the all male crew watch films from an old style projector, thread their own reader tapes, and spend hours in the ship's laboratory testing and calibrating with nary a computer in sight; the ship's photographer must keep his eye to the viewfinder while his camera "grinds away." These anachronisms are jarring and detract from what would otherwise be an enjoyable adventure story.

The plotting is typical of Nourse, tight and fast moving. If someone had taken the time to modernize this novel it

could be recommended; however, as it is, the sophisticated young readers of today might find it laughable.

> *Patricia Altner, "Outdated Nourse," in* Fantasy Review, *Vol. 9, No. 11, December, 1986, p. 41.*

So You Want to Be a Doctor (1957)

Dr. Nourse, who recently became a doctor, makes the rounds of the years of preparation which face the high school or college graduate who has chosen this profession and points out the restrictions and responsibilities ahead, as well as the 9 years and $15,000 it will entail. The requirements of the courses taken in the premedical years and why they are important; admission to medical schools (only roughly a third of all applicants qualify); the four years of medical school—year by year—and basic program of instruction; internship. This is summed up in practical, tangible terms—as against Dr. Alan Gregg's more philosophic guidance in *For Future Doctors.* The market is as sharply defined as the intentions.

> *A review of "So You Want to Be a Doctor," in* Virginia Kirkus' Service, *Vol. XXV, No. 19, October 1, 1957, p. 760.*

So You Want to Be a Lawyer (with William B. Nourse, 1958)

This is an explanation of what the law is, what a lawyer does, addressed particularly to students considering the law as a profession. The authors discuss: pre-law education, stressing the importance of a general, liberal undergraduate background; the courses given each year in law school; the case work method; legal research and writing; the bar examination; the gaps between textbook theory and actual practice; special problems in early practice; the several professional opportunities and directions within the profession; the advantages of a legal education for non-lawyers. A useful manual.

> *A review of "So You Want to Be a Lawyer," in* Virginia Kirkus' Service, *Vol. XXVI, No. 21, November 1, 1958, p. 839.*

Scavengers in Space (1959)

The threat of over-population is one which has alarmed even the most ardent realists. In this fantasy, projected many years into the future, earth, having become over-populated, has already expanded to other planets. And it is on Mars, a base from which man conducts his interplanetary mining expeditions, that earth's hope for expansion are nearly defeated. Into the battle for living-space come Greg and Tom, the twin sons of a famous scientist-prospector, who rescue their father's discovery of a vehicle to the stars from the hands of unscrupulous opportunists. A well conceived, if rather bleakly mechanical, universe is provided here for those who like their who-dun-its colored by astral rays and reflections from outer space.

> *A review of "Scavengers in Space," in* Virginia

Kirkus' Service, *Vol. XXVII, No. 2, January 15, 1959, p. 43.*

Most of the spacemen in Alan Nourse's latest piece of science-fiction prefer to use the term "miners" when referring to themselves, instead of the less attractive word used in the title. Although based on Mars, they have individual space ships in which they can cruise through the asteroid belt, landing on the burned-out fragments of rock in orbit there and prospecting for rare metals. The story concerns twin brothers who try to find the rich claim they are sure their father had found before he met with a mysterious accident. Well-sustained suspense and swiftly paced action combine to make this a fine adventure novel, but its best feature is the ease with which the author moves around in the world of the future, describing potential scientific marvels as vividly as if they were already here.

> *Marion West Stoer, "Almost Adults," in* The Christian Science Monitor, *May 14, 1959, p. 13.*

Mr. Nourse is already a successful member of the Faber S.F. team but he has not taken himself for granted in composing the background of this story of space criminals. The idea that the time will come when men will prospect for minerals in space—and even "scavenge" them from the débris of the Asteroid Belt—is a very good one. That Tom and Greg Hunter's prospecting father should be killed because a monopolistic organisation seeks the secret of his latest "strike" seems slightly old-fashioned, but the efforts of his sons to recover his secret and defeat the Jupiter Equilateral Mining Combine, which bids fair to become a threat to the authority of the U.N., lead them into tense situations which remind one, though more convincing, of Bond's adventures in the toils of *Dr. No*. The technical embellishments of the story reinforce its sound plot, however much one may boggle at the idea of a human being journeying through space while clinging to the *outside* of a space-craft.

> *A review of "Scavengers in Space," in* The Junior Bookshelf, *Vol. 28, No. 6, December, 1964, p. 385.*

So You Want to Be a Scientist   (1960)

The author of **So You Want to be a Doctor** and **So You Want to be a Lawyer** here describes the work of a scientist, emphasizing pure rather than applied science. He discusses personal and educational qualifications for research scientist. Three areas of work are considered: academic careers, government service, and industry. Since information regarding both jobs and training is general rather than specific, books with more detailed and practical information, such as those by Pollack, will be needed to supplement it. In his attempt to describe the attitude of mind of a scientist and the nature of his work, the author is often wordy and repetitious, but he does convey a sense of the distinctive character of scientific research. Good general introduction to the science field. Recommended.

> *Dorothy Schumacher, in a review of "So You*

Want to Be a Scientist," in Junior Libraries, *Vol. 6, No. 6, February, 1960, p. 58.*

[This] is a good informal introduction to careers in science. Stressing pure rather than applied science, the writer first pictures the kind of person a scientist is, explores the nature and scope of science itself, and outlines the general education required for various levels of scientific work. He then takes up the major fields of science, discussing the qualifications, special training, vocational opportunities, and rewards of each, and indicates some of the challenging scientific frontiers of the future.

> *A review of "So You Want to Be a Scientist," in* The Booklist and Subscription Books Bulletin, *Vol. 56, No. 15, April 1, 1960, p. 484.*

Star Surgeon   (1960)

Dal Timgar, not of this earth, not even of this galaxy, has wanted all his life to be a doctor. But his ambition places in jeopardy the right of the earth members of the Galactic Confederation to stay within the organization since membership is allowed only to the productive, and it is only in the field of medical society that humans excel. If Dal can be used as a test case proving that other galaxies are equally capable in medicine, the earth may well be ousted. Dal's struggle to win the status of a surgeon involves much imaginative manipulation of medical and astronomical detail in a story which is suspenseful from start to finish.

> *A review of "Star Surgeon," in* Virginia Kirkus' Service, *Vol. XXVIII, No. 13, July 1, 1960, p. 507.*

The really satisfying books of teen-age science fiction come from the regular creators of adult s. f. and not (with the sole exception of Andre Norton) from specialists in writing for the young. Youthful s. f. addicts do, apparently, like a hero near their own age; but otherwise they want fiction that meets the standards of the better adult s. f. magazines (which they also read)—and that's just what Alan E. Nourse gives them in **Star Surgeon.**

There's been far too little medical s. f. written for young or old; but Nourse, himself a physician in active practice, does much to remedy that defect. In this story of the deep-space probation of the first M.D. who is not an Earthman, in a future in which Earth is the hospital and clinic of the Galaxy, he combines the attractions of the medical career novel, the exciting adventure tale, and the genuine article in science fictional extrapolation, with a fascinating picture of the future of organized medicine and the puzzles of planet-hopping General Practice.

> *H.H. Holmer, in a review of "Star Surgeon," in* Books, New York, *May 14, 1961, p. 26.*

The important theme of racial tolerance is freshly illuminated in an exciting and ingenious story about Dal Timgar, from the planet Garv, a be-furred person sufficiently like earth men to be able to work with them, but different enough to suffer persecution as he serves a probationary period in a hospital ship cruising in space from medically-expert Earth. A closely argued prediction of the world of

2375 with a severe application to the world as we know it; also, most important, a well-written story.

Margery Fisher, in a review of "Star Surgeon," in Growing Point, *Vol. 1, No. 5, November, 1962, p. 79.*

Mr. Nourse's novel of space activity envisages an international or intergalactic health service of some one hundred years ahead. There are the usual space travel trimmings and technicalities, handled well enough, and one or two ingenious medical problems posed and solved. In fact the suspense attending on the latter is effective and novel in the best sense. A further element which affords tension and expectation is posed as a racial problem of the future. One of the doctors who makes up the team of medicos on whose tours of duty the story turns is a "native" of another planet; he looks different and feels different from an earthman and the differences are resented to the point of prejudice even by a powerful official of the medical service. Dal Tingmar has, therefore, to prove himself as a "man" as well as a doctor and does so, thank goodness, in a good old-fashioned dramatic way. Thus there is a strong thread of personal as well as material conflict running through the story.

A review of "Star Surgeon," in The Junior Bookshelf, *Vol. 26, No. 5, November, 1962, p. 274.*

Tiger by the Tail: And Other Science Fiction Stories (1961)

With space legs well oiled and antennae vibrating, prepare for another breathless journey into the world of science fiction, transported deluxe via Alan Nourse's stories gathered from the pages of the leading science fiction magazines. Here we encounter an aluminum-thirsty pocketbook with a strange universe attached, a remarkable cure for the common cold, frightening invasions of earth, a starship pilot-to-be and a full range of additional fabricated intrigue to make an escape from reality utterly delicious within the safety of paper pages.

A review of "Tiger by the Tail," in Kirkus Reviews, *Vol. XXIX, No. 3, February 1, 1961, p. 110.*

A collection of Nourse's shorter stories . . . , all from adult magazines, is nicely calculated to attract the younger reader. These are ingenious but relatively simple and often humorous tales, attractive to the reader without a postgraduate background in s. f. The stimulating **"Family Resemblance,"** in particular, should set bright young minds really worrying about the origin of man.

H. H. Holmes, in a review of "Tiger by the Tail," in Books, *New York, May 14, 1961, p. 26.*

A highly readable group of short stories, reprinted from science fiction magazines, on subjects ranging from an uncommon cure for the common cold to a liar's contest on another planet. Mr. Nourse is an imaginative craftsman, sometimes humorous and always thought-provoking, who

wastes no time in getting to the point. Almost invariably, that point is very sharp indeed. For examples, see **"PRoblem"** *(sic)* or **"Brightside Crossing."**

A review of "Tiger by the Tail," in The New York Times Book Review, *June 11, 1961, p. 34.*

Most of these stories play with a single idea; since the ideas are usually good and the stories short, there is little danger of shipwreck on complications. Mr. Nourse has a particular gift for inimical natural surroundings; here are two winners, **"Brightside Crossing"**, which recalls an exploration of Mercury that might daunt Sir Edmund Hillary, and **"The Native Soil"**, where prospectors for antibiotics in the universal mud of Venus are driven almost to death by the willing stupidity of the natives. The other fantasies are more lightweight. But the jokes come off and the title-story at least leaves one wondering uncomfortably what will happen two paragraphs after the end.

"Alien Worlds," in The Times Literary Supplement, *No. 3146, June 15, 1962, p. 449.*

So You Want to Be an Engineer (with James C. Webbert, 1962)

After explaining what engineering is and the kind of work done by a professional engineer the authors survey the major fields of engineering, discuss personal qualifications, and outline educational requirements. They then consider some of the problems involved in job hunting, the choice of field training, and professional accreditation and conclude with a look at the future of engineering. A useful career book, informally written and enlivened by case examples, for interested readers from junior high age up.

A review of "So You Want to Be an Engineer," in The Booklist and Subscription Books Bulletin, *Vol. 58, No. 20, June 15, 1962, p. 725.*

Raiders from the Rings (1962)

[This is a] story of total war between the inhabitants of Earth and a race of outlaws who have been banished to Outer Space and live a semi-nomadic Viking life between the planets and asteroids. Because of radiation-mutation these Spacers are incapable of breeding females, and so are compelled to make intermittent raids on Earth to snatch their mates. In the course of one of these raids a Terran male is inadvertently included in the bag, and it is his eventual conversion to the Spacer ethic which predetermines the somewhat mystical ending of the age-long war. Mr. Nourse manages to pack into his scientific framework some quite advanced genetics, alongside the original elves, the song of the sirens, and some naval battles in space which sound like something from the Odyssey. But all is here to elevate and instruct.

"Hi Sci Fi," in The Times Literary Supplement, *No. 3320, October 14, 1965, p. 925.*

Mr. Nourse is now nearly a veteran member of an exceptional team of space fiction writers and shows no sign of flagging. **Raiders from the Rings** has several good ideas about the possible effects of space colonisation as well as a plot well nourished with suspense. The "Dr. Who" series has possibly tended to make people believe that almost anything is possible but Mr. Nourse is if anything more convincing, though to demonstrate it would be to give the game away. One thing is worth mentioning, and that is the author's contention that the suspicion which promotes the continuing enmity between earthmen and "spacers" is largely the result of ignorance and myth—as is much of the suspicion between peoples in the real world of today. The other is that perhaps it is high time science fiction writers in general caught up with the technological revolution in the formation and shaping of materials which is well on its way and applied it more thoroughly to the details of their fantasy worlds and peoples instead of relying on vague indications of how things are driven, manufactured or repaired in the outer worlds. Mr. Nourse is good on relationships between beings; he could polish up on this.

> *A review of "Raiders from the Rings," in* The Junior Bookshelf, *Vol. 29, No. 6, December, 1965, p. 380.*

The Counterfeit Man: More Science Fiction Stories (1963)

The favorite theme in this collection of SF short stories is the mind invaded or controlled by a superforce emanating from either unknown galaxies or earthbound science/psychology cabals. The conceptions are not new and the presentation is by way of hackney rather than rocket-swift writing. They take a less than optimistic view of the future average man's general capabilities and chances of resistance to mental assault.

> *A review of "The Counterfeit Man: More Science Fiction Stories," in* Virginia Kirkus' Service, *Vol. XXXI, No. 11, June 1, 1963, p. 521.*

A collection of science fiction short stories, all but one of the fourteen having been previously published. The writing is better than average science fiction, and the collection should be useful, since most of the material was originally printed in magazines. The one new tale, **"Circus,"** is a variant on the non-human on our planet; the visitor, desperate because nobody believes that he comes from another planet, goes to a science fiction writer—a story with a poignant note and a neat ending.

> *Zena Sutherland, in a review of "The Counterfeit Man," in* Bulletin of the Center for Children's Books, *Vol. XVII, No. 6, February, 1964, p. 99.*

So You Want to Be a Chemist (with James C. Webbert, 1964)

As the title suggests, this is an invitation to young people to explore the possibilities of chemistry as a career. Not only does it give a succinct account of what the founders of chemistry, for example, Priestley, Cavendish, and La-

voisier did, but it succeeds in imparting a glimpse of what a career in chemistry consists of. More up to date than Pollack's *Careers and Opportunities in Chemistry* (Dutton, 1960) and Batista's *The Challenge of Chemistry* (Holt, 1959), the distinction of this book lies in its emphasis on what becoming a chemist involves, the decisions that must be made in high school and college in order to prepare for a career in this field.

> *Thomas B. Grave, in a review of "So You Want to Be a Chemist," in* School Library Journal, *Vol. 11, No. 3, November, 1964, p. 77.*

The Body (1964)

The subject of this volume is one of abiding interest, and the way in which it is here treated should prove popular. The book is cast as a series of eight picture essays, on changing views of the body, general anatomy, bone and muscle, blood circulation, the digestive system, lungs and kidney, nerves and sense organs, and hormones. The writing is journalistic, and the illustrations are superb. Old prints and documents show the changing concepts of the body during the ages, vivid photographs enliven the dry bones of the skeleton by comparisons with engineering structures, and a whole variety of plain and coloured pictures and diagrams bring out special aspects of the body. The overall feeling engendered is one of reverence; the range of individual variations is emphasized; illustrations of some medical techniques stop the book from falling into sentimentality. It is not a comprehensive textbook, but the extensive index gives it reference value. A readership range from teenage to dotage may be anticipated.

> *H. M. Thomas, in a review of "The Body," in* The School Librarian and School Library Review, *Vol. 14, No. 2, July, 1966, p. 211.*

The Universe Between (1965)

One of the most interesting books in this year's crop of juvenile science fiction . . . The sensitive had better read the first two or three pages with their eyes shut, but after that all is well. This book is genuine science fiction. It has a youthful hero and heroine and plenty of quick colorful action; but always at the center of the stage is the scientific concept on which the book is built, that of other and multi-dimensional worlds making contact with our three-dimensional world.

> *Peter J. Henniker-Heaton, "Dreams about Tomorrow's Facts," in* The Christian Science Monitor, *November 4, 1965, p. B8.*

On an Earth desperate for natural resources, Dr. Hank Merry's transmatter machine wrenches material through a parallel four-dimensional universe forcing the Threshold inhabitants to retaliate. Seventeen-year-old Robert Benedict, trained from birth to familiarity with both worlds, must make contact with the Thresholders if Earth is to survive. Highly imaginative, above average science-fiction which deals with the relativity of space and time and explores the problems in developing understanding between two alien cultures. Based on two short stories originally published in *Astounding Science Fiction.*

A review of "The Universe Between," in The Booklist and Subscription Books Bulletin, *Vol. 62, No. 7, December 1, 1965, p. 358.*

Alan Nourse's **The Universe Between** tries to make dramatically meaningful a theoretical concept that has intrigued physicists since Descartes: the concept of a fourth linear dimension. In the novel, Earthmen of 2017 are faced with the problem of a dwindling supply of natural resources. Dr. Hank Merry reopens a project of building a device to transmit matter from one planet to another. As early as the 1960s, Dr. John McEvoy had experimented with a similar project but had abandoned it when only Ruth Benedict had survived the psychological shock of peering into "the universe between"—the fourth linear dimension existing parallel and contiguous with the known universe. In 2017, Robert Benedict, who has been raised in both his own universe and the Thresholder's universe of the fourth dimension, discovers that Merry's crudely constructed "transmatter" wreaks havoc with the Thresholder's four-dimensional world. Together with Sharnan, a girl from the parallel universe, Robert finds a solution which will permit the universes to co-exist without the destruction of either.

As often happens in science fiction, Nourse necessarily falsifies when he tries to render in terms of concrete experience what may be intelligible at the moment only in mathematical terms. Yet this fact does not vitiate an exciting and thought-provoking story. Nourse does a commendable job of delineating the emotional turmoil of a boy facing a psychological crisis.

Alan Madsen, "In the Future Tense," in Book Week—New York Herald Tribune, *February 27, 1966, p. 10.*

So You Want to Be a Surgeon   (1966)

The author gives a brief history of surgery, an idea of its broad scope today, a general surgeon's "typical day," and information about surgical training (including college, medical school, internship, and residency). Surgical specialties are only briefly mentioned. If sample patients and procedures had been used more in the chapters on medical school and hospital training, these would have seemed less dry. The style is often wordy and repetitive. Subjective generalizations also mar the book's value (e.g. "For most students pathology is the most fascinating course of all in the four years of medical school."). This book probably will be of very limited use. General books on becoming a doctor are already available and by the time a medical student needs information on surgical training, he can get it from those in the medical world around him. High school youth interested in surgery would probably find something like Sarah Riedman's *Masters of the Scalpel* (Rand, 1962) much more interesting. (pp. 204, 206)

Isadora Kunitz, in a review of "So You Want to Be a Surgeon," in School Library Journal, *Vol. 13, No. 1, September, 1966, pp. 204, 206.*

Similar to the author's **So You Want to be a Doctor,** this addition to the publisher's series of career books briefly recounts the history of surgery, surveys the work of surgical interns and surgical residents, mentions some of the specialities, and summarizes the necessary education and training. Although the good index improves the book's usefulness, it should have included a list of selected readings that would afford additional background.

A review of "So You Want to Be a Surgeon," in Science Books: A Quarterly Review, *Vol. 2, No. 3, December, 1966, p. 216.*

Psi High and Others   (1967)

While "The Watchers" from the Galactic Confederation patiently await the verdict—freedom or "Quarantine" for earth, they review man's reaction to three past crises. In **"The Martyr"** we have a portrait of a civilization on the brink of immortality through the discovery of a rejuvenation process. The story moves beautifully toward its climax as the Senator who has been pushing a universal rejuvenation program slowly discovers that the cost is psychological suicide—man loses that drive that has brought him so close to the stars. In **"Psi High"** high Psis have become social pariahs, stigmatized and controlled until an enemy alien telepath arrives. Don't anticipate . . . this one has a real Hitchcockian twist. Finally **"Mirror Mirror"** shows humanity engaged in an unusual war with an elusive enemy. The solution lies in reflection . . . and in a very human weakness. Intelligent postulates; skillful storytelling which challenges, entertains.

A review of "Psi High and Others," in Kirkus Service, *Vol. XXXV, No. 3, February 1, 1967, p. 144.*

One of America's most outstanding writers of science fiction presents three short stories within this one volume— **"Psi High," "The Martyr,"** and **"Mirror, Mirror."** The stories represent a two-century span during which "watchers" from outer space observed the intelligent creatures of the planet Earth who were ready to break the shackles that bound them to the planet and to leap into outer space. There is more truth than fiction in these stories. Highly recommended.

Sister Regina Richter, in a review of "Psi High and Others," in Catholic Library World, *Vol. 39, No. 2, October, 1967, p. 171.*

The Mercy Men   (1968)

The "Mercy Men" are medical mercenaries . . . desperate, derelict human beings who have sold their brains to science in the hope that if they survive with some degree of sanity, they can return to the normal world with a fortune. But even the world outside the Hoffman Medical Center is becoming filled with a disproportionate number of neurotics. This, supposedly has little to do with young Jeff Meyer who has been obsessed for three years by a face and the knowledge that this stranger by the name of Paul Conroe, once, somehow, killed his father. Jeff, who suffers from a strange, painful blank space in his memory knows that there is a tie-up and is determined to catch the illusive Conroe and question him. But Conroe disappears again, this time into the guarded and secretive depths of the Medical Center and Jeff follows, pretending to be a candidate as a Mercy Man. It's all very ingenious and intricate suspense as Jeff slowly learns the truth about his father and his own, unsuspected nature. A real brain twister. (pp. 272-73)

> *A review of "The Mercy Men," in* Kirkus Service, *Vol. XXXVI, No. 5, March 1, 1968, pp. 272-73.*

The characterizations in this novel barely deserve the term, but they serve to keep the plot moving rapidly through a succession of twists in which Jeff learns that he—not Conroe,—is really the hunted, discovers the truth about his father and himself, and helps the scientists conquer the mental disease which has been attacking increasingly large segments of the population. It's all good science fiction fun by a knowledgeable, practiced hand. (p. 142)

> *Margaret A. Dorsey, in a review of "The Mercy Men," in* School Library Journal, *Vol. 14, No. 8, April, 1968, pp. 141-42.*

The Mercy Men is . . . [very] alarming potentially because the dangers in this story are mental rather than physical. In fact it is a book which could well belong to the 'thirties' as an indictment of Fascism. Frightening too is the author's Kafkaesque approach to his characters. All are anonymous, though some have names; enemies prove friends, friends enemies, without warning. Ostensibly this is the story of Jeff Meyer's attempts to catch Paul Conroe, whom he suspects of murdering his father. He can only catch him by following him into a Medical Centre where humans are used for brain research. In a terrifying progress through underground corridors full of masked figures Jeff slowly discovers that the danger is in himself, that a rogue chromosome is the key to the mystery and the threat to mankind. The author expresses his fear of mental collapse so strongly that it is difficult to believe his hero's last-minute escape from tragedy; I almost wish this book had been written still more forcefully. (pp. 1395-96)

> *Margery Fisher, in a review of "The Mercy Men," in* Growing Point, *Vol. 8, No. 4, October, 1969, pp. 1395-96.*

Rx for Tomorrow: Tales of Science Fiction, Fantasy, and Medicine (1971)

There are eleven unique prescriptions in this package. Dr. Nourse presents a medicine man from an alternate world where white witchery is the general practice who learns our medical techniques in exchange for his unusual method of practicing psychiatry. Then there's a real doctor's dilemma in a *Rosemary's Baby* short shocker; a man confronted with a new life in a new body in an old world that he can no longer adapt to; a tale of an unlucky transplant in which the recipient finds himself with a new ulcer; a sad comment on over-mechanization in medicine when an

aging physician finds himself forced to make **"The Last Housecall";** and a frolic of a diagnosis where a pompous physician is confronted with a man who has all the symptoms of pregnancy. Good for the whole family, especially young M.D.'s, whether taken in small doses or in one satisfying lump.

> *A review of "Rx for Tomorrow," in* Kirkus Reviews, *Vol. XXXIX, No. 7, April 1, 1971, p. 381.*

Space medicine is one of the challenges of science today, and in these tales Alan Nourse turns his imagination to situations and problems that may arise. While fantasy plays a part in some of these stories, most of them are quite within the realm of possibility: computerized diagnosis is, for example, already on the horizon. The style is tight, the stories have a variety of plot and mood, the theme of medicine in an advanced technological world of the future is intriguing, and—as all Nourse fans know—the technical and medical details are accurate.

> *Zena Sutherland, in a review of "Rx for Tomorrow: Tales of Science Fiction, Fantasy, and Medicine," in* Saturday Review, *Vol. LIV, No. 38, September 18, 1971, p. 49.*

Eleven stories, all of which have been previously published in science fiction magazines, are included in this collection. Most of the stories are concerned with the medical problems that may be created by scientific and technological progress in the future, and several have settings that will be familiar to readers of Nourse's novels. As in those novels, the greatest appeal is the capable and authoritative handling of the medical details; the plots are varied and the style competent, with the fantastic element used sparingly.

> *Zena Sutherland, in a review of "Rx for Tomorrow," in* Bulletin of the Center for Children's Books, *Vol. 25, No. 2, October, 1971, p. 29.*

Venus and Mercury (1972)

This book deals with the two planets closest to the sun, and it includes observations and speculations made by astronomers as to their orbital patterns, probable composition, and their future exploration. It touches on just about every aspect of concern to a student interested in what actual information we have ascertained about Venus and Mercury and debunks several old myths surrounding them. The book seems to have included the most recent findings on the subject, and it describes the space exploration program's probable plans in the forseeable future. The black-and-white photographs and diagrams are very clear and informational but uninspired and uninspiring. This is the general tone of the whole book. It is on a subject of definite interest to students and could be most serviceable in filling this need. It is well done, and the information is lucidly presented, but it is definitely not a book to warm anyone's heart.

> *Sonja M. Wieta, in a review of "Venus and*

Mercury," in Appraisal: Children's Science Books, Vol. 6, No. 2, Spring, 1973, p. 25.

Besides being rather repetitious in its descriptions of the solar system and particularly the two innermost planets, several things prevent this book from scoring higher [than a rating of "good"]. Apparently conflicting statements as to the number of "wandering stars" are made in figure captions and the text. Also the figures showing photos of a solar transit of Mercury are negatives while those a few pages later showing a transit of Venus are positives without comment and with no explanations. What the author means by saying that Mercury occupies "less than one-tenth the space the earth does" is not clear. On an area basis the earth is seven times bigger than Mercury; on a volume basis it is eighteen times bigger. It is stated that Venus comes as close to us as "only a thousand times more distant than our moon." The true figure of 100 times is more dramatic yet! The author can be excused, perhaps, of being unaware of our Pioneer probe on the way to Jupiter or that two of the Soviet Venera Spacecrafts did broadcast for a considerable time from the surface of Venus. In this reviewer's judgment, however, he is much too optimistic about future landings on Mercury and Venus, both of which are forbiddingly hot. Except for these flaws, the book is rather well done. It has a really good index that works! (pp. 25-6)

David G. Hoag, in a review of "Venus and Mercury," in Appraisal: Children's Science Books, *Vol. 6, No. 2, Spring, 1973, pp. 25-6.*

The Backyard Astronomer   (1973)

After a general discussion of astronomy and standard tips on observation, Nourse devotes separate chapters to unaided eye observation, binocular observation, and telescopes. The section on viewing the moon with binoculars is especially good, but the star maps are below par. The treatment of telescopes is concerned more with the instruments, themselves than with objects to be viewed. A short but good list of additional reading is included along with an excellent index. Overall, this is a better than average guide to star gazing, though it's not as detailed and attractive as Leslie Peltier's *Guideposts to the Stars: Exploring the Skies Through the Year* (Macmillan, 1972), R. Newton Mayall's *The Sky Observer's Guide* (Golden, pap. 1965), or Joseph M. Joseph and Sarah L. Lippincott's *Point to the Stars* (McGraw, rev. ed. 1972).

René Jordan, in a review of "The Backyard Astronomer," in School Library Journal, *Vol. 20, No. 4, December, 1973, p. 56.*

This is an excellent book for those who like to engage in "backyard astronomy" or the kind of astronomy which can be pursued with the naked eye or a good pair of binoculars. The illustrations are excellent and the text clear and interesting. Directions for location and identification of constellations are especially well done. The author does not attempt to review or cover modern astronomy. He sticks to the limitations imposed by his purpose but demonstrates how absorbing the subject can be for a good observer with little or no investment in auxiliary instruments.

A review of "The Backyard Astronomer," in Science Books: A Quarterly Review, *Vol. X, No. 1, May, 1974, p. 28.*

Aimed essentially at the beginner and very appropriately titled, this volume will be of little value to the advanced amateur or professional astronomer. It is intended for anyone, any age, interested in astronomy but with little or no experience in naked-eye observations of the moon, planets and stars, or in identifying the constellations and phenomena peculiar to them.

Chapter 1, the "Incredible Sky," is a familiar replay on the splendors of the sky as seen by the unaided eye: how to adapt our eyes for observing at night, and general information on the solar system and star patterns. Next, the author describes the northern constellations and touches on their mythology. Arrows on the sectional star maps point from constellation to constellation or star to star to aid in visualizing the sky. This system, sometimes employed by other authors, is certainly to be encouraged. The naked-eye sections conclude with solar and lunar eclipses, precautions against injuring one's eyes during solar eclipses, when to observe the planets, and descriptions of comets and meteors.

In Chapter 4, which is especially good, author Nourse describes the advantages and disadvantages of binocular observing. He illustrates (in four quadrants) the approximate appearance of the lunar surface in high-power binoculars and describes the overall physiography of the moon. Then he turns to binocular studies of the Milky Way, the constellations, and various kinds of stars and clusters.

Finally, "The Universe by Telescope" covers the use of refractors and reflectors. Here we learn how to construct simple altazimuth and equatorial mountings for each type, what eyepieces to employ, how to purchase a telescope, and what to look for in the heavens with it.

Nourse is up to date in his astronomy, and I have found few serious errors. He wrongly implies that totality at a solar eclipse can last from two to seven minutes, whereas totality may actually appear for only a brief instant (at an annular-total eclipse). Except for proving that the moon has no appreciable atmosphere, star occultations seem to this reviewer to deserve less attention than Nourse gives them. He cannot be forgiven for saying that the Andromeda galaxy will stand out in "exciting detail" using a modest amateur instrument. Actually, Messier 31 cannot be viewed in any real detail even with a 12-inch reflector—it looks like an elliptical blob of nebulosity.

Illustrations might have been included comparing the apparent sizes of the moon and planets as observed through telescopes of different apertures and magnifications. The star maps, with black stars on white paper, would be more impressive with white stars on a blue background. For the beginner, especially curious young people, there ought to be some color pictures of the planets and other celestial objects. There should also be a key chart showing where the constellations described in the sectional illustrations fit into the overall scheme of the sky.

I like Nourse's book. It is not written amateurishly, but neither is it sophisticated. It can be used as a junior high school text in astronomy, and it is ideal for boy and girl scouts and hobby clubs, as well as the teenager whose parents gave him a pair of binoculars or telescope for Christmas. (pp. 328-29)

> *William R. Benton, in a review of "The Backyard Astronomer," in* Sky and Telescope, *Vol. 47, No. 5, May, 1974, pp. 328-29.*

The Giant Planets (1974)

Although technically a "First Book", **The Giant Planets** is not for the young beginner. The text is clear and simply written, but the amount of material is so vast as to be assimilated only by the more advanced student. That I could understand what was being described attests to the excellence of the presentation, but even so I was overwhelmed by the amount of information. The author, one of our foremost writers on astronomy for young people, vividly portrays the enormous concepts of size and distance in the outer realms of the "Gas Giants" as compared to Earth. Also scientifically explored is the intriguing question of the possibility of life as we know it on these planets. Past historical theories are discussed and the future expectations of exploration are considered. I recommend this little book as valuable source material for all ages. (pp. 31-2)

> *Sallie Hope Erhard, in a review of "The Giant Planets," in* Appraisal: Children's Science Books, *Vol. 7, No. 3, Fall, 1974, pp. 31-2.*

This presentation of man's knowledge of the planets Jupiter, Saturn, Uranus, Neptune, and Pluto was carefully done by an author who thoroughly researched his facts and has a clear and interesting style of presenting them. It is difficult in these times to stay up to date in science. The book, although copyrighted in 1974, did miss including the results of the Pioneer 10 spacecraft passage by Jupiter in December, 1973. The photographs and diagrams are, for the most part, excellent, although in one diagram the arrow pointing to one of Saturn's rings gets lost in the darkness of printing ink. The index is complete and easy to use. This book is recommended.

> *David G. Hoag, in a review of "The Giant Planets," in* Appraisal: Children's Science Books, *Vol. 7, No. 3, Fall, 1974, p. 32.*

[*The following excerpt is from a review of the revised edition published in 1982.*]

Astronomy collections will be enhanced by this edition of Nourse's book. A brief astronomical orientation with historical highlights constitute the introduction. Concept words are printed in bold face type and also are in the glossary. Introductory chapters are based on widely available data. Nourse's significant contribution presented here is his competent interpretation of the findings from the *Pioneer* and *Voyager* missions. Noteworthy discoveries mentioned are Jupiter's previously unsighted ring and two ad-

ditional moons. Students will appreciate the beautiful color photographs that display the startling contrasts among four of Jupiter's moons. NASA's *Voyager* 1 also discovered seven more saturnian moons. *Voyager* 1 graphically demonstrated to astronomers that Saturn has not only three or four but possibly thousands of rings. Chapters on Uranus, Neptune, and Pluto are also well written but contain no updated information. I hope that the results of the anticipated Voyager visits to Uranus in 1986 and Neptune in 1989 will provide the basis for the next revision of this book.

> *Philip E. Rose, in a review of "The Giant Planets," in* Science Books & Films, *Vol. 18, No. 3, January-February, 1983, p. 145.*

The Bladerunner (1974)

Overpopulation and new, uncontrolled strains of disease—both by-products of the medical science of the 1900's—have become the major problems of this eastern megalopolis in the first quarter of the next century. A National Health Control enforces rigid eugenics laws, and it is illegal for doctors to treat people who have not had themselves sterilized, but many rebel, and an intricate, underground medical black market develops. Against this background of routine transplants, programmed robot surgery and systematic electronic eavesdropping, Alan Nourse weaves the tense, rapid-paced subterfuges of Doc, an old-time idealist, and his medical supplier, or "bladerunner," Billy Gimp—who cope with an epidemic and thus prove their indispensability when the National Health breaks down. It all turns out better than it has any right to, but Nourse skimps neither on physical confrontation nor on his detailed scenario of technological nightmare.

> *A review of "The Bladerunner," in* Kirkus Reviews, *Vol. XLII, No. 22, November 15, 1974, p. 1202.*

A novel about a future world in which medical services are obtainable only under government supervision (with compulsory sterilization the price for treatment on a long-term basis, robot-surgery, etc.) focuses on the illegal practices of the medical underground. . . . Nourse's medically-oriented science fiction always has adequate characterization, authoritative details (he is a physician) and competently constructed plots. Here, although the medical situation of an imagined 21st century is nicely conceived if biased, the book is weakened by many long passages of medical details. A sample sentence within such a passage: "In theory, by repetitive neuropantographic scan of the same surgeon doing the same kind of procedure multitudes of different times, the number of surgical eventualities that the computer could be programmed to face and act upon would be increased exponentially until, in the end, the risk that the computer might encounter a problem or complication it could not handle was reduced to the point of the negligible."

> *Zena Sutherland, in a review of "The Bladerunner," in* Bulletin of the Center for

Children's Books, *Vol. 28, No. 9, May, 1975, p. 152.*

The Asteroids   (1975)

Nourse predicts that scientists' new interest in asteroids will lead to the launching of space probes to study them at close range. He describes how asteroids were discovered, what is known about them, current theories of their origin, and the hope that asteroids will yield evidence about the origin of the solar system. Similar to the author's **The Great Planets** and **Venus and Mercury** this is an accurate and readable introductory book on astronomy.

> *Ovide V. Fortier, in a review of "The Asteroids," in* School Library Journal, *Vol. 21, No. 8, April, 1975, p. 56.*

The origins of asteroids still remain a mystery; Nourse describes the flurry of excitement that surrounded their discovery in the nineteenth century and notes the current rekindling of scientific interest in these minor planets. He clarifies popular misconceptions about the dangers presented by asteroid belts and reassures us that though a collision between earth and an asteroid is possible, the possibility is remote. Theories of origin and the potential of further space exploration to uncover new information about these bodies round out the straightforward account, and a few books for additional reading are listed. Illustrated with black-and-white drawings and diagrams.

> *A review of "The Asteroids," in* The Booklist, *Vol. 71, No. 19, June 1, 1975, p. 1015.*

Dr. Nourse has written an excellent, interesting book about a very specialized topic. Junior high students who hear about the asteroids when reading or hearing about space probes to Jupiter and Saturn will find out all they want to know about these little planets. A prior interest in astronomy might help the reader a little, but a new student to astronomy should have no trouble following this book. Dr. Nourse, a well-known author of science fiction and popular astronomy, has written an outstanding book with clear, interesting examples and analogies. This book makes clear the great open space between the asteroids, countering the cliché of the hazards of spacecraft crossing it. Students I tried it on had difficulty with the typeface. The "j's" and "q's" gave them a little trouble because of their unusual design, but this was by no means an insurmountable difficulty. Every middle and junior high library should have this book. (pp. 24-5)

> *Edmund R. Meskys, in a review of "The Asteroids," in* Appraisal: Children's Science Books, *Vol. 8, No. 3, Fall, 1975, p. 24-5.*

Viruses   (1976)

An informative introduction to viruses, touching upon history, identification, vaccines, and—very briefly—on research. Difficult terms are given parenthetically or italicized. A bibliography and very detailed index are included. Sound and suitable for middle graders not yet ready for more exhaustive books on the subject—Rosenberg and

Cooper's *Vaccines and Viruses* (Grosset, 1971), Stanley and Valens' *Viruses and the Nature of Life* (Dutton, 1961), and Thompson's *Virus Realm* (Lippincott, 1968).

> *Charles Rusiewski, in a review of "Viruses," in* School Library Journal, *Vol. 22, No. 8, April, 1976, p. 77.*

Nourse's new book is an informative delight, readable both by youngsters and adults who have some science background. Nourse ranges from the 18th century (Jenner's work with smallpox and Pasteur's with rabies) to present-day knowledge and research. In an introductory fashion, he discusses the discovery and study of viruses, viral diseases and their effect on humans, and the search for vaccines (including how immunity works, the antigen-antibody reaction and the uses of gamma globulin). Modern virus research is presented in a rational fashion, current ideas are discussed in the light of supporting evidence, and the author makes it clear that further research may alter or disprove present theories. There is a good index and an additional reading list, and the text is interspersed with photographs and excellent explanatory diagrams. This is a most recommendable book for the students interested in medical science.

> *Dorothy Bickerton, in a review of "Viruses," in* Science Books & Films, *Vol. XII, No. 3, December, 1976, p. 162.*

[*The following excerpts are from reviews of the revised edition published in 1983.*]

The mechanism of viruses and the history of viral disease and research are covered in this revision of Nourse's 1975 work. The text is basically the same, though sections on herpes and hepititis B have been added, along with a glossary. The bibliography has also been updated. Unfortunately, some useful diagrams of the first edition have been dropped. The writing is clear. Illustrations are black-and-white photographs of virologists and/or their prey. An adequate update for school and public library collections.

> *Symme J. Benoff, in a review of "Viruses," in* School Library Journal, *Vol. 29, No. 9, May, 1983, p. 75.*

What can you possibly cover in a scientific topic in 56 pages and in fewer than 13,000 words of text? Plenty, as Nourse proves. In clear prose, he introduces readers to Jenner's and Pasteur's discovery of vaccination. A short history that emphasizes the role of methodology in scientific progress brings us to the present use of vaccines and the reason for the difficulty in producing a universal flu vaccine. Patterns of viral infection, including portals of entry, symptoms, and treatment are discussed. The meaning and mechanism of immunity is simply, but thoroughly described. This is followed by a review of current virus research, including the functions of the nucleic acids and the relationship between viruses and cancer. The opening paragraphs of the book, which raised questions about Jenner's ethics, troubled me but these introduce readers to a general discussion of medical ethics. Aside from this and the use of "living virus" after an indication that "living" may not be applicable to viruses—both minor objections—this book provides an excellent introduction to the field. The glossary and index are highly useful. Several sixth graders found the book fascinating and not at all too difficult.

> *Fred Goodman, in a review of "Viruses," in* Science Books & Films, *Vol. 19, No. 2, November-December, 1983, p. 88.*

Lumps, Bumps, and Rashes: A Look at Kids' Diseases (1976)

Nourse does a fine job describing the symptoms and treatments of common childhood diseases. Explanations of the inoculation process and of the body's natural defense system are exceptionally clear. He also discusses the history of medicine, making readers aware of the importance of immunization. An excellent companion to the author's **Viruses,** this is well illustrated with drawings, cartoons, and photographs and includes a glossary and a comprehensive index.

> *Charles Rusiewski, in a review of "Lumps, Bumps, and Rashes: A Look at Kids' Diseases," in* School Library Journal, *Vol. 22, No. 9, May, 1976, p. 62.*

This medical book for young people overlaps and extends Nourse's **Viruses.** Here, he extends his coverage of all common childhood diseases and infections to include those caused by bacteria as well as viruses. He divides his material logically into the measles diseases, the strep and staph infections, virus diseases, and the preventable destroyers (pertussis, poliomyelitis, diphtheria, smallpox, tetanus). Then he covers vaccines and how they work and immunization programs. He describes the symptoms and treatment of each of these common childhood diseases and infections and lists basic immunization vaccines. Photographs, diagrams and cartoons are used effectively as an adjunct to the text. There is an excellent glossary and the book is indexed. It should find a wide readership among young people interested in medical science, and perhaps also among parents who are experiencing these lumps, bumps and rashes firsthand.

> *Dorothy Bickerton, in a review of "Lumps, Bumps, and Rashes: A Look at Kid's Diseases," in* Science Books & Films, *Vol. XII, No. 3, December, 1976, p. 162.*

[The following excerpts are from reviews of the revised edition published in 1990.]

This is a very basic book describing childhood diseases of viral and bacterial etiology including the most common symptoms, causes, treatments, and methods of prevention. Importantly, the use of vaccines and childhood immunization is stressed, with an immunization schedule (adapted from the Centers for Disease Control) presented on page fifty-four. Unfortunately, even though many childhood diseases are caused by viruses, no electronmicrographs of viruses are presented. Likewise, the micrograph of the streptococci is of poor quality, and those individuals unfamiliar with the subject may need the streptococci pointed out in the photograph. Further, as rotaviral infections and enteropathogenic bacterial infections are important agents of childhood diarrhea, these agents should be represented in a text of this nature. (pp. 40-1)

> *Richard M. Bauer, in a review of "Lumps, Bumps and Rashes," in* Appraisal: Science Books for Young People, *Vol. 24, No. 1, Winter, 1991, pp. 40-1.*

This is an attractive, serviceable book that has an oddly misleading title; it is not about skin diseases, but rather the range of common, communicable childhood illnesses. Nice layout and color photographs help make the subject of colds, strep, measles, and chicken pox more interesting than it might otherwise be. There is an explanation of the role of bacteria and viruses and historical information on illnesses that have been nearly eradicated by vaccinations. A table of contents, an index, and a glossary make this useful for report writers. Libraries that already have Melvin Berger's *Germs Make Me Sick* (Crowell, 1985), and Dorothy Hinshaw Patent's *Germs!* (Holiday House, 1983) will consider this a good supplemental purchase.

> *Suzanne S. Sullivan, in a review of "Lumps, Bumps and Rashes," in* Appraisal: Science Books for Young People, *Vol. 24, No. 1, Winter, 1991, p. 40.*

Although this book is written primarily, it seems, for those in grades six and lower, it would not hurt general adult audiences to read it. Mainly about immunization and the good it can do—although there are those who honestly disagree—the book (so like a *Golden Book* of yore) covers most of the illnesses a young boy or girl is subject to and what to do about them. The pictures are clear and useful, and the way the subject is presented should make the book easy to read—to oneself or, out loud, to others. The book should give children confidence and encouragement, as well as ease fears about the topic. There is a glossary at the end, but most of the words requiring understanding are explained or defined in the story itself. This book could help prevent a great deal of infections in a child's future, and that is its emphasis. In addition to the usual skin diseases, ear and upper respiratory infections are also covered, making the text fairly complete, as well as accurate. This is one of the best books of its kind.

> *Edward R. Pinckney, in a review of "Lumps, Bumps, and Rashes," in* Science Books & Films, *Vol. 27, No. 2, March, 1991, p. 52.*

A revision of an earlier book. It's essentially the same coverage of childhood diseases: chicken pox, mumps, measles, etc., with mention of whooping cough (or "whopping cough" in one index entry), diphtheria, and scarlet fever as more common in bygone days. The first edition briefly discussed smallpox vaccination; the new one asserts that smallpox has been eradicated. The cartoons and murky, black-and-white photographs have been replaced by full-color photographs. While it's a good primer on the subject, there is no key (or apparent logic) to the in-text use of italics and bold type. Some nonbolded terms get indexed, most do not; italicized terms may be picked up in the index, the glossary, both, or neither; and the same goes for bold-type words. A could-be useful addition is a list for further reading, but five of the eight titles are out of print.

George Gleason, in a review of "Lumps, Bumps, and Rashes," in School Library Journal, *Vol. 37, No. 7, July, 1991, p. 84.*

Clear Skin, Healthy Skin (1976)

This clear, sensible approach to . . . *Healthy Skin* offers simple, brief explanations of the causes of skin problems as well as methods of controlling them, including home and medical treatment. The diagrams are accurate when describing the structure of the skin but often are on the cute side when illustrating treatments and care; however, they do not distract from the otherwise fine, practical text. Not as technical as Sternberg's *More Than Skin Deep* (Doubleday, 1970) or Lubowe's *The Modern Guide to Skin Care and Beauty* (Dutton, 1973), Nourse's text will be read more easily and will give teenagers the reassurance they need about what is to them an extremely sensitive subject.

Ann Spindel, in a review of "Clear Skin, Healthy Skin," in School Library Journal, *Vol. 23, No. 3, November, 1976, p. 72.*

Alan Nourse returns from SF to describe understandingly, unpatronisingly and often hilariously acne and related problems, substituting for old-wives' tales medical explanations and information on home-and more drastic treatments. Ric Estrada's very funny drawings and diagrams further help to take the sting out of the subject.

M. Hobbs, in a review of "Clear Skin, Healthy Skin," in The Junior Bookshelf, *Vol. 42, No. 4, August, 1978, p. 208.*

Vitamins (1977)

There's nothing new in this straightforward explanation of the discovery, uses, and benefits of the 13 vitamins humans need. Historical background is given on the scientists who discovered vitamins A, B, and C, and the current controversy over the use of megavitamins is very briefly discussed. Faber's *The Miracle of Vitamins* (Putnam, 1964) is a more stimulating presentation of the same material, as is Asimov's simpler *How Did We Find Out About Vitamins?* (Walker, 1974). (pp. 116-17)

Shirley A. Smith, in a review of "Vitamins," in School Library Journal, *Vol. 24, No. 2, October, 1977, pp. 116-17.*

For older readers than the audience for the Malcolm Weiss or Hettie Jones books on the subject, this is serious and authoritative, yet written in a direct style. Nourse, a physician (probably best known to readers as a writer of science fiction), is objective about controversial topics such as the value of massive doses of vitamin C, his material is organized well, and he includes a brief list of books for further reading and an index. The text balances nicely such aspects as early research, the nature of vitamins, the causes and cures of dietary deficiencies, the various kinds of foodstuffs and the ways in which the human body uses them, and some sensible advice about use of vitamins. Diagrams are adequate; photographs—especially those paired

pictures of before-and-after patients—are dramatic. (pp. 64-5)

Zena Sutherland, in a review of "Vitamins," in Bulletin of the Center for Children's Books, *Vol. 31, No. 4, December, 1977, pp. 64-5.*

An experienced science writer who was once a practicing physician here presents a clear sketch of the vitamins. A reasonable if distant analogy is suggested for the work of enzymes and coenzymes, and there are some chemical formulas. All the vitamins of the Recommended Daily Allowance tables are discussed: their discovery, the results of deficiency, their various sources. In a very brief account we can read of the triumphant failure of the experiments of Christiaan Eijkman with sick chickens (his controls sickened too, since all of them were being fed on polished rice), of James Lind and the able seamen who daily got two oranges and a lemon (the lime juice came later, for economy) and no scurvy, and the rest of nutrition's heroes. We see their portraits and also a few clinical before-and-after pairs.

The most surprising story is that of the blood-clotting requisite, vitamin K. It is rare in foods, but adults get quite enough from the normal intestinal flora; made by our symbionts there, it enters directly through the gut. Newborns, all of whom have sterile intestinal tracts, tend to be bleeders, so that the vitamin is normally injected into the mother's or the infant's bloodstream just before or after birth. The massive-dose enthusiasm, particularly for vitamin C, is viewed conservatively by Dr. Nourse, but not dogmatically. The list of references is brief but excellent, and it includes Linus Pauling's contrariwise book on vitamin C and the common cold. This small work is an uncommonly straightforward and compact summary for readers in the middle grades.

Philip Morrison and Phyllis Morrison, in a review of "Vitamins," in Scientific American, *Vol. 237, No. 6, December, 1977, p. 32.*

The Tooth Book (1977)

George Washington, Ug the Caveman, and Rameses II appear here as toothache sufferers. Nourse's prose style is straightforward and clear; however, the text is sparsely illustrated, a lack felt particularly in the discussion of the characteristics of incisors, cuspids, and molars. The author concentrates on preventive care and the benefits of prompt treatment. His explanations of the processes involved in orthodontia should be especially welcome to the braces set. Valuable for the human body section of school libraries as well as a useful source for junior high health classes.

Sue Bottigheimer, in a review of "The Tooth Book," in School Library Journal, *Vol. 24, No. 6, February, 1978, p. 66.*

In this practical, well organized introduction to teeth and their care, Nourse effectively explains why everyday upkeep and regular dental checks are so important to keeping a whole and healthy set of teeth. Tooth structure, the decay process, and particulars of proper brushing and flossing are well covered; but beyond this Nourse has taken time to explain the hows and whys of various dental problems; brace wearers might find the discussion of alignment problems particularly interesting and appreciate Nourse's acknowledgment that braces are "not very attractive, never have been, never will be" but are not in vain. Format is unexceptional, and diagrams seem harshly reproduced, but content definitely compensates.

> *Denise M. Wilms, in a review of "The Tooth Book," in* Booklist, *Vol. 74, No. 8, December 15, 1978, p. 685.*

Fractures, Dislocations, and Sprains   (1978)

The nature of these relatively common injuries is made clear in the course of Nourse's elementary explanations. The first chapter's repetitive quality as accident scenes are sketched ("You've been skiing since nine in the morning, hardly even stopping for lunch.") gets things off to a dubious, clichéd start, but once Nourse settles into explaining bone and muscle configurations and how they commonly go awry in breaks, sprains, and dislocations, the information flows smoothly. There are diagrams aplenty, photographs, and first aid pointers. Good introductory material, especially useful in health or first aid units.

> *Denise M. Wilms, in a review of "Fractures, Dislocations, and Sprains," in* Booklist, *Vol. 75, No. 7, December 1, 1978, p. 618.*

Hormones   (1979)

Nourse introduces several common hormones (chemicals which stimulate bodily functions) and describes their effects. Unfortunately, the scope of this book does not match the scope of this subject, and only a few hormones (thyroxine, adrenalin, and insulin) are given thorough treatment. Many others are mentioned briefly. What text there is makes interesting reading, but one wishes for more. There is also a problem with some of the illustrations—one drawing suggests that the adrenal cortex is located in the chest rather than on top of the kidney, and two diagrams are reversed. Libraries needing additional material may want this title, but Sarah Riedman's *Hormones: How They Work* (Abelard, 1973) is more detailed.

> *Kathryn Weisman, in a review of "Hormones," in* School Library Journal, *Vol. 26, No. 6, February, 1980, p. 70.*

A short but effective description of how chemical substances in the human body function, this introduction to hormones is a good source of information for grades 7-9, and because of the format, not content, for slower high school students. Clear explanations of the thyroid and pituitary functions, the use of insulin and cortisone, sex hormones and their role in reproduction, and dysfunctions of thyroid hormones are emphasized by informative illustrations. The cover lists clinical-sounding terms, however no glossary is provided; these words are italicized in the text, some are found in the index. This is no real hardship, but

may discourage the slower reader who has no quick access to definitions. Recommended as a basic presentation.

> *Hilary King, in a review of "Hormones," in* Voice of Youth Advocates, *Vol. 2, No. 6, February, 1980, p. 45.*

Hormones are powerful chemical regulators of the human body. They control almost every aspect of our metabolism. The author surveys the various endocrine glands and discusses the hormones they produce and their related diseases. This scientifically accurate book is up-to-date and includes such topics as the releasing factors of the hypothalamus, the role of cyclic AMP and hormone action, prostaglandins, and the involvement of hormones and cancer. Although there are many technical words, all are clearly defined. The style of writing is interesting, simple, and easy to understand. Unfortunately, some of the excitement of the discoveries of the various hormones is lacking. Also, the illustrations and photographs are only fair. (pp. 57-8)

> *Herbert J. Stolz, in a review of "Hormones," in* Appraisal: Children's Science Books, *Vol. 13, No. 2, Spring, 1980, pp. 57-8.*

This is a very simplistic text on hormones by a retired physician whose earlier books concerned skin conditions and fractures. *Hormones* seems to be intended for general audiences who have achieved a high school reading level. It is not entirely up-to-date as it does not discuss the newer concepts relating to the hypothalamic stalk. The book is rather sketchy in content. Its pictures are barely adequate and the bibliography is very poor.

> *Austin T. Hyde, Jr., in a review of "Hormones," in* Science Books & Films, *Vol. XV, No. 5, May, 1980, p. 269.*

Menstruation: Just Plain Talk   (1980)

For girls about to reach sexual maturity and for many who already have done so, this discussion of menstruation will prove both enlightening and comforting. Nourse carefully delineates the differences between normal and abnormal sexual development, explaining away many common fears, offering advice on coping with common accompanying symptoms related to menstruation, and directing readers on when to seek medical advice. In addition, a description of a pelvic examination, a transcript of a discussion between the author and several college-age women, and a glossary are included. Although the current controversy over tampons is not mentioned, this is, on the whole, an open, helpful book.

> *Judith Goldberger, in a review of "Menstruation: Just Plain Talk," in* Booklist, *Vol. 77, No. 13, March 1, 1981, p. 966.*

[The following excerpts are from reviews of the revised edition published in 1987.]

A revision of the 1980 edition. A thorough, albeit dry discussion of the subject, including the latest word on Toxic Shock Syndrome, a condition discovered in 1979, which makes older books on the subject incomplete. The text, for the most part, seems to be aimed as much at parents as at young people. For readability, Voelckers' *Girls' Guide to Menstruation* (Rosen, 1975) is preferable, except for the omission of TSS. Some of the illustrations are clearer in this edition than in the older one, but most are about the same. The emotional aspects of menstruation are only briefly touched upon in a final chapter, where Nourse, a male physician, interviews several college girls as to how they felt when they first got their periods. Recommended for libraries needing to update information on menstruation; otherwise it's an additional purchase.

> *Ann Scarpellino, in a review of "Menstruation," in* School Library Journal, *Vol. 33, No. 11, August, 1987, p. 97.*

This book is a good introduction to how the female body works. It also provides a well-organized, accurate description of the specific biological changes that occur during and after puberty. The subject matter and illustrations are best suited to ninth graders. However, because of the simplified language, this book may prove useful as a teaching aid for a seventh-grade audience. If used with seventh graders, careful supervision is necessary as some of the illustrations—especially the one depicting a gynecological exam—might be disturbing. In general, the book is designed to stimulate discussion between teacher and student and even parent and child. It attempts to dispel common myths about menstruation by answering the questions most often asked. Diseases, such as endometriosis and toxic shock syndrome, are explained in a simplified manner to allow for a basic understanding of what occurs and how to best treat it. I recommend this accurate, well-organized book both as a teaching aid and general-awareness reference.

> *Karen Fassuliotis, in a review of "Menstruation," in* Science Books & Films, *Vol. 23, No. 2, November-December, 1987, p. 95.*

This informative presentation by a physician is thorough and well organized. . . . Rather homely, simple pencil drawings quite adequately diagram the physiology and include a patient in position for a pelvic examination along with a picture of the speculum. A glossary and index are included. The text is clear though a bit clinical in tone and is geared to very capable readers. The series title—"First Books"—is a serious misnomer. The plain tan cover and slightly wide pages give the book a very utilitarian appearance though the wide margins and good type face are pleasant. This is a very serviceable information source for collections needing more material.

> *Margaret Bush, in a review of "Menstruation," in* Appraisal: Science Books for Young People, *Vol. 21, No. 1, Winter, 1988, p. 46.*

Your Immune System (1980)

Nourse presents a lively and comprehendable discussion of the body's immune defense system (including sections on antigens and antibodies, allergies, vaccination and immunization, organ transplants and cancer). This book is highlighted by down-to-earth case study examples; clear

and interesting picture and chart illustrations; a multitude of biographical sketches on important scientists/researchers/explorers in the field of immunology. Nourse successfully uses analogy to present more complex ideas, i.e., lymphocytes as "soldiers on patrol" and body cells and dangerous bacterial cells as "self " and "not self." *Your Immune System* contains information that can be found in other works for this age group, i.e., Joan Arehart-Treichel's *Immunity* (Holiday, o.p.). However, this title is better at breaking down scientific/technical barriers and creating an interesting background to basic but complex concepts. While Nourse does not focus on related current research, he does bring readers briefly up-to-date on cancer research and new vaccines. A glossary, additional reading list and index are useful bonuses.

> *Laurie Bowden, in a review of "Your Immune System," in* School Library Journal, *Vol. 29, No. 7, March, 1983, p. 182.*

Immunity is not an easy topic to present to young readers. In this book, Nourse discusses in simple terms the body's defense mechanisms against harmful agents, chiefly infectious microorganisms that threaten us constantly. Chapters deal with antigens, antibodies, lymphocytes, phagocytes, complement and hyperimmune states. He presents the information in a style to stimulate readers' interest. Unfortunately, the illustrations are not very good, and some photographs are useless and unrelated to the topic. More diagrams that show the structures of the various immunoglobulins and how they interact with the antigens should be provided. Some examples of diagnostic antien-antibody reactions also would be helpful. A few terms, especially words used for the first time in the text, could be defined in more detail for better understanding. In a good introduction Nourse cites actual cases of immunological problems. In general, the information given is accurate. The glossary and index could serve as quick reference sources.

> *Lucia Anderson, in a review of "Your Immune System," in* Science Books & Films, *Vol. 18, No. 5, May-June, 1983, p. 264.*

[The following excerpts are from reviews of the revised edition published in 1989.]

It is obvious from the new material included here that much has been discovered over the last decade in the field of immunology. While a good part of the text is a word for word reprint of Nourse's earlier work, this book does include new information on AIDS, antibodies, and lymphocytes, giving readers a clearer understanding of this essential body function. Background information is offered in five basic areas: how the immune system works, benefits to the body, effects on the body when the system works improperly (e.g. allergies), AIDS, and current research. The text is well written, including rephrasing of some of the original text, offering a clear, easily understood factual base. The glossary has been expanded by 50 percent, defining both terms from the additional text and picking up several from the original body that were previously undefined. The inclusion of several case studies of patients with immunity problems lightens the tone and adds interest. There is one false note here: when relating the story of an asthmatic, Nourse states that "his asthma attacks are never life-threatening," a statement that could be misconstrued by readers as an inference that asthma hasn't the potential to be fatal. For those who own the first edition, this update is worthwhile. For those who don't, it would be a good complement to current titles on AIDS, and should be considered.

Denise L. Moll, in a review of "Your Immune System," in School Library Journal, *Vol. 35, No. 13, September, 1989, p. 282.*

This revised edition of Nourse's earlier work includes much new information. The author discusses recent discoveries about IgE (immunoglobulin E, an antibody that seems to be connected with allergic reactions), B-cells and T-cells and their role in the immune response, immunosuppressive drugs used in transplant therapy, new vaccines for malaria and hepatitis B, and the possibility that juvenile diabetes may be an autoimmune response. A new chapter on AIDS has also been added, and the glossary, bibliography, index, and illustrations have been redone and expanded. Nourse's style remains very readable in spite of his difficult subject, and his analogy of the body as a battlefield, with the various members of the immune system operating as soldiers, is appropriate. Designed for a slightly older audience than the first edition, with a more mature format to match, this will be a useful and worthwhile purchase. (p. 674)

Kay Weisman, in a review of "Your Immune System," in Booklist, *Vol. 86, No. 6, November 15, 1989, pp. 673-74.*

Although not devoted entirely to the AIDS epidemic, a book on the immune system and how it functions must be considered timely. This revision of the 1982 edition contains new information, in a chapter titled, "The Immune System Destroyed," on the use of zudovidine (AZT) for the treatment of AIDS. Without a copy of the original, it was not possible to determine other areas of revision. A few excursions into anthropomorphism such as, "the immune system learns" occur, but where these appear the author usually uses quotation marks around them. Therefore, the interest grabbing nature of things, like the battle inside of us against foreign invaders, can be used without diluting the message and indicating to young readers that the immune system reacts in thoughtful, purposeful ways. Further support for the scientific workings of the system comes from sections on people born with no immune system, auto-immune diseases and allergic reactions.

In less than one hundred pages, Dr. Nourse gives young readers, from junior through senior high school, an excellent introduction to the human immune system. The logical organization of the book, beginning with the immune defense system and ending with frontiers in immunology, helps readers build their knowledge on the foundations of previous information. The author interrelates the material, providing a framework for a great deal of science content. A useful glossary will aid readers. The list of six additional reading books should also include articles so that students become aware of their use in studying any topic. Whether read as a supplement to work in life science, health, and biology classes, or simply for interest, adoles-

cents through young adult readers will be enriched. (pp. 47-8)

Leonard J. Garigliano, in a review of "Your Immune System," in Appraisal: Science Books for Young People, *Vol. 23, No. 2, Spring, 1990, pp. 47-8.*

Herpes (1985)

Nourse enlivens an otherwise straightforward account of the five forms of the herpes virus by comparing pathogenic microbes to the James Gang of the old West—both active, troublesome and of little use to anyone. His style, clarity and succinct definitions make the book suitable for reports, but the lackluster cover, small print and a few grainy microphotographs eliminate any interest it may have for non-assignment reading. Genital herpes is the most rapidly spreading sexually transmitted disease in the U.S. There is no cure yet discovered, but Nourse discusses the antibiotic ointment acyclovir that offers some relief from the two Herpes Simplex strains. The address of the Herpes Resource Center in Palo Alto and the 800 number of the American Social Health Association are included. Aside from these timely tips, most of this data can be found in an encyclopedia. No attempt is made to relate exposure to the virus to a teenager's life style. The last half of this brief book nearly repeats the first, adding a look at other STDs, but with only two pages on AIDS, outdated already. No new information has been added beyond that in *Living with Herpes* (Doubleday, 1983) by Deborah P. Langston, *Herpes* (Running Pr, 1982) by Frank Freudberg and E. Stephen Emmanuel or *The Truth About STD* (Morrow, 1983) by Allan Chase.

Anne Osborn, in a review of "Herpes," in School Library Journal, *Vol. 32, No. 4, December, 1985, p. 104.*

Although the text contains chapters devoted to other forms of herpes and to other sexually transmitted diseases, it is primarily concerned with genital herpes, a fact not made clear by the title of the book. Nourse describes the several forms of herpes; unfortunately, he begins with a cute and patronizing bit about the "Herpes gang" as bandits. Information about causes, effects, and treatments is authoritative, but the book is weakened by a good bit of repetition and by some careless writing: a definition of prophylaxis (singular) that is plural, a reference to nephritis as "kidney damage," the use of the word "overexaggerated."

A review of "Herpes," in Bulletin of the Center for Children's Books, *Vol. 39, No. 5, January, 1986, p. 93.*

An up-to-date, well-researched, accurate text, written with charm, wit and appeal at the right age level, devoted to a topic of great significance to adolescents and adults alike. What higher expectations could one have of a children's science book? Yet, *Herpes* satisfies these expectations in every respect. The author is obviously knowledgeable about his subject and capable of communicating his knowledge to teen-age readers in an interesting way. I would think that this book is an absolute *must* for every school library in the country.

Two relatively minor problems detract from an otherwise fine product. First, some of the illustrations are confusing and less-than-helpful. The photograph of the Epstein-Barr virus facing page 12, for example, is unlabeled so that the reader can never really know which of the many structures shown is, in fact, the virus.

Second, the book appears to be too long by about two chapters. Chapter 4, "Questions and Answers about Genital Herpes," although a nice idea, repeats too much information presented earlier. And Chapter 5 takes on the impossibly difficult task of outlining all "Other Sexually Transmitted Diseases" in only nine pages! Hardly surprising that this chapter falls so short of its admirable, but unrealistic, goal. I'm especially disturbed that the information on AIDS is so incomplete and out-of-date, even given the copyright date for the text.

Just in case you missed the point of the first paragraph of this review, however: Buy this book!

> *David E. Newton, in a review of "Herpes," in* Appraisal: Science Books for Young People, *Vol. 19, No. 4, Fall, 1986, p. 72.*

AIDS (1986)

Nourse updates information found in the Silversteins' *AIDS: the Deadly Threat* (Enslow, 1986) and Margaret Hyde's *AIDS: What Does It Mean to You?* (Walker, 1986). His prose is graceful and vivid; his approach is to the medical rather than the social aspects of the disease. The charts and graphs (which cite statistics published as recently as June, 1986) are hard to read; the only photographs are microphotographs of the virus itself. The text employs many terms (such as adenopathy, HTLV-III, lymphadenopathy) that are clearly defined there and in the glossary and listed in the thorough index. Nourse's non-judgmental advice is to live defensively, and he sensibly outlines methods of doing so without using graphic sexual terms. His scenarios of sick and dying young men add emotional impact to his objective tone. Nourse includes information not in other books for young people—for example, how blood banks screen donors for the AIDS virus. The Silversteins' title is still the first choice in this area because of its thorough look at both the social and medical impact of AIDS, and for its compelling readability. Nourse provides an update that will be more useful for curriculum support than for general-interest reading. (pp. 173-74)

> *Anne Osborn, in a review of "AIDS," in* School Library Journal, *Vol. 33, No. 7, March, 1987, pp. 173-74.*

AIDS is certainly on the minds of children's book publishers these days, reflecting a tremendous concern in the public-at-large. This title is a reasonable offering, moderate in tone. Perhaps its best feature is the way scientific principles are explained in everyday terminology, so that an imaginative reader can then easily picture the cell or virus or whatever doing its thing. Lots of comparisons to examples in ordinary life are presented about scientific concepts. Specific health and sexual terms are simply explained in a clear parenthetical nonchalant way, not to arouse prurient sensibilities. The reader may be assumed to be young or simply ignorant, yet once the terminology is defined, the text proceeds matter of factly, without repetition. The author defines "promiscuous" simply as "having intimate sexual relations with a lot of different persons on a casual basis." Several pages of text explore the use of this word in terms of behavior as contrasted to any emotionally loaded tone. Patterns of sexual activity in the 40s, 50s, and 60s are described socio-culturally, showing trends and major changes. The challenges of the risk of intimacy are presented in a comprehensive and thoughtful way. The emphasis is on featuring "lowest risk groups:" those who are not sexually active male homosexuals, and who are not intravenous drug users, not promiscuous, use only safe blood transfusions, and who have never traveled to central Africa or Haiti. This intelligent and reassuring tone will do much to quash AIDS hysteria.

> *Leslie Chamberlin, in a review of "AIDS," in* Voice of Youth Advocates, *Vol. 10, No. 1, April, 1987, p. 46.*

Here is a new book that gives the background information that young people need to understand a very current event. It is unfortunate that the format of these "Impact Books", i.e. pages of black and white text broken up only occasionally by charts and tables, is almost as depressing as the subject matter. However, the author, who is a physician with a good deal of experience writing for young people, has covered all the main ideas: identification of the virus, how it affects the human immunity system, and what is being done to combat this serious threat to society.

I found the writing of the text to be a little uneven. For the most part the author is very direct, forceful and interesting; only occasionally he seemed to bog down in details with a slight sense of "writing down" to the reader. However the serious student will find the subject very timely, the information up-to-date, and the advice cautious but sound without sensationalism. Highly recommended as resource material to back up newspaper and magazine articles. (pp. 65-6)

> *Sallie Hope Erhard, in a review of "AIDS," in* Appraisal: Science Books for Young People, *Vol. 20, No. 3, Summer, 1987, pp. 65-6.*

A friend at the San Francisco AIDS Foundation informs me that more than two dozen popular books on AIDS now exist. In the ones I've seen, the emphasis ranges from the scientific and technological to those with a more holistic view, examining the personal, social, political, and economic issues arising out of the epidemic. This book tends to fall toward the "hard-science" end of the spectrum. Written by a retired physician, *AIDS* provides a relatively accurate, up-to-date review of most of the scientific information about the disease available at the time the book was written.

I have one major concern and a number of minor ones about the book. Most important, the author consistently refers to "homosexual males" in the text. That, of course, is not unusual for a book on AIDS. Most authors tend to perpetuate the notion that humans fall into two (or perhaps three) distinct sexual categories: heterosexual and homosexual (and, perhaps, bisexual).

But, of course, we have known since the Kinsey studies of the late 1940's that this view is much oversimplified. Humans display a much wider range of sexual behavior than this dichotomy (or trichotomy) suggests. Kinsey himself suggested a 7-point scale as a closer approximation of reality.

The reason this concept is important is that AIDS is so commonly identified as a *gay* disease. Some religious leaders have hit hard on the notion that AIDS is God's punishment for a particular lifestyle. Non-gays may feel, then, that only "those" people will catch the disease and that "we" are fairly safe. When we begin to understand that homosexual *behavior,* not "the male homosexual" is responsible for disease transmission, education about AIDS may move forward.

Now the minor points: The author opens the book with a rather extended discussion of one possible way in which AIDS may have originated as a human disease. Since he himself admits that this scenario is only one of many possibilities, I'm not clear as to the reason for the prolonged discussion of this particular possibility, especially when it is likely to offend a lot of people who already feel that they're being unfairly accused of "originating" the disease.

I also wish the author would have used the currently preferred term, human immunodeficiency virus (HIV), for the AIDS-causing virus. His description of RNA as "incomplete DNA" is also misleading and probably incorrect. I further regret that the author did not use the expression "safe sex" although he did spend some time talking about the concept.

Finally, I wonder who could have approved the cover—a scarlet "A" that appears to have been sewn to the dust jacket!—for this book. A terrible choice on someone's part!

In spite of some disturbing minor points such as these, the book is a valuable, useful resource for someone who wants to learn about the technical aspects of AIDS.

> *David E. Newton, in a review of "AIDS," in* Appraisal: Science Books for Young People, *Vol. 20, No. 3, Summer, 1987, p. 66.*

[*The following excerpts are from reviews of the revised edition published in 1989.*]

While the chapter titles and the bulk of the text remain the same, a number of important changes have been made in this new edition of Nourse's 1986 book. The most apparent include a new dust jacket illustration (an improvement over the stark red *A* that adorned the previous volume), revised charts and statistics, the substitution of the now universally accepted term *HIV* for *HTLV-III,* and the addition of footnotes. Nourse has also provided updated information about ARC, a lengthy discussion about the safety of the blood bank supply, consideration of the controversy over mandatory testing, and step-by-step instruc-

tions for using condoms. The text is still one of the strongest on medical aspects of the virus, and its acceptance of AIDS as a concern for the many, not simply the few, is of great importance to teens.

> *Stephanie Zvirin, in a review of "AIDS," in* Booklist, *Vol. 85, No. 19, June 1, 1989, p. 1715.*

This update is a great improvement on the 1986 edition, with changes on nearly every page. There is more certainty on the signs and symptoms to look for in diagnosing AIDS, and clearer distinctions made between AIDS, ARC, and LAS, as well as HTLV-III, HIV and HIV-2. Visually, also, this edition is much improved: larger, darker print on whiter paper in a better layout. The ten pages of charts and illustrations, although clearer, are mostly the same as the 1986 edition. The text is punchier, with fewer hedging qualifiers. The only section that seems unchanged is the clear explanation of the immune system. Statistics from the Centers for Disease Control are current up to 1989. The results of ongoing surveys by public health authorities on the spread of the disease are discussed. Predictions are updated and changed considerably, because "virtually all our questions about AIDS have been answered except how to cure it and how to make a vaccine to prevent it." Overall, this edition is more accessible, its tone more conversational—although, with current research findings, more alarming. Nourse adds far more detailed recommendations on condom use (still no illustrations) and outlines drugs being tested (acyclovir; zidovudine; AL-721) that might help. There is more on social and health aspects (i.e., whether to use prophylactic drugs as preventives), on the formidable obstacles to the development of a vaccine, and on the staggering cost of medical care for sufferers. Vocabulary will put this out of the range of most junior high readers, for whom *Lynda Madaras Talks to Teens about AIDS* (Newmarket, 1988) is still the best in the field. (p. 97)

> *Anne Osborn, in a review of "AIDS," in* School Library Journal, *Vol. 35, No. 11, July, 1989, pp. 96-7.*

Birth Control (1988)

With the book jacket adorned only by title and author (somewhat akin to a plain brown wrapper?), Nourse's latest nonfiction is one of the most thorough considerations of birth control yet published for a teenage audience. Although the book's dense format won't attract young adults who need a quick contraceptive reference, students and teenagers wanting a fuller picture will certainly find it: the author covers everything from the structure of the male and female reproductive systems to new approaches to contraception that may lead to more reliable birth control in the future. Introducing medical terminology in boldface, Nourse is both clear and explicit in his discussion of the advantages and drawbacks of birth control methods, which he divides into eight categories—natural, barrier, the pill, other hormone methods, etc. While he includes abortion in this contraceptive "menu," he stresses that it is "not truly a form of birth control"; it is rather a "*failure* of birth control—a last resort procedure" that is, "right or wrong, . . . a fact in the world today." His discussion of the rhythm method, which he describes as not only chancy but also rigid in its requirements, includes well-detailed explanations of the three means used to determine ovulation. In addition, he considers several kinds of contraceptive pills now available, discusses the problems plaguing the IUD, offers information on the still controversial contraceptive sponge, and explains sterilization for both men and women. Black-and-white drawings are included as are an extensive glossary and an index. Unfortunately, there are neither footnotes nor a bibliography.

> *Stephanie Zvirin, in a review of "Birth Control," in* Booklist, *Vol. 84, No. 18, May 15, 1988, p. 1594.*

A serviceable discussion of the array of birth control methods currently used, this book is useful for term papers on the subject but less so for advice to young people on which method to use. Sixteen pages treat "natural" methods of birth control, i.e., coitis interruptus, rhythm, and extended nursing, none of which are really effective methods for young couples. Fifteen pages discuss barrier methods such as the diaphragm, condom, spermicidals, and the sponge. Nowhere is there a suggestion that two barrier methods, the condom and the diaphragm, would, when used together, virtually eliminate the chance of an unwanted pregnancy. The other virtually certain method is the pill, which is discussed exhaustively in a separate chapter. The section on the rhythm method is unique in a book for young people, as it goes into detail about how to determine the time of ovulation. Illustrations are excellent, as is the organization of the book. The style is rather dry and academic. This is the only up-to-date book exclusively on this subject for this audience. For practical advice to young people, see chapters in Bell's *Changing Bodies, Changing Lives* (Vintage, 1988).

> *Ann Scarpellino, in a review of "Birth Control," in* School Library Journal, *Vol. 35, No. 9, June-July, 1988, p. 125.*

This low-key, objective, factual presentation of the wide variety of birth control methods is outstanding. Nourse presents the information in a logical manner, explanations are clear, and bias is avoided. After introductory chapters on what birth control is, why it is necessary in many different situations, and how pregnancy takes place, specifics are provided on the various methods of birth control, with chapters on "natural" methods, barrier methods, the pill, other hormonal methods, IUDs, sterilization, abortion, and possible future methods of birth control.

Each method is explained clearly and completely, including who might choose it and why, precise instructions on how to use it, the advantages and disadvantages it has compared to other methods, and some information on its development and the history of its use. The drawings illustrating the male and female sexual organs and how to use or apply several of the methods are usually cutaway side views, which can be hard to understand when trying to visualize one's own body or oneself using a particular item. However, they are not impossible to understand, and are very accurate and in no way titillating.

The book is complete, gives information on which methods to use to prevent diseases, including AIDS, as well as pregnancy. The tone is objective and straightforward, and while the text is not simplistic, it is also not difficult to understand. It would be a choice as a test for a sexual education class. All in all, it is an excellent presentation, and is recommended for all public and school libraries that serve adolescents and preadolescents.

> *Joni Bodart-Talbot, in a review of "Birth Control," in* Voice of Youth Advocates, *Vol. 11, No. 3, August, 1988, p. 149.*

The precise audience for which [**Birth Control**] was written is not clear. In early chapters, Nourse seems to be addressing adolescents as he discusses in simple terms reproductive anatomy and physiology and changes that occur during puberty. However, the rest of the book seems aimed at a general adult audience. Covered in reasonably good detail are most of the birth control methods currently available in this country plus a number of others still considered "experimental" (such as skin patches, male pill, antipregnancy vaccines). A brief chapter is also devoted to abortion. A useful glossary and index are included. Early-on, Nourse presents examples of four individuals who need birth control. One is a 14-year-old girl under pressure from her boyfriend to have sex. Never mentioned is that the best birth control method for this girl might be to say "no." Another method of birth control not covered in detail is the cervical mucus method; it is mentioned but not adequately described. Also, a few sentences are misleading and may result in problems for the reader who does not read an entire chapter. For example, "natural methods" are defined as "controlling or ordering intercourse in one way or another so that fertilization can't occur." Included under this heading are coitus interruptus, the rhythm method, and extended nursing, in all of which fertilization certainly can occur. It is also stated that the contraceptive pill "provides protection against some forms of sexually transmitted diseases." Later it is apparent that Nourse is referring only to pelvic inflammatory disease. The comment is made that "most doctors today believe the Pill is effective immediately as you begin using it, providing instant contraception." I don't know what "most doctors" believe, but I certainly would not want to assure women that they could start the pill today and be protected tonight or even tomorrow. Finally, a significant typographic error appears where the word "hysterectomy" is used when "hysterotomy" apparently is meant. In summary, although this is a reasonably complete and accurate presentation of available methods of birth control and their advantages and disadvantages, I fail to see what it offers over scores of other, similar books available.

> *Ronald K. McGraw, in a review of "Birth Control," in* Science Books & Films, *Vol. 25, No. 1, September-October, 1989, p. 29.*

Teen Guide to Birth Control; Teen Guide to Safe Sex (1988)

With a simplified format featuring numerous color photographs and drawings to attract reluctant readers or teenagers unable to manage more complex materials, [*Teen Guide to Birth Control,* an] entry in a new Watts series of teen guides is a competent distillation of Nourse's more comprehensive treatment in *Birth Control.* Keeping medical terminology to a necessary minimum, he provides clear, simplified explanations of reproductive anatomy and the ovulation and fertilization processes before introducing particular methods of birth control. Realistic about sexual abstinence as a workable method of birth control for teenagers, he suggests that even individuals who have decided not to have sex prepare for the unexpected by having an alternate method of contraception. Although more information about the disadvantages of the mini-pill and the use of nonoxynol-9 as a potential deterrent to the spread of AIDS would have been valuable. Nourse's approach is concise, his information up-to-date, and his presentation evenhanded, as in his consideration of the controversy over the IUD. No notes, no bibliography, although a glossary and an index are appended.

> *Stephanie Zvirin, in a review of "Teen Guide to Birth Control," in* Booklist, *Vol. 85, No. 10, January 15, 1989, p. 857.*

[*Teen Guide to Safe Sex*] borrows some photos and diagrams from the "Understanding Drugs" series and some explanations from Nourse's *AIDS.* Nourse's reliable clarity is enhanced by photos of teenagers, as well as microphotographs of viruses. Pronunciation guides in the text help with often-mispronounced names of sexually-transmitted diseases. The most helpful sections show how to use a condom and what symptoms to look for with each STD. Captions are thorough and repeat much of the text, making this informative for browsers. The attractive layout, boldtext scientific terms, and brevity will make the book appealing to reluctant readers. It's important that Nourse gives equal space to 12 STDs as well as AIDS. Yet in discussing preventative measures, he describes sexual abstinence and the use of condoms, but not alternatives to intercourse. This is not written in the teen idiom as is *Lynda Madaras Talks To Teens About AIDS* (Newmarket, 1988), nor as thorough as Nourse's own book on AIDS, but its format makes it likely to be the only book about STDs that sexually active teenagers will actually pick up and read.

> *Anne Osborn, in a review of "Teen Guide to Safe Sex," in* School Library Journal, *Vol. 35, No. 6, February, 1989, p. 107.*

Teen Guide to Safe Sex by Nourse is [a] pertinent text for today's young people. AIDS is here to stay; its consequences are irreversible. With the stakes so high, it is only fitting that young people have the necessary information to avoid contracting this disease or other sexually transmitted diseases. Once again, the best course of action is abstinence. Waiting until marriage to become sexually active and remaining faithful to the marriage partner is the best way to avoid these dangerous diseases. However, since so many young people are engaging in sex, they need to know what is involved when they make that decision.

Nourse begins *Teen Guide to Safe Sex* with an overall explanation of what STDs are. He then describes the bacterial and viral infections that are sexually transmitted. Next he outlines gonorrhea and syphilis, their causes, symptoms, and cures. He stresses throughout the book the necessity of getting early treatment and underlines the serious consequences of ignoring the warning signs of these infections. Sexually transmitted diseases will not go away if they are ignored; they will only get worse.

Chlamydia, a disease virtually unknown ten years ago, is the next subject in the book. Difficult to diagnose, it can cause permanent infertility if left untreated. Other widespread STDs receive individual treatment as well.

Last, *Teen Guide to Safe Sex* discusses genital herpes, AIDS, and how to prevent STDs. The wise young person will read and digest this material before making a decision concerning sexually activity. Nourse provides the facts to young people and is unafraid to discuss the consequences of indiscriminate sexual activity. I highly recommend it for a senior high school library.

> *Susan N. Bridson, in a review of "Teen Guide to Safe Sex," in* Voice of Youth Advocates, *Vol. 12, No. 2, April, 1989, p. 63.*

The Teen Guide to Birth Control is a short, readable account of different forms of birth control. Use of plain English is an important and appealing feature of the guide, adding to its overall effectiveness. Each chapter is a self-contained unit designed to answer the sort of questions and worries young people may have about contraception. Methods explained range from the rhythm method to the pill and sterilization. Controversial issues such as abortion are discussed in a balanced and unemotive way.

The guide aims to give young adults information about their bodies and the range of choices available to them. It achieves this purpose admirably, though the few references to young men and their share of the responsibility seem to occur as an afterthought.

Health educators may take issue with some of the language used in the text, especially when two of the opening assertions read "Almost all girls daydream once in a while about someday having babies and raising their own families. Most boys think about becoming fathers someday, too, though they may not admit it." An underlying, if unintentional, message in this extract may be that girls daydream and boys think!

Similarly, strong sexual feelings are attributed only to men and there is little indication that women may also experience them and it is OK if they do. The guide is certainly a useful resource for teachers faced with older students who need more specific information.

The Teen Guide to Safe Sex is a comprehensive guide to sexually transmitted diseases and ways of avoiding them. It is a useful, simply-written reference book for schools and individuals.

The opening chapter, "The Tiny Troublemakers", is a particularly lucid and interesting account of the nature of infections, micro-organisms, bacteria and viruses. It forms an excellent foundation for the discussion of specifically transmitted diseases in subsequent chapters.

The author makes the important and often ignored point

that safe sex is important in avoiding all sexually transmitted diseases, not just HIV, the AIDS virus, though it is a vital precaution in this respect.

Each sexually transmitted disease is discussed frankly and in straightforward terms. Advice about how to seek help and treatment is given in a reassuring and friendly manner. The approach is non-alarmist, yet confirms the need for quick action should symptoms become obvious.

Most of the photographs enhance the message, but a few raise a number of questions. One shows an AIDS victim and doctor alongside a text which clarifies that AIDS is an issue for all sections of the population. In this instance the image shown is perhaps rather stereotypical.

Equally, in the chapter "Protecting Yourself Against STDs" the photograph is of two young women sorting through a selection of condoms. One or two young men wouldn't have been out of place in such a crucial section of the book.

Although the book is about defence mechanisms, it could have included some more positive statements about the value of good sexual relationships. Sex needn't become a minefield or a battleground if commonsense and responsibility to self and others prevail.

> *Anne Hovey, "Safety First," in* The Times Educational Supplement, *No. 3797, April 7, 1989, p. B17.*

Radio Astronomy   (1989)

Beginning with Jansky's accidental discovery of "whispers from the sky" (radio waves from space), Nourse traces the invention of the radio telescope and the development of radio astronomy as a way to unlock the secrets of the invisible depths of outer space. Brief chapters deal with the discovery of quasars, pulsars, neutron stars, and black holes. There is a glossary, although many of the terms are explained in the text. The presentation is nicely organized, and Nourse's writing is informal enough to be inviting without sacrificing clarity. Reminiscent of Asimov's *How Did We Find Out About . . .* series, this should appeal to astronomy buffs and report writers alike.

> *Elaine Fort Weischedel, in a review of "Radio Astronomy," in* School Library Journal, *Vol. 35, No. 15, November, 1989, p. 132.*

This enjoyable book covers the topic of radio astronomy in a clear, concise, and easy-to-read format. A variety of subjects are covered, ranging from the first telescopes and their users to pulsars and quasars. The scientific information is conveyed in clear terminology, and diagrams are used to assist in the descriptions. Black-and-white pictures are found on nearly every page, which help lead the reader from historical times to present-day research. Some complex topics, such as gravitational collapse, are described with an eye toward future study. A complete glossary is included, as well as a list for further reading. Overall, this is an exceptional book that describes a complex subject in a clear and exciting way, with ample pictures to appeal to all readers.

> *D'Arlyn G. Fromme, in a review of "Radio Astronomy," in* Science Books & Films, *Vol. 25, No. 5, May-June, 1990, p. 256.*

I wish that I could be enthusiastic about this book. Its six chapters certainly cover the range of topics within radio astronomy. However, there are a number of details in which the book is technically incorrect or at least misleading.

For example, in a diagram of a reflecting telescope, the prism shown within a Newtonian focal arrangement is incorrectly labeled as an "objective lens." Elsewhere, cosmic rays are described as part of the electromagnetic spectrum, the nearest star is indicated as being 3.5 (not 4.3) light years distant, and there is an implication that the most conventional cosmology has individual objects continually increasing their recessional speeds.

These and other flaws occur amidst much good material, but it is frustrating to see them. Science books for young people need to present simplified, but not oversimplified or inaccurate, accounts. (pp. 38-9)

> *William H. Ingham, in a review of "Radio Astronomy," in* Appraisal: Science Books for Young People, *Vol. 23, No. 3, Summer, 1990, pp. 38-9.*

Teen Guide to AIDS Prevention   (1990)

This is a fine, straightforward, useful book. It is clear, detailed, and no-nonsense in tone. It gives an excellent description of the great deal that is known about the AIDS virus, and then provides a chapter on how teenagers can protect themselves. The major focus is on abstention, from IV drugs and sexual activity, but there is clear information about condoms for those who choose not to take that advice. Color photographs help offset the fact that the text is cramped into small pages with narrow margins. The guides to pronunciation throughout the text are a thoughtful addition. This is an excellent choice, both for report writers and the general reading public, from middle-schoolers (seventh grade) on up. (pp. 39-40)

> *Suzanne S. Sullivan, in a review of "AIDS Prevention," in* Appraisal: Science Books for Young People, *Vol. 24, No. 1, Winter, 1991, pp. 39-40.*

Nourse has done a commendable job of presenting a very complex scientific and health issue in an understandable and informative manner geared to adolescents. Some of the difficulty in discussing subjects such as AIDS is due to the general lack of basic scientific understanding in our society today. The book presents explanations of fundamental microbiological (such as the difference between bacteria and viruses) and immunological concepts and relates them to the medical manifestations of the disease. The book is organized from the recognition of the illness to the identification of the virus, the mechanisms of the disease process, the modes of transmission, the ways to avoid infection, and finally, what happens if one is infected. The information is as accurate as can be expected with a rapidly evolving story. One minor error on page twenty-one is the citation of AIDS cases as of April 1990 that references CDC statistics from 1988. One noteworthy touch is the inclusion of pronunciation aids for some medical terms. This method helps people to remember and feel comfortable talking about the topics.

The book includes frank discussions of homosexuality, sexually transmitted diseases, and intravenous drug use. Knowledgeable adults should be prepared to assist adolescents in thoughtful discussions on various aspects of the book. Of particular note is the lack of mention of social policy aspects of the disease. Discrimination and health care policy issues are not discussed. These would be areas to explore further with teenagers.

Finally, it must be emphasized that AIDS is a rapidly evolving scientific, social, and medical problem. Education about AIDS needs constant updating and revision. This book is a very good basis for valuable information, but should not be viewed as the final word.

> *Michael G. Kurilla, in a review of "AIDS Prevention," in* Appraisal: Science Books for Young People, *Vol. 24, No. 1, Winter, 1991, p. 40.*

A standard overview, imported from England. Nourse includes his usual good introduction to the complexities of the immune system, much summarized from his previous titles such as *AIDS* (1989) and *Teen Guide to Safe Sex* (1988, both Watts). For collections with these titles, this one adds little of significance. Statistics are updated to April 1990. Some of the social movements that have arisen since the virus was first discovered are mentioned, such as the NAMES Quilt and the Condoms for Prisoners campaign. Typical of this series are full-color photos and drawings (including one of condom use) and a handsome open format. Pronunciations are in the text, and bold type indicates a glossary definition. There are clear instructions for cutting down the risk of infection. This is not as outstanding as Nourse's previous AIDS books, and nothing yet published outshines *Lynda Madaras Talks to Teens about AIDS* (Newmarket, 1988) as the premiere book in the field.

> *Anne Osborn, in a review of "Teen Guide to AIDS Prevention," in* School Library Journal, *Vol. 37, No. 2, February, 1991, p. 98.*

Teen Guide to Survival   (1990)

Written in simple, direct language, and arranged with short chapters offering clear and concise information, this book briefly addresses the topics of alcohol, physical violence, depression, tobacco, drugs, and sex. Intended as a quick reference, the book includes a list of additional readings for the teen who wishes to explore a specific topic in-depth.

One weakness of the book is the staged photographs. For example, a "teacher" appearing in one photo is portrayed in the accompanying text as an adult one can rely on. In a later photo, this same "teacher" wearing the same clothes is shown "shooting up." The brief stories which appear in the opening paragraph of each of four chapters

are not necessary. The point of each story and its relevance to the topic at hand are not direct enough to be useful. The text in the remaining chapters flows much better without these stories. Another difficulty is the author's style and tone that wavers from preachy to objective. Included after the glossary are seven toll-free hotline numbers as well as brief explanations of how each agency or organization can be of service to the reader.

> *Mary Ann Capan, in a review of "Teen Guide to Survival," in* Voice of Youth Advocates, *Vol. 13, No. 6, February, 1991, p. 379.*

Survival is a less successful text [than Nourse's *AIDS Prevention*] being of thematically poor coherence, the key issue of survival inadequately connecting discussion on drunk-driving, drugs, violence, sex and teen suicide. The text tends to adopt a prohibitive stance on a number of issues without adequate explanation and in some cases with misleading advice. In the "Drinking, Driving and Disaster" section, unlicensed teens are encouraged to drive home rather than risk a ride with their licensed but drunk friends. This advice is given in the absence of more obvious suggestions such as taxis and public transport. Gender-based role casting appears in a number of instances and sections on drink-driving and violence seem particularly directed at boys. The final sections are hurried and the book is unsatisfactorily concluded. While *Survival* offers some useful introductory ideas, it is not a book that can be used alone for any of the topics it discusses.

> *Nola Cavallaro, in a review of "AIDS Prevention," in* Magpies, *Vol. 6, No. 2, May, 1991, p. 36.*

Sexually Transmitted Diseases   (1992)

For the teenager who is interested in knowing more about sexually transmitted diseases (STDs), this book offers a thorough explanation of the common STDs that plague them. Written in a conversational tone, the book matter-of-factly discusses how STDs are contracted, treated, and prevented.

Nourse starts with describing the differences between viruses, bacteria, yeasts, and protozoans, then moves on to talk about the particulars of individual STDs. The discussion on condom use is complete and to the point. The section on choosing abstinence as a way to avoid sexually transmitted diseases is also very good. However, I particularly liked how the author handled the chapter on the prevention of sexually transmitted disease; he doesn't give simplistic "just say no" advice nor does he tout condom usage as the only way to prevent STDs. Rather he gives a solid, nonjudgmental commentary on the benefits of postponing sexual intercourse at least until a rational assessment of a future sexual partner is made. "A fairly lengthy and intimate nonsexual relationship with a person before actually having sex is probably a better guide to his or her actual sexual history than any amount of impulse driven, under-the-gun, now or never conversation."

The book does not deny young adults' sexual feelings; but it advises them to proceed cautiously when making a sexual decision. I would have liked more discussion on "outer-course"—sexual activities that are alternatives to intercourse. Many teens still do not have a good understanding of which sexual behaviors (other than intercourse) are more likely to transmit disease.

The chapters are short and to the point and unfamiliar terms are described simply. All of these qualities make this book useful for the teen who is writing a report on the topic or wants to learn more for personal reference.

Mary Singler, in a review of "Sexually Transmitted Diseases," in Voice of Youth Advocates, *Vol. 15, No. 2, June, 1992, p. 131.*

Comparing today's world to a war zone, Nourse describes symptoms, treatment, and prevention of a gamut of sexually transmitted diseases. In addition to self-esteem as the basis for defensive living, he recommends avoidance of drugs and intravenous drug users; monogamy; protection with condoms and spermacides at all times; or abstaining from sex altogether. The straightforward text is factual, nonjudgmental, and persuasive. Content is similar to Elaine Landau's *Sexually Transmitted Diseases* (Enslow, 1986). Other good sources on individual diseases are available, such as Alvin and Virginia Silversteins' extensively revised *AIDS* (Enslow, 1991) and the very frank *Lynda Madaras Talks to Teens about AIDS* (Newmarket, 1988). Nourse's title should be considered for purchase because of its clarity and comprehensiveness. A possible drawback is the lack of a list of places to go for help, but Nourse does emphasize the importance of seeking medical advice and the need for young adults to take their concerns to parents and professional counselors.

Sue A. Norkeliunas, in a review of "Sexually Transmitted Diseases," in School Library Journal, *Vol. 38, No. 7, July, 1992, p. 95.*

As the range of sexually transmitted diseases has expanded from bacterial diseases such as syphilis and gonorrhea to viral diseases such as genital herpes, genital warts, and HIV infection, the concerns and fears of the general public have increased accordingly. *Sexually Transmitted Diseases* attempts to provide an overall view of these diseases and the microorganisms that cause them. Unfortunately, the publication contains a number of errors, misconceptions, incorrect uses of terms, and misleading definitions. Examples of error may be found in the coverage of viruses and the nucleic acids DNA and RNA. While viruses attach to receptor sites on susceptible cells, animal viruses gain entrance into the interior of cells by variations of pinocytosis or other mechanisms of engulfment. Several bacterial viruses generally inject their nucleic acids into susceptible bacteria. By contrast, the author generalizes and implies that all viruses carry out their infection cycle in the manner of bacterial viruses. In addition, he mistakenly describes RNA as "essentially just a small segment of DNA." Descriptions of the immune system are

lacking, especially in regard to the functions of its various parts. Several misconceptions also stand out. For example, Chlamydia are referred to as germs in one case and then described as "a sexually transmitted infection caused by a tiny germ known as *Chlamydia trichomatous.*" In addition, from a scientific standpoint, the overuse of the term *germ* instead of specific terms such as disease agent or infectious microorganism detracts from the presentation of the subject matter. Various portions of the text and the accompanying glossary contain misleading definitions or descriptions that are very limited. Among the poorest definitions are those for the terms *antibiotics, erection, hepatitis B virus, Herxheimer reaction* (which is correctly known as the Jarisch-Herxhcimcr reaction), *immune system, labia, ovaries,* and *pelvic inflammatory disease.* Some definitions even contradict illustrations in the book. For example, a scrotum is wrongly described as "the small sac *behind* [italics added] the boy's penis." While the book provides an overview of the better known sexually transmitted diseases, it is interesting to note that there are no photographs showing signs and symptoms of infections in adults. Only a case of oral herpes and a baby born to a woman infected with herpes are depicted. *Sexually Transmitted Diseases* also covers topics such as attitudes and prevention. It is regrettable that this book has so many problems, that it loses its effectiveness in presenting a most important subject.

George A. Wistreich, in a review of "Sexually Transmitted Diseases," in Science Books & Films, *Vol. 28, No. 6, August-September, 1992, p. 172.*

The Virus Invaders   (1992)

Nourse describes the discovery of viruses and their nature, and discusses the variety of viral diseases, vaccines and immunity, and recent research. He presents a wide scope of information; detailed, complex explanations about such topics as DNA and RNA; and focuses on AIDS and HIV. Likewise, hepatitis A, B, and C are dealt with separately. An excellent double-page chart details in outline form the viruses, diseases caused, organs attacked, symptoms, usual outcomes, and possibilities of an available vaccine. Students and teachers will love this feature. Variable-quality black-and-white photographs and diagrams aid in understanding topics under discussion. While the explanations of DNA and RNA are complex at times, this will serve as a useful introduction. Knight's *Viruses* (Morrow, 1981; o.p.) is a simpler treatment for younger audiences.

Lois McCulley, in a review of "The Virus Invaders," in School Library Journal, *Vol. 38, No. 7, July, 1992, p. 95.*

(Sir) Charles G(eorge) D(ouglas) Roberts

1860-1943

Canadian author of fiction, poetry, and nonfiction.

Major works include *Earth's Enigmas: A Book of Animal and Nature Life* (1896), *The Kindred of the Wild: A Book of Animal Life* (1902), *The Watchers of the Trails: A Book of Animal Life* (1904), *Red Fox: The Story of His Adventurous Career in the Ringwaak Wilds, and of His Final Triumph over the Enemies of His Kind* (1905), *The Lure of the Wild: The Last Three Animal Stories* (1980).

Major works about the author include *Sir Charles G. D. Roberts: A Biography* (by Elsie M. Pomeroy, 1943), *Sir Charles God-Damn: The Life of Sir Charles G. D. Roberts* (by John Coldwell Adams, 1986).

INTRODUCTION

Renowned as a seminal figure in Canadian literature, Roberts is the creator of poetry and prose which are praised as both reflective of his homeland and universal; J. D. Logan and Donald G. French note, "Of a certainty he was the first native-born Canadian to take the leading role in making real and permanent . . . a native and natural literature in Canada." Called the father of his country's poetry, he influenced an entire school of early twentieth-century Canadian writers and initiated what is known as the Canadian Renaissance through his contributions to the genre, which include romantic and meditative pieces and nature poems. Roberts, along with fellow Canadian Ernest Thompson Seton, is also credited as the creator of realistic animal fiction, the first internationally recognized literary genre to originate in Canada. Prior to the writings of Roberts and Seton, animal fiction was limited to fables; fantasies about clothed, anthropomorphic animals; and sentimental stories in which domestic animals enjoy the benevolence of, or suffer mistreatment from, humans. Basing his twelve novels and several short stories on close observation of animals and nature, Roberts pays homage to the bravery of his animal characters, glorifying their primal struggle for life. Unlike his poetry, in which nature figures as a positive force of change and inspiration, Roberts's fiction portrays the savage aspect of nature; in these works the survival of the fittest is enacted repeatedly. Although he occasionally features human protagonists, Roberts generally presents dignified, often heroic, animal characters from the Canadian wilds, such as the fox, the bear, the wolf, and the eagle. Motivated almost exclusively by their search for food or their attempts to escape their fate as prey, the animals valiantly confront danger and death, illustrating the immutable cycle of life that underscores Roberts's works. His stories, stark in their depiction of violence and tragedy, begin and end with set pieces of landscape description, abounding with lush language that details sounds, smells, and vibrant colors and plays of light. Throughout his works, Roberts uses this poetic prose to describe the lives and deaths of the animals. Although the content of his fiction is sometimes graphic and

fatalistic in its depiction of predatory behavior, Roberts shows an unabashed admiration for his characters as well as a profound respect for the dignity of the natural world.

Born in New Brunswick, Roberts was raised in the Tantramar marsh country located near Sackville, an area he often praises for its natural beauty in his poetry. As a young boy, he spent a great deal of time outdoors, often with an uncle who taught him about wildlife. By the age of twelve, Roberts was writing articles on agriculture; he became headmaster of a grammar school at nineteen and published his first book of poetry at twenty. More than a decade later, after becoming a professor of English, French, and economics and working as an editor, he wrote his first animal story, "Do Seek Their Meat from God" (1892), in which a young boy is terrorized by two panthers who confront him in an isolated cabin; after the boy's father has come to his rescue and shot the panthers at the end of the story, Roberts shows the reader that the panthers' cubs have starved to death because their parents have not returned with food for them. Roberts had difficulty finding a publisher for a story that ends so grimly and shows such sympathy for savage predators. However, the success of Ernest Thompson Seton's collection *Wild*

Animals I Have Known (1898) caused Roberts to return to his fiction with fervor, publishing nearly two hundred stories over the course of the next half century. Influenced by both the traditional hunting tale and beast fable as well as by his youthful observations of the Canadian woods and the camping trips he took along the rivers of New Brunswick, Roberts wrote his stories from the point of view of his animal characters and from his conviction that they could reason. The tales also blend two popular concepts of the time, Darwinism and romanticism. The near-Edenic settings and the heart-rending pathos of the inevitability of death make Roberts's works apt examples of romantic fiction, but they do not evade the prevalent scientific views of his day. Both his animal and human characters battle to survive, and nature is shown most emphatically as "red in tooth and claw." In *The Kindred of the Wild,* Roberts calls the Canadian animal story "a psychological romance constructed on a foundation of natural science"; it is this latter attribute that brought Roberts the most controversy regarding his own work.

At the beginning of the twentieth century one of the greatest debates in science was whether animals acted by use of reason or instinct; Robert H. MacDonald writes that Roberts informs his readers that animals "could reason, that they could and did educate their young, and that they possessed and obeyed laws of their own." One of Roberts's best known works, *Red Fox,* chronicles a fox's brushes with death and his battles with various predators, including a young boy who hunts the fox despite his admiration for him. Reviewing this work in 1906, noted naturalist John Burroughs wrote, "As literature, the work has many merits, but as natural history, it is erroneous and misleading in many particulars." Following the publication of *The Kindred of the Wild,* Burroughs wrote the short essay "Real and Sham Natural History" (1903), in which he maintains that Roberts's book, although admirable, features characters who "are simply human beings described as animals, they think, feel, plan, suffer, as we do; in fact, exhibit almost the whole human psychology." The next year, Roberts wrote a prefatory note to *The Watchers of the Trails* in which he counters Burroughs's claims, stating that he tries to write from the animals' point of view and ascribes to their actions "the motive which I have here assumed affords the most reasonable, if not the only reasonable, explanation of that action." The controversy continued to ensue: for example, in *Everybody's Magazine* (June 1907), Theodore Roosevelt accused Roberts of being a "nature faker." After the first World War, Roberts's popularity tended to diminish even as his works continued to be evaluated on the basis of the authenticity of their animal characters. However, Roberts's stories appealed to a wide range of readers during his lifetime; at present, they are read primarily by readers in the middle and upper grades, for whom the stirring adventures and educational view of wildlife offer a distinctive reading experience. In addition, the greater issues Roberts addresses in his fiction remain relevant; the animal stories have been recently republished and continue to find an audience among the young. Recent critics have also begun to re-evaluate Roberts. Thomas R. Dunlap writes: "It was Roberts's genius to subsume older Romantic ideas about nature within the framework of the popular notion of a Dar-

winian struggle, to show within that seeming chaos continuity, order, and a place for man; to explain nature to his generation; and to give emotional content to a scientific explanation of man and nature in a coherent world view." David McCord adds that "Roberts stood head and shoulders above his few North American contemporaries, such as Ernest Thompson Seton, as a nature writer who made the wild animals, birds, fish, and even dragonflies of backwoods New Brunswick come alive on the printed page." In addition to his animal fiction and poetry, Roberts wrote a history of Canada and several historical romances set in eighteenth-century Nova Scotia, as well as several novels in which human characters strive to live in harmony with nature. In 1926, he was awarded the first Lorne Pierce Medal for outstanding achievements in imaginative literature; he was knighted for his services to Canadian letters in 1935. Roberts was also named a member of the Royal Society of Canada and the Royal Society of Literature as well as the American Academy.

(See also *Twentieth-Century Literary Criticism,* Vol. 8; *Something about the Author,* Vol. 29; and *Contemporary Authors,* Vol. 105.)

AUTHOR'S COMMENTARY

Alike in matter and in method, the animal story, as we have it to-day, may be regarded as a culmination. The animal story, of course, in one form or another, is as old as the beginnings of literature. Perhaps the most engrossing part in the life-drama of primitive man was that played by the beasts which he hunted, and by those which hunted him. They pressed incessantly upon his perceptions. They furnished both material and impulse for his first gropings toward pictorial art. When he acquired the kindred art of telling a story, they supplied his earliest themes; and they suggested the hieroglyphs by means of which, on carved bone or painted rock, he first gave his narrative a form to outlast the spoken breath. We may not unreasonably infer that the first animal story—the remote but authentic ancestor of "Mowgli" and "Lobo" and "Krag"—was a story of some successful hunt, when success meant life to the starving family; or of some desperate escape, when the truth of the narrative was attested, to the hearers squatted trembling about their fire, by the sniffings of the baffled bear or tiger at the rock-barred mouth of the cave. Such first animal stories had at least one merit of prime literary importance. They were convincing. The first critic, however supercilious, would be little likely to cavil at their verisimilitude. (pp. 15-16)

With the spread of freedom and the broadening out of all intellectual interests which characterise these modern days, the lower kindreds began to regain their old place in the concern of man. The revival of interest in the animals found literary expression (to classify roughly) in two forms, which necessarily overlap each other now and then, viz., the story of adventure and the anecdote of observation. Hunting as a recreation, pursued with zest from pole to tropics by restless seekers after the new, supplied a species of narrative singularly akin to what the first animal stories must have been,—narratives of desperate encounter, strange peril, and hairbreadth escape. Such hunters' stories and travellers' tales are rarely conspicuous for the exactitude of their observation; but that was not the quality at first demanded of them by fireside readers. The attention of the writer was focussed, not upon the peculiarities or the emotions of the beast protagonist in each fierce, brief drama, but upon the thrill of the action, the final triumph of the human actor. The inevitable tendency of these stories of adventure with beasts was to awaken interest in animals, and to excite a desire for exact knowledge of their traits and habits. The interest and the desire evoked the natural historian, the inheritor of the half-forgotten mantle of Pliny. Precise and patient scientists made the animals their care, observing with microscope and measure, comparing bones, assorting families, subdividing subdivisions, till at length all the beasts of significance to man were ticketed neatly, and laid bare, as far as the inmost fibre of their material substance was concerned, to the eye of popular information.

Altogether admirable and necessary as was this development at large, another, of richer or at least more spiritual significance, was going on at home. Folk who loved their animal comrades—their dogs, horses, cats, parrots, elephants—were observing, with the wonder and interest of discoverers, the astonishing fashion in which the mere instincts of these so-called irrational creatures were able to simulate the operations of reason. The results of this observation were written down, till "anecdotes of animals" came to form a not inconsiderable body of literature. The drift of all these data was overwhelmingly toward one conclusion. The mental processes of the animals observed were seen to be far more complex than the observers had supposed. Where instinct was called in to account for the elaborate ingenuity with which a dog would plan and accomplish the outwitting of a rival, or the nice judgment with which an elephant, with no nestbuilding ancestors behind him to instruct his brain, would choose and adjust the teak-logs which he was set to pile, it began to seem as if that faithful faculty was being overworked. To explain yet other cases, which no accepted theory seemed to fit, coincidence was invoked, till that rare and elusive phenomenon threatened to become as customary as buttercups. But when instinct and coincidence had done all that could be asked of them, there remained a great unaccounted-for body of facts; and men were forced at last to accept the proposition that, within their varying limitations, animals can and do reason. As far, at least, as the mental intelligence is concerned, the gulf dividing the lowest of the human species from the highest of the animals has in these latter days been reduced to a very narrow psychological fissure.

Whether avowedly or not, it is with the psychology of animal life that the representative animal stories of to-day are first of all concerned. Looking deep into the eyes of certain of the four-footed kindred, we have been startled to see therein a something, before unrecognised, that answered to our inner and intellectual, if not spiritual selves. We have suddenly attained a new and clearer vision. We have come face to face with personality, where we were blindly wont to predicate mere instinct and automatism. It is as if one should step carelessly out of one's back door, and

marvel to see unrolling before his new-awakened eyes the peaks and seas and misty valleys of an unknown world. Our chief writers of animal stories at the present day may be regarded as explorers of this unknown world, absorbed in charting its topography. They work, indeed, upon a substantial foundation of known facts. They are minutely scrupulous as to their natural history, and assiduous contributors to that science. But above all are they diligent in their search for the motive beneath the action. Their care is to catch the varying, elusive personalities which dwell back of the luminous brain windows of the dog, the horse, the deer, or wrap themselves in reserve behind the inscrutable eyes of all the cats, or sit aloof in the gaze of the hawk and the eagle. The animal story at its highest point of development is a psychological romance constructed on a framework of natural science.

The real psychology of the animals, so far as we are able to grope our way toward it by deduction and induction combined, is a very different thing from the psychology of certain stories of animals which paved the way for the present vogue. Of these, such books as *Beautiful Joe* and *Black Beauty* are deservedly conspicuous examples. It is no detraction from the merit of these books, which have done great service in awakening a sympathetic understanding of the animals and sharpening our sense of kinship with all that breathe, to say that their psychology is human. Their animal characters think and feel as human beings would think and feel under like conditions. This marks the stage which these works occupy in the development of the animal story.

The next stage must be regarded as, in literature, a climax indeed, but not the climax in this genre. I refer to the "Mowgli" stories of Mr. Kipling. In these tales the animals are frankly humanised. Their individualisation is distinctly human, as are also their mental and emotional processes, and their highly elaborate powers of expression. Their notions are complex; whereas the motives of real animals, so far as we have hitherto been able to judge them, seem to be essentially simple, in the sense that the motive dominant at a given moment quite obliterates, for the time, all secondary motives. Their reasoning powers and their constructive imagination are far beyond anything which present knowledge justifies us in ascribing to the inarticulate kindreds. To say this is in no way to depreciate such work, but merely to classify it. There are stories being written now which, for interest and artistic value, are not to be mentioned in the same breath with the "Mowgli" tales, but which nevertheless occupy a more advanced stage in the evolution of this genre.

It seems to me fairly safe to say that this evolution is not likely to go beyond the point to which it has been carried to-day. In such a story, for instance, as that of *Krag, the Kootenay Ram,* by Mr. Ernest Seton, the interest centres about the personality, individuality, mentality, of an animal, as well as its purely physical characteristics. The field of animal psychology so admirably opened is an inexhaustible world of wonder. Sympathetic exploration may advance its boundaries to a degree of which we hardly dare to dream; but such expansion cannot be called evolution. There would seem to be no further evolution possible, unless based upon a hypothesis that animals have souls. As souls are apt to elude exact observation, to forecast any such development would seem to be at best merely fanciful.

The animal story, as we now have it, is a potent emancipator. It frees us for a little from the world of shop-worn utilities, and from the mean tenement of self of which we do well to grow weary. It helps us to return to nature, without requiring that we at the same time return to barbarism. It leads us back to the old kinship of earth, without asking us to relinquish by way of toll any part of the wisdom of the ages, any fine essential of the "large result of time." The clear and candid life to which it reinitiates us, far behind though it lies in the long upward march of being, holds for us this quality. It has ever the more significance, it has ever the richer gift of refreshment and renewal, the more humane the heart and spiritual the understanding which we bring to the intimacy of it. (pp. 21-9)

> Charles G. D. Roberts, "The Animal Story," in his The Watchers of the Trails: A Book of Animal Life, L. C. Page & Company, 1904, pp. 15-29.

[*The following excerpt includes a reference to John Burroughs's review of* The Kindred of the Wild. *An excerpt from the review, published in* The Atlantic Monthly *in March 1903, appears later in this entry.*]

The stories of which [***The Watchers of the Trails***] is made up are avowedly fiction. They are, at the same time, true, in that the material of which they are moulded consists of facts,—facts as precise as painstaking observation and anxious regard for truth can make them. Certain of the stories, of course, are true literally. Literal truth may be attained by stories which treat of a single incident, or of action so restricted as to lie within the scope of a single observation. When, on the other hand, a story follows the career of a wild creature of the wood or air or water through wide intervals of time and space, it is obvious that the truth of that story must be of a different kind. The complete picture which such a story presents is built up from observation necessarily detached and scattered; so that the utmost it can achieve as a whole is consistency with truth. If a writer has, by temperament, any sympathetic understanding of the wild kindreds; if he has any intimate knowledge of their habits, with any sensitiveness to the infinite variation of their personalities; and if he has chanced to live much among them during the impressionable periods of his life, and so become saturated in their atmosphere and their environment;—then he may hope to make his most elaborate piece of animal biography not less true to nature than his transcript of an isolated fact. The present writer, having spent most of his boyhood on the fringes of the forest, with few interests save those which the forest afforded, may claim to have had the intimacies of the wilderness as it were thrust upon him. The earliest enthusiasms which he can recollect are connected with some of the furred or feathered kindred; and the first thrills strong enough to leave a lasting mark on his memory are those with which he used to follow—furtive, apprehensive, expectant, breathlessly watchful—the lure of an unknown trail.

There is one more point which may seem to claim a word. A very distinguished author—to whom all contemporary writers on nature are indebted, and from whom it is only with the utmost diffidence that I venture to dissent at all—has gently called me to account on the charge of ascribing to my animals human motives and the mental processes of man. The fact is, however, that this fault is one which I have been at particular pains to guard against. The psychological processes of the animals are so simple, so obvious, in comparison with those of man, their actions flow so directly from their springs of impulse, that it is, as a rule, an easy matter to infer the motives which are at any one moment impelling them. In my desire to avoid alike the melodramatic, the visionary, and the sentimental, I have studied to keep well within the limits of safe inference. Where I may have seemed to state too confidently the motives underlying the special action of this or that animal, it will usually be found that the action itself is very fully presented; and it will, I think, be further found that the motive which I have here assumed affords the most reasonable, if not the only reasonable, explanation of that action. (pp. vii-ix)

> Charles G. D. Roberts, in a preface to The Kindred of the Wild: A Book of Animal Life, L. C. Page & Company, 1904, pp. vii-ix.

GENERAL COMMENTARY

Michel Poirier

[Between 1892 and 1894, Roberts published] a group of three stories: **"Do Seek their Meat from God"**, followed by **"The Young Ravens that cry upon Him"** and **"Strayed."** As most of Roberts' works, they first appeared in periodicals and were then collected in book form, together with other short stories depicting life in the backwoods or relating some weird dreams, under the title ***Earth's Enigmas.*** The importance of these three tales in the history of the animal story is considerable. Firstly, the date of their publication proves that Roberts was working in that vein before the publication of *The Jungle Book* (1894), the conception of which is, besides, altogether different. Impersonal accounts of imaginary adventures, they gain in vividness what they may lose in accuracy, give the reader an impression of direct contact with the animals, no longer seen through the writer's eyes. C. D. Warner was the only previous author to apply that method, which was to be that of all Roberts' ulterior animal stories and which, with the true instinct of a great writer, he chose so unhesitatingly. It is equally remarkable that he almost at once reached the highest watermark of his production. In **"Do Seek their Meat from God,"** a tale relating how a little boy is saved from two hungry panthers by his father's providential intervention, he tries to kindle the emotions by means of all the stock devices of sensational stories such as coincidences and unexpected meetings. The next two tales, however, rank among his finest achievements. In **"The Young Ravens that cry upon Him,"** a family of eagles is shown awaking at dawn, racked with hunger. The male soars in the morning sky, decries the landscape until he sees an ewe grazing with her new-born lamb. Like an arrow, he shoots down towards them and, when he flies upwards, he holds the lamb in his iron claws, while its helpless mother bleats pitifully. Besides its soberness and dignity, this tale, one of the most poetical in all Roberts' works, possesses a symbolic value: it is representative of the struggle for life which goes on ceaselessly in every corner of the universe and upon which Roberts looks with a serene acceptance of the inevitable. . . . Although without the broad significance of the latter tale, the third one, **"Strayed,"** is a fine realistic picture of wild life from which man is similarly absent: an ox, impelled by a sudden desire of freedom, leaves the camp and wanders in the wilderness until he falls prey to a roving panther. (pp. 398-99)

Roberts' next animal story appeared in 1896 (**"Savoury Meats"**), and was followed by a group of tales published in various magazines and gathered in May, 1902, under the title, *The Kindred of the Wild.* A collection of twelve tales, this book retains a certain unity as all deal with the dwellers in the New Brunswick wilderness and the stories present a general picture of life in these remote districts. The enthusiastic reception that that book met in Canada encouraged Roberts to persevere in the same *genre*: from that time, volume after volume of animal stories appeared under his name. A new tendency of enlarging the field described is manifested in the next one: in *The Watchers of the Trail,* the scene is again laid in New Brunswick, but while large mammals and birds were the only heroes of the tales in *The Kindred of the Wild,* the second collection deals also with smaller animals (muskrat, field-mouse), even fishes and insects (trout, dragon-fly). That extension is carried on further still in *The Haunters of the Silences*: Roberts quits his native province to relate incidents taken from the lives of arctic animals (polar bear and narwhal), of dwellers of the tropical seas (shark, cuttle-fish), and even the doings of the sarracenia or pitcher-plant. More collections follow, dealing mainly with the larger wild animals of the New Brunswick forest, including also occasional excursions to other spheres of wild life. They have no unity of subject or of tone save *Kings in Exile,* in which most of the tales are concerned with wild animals captured alive who either recover their freedom in one way or another or die in captivity. Many pages dating from that middle part of Roberts' career give the impression of having been written on the spur of the moment; composition and style no longer attain such excellency as in his first few volumes. (p. 400)

The extent of Roberts' production with the corresponding decline in its quality cannot be but a source of regret to the student of his works. As he himself confessed, it is to be accounted for by the necessity of earning a livelihood. "I write always," he said once, "of what has passed into my blood and my bones. I never write for any other reason—except sometimes for the necessary pocket-book reason." The ease with which his imagination creates incidents, coupled with repeated offers from editors who, since Thompson Seton's first success, had always an uncritical public ready for such tales, also contributed to produce that prolificness, various consequences of which appear in his works. In the first place, the desire of catering for not too fastidious a public led him to tell melodramatic stories devoid of all verisimilitude and to seek to rouse the reader's interest and emotions by vulgar means. **"The**

Truce" is a specimen of that class: an unarmed trapper pursued by a hungry bear reached a frozen river. Although it had begun to thaw, the man had no choice but to walk across, still followed by his enemy. Suddenly, the ice broke into floes. Now, it happens that this uncommon occurrence took place a few miles above big falls where a certain death awaited both man and beast. Fortunately, the floe supporting the man ran aground on an islet providentially situated in the middle of the river and overhanging the falls. As the bear struggled to reach the same shelter, the trapper, out of sympathy, pulled him ashore! Alone with the hungry beast, he soon repented his rash deed, when another miracle happened: big logs and blocks of ice formed a temporary bridge over which the man and then the beast passed on their way to safety. The introduction of such fortuitous means of salvation is a convenient device appearing in many tales.

In an attempt to sustain the interest, other numerous incidents are crowded into a short period, following one another with true cinematographic speed (**"The Fisher in the Chutes"**). Various animals sometimes appear in such rapid succession that the wilderness seems as densely populated as a town. (pp. 401-02)

Roberts' great prolificness carries another consequence with it, the repetition of the same theme with slight variations in several stories. In two of them, (**"The Passing of the Black Whelps,"**; **"The Invaders,"**) a female mongrel meets a wolf, follows him, gives birth to hybrids, but, hearing a man's voice, takes the latter's side in a fight. (p. 402)

But the most important group, both from the standpoint of number and of originality, deals with life in the wilderness, far away from man's haunts. Some of these tales may be looked upon as psychological studies while those that relate actions of the smaller animals appear as records of observations taken by a naturalist. Sometimes, one single episode, generally dealing with the search for food, the killing of a prey, is related; such is the case in **"The Young Ravens that cry upon Him."** Sometimes, the writer follows his hero from his birth throughout his existence or the greater part of it. Roberts has made a very limited use of biography, probably because he realizes the difficulties inherent to that form. *Red Fox,* the longest and most elaborate of his life-histories of animals, contains pages that rank among his best, but there is not more unity in it than in Seton's writings. It is nothing more than a *roman à tiroir,* a succession of unconnected episodes, so much so that some chapters appeared separately in several magazines before the publication of the book. The few biographies that Roberts has written besides *Red Fox* are short; at their close, the animal is still strong, victorious after a strenuous battle which constitutes a climax. *Red Fox* ends with the hero's escape, representing the triumph of the wild animals, the glorification of their freedom and strength.

Occasionally, Roberts takes a medium course between these extreme forms, the anecdote and the biography, and relates all the incidents befalling an individual or a family during a given period. This method also is open to criticism: there can be no logical link between the events that succeed one another; the personality of the hero is the sole factor making for unity and it is hardly sufficient. The reader is given a sense of completeness in **"The Winged Scourge of the Dark"**, relating the happenings of a single night and ending with the owl's death, or in **"The Watchers of the Swamp"**, describing one day of a bittern's life, with the song of the hermit thrush as the opening and closing note. On the other hand, there are cases when the "slice of life" is cut arbitrarily, the action left in suspense.

Most of Roberts' stories begin with a description of the scenery. An animal is then shown, doing some particular act. A brief description of that hero, never long enough to appear tedious, follows and the action is resumed. Often, Roberts withholds the name of the animal until the end of the description or even, in a few cases, until the end of the first episode, thus exciting the reader's curiosity. The action then proceeds, generally along a single line. In a few stories, each chapter takes up a separate succession of events and these various threads meet in the last chapter, by means of a coincidence. Roberts does not make an excessive use of this device; nearly always, he endeavours to justify its use and make it acceptable by means of a few remarks.

His tales deal mostly with questions of life and death; fights between animals are given a prominent place in many of them. Aware of their dramatic value, he generally selects combatants of fairly equal strength and, until the last instant, leaves the reader in suspense as to the issue. On the other hand, he occasionally relieves the sombre atmosphere by amusing episodes and humorous remarks; the comical and tragical elements are cleverly blended in stories such as **"Up a Tree"**. (pp. 403-05)

[Roberts had] partiality for the objective method. All his works do not contain more than two stories told in the first person: **"Bear versus Birchbark"** . . . and **"The Bear's Face"**, in which the hero himself relates his own adventure with a beast. This form makes it possible to add to the narrative a psychological sketch of the speaker as Kipling has done in *Bertran and Bimi,* but Roberts did not use that possibility to any great extent. *The House in the Water* is mainly an account of what a boy witnesses while watching a colony of beavers at several moments, but it includes two chapters (III and VII) that depict incidents happening in the beavers' houses and under the icy surface of the pond, which no man can have seen; although each method is perfectly legitimate, their union is questionable.

In the course of his boyhood, mostly spent in the country, close to the "forest primeval" of the land of Evangeline, Roberts acquired a thorough first-hand knowledge of Canadian wild animals which was an excellent asset for his later task. He also developed a sympathy towards them which is the keynote of his tales, but which never renders him blind to the deficiencies of his heroes, never makes him idealize them. Aiming at the faithful representation of nature, he does not hesitate to correct the first impression given by the moose's call, even though his remarks destroy the idyllic character of the scene:

> To one listening far down the lake, the call would have sounded beautiful in its way, though lugubrious—a wild, vast, incomprehensible voice, appropriate to the solitude. But to a near-
> by listener, it must have sounded both monstrous and absurd—like nothing else so much as the effort of a young farmyard bull to mimic the braying of an ass. Nevertheless, to one who could hear aright, it was a noble and splendid call, vital with all sincerity of response and love and elemental passion.

Nor does he ascribe to animals a moral perfection they do not possess; of a mother rabbit, he says:

> She loved her young ones; but she loved life better. She had but one life, and she had had, and with luck could go on having many young.

Like Seton, he assumes that animals can reason to a certain extent: . . . . Were not this taken for granted, it would be difficult to conceive stories such as his, for animals, as heroes of tales, can only interest us in proportion as they share some of man's attributes. But . . . the greatest difficulty that besets realistic nature-writers is to resist the anthropomorphic tendency, to endow animals with a certain amount of intelligence, but not to present them as disguised human beings.

Whether Roberts has always escaped that danger is a very difficult question to answer. Very little is known about the life of the wild; even naturalists disagree among themselves as to the degree of intelligence to be ascribed to animals. "It is mainly guess work how far our psychology applies to the lower animals," Burroughs wrote at the end of a life devoted to the observation of nature. Hence, extreme prudence is necessary and the ideas expressed on that subject are to be looked upon as mere opinions.

Roberts denies the faculty of speculating to animals, but believes they can use reason in the pursuit of the few primary desires that constitute all their life. Even Burroughs, who was in no way favourable to animal story writers, said: "In *The Kindred of the Wild,* one finds much to admire and commend, and but little to take exception to. The volume is in many ways the most brilliant collection of animal stories that has appeared." Only in a proportionally small number of cases does Roberts seem to forget he is speaking of animals, not of men. The panthers, in **"Do Seek their Meat from God,"** "knew the voice was the voice of a child, and something in the voice told them the child was solitary." It seems most doubtful whether animals can thus distinguish the various shades of emotion exposed in a human cry. (pp. 405-07)

Among the higher animals, the fox has a reputation of extraordinary cunning, handed down from time immemorial; in Roberts' works are retold old tricks of his, to the support of which no authentic evidence could probably be offered. Twice, when caught, he pretends to be dead and succeeds the first time in deceiving men. On another occasion, he uncovers a trap, soils it and leaves it exposed "so that no other of the forest dwellers might be betrayed by it." It is all the more difficult to admit that he acts on altruistic motives as, a few pages further on, we are told that Red Fox takes home and eats a rabbit killed in a trap!

Still more incredible are some passages about communications between animals. Of course, Roberts never makes them speak as fabulists do: that would be in flat contradiction with his realistic conception of the animal story. Although he generally shows more reserve than Seton in that respect and merely ascribes to them the power of expressing a few simple ideas such as danger, joy, etc., his works contain some absolutely unaccountable facts [Editor's note: The following quotes are from two pages of *Red Fox.*]:

> In some way, partly by example and partly no doubt by a simple language whose subtleties evade human observation, she (the mother fox) had striven to impress upon them the suicidal folly of intervening with the man-people's possessions. Easy hunting, she conveyed to them, was not always good hunting.

> She (his mate) gave him to understand that this (a trap) was one of the cunningest and most deadly of all the devices which that incomprehensible creature, man, was wont to employ against the wild kindreds. And she also made him understand that unexpected blessings, like the chicken head, or other unusual dainties, when found scattered with seeming generosity about the forest ways, were pretty sure to indicate at least one trap in the immediate neighbourhood.

Such are Roberts' departures from verisimilitude in the psychology of beasts. Like Thompson Seton's, they are fortunately offset by incidents that illustrate the limitations of animal intelligence. The dim reasoning power of the moose is well shown in the passage quoted below; a bull, answering a moose-call, sees a man instead of the expected female; then a bear, also attracted by the call, limbers forward:

> He dimly felt that the mystery which had been tormenting him was the fault of this particular bear. The man was forgotten. A cow had been calling to him. She had disappeared. Here was the bear. The bear had probably done away with the cow. The cow should be terribly avenged.
>
> (pp. 407-09)

A second way of counterbalancing the humanization is found in the introduction of instinct under various forms. The mother's instinctive love of her young leads her to fight most dangerous battles and even to sacrifice herself for them. The sexual instinct overpowers all suspicions in the moose, when he hears a female calling, and occasionally carries him to his doom. More important still in Roberts' stories is the impulse that calls back animals to their natural surroundings; such is the migrating instinct, in one case in conflict with sexual love. Wild animals born in captivity are shown longing for a life they have never experienced, but Roberts often gives to such tales a romantic ending, somewhat unlikely: feeling lonely, they finally return to man, preferring society to freedom.

Even some domesticated animals are subject to that longing for freedom which reappears after many generations. One of the most subtle and clever psychological studies in Roberts' works comes under that head. In Bran's mind clash conflicting tendencies inherited from his various ancestors. Some were tame dogs who have handed down to him the impulse of watching over his master's sheep; oth-

ers lived free from man's domination and have left a blood-lust that sometimes emerges in Bran's feelings. When, one day, a dog slew sheep of his flock, he attacked and killed the murderer, but the sight of blood roused all the instincts of his race. His sense of ownership still surviving, he went to a stranger's flock and killed a lamb; at once the taste of blood disgusted him and restored him to sanity. Ashamed and afraid, he returned to his old occupation in perfect submission. It is true that Bran shows a complexity of reasoning processes most unusual in an animal, but every act of his is well accounted for and the tale offers no absurdity.

When one comes to examine the psychology of inferior animals, the defects already mentioned appear far more grievous. It is difficult to subscribe to the attribution by Roberts of feelings to an octopus, memory to a fish, clear consciousness to a bee or an ant. Indeed, it seems almost impossible to build successful stories on the adventures of such beings. Either the author gives them feelings and thoughts, i.e. humanizes them to a certain extent, which cannot be accepted so easily as in the case of the higher mammals; or they are treated from outside, the story being a mere record of what an observer might see of their actions. The facts related are then typical not of the individual but of the species. There is no longer any psychology, any individuality: it is science, not literature. Such is the case with several other tales, open to different but equally serious objections as those referred to above.

As for the education of animals by their parents, Roberts, while recognizing its existence and importance, gives it a much smaller place in his stories than Seton in tales such as *The Biography of a Grizzly,* or *Krag,* for he is not so much interested in the development of the animals' powers as in the dramatic conflicts in their mature life.

Roberts chooses his heroes in a number of species which may be convenient divided into three classes. Firstly, the creatures of the sea, especially the larger and more formidable ones: the ravenous shark, prowling round with his fixed stare on his human prey,—the saw-fish, surging from the depths and raking his opponent's belly with his terrible weapon,—the loathsome octopus, a living nightmare and a fearful antagonist. A second group is formed by the dwellers of the arctic regions: the harmless seal, frolicking in the waters or basking on rocky ledges; the walrus, whose long tusks make him a dreaded enemy; the polar bear, the acknowledged master of these white solitudes. But the place of honour is reserved to the wild beasts of New Brunswick whose ways Roberts knows much more intimately: creatures of the air like the hawk, the migrating wild goose, and the lordly eagle;—inhabitants of the water, the muskrat, the snake-like and sleek otter and her enemy the beaver, whose wonderful dam-building, tree-felling and house-repairing fill many pages;—lastly, inhabitants of the woods and fields, the invulnerable porcupine, the chipmunk, the field mouse, the snowshoe rabbit and their bloodthirsty destroyer the weasel; the cruel lynx, the sly fox, the antlered moose and the bear, most powerful of them all.

With so many animals constantly in the foreground, man's place is necessarily restricted. In many tales, he is

A watercolor sketch of Westcock Parsonage, Roberts's birthplace. Roberts spent his first thirteen years at the parsonage, which is located near Fredericton, New Brunswick.

not seen at all; in others, he appears as an intruder in a world not his own, often crossing the stage too quickly for us to perceive more than a mere shadow, the silhouette of a hunter or animal lover. And yet, no sooner has his axe broken the silence of the wooded solitudes that the animals look upon him as a weird being, to whose powers no clear bounds can be set. Roberts' sympathy for animals does not make him forget the overwhelming superiority of man. In his tales, the latter appears as the ruler of the world, the ultimate victor in his struggles with other beings, and those, if they have any opportunity of watching him, motionless behind a thick screen of foliage, respect and fear his lordship. Only when the wolf pack has hunted in vain for days or when the panther's cub has been stolen from her do they dare to attack him. They are daunted by his masterful voice; his very laugh dismays them. Some, the more intelligent, have indistinct ideas concerning his property and are aware of the advisability of keeping away from his dwellings and possessions, to avoid drawing down his vengeance upon them.

How does he look upon them in his turn? Typical hunters are merely sketched and Roberts seldom condemns their doings. Most frequently, the hunting instinct appears in

his tales as a temporary crisis, an emergence of the old bed-rock covered by civilization. Some human characters are "backwoodsmen," either woodcutters or trappers, simple sturdy beings, always unwilling to admit that their woodcraft has been foiled, lest their reputation should receive a blemish. They do not devote much thought to animals, a part of their natural surroundings and sometimes their very livelihood. They do not yield to sentimentality, yet they are human. They chivalrously intervene in battles between animals, killing in order to spare cruel sufferings to the weaker one. If a beast that they intended to destroy saves their life, even unwittingly, if one performs an unusual exploit before their eyes, their gratefulness or their admiration overcomes their interest. The old Jabe, who appears in *The House in the Water* and in other tales, is the most representative specimen of that class.

Roberts often endows dwellers of the woods with the consciousness of being watched or followed by some being, on occasions when their senses do not inform them of it; in no less than ten different passages is that faculty shown, mostly in men, sometimes in animals. Does it correspond to a reality? Would it develop in dwellers of the wild, men or beasts, so alert that their subconscious self might perceive dim sensations, normally unheeded? Or is it merely a device meant to make the story more thrilling and increase its interest gradually?

Another class is composed of young people deeply engrossed by the study of the wild creatures and averse to their destruction. Some of them, and particularly "the Boy," who is portrait of the author as he was in his early teens, represent Roberts' attitude fairly well.

Roberts looks upon nature as the scene of the dramas, generally depicted before the beginning of the action. Like a playwright giving brief indications of the scenery before the text of his play, he once described it solely by means of sentences without verbs:—

> A perfect dome of palest blue, vaporous but luminous. To northward and south-eastward a horizon line of low uplands, misty purple. Along the farthest west a glimmer and sparkle of the sea.
>
> (pp. 409-13)

More seldom, a little touch of scenery may be found at the end, after a fight to the death, as a contrast between the fleeting violence of animal life and the impassibility of nature. . . .

He lays a particular stress on the transient features of the landscape, the changes due to the season or the hour. He knows how light transforms the whole aspect of the scenery, how in particular the moon can work a weird enchantment on the most trivial objects, giving beauty and an air of unreality to everything upon which she throws her silver beams. . . . (p. 413)

His perception of smells is equally keen. . . .

> This air seemed to carry with reluctance a certain fluctuating chill, caught from the icy water. But in the main, its burden was the breath of willow catkin and sprouting grass and the first shy bloom on the open edges of the uplands. It was the characteristic smell of the northern spring, tender and elusive, yet keenly penetrating. If gems had perfumes, just so might the opal smell.

Nor does he neglect sounds. Moving with a furtive wariness, wild animals always observe the law of silence, upon which depend the success of their hunts and their very safety; thus, in spite of the abundant life they hide, the wild regions are always still, and if, from time to time, a noise is heard, it intensifies the silence rather than disturbs it.

> In the heart of the cedar swamp the silence was thick, brooding, imperishable. One felt that if ever any wandering sound, any bird's cry or call of wayfaring beast should drop into it, the intruding voice would be straight away engulfed, smothered and forgotten.

All these descriptive passages, more patiently wrought than the ordinary warp of the narrative, remind the reader that the author is a poet who knows how to convey the beauty of the scenes he depicts, and at the same time manifest the individuality of his tastes and impressions.

One cannot but be struck by the extreme accuracy and viv-

idness of many passages in which Roberts excels in discovering the salient features of the objects described, at emphasizing those by means of a short, well chosen and often original comparison:

> The roots of the trees were half uncovered,—immense, coiled, uncouth, dull-coloured shapes, like monsters struggling up from the teeming primeval slime.
>
> (pp. 414-15)

His descriptions, frequent but sober, never stop the progress of the tale; aiming at the essential, he condenses his pictures to the few most interesting features. The narrative element is naturally predominant. Aware that it requires a different method, Roberts replaces the minute selection and delicate chiselling of details by a broader treatment. No longer important in themselves, words and sentences of a classical simplicity are nothing but the most direct and limpid expression of the ideas that the author wishes to convey, and they flow in a current as swift as the stream of events they tell. (p. 416)

Although the reader may derive some information from Roberts' books, [he] is not concerned with their educational value. Only one of his tales, *The House in the Water,* has a truly didactic character. It might be called a treatise presenting, under the form of observations and dialogues, the beaver's habits, their mode of building and repairing houses, dams and canals, of felling trees and accumulating winter supplies, etc. The scientific interest predominates and the author's first aim has undoubtedly been to make his readers familiar with beavers. In all his other writings he may impart knowledge incidentally but never designedly.

In many stories, particularly in those where man does not appear, Roberts does not side with the most important hero but presents the events in an impartial way. At first sight, this might be thought to lessen the interest; yet, it sometimes produces very striking effects and imparts to the tale a wider significance. . . . It helps Roberts to impress his readers repeatedly with the idea that, apart from a few exceptions (weasel, mink, horned owl), wild animals do not fight and kill for the sake of fighting and killing, not to satisfy any blood-lust, but merely because such is the law of their life, nay of all life.

In spite of this, killing is a common occurrence in Roberts' pages as well as in the wilderness. Man himself, urged for the need for meat, is sometimes seen fighting the wild kindred, though reluctantly. That necessity is a law of nature: such is the great truth that underlies so many episodes, yet has been expressed only once by Roberts, in the picturesque backwoods vernacular:

> Nature's nature (Dave says), an' ye can't do much by buckin' up agin her. Look now, ye told me to shoot the lou'-cerfie coz he killed the deer kid. But he didn't go to kill it for ugliness, nor jest for himself to make a dinner off of—you know that. He killed it for his mate too. Lou'—cerfie ain't built so's they can eat grass. If the she lou'-cerfie didn't get the meat she needed, her kittens 'd starve. She's just *got* to kill. Nature's put that law onto her, an' onto the painters, an'

the foxes an' wolves, the 'coons an' the weasels. An' she's put the same law, only not so heavy, onto the bears, an' also onto humans, what's all built to live on all kinds of food, meat among the rest. An' to live right, an' be their proper selves, they've all got to eat meat sometimes, for Nature don't stand much foolin' with her laws! . . . I've thought about it a heap, alone in camp, an' I can noways see through it. Oftentimes, it's seemed to me all life was jest like a few butterflies flitterin' over a graveyard.

(pp. 417-18)

Michel Poirier, "The Animal Story in Canadian Literature: Part II—C. G. D. Roberts," in Queen's Quarterly, *Vol. XXXIV, No. 4, April-June, 1927, pp. 398-419.*

Pelham Edgar

[The] future will recognize even more than we are willing to do that Roberts was a pivotal figure, a musical hinge around which our poetry first began to revolve. (p. 117)

[Nonetheless, his] formal fiction is not quite first-rate. His constructive skill is not of the highest order, and humanly speaking his power of invention is weak and his command of incident limited. But books that we might call "near novels," like **The Heart of the Ancient Wood** and **In the Morning of Time** have an enduring fascination. And some of the stories appearing in the animal volumes, but deviating from the theme, are works of the highest art. **"The Perdu,"** of **Earth's Enigmas,** is such a piece, and others might be named that possess the same haunting suggestiveness, and the same deftness of touch and unerring quality of observation.

As for the animal stories themselves it must be admitted that their never ending flow makes for monotony. While the vogue lasted their influence operated, but that influence is now dead and the modern short story has taken on a totally new character. (pp. 123-24)

Pelham Edgar, "Sir Charles G. D. Roberts and His Time," in University of Toronto Quarterly, *Vol. XIII, No. 1, October, 1943, pp. 117-26.*

William H. Magee

In art realistic animals are as old as the caveman drawing on his stone wall, but in the novel and short story they are as new as the theory of evolution. A direct if minor effect on literature of the controversy over that theory appeared in the sudden creation of animal heroes in the closing quarters of the nineteenth century. Although a consciousness of such an inspiration would probably have shocked some of the first modern writers with four-legged heroes, particularly moralists who made a cause of the prevention of cruelty to animals, Sir Charles G. D. Roberts made the connection. He also described the first consistently realistic animals in literature, thus giving Canada a founding influence in this development in modern literature. (p. 156)

The widespread use of animals in modern literature dates from the last quarter of the nineteenth century. In 1877 Anna Sewell began the vogue with *Black Beauty,* the best-selling horse story which pleaded for more humane treatment of domestic animals. Through her philanthropy,

Miss Sewell had hit on a purpose for her story which distinguishes animal characters from man, instead of stressing similarities. The artistic appeal for human readers is genuinely indirect, a good will based perhaps on the misery and cruelty suffered by all living creatures and caused by bad men. For the first time in literary history it was no longer desirable or even artistically sensible to draw man-like animals. Any failure to make the domestic animals credible on the part of Anna Sewell or her followers is the result only of failures in technique.

Pets can beguile readers into tears even more readily than horses can, and so it is that the Canadian contribution to Anna Sewell's type of animal story is even more sentimental than *Black Beauty.* When Margaret Marshall Saunders wrote her famous dog story, *Beautiful Joe* (1894), she won a competition for a companion piece to *Black Beauty.* Again the animal is at the centre of the scene, and again the author stresses needs peculiar to it rather than common with man. Indeed *Beautiful Joe* seems for chapters at a time to be less a story than a manual in the care of animals. . . . The characterization of Beautiful Joe takes on a clarity of outline through its new, nonhuman perspective, and some continuing credibility results from the marked simplicity of the dog's reflections and its lack of dialogue. Miss Saunders's failure came in the more advanced challenge of devising a credible plot for her dog hero. Confronted with the need to develop a conflict, she borrowed a melodramatic villain and weeping young women from the traditions of nineteenth-century human fiction. . . . The constant Christian didacticism in the book suggests another literary tradition of the times. As a result, the story which begins from a distinctive and credible nonhuman point of view ends in a medley of long popular conventions of fiction. (pp. 157-58)

Also in 1894, Rudyard Kipling introduced a different widespread use of animals in modern literature with his first *Jungle Book.* It is a pure romance of man living among the beasts of the jungle, with the boy Mowgli as the typical hero of an adventure which differs from the hackneyed only because of the rest of the cast. Sometimes Kipling reverted to the primitive use of animals as antagonists of man, sometimes his characters echo human virtues and vices. The animals would suit Kipling's purpose at least as well if they were characterized realistically. As with Miss Sewell and Miss Saunders, the old hybrid characters no longer were essential to the purpose, and the incredible humanness is merely a difficulty of technique. The chief literary advance in Kipling's animal stories results from the more unified atmosphere provided by his romantic approach. Kipling subdued the attendant artistic dangers of triviality, sentimentality, and melodrama, although his sprawling progeny of Tarzan and other yarns of men living among somewhat nonhuman beasts has carried the art of fiction close to its nadir. Sir Charles G. D. Roberts objected to the falsified animals of both traditions and started a third and accurate one in **Earth's Enigmas.**

When Roberts turned to the animal world to populate his stories, he tried to look at life from the animals' point of view. To do so, he would choose an animal or animal family going about its daily business of searching for food, the most common concern of such creatures, Roberts felt. Their chief obstacle is the threat of danger or death from the intended victim or from another hungry animal. Consequently the typical character has a serious outlook on life, with no time for fun, no concern for outsiders, and the stories seethe with this solemnity. When the simple wants of two such hungry animals clash, when the one eats the other, or more often the young of the other, the irreconcilable conflict creates an effect of stark tragedy. Roberts usually increased the poignancy of this effect by making the animals either pregnant or starving from trying to feed their young. In **"The Young Ravens That Call upon Him"** (*Earth's Enigmas*), a starving eagle seizes a newborn lamb to feed the starving eaglets, bringing momentary contentment to the nest but leaving the wandering ewe utterly forlorn. Such a juxtaposition can make the animal story a profound comment on the tragedy of life on earth.

Having focused his animal characters on the central concern of their lives, Roberts went on to draw them as convincingly nonhuman. Anna Sewell and Miss Saunders had chosen a special rather than a central problem of animals in the world, one in which man plays a unique and godlike rather than a similar role. Without any men at all in some of his stories, Roberts was driven back to consider the first principles of animal characterization. His animals do not talk, and their thoughts are single, immediate, and simple. Most of the time their behaviour is habitual or instinctive, as when the male eagle always hunts the Squatook Lakes and his mate hunts the Tuladi in **"The Lord of the Air"** (from *The Kindred of the Wild*). When the environment changes, as when an Indian trapper regularly leaves food for the male eagle, and later a net under the food, the eagle comes to accept the change as habitual too. After being captured, the bird can think of one quick move to escape, but only pride provides the continuing urge to escape, and an unexpected ferocity makes it succeed. As the story closes, the eagle has returned to its habitual perch over the Squatooks. The dominion of the eagle, and his determination, make the character heroic, but the simplicity of his outlook helps retain the conviction of reality.

At best Roberts developed a powerful new literary form out of the simple stories of such realistic animals. The climax of two stories of starving animals in the same incident lends depth to the view of the world, and the joining at the climax turns their innocent wants into pathetic tragedy. A rare irony deepens the effect still further at the end of **"When Twilight Falls on the Stump Lots"** (*The Kindred of the Wild*), after a mother cow has fatally gored a bear looking for food for its cubs:

> The merry little cubs within the den were beginning to expect her, and getting restless. As the night wore on, and no mother came, they ceased to be merry. By morning they were shivering with hunger and desolate fear. But the doom of the ancient wood was less harsh than its wont, and spared them some days of starving anguish; for about noon a pair of foxes discovered the dead mother, astutely estimated the situation, and then, with the boldness of good appetite, made their way into the unguarded den.

> As for the red calf, its fortune was ordinary. Its

mother, for all her wounds, was able to nurse and cherish it through the night; and with morning came a searcher from the farm and took it, with the bleeding mother, safely back to the settlement. There it was tended and fattened, and within a few weeks found its way to the cool marble slabs of a city market.

The curtailed lives of both groups in the conflict, dams and offspring alike, add a perspective of the futility of survival that makes this Roberts' most moving story. Perhaps a less conscious irony underlies the treatment of man as just another animal with the same hunger to satisfy. In **"Savoury Meats"** (*The Kindred of the Wild*) a man shoots a doe to give his invalid father the red food to live, but a wildcat eats the abandoned fawn. In **"Wild Motherhood"** (*The Kindred of the Wild*), which tells three parallel stories, a man with a meat-hungry wife and son shoots not only a wolf who is trying to feed a pregnant mate who cannot hunt because of missing a paw, but also the moose that the wolf is hunting. In stories like these man is an animal competing with his fellows in satisfying the same wants, and succeeding because he is the most fit.

Other variations on the basic characters and plots proved less rewarding. Stories of men trapping tended to distract Roberts into sentimental studies of tender-hearted human beings. **"The Moonlight Trails"** (*The Kindred of the Wild*) ends with a boy, who has excitedly been snaring rabbits, repenting at the sight of dead rabbits hanging in the noose. . . . Once in a while man even enters as a god looking after animals like a puppet master. In **"The Watchers of the Camp-Fire"** (*The Kindred of the Wild*) the man shoots a hungry panther just to save a doe which has been attracted to the site by the light of his campfire. In casting around for the necessary variety in the development of his plots, Roberts fell back more and more on the repertoire of human fiction, particularly in his later volumes. Roberts also had an instinctive bent towards romantic justice which clashed with the air of objectivity so important to his best effects. In **"The Haunter of the Pine Gloom"** (*The Kindred of the Wild*) the animal-loving young boy of **"The Moonlight Trails"** turns out to hate lynx while loving all other creatures. With romance entered nostalgia, with nostalgia sentimentality. A heightened scene produces a heightened emotion, and so melodrama was pressed into service.

Ultimately Roberts was unable to develop a general repertoire of fresh characters and situations for his new genre. Deliberately giving up the dialogue, the extended descriptions, and the casual plotting of traditional fiction, he found it difficult to fill up his stories without repetition. The juxtaposition of two or even three parallel searches for food, climaxing in tragedy for at least one, eked out the material for several well-rounded stories, but it did not provide a pattern which was repeatedly reusable and fresh. The restriction to simple wants also worked against variety. In effect Roberts seldom wrote well with any other want for his heroes than food. In **"The King of the Mamozekel"** (*The Kindred of the Wild*), the long biography of a bull moose from birth to adult domination of a herd is tied together only by the dubious psychological dread of bears suggested as unique to this moose. The wintertime longing of a young ox for the dream pastures of the previous June makes **"Strayed"** (*Earth's Enigmas*) an untypical romance of minimal interest. Roberts developed a new literary form, but then he found no reliable means to give it variety.

"Alike in matter and in method, the animal story, as we have it to-day, may be regarded as a culmination." When Roberts began his essay on **"The Animal Story"** (in *The Kindred of the Wild*) with these words, he was recording his technical frustration. He was also rejoicing in the sense of his own accomplishment and his new recognition of the significance of the history of animals in literature. He saw that the keys to his discovery were the recent advances in psychology and the biological sciences, declaring that "the animal story at its highest point of development is a psychological romance constructed on a framework of natural science." Consequently he sets his own stories and those of Ernest Thompson Seton against those of Anna Sewell, Marshall Saunders, and Kipling, pointing out their errors in the representation of animals. Although he is rather distressed that Christianity with its "Dispensation of Love" had not stimulated this advance long before, he rejoices ultimately that his stories appeal to the heart and the spirit of evolutionary man after "the long upward march of being." Perhaps the delight in this "potent emancipation" provided the stimulus for Roberts to produce a score of animal story books despite his conviction that he had reached the culmination of the genre: "There would seem to be no further evolution possible." (pp. 158-62)

> *William H. Magee, "The Animal Story: A Challenge in Technique," in* The Dalhousie Review, *Vol. 44, No. 2, Summer, 1964, pp. 156-64.*

Joseph Gold

Roberts' animal stories constitute, as far as I can ascertain, the only sustained attempt to use the materials of the Canadian Wilderness for the purpose of expressing a coherent view of the world that man inhabits. Roberts has created a Canadian mythology, in which animals, rather than gods, play out a systematic drama of conflict and resolution. This is all done, of course, within the framework of an accurate survey of natural history, and it is a brave man who would casually question Roberts' knowledge of the wilderness. Nevertheless it would be as pointless to apply standards of "realism" to these stories as it would be to question the size and character of William Faulkner's bear, in any discussion of its ultimate significance. Roberts' bear, fox, moose and porcupine are distillations of certain instincts and concretizations of certain abstractions. There are no centaurs or griffins but there are many other creatures who emerge from the author's poetic imagination with equal meaning and consistency and with a similarly forceful effect. This mythology is, at its best, a carefully designed metaphor for the order and structure of nature, as in the story **"In the Deep of the Silences"**. The title itself suggests not just a location but a dynamic force at the heart of things. In the story the elements, land, air and water are represented by a bear, an eagle and a lake trout. Each is king, or god of his domain. This almost Classic arrangement, far from being vague or accidental,

is clearly intended. Not only is the story divided into four parts, one to each of the elements, and the last to the conflict between their "gods", but the descriptions themselves indicate Roberts' attitude:

> His fierce yellow eyes, unwavering, brilliant, and clear like crystal, deep set beneath straight, overhanging brows, searched the far panorama with an incredibly piercing gaze. At such a distance that the most penetrating human eye—the eye of a sailor, a plains' ranger, a backwoods' huntsman, or an enumerator of the stars—could not discern him in his soundless altitude, he could mark the fall of a leaf or the scurry of a mouse in the sedge-grass.

What could be more suggestive of an invisible sky-god, who unseen himself, sees all beneath him? And when he does descend he comes like a thunderbolt:

> There was a harsh, strong hissing in the air, and a dark body fell out of the sky. Fell? Rather it seemed to have been shot downward from a catapult. No mere falling could be so swift as that sheer yet governed descent.

This aura of design, pattern, structure, in a world peopled by creatures pursuing a highly dramatic and meaningful action pervades all the best Roberts' stories, and there are many of them. . . . In an interesting essay, **"The Animal Story"**, Roberts states with admirable candour that the animal story of his time, and as he writes it, is a "culmination". He surveys the history of this mode of writing from its "fabulous" origins up to Kipling and Seton and he asserts that the "psychological" animal story, in which the "personality, individuality, mentality" of an animal is pursued, has evolved fully and can go no further. Roberts clearly does not see himself as writing this kind of story at all. He believes rather that through the animal the writer can approach some larger vision of basic human drives and some understanding of the transcendent universal design to which all things contribute. He says of the animal story:

> It leads us back to the old kinship of earth, without asking us to relinquish by way of toll any part of the wisdom of the ages, any fine essential of the 'large result of time'.

By this Roberts means that the artist can use animals to make sense of the world of which man is part and from which he grew, that we are given a detachment and perspective from which to examine the fundamental base on which we rest. (pp. 23-4)

Roberts' animal world amounts . . . to an affirmative vision in which the conditions of a wilderness struggle for survival are accepted and confirmed. . . . Roberts was born in 1860 and inherited the full force of nineteenth-century disillusion. The period which saw a search for answers to a godless world culminate in Existentialism made it necessary for Roberts also to seek some positive confrontation with the problem of man's apparent lonely helplessness. Being an artist, not a philosopher, Roberts sought the kind of imaginative understanding that Blake and Shelley and Wordsworth had sought before him. The terms of his clerical background were not acceptable, the raw materials of a New Brunswick wilderness were to hand, and so Roberts brought his imagination to bear on nature and animals and produced his own Canadian mythology. The principal feature of this myth is that, while individual creatures constantly lose the struggle for survival, life itself persists. In the long run death itself has no sting and is ironically defeated by the uses nature makes of its processes. All things conspire to sustain life and the stories create a very strong sense of rhythmic pattern and cycle, of the seasons, of birth and death, of mating and separating, and these patterns persist no matter what the creatures, what the setting or what human interference is attempted. This may not seem like a great deal by which to celebrate some meaning to existence, but after all has man ever been honoured for doing more than living, to the best of his ability?

Roberts is, to my knowledge, the only writer who has used animals to illustrate such a vision. But the effect of his writing is frequently and strongly like that experienced with Becket's *Godot,* or Faulkner's *Dilsey,* or Brecht's *Mother Courage.* It may sound ludicrous to put, say, Red Fox in such company, but when one has actually read about him the comparison is not nearly so laughable. Certainly it is true to say that Roberts' animals are more dignified and lead more meaningful lives than the characters in the writings of Zola and Dreiser, who were contemporaries of Roberts and whose creatures are infinitely more "animal". "Human" and "animal" are labels earned by the quality of behaviour so that a writer may humanize an animal world or animalize a human one. Roberts is after all a poet, which is to say that his imagination makes definition and his human version of the animal world dignifies and ennobles that world. Roberts celebrates courage and endurance and for this reason his stories of defeat and death produce not despair but a sense of elevation, and often something akin to catharsis. His animals and birds and fishes confront overwhelming odds. Every second is a challenge to life itself. The combatants in man's conflict, when not hunger and cold, are accident and disease. For the animal, in exactly the same way, they are the innumerable enemies who see him as food and wait for him in silence. The animal who guards his life best survives longest, but there is never any guarantee that the next moment will not be the last. It is precisely because the contest is always finally lost that the struggle is meaningful. Roberts' animal world, like ours, is a fallen world and the best that can be achieved in it is a persistent denial of death, hunger and fear. Every moment wrenched from time is a major victory and every meal is a conquest over an indifferent universe. Roberts would agree with Blake that "everything that lives is holy" but he would add, I suspect, "And holy because it lives."

The techniques Roberts employs are simple and it is the retention of simplicity that is his greatest strength. There is no commentary, no moralizing, but a stark presentation of animal impulses and success or defeat. *The Last Barrier* is by no means a collection of the best of Roberts' stories, but since it is readily available we must confine ourselves to it. The title story illustrates the Roberts' theme and technique most clearly. The salmon is born, miraculously grows up and dies in the paws of a bear after a hopeless struggle to climb a waterfall. This is the archetypal pattern of the birth-death cycle for all living creatures. But Roberts conveys to the reader a clear sense of his own awe at the fact that the process takes place at all. Survival itself is a miracle and even before this, gestation and birth. (pp. 25-6)

The strong sense of the infinite scale of size in the universe, from the minute forces of energy to the unconquerable seasons, is characteristic of Roberts' awareness. The salmon is not only born but turns into something animate, complete, perfect and volatile and for the humanizing, poetic imagination of Roberts, this is a supreme and even divine achievement:

> The deep hollow in the gravel sheltered the moving atoms, so that they were not swept away by the current streaming over them. But minute as they were, they speedily gathered a strength altogether miraculous for their size, as they absorbed the clinging sacs of egg-substance and assumed the forms of fish, almost microscopic, but perfect.
>
> (p. 27)

One has the sense of reading the commentary of a man peering through a microscope at the astonishing activities of a new world. Certainly, if this writer may judge from his own and from his students' responses, a reading of Roberts produces a different, a more sensitive and a more aware encounter with a world that was originally taken much more for granted. It is unnecessary here to record the progress of the salmon through all its stages, from Parr to Smelt to Grilse to Salmon, or to summarize its ocean voyages and its change from a new born "speck of life" to parenthood in its turn. Roberts writes a history of one sample of myriad life that inevitably ends in defeat, and yet he writes it in such a way as to indicate, not a despairing or cynical view of the natural process, but a celebration of the struggle itself, as a careful look at his wording indicates, "the pioneer of the shoal found all his ability taxed to guard the speck of life which he had so lately achieved."

The ending to the *The Last Barrier* is full of meaning. During one of the salmon's annual absences the falls of his stream have greatly changed by virtue of a shift in formation that makes them now insurmountable. The salmon ends itself in vain leaps and is finally injured and exhausted:

> When, at last, the salmon came blindly into the eddy and turned upon his side, the bear was but a few feet distant. She crept forward like a cat, crouched—and a great black paw shot around with a clutching sweep. Gasping and quivering, the salmon was thrown up upon the rocks. Then white teeth, savage but merciful, bit through the back of his neck; and unstruggling he was carried to a thicket above the Falls.

The use of the word "unstruggling" is curious here. More than a mechanical description is intended and the word in this context suggests acceptance, resolution, completion. When the fish can struggle no longer it is ready to give up its life, for life and struggle have become synonymous. Nature fulfills itself in many ways and the writer provides a curiously ironic ending in which the fish, unable to master the falls alive is carried to their summit in death, as food in the mouth of the bear. A greater harmony, accessible only to the human imagination, is thus illustrated by the writer. The final victory is paradoxically that of life itself, and many deaths go to its making. In spite of the reiterated patterns of the stronger eating the weaker and cunning or speed eluding the dull or slow, Roberts is not interested in labouring a cliché. He goes to some pains to indicate that not even the fittest survive. . . . [What] we see is the survival of life and the process of cycle, of forces struggling against matter and matter itself altered by the operation of natural laws. All things are fit for some time and place. The waterfalls will be mastered one way, if not another.

It is interesting at this point to consider more precisely the basis for the inevitable discussion of Wordsworth's influence on Roberts. To suggest the areas of similarity would require a discussion of Wordsworth beyond the scope of this paper. However the Mutability Sonnet is at the centre of Wordsworth's outlook, and it is curious that it reflects so accurately the themes illustrated everywhere in Roberts' prose,

> From low to high doth dissolution climb,
> And sink from high to low, along a scale
> Of awful notes, whose concord shall not fail . . .

"Concord shall not fail," Wordsworth says, and later he writes "Truth fails not." Concord is Truth and Truth is Concord; that is all you know on earth and perhaps all you need to know, and this hypothetical dictum might stand as well for Roberts as for Wordsworth. The animal stories also amount to a hymn to concord and harmony, and this "scale of awful notes" along which life and death and change harmoniously run is to be perceived by the imagination of a detached artist, a man possessed of heightened sensibility, who is not confused by spiritual myopia. When this "scale" is heard it produces not despair but a transcendent understanding.

> A musical but melancholy chime,
> Which they can hear who meddle not with crime
> Nor avarice, nor over-anxious care.

Roberts says of the animal story that it might, if used as he tries to use it, aid us in attaining such an awareness, "It frees us for a little from the world of shopworn utilities, and from the mean tenement of self of which we do well to grow weary." Roberts quite deliberately seeks to produce a detached awareness in his reader by creating metaphor free from discourse or commentary. The effect is to hold the reader at a kind of intellectual distance whence he may apprehend the vast process of dissolution and regeneration, even unconsciously. (pp. 27-9)

One of the surest marks of Roberts' genius and an indication of the degree of conscious control usually employed, is his complete freedom from sentiment. Roberts' animals never become pets, the reader is never allowed to lose his detachment and there is no compromise in the recorded events with the bloody processes of universal natural law. There is too, the mastery of perspective, the ability, almost

Swiftian, to construct whole worlds scaled to the size of ants as in **"The Prisoners of the Pitcher-Plant"** or to the world of giant moose and bear as in **"The King of the Mamozekel"**. Nor is there space to pursue the brilliance of poetic description, always used for specific and often symbolic purposes, or to comment on the division of the whole work into groups or types that follow definable patterns. For instance, Roberts varies his stories so as to produce a strong sense of the individual animal personality, as with the King moose or with Kehonka the wild goose, or he carefully avoids any suggestion of personality and constructs the type, where this seems appropriate, as with the salmon or the ant. The former is achieved by introducing some peculiar circumstance into the individual life, the capture and clipping of Kehonka or the bear's attack on the King of the Mamozekel. . . .

I know of no other Canadian writer who has left a body of work so consistently arranged about a clear idea of the order of life itself, or a writer of animal stories who has been at one and the same time so true to the characteristics of his actors and able to produce a genuine, unsentimentalized or dynamic fiction. (p. 31)

> *Joseph Gold, "The Precious Speck of Life," in* Canadian Literature, *No. 26, Autumn, 1965, pp. 22-32.*

Alec Lucas

Roberts originated the animal short story with **"Do Seek their Meat from God"**, a "sketch," as he called it, which, with two like it, he published among the fifteen stories of *Earth's Enigmas.* (p. 383)

The background of Roberts's new genre includes both literature and science. Roberts had already written articles for *Forest and Stream* (in the 1880's) before **"Do Seek their Meat from God"** appeared. Moreover, the short story was a prominent form at the time, and Roberts simply adapted it to a whole new subject. As for the influence of science, the spread of Darwinism, positing man's evolution from animals, and the increasing number of books on the subject, refocused man's mind on the interrelationship of man and nature.

Roberts's life was also influential on his work. Like Seton, who spent his boyhood . . . roaming the countryside near Lindsay and Toronto, Roberts owed his interest in nature to his childhood "passed in the backwoods" in New Brunswick. He was not, however, a naturalist of Seton's stature—was, in fact, not a naturalist but a casual observer. Despite his realism, he did not write his "true" stories like Seton out of his experiences but, in large part, from hearsay and his reading. Consequently, his two hundred or so stories on almost every living creature are often inaccurate and lack something of the attractive intimacy of Seton's. No salmon parr ever matured as rapidly as the one in **"The Last Barrier"** (*The Haunters of the Silences*), and no mallard ever flew so fast as the one in **"The Nest of the Mallard"** (*The Backwoodsmen*). Yet if he is guilty of misrepresenting facts he is not of misinterpreting them in the wider orientation of the "laws" of nature.

Although free from Seton's practice of upstage comment

and generally less subjective, Roberts can be excessively anthropomorphic. In the name of animal "personality," a fox may "fling dignity to the winds," a moose "look with longing eyes," a rabbit "wave long ears of admiration" at a "comely" mate. Again he may present an animal hero almost allegorically as in *Wisdom of the Wilderness* (1922), when **"The Little Homeless One"** lays down his life during a "moonlit revel" to save the other rabbits. Normally, however, he lets nature speak dramatically through the interplay of protagonist and incident.

Roberts's stories fall into three groups—the animal biography, the story of action, and the "sketch." The first of these, as Roberts handled it, uses event less to present animal habits than to examine animal "conduct." **"The Keeper of the Water Gate"** in *The Watchers of the Trails* is typical in its stress on the motives and reactions of its muskrat protagonists. The second kind of story subordinates animal personality and natural history to incident and plot as in **"The White-slashed Bull"** (*The House in the Water*), an episode in which a moose escapes death through a hunter's mercy. Men almost always appear in these stories, as participants or as choric observers. The third type, the graphic sketch-like story, isolates and dramatizes a single episode that suggests an elemental force governing the natural world from without, rather than within, or "Fate," as Roberts calls it in **"The Iron Edge of Winter"** (*The Backwoodsmen*). Here a weasel, about to seize a squirrel, is itself seized and carried off by a hawk. Stories of this kind often read as if Chance were a whimsical god playing jokes on his children of the wild, or having a game in which the rule of "survival of the fittest" no longer holds. The "sketch" Roberts wrote less and less frequently and in his later books not at all.

As an artist Roberts has many merits. He writes a fluent prose. He knows how to create suspense by hinting, withholding information, and working toward a major climax—techniques that **"The Haunter of the Pine Gloom"** (*The Kindred of the Wild*) admirably demonstrates. He gives individuality to essentially type characters by selecting the fleetest, strongest, and wisest as heroes—the "kings" of the species. Unfortunately this practice tends to turn his protagonists into noble savages, thus detracting from his work as natural history. He knows, also, how to unify his stories, opening and closing them with descriptions as if they were the curtains of a play. Yet the descriptions are not separate from the narrative. They are not simply realistic settings, the curtains of a play, or prose lyrics framing a story. They are his way of disclosing, within the transitory, something of the permanence of the natural world. Or again he begins *in medias res* and ends with a denouement that brings the narrative full circle. Even the longer animal biographies he can keep from sprawling by shaping them around some centre as in **"The Last Barrier"** (*Haunters of the Silences*). This starts and finishes at a falls that a salmon parr descends on his way to the sea and to which he returns years later.

Whatever the story, it also has a unifying theme: the amorality of nature, the struggle for survival, the cyclical aspect of time. This is as true of the longer as of the shorter stories. **"The King of Mamozekel"** and **"The Lord of the**

Air" (*The Kindred of the Wild*) both depend greatly on narrative and on the facts of life history for their interest, but neither is unified solely as biography. In the one a moose reveals the power of the instinct for the preservation of species; in the other an eagle becomes the embodiment of nature's freedom of spirit forever reasserting itself in defiance of man's attempts to destroy it.

Roberts's adherence to the concept of the animal hero and of nature as conflict frequently leads to the sensational and spectacular. His stories abound in "desperate encounters" (or duels) of courageous beasts, like epic heroes, battling to the death. At times, however, he resolves plot conflict in a conclusion that has wider and subtler implications.

> Just about this time a visitor from the hills had come shambling down to the river's edge—one of the great black bears of the Quahdavic valley. Sitting contemplatively on her haunches, her little, cunning eyes had watched the vain leaps of the salmon. She knew a good deal about salmon and her watching was not mere curiosity. As the efforts of the brave fish grew feebler and feebler she drew down closer and closer to the edge of the water, till it frothed about her feet. When, at last, the salmon came blindly into the eddy and turned upon his side, the bear was but a few feet distant. She crept forward like a cat, crouched,—and a great black paw shot around with a clutching sweep. Gasping and quivering, the salmon was thrown upon the rocks. Then white teeth, savage but merciful, bit through the back of his neck; and unstruggling he was carried to a thicket above the Falls.

This has some of the pathos so typical of Seton's endings, but it has more than pathos. It contains Roberts's comment on the grim irony and amorality of life in the world of nature.

As Roberts continued to add more and more animals to his "ark" with *Kings in Exile, Neighbours Unknown* (1911), *More Kindred of the Wild* (1911), *The Feet of the Furtive, Hoof and Claw, Children of the Wild* (1913), *Secret Trails* (1916), *They Who Walk in the Wild* (1924), to list some not already mentioned, he tended, in the cause of entertainment, to resort to more derring-do and farfetched incident and to reduce his stories to formula. This latter development was almost inevitable since there is a sameness about the situations and themes available to him. His grumpy bears and wary foxes and other animals, despite their personalities, of necessity become types—within a species one creature's habits scarcely differ from another's. Consequently many later stories become monotonous variations in terms of species or situation on his fresh and original early work. Yet at their best, whenever written, they are an impressive fusion of art, fiction, and natural history. (pp. 384-86)

Alec Lucas, "Nature Writers and the Animal Story," in Literary History of Canada: Canadian Literature in English, *edited by Carl F. Klinck and others, University of Toronto Press, 1965, pp. 364-88.*

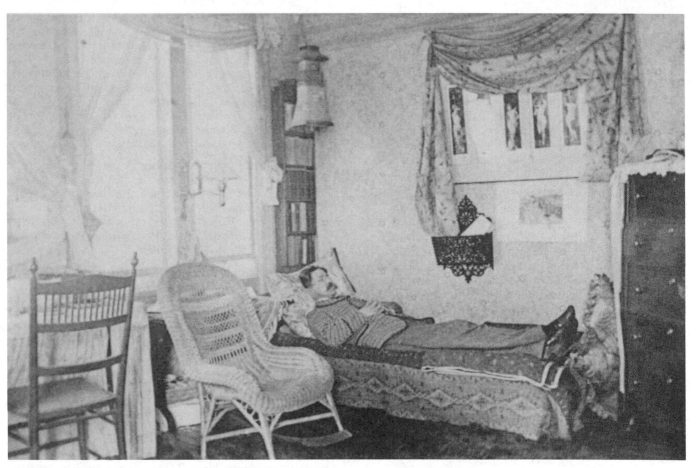

Roberts reclining in his dressing room at Kingscroft, his home at King's College, Windsor, Nova Scotia, 1893. Roberts taught English, French, and economics at the college, which allowed him his mornings free to write.

Sheila Egoff

In the late nineteenth and early twentieth centuries, when most writers of fiction were slavishly following the accepted English literary tradition, the realistic animal story appeared in Canada as a genuine native product and spread outward to influence the animal story around the world. It was the creation of two Canadians, Ernest Thompson Seton and Sir Charles G. D. Roberts, and it was their works that gave it both its definition and its highest form.

The realistic animal story can best be described as animal biography in fictional form. Although it can vary greatly in the amount of fiction purposefully used, it is founded upon scientific observation and a profound knowledge of animals. Using his knowledge, and with affection and respect, the writer brings his animal hero alive in its own world and in complete harmony with its own nature. The realistic animal story is not concerned with talking-animal fantasies and fables or with satires based on animals, such as George Orwell's *Animal Farm:* these genres do not really contain works about animals but about human actions and aspirations. Neither should it be confused with the kind of story in which a child's adventure is the main subject, and an animal, usually a horse or a dog, plays an auxiliary role: the horse is stolen or the pet dog is blamed for killing sheep. The realistic animal story under discus-

sion here has its closest link with the writings of naturalists like Raymond L. Ditmars, Gerald Durrell, and Jean Henri Fabre.

It is obvious that the naturalist would not indulge in anthropomorphism—the endowment of animals with human traits. It is not so clear that the writers of even the best animal stories should not or do not do so. Some transfer of human intelligence and emotion to the animal character can, in good hands, heighten the emotional impact of a story and strengthen the rapport between writer and reader. Animal lovers, both children and adults, often ascribe super-animal qualities to their pets and it should be no surprise that some of this feeling has worked its way into animal literature. But it takes a sure sense of the limits of credibility to keep the realistic animal story from being maudlin or, worse, so confused as to be neither animal story nor outright fantasy. Seton and Roberts trod this line closely, but in the main successfully. . . . (pp. 105-07)

That the realistic animal story should first have appeared and developed in Canada is not entirely the result of chance. When Seton and Roberts wrote, knowledge of animals, especially wild animals, was still a necessity for Indians, who depended upon them for food, for those who hunted for profit, and for those concerned with conservation; and of course protection and interest have always made some knowledge essential. In a sparsely populated country the forces of nature still played a major role, as indeed they do today in many parts of Canada. Probably in no other part of the world were the cities so close to the forests. In Canadian art, in Canadian novels, in Canadian poetry there was still an intense concentration on descriptions of nature. Seton and Roberts maintained this emphasis, but added to it a new dimension—a genuine insight into the nature of the animals that roam our woods and forests. (pp. 107-08)

For the moralizing and sentimentality of their predecessors, Seton and Roberts substituted a rigorous naturalism. They were interested in their animal subjects as animals, not as devices. They assumed that their animal heroes were as intrinsically worthy of interest as any human being might be and they created, in effect, 'animal biographies'. Like the biographer, then, they undertook an analysis of character that was based on the influence of environment, youthful training, and education, with a selection of facts and events to make the portrait emerge clearly. Their animals are not mere automatons, led by blind instinct; they are creatures that possess the faculty of reason—but not human reason. The plots are chiefly life-and-death struggles in the wilderness. Most of the animals fall to the laws of nature, and usually if man is pitted against them, man is the victor. As Seton put it, 'The fact that these stories are true is the reason why all are tragic. The life of a wild animal always has a tragic end.' (*Wild Animals I Have Known.*) Roberts, with his greater poetic skill, put it thus, 'And death stalks joy forever among the kindred of the wild.' (*Kindred of the Wild.*)

Both Seton and Roberts frequently used composite animal characters. That is, although the incidents related happened to an animal, they would not all have happened to the same animal or in the sequence presented. Both writers wisely used the short-story form and the novella. Lengthy animal stories, especially those about wild animals, can easily become repetitious, and a preponderance of gory detail can surfeit the reader and break the dramatic impact. (pp. 109-10)

Seton was a professional naturalist and his stories were based on the scientific observations of an adult. The stories of Charles G. D. Roberts derived from recollections of his boyhood in the forests of New Brunswick. This approach gives Roberts's work a romantic cast, in contrast with Seton's more matter-of-fact approach to the wilderness. Here, in two sentences, he sets the stage and mood of '**The Boy and the Hushwing**' in *The Kindred of the Wild:*

> A hollow, booming, ominous cry, a great voice of shadowy doom rang out suddenly and startled the dark edges of the forest. It sounded across the glimmering pastures, vibrating the brown-velvet dusk, and made the lame old woman in the cabin on the other side of the clearing shiver with vague fears.

Roberts can write with equal excitement of the largest animal (and his favourite), the bear, in a group of stories brought together in 1947, *Thirteen Bears,* and of the tiny ant in '**The Prisoners of the Pitcher Plant**' (*The Haunters*

of the Silences). Roberts often became intoxicated with words. Phrases such as 'the intense sapphire of the zenith thrilled and melted' (*The Haunters of the Silences*) and 'his baby face of tenderest cream and pink . . . the hair . . . like a fleece all over his head, enmeshing the sunlight in its silken tangle' (*Jim, the Story of a Backwoods Police Dog*) suggest nineteenth-century floridity. But in books such as *Red Fox, Thirteen Bears,* and *The Feet of the Furtive,* the description adds beauty to the stories and gives them individuality and distinction.

There is infinite variety in Roberts's nature themes. Fate or preordained doom, mother love, the tragedy of growing old in the wilderness, the balance of nature and the chain of events resulting from killing, by animal or man, are only a few examples. Roberts ranged much further than Seton in the kinds of animals he treated, writing about tropical creatures as well as the inhabitants of Canadian forests.

Roberts's animal stories have been criticized more harshly than those of Seton. His book-length story, *Red Fox,* for example, is not as scientifically presented as are most of the works of Seton. In his attempts to bring drama to his stories and to emphasize the personality and cunning of his hero, he often strains credulity. That animals are instinctively on guard against man-made traps is a fact of hunting. But when Roberts has Red Fox and his mate deliberately leave the trap uncovered 'so that no other of the forest dwellers might be betrayed by it', and then go off to find out what other treasons man had plotted against the wild folk, he leaves reality for fantasy. However, as Frank Underhill once pointed out, 'biography only becomes interesting and alive when the biographer is partisan', and perhaps this is Roberts's way of being partisan to *his* hero. The story of Red Fox is spellbinding. He is shown as the strongest and most intelligent of the litter and is the only one to survive, even outwitting his human captors twice by playing 'dead'. At the end of the story he has triumphed over the hunters and the hounds and finds a home in a new wilderness. This ending represented to Roberts the triumph of the wild animal and a glorification of its freedom and strength.

Not all of Roberts's animals are endowed with the intelligence of Red Fox. Sometimes a beast's limitations are humorous: a young muskrat belonging to a litter of nine is killed by a duck. 'The attention of the little mother was just then occupied, and never having learned to count up to nine, she, apparently, never realized her loss.' ('**The Calling of the Lop-Horned Bull**' in *The Secret Trails.*)

Many of the stories of Seton and Roberts would be wearisome if they had been dragged out to a full-length book, and the reader would be far more conscious of, and probably repelled by, the wholesale slaughter animals inflict on one another and man inflicts on animals. As it is, they preserve suspense which, together with the genuine emotions they arouse for their animal heroes, has kept them very much alive. (pp. 114-16)

Sheila Egoff, "The Realistic Animal Story," in her The Republic of Childhood: A Critical Guide to Canadian Children's Literature in English, *Oxford University Press, Canada, 1967, pp. 105-30.*

W. J. Keith

Both Roberts and Seton, as a result of their personal experiences as observers in the wild, believed that animals (at least in the higher forms) displayed qualities that could not be explained away by the convenient but notoriously vague term "instinct." Both saw themselves, in W. H. Hudson's terms, as field-naturalists rather than closet-naturalists (Roberts distinguishes between the "true naturalist" and the "mere dry-as-dust cataloguer of bones and teeth"), and both insisted upon the need for going beyond the descriptive, classificatory boundaries of traditional science. Roberts has presented his own position most clearly and reasonably in the introduction to *Eyes of the Wilderness*. . . .

> To me it seems not enough to approach this fascinating study with merely the curious eyes of the naturalist. To really know the wild creatures something more is necessary than to note their forms and colours, their seasons and their habits, their food, their tracks, their dwellings and their matings. . . . [The] exciting adventure lies in the effort to "get under the skins," so to speak, of these shy and elusive beings, to discern their motives, to uncover and chart their simple mental processes, to learn to differentiate between those of their actions which are the results of blind, inherited instinct, and those which spring from something definitely akin to reason; for I am absolutely convinced that, within their widely varied yet strictly set limitations, the more advanced of the furred and feathered folk do reason. In other words, there is a psychology of the creatures lower in the scale of creation than ourselves. It is profoundly different from human psychology, however, that to forget the difference is to go hopelessly astray in one's deductions. To investigate that psychology, and to interpret it, is one of the most fascinating of enterprises for the Nature lover.
>
> (pp. 88-90)

One can appreciate, and have sympathy with, this method of approach while at the same time being aware of the dangers inherent within it. The problems are considerable. Even if we accept an observer as reliable, for instance, how can we be sure that he correctly interprets what he sees? How is it possible to use words that are originally descriptive of human behaviour and apply them to animals without carrying over, wittingly or unwittingly, the associations of human psychology? In other words, is not anthropomorphism as much a feature of the stories of Roberts and Seton as it was, albeit more obviously, in the fables of Aesop? Many contemporary naturalists were disturbed by these questions, and were particularly aware of the sentimentalizing effect of such writing on the thinking of the unsophisticated and unsuspecting reading public. (pp. 90-1)

It is tempting to dismiss the whole controversy as irrelevant to a literary appreciation of Roberts as imaginative artist, but this is not, I think, legitimate. Thus I cannot wholly agree with Joseph Gold when he observes: "Whether the interpretation of animal psychology is 'realistic' is beside the point, for Roberts' intention is to make his characters humanly comprehensible and convincing and this he does with unmatched skill." But the stories are convincing only in so far as they can be accepted as at least possible within the world of nature. We read them for information as well as for enjoyment, and part of the resulting pleasure depends upon their possessing a reasonable foundation in fact. If we are convinced that an incident is not only improbable but impossible, our appreciation is severely qualified. Admittedly, no hard and fast line can be drawn, but at some point any sophisticated reader will begin to have doubts. It is not difficult to accept a capacity for "something definitely akin to reason" in a fox or a bear; it is a little more difficult in, say, a skunk or a goose, and more difficult still in a fish or an insect. This is not merely a matter of judgment concerning the respective qualities of species, genera or classes. It is connected also with an awareness of the writer's ability to make the necessary preliminary observation. Roberts himself draws attention to the problem in his introduction to *The Haunters of the Silences* when he asserts, as if in a tone of wide-eyed innocence: "It is not easy for any observer to be intimate with a sawfish". But how, the reader may legitimately ask, could Roberts obtain any information upon this subject? Part of the effectiveness of the backwoods stories derives . . . from the fact that they contain answers to such a question. As we read, we begin to understand not only what life in the wilds is like, but how this information is gained. However, when Roberts extends his range to include such unlikely settings as the ocean depths, when we are aware that his assertions are not and could not be backed up by intimate and detailed knowledge, then he has crossed the boundary that divides the "new" natural history from what we have learned to call science fiction. In such cases, no allegedly first-hand report is acceptable. We are at liberty to grant him our willing suspension of disbelief, but this will be an artistic, not a scientific judgment.

At the same time, it may be granted that there are many instances in which there is no clear division between an artistic and a scientific judgment, in which acceptance or rejection depends upon the actual words used. The problem is as often as not one of literary tact rather than scientific reliability. In one story, for example, Roberts writes of a wild goose: "As leader, for two seasons, of his own flock, he had necessarily learned certain simple processes of deduction". This is unconvincing because the clumsy and inappropriate last phrase raises the wrong associations. Roberts has thus drawn attention to a weakness when a more judicious expression might have smoothed over the difficulty or even removed it entirely. . . . And in a late story, **"The Citadel in the Grass,"** he has to fall back on direct assertion to persuade us of the capacities of his ant world: "Prudent forethought and a fine directing intelligence, as distinguished from mere instinct, or what the scientists call reflex action, were most unmistakably stamped upon it". The diction here bears witness to Roberts' failure to recreate the ant community in convincing imaginative terms. But these are exceptions. In general, Roberts presents the animal world with a combination of authority and finesse which carries complete conviction. This conviction derives ultimately from the same acceptance we give to the behaviour of a human character. The actions of Red Fox, for example, should be no more and no less credible than those of Luella Warden in *The Heart That Knows.* We judge his actions according to our knowledge of animal behaviour just as we judge Luella's by what we know of human nature. Our standards of "realism" apply to both. Read as works of literature, then, not as natural-history textbooks, Roberts' animal-stories may be accepted on the same level of truth as his novels and poems.

In the animal-stories, the two sides of Roberts' nature—his fascination with wild life and his ambition to be a writer—blend happily together. In his early years he learned much about animal behaviour through careful and patient observation in the wilds of New Brunswick; later, he found that this investigation could be continued at the writing desk. He probed the mind and attitude of the observer as well as the actions and impulses of the animals observed. His stories concern the world of nature, the struggle for existence within nature, and the attempts of men to survive, and come to terms with, a world which is hostile and in which they are themselves recognized as enemies. What is this world like? How do men enter into its mysteries and comprehend its realities? These are the basic questions that underlie Roberts' work. (pp. 93-6)

A number of his most successful stories of the wild are linked by the character known simply as "the Boy." For the most part these are based on Roberts' own early experiences; they are important because they demonstrate, even embody, one human being's method of approaching the natural world. Though primarily an observer, he employs the methods of the hunter. "He would know the wild folk living, not dead", but he learns from his trapper-friend Jabe Smith that "there's some things ye learn about wild critters in trying to git the better of 'em that ye can't learn no other way". The Boy (and through him, the reader) gains knowledge and awareness, but this awareness often concerns himself as much as the creatures he is observing. Moreover, in denying him a proper name, Roberts deliberately places him on the same footing as the animals. He is representative of human beings just as Red Fox is representative of his own species. This is Roberts' way of preparing us for more striking similarities between man and animal in the stories that follow.

The Boy's most characteristic feature is his enthusiastic curiosity: "His appetite for knowledge of all the wild creatures of the woods was insatiable". He makes himself familiar with every square foot of wilderness within reach of his home. He learns how to observe, how to anticipate the actions of his quarry, how to become the intellectual monarch of all he surveys. His aim, we might say, is to be a camera, but he soon realizes that his own responses, rational or irrational, necessarily affect his observations. In other words, he demonstrates Roberts' own awareness of the dangers that Burroughs had pointed out. Roberts was by no means ignorant of the inevitable subjectivity of the observer; moreover—and this perhaps is an insight that only an imaginative artist could provide—he realizes that these subjective responses are themselves an inheritance from the world he is scrutinizing. Thus in **"The Haunter of the Pine Gloom,"** the Boy one day experiences a strange sense of uneasiness in the woods in which he usually feels

at home. His first attempt to fathom the mystery is described as follows:

> Standing motionless as a stump, and breathing with perfect soundlessness, he strained his ears to help his eyes in their questioning of this obscure menace. He could see nothing. He could hear nothing. Yet he knew his eyes and ears were cunning to pierce all the wilderness disguises. But stay—was that a deeper shadow, merely, far among the pine trunks? And—did it move? He stole forward; but even as he did so, whatever of unusual he saw or fancied in the object upon which his eyes were fixed, melted away. It became but a shadow among other shadows, and motionless as they—all motionless in the calm of the tranquil sunset. He ran forward now, impatient to satisfy himself beyond suspicion. Yes—of course—it was just this gray spruce stump! He turned away, a little puzzled and annoyed in spite of himself.

Later he discovers that he was being watched by a lynx. Roberts changes his viewpoint from human being to animal, and at once the positions are reversed. This time it is the lynx who is disturbed, having smelt traces of the Boy:

> Now, judging by the scent, the object of [the lynx's] curiosity was close at hand—yet incomprehensibly invisible. After sniffing and peering for some minutes he came out from behind the log and crept forward, moving like a shadow, and following up the scent. . . .

> At length the animal, on a stronger puff of air, located the scent more closely. This was obvious from a sudden stiffening of his muscles. His eyes began to discern a peculiarity in the pine trunk some twenty paces ahead. Surely that was no ordinary pine trunk, that! No, indeed, that was where the scent of the Boy came from—and the hair on his back bristled fiercely. In fact, it *was* the Boy!

This is more than a mere structural formula—the tracker tracked instead of the biter bit. Roberts is deliberately drawing attention to the similarity between the actions of man and animal when in the wild. (pp. 96-9)

Many commentators have noted how Roberts' animals are described in terms usually reserved for human beings; few if any have drawn attention to the converse effect in which his human beings are seen in terms of the animal world. This is especially true of the Boy since he makes a particular effort to act and move imperceptibly in order to observe the wild life that so fascinates him. In a story called **"The Boy and Hushwing,"** for example, the similes used for the Boy are invariably drawn from the wild creatures he stalks. He creeps "soundless as a snake," his eyes are "keen as a fish-hawk's," and he "lay still as a watching lynx". But it is also true of Roberts' hunters and trappers. . . . Indeed, whenever in a Roberts story a man faces a sudden emergency, he invariably reverts to instinct, and acts just as an animal would in a similar situation. (pp. 99-100)

These backwoodsmen are rarely characterized in any detail since their unique qualities are less important than their functions as trapper, hunter or lumberman. They are no more and no less individualized than the bears and foxes and squirrels with which they are in such close contact. In many of Roberts' stories (**"On the Roof of the World"**, for example), the human hunter is in competition with animal hunters, and thus inevitably becomes a part of the animal world. In others he displays the same abilities. In **"The Theft,"** which concerns the robbing of a panther's cubs by a squatter and their subsequent recovery by their mother, both man and panther are able to distinguish a trail as "a good half hour old". These are all inheritances from the world that Roberts explored in *In the Morning of Time,* a world where man is only too obviously a denizen of the world of nature. But in the world of Roberts' animal-stories the link, though less obvious and less clear, is still discernible. Often enough, it leads the characters into inconsistency. Thus we are told that Jabe Smith, the Boy's friend and companion in the wild, "loved all animals, even those which, in the fierce joy of the hunt, he loved to kill." (pp. 100-01)

Like most writers on wild nature, Roberts treads a middle path with respect to hunting, which often must have seemed to him, as it seemed to the Boy and Jabe Smith in *Red Fox,* "a regulated and long-drawn cruelty". He naturally deplores indiscriminate and unnecessary slaughter, but at the same time he is aware that hunting and being hunted are the unvarying and unending conditions of animal life. The link between man and the wild, as his stories continually demonstrate, is essentially one of blood.

The adventures of the Boy tell us much about man's difficulty in approaching and comprehending the wilderness. But woodcraft, though difficult to learn, can enable us eventually to pass into what is otherwise a closed and mysterious world. In scores of other tales, Roberts endeavours to show what this new world is like. Any comfortable illusions we may have are quickly shattered. There is nothing sentimental about Roberts' view of Nature. Indeed, much of the didactic purpose of *Babes of the Wild* is concerned with demonstrating that there is no room for either sentiment or compassion in the natural world. We cannot read many of the animal-stories without realizing the truth of his observation that "death stalks joy forever among the kindred of the wild." . . . Despite the title of his first animal-story, **"Do Seek Their Meat From God,"** the divinity that reigns over the wilderness is not God but Fate. And although there are occasional references suggestive of a Classical trinity—when, for example, the "antic forest Fates" are presented as "giggling in their cloaks of ancient moss"—this is once again more a problem of language than of concept. For the most part Roberts' Fate, whether stern or apparently whimsical, is strictly impartial.

It is also implacable, and is not to be deterred from its fatal and obscure purpose by any accidental or fortunate escape. "When the doom of the wild has once snatched at its prey," he writes in **"The Leader of the Run,"** "and, in part, missed its grip, the unhappy victim seems marked for every stroke of Fate". Many of the stories gain a sinister tension from this remorseless principle. (pp. 102-03)

But this principle (which, like Hardy's "Immanent Will,"

one is tempted to refer to as a capitalized "It") can also, in its own rough way, act in a manner that seems almost merciful. In the fine story **"When Twilight Falls on the Stump Lots,"** the "doom" is kind to the dead bear's cubs since they are quickly devoured by foxes instead of being left to die painfully through slow starvation. This story, in fact, underlines the argument of Young Dave in *The Heart of the Ancient Wood.* It reminds us that Roberts' world is essentially Darwinistic, one in which the struggle for existence is constant and where only the fittest (and Roberts' animal heroes are invariably princes of their kind) survive. But even the fittest reach a stage when their strength begins to decline, and "the wild wood Fates" are presented as kind rather than stern in abruptly cutting off an inevitable descent. As Seton has written, "for the wild animal there is no such thing as a gentle decline in peaceful old age."

Many of Roberts' animal-stories depend for their effect on the remorseless presentation of the life in nature. . . . [**"Mothers of the North"**], despite the sentimental suggestions of its title, presents a bleakly effective incident in which a mother polar bear kills a baby walrus for the good of her own cub. The loss of the walrus, the gain of the bear, the sacrifice of one creature that another may live—these are the unavoidable facts of wild life which the story presents with all the detached inevitability of a historic chronicle.

The endings of Roberts' stories are especially important in this respect. Whether the subject dies or escapes, Roberts is too much of a realist to underplay the constant danger of life in the wild, and we are generally left with an impression that is both sobering and uncomfortable. . . . Absence of emotion is an essential part of Roberts' effect; Nature, he is saying with a brutal simplicity, is like that. The same is true of many of the stories in which man intrudes upon the life of the wild. **"When Twilight Falls on the Stump Lots"** concerns a strayed cow that valiantly defends her calf against a black bear. But her success in this venture is severely qualified by Roberts' final paragraph which he writes in the role of detached and neutral commentator:

> As for the red calf, its fortune was ordinary. Its mother, for all her wounds, was able to nurse and cherish it through the night; and with morning came a searcher from the farm and took it, with the bleeding mother, safely back to the settlement. There it was tended and fattened, and within a few weeks found its way to the cool marble slabs of a city market.

Out of context, this might be interpreted as an attack upon man's treatment of the lower animals, but a fuller experience of Roberts' art will convince us that he is deliberately demonstrating the fact of man's connection with, and reliance upon, the world of nature. Just as the baby walrus must die so that the bear cub may live, so the life of the calf is sacrificed to the life of man. Once again, Nature is like that.

In his prose Roberts never pontificated; he made no attempt to impose his view of the world upon his readers. None the less we have been able to extract from the short stories a coherent position which may without undue pretentiousness be called a vision of nature. Joseph Gold describes it as "an affirmative vision in which the conditions of a wilderness struggle for survival are accepted and confirmed." Roberts created, he argues, a genuine Canadian mythology: "The principal feature of this myth is that, while individual creatures constantly lose the struggle for survival, life itself persists." This, of course, is neither an original nor a profound position; moreover, as we have already noted, it differs in many important respects from the world-view presented in his poetry. Where the latter reflects the religious orthodoxy of Westcock parsonage, the prose mirrors the a-moral, a-religious "Nature red in tooth and claw" of the backwoods. . . . I prefer the prose because I believe it to attain a noticeably higher degree of artistic success than the poetry. . . .

Roberts was well aware of the formal problems that confronted him. By a deft selection of material and incident, he tried, without sacrificing his claim to realistic accuracy, to suggest—at least for artistic purposes—an ordered pattern beneath the apparent anarchy of the natural world. In other words, he attempted to create the illusion of form in what is seemingly formless, to maintain a balance between the demands of his subject-matter and the requirements of art. (pp. 103-08)

He distinguished two kinds in his own work, "the story of adventure and the anecdote of observation". We may add a third which I shall call the representative chronicle. These three kinds necessarily overlap to some extent, but the distinctions are none the less useful, and it may be helpful to separate their characteristic features.

The story of adventure is at once the most familiar and the least "natural." It has, in the traditional sense, a beginning, a middle and an end. **"The Isle of Birds"** . . . is an example. We are aware that Roberts has deliberately shaped the material, tied the loose ends together, and produced a convincing and satisfying story. At the same time we realize that the natural world rarely if ever provides so neat a plot. The danger with the story of adventure is that the overall pattern may become little more than an empty formula. Since Roberts published well over two hundred animal-stories, and since the majority of them fall into this category, it is scarcely surprising that certain basic situations recur again and again. A distraught mother avenges the death of her young; an animal is killed at the moment of its triumph over another; a human hunter spares his victim at the last moment when the creature distinguishes itself in its efforts to evade capture. One cannot read for long in Roberts without encountering one or other of these basic stories, and I have no wish to underestimate the artistic dangers involved. At the same time, we should not be disturbed unduly, since in most instances Roberts is merely being true to his subject matter in underlining the repetitive patterns of Nature. . . . "It is the exceptions rather than the rules," he says, "which make the life of the wilderness exciting"—and his insistence upon this almost becomes a formula in itself. But we cannot criticize him on the one hand for anthropomorphizing his animals and on the other for failing to provide variety and originality within the monotonous routine of the natural world. His

strength, indeed, is that he is usually able to maintain an acceptable balance between the two.

The representative chronicle, in contrast, finds a unity in subject rather than in plot. Here we follow the fortunes of a single creature over an extended period of time and so witness a collection of individual adventures which accumulate to become representative of the species. . . . **Red Fox** is his most extended and ambitious attempt. . . . Roberts tended to employ this kind more often as he grew older. It avoids many of the dangers of the more tightly-constructed tale of adventure. The story is shaped by the natural exigencies of time and place, and there is less pressure to fall back on a stock formula to provide a climax; moreover, emphasis on the typical rather than the individual life neatly sidesteps some of the objections of the traditional naturalists.

The anecdote of observation is a sketch rather than a story and attempts no more than a straightforward presentation of a simple natural occurrence. It differs from the other kinds in that it is almost always "true literally" while the story of adventure and the representative chronicle can only partake of a more general, eclectic truth. . . . In the anecdote of observation (and, to some extent, in the representative chronicle) the intrusion of the author into the story is less noticeable. He is inevitably a selector of incident, but he is not necessarily a manipulator, and when literal truth is at a premium, an exciting climax to a thrilling tale of adventure may be less acceptable than a "slice of (wild) life" which includes nothing unusual or unexpected. . . . [Although] there is often no climax and no resolution, these can rank among Roberts' most impressive and satisfying creations. **"The Keepers of the Nest,"** for example, is merely an account of how on two occasions a pair of swans guard their nest—once from a fisher, once from a lynx. There is no thematic connection between the two incidents, and therefore no plot in the precise sense, but as a vignette of wild life the anecdote is both credible and successful.

We have seen, then, that Roberts distinguished and used a number of forms of the animal-story. In addition, he employed various formal devices to hold his anecdotes and chronicles together. These are for the most part the standard patterns that are always available to literature—the traditional elements of earth, air and water, the daily cycle from dawn to sunset, the seasonal cycle from spring to winter. Other patterns, more limited but particularly appropriate to Roberts' subject-matter, include those provided by animal hibernation and the continual process of mating and separation. . . . [Similar] patterns are to be found in Roberts' diction. (pp. 108-12)

Even a casual reading of Roberts will reveal an unusual number of repeated words and phrases. "The wild kindred," "the furtive folk," "the Fate of the wilderness," "the savage and implacable sternness of the wild"—these and others occur so frequently as to recall the repeated patterns of oral formulaic that are now recognized as a characteristic feature of primitive poetry. This effect in Roberts has sometimes been attributed to lack of originality or the carelessness of haste, but it is clearly deliberate and carries considerable literary significance. Just as the

Anglo-Saxon poets, members of small human communities surrounded by the vast unknowns of nature, evolved a poetry that reflected a world in which Law and Rule were omnipotent though often mysterious, so here Roberts has made use of related rhetorical devices that appropriately embody the rules of the wilderness itself. They continually remind us of continuity behind the ever-changing face of nature, the impersonality that endures and is eternal. Individuals die but "life itself persists"; the single life is expendable, but the type remains. Through reiterated words and phrases, these natural patterns and rhythms are made manifest.

Moreover, the effect is not confined to diction; it extends to image and metaphor. Joseph Gold has quoted with approval a passage from **"The Aigrette"** where the birds "looked like bits of Japanese screen brought to life" and has shown how the image suggests "a civilized pattern in the midst of wilderness." But this image is repeated on several occasions by Roberts in almost identical words. In this way he emphasizes the motif, inviting us to go further and see the "civilized pattern" as itself the reflection of a larger natural one. The stillness of the screen is representative of the stillness of nature; it suggests not so much an artistic stasis as what Roberts calls "the stillness of vast, untraversed solitude". The pattern which the Japanese painter transforms into art is, like that which Roberts portrays in words, a distillation of the recurrent, instinctive actions constantly repeated in the wild.

Once we become aware of the presence and effect of these formal and technical devices, we are in a better position to appreciate the unquestioned but curiously elusive merits of Roberts' prose style. Perhaps its most remarkable quality is a consistent competence that enables him to describe any scene, express any idea, evoke any response with accuracy, vividness and economy. He is not a "stylist"; that is to say, he does not use words as either ornament or veneer. He is in command of words without being self-consciously aware of his power over them. We never feel that he is deliberately striving for an effect. (pp. 112-13)

Characteristically, there is nothing ostentatious about this prose. The diction is simple, the rhythms conventional. Its prime virtue lies in its transparent naturalness; it never intrudes between reader and subject-matter. (p. 116)

Roberts' chief claim to our attention would seem to lie. . . . in his mastery of the animal-story. If both critics and serious readers have hitherto been reluctant to admit this, the reasons are not far to seek. It must be granted that the animal-story is not generally considered an important—or even a dignified—form. We think of *Black Beauty* or *Bambi,* assume that sentimentality or cuteness are necessary ingredients, and refuse to recognize it as an "adult" or sophisticated taste. Such a verdict cannot be defended, however, upon rational grounds. When the debate is argued in general terms, few (one assumes) would be prepared to assert that some subjects are automatically beyond the pale of art. In principle, then, there is no reason why, if modern poets are free to write about such conventionally unpoetic objects as trains and aeroplanes, Roberts should not be at liberty to take the animal world

as his province. Ironically, this is a traditionally-sanctioned subject, and it might well be argued that Roberts' fresh and challenging approach is especially deserving of literary praise. For the artist must ultimately be judged, not on his choice of subject-matter, but on what he has created out of it. (pp. 119-20)

Roberts, in his animal-stories, has confined himself to a limited area which, when, viewed as a microcosm, is seen to expand in application and become relevant to the whole world of man. He takes as his major theme the age-old problem of man's relation to the earth upon which he lives, but the questions he raises are as challenging as ever and are phrased in a new way. Where Tennyson looked forward (however tentatively) to a time when future generations would read Nature "like an open book," when inheritances from the jungle would be outgrown and man no more be classified as "half-akin to brute," the post-Darwinian Roberts is more doubtful. For him, the book of nature communicates a different message. It questions the possibility of "working out the beast" in terms, not of ape and tiger, but of wolf and lynx. Man, he tells us, may well emerge triumphant, but his triumph will be that of the hunter. In Roberts' animal-stories, man is always seen *within* the context of an all-embracing struggle for existence. To quote Joseph Gold, he attains his humanity "only by his supremacy as an animal." This may not constitute Roberts' firm "philosophy of life." He was not, after all, a philosopher, and his poems present a far more optimistic picture. But it is a meaningful possibility, and Roberts presents it dramatically and acutely. We may freely grant that he wrote too much, that his weakness for both the sensational and the exotic is a blemish. In his prose, as in his verse, a winnowing process is required. But whereas we are left in his poetry with a number of skillful, satisfying but unallied poems, in his animal-stories we find a distinct body of work that can ultimately stand as representative of the "world" of Charles G. D. Roberts. This is a generally unrecognized but none the less substantial achievement that deserves to be accepted as a permanent contribution to a specifically Canadian literature. (pp. 120-21)

> *W. J. Keith, in his* Charles G. D. Roberts, *The Copp Clark Publishing Company, 1969, 134 p.*

James Polk

[Charles Roberts] grew up in Westcock Parsonage, New Brunswick, where his father was in charge of a large parish which included the town of Sackville. (p. 67)

Westcock is in the Tantramar marsh country, where long dikes hold back the powerful tides of the Bay of Fundy from flooding the lush acreage of grassland. The lonely, haunting beauty of this landscape was to be described often in Roberts' poetic works, as in his famous poem, **"Tantramar Revisited."** (pp. 67-8)

Despite the many travels of his later life, Roberts never really left the Tantramar as far as his imagination was concerned, and much of his best writing may be traced back to his youthful experience in the area.

He often explored the woods and marshes with his uncle,

Roberts in camp on the Nictau, northern New Brunswick, 1905. In this year, he published his most famous book, Red Fox.

Dr Edward Roberts, an avid fisherman who taught Charlie a great deal about plants and animals. Edward is probably the original of Uncle Andy in *Babes of the Wild* (published in the United States as *Children of the Wild*), in which an older man tells tales about animals and their young to a boy named Babe. (p. 68)

Wandering through the woods and marshland, [Roberts] observed the animals which featured in his writing many years afterwards. [It] is likely that many of Roberts' stories involving the Boy and an animal had some basis in his Tantramar days.

One evening in the forest, for example, he ran smack into a now-rare Eastern Canadian lynx, which the New Brunswickers called a "lucifee". Charlie stood stockstill in terror as the big smoke-coloured cat padded around him, examining the alien human with glittering eyes. A sudden squeak from a new pair of shoes made the creature vanish, and for weeks afterwards Charlie tested his knowledge of woodcraft by playing a dangerous game of hide-and-seek with the elusive lynx. This was to be the kernel of one of Roberts' finest tales, **"The Haunter of the Pine Gloom".** (pp. 70-1)

[His] first book of poetry appeared in the autumn of 1880. He was just twenty years old.

The book was **Orion and Other Poems,** one of the most important books of poetry ever to appear in Canada, not so much for its content as for its influence on other poets in the young nation. Archibald Lampman, for example, stayed up all night reading and rereading **Orion,** and later wrote:

It seemed to me a wonderful thing that such a

work could be done by a Canadian, by a young man, one of ourselves. It was like a voice from some new paradise of art calling to us to be up and doing.

Archibald Lampman, along with Bliss Carman and Duncan Campbell Scott, were among the "Confederation Poets" to be inspired by Roberts' example. **Orion** proved to them that a poet did not have to be British or American to write well, that a Canadian literature was possible, and that the new nation should be able to produce a fresh and characteristic kind of poetry. (pp. 75-6)

Almost all the things Roberts ever wrote, from nature poems to histories to tourist guidebooks, were united by one common theme: Canada. His patriotism went far beyond his fervent interest in the nation's political future, for he was fascinated by the land as a unique place with its own special spirit and beauty. He hoped to capture this special quality in his writing.

His chest-thumping imperialist verses couldn't be more out of style today, most readers preferring the quiet poems on New Brunswick landscapes. Even these seem old-fashioned to some, but whatever is decided about the value of Roberts' poetry, there can be no doubt about his importance as the first poet to see the possibilities of Canada as a literary subject. (p. 82)

For many readers, the most important thing Roberts wrote during his years at King's College was his first animal story, **"Do Seek Their Meat From God".** In it, a five-year-old boy is threatened by two hungry panthers in an empty cabin. The boy's father saves him in the nick of time, and shoots the beasts, although Roberts shows us that the panthers are not evil monsters, but natural parents searching for food. Several weeks later, the father finds the panther's cave and the bodies of the two cubs who starved to death because their parents had not returned. This short, gripping tale suggests the hard laws of nature: a human child is saved, but only at the expense of two animal children.

Roberts had trouble getting the story published, since its bleak ending and its sympathy for dangerous animals were unusual at the time. Cautious editors returned it with puzzled comments, and *Harper's* magazine only accepted it at last with many doubts and misgivings. He tried a few more tales of the kind but stopped when editors offered no encouragement. It was much later, after the success of Seton's *Wild Animals I Have Known,* that Roberts began writing animal stories in quantity. (pp. 83-4)

In 1903, [Roberts] lectured in Toronto on Canadian literature—pointing out how few people realized that the man who was making nature stories popular, Ernest Thompson Seton, was a Canadian. The following year, the first of Roberts' own animal-story collections, **Kindred of the Wild,** appeared. There is a good preface to this book, in which Roberts surveyed the development of the animal story through the ages, and emphasized that realism and the psychology of the animal had become a leading concern. Animals and men both reason, but not necessarily in the same way. He ended by praising the animal story for offering readers escape from the workaday world, since such fiction allows us "to return to nature, without requiring that we at the same time return to barbarism."

In *Kindred of the Wild,* as in most of Roberts' animal-story collections, the theme is the conflict everpresent in nature. Roberts was especially interested in describing fights between animals over food or territory—following Darwin's idea that there is a continual struggle for survival in the natural world. Man is included in this struggle, and many stories measure the rights of animals against the assumptions of the human beings who hunt them.

Roberts was noted for describing the natural world in a more artistic manner than was expected for wilderness narratives. He never pretended to be a professional naturalist and he respected the scientific detail Seton was able to bring to his material. Several of Roberts' works are frankly unrealistic, such as *The Heart of the Ancient Wood,* which tells of a young girl who is brought up by a bear. She lives among the animals until she falls in love with a hunter; at the end her hunter is treed by the very bear that brought her up. The girl must face the dilemma of which one to save.

Dramatically it is a choice between nature and civilization. She chooses civilization by shooting the bear, but then blames her human lover for making her kill the wilderness mother. This is a far cry from the kind of work Seton was doing, but Seton admired Roberts' talent for meaningful fantasy. When a boy asked Seton, "Why don't you write something as good as *The Heart of the Ancient Wood*?" Seton answered, "I would if I could but I can't."

Most of Roberts' scientific facts are correct, however, and he had vivid memories of his own early experiences in the woods. When a friend told him it was a shame he was forced to write so many "beasties" to make a living, Roberts protested. "There's no shame about it. I'm just lucky that the kind of story I've always wanted to write should be fashionable today. All my recollections of animals and the wild country of my childhood were there just waiting to be written about."

But he had to endure an attack on the truth of his natural history, just as Seton did. In 1907, *Everybody's Magazine* in New York ran an article called "Roosevelt on the Nature Fakirs", in which the American President claimed that Roberts was a charming writer, but that most of his stories were really only fairy tales. Theodore Roosevelt, an amateur naturalist, was particularly disturbed by the fight between a lynx and some wolves described in Roberts' **"On the Night Trail"**. Roberts replied that Roosevelt was thinking of the large Rocky Mountain animals, whereas he had written about the Canadian lynx and the small, eastern wolf.

The New York newspapers had a field day with the argument, and a parody of a typical animal story appeared in *The New York World* with comments supposedly added by Roosevelt ("TR") and Roberts ("CGDR"), which began this way:

> It was night.
>
> Bill, the trapper, saw two green orbs. He knew

they were the eyes of a lynx caught in his steel trap.

> TR: A mendacious mis-statement of fact. A lynx has not green eyes.
>
> CGDR: This was a Canadian lynx; they are greener than the Manhattan kind.

The whole controversy was a friendly affair, little more than a joke, and Roberts and President Roosevelt became good friends after it had blown over.

By 1936, Roberts had published over two hundred nature stories. Perhaps his most well-known collections are *The Kindred of the Wild, The Haunters of the Silences,* and *Wisdom of the Wilderness.* Another good one, *Kings in Exile,* is about animals who are taken out of their natural habitat and are made into pets or put in zoos—a group of stories which has some bitter things to say about man's mistreatment of animals. (pp. 89-91)

These stories did not match the popularity of Seton's, but they sold well. So did Roberts' historical fiction, especially *Barbara Ladd,* an adventure set in the American Revolution. This novel was published in 1902, the same year as *The Kindred of the Wild.* Not many people read Roberts' historical romances any more, although they contain plenty of action, and have exciting—if somewhat preposterous—plots. Most of them, like *A Sister to Evangeline,* are set in Canada during the French and English conflicts of the eighteenth century. They come complete with noble, unhappy lovers (one French and the other English, naturally) and a horde of evil Indians, mad witches, plotting priests, exiled Acadians, and faithful backwoodsmen, all rushing about the forests bent on secret missions. Even these books have their origins in the Tantramar days, for Roberts used to play near the ruined French fort of Beauséjour on visits to an uncle, and hear the sad legends of Acadian history.

The historical romances are not Roberts at his best. . . . (p. 93)

Roberts will always be important as the Father of Canadian Poetry, and some people are surprised to find that he wrote animal stories at all. But in the stories, his deep feeling for the Canadian land is expressed as much as in his most resounding patriotic poem. A Maritimer never forgets, and throughout his active and restless life Roberts was always true to his early education in the ways of nature and to the familiar marshes and woodlands of his New Brunswick home. (p. 99)

> *James Polk, "Sir Charles G. D. Roberts," in his* Wilderness Writers: Ernest Thompson Seton, Charles G. D. Roberts, Grey Owl, *Clarke, Irwin & Company Limited, 1972, pp. 62-99.*

Tim Murray

When critics first started to direct their attention to Charles Roberts' animal stories in the early 1900's, they tended to view the stories in terms of the level of realism that Roberts achieved in portraying animals in their wild environment. Back and forth went the discussions of whether Roberts was describing animals or humans disguised as animals. Roberts himself tried to define the genre he was working in as "psychological romance constructed on a framework of natural science." He disassociated his stories from such works as *Black Beauty* and Kipling's "Mowgli" stories. Roberts also replied directly to the charges of John Burroughs, a crony of Theodore Roosevelt and self appointed Dean of nature writers, who faulted Roberts for assigning human motives to animals. In a prefatory note to *The Watchers of the Trail* Roberts stated:

> The fact is, however, that this fault is one which I have been at particular pains to guard against . . . In my desire to avoid alike the melodramatic, the visionary, and the sentimental, I have studied to keep well within the limits of safe inference. Where I may have seemed to state too confidently the motives underlying the special action of this or that animal, it will usually be found that the action itself is very fully presented; and it will, I think, be further found that the motive which I have here assumed affords the most reasonable, if not the only reasonable, explanation of that action.

However, critics still debated whether or not Roberts was successful in meeting his own criteria.

In 1911, an anonymous writer in the *Edinburgh Review* tried to settle the question once and for all. He was reviewing a number of contemporary books that were classified as animal stories (two books by Roberts were included). He traced the animal story from its historical beginnings and came to the conclusion that what typified the modern, realistic animal story that Roberts was writing was that the animal was the central point of study. He saw the work of Roberts as an "attempt not to humanize but to individualize the animal," and considered Roberts to be successful in this attempt. He agreed with Roberts' view that previous fable animals bear little resemblance to the "true" animals in the latter's stories and saw Roberts' detractors as being aware of this difference, but also recognized that "libels disproved retain their vitality." The anonymous writer's analysis is extremely thorough and the question of the realism of Roberts' characters would seem to have been answered.

After this initial heyday, critical attention to Roberts' animal stories lessened. However, most of what little criticism there was in the next fifty years tended to continue the original controversy, and dealt with the stories in terms of the realism of Roberts' characters. Finally, when Canadian critics started to evaluate the literature of their past in terms of its relation to the growth of a truly Canadian literature, Roberts' animal stories began to get more thorough critical attention. However, many of these critics still felt compelled to analyze the level of realism that Roberts achieved and to apologize if they found him lacking. (pp. 23-4)

Thus the question that the anonymous writer in the *Edinburgh Review* tried to settle in 1911 is still being kept alive. Margaret Atwood, in *Survival,* gets to the heart of this question and answers it, one hopes finally, with a simplicity that previous writers have overlooked. "However, 'real-

ism' in connection with animal stories must always be a somewhat false claim, for the simple reason that animals do not speak a human language; nor do they write stories. It's impossible to get the real inside story, from the horse's mouth so to speak." Thus a writer of animal stories will always project some human qualities into his animals if he wants to try to portray animal behavior from an animal's point of view. However, as Ms. Atwood shows, there is a world of difference between Roberts' animals and those of Kipling or Kenneth Grahame. Roberts is trying to portray animal behavior, and when he sometimes injects a human quality into a character, it is not because he is trying to humanize it but rather because he is attempting to describe how and why an animal behaves in a certain way.

Roberts, of course, was an experienced woodsman and had an intimate knowledge of the wilderness and of the animals that lived in it. This knowledge, together with his interest in the evolutionary discoveries made by Darwin and his followers, is what formed the basis for Roberts' animal stories. He wanted to portray animals in their natural environment as accurately as he could. Since he was familiar with their habits, he had no trouble describing *what* animals did. What made Roberts' work different from that of a naturalist like John Burroughs, however, was that he wanted to also try to show *why* animals behaved the way they did. Roberts accepted the Darwinian notion that the prime force behind animal behavior was the preservation of the species. The basic law of Roberts' wilderness world is the survival of the fittest. Thus the animals in his stories reflect this in their behavior. (p. 24)

In **"The Animal Story,"** Roberts' Introduction to *The Kindred of the Wild,* he states that "As far, at least, as the mental intelligence is concerned, the gulf dividing the lowest of the human species from the highest of the animals has in these latter days been reduced to a very narrow psychological fissure." I hope to show that Roberts' animal stories represent an attempt to dramatize the infinite possibilities that this statement suggests. In this analysis, I am trying to reveal the motives behind Roberts' stories and, as a result, show that criticism directed at the level of realism Roberts' characters achieve is critical nit-picking and ultimately a waste of time.

In my analysis of Roberts' animal stories, I separate them into three basic thematic types. My criterion for establishing these types has been the degree of human intrusion into the stories. For this principle to be operative and, at the same time, consistent with the definition of an animal story, one must remember Roberts' statement, quoted above, in which he considers the line between humans and animals to be very fine. Thus I am considering, as animal stories, many stories that focus on man in the wilderness. Roberts treats the men (and women) in these stories, however, the same as he does his animal characters. While the human approach to some situations may be more sophisticated than an animal's, the motivation behind basic behavior is the same. Man is striving to survive and it is his superior intelligence that makes him the fittest animal of all.

The first type of story that I will consider is that which depicts animals in the wild, with almost no human intrusion.

I say almost because man's unseen presence is sometimes felt in the form of traps, logjams, etc. The focus, however, is totally on the animal and if men do enter the story, they are seen only as one more wilderness hazard. In this type of story Roberts tries to show how his characters respond to various life situations. One of the things that makes Roberts so successful in these stories is his ability to create different situations for his characters. Since he remains faithful to the basic Darwinian axiom of behavior, his characters' prime motivation is survival. Thus every action of his characters, whether it be gathering food, building a nest, mating, or protecting their young, is governed by this rule. With this seeming limitation placed on his work, it would seem that the number of situations Roberts could create would not be very great. However, he is able to work effectively and with variety under this rule. I do not agree with William Magee's statement that, "In effect, Roberts seldom wrote well with any other want for his heroes than food." Roberts works consistently with all his animals' basic wants.

When Roberts is portraying his animal characters, he uses two basic structural techniques. The first involves focusing on an animal or a group of animals and following it, or them, over a period of time. The period of time may vary from an entire life cycle to a matter of hours. In portraying an animal over an extended period of time, Roberts is able to show various responses to different situations. He is also able to show the interrelation of such responses and show how everything goes back to the prime rule of preservation of the species. Three good examples of this structural type which effectively illustrate the range of Roberts' ability are **"The King of the Mamozekel," "Queen Bomba of the Honey-Pots,"** and **"The Last Barrier."** (pp. 25-6)

[In] what may be called animal biographies, whether Roberts gives his readers a sustained view of an animal's life or whether he just focuses on a critical moment, he is doing basically the same thing. He is depicting animals in their natural habitats and showing their responses to various life situations from their point of view. And, whether he's showing the individualistic antics of the "King" or the predetermined life of Bomba, his characters all have one goal, survival.

Roberts approaches the subject of animals in the wild from a situational viewpoint as well as from the viewpoint of individual animals. He either creates a situation that may attract a number of animals to a specific area, or he focuses on a specific area and portrays a number of animals engaged in typical activities in that area. This sort of approach does not really allow any sustained development, since that would involve extensive character development and Roberts is mainly concerned with portraying typical life-death struggles that are common to a situation or area. (pp. 27-8)

At times, Roberts manages to combine the situational approach with fairly developed characters. **"The Keeper of the Watergate"** and **"In the Moose-Yard"** are good examples. In the former, the character of the muskrat is developed to some extent, but his behavior is examined in terms of how he responds to environmental influences which take on an importance equal to that of his character. In

the latter story, a moose family is described in some detail at their winter quarters. But, it is the effect of the harsh winter itself which brings other animals to the scene, including a wolf pack and a bear which attack the moose family. Here, too, the environmental conditions and the behavior of a number of animals are just as important to the understanding of the story as the portrayal of the moose family. One can compare **"In the Moose-Yard"** with **"The King of the Mamozekel"** and clearly see the difference in emphasis between them. In the latter the reader is concerned primarily with the development of the "King." He is seen responding to environmental influences, but they are important only to the extent that they help mold his character. In the former story the environmental situation is just as important, and at times more important, than the moose family itself.

All of the above stories, no matter what approach Roberts used, were totally concerned with animals in their wild environment. And, no matter what the immediate stimulus was that caused an animal to behave in a certain way, the basic motivation behind any action was survival. Roberts has not deviated from this fundamental theme in any of these stories. There is another group of stories which, while it keeps the basic theme of survival, really belongs to a different thematic grouping. I mentioned above that the criterion for determining these groupings has been the degree of human intrusion into the stories. The next type of animal story that I am going to look at deals with animals who are caught between two worlds, the wilderness world and the domestic world of man, and are forced to "choose" between the two.

Margaret Atwood, in *Survival,* distinguishes between American and Canadian "realistic" animal stories by trying to show that the former are usually animal success stories, "success being measured in terms of the animal's adjustment to people." She cites London's *White Fang* as an example. She concludes that Canadian animal stories work in just the opposite way. They deal with the death and failure of animals, which become tragic events "because the stories are told from the point of view of the animal". I mention this because I feel that Roberts does not comfortably fit this limited, categorical description that Ms. Atwood applies to the Canadian animal story. Roberts has written a number of stories, still from the animal's viewpoint, that deal with animals moving not only from domestication to the wild, but also from the wild to domestication. And, Roberts' characters that exhibit this movement do so in varying degrees of success and failure. In other words there is no consistent pattern as Atwood tries to suggest.

In his "domestic" stories Roberts is still concerned with the motivation behind animal behavior, and his characters are still governed by the law of survival. But the world of man represents another path to achieving survival, and in these stories Roberts is analyzing the difference between the two paths. He shows that no matter how domesticated an animal is, the instinctual forces that guided its remote ancestors are still present and can surface at any time. Roberts, however, is not just content with dealing with this "call of the wild" theme. He also depicts animals in the wild who find themselves, for one reason or another, drawn to man. He is trying to approximate the conditions that led wild animals to become domesticated in the first place. There are also a number of stories that exhibit two-way movement (wild domestic wild, and domestic wild domestic). (pp. 28-9)

In **"The Homesickness of Kehonka"**, Roberts traces movement from the wilderness to domestication, in this case forced domestication. Kehonka was one of several wild goose eggs that a farmer had taken and hatched with his domestic geese. Two of the wild geese reach adulthood and, with their wings clipped, find themselves living in domestication. The first goose adapts to this life; he is content with domestication. Kehonka, however, never becomes fully domesticated. He responds to the calls of the migrating wild geese and, when his wings grow back to the point where he can fly a limited distance, he attempts to follow them north. His wings fail him but he keeps on, even when he has to walk. Though "In his heart was the hunger of the quest" he is killed by a fox. Kehonka has been unable to adjust to domestication but he has also been rendered ineffective for life in the wild. Thus he does not survive.

In **"A Gentleman in Feathers"**, Roberts portrays a wild goose who is able to adapt successfully to domesticated life. Michael, the goose in this story, has been shot down by a farmer. Like Kehonka, he has had his wings clipped. Michael takes to civilization a little better than did the other goose; he even finds a domestic mate, though they do live aloof from the rest of the flock. But when he hears the sound of the migrating geese, he, like Kehonka, responds to their call. Michael's wings fully grow back and he can join them. However, his mate cannot make so strenuous a journey, and "rather than forsake her he would forget the blue lagoons and the golden reed-beds". In the end Michael rejects life in the wild and returns to the farm and his mate.

"Mishi of Timberline" has a similar theme. Mishi, a panther, has been raised amidst humans since he was a cub. Early in the story Roberts mentions that Mishi functions quite well in this society, "his savage inherited instincts having been lulled to sleep or else never awakened." When an accident occurs, Mishi is forced into the woods and these instincts do awaken, and he functions quite well in the wild. It appears that he, unlike Kehonka, can function on instinct alone. However, Mishi is not content in the wilderness and "chooses" to return to civilization. At the end of the story he accepts civilization in the form of a plate of pancakes. "Mishi devoured them politely, though he would have preferred a chicken." Though the wild animal can function in civilization, his wild instincts are always present.

The story of Mishi actually belongs to another group of stories that exhibit what I have referred to as two-way movement. The animals can function equally well in the wilderness or in the society of man. In **"The Freedom of the Black Faced Ram"**, the "call of the wild" enters a domestic ram who escapes into the wild and functions quite well, though awkwardly, there. He eventually finds a mate and fights off a bear. Finally his former master appears on the scene:

> He had no mind to go again into captivity. But on the other hand, for all his lordliness of spirit, he felt that the man was his master. At first he lowered his head threateningly, as if about to attack; but when the backwoodsman shouted at him there was an authority he could not withstand.

In the end the ram follows the man home. In the characters of Mishi and the ram, Roberts has tried to show the effect man has on animal behavior, both short and long range. Mishi, whose acquired skills have been received entirely from man, still retains the basic wants that are common to all panthers. Though he will eat pancakes and accept society, he still would prefer a chicken. The ram, on the other hand, when he finds himself in the wilderness, finds heretofore unknown instincts awakening in him. But the centuries of domestication that are present in his blood are responsible for instincts, just as strong as the wild ones of Mishi, that tell him that man is his master. A character like Kroof, the she-bear in *The Heart of the Ancient Wood,* is another good example of an animal who can function in the world of man or in the wild. However, in the end she turns on man and is true to her own wild nature.

Roberts' main point in all these stories is to get at the ultimate difference between wild and domestic animals. In a story like **"Mishi"** Roberts shows that though the wild animal can be domesticated, the wild instinct never dies out. In the case of Kroof, it surfaces unexpectedly and the bear turns on man. Conversely, domestic animals can respond to the "call of the wild" but the centuries of domestication in their blood also exert an influence. **"The Passing of the Black Whelps"** perfectly exemplifies Roberts' feelings. The wolf and the dog unite against their unnatural offspring, but in the end the dog dies for the man and the wolf returns to the wild. Ultimately Roberts differentiates between domestic and wild animals, though the difference is not so clear at times at the individual level. At the species level, as **"The Passing of the Black Whelps"** symbolically illustrates, animals are true to their natures. And, the influence of man on animals has been great enough to actually create a domestic nature with its own powerful instinctual drives.

Roberts' third major group of animal stories contains the highest degree of human intrusion of all. In this type of story Roberts actually focuses on man. Man is not just another wilderness hazard, nor is he just a domesticating force. But these stories are still animal stories. Roberts is examining man's behavior in the same fashion as he did that of his animal characters. One must be careful, however, not to include all of Roberts' stories that deal with man in the wilderness in the category of animal stories. *The Heart of the Ancient Wood,* for example, is not an animal story; it is a romance. Though Roberts defined the animal story as "a psychological romance constructed on a framework of natural science," *Heart of the Ancient Wood* ultimately represents the more sentimentalized, conventional traditions of romance. Roberts' "human animal" stories, with a few exceptions, are not concerned with human relationships, rather they deal with man in relation to the wilderness. Men are found avoiding predators, hunting, and simply trying to survive in the harsh natural world. In other words, Roberts is depicting humans functioning in the same situations as his animals do. And, just as Roberts was trying to get at the difference between wild and domestic animals, in this group of stories he is trying to analyze what exactly makes man different from animals.

Probably the best place to begin an analysis of Roberts' "human animals" is the novel *In the Morning of Time.* In this book Roberts goes back and takes a look at man in his most primitive state. At the beginning of the novel, the cave men that Roberts depicts are not much different from animals. In Chapter II, a sort of prologue to the book, Roberts recounts what he feels to be the crucial moment in man's development, his first use of intelligence to defeat animals. The "man-creature" defeats two groups of animals by leading them into conflict with each other. Through this action the man realizes his superiority over all other animals and he comes down from the trees. Roberts spends the rest of the novel focusing on a specific tribe of men, and more particularly on the character of Grôm. He follows Grôm as he discovers fire, the bow, the boat, and a number of other important items. Through the archetypal character of Grôm, Roberts clearly illustrates the basic differences between man and animals. Grôm is seen responding to the same behavior situations as animals, but his methods are much more sophisticated, even at this primitive stage. The difference then is in degree rather than kind; man responds differently but is motivated by the same basic needs.

When looking at Roberts' cave men in comparison with some of his more advanced, modern "human animals," one notices that the gap between the two groups is not very great . . . [In] Roberts' opinion, man is not that far removed from his remote ancestors, and that his primitive instincts can surface very quickly.

The Boy, a figure found in a number of Roberts' stories, is a good example of a character in whom these instincts surface. *The Kindred of the Wild* contains a trilogy of stories structured around this character. The reader first encounters the Boy in **"The Moonlight Trails."** He seems to be a highly sensitive character. "Animals he loved, and of all cruelty toward them he was fiercely intolerant." The Boy even goes against "Biblical injunction" and defends the snake against human cruelty. However, when Andy, the hired man, suggests they go rabbit snaring, a change comes over the Boy:

> The silent and mysterious winter woods, the shining spaces of the snow marked here and there with strange footprints leading to unknown lairs, the clear glooms, the awe and the sense of unseen presences—these were what came thronging into the boy's mind at Andy's suggestion. All the wonderful possibilities of it! The wild spirit of adventure, the hunting zest of elemental man, stirred in his veins at the idea. Had he seen a rabbit being hurt he would have rushed with indignant pity to the rescue. But the idea of rabbit-snaring, as presented by Andy's exciting words, fired a side of his imagination so

remote from pity as to have no communication with it whatever along the nerves of sympathy or association.

The instincts of his primitive ancestors have been awakened. To go along with the instincts, the Boy has the ability to recognize and interpret animal tracks, the most primitive sort of reading. When they set the snares, "His tenderness of heart, his enlightened sympathy with the four-footed kindred, much of his civilization, in fact, had vanished for the moment, burnt out in the flame of an instinct handed down to him from his primeval ancestors." At the story's end he repents, not really just for killing the rabbits, but for the cruelty of his actions. He realizes that he has descended to the level of the weasel who seems to kill for no other reason than the sake of killing.

The second part of the trilogy is **"The Boy and Hushwing."** When we encounter the Boy at the start of the story he is planning to capture an owl. "He might have shot the bird easily, but wanton slaughter was not his object." He is merely trying, "first of all, to test his own woodcraft; and, second, to get the bird under his close observation." He succeeds in capturing the owl by outwitting it. In the end the bird escapes back to the wilderness, but the Boy realizes that that is where the bird belongs.

The final story is **"The Haunter of the Pine Gloom."** By this time the Boy has become an accomplished woodsman. "He had a pet theory that the human animal was more competent, as a mere animal, than it gets credit of being; and it was his particular pride to outdo the wild creatures at their own games". However, he has still retained his ethical standard and does not kill the animals. Roberts shows that the Boy is not a romantic though. When a lynx family migrates into the area and starts killing his father's stock, the Boy does what is necessary. "His primeval hunting instincts were now aroused, and he was no longer merely the tender-hearted and sympathetic observer. It was only toward the marauding lucifers, however, that his feelings had changed." He eventually kills the lynxes. The trilogy ends on an ironic note, with a lynx hanging dead in the Boy's snare. Underneath the dead lynx a group of rabbits play. This neat twist brings the reader back to the first story, in which the Boy snared rabbits in the same fashion. By the end of the trilogy the Boy has blended his useful primeval instincts with his ethical standard. Thus the rabbits have nothing to fear from him, but the lynxes, who pose a threat to the Boy, are killed. (pp. 30-4)

In **"The Kill"**, Roberts portrays a man who, like the Boy, can accept nature's harsh realities. But, unlike the Boy, he accepts them a little too eagerly. He shoots a moose and, "elated and fiercely glad," the man surges forward to complete the kill. He stumbles and just as the moose is about to trample him, the animal dies and the man is saved. However, instead of giving thanks for his good fortune, the hunter "sprang up, rushed forward with a shout, and drew his knife across the outstretched [moose's] throat." He has sunk to the level of the weasel and kills for pleasure. The Boy has distinguished between wanton killing (snaring the rabbits) and necessary killing (the lynxes), and thus imposes an ethical standard upon himself. Roberts clearly sees this standard as a basic part of man's nature. When man shirks this standard and descends to the level of the animals. . . . (pp. 34-5)

What Roberts is trying to show in all these "human animal" stories is that although man is motivated by the same wants and needs as animals, he is still different. Man is more than just an animal; further along the evolutionary line, he has moral responsibilities that are equal to, and sometimes take priority over, the mere satisfying of biological drives. A story like **"The Truce"** clearly illustrates this idea. A woodsman finds himself caught on an ice floe, heading towards a waterfall, with a bear who only moments before was trying to attack him. The woodsman can stoically accept the situation. But, when the opportunity arises, he makes his way ashore. Though he had earlier thought that, perhaps, the bear would find a way out, he realizes "that if he didn't know more than a bear he'd no business in the woods." And, not only is he aware of his own superiority over the bear, he also accepts the moral responsibility for the bear's life, and rescues him. This is basically the same conclusion that the Boy reaches. The Boy feels that "the human animal was more competent, as a mere animal, than it gets the credit of being," but he still realizes that he is fundamentally different from "mere animals." The woodsman, though he is a hunter and can regard the wild creatures as his prey at times, can also accept a moral responsibility for the bear's life, something the bear would never have done for him. When Roberts' "human animal" stories are read with these ideas in mind, a fundamental fallacy is perceived in the sort of argument that Desmond Pacey puts forth. Pacey feels that when Roberts "introduces human characters his touch falters and the wildest melodrama occurs." What Pacey considers to be melodrama is usually just man's ethical responsibilities surfacing amidst the wilderness struggle for survival.

In my treatment of Roberts' animal stories, one of my main concerns, and one that I dealt with specifically in the beginning of this article, is that critics have focused on mistaken and irrelevant aspects of Roberts' animal stories. Pacey's above statement is typical of this. Roberts himself talked of the proper function of the animal story:

> The animal story, as we now have it, is a potent emancipator. It frees us for a little while from the world of shop-worn utilities, and from the mean tenement of self of which we do well to grow weary. It helps us to return to nature, without requiring that we at the same time return to barbarism. It leads us back to the old kinship of earth, without asking us to relinquish by way of toll any part of the wisdom of the ages, any fine essential of the 'large result of time.'

By arranging the stories into three general thematic groups, I have, in a sense, viewed the stories in terms of this statement. Though my specific examples are ones that best exemplify the qualities I have tried to illustrate, all of Roberts' animal stories fall into one of these three groups. They either deal with animals in the wild, apart from man; with animals in relation to man; or with the "human animal." Joseph Gold has stated that Roberts, through the animal story, was "trying to approach some larger vision of basic human drives and some understanding of the tran-

scendent universal design to which all things contribute." This larger vision can be perceived only when Roberts' animal stories are seen as a unified whole. I have tried to show that one way of perceiving this unity is to view the stories in terms of thematic groupings based on the degree of human intrusion. In each group Roberts is portraying a different aspect of animal behavior, ranging from animals in the wild to "human animals." When viewed as a whole, Roberts' animal stories are revealed to be an attempt to define man's relation to the wilderness and to the animal kingdom. (pp. 35-6)

> *Tim Murray, "Charles Roberts' Animal Stories," in* Canadian Children's Literature, *No. 2, 1975, pp. 23-37.*

George Woodcock

The outdoors story and the animal story became very popular around 1900, and this was the first period in which Canadian writers began to draw the attention of the whole English-reading world. For a considerable period, such fiction was one of the main streams in Canadian writing, and, although the vogue tended to die away about the time of the Great War, a steady interest in outdoors writing has sustained later exponents, such as the ambiguous Archie Belaney who gained celebrity as Grey Owl and the British Columbian fisherman, naturalist, and novelist, Roderick Haig-Brown, who died as recently as 1976.

Of the two leading exponents of the animal story, Seton was the better naturalist and tended to be the more didactic, striving—with many lapses into pathos—to portray the actual lives of animals as nearly as possible and in this sense he was a realist. Roberts was the more philosophic and also the more melodramatic writer, tending to portray his animal heroes in extreme situations where they could be displayed as the tragic victims of destiny in an indifferent universe. His views are impregnated with the fashionable evolutionism of his time, but it is Huxley's pessimistic interpretation of Darwinism rather than Kropotkin's optimistic one that shadows his stories.

In seeking the common themes of Canadian writing and the myths that underlie them, contemporary Canadian critics have been inclined to make much of these turn-of-the-century creators of animal stories, and from their special viewpoint of cultural nationalism they are right, since here for the first time are writers working in Canada whom it is difficult to relegate to the fringes of more dominant literary traditions such as the English and the American. One may perhaps consider Duncan a lesser Edith Wharton, dismiss Niven as a minor Robert Louis Stevenson, but the Canadian animal writers were doing something quite different from either their British or their American counterparts. British animal stories have almost always been thinly disguised fables, acted out by men in animal skins to illuminate essentially human problems. (George Orwell's *Animal Farm* is an outstanding example, but even less obviously didactic works like *The Wind in the Willows* are just as essentially anthropomorphic.) American animal stories, like Faulkner's "The Bear" or Hemingway's *The Old Man and the Sea,* are almost invariably stories of antagonism and confrontation, man pitting himself against the animal who becomes the symbol of all that is hostile in nature. But Canadian animal stories are really about animals, and they are about animals with whom we are invited to empathize. We are invited to empathize with them—critics such as Margaret Atwood are likely to claim—because they are invariably portrayed as victims, and we, a multiply colonialized people, are victims, too.

It does not, however, require any such deference to literary theory to recognize that in such fiction the Canadian writer is at last beginning to respond to and utilize his environment directly and without fear; it is no longer necessary to interpose the screen of European forms and values between him and the world in which he is destined to live. It is Canada's own myths that Canadians must recognize, mediated through the images which at last can begin to be recognized in their true shapes. But even the animal writers of the turn of the century present us with the reality of the specific Canadian existence at one remove. For all his skill in evoking the lives of wild animals, Roberts failed when, in *The Heart of the Ancient Wood,* he attempted to establish a meaningful relationship between human beings and the wilderness. Roberts failed because he created a sentimental identification of man with untamed nature rather than an organic link. (pp. 78-80)

> *George Woodcock, "Possessing the Land: Notes on Canadian Fiction," in* The Canadian Imagination: Dimensions of a Literary Culture, *edited by David Staines, Cambridge, Mass.: Harvard University Press, 1977, pp. 69-96.*

Robert H. MacDonald

In his introduction to *Kindred of the Wild*—a chapter that stands as a succinct apologia for the animal story—Sir Charles Roberts in 1902 explained the particular inspiration of the new genre practised by Ernest Thompson Seton and himself. Animals and men, he said, were not so separate as had been supposed, for animals, far from being mere creatures of instinct, could and did reason, and what is more, frequently displayed to the discerning observer signs not only of their psychologies, but also of something which might appeal to man's spiritual self. "We have come face to face with personality, where we were blindly wont to predicate mere instinct and automatism." The animal story, Roberts concluded, was thus a "potent emancipator," freeing us from "shop-worn utilities" and restoring to us the "old kinship of earth," a spiritual and uplifting union with nature.

These statements can be labelled "romantic," or "transcendental," and dismissed as a rather sentimental defence of the "inarticulate kindred" of the wild, who are distinguished from Black Beauty and Beautiful Joe only by the fact that they live in the woods. I propose, however, to take Roberts at his word, and to examine his and Seton's stories in the light of his crucial distinction between instinct and reason. The animal story, I shall show, is part of a popular revolt against Darwinian determinism, and is an affirmation of man's need for moral and spiritual values. The animal world provides models of virtue, and exemplifies the order of nature. The works of Seton and Roberts are thus celebrations of rational, ethical animals, who, as they rise above instinct, reach towards the spiritual. This theme, inspired as it is by a vision of a better world, provides a mythic structure for what is at first sight, realistic fiction.

At the popular level, the chief implication of Darwin's theories of evolution and the principle of natural selection

Roberts at Hubbards Cove, Nova Scotia, 1930.

had been to diminish the distinction between man and the animals. We were descended from the apes, and if the apes were mere brutes, could we be very much different? All creatures, it seemed, owed their present form to certain inherited characteristics, which together with environmental influences, dictated their ability to survive. Nature was amoral; life was a power-struggle in which only the fittest survived. Instinct, to a large extent, seemed to govern animal behaviour; there was little place in nature for ethics or spirituality. Though man traditionally had been separated from the animals by his unique power of reason, could it now now be that man himself was little more than a brute beast?

By 1900 one of the most important controversies in the biological sciences was the question of animal behaviour: did animals act instinctively, or were they capable of learning? What was the nature of an animal's knowledge: was it inherited, or was it acquired? Were animals capable of reason? Did they learn from experience, did they teach each other? The weight of opinion, at least from the biologists, seemed to favour instinct and inheritance. In their reaction to this controversy (and in a larger sense to the whole impetus of Darwinism), Seton, Roberts and their fellow nature writers rescued their public from the awful amorality of Darwinian nature. They reassured their readers, not so much that man was superior to animals, but that animals were superior in themselves, that they could reason, that they could and did educate their young, and that they possessed and obeyed laws of their own. Judging by the commercial success of their stories, this was a popular and much-needed antidote to Darwinian pessimism.

"The life of a wild animal," said Seton in *Wild Animals I Have Known* (1899), *"always has a tragic end."* By that he meant that all animals die, and since most of them prey upon each other, they frequently die violently. Both Seton and Roberts refused to evade this unpleasant fact: kill or be killed is the natural law. To this extent they were both Darwinians: nature was indeed red in tooth and claw, and only the best escaped for a time. (pp. 18-19)

In their biographies of animal heroes, both men repeatedly illustrate this central fact of the evolutionary theory. Their animals are not ordinary animals, but superior animals, distinguished by their size, skill, wisdom and moral sense. These animals have all learned to cope with a hostile environment; they endure. They are the leaders of their kind. Thus Wahb is the largest and most intelligent grizzly, Krag the noblest mountain sheep, Lobo a giant among wolves, Raggylugs a most sagacious rabbit, and so on. From the first Red Fox is the pick of his litter, larger, livelier, more intelligent, and, curiously, redder. (p. 19)

Both Seton and Roberts took pains to establish that everything they wrote was within the bounds of truth. Their animal biographies were frequently "composite" biographies; that is, they included everything that had been done, or might have been done, by a crow, or a wolf, or a fox, but they contained nothing that was not possible. Thus Seton, in his preface to *Wild Animals I Have Known,* acknowledges having "pieced together some of the characters," but claims that there was, in at least three of the lives, "almost no deviation from the truth." Roberts, in-

troducing Red Fox, makes the same point saying that in the life of his hero, "every one of these experiences has befallen some red fox in the past, and may befall other red foxes in the future." He has been, he assures his readers, "careful to keep well within the boundaries of fact." We may take these statements at face value: by and large, both men were astute and careful observers of nature, and in most of their writing give realistic, though fictionalized, descriptions of animal life. Both also claim that though they have given their animals language and emotions, these are, within the demands of the genre, realistic, and not anthropomorphized.

However it is not realism that entirely inspires the art of Seton and Roberts, whatever strength that lends to their work, but certain ideas which frame and condition the realism, and which give to it symbolic form. The animal heroes may live and die in the wild, being only interesting specimens of their race, but their biographies, as literature, belong in the world of myth. What matters is not that everything that is told *could* have happened to a fox, or a grizzly, but that it *did* happen, and that, for the author, the life of the animal was organized according to certain basic ideas, and that in its living it demonstrated certain fundamental truths. At the heart of the myth that gives structure to the work of both Seton and Roberts is their belief that animals are rational and ethical beings, and that they rise above instinct. This is demonstrated most clearly in the ways the animals train their young to survive, and the ways in which their young respond to the challenge. (p. 20)

Seton, as a careful naturalist, frequently describes instinctive (or innate) behaviour in animals. In most cases, he regards it as an inherited substratum, a built-in defence against the early dangers of life. He speaks of an animal's "native instincts," which are supplemented by the twin teachers of life, experience and the example of fellow animals. The little mountain lambs in *Lives of the Hunted,* surprised and chased by a hunter just after birth, are able to dodge and escape, for "Nature had equipped them with a set of valuable instincts." Instinct, however, takes an animal only just so far. Its role in survival is subsidiary to reason. In the story of the Don Valley partridge, for instance, Seton tells us that the partridge chicks soon graduate from instinctive to rational behaviour: "their start in life was a good mother, good legs, a few reliable instincts, and a germ of reason. It was instinct, that is, inherited habit, which taught them to hide at the word from their mother; it was instinct that taught them to follow her, but it was reason which made them keep under the shadow of her tail when the sun was smiting down. . . ." And, Seton concludes, "from that day reason entered more and more into their expanding lives."

Roberts treats instinct in much the same way, as a valuable though necessarily limited body of inherited knowledge. Thus Red Fox, as befits a superior animal, has an extra amount: "he seemed to inherit with special fulness and effectiveness that endowment of ancestral knowledge which goes by the name of instinct." At the same time, of course, we are told that he is more intelligent, that he can reason, and that he is "peculiarly apt in learning from his mother." Instinct is, too, a latent skill, which can surface when necessary: in the story of **"Lone Wolf "** (*Neighbours Unknown*), the tame circus wolf who escapes to the wilds, Roberts shows us its hero rediscovering "long buried memories" of how a wolf kills. "It was as if all his life Lone Wolf had been killing bulls, so unerring was that terrible chopping snap at the great beast's throat." These are perhaps unexceptionable ideas, yet elsewhere in Roberts' work there is the definite implication that instinct is a primitive force which must be controlled and subdued by reason. This is especially true when applied to man himself (though as the highest of the "kindred" what is true for man is also true for animals). In **"The Moonlight Trails"** (*Kindred of the Wild*), we are told of a boy who loves animals and is sensitive to their feelings, who accompanies the hired man on an expedition to the woods to snare rabbits. As they set the snares the boy is moved by the primitive lust of the hunter; he feels "stirrings of a wild, predatory instinct." When they return in the morning to see what they have caught the boy is still at first in the grip of the hunting passion, but when he sees the cruel tragedy of death his more civilized feelings come to the surface. "We won't snare any more rabbits, Andy," he tells the hired man.

The gap between man and the animals, Roberts insists, is very narrow. Animals "can and do reason." **Red Fox** illustrates this thesis: the whole novel is a celebration of one animal's cunning and sagacity. We are repeatedly told of Red Fox's cunning, his "nimble wits," his ingenious and deliberate schemes for evading his enemies, his prodigious memory, his ability to study a situation, to make plans, to reason. We hear how he outwits "the Boy," how he leads the hounds to their destruction, how he fools his enemy Jabe Smith. His qualities are quite obvious: "look at that cool and cunning eye," says one of his American captors. "He's got brains."

In his early education, Red Fox shows that instinct is subservient to reason. Red Fox must learn both from his mother and from experience. "It is possible (though some say otherwise!) to expect too much of instinct," Roberts tells us, and explains how a successful fox will learn his lessons, "partly by example and partly no doubt by a simple language whose subtleties evade human observation." Yet we notice that when instinct gets Red Fox into trouble, it is instinct that rescues him. His nose tells him to dig in a bees' nest for honey, and when they sting him, he runs blindly for a thicket, and automatically cools his smarting nose in the mud. These are inconsistencies: Roberts' dominant theme is the supremacy and efficacy of his hero's reason. The vixen's instructions to leave men alone have "their effect on [Red Fox's] sagacious brain," whereas his stupider brother thinks he knows better, and pays the price with his life. This incident, one should note, is at the same time an apt illustration of Darwinian theory, for it is the better animal that survives.

The intelligent young animal is also the obedient young animal. In the School of the Woods, obedience is a primary virtue. The child must obey the parent. "For a young animal," Seton said, "there is no better gift than obedience," and he demonstrated this again and again by show-

ing us the fate of the disobedient, the young lambs who do not come when they are called, and are caught and killed, or the foolish partridge chicks who refuse to stay close to mother. The fate of Red Fox's siblings again makes the point: the weak and the foolish will not survive, but the disobedient bring trouble upon all.

The essential argument of this article should be clear by now: the fiction of both Seton and Roberts is inspired by their desire to present a moral and coherent order in the life of the wild, which is part of the greater order of the cosmos. That many of their observations of animal life are accurate is undeniable—animals do learn, they are intelligent in their way, and they are probably even capable of reason. Yet what is important in Seton and Roberts is the way the details are presented. Animals, we are told, are very much like ourselves. They obey certain laws, they demonstrate qualities we would do well to admire, they are our own kin. They inhabit what is often clearly a mythic world; they are symbols in our own ontological system. Nowhere is this more obvious than in the context of morality.

Each animal, first of all, must learn to obey the laws of its kind. Morality is not a human invention, but an integral part of all nature. "It is quite common," says Seton in *Lives of the Hunted,* "to hear conventionality and social rules derided as though they were silly man-made tyrannies. They are really important laws that, like gravitation, were here before human society began, and shaped it when it came. In all wild animals we see them grown with the mental growth of the species." The higher the animal, the more clearly developed the moral system. The better the animal—the more successful, or superior specimen—the more moral the animal. Thus superior animals fight fair, but the weak, the cowards, and the mean may well resort to dirty tricks. Krag the mountain sheep, whose strength, and size, and curling horns make him appear like a "demigod" to his ewes, has to beat off two other rams to defend his rights to his harem. One ram fights fair and meets Krag horn to horn; the other fights foul, and attacks from the side. It is important that in this moral world the immoral ram "works his own destruction," running himself over a two hundred foot cliff to his death.

These animal laws would appear to be somewhat flexible, coloured as they are by the vision of the human observer, since occasionally even a "good" animal will break the rule of his kind to preserve himself or another. This is always done for a reason: the law may be broken in the name of the higher good. We are told, in **"Raggylugs,"** that "all good rabbits forget their feuds when their common enemy appears." Rag's rival, the stranger, ignores this basic rule of rabbit society, trying to drive Rag into the reach of a goshawk. This is bad. Yet one sentence later we find Rag playing the same game to save himself and his mother, as he successfully lures old Thunder the hound into the nest of "the stranger." This, we infer, is good.

It is at moments like this that it is most evident that the animal story belongs not to the world of natural science, but to the world of literature. There are good animals and bad animals, and we, as readers, are always expected to be on the side of morality. Seton, however, is usually careful not to denigrate a species: each animal, of whatever kind, has some quality that a man might admire. Even the hated rat is courageous. Roberts, on the other hand, lets his sympathies show: there are some species who exhibit only the worst. Such are lynx. In **"Grey Lynx's Last Hunting"** we are shown a portrait of animal cruelty, selfishness and marital hatred, whose appropriate outcome is the sordid death of the male, killed by his savage and mad mate. Both writers, in their desire to make a moral point, cross from realism into romance. Seton has a story of wolves who lynch an apparent cheat and liar, and Roberts the fanciful tale of a society of animals who voluntarily resolve not to kill "within eyeshot" of a sensitive and disapproving child.

Throughout Roberts' work there is an insistence on the meaning, the vitality, the harmony and the morality of the struggle of life, and in Seton, of the fairness and ultimate order of nature. Perhaps the most dramatic illustration of their essentially similar moral philosophy is Seton's short *The Natural History of the Ten Commandments* (1907), in which he finds that the Mosaic laws are not "arbitrary laws given to man, but are fundamental laws of all highly developed animals." Animals, in their own way, observe the last six of the ten commandments, and in their occasional willingness to "throw themselves on the mercy of some other power," manifest the beginnings of a spiritual life. Man, obeying the first four commandments, acknowledges the Deity; the higher animals acknowledge man. (pp. 22-5)

[The] lives of the animals resemble, in their structure, the life of the mythic hero: they are born, go through early trials, win their kingdom and die. Some, like Seton's Krag, who returns after death to haunt his murderer, even have an apotheosis. Fate in the shape of a Darwinian catastrophe ensures in the evitable death of the hero a technical tragedy, though the prevailing note in both Seton and Roberts is one of life ever renewed. Man, especially in Seton's stories, may be part of a corrupt and decadent postlapsarian world. In Roberts, man's ignorance and callousness are crimes against nature, though innocence and goodness are often represented by a child or youth, the sensitive girl or boy who knows and loves the creatures of the woods. In Roberts also, the landscape is often magical or enchanted.

In all these details it is clear that the animal tales of both Seton and Roberts take their inspiration and structure as much from literature as from life. In their use of the conventions of the romance, in their echoing of a mythic pattern, and in their quite definite symbolic treatment of animal character, both men translate the indiscriminate facts of nature into the ordered patterns of art. At the centre of their fiction is their belief in moral and rational animals, which in its extensiveness and pervasive force, takes on the quality of an organizing myth. It is ironic that at a time when the forces of instinct, intuition and the unconscious were being rediscovered in man, the power of the Logos was found in the kingdoms of the brute beasts. (pp. 27-8)

Robert H. MacDonald, "The Revolt against Instinct: The Animal Stories of Seton and Rob-

erts," in Canadian Literature, *No. 84, Spring, 1980, pp. 18-29.*

Joan McGrath

Sir Charles G. D. Roberts, knighted for his work in the field, pioneered a sort of animal story-cum-fairy tale style that is now more amusing than it is moving, though certainly that was not his intention. His animal heroes and villains are forever plotting revenge or burning with resentment: their eyes flash and dart; they behave, in fact, like furry human beings. Notwithstanding this inappropriate attribution of human emotions and motivation, Roberts had a keen eye for the detail of animal lives. At a time when wild animals were too often regarded merely as targets for sportsmen or prey for trappers, such titles as *Kindred of the Wild* and *Red Fox* did good service in fostering awareness of the irreplaceable qualities and interdependence of all forms of animal life. (pp. 41-2)

Joan McGrath, "The Red & the White: Canadian Books for Children," in School Library Journal, *Vol. 27, No. 1, September, 1980, pp. 41-3.*

Michael Hornyansky

The chief sin, in writing for children, is archness. I shall examine in this light three books by Charles G. D. Roberts: *Children of the Wild, The Heart of the Ancient Wood,* and *In the Morning of Time.* I choose these three because they are sufficient to show how far the sin afflicts him, and how he overcomes it; because they have a focus that should be of enduring interest and profit to children; and because each of them is (more or less) a complete and connected whole. I could make the same case for a great many individual stories in various collections, but it would have to be in a scattered way.

What I mean by archness is the knowing, the waggish, the roguish: the posture or tone that conveys, with cocked eyebrow or rolled eye, that you and I know there is more to a matter than what we speak. Between adults or equals it may be harmless, an invitation to share a tacit joke; though it is always coy, and usually (to my taste) a bit sickening. Between adult and child it is inexcusable, and fatal to honest dealing . . . When we condescend . . . , to our inferiors in age or learning or social degree, it is an overt stooping, doffing for the moment our proper worth. Children shy away from this, as they do from all manner of adult pomposity. Perhaps I should add that by "children" I mean people up to the age of twelve or so—before the tribal laws of the teenager muffle their directness and mask their true feelings.

Condescension in books for children occurs when we call them Kiddie Lit, and when we treat or practise them accordingly. Two forms of it are obvious. First we scale down our vocabulary, if not to outright goo-goos and choo-choos, at least to a Dick-and-Jane level of primer chat that the poor dears can be expected to follow. Second, we don the pink glasses of sentimentality, and distort the child's world into a cute, sugary never-never-land. (pp. 163-64)

Surprisingly, the grossest pitfall is the one to give Charles

Roberts most trouble. We have almost the sense of a man so skilled in solitary forest walking that he proves gauche in human company. *Children of the Wild* is a collection of stories about young animals, mostly such as might be met with in New Brunswick eighty years ago. Risky territory, one might think, inviting coy anthropomorphism. But Roberts has Darwin's eye, and Darwin drives out Disney. What causes difficulties is the frame story: Uncle Andy is telling these short tales, *in situ,* by way of instructing his nephew in natural science. A useful device, on the face of it, to mediate between the object lessons and the pupil, the wild world and our own. But the fact is, it gets in the way. One problem is with diction: properly launched on a narrative, Roberts allows himself the full amplitude of his own style: but at the beginning of each tale, and occasionally along the way, he recalls Andy and the nephew, and becomes momentarily self-conscious. For instance:

> "[The two young crows] had inherited from their eccentric parents an altogether surprising amount of originality. Their feathers were beautifully firm and black and glossy, their beaks sharp and polished; and in their full, dark, intelligent eyes there was an impishness that even a crow might regard as especially impish."

> "What's *impish?*" demanded the Babe.

> "Goodness me! Don't you know that *impish* is?" exclaimed Uncle Andy. He thought a moment, and then, finding it a little difficult to explain, he added with convenient severity: "If you listen, you'll find out, perhaps."

Yet here is Andy a moment later:

> ". . . before their parents had realized at all what precocious youngsters they were, they had climbed out upon the edge of the nest. . . . With hoarse expostulations their father tried to persuade them back. But their mother . . . chuckled her approval and flew off to hunt young mice for them. Thus encouraged, they ignored their father's prudent counsels, and hopped out, with elated squawks, upon the branch."

I blame Roberts not for being grandiloquent—though he is that, as most nineteenth century story-tellers are for the post-Hemingway reader—but for virtually apologizing, and thereby reminding us that this is meant to be oral delivery.

The same passage illustrates other oddities. You will have noticed that the nephew is called the Babe: as he is throughout, with a capital B, except when younger infants intervene and the nephew becomes temporarily the Child. We can hardly scold Roberts for not knowing the later history of "babe" as an endearment; but all the same it becomes obtrusive, like a continual pat on the head, and we wonder why the lad doesn't deserve a proper name. We have also seen Uncle Andy get a comeuppance, for being unready to define *impish*—as he does at several points in the book, and as he deserves, for he is unreasonably stern about interruptions, jealous of being upstaged, and quite inhuman about fidgeting. The last lesson is happily justi-

fied later on, when the boy learns that by keeping heroically still in the woods he can grow invisible to animals, and witness all sorts of wonders instead of hearing about them.

The frame story, in fact, works best when it stops being a device and comes alive in itself, as Chaucer had discovered some time before. Roberts achieves this, rather mechanically, by having the Babe fall asleep on an unmoored raft in a much later chapter, and drift into adventure; he manages it more organically in the "keeping still" chapter already cited; and most subtly and far-reachingly by an unobtrusive comment on Andy near the start. Is it strange that he should begin with the subtlest method and hit upon the most obvious at the last? Only, I think, if we expect him to take more care with narrative tidiness than with telling the truth. Here is the comment from Chapter I:

> "And she could never come!" murmured the Babe thoughtfully.

> "Well, she didn't," snorted Uncle Andy, the discourager of sentiment. Fairly reeking with sentiment himself, at heart, he disliked all manifestation of it in himself or others. He liked it left to the imagination.

This serves first to humanize the uncle, and to discount the pedestal from which he addresses the Babe. Second, it explains what otherwise would seem lapses in Andy's outlook, veerings away from Darwin towards Disney: for example, a woodchuck called Young Grumpy and treated accordingly (Chap. III), and a young bear in search of honey guarded by bees, who is treated far more realistically than Winnie-the-Pooh but is nevertheless called Teddy Bear (VI). For the overriding aim in this series of lessons is of course quite the contrary—to teach the Babe, and all children, to see the natural world with unsentimental clarity, as governed by inexorable laws far from our heart's desire. Thus, the mother of that grumpy woodchuck has already gnawed off her own paw to escape from a steel trap; and Uncle Andy confesses to the accidental murder of a historical woodchuck who, startled by the onrush of a big red automobile, "jumped straight on the front wheel and bit wildly at the tire." (pp. 165-67)

The Heart of the Ancient Wood is more complicated, both in narrative and in perspective. It is a single unified story, extended in time and carefully plotted, and its focus is human—indeed, at its centre is a young girl, growing up in much the same territory that the Babe was visiting on a summer holiday. Since the child has been thus shifted from observer to protagonist, the difference between the human world and the wild likewise shifts, from a perceived contrast to a conflict directly experienced. And if there is to be any patronizing of the child, the author supplies no Uncle Andy to take the rap.

To a remote cabin in the heart of the New Brunswick wood comes Kirstie Craig, a strong young woman abandoned by her indolent husband (a frail artist from the city) and exiled from the Settlement by the "bitter tongues" of gossip. She brings with her two named steers, a cow, some chickens, and a five-year-old daughter. They are escorted by young Davey Titus (torn between personal loyalty and fear of social disapproval), and received by his father Old Dave, who has repaired the abandoned cabin and clearing as their refuge. Once the party is settled in, the two men depart, and we are left with Kirstie and young Miranda facing a new life far from humankind. The child's name and other hints point us toward Shakespeare's *Tempest;* but no sooner has Roberts confirmed the parallel than he transforms it. We realize, within moments of the arrival, that Miranda will be the Prospero of this version. It is her fresh young eye that sees the brave newness of this world, and the fascinating creatures in it—which are quite invisible to the others; her inexperience leads her to confuse Kroof the she-bear with a "nice, great big dog," but she learns otherwise without damage, having got her hand in by quelling a bumptious rooster. The history of the next months unfolds her astonishing skill and rapport with the wildlings, above all with the bear, and her establishing of a "pax Mirandae" over the environing wood. The difficult lesson that remains is to learn that she is human, to resolve the conflicting claims of the wild and her own emerging nature—the latter being poignantly reinforced by the return of young Dave, now a full-grown hunter and trapper.

It is clear from the start that there will be no condescending to the child reader in this book. The language makes no concessions; even the first words heard from Old Dave the lumberman are almost incomprehensible. But a child who can read at all must surely be ensnared by the skill of the narrative: the undisturbed forest, pursuing its own affairs; the entry of Old Dave, slouching along the trail unaware of all the watchers; the appeal of the haven he rebuilds in the clearing; and the delayed entry of the main characters, Miranda above all. Her ability to see and gradually to master the wild creatures, witnessed by a half-fearful, half-baffled mother, makes Miranda irresistible—magical and yet credible. Her virtual adoption by Kroof is exciting as well as entrancing. Kroof has lost her only cub to a deadfall trap set by a man; and when the child's overconfidence leaves her lost in the forest at peril from a marauding "panther," it seems wholly natural that the bear should rescue her and treat her as a surrogate. The bear has a dim hope that her new cub will ease the aching of her swollen teats. This detail does a lot to dispel a sentimental reading; and of course the child doesn't oblige—worn out by her ordeal, she goes to sleep on Kroof's belly instead. (pp. 167-68)

In all this, the only risk of archness is that Roberts might slip into sentimentalizing either the animals or the child. We can trust him with the animals; slight hints of anthropomorphism can be taken as forgivable translations of non-human feelings, *e.g.,* Kroof's blind grief over her dead cub, and otherwise the predators and their quarry move unconsciously through their own dooms. The crux, the entente between bear and child, I have already argued Roberts makes credible. He preserves Miranda from cuteness partly by placing her amid unexaggerated dangers, partly by presenting her as a holy fool, the object of ironies she cannot yet see. One example is the question of Kroof's diet. As long as the bear pursues berries and roots Miranda approves; but when Kroof craves meat and kills a hare, the appalled child gives her hell. The she-bear, perplexed by a habit of tender regard and an uneasy recognition of

Miranda's human authority, watches as the hare is buried. After Miranda goes home to the cabin, Kroof returns to dig up the hare and enjoy a guiltless supper. This amiable clash of values, animal and human, foreshadows several others, before the far-off climax in which Miranda, now a young woman caught between forest loyalties and the call of her own kind, must choose in the starkest circumstances between Kroof and Dave, the meat-eating trapper. This passage would seem melodramatic in summary; in reading, it is entirely satisfactory.

In the Morning of Time is a tale of prehistory, with no room for a child. In fact through the first chapter there is no room for humans at all, as Roberts paints with some gusto a broad picture of colossal saurians tearing each other in the primeval slime. Chapter II opens a quarter million years later, with a set-to between an obsolescent dinosaur and a giant black mammal resembling a six-horned mammoth (Roberts calls him Dinoceras; we know him as Uintatherium, having found his bones in Wyoming); among the spectators we discover a furry anthropoid with an opposed thumb and a sagacious gleam in his eye. He is too early a starter to show much more than promise, but this he does splendidly in revenging himself on the dinosaur who has casually slaughtered his mate and baby. The chapter ends with him groping dimly after the idea of new sons, as inquiring and resourceful as himself, to start the long work. To find continuous action on the hominid plane, we must leap forward again to Chapter III, and zero in on the people of the Little Hills at their takingoff point, **"The Finding of Fire."** Here we meet the admirable hero Grôm, whose saga fills the rest of the book. Not the least of his qualities is his readiness to leave politics to his chief, Bawr—whom he serves as fighter, counsellor, strategist, explorer, and inventor. It is Grôm who learns by rapid trial and error how to deploy, and ultimately to transport, the dancing flames offered by volcanic fumaroles. Not long afterwards he invents and refines another weapon, the bow, from a baby's toy accidentally devised by his wife A-ya. . . . (pp. 168-69)

There is no condescension here, in either language or content. If vestiges of archness crop up in his style, they belong to the type customary with Dickens or Conan Doyle:

> "This is a country of very great beasts," Grôm remarked, with the air of one announcing a discovery. As A-ya showed no inclination to dissent from this statement, he presently went on to his conclusion, leaving her to infer his minor premise.

And sentimentality can hardly infect this scene: quite the contrary—animals and proto-humans slaughter each other with such ferocity that one suspects Roberts has been restraining an urge to do full justice to this aspect of the Darwinian struggle. Nothing hampers him here. Since the animals are monstrous, predatory, or edible, no child will mourn their passing, however gory; and most of the *human* enemies are alien and brutish—squat, bowlegged, and regrettably yellow-skinned. . . . But who can cavil at Grôm's basic decency? In early days, the girl A-ya by excess zeal has smothered their portable fire, while her mighty hunter sleeps.

She expected a merciless beating, according to the rough-and-ready customs of their tribe. But Grôm had always been held a little peculiar, especially in his aversion to the beating of women, so that certain females of the tribe had even been known to question his manhood on that account.

(The use of "women" and "females" is deft, and the irony resonates even today.) And if A-ya reacts by feeling quite sure he is a god—well, after all, she's a child of her times; and she'll have her innings later.

But our wise smiles do Roberts less than justice. In Grôm, he has created something far more impressive than Ug the clever cave-man. Above those shaggy brows lies an ample forehead, and beneath them a brooding face whose "calm, reasoning eyes" are apt to be clouded with visions. He finds mystery a magnet, and takes supreme delight in utterly new experience. His feeling for A-ya ("a kind of thrilling tenderness, such as he had never felt toward a woman before"—too soon to call it love, Roberts notes, but it's a start) is of a piece with his "compunction" in questioning a wounded foreigner (Chap. IX): clear tokens of the emerging humane. A-ya likewise is much more than a savage mate; help meet for this Adam, she saves his life more than once and brings a practical wisdom to share his dreams (she soon surpasses him with bow and arrow; and remarks approvingly that he has "not grown too divine to be ready to run away on fitting occasion"). In these two, nature has cast up the virtual founders of a race that will find its values in a realm above nature.

In short, Darwinism is not enough. The struggle for existence, ruled by mechanism and chance, offers no foundation for purpose and ideals. Some fitter must be sought. If the universe offers no God, we must trust to what divinity we can find. Darwin's astute front man, T. H. Huxley, had taken this road in *Evolution and Ethics* (1894): firmly championing natural selection against the bishops (and showing by the way that "survival of the fittest" held no hope for progressionists), he insisted with equal force that the human world is not part of this wilderness, but a walled garden responsive to the care and purpose of its gardeners. Human truth is not natural truth; and we must learn to hold it against the world—a stance remarkably close to modern existentialism.

Now, younger readers of Roberts might have trouble digesting such an argument, but they cannot miss the hints and signposts he provides. Of Grôm, mastering the gods of fire, he comments explicitly: "then still more of the god was there in his own intelligence." To the Bow-legs, their sub-human enemies, Grôm's people are "a tribe of tall, fair-skinned demons"—demons being gods inimically viewed. The apparent racism of Roberts' account falls into clearer perspective. Grôm's race should not be taken as primal shoulderers of the white man's burden, but as a giant stride above the beast. In Mawg the renegade there are still signs of "the mere brute from which the race had mounted." And when Grôm's folk in their great trek westward are menaced by unevolved apes, what sickens A-ya is not the peril but the "hideous caricature of man" they present. (pp. 169-71)

Roberts comes nearest to being arch in *Children of the Wild,* where he invents a narrator telling the stories to a child. In *The Heart of the Ancient Wood* he solves most of the difficulty by getting rid of the narrator and by moving the child into the centre of the story. Finally (*In the Morning of Time*) he avoids all risk of sentimentality by taking a full-scale Darwinian romp through prehistory, and starring a proto-human who is far too noble and ingenious to patronize.

It might be observed that these books are presented in the wrong order: *The Heart of the Ancient Wood,* which I have represented as a considerable advance on *Children of the Wild,* actually pre-dates it by some thirteen years. Need this fact damage my case? Surely not. I have been teaching (and learning) long enough to know that wisdom doesn't grow in a smooth logical order. (p. 171)

> *Michael Hornyansky, "Roberts for Children,"*
> *in* The Sir Charles G. D. Roberts Symposium,
> *edited by Glenn Clever, University of Ottawa*
> *Press, 1984, pp. 163-71.*

Thomas R. Dunlap

Roberts believed that the "animal story, as we now have it is a potent emancipator. . . . It helps us to return to nature, without requiring that we at the same time return to barbarism. It leads us back to the old kinship of earth, without asking us to relinquish by way of toll any part of the wisdom of the ages, any fine essential of the 'large result of time.' " Our life in nature, "far behind though it lies in the long upward march of being," is nevertheless a touchstone, a life to which we can and must return for refreshment and even wisdom, and the animal story will be our guide.

Modern critical work has, while recognizing the importance of the animal story, neglected or distorted a vital element—the science that made the stories plausible as realistic fiction and shaped their form and message. . . .

The ideology of Roberts's animal stories owed as much to nineteenth-century biology, particularly to Darwinian evolution, as it did to Romanticism or the Canadian wilderness. Science, by Roberts's own admission, justified the stories as realistic fiction. The key feature of the genre, and a mark of Roberts's stories—the use of a point of view interior to the animal—was plausible only if one accepted the animal psychology of the period, and that science had been stimulated by Darwinian ideas. Major elements of the world view owed much to Darwinian ideas: the constant struggle of one animal with another; the ambiguous place of man in the natural world; and . . . death as the price of life, necessary to the continuance of the world. Roberts was not revolting against a Darwinian determinism; far from it. He used the new biology, fusing it with older, Romantic conceptions to make an emotionally satisfying and scientifically correct vision of nature and of man's place in it. He constructed a new nature myth for an industrial, urban society that sought the authority of science for its views of humanity and of the world around it. (p. 105)

The realistic animal story Seton and Roberts invented in

the 1890s differed from earlier nature literature in its authors' insistence that not only the natural history but the mental life they ascribed to animals was scientifically accurate. The modern animal story, Roberts said, was "a psychological romance constructed on the framework of natural science." We have, he went on, tried to explain animal behaviour on the basis of instinct and coincidence, but we have stretched these to their limits and they have failed. We now believe that "animals can and do reason." They have a mental life, like our own but simpler, and "the gulf dividing the lowest of the human species from the highest of the animals has . . . been reduced to a very narrow psychological fissure."

It was this claim—that animals "can and do reason"—that made the stories credible as realistic fiction. Without the "framework of natural science" they were fantasy, entertaining but inconsequential; with it they were powerful, emotionally compelling (so far as art made them so) dramas of the natural world surrounding man and a means of explaining man's place in it. It was the animal psychology stimulated by Darwin that furnished the "framework." (pp. 106-07)

[For] Roberts and his contemporaries the result of scientific study was a license to depict animals with many human qualities, abilities, and emotions.

Making animals the central figures of fiction, realized from within, implied that they felt and thought, but Roberts used plots and incidents to reinforce that conclusion. Evidence of animal emotion runs through the stories. His subjects are curious, interested, brave, angry, or fearful. In some cases the emotions are the result of the constitution of the species; the weasel has an "inherited bloodlust" which drives him to spasms of slaughter. Roberts even appeals to a kind of racial memory. "Last Bull," a zoo buffalo, has never known freedom, but he is restless. He escapes, and is killed by the keeper when he charges a group of children. Dying, "he saw once more, perhaps—or so the heavy-hearted keeper would have us believe—the shadowy plains unrolling under the wild sky, and the hosts of his vanished kindred drifting past into the dark."

Roberts shows other reactions that are "higher," and more "human." Captive animals yearn for freedom. "Lone Wolf" looks for "delights which he had never known, for a freedom which he had never learned or guessed." In **"The Summons of the North"** a captured polar bear dies, apparently of a heart attack, during the first snowstorm he experiences in the zoo. Animals defend their young, even at the sacrifice of their lives. This is Romanticism, certainly, but Romanticism justified by science. Without animal psychology, the pathos of captivity dissolves into fantasy, and the self-sacrifice of mother love gains its emotional power only as a conscious, not instinctive, reaction.

Animals also think. Sometimes Roberts is tentative in his assessments: a bear, if he is "capable of reflection—a point on which the doctors differ with some acrimony—he perhaps reflected that. . . ." The "Boy," an autobiographical figure, surveys a beaver dam and smiles as "he thought how inadequate what men call instinct would be to such

a piece of work as this." More often, and more characteristically, Roberts takes a bolder stand. "The Ringwaak Buck" has instinct as his "first, and most important, source" of knowledge. Beyond that is

> . . . experience, which teaches varying lore, according to variation in circumstances and surroundings. . . . But, after instinct and experience have accounted for everything that can reasonably be credited to them, there remains a considerable and well authenticated residuum of instances where wild creatures have displayed a knowledge which neither instinct nor experience could well furnish them with. In such cases observation and inference seem to agree in ascribing the knowledge to parental teaching.
>
> (pp. 107-08)

Attributing emotions and thought to animals was not, for Roberts, a literary device or a concession to anthropomorphism. It was a recognition that the mental life of animals resembled that of man. The opposite was also true: man was an animal, a creature of nature. Roberts pursued this theme in several ways—emphasizing the common emotional life of man and animals; portraying man as an animal, or civilized man as the inheritor of more "primitive" "instincts"; and emphasizing the ties that bound man, as they did animals, to the economy of life and death that drove the world. All these themes were affected by Romanticism and a glorification of the primitive, but they also drew on scientific theories.

Man and animal shared an emotional life. "Insofar as man is himself an animal," Roberts said, "he is subject to and impelled by many emotions which he must share with not a few other members of the animal kingdom." The aim of the stories was to show that animals felt—that they suffered, feared, and rejoiced like people. Roberts made this point in all the stories, but most dramatically in **"The Kill."** Here he inverted the usual hunting story, telling it from the point of view of the hunted, wounded, and ultimately slain moose, replacing the usual emotions of excitement and ultimate triumph with the animal's suffering, pain, fear, and death. (p. 109)

Roberts was fascinated with the backwoodsmen, the lumberjacks, trappers, and hunters of his youth, and they appear in his stories as figures of man's ability to live, in one sense, within and without nature. Roberts showed man as an animal—a very Darwinian animal—in a story about a castaway on the New Guinea coast. The man, civilized, helpless, out of his element, nevertheless establishes his dominion over the jungle. He is sustained by the "old faith in man as the master animal" and by his wild heritage. In the end he kills a tiger, thus taking his rightful place as the "King of Beasts" (and is then rescued, bringing his saga to an appropriately civilized conclusion). In the struggle for survival, man—even civilized man—is the fitter animal.

Frequently Roberts emphasized the links that bound man with the animals in a common natural economy—the round of life and death which was the fabric of the world—and here his ideas were closely tied to popular conceptions of a dark, Darwinian world in which the price

Roberts at his desk.

of life is the death of others. The theme dominates his first story, **"Do Seek their Meat from God."** Like **"The Kill,"** it inverts a literary form for effect, which may account for the baffled reactions of several editors. The story begins with two "panthers" (eastern mountain lions) leaving their cubs in the den and setting out on a night's hunt. They hear a child crying and move toward the sound. The child, we learn, has been seeking his playmate, but the family has, that very day, abandoned their farm, leaving only the empty cabin with a broken door. The child's father, coming home from town, almost passes by, thinking it is only the "squatter's brat" crying. Then, moved by pity, he decides to see what is wrong.

So far we see the standard wilderness adventure, man against beast, with everything set for a confrontation between father and panthers at the cabin—but Roberts pauses here to disabuse the reader of his prejudices, and to drive home the moral implicit in the title. "Theirs," he says, "was no hideous or unnatural rage, as it is the custom to describe it. They were but seeking with the strength, the cunning, the deadly swiftness given them to that end, the food convenient to them." The father and the panthers arrive at the clearing together, and he kills them, one in hand-to-hand combat. Only when he finds the child does he realize it is his own son he has saved. This is a melodramatic climax, but the story does not end there. It

ends "not many weeks afterward" when the farmer, following a bear that has killed one of his sheep, finds a wild animal's den, and, in the back, "the dead bodies, now rapidly decaying, of two small panther cubs." (pp. 110-11)

Roberts's stories tied man to the natural world but they also showed him separated from it. He was more than the "King of Beasts," more than a superior animal; he had a life above nature, beyond its round of life and death. Polk saw Roberts's ambivalence as "the romantic dilemma—nature good but uncivilized, civilization good but unnatural." This is true, but it is the Romantic dilemma in a particular setting. Roberts had not only to reconcile his experience of the Canadian wilderness with Romantic ideas about nature, but to accommodate his vision of nature to that of science. Darwinism, fortunately, lent itself to the vision of man within, but not part of, nature. It showed him as a creature of the animal kingdom but it also, in its emphasis on change, suggested that he had "evolved" beyond nature. People could, and did, see in science a warrant for struggle, even struggle within society, and for the conquest of nature, but others could find warrant for the Romantic identification of man with the great world of nature and arguments for the humane treatment of animals. (p. 111)

Roberts emphasized man's divided nature in several ways,

beginning with his defense of the animal story. Its particular virtue, he wrote, was that it allowed us to go back to nature "without requiring that we at the same time return to barbarism." The animal story lifted man out of himself and out of his ordinary life. Man had to go back to nature, be freed "from the mean tenement of self." The stories allowed him to do that without paying "by way of toll any part of the wisdom of the ages."

The form of the stories reinforced this ambiguity. Roberts commonly framed bloody dramas of the struggle for existence with Romantic descriptions of the beauties of nature. **"When Twilight Falls on the Stump Lots"** begins with a lyrical description of the spring. **"The Watchers in the Swamp,"** a chronicle of danger faced and defeated by a pair of nesting bitterns, begins and ends with the song of a hermit thrush, one of the most beautiful sounds of the woods. . . . Both the struggle and the Romantic vision are real; it is man's heritage to see them both and to know both.

Roberts also makes it clear that man, even when acting as an animal, is not natural. The hero of **"King of Beasts"** forges tools, and his victory, his crowning, does not lead him to life in the jungle. He is a king who cannot live in his kingdom. On a deeper level, too, man's skills as a hunter, his primitive heritage, are not part of the order of nature. In a story about moose hunting, for instance, we have two hunters, an older man wielding a birchbark horn to call a bull, the other a young man after his first moose. The older man is a master woodsman, able to outdo the animals at their own game and to "slay the cunning kindred of the wild by a craft finer than their own." He can mimic with complete fidelity the call of the cow moose, that "noble and splendid call, vital with all the sincerity of response and love and elemental passion," and he uses that skill to lure the bull to his death. The final call, which overcomes the animal's suspicions, contains all the "yearning of all the mating ardour that had triumphed over insatiable death and kept the wilderness peopled from the first. . . . " The story is entitled **"A Treason of Nature."**

Roberts addressed the theme of man's separation from nature in a less direct fashion as well, in some dozen stories dealing with man's animals—strayed, lost, or feral—and the wildlings he captured. They have a consistent theme: man has made a separate world.

Domesticated animals are strangers. They may win a battle, as the cock in **"Cock Crow"** or the black-faced ram enjoying his day of freedom, but they cannot survive in the wild. The ox in **"Strayed,"** escaping from a winter lumber camp, looking for the pastures of summer, falls victim to a panther. The surviving ox in **"Brothers of the Yoke,"** the horses in **"A Stranger to the Wild"** and **"In the Unknown Dark,"** and the central figure in **"How a Cat Played Robinson Crusoe"** are glad to return to man, for life in the wild is beyond them.

More striking, man can command his animals. **"The Freedom of the Black-Faced Ram,"** a day-long adventure, ends when he is found by a man. He comes when called, for there was in the man's voice "an authority . . . which [the ram] could not withstand," and without whom the world was "empty and desolate." This is true even for the bitches who, in two stories, run off with wolves and raise a litter of half-bred whelps (the two are actually one, Roberts having thriftily recycled plot material by changing the locale and some of the action). The climax of both stories comes when the wolf, the bitch, and the cubs attack man, and the bitches cannot resist his shouted order. In **"The Passing of the Black Whelps"** the grown cubs tear their mother apart for this treason and are themselves killed by their wolf father and the man. In **"The Invaders"** the bitch survives, better and stauncher, the old hunter says, for her fling with the wild. In both stories the half-breed offspring are worse than either parent, with an implacable hostility to man and treacherous dispositions—another indication of the unnatural nature of the crossing of wild and tame. (pp. 111-13)

Man's separate world would seem to mock Roberts's statement that the animal story will "lead us back to the old kinship of earth," but our kinship, for Roberts, does not involve a complete identification with nature. Indeed, he explicitly rejected that in an early novel, *The Heart of the Ancient Wood.* The vision of a Romantic life in nature, the book says, can come only at the sacrifice of full humanity and of a real understanding of nature. The heroine, Miranda, has been raised by her mother, self-exiled from her town, in the heart of the ancient wood. . . .

She is separated from nature only by her inability to appreciate the silent struggle which goes on around her. Marked off by her red kerchief and surrounded by a charmed circle, the "Pax Mirandae," she sees little of the bloodshed of the wood, and comes to regard "the folk of the ancient wood as a gentle people, living for the most part in voiceless amity. Her seeing eyes quite failed to see the unceasing tragedy of the stillness. . . . She little dreamed that for most of them, the very price of life itself was the ceaseless extinguishing of life." The plot concerns the efforts of a trapper, young Dave, to win Miranda back to humanity. In the end, she must not only recognize the place of death in the life of nature, she must participate in it; she has to shoot the old she-bear to save Dave. The last scene has Miranda, her mother, and Dave burying the dead bear, and with it Miranda's life in nature. Buried, too, is Roberts's fling with allegory, "elvish" people raised in the woods, and tutelary deities in the form of animals.

Miranda's "solution," or young Dave's solution, one Roberts endorsed, was a balance between the life of civilization and the world of nature, a balance reached by the tension between two worlds, not by a resolution. Dave appreciates and understands the cruelty and death that lie below the surface of the life of the ancient woods, but he is not repelled by them. He has a place within nature, but also one outside it. (p. 114)

Roberts's vision of nature struck a chord with the late Victorian reading public. In 1892 he had difficulty placing **"Do Seek Their Meat from God,"** but by the end of the decade he could sell everything he could write. *Outing* alone printed five of his stories in a two-year period (1901-1903), and up to World War I he published almost annually books filled with stories which first appeared in magazines. Roberts's production and popularity fell off after that. . . . Roberts's stories were less in demand because the general educated public, to which he spoke, had assimilated Darwinism. This argument gains more force when we consider that nature essays and nature stories did not go out of fashion, but shifted focus. Especially after 1940, with such works as Rachel Carson's *Under the Sea Wind,* Sally Carrigher's *One Day on Beetle Rock,* Fred Bodsworth's *The Last of the Curlews,* and Farley Mowat's *Never Cry Wolf,* new themes appeared—the intricate connections within the web of life and man's enormous destructive powers—themes that reflected and explained our new knowledge of the science of ecology and of human impact on the ecosystem.

Viewing Roberts in this light, as an author explaining and giving emotional content to a scientific view, also makes it apparent why he was so popular beyond Canada. The issues he addressed in his fiction were part of the situation of Western civilization. Science was providing a new understanding of nature and man's place in it. Industrialization was giving man new powers, making humans, for the first time, independent of nature, or at least not immediately exposed to its dangers. That the Canadian wilderness was not conquered, even that it could not be conquered, was irrelevant. The civilization of which Canada was a part and Canada itself were insulated from the horrors of life in nature. That, with our new understanding of nature, compelled a new perspective. It was Roberts's genius to subsume older Romantic ideas about nature within the framework of the popular notion of a Darwinian struggle; to show within that seeming chaos continuity, order, and a place for man; to explain nature to his generation; and to give emotional content to a scientific explanation of man and nature in a coherent world view. (p. 116)

> *Thomas R. Dunlap, " 'The Old Kinship of Earth': Science, Man and Nature in the Animal Stories of Charles G. D. Roberts," in* Journal of Canadian Studies/Revue d'etudes canadiennes, *Vol. 22, No. 1, Spring, 1987, pp. 104-20.*

TITLE COMMENTARY

Earth's Enigmas: A Book of Animal and Nature Life (1896)

In the silent Canadian forests and sea-born Tantramar marshes one might hope, if anywhere, to be rid of 'Earth's Enigmas,' but it is just in these lonely, lovely places that Mr. Roberts has found riddles plentiful and profound: why unconsidered trifles are mile stones of destiny; why gratified ambition turns out Dead Sea fruit; why the happiness of young love is smitten in an instant by tragedy; why superstitions are often justified by facts, and why no man can always believe his own eyes or any evidence of his senses. Fortunately Mr. Roberts has not attempted to analyze the inscrutable or to explain the inexplicable. His tales are objective, tales of moral and physical courage, of accident from floods and high tides, of fights for life with wild beasts, and of terror, of supernatural omens and portents. His questions are matters of inference, and it is pos-

sible to read the tales without suspecting any far-reaching speculation. The incidents and scenes fit each other admirably, and the characterization is strong, clear, and interesting. Sometimes the beauties and wonders of nature are overwrought, but the defect is excused when we remember that a poet of nature is struggling with the limitations of a plain prose tale. Much more surprising than decorative excursions are the vivid presentation of rough and primitive people, and a vigorous directness at critical moments which we are accustomed to find only in very accomplished writers of prose fiction.

> *A review of "Earth's Enigmas," in* The Nation, *New York, Vol. LXII, No. 1612, May 21, 1896, p. 399.*

We have long known Professor C. G. D. Roberts for the foremost of Canadian poets, and the publication of *Earth's Enigmas* now calls upon us to recognize him as a writer of a high order of imaginative prose. Slight as these stories are—for no less than fifteen of them are crowded within the limits of a very small volume—they are noteworthy for their artistic finish and poetic feeling, no less than for the fidelity with which they picture Canadian landscape and character. There are beautiful dreamy pages in this little book, a fine sense of life under primitive conditions and enveloped in the atmosphere of romance. **"A Tragedy of the Tides"** is perhaps the gem of the collection.

> *William Morton Payne, in a review of "Earth's Enigmas," in* The Dial, *Chicago, Vol. XX, No. 239, June 1, 1896, p. 338.*

The Kindred of the Wild: A Book of Animal Life (1902)

Despite the presage of his ambiguous title and the rather labored introductory chapter, the reader of Prof. Roberts's book, as he proceeds, cannot avoid the conviction that it is a masterpiece of its kind. An earlier volume by the same hand, *The Heart of the Ancient Wood,* showed a most intimate and appreciative acquaintance with the habits and motives of the animal life of the woods. This one, which describes the life histories of various wild animals, does so with most extraordinary fidelity and breadth of knowledge. The author makes it evident that he knows whereof he writes, and writes from the fulness of his knowledge and interest, and for a public which can detect such errors of fact and flights of egotistic fancy as embellish the popular narratives of a certain favorite author on wild life and natural history.

The book begins with a story—in fact, all its chapters are stories—entitled, **"The Moonlight Trails."** These were the paths, regular and irregular, of rabbits (hares?) in the snow among the firs, where they were wont to have social gatherings in the winter nights.

> From time to time two of these harmonious shapes would halt, sit upon their hind-quarters, erect their long, attentive ears, glance about warily with their bulging eyes (which, in this position, could see behind as well as in front of their narrow heads), wrinkle those deft nostrils which were cunning to differentiate every scent upon the sharp air, and then browse hastily but with

a cheerful relish at the spicy shoots of the young yellow birch. Feeding, however, was plainly not their chief purpose. Always within a few moments they would resume their leaping progress through the white glitter and the hard, black shadows. . . . Long ears, twinkling, round eyes softly shining, they leaped lightly hither and thither, pausing every now and then to touch each other with their sensitive noses or to pound on the snow with their strong hind legs in mock challenge.

The story goes on to tell in what manner these rabbits were trapped, and gives an idea of the cruelty of that process of securing them.

"The Lord of the Air" is a tale of an eagle which, with his mate, had an eyrie on the top of a high mountain peak from which watch-tower he made forays on the surrounding country for food for himself and his young family. He is thus described:

> His powerful beak, long and scyth-edged, curved over sharply at the end in a rending hook. His eyes, clear, direct, unacquainted with fear, had a certain hardness in their vitreous brilliancy, perhaps by reason of the sharp contrast between the bright gold iris and the unfathomable pupil, and the straight line of the low, overhanging brow gave them a savage intensity of penetration. His neck and tail were of the same snowy whiteness as his snake-like head, while the rest of his body was a deep shadowy brown close kin to black.

There follow most vivid descriptions of the eagle's manner of pursuit and overtaking of the various weaker creatures among which he sought his prey, and of his final capture by an ingenious trick, conceived and carried out by a half-breed. For a few weeks the bird remained in captivity, chained by the leg in an open shed that looked out on the river, whence, "across the forest hills, further than any human eye could see, a dim summit, as it were a faint blue cloud on the horizon, he could perceive—his own lost realm of Sugar Loaf. Hour after hour he would sit upon his rude perch, unstirring, unwinking, and gaze upon this faint blue cloud of his desire." The eagle finally escaped. "The air, as he bounded upward, whistled under his tremendous wing strokes. Up, up he mounted, leaving the men to gape after him flushed and foolish. Then he headed his flight for that faint blue cloud beyond the hills."

There are chapters on the moose, the wild goose, the cougar, the owl, the lynx, and other denizens of the forest and air, and the uniform and sustained excellence of all these cannot fail to excite the reader's admiration, especially of such as share the author's sympathetic feeling for animate Nature, and can realize from intimate contact with her how true an interpreter he is who writes this charming book. (pp. 16-17)

A review of "The Kindred of the Wild: Book of Animal Life," in The Nation, *New York, Vol. LXXV, No. 1931, July 3, 1902, pp. 16-17.*

Naturalists have no quarrel with the romances of animal psychology. They enjoy the stories as much, if not more, than do other folk. When, however, the romancers claim to be explorers in animal psychology and assiduous contributors to natural history the startled scientist scans in vain the unpaid pages of the chronicles of research in these fields for some revelation of their discoveries. The credulous public as well as the naturalist will have difficulty in separating the fabric of romance from the framework of facts in any contribution prepared to meet the demands and rewards of the popular animal story.

Just as the historical play or novel rests on some knowledge of the times and places in which the drama or romance was enacted, so the animal story requires a background of facts drawn from science for its setting. The success of all three types of literature depends much less on their faithful portrayal of historical or scientific fact than on their form and action. The play and the novel are not history, nor is the animal story primarily animal psychology. It is not the psychology of it but the simple romance or tragedy of it which makes it interesting to most readers.

It would be unjust to Mr. Roberts to impute to his tales any breath of suspicion that he has distorted the facts of science. Of all recent stories his carry to the skeptical the most conviction of scrupulous faithfulness in detail of fact. It would be equally unfair to him not to recognize that his great success lies primarily not in this phase of the work, but in the technique of its presentation and in the tragedy or comedy which runs through his simple narrative. Mr. Roberts should not throw dust in the eyes of his readers.

The most of the stories combined in this volume have appeared in periodical literature prior to their collection here. They will bear rereading many times. In purity and delicacy of diction, in wholesomeness and absence of the shadows of coarseness or brutality which have crept into some animal stories, and in lightness and freedom of action, Mr. Roberts's animal stories are unsurpassed. (p. 240)

Charles Atwood Kofaid, "Beasts, Birds, and Fishes," in The Dial, *Chicago, Vol. XXXIII, No. 342, October 16, 1902, pp. 240-42.*

The growing demand for nature-books within the past few years has called forth a very large crop of these books, good, bad, and indifferent,—books on our flowers, our birds, our animals, our butterflies, our ferns, our trees; books of animal stories, animal romances, nature-study books, and what not. There is a long list of them. Some of these books, a very small number, are valuable contributions to our natural history literature. Some are written to meet a fancied popular demand. The current is setting that way; these writers seem to say to themselves, Let us take advantage of it, and float into public favor and into pecuniary profit with a nature-book. The popular love for stories is also catered to, and the two loves, the love of nature and the love of fiction, are sought to be blended in the animal story-books, such as Mr. Charles G. D. Roberts's **Kindred of the Wild,** Mr. William Davenport Hulbert's *Forest Neighbors,* Mr. Thompson Seton's *Wild Animals I Have Known,* and the Rev. William J. Long's *School of the Woods.* Only the last two writers seem to seek to profit by the popular love for the sensational and the improbable, Mr. Long, in this respect, quite throwing Mr. Thompson Seton in the shade. It is Mr. Long's book, more than any of the others, that justifies the phrase "Sham Natural History." (p. 298)

In Mr. Charles G. D. Roberts's *Kindred of the Wild* one finds much to admire and commend, and but little to take exception to. The volume is in many ways the most brilliant collection of animal stories that has appeared. It reaches a high order of literary merit. Many of the descriptive passages in it of winter in the Canadian woods are of great beauty. The story called **"A Treason of Nature,"** describing the betrayal and death of a bull moose by hunters who imitated the call of the cow moose, is most striking and effective. True it is that all the animals whose lives are portrayed—the bear, the panther, the lynx, the hare, the moose, and others—are simply human beings disguised as animals; they think, feel, plan, suffer, as we do; in fact, exhibit almost the entire human psychology. But in other respects they follow closely the facts of natural history, and the reader is not deceived; he knows where he stands. Of course it is mainly guesswork how far our psychology applies to the lower animals. That they experience many of our emotions there can be no doubt, but that they have intellectual and reasoning processes like our own, except in a very rudimentary form, admits of grave doubt. But I need not go into that vexed subject here. They are certainly in any broad generalization our kin, and Mr. Roberts's book is well named and well done. (pp. 299-300)

> *John Burroughs, "Real and Sham Natural History," in* The Atlantic Monthly, *Vol. XCI, No. 3, March, 1903, pp. 298-309.*

The Watchers of the Trails: A Book of Animal Life (1904)

The Watchers of the Trails, by Charles G. D. Roberts, is certainly the book of the month. . . .

Mr. Roberts claims to have written animal stories before Mr. Thompson Seton, and there is sufficient evidence to give the contention the appearance of truth. Both write well and both are a credit to Canadian letters and Canadian culture. Were it not that Mr. Roberts has marred his life by some features which prevent his becoming a popular hero, he would undoubtedly stand among the first two or three writers whom this country has produced. His art as evidenced in his poetry and his prose is undoubtedly of a high order. Perhaps when the final verdict is given his work will be placed above that of Sir Gilbert Parker, Mr. Seton, Mr. Fraser or the other prominent Canadian writers. It may be that his limpid style and mastery of poetical phrase are greater than his story-telling ability, but the latter is good enough to round out his other qualities in producing work which will some day be classics in Canadian literature. The day will come, no doubt, when his prose will be used as models by high schools and universities. It might be even now, were our professors of English disposed to give the credit which is due him. This provincialism will be overcome in time.

These stories "are avowedly fiction" as the author says in his prefatory note, yet they consist of facts gathered and grouped in such a way as to give life to the story of each animal. Mr. Roberts spent most of his boyhood on the fringes of the forest and claims to have had those "intimacies of the wilderness" which enable him to translate into words the simple psychological processes of the animals without ascribing to them human motives and the mental processes of man. He says himself, "I have studied to keep well within the limits of safe inference."

> *"Animal Stories," in* The Canadian Magazine of Politics, Science, Art and Literature, *Vol. XXIII, No. 4, August, 1904, p. 381.*

Mr. Roberts cannot complain if his stories are examined in the light of [his declarations in the Prefatory Note to *The Watchers of the Trail*]. Take **"The Truce,"** for example. Here we are told how a trapper (who happens to be armed only with a hunting-knife) is chased by a bear. Naturalists and hunters agree that a bear will invariably flee from a man, unless he is cornered, or thinks he is cornered. Mr. Roberts evidently is aware of this, for he says of this particular bear that "at almost any other time he would have taken the first whiff of that ominous man-smell as a signal to efface himself and make off noiselessly down the wind." But Bruin, in this instance, is trying to dig a chipmunk out of a decayed tree, and, as he is very hungry, the interruption promised by the "man-smell" so angers him that he sets off after the cause thereof. (This, we assume, is what Mr. Roberts would have us consider "obvious animal psychology.") There is a long chase, and the hunter is so hard pressed that he is obliged to throw away his pack, which contains bacon and sugar. But the hungry bear pays no attention to these delicacies, and continues his relentless pursuit, so wroth is he at having been disturbed in his hunt for the chipmunk. (Is this, too, "obvious animal psychology"?) The upshot of the chase is that, as a result of the sudden breaking up of the ice on a river which the pursued and the pursuer are attempting to cross, they find themselves stranded on a small island just above a thundering waterfall. The hunter got there by leaping from one cake of ice to another, and then, filled with admiration for the determination of the bear, he pulls Bruin from the water as he is being swept by toward certain death. As might have been expected of such a bear, gratitude to his preserver quite overcomes his wrath at having had his chipmunk hunt interrupted, and when the hunter makes his way ashore on a timely ice jam, Bruin follows and very meekly disappears in the woods.

Then there is another bear story, **"The Return to the Trails,"** in which Mr. Roberts gives us an elaborate study of complicated animal psychology and spasmodically atrophied instinct. To begin with, this bear receives a series of confused and contradictory impressions about mankind, through having seen his mother killed by a dead-fall, when he was a cub, and through having spent five years or so with a traveling circus as a trick bear, in which capacity he was treated kindly, or cruelly, by the various people who had to do with him. All this psychology is described in considerable detail by Mr. Roberts. "Instinct," prompted the bear to knock his keeper down and take to the woods, when the circus happens to come again to the region where he was born; and presently he had made his way back to his ancestral mountain, intent upon resuming his natural life. But once again in the woods this same "instinct" plays him false when it should be his surest guide.

He blunders around in the forest making so much noise that woodchucks, squirrels and other small animals have an easy time avoiding him. He doesn't know the difference between food and poison, and consequently eats a poisonous fungus which "gave him excruciating cramps." And—the final and fatal flaw in his instinct—he wakes up in the middle of winter, and goes roaming half starved through the woods. But, prompted by recollections of the *kind* treatment he had received from man, he at last follows a human trail into a lumber camp, where he is shot.

Such are a few of this bear's adventures, based upon "facts as precise as painstaking observation and anxious regard for truth can make them," and of such are his "obvious psychological operations," which are "well within the limits of safe inference."

Scarcely less remarkable is the story of **"The Rivals of Ringwaak"**—the "rivals" being a "catamount" (puma?) and a lynx. The catamount's psychological states include wrath because lumbermen have come into his country with their screeching sawmills, and have driven the fish away with their sawdust. Wherefore the catamount takes revenge upon the lumbermen by chewing up their dog. (Here we have an impulse to take vicarious revenge, as "obvious animal psychology.") The lynx's psychology likewise includes wrath, because he finds the marks on a tree of the catamount's claws, two inches higher than he can reach. Then the two animals meet and have a duel in which the catamount is killed. On this subject of duels to the death between animals, Mr. W. T. Hornaday, in his *American Natural History,* says: "A fight between two wild animals is usually a very brief event—so say reliable men who have seen them in the wilds—and unless there is an accidental death-lock of antlers, the vanquished party usually shows his heels long before he is seriously wounded."

Mr. Roberts' birds are no less intellectual than his quadrupeds. **"The Decoy,"** for example, is the story of a wild goose, captured alive after having had its wing broken by a hunter's shot, and used by the hunter as a stool. But the bird, after seeing two of its kind shot as the result of having responded to its call, refuses to be a party to any further deception. Then there are a pair of kingbirds, of very complicated psychological processes, who have a series of exciting adventures, including the fighting off of a black snake, whose "fangs" they manage to avoid—although a black snake is a non-poisonous serpent, and as such has no *fangs.*

As we have said, there would be little, if any, reason for the implication connoted by these quotations, but for the declarations which Mr. Roberts is at pains to make concerning the natural history of his stories. And the same would be true as to the criticisms of the stories of Mr. Ernest Thompson Seton and the Rev. William J. Long. But, although Mr. Roberts presumably may be convinced of the essential accuracy of his stories, he cannot blame some of his readers if they smile politely and at the same time fail to conceal their incredulity as he describes the psychological operations of his animals. A man's study of "trails" may have extended no further than the scrutiny of the trail of a North River ferryboat, but he may, at the same time,

have a sense of humor, and this sense may arouse the suspicion that Mr. Roberts' authenticated animals—like Cassius—"think too much"—altogether too much. Obviously, it is this kind of writing to which Mr. Hornaday refers when he says: "The tendency of the present is to idealize the higher animals, to ascribe to them intelligence and reasoning power which they do not possess, and in some instances to 'observe' wonderful manifestations that take place chiefly in the imagination of the beholder." And again: "The virtues of the higher animals have been extolled unduly, and their intelligence has been magnified about ten diameters." And yet again: "You and I may spend years in the forests and fields, observing and collecting wild creatures, and see only a very few of the acts of the wild folks which we can call wonderful. But then, somehow, our animals have rarely been as large, or as well educated, as those of some other observers." (*The American Natural History.*)

Whether any actual harm is done by such stories is a question which will be considered seriously or otherwise, according to the temperament and the point of view of the reader. That many of the tales of Mr. Seton and Mr. Long and Mr. Roberts which excite the ridicule of naturalists as such, are interesting and cleverly written, cannot be denied. And that they do good to the extent that they inculcate a friendly attitude toward animals, is also true. On the other hand, that they spread much misinformation about animals is becoming more and more apparent. A young naturalist acquaintance of the present writer says that, in conducting a series of nature classes, he occasionally has much difficulty with those of his pupils, juvenile and adult, who have followed in good faith such "trails" as Mr. Roberts describes. He finds that, in not a few instances, such pupils have a point of view which makes them almost unwilling to accept plain facts of natural history. The question which naturally arises, therefore, is whether the entertainment furnished by these stories, and the kindliness toward animals which they prompt, are overbalanced by the actual amount of misinformation which they spread.

As to Mr. Roberts' literary style and general form of presentation, candor compels the further criticism that, in this volume, at least, neither is of a kind calculated to enhance the plausibility of his stories. His tendency to multiply unessential details—to over-explain—and a more than occasional floundering in the bog of verbosity, bespeak the lack of careful editing. (pp. 161-64)

George Gladden, "Natural History—or Imagination?" in *Current Literature, Vol. XXXVII, No. 2, August, 1904, pp. 161-64.*

All lovers of nature and the wild creatures of forest and field cannot fail to be delighted with this new volume of nature stories. Mr. Roberts does not belong to that class of authors who endow animals and birds with absolutely human powers of reasoning; neither does he belong to that other but smaller class who seem to regard them as devoid of all reasoning faculty. The author spent much of his early youth on the outskirts of a great forest, where he learned to know and love the denizens of the wood; to understand their habits and mental processes. Animals have personalities differing as widely as do those of human beings, and he who lives much among them will come to recognize these differences of temperament and understand the motives which underlie their various actions. And in these tales, many of which are vouched for as absolutely true in detail, while all are true in essence, Mr. Roberts has endeavored to make clear these motives and mental processes of the "kindred of the wild." (p. 340)

> *A review of "The Watchers of the Trails,"* in The Arena, *Boston, Vol. XXXII, No. CLXXVIII, September, 1904, pp. 340-41.*

A welcome reprint of stories, first published in 1904, which set a standard for straight animal reportage warmed by sympathy and supported by sharp observation. Each tale has its climax, some offering almost a life-history in brief (of porcupine, wild goose, lynx and so on) while others contain a single, striking scene—for instance, a bear and a man trapped on an islet in a frozen river with breaking ice all round them, a dragonfly nymph killing a minnow. Rich, rolling prose, elaborate detail of weather and terrain, sympathy without humanisation.

> *Margery Fisher, in a review of "Watchers of the Trails," in* Growing Point, *Vol. 14, No. 9, April, 1976, p. 2855.*

Red Fox: The Story of His Adventurous Career in the Ringwaak Wilds, and of His Final Triumph over the Enemies of His Kind (1905)

AUTHOR'S COMMENTARY

[The following excerpt is from Roberts's introduction to Red Fox *dated August, 1905.]*

In the following story I have tried to trace the career of a fox of the backwoods districts of Eastern Canada. The hero of the story, Red Fox, may be taken as fairly typical, both in his characteristics and in the experiences that befall him, in spite of the fact that he is stronger and cleverer than the average run of foxes. This fact does not detract from his authenticity as a type of his kind. He simply represents the best, in physical and mental development, of which the tribe of the foxes has shown itself capable. In a litter of young foxes there is usually one that is larger and stronger, and of more finely coloured fur, than his fellows. There is not infrequently, also, one that proves to be much more sagacious and adaptable than his fellows. Once in a while such exceptional strength and such exceptional intelligence may be combined in one individual. This combination is apt to result in just such a fox as I have made the hero of my story.

The incidents in the career of this particular fox are not only consistent with the known characteristics and capacities of the fox family, but there is authentic record of them all in the accounts of careful observers. Every one of these experiences has befallen some red fox in the past, and may befall other red foxes in the future. There is no instance of intelligence, adaptability, or foresight given here that is not abundantly attested by the observations of persons who know how to observe accurately. In regard to such points, I have been careful to keep well within the boundaries of fact. As for any emotions which Red Fox may once

in a great while seem to display, these may safely be accepted by the most cautious as fox emotions, not as human emotions. Insofar as man is himself an animal, he is subject to and impelled by many emotions which he must share with not a few other members of the animal kingdom. Any full presentation of an individual animal of one of the more highly developed species must depict certain emotions not altogether unlike those which a human being might experience under like conditions. To do this is not by any means, as some hasty critics would have it, to ascribe human emotions to the lower animals.

> *Charles G. D. Roberts, "Preface," in* The Horn Book Magazine, *Vol. XLVIII, No. 3, June, 1972, p. 258.*

Among the many writers of nature-books none is more satisfactory than Mr. Roberts. He does not endow his animals with absolutely human faculties and reasoning powers, but he does perceive and express clearly the mental processes of the wild creatures and the impulses which underlie their various actions.

In the present volume he has taken a remarkably intelligent and sagacious member of the fox family—a fox who may serve as the type of all that is best in the breed—and has traced the course of his life through several years. Mr. Roberts in his preface states that Red Fox "simply represents the best in physical and mental development of which the tribe of foxes has shown itself capable." He further adds that every adventure which befalls him has befallen some fox in the past and may come within the experience of other foxes in the future, and that the emotions which Red Fox manifests may safely be accepted as fox emotions and not as human emotions.

Incidentally we learn much about the habits of the other denizens of the forest and field with whom Red Fox comes in contact in various ways, and one chapter contains a wonderfully graphic description of a forest fire—that devastating scourge following a long-continued drought.

> *Amy C. Rich, in a review of "Red Fox," in* The Arena, *Boston, Vol. XXXV, No. CXCIV, January, 1906, p. 105.*

[**Red Fox**] isn't a sincere piece of work. Mr. Roberts knows the thing cannot be done to last over night. There isn't enough to a fox; his psychology, his interests, his daily round is too limited to sustain him throughout a volume. The author has tried to meet the lack of substance with style. The fox makes raids on barnyards in "violet sunsets," he fights woodchucks in "rose-lit grass"—atmosphere this, purple patches, that do not convince, but only emphasize the smallness of Red Fox and the largeness of the story. Not a page of it comes from the woods direct. Of the incidents, to quote the preface, "there is authentic record of them all in accounts of careful observers"—of Red Fox playing dead, running the sheep's backs, and jumping into a cart (the climax of the story) to escape the dogs,—these records are in our nursery-books. What we haven't read before we cannot quite believe—the bees, for instance, driving Red Fox from his fetid den to go into the honey business there! But all this we could take, for we are boys enough to like the fighting (there is a deal of this, for there is a fight on every page), were it not for the anthropomorphizing of the beast—as extreme and unreal as the rose-lit treatment of the grass. (pp. 122-23)

Dallas Lore Sharp, "Out-of-Doors from Labrador to Africa," in The Critic, *New York, Vol. XLVIII, No. 2, February, 1906, pp. 121-23.*

There has been so much criticism lately of the methods of the writers of "animal stories," and more particularly of their "pernicious" habit of investing their four-footed heroes and heroines with human, if not superhuman attributes, that the appearance of this new volume by Mr. C. G. D. Roberts aroused in us a lively curiosity. Mr. Roberts is an old offender in the eyes of the naturalists, and the question immediately rose—had he mended his ways in consequence of the scathing rebukes administered by those who believe that animals are not proper subjects for idealization? Secretly, it must be confessed, we hoped he had not, for we are still old-fashioned enough to cherish fairytales and desire "animal stories" of the imaginative variety. For a moment we feared that the shafts of the critics had struck home. "The incidents in the career of this particular fox," says Mr. Roberts in a prefatory note, "are not only consistent with the known characteristics and capacities of the fox family, but there is authentic record of them all in the accounts of careful observers." Immediately we had visions of foot-notes, textual references, even of a critical bibliography. But, a few lines more and confidence returned. "As for any emotions which Red Fox may once in a great while seem to display, these may safely be accepted by the most cautious as fox emotions, not as human emotions." Then, after all, there were to be emotions? We hurriedly turned the page and plunged into one of the most delightful tales of wood-life and wood-craft we have come across in many a day.

It is simply the story of the career of a Canadian fox. But as it is told, with the whirring of insects in the calm summer air, the crackling of branches snapping in the winter frost, the meetings—friendly and otherwise—of the small folk and the great folk of the forest, it is enough to send any healthy boy to the nearest patch of woods to study the ways of nature, while in every man it must arouse pleasant memories of the days when he was a boy and lived in the fairyland which boys forget all too soon. *The Athenæum* is none too eulogistic when it says of *Red Fox*: "It has the fascination of a real jungle story, without owing any apparent debt to Mr. Kipling. . . . There are scores of touches of real nature—touches only possible as the result of close and patient watching—in the story of Red Fox's puppyhood and in such incidents as his captivity and hunting methods." Even the staid *Nation* is moved to declare: "We accept Red Fox as the flower of his race, even though he may belong to the order Compositæ." And, with *The Nation*, we would add that "Mr. Roberts appears to tell his story chiefly for its own sake, but he impresses us quite as deeply as if he had tried to enforce it by didacticism. We feel, for instance, with the rabbit and mink, the barbarity of trapping, and take the fox's point of view when we see the field of scarlet riders and hear the loud-mouthed pack on the trail."

This last is the final incident of the tale, and it leaves us with a strong hope that some day Mr. Roberts will give us more of the adventures of Red Fox. For we cannot believe that Red Fox will linger in the barren mountain regions. He is certain, ultimately, to make his way back to the forests, the meadows and the farms of the Ringwaak country. And when he does return we shall expect to hear again of him and his mate, and of Jabe Smith and the Boy.

"The Fairy World of Foxdom," in The Literary Digest, *New York, Vol. XXXII, No. 9, March 3, 1906, p. 332.*

I have thought it would be interesting and possibly amusing to go through Mr. Roberts' **Red Fox** and see when and where one could detect the man under the fur, or point out wherein his hero is nearer akin to the human than to the vulpine. I have genuine admiration for Mr. Roberts' genius, and when I read his animal stories I am so in sympathy with the writer and his subject, and so taken by the fine description and the wild flavor of it all, that I have to make a special effort to keep an eye on his natural history. I have constantly to nudge myself and say, "Look out! you are being hoodwinked, it is the author himself who is playing the part of Red Fox now." Mr. Roberts says in his preface and thereby, as it were, challenges the acumen of his reader, that his Red Fox is a real fox, that he is fairly typical of his kind, though "stronger and cleverer than the average run of foxes." But I am bound to say that he is cleverer than I believe it possible for any fox to be, and that Mr. Roberts puts himself in his place time after time.

Most of the lower animals we know share our emotion, but they do not share our intellectual powers, they do not put this and that together and draw reasonable conclusions. Our complex psychology has no room to turn around inside their small brains. The animal-story writer is constantly in danger of endowing them with his own faculties and motives in order to account for their conduct. He reasons for them and imputes to them his own knowledge. Mr. Roberts does this repeatedly in **Red Fox.** The mother fox, for instance, was too wary, too prudent, to molest poultry near home. She did not wish notoriety in her own neighborhood. "She would pass a flock of waddling ducks, near home, without condescending to notice their attractions." "She had no wish to advertise herself." And she succeeded in impressing this policy upon young Red Fox. She taught him the subtle wisdom of this saying, "that easy hunting is not always good hunting." Where and how the mother fox learned so much human nature does not appear. I know that country people sometimes fool themselves with the belief that, for prudential reasons, the fox will not molest poultry on the farms near its den. But there is no proof of the soundness of such an opinion. . . . A man in my neighborhood who lives near the woods frequently had his chickens caught by foxes in the daytime. Is there any reason to suppose those foxes do not live in the immediate vicinity? No, the reasoned cunning which Mr. Roberts ascribes to his fox is human and not vulpine.

I can think of but one reason why a fox should go to a distant farm for its poultry: it is afraid to invade the hen-roosts near at hand. It sees so much life there during the day and early evening—human voices, the barking of dogs, the firing of guns, etc.—that it becomes shy of the place, while distant farms, which it would be likely to pass through only late at night, would seem comparatively safe. Or has the fox this human trait, that it looks for rich finds only far from home? Whatever may be the fact, it is unwise to seek to account for an animal's conduct on difficult and complex grounds when a simple explanation serves better.

I do not think Mr. Roberts is within the truth of natural history when he makes his foxes pair and the male assist in caring for the young. So far as is known, foxes do not differ in this respect from the habits of the domestic dog. The two sexes appear to live quite apart except in the mating season in February. There is no conjugal union between them lasting through the year, as Mr. Roberts sets forth. According to all the evidence I have been able to collect, the female lives alone with her young and brings them up without aid from the male. It is possible of course that the male may visit the den at night, but how shall we prove or disprove a statement of this kind? In fact, I cannot now recall one case among our mammals where there is anything like a permanent union between the sexes or where the males aid in rearing the young. If the mother bird had nursed her young, it is probable that the male would be as indifferent to his family as the male mammals now are indifferent to theirs. But Mr. Roberts makes his foxes live together and hunt together and share equally in the cares of the family from year to year. (pp. 512a-512b)

If Mr. Roberts had been a fox hunter, he would have known that a wounded fox takes to hole as soon as possible, and does not stop and wait for the hounds to come up and grapple with it. Of course a fox may be so sorely wounded that it cannot reach its den, but in this case the fox stops amid the rocks and awaits the dogs. Think, too, of a fox, in trying to lead the hounds away from its den, knowing enough to stop upon its old trail and stand there deliberately, having thought the matter all out, long enough for the new scent to overpower the old so that the hounds would be switched off when they reached that point! Is not Mr. Roberts again in the fox's place?

A little further along in the story we come upon the old fable of the fox baffling his pursuers by running across the backs of a flock of sheep. Fancy such a thing! Even if Reynard were astute enough to try such a trick, fancy a flock of sheep standing in a compact body with a wild animal racing across their backs! Both sheep and foxes are misrepresented in this incident. Again, he makes his fox show an interest in, and a curiosity about, the first snow and ice that it saw quite equal to that which a person from the tropics might show. Now I think it quite certain that the animals, wild or domestic, are not at all curious about the general phenomena of nature nor disturbed by them. A sudden change from a brown world to a white world does not apparently attract their attention at all. But Red Fox was startled and alarmed by the change and dared not venture out from his den. He at first thought it was feathers and that there had been a great hunting, and not till he had smelled of it and took some of it in his mouth, was he convinced that it was not feathers! Is not this putting one's self in the fox's place?

Twice in the course of this story Red Fox "plays possum," feigns death and thereby effects his escape from his captors. I do not take any stock at all in this legend of the fox playing possum. I do not believe it ever happens. I can gather no evidence of it among trappers and hunters, but I freely admit that such a fox as Mr. Roberts describes might easily be capable of the trick—a fox so wise that he knew a certain farmer in the valley below was no adept with the gun and therefore did not fear him; that knew another farmer was not at home one day when he approached his wagon shed because the wagon was gone; that, in order to escape the hounds when the pursuit became too hot, jumped into the hind end of a wagon that was passing along the road and curled up in it behind a bag of feed; that knew that a strangely acting muskrat had gone mad, and that therefore its bite would be fatal to her young; that knew a small dark cloud moving up the slope toward him as he sat on the ridge to be a swarm of bees and that the bees were probably bound for a hollow tree in the mountain—and so on through a long list of things that men alone are supposed to know and to do.

Mr. Roberts would not have exposed his **Red Fox** to this kind of criticism if he had not taken pains to assure his reader that his story was substantially true, and that there is abundant evidence that the fox may and does show all the intelligence, adaptability and foresight that he ascribes to his hero in this book.

As literature, the work has many merits, but as natural history, it is erroneous and misleading in many particulars. (p. 512b)

> *John Burroughs, "Mr. Roberts' 'Red Fox',," in* The Outing, *Vol. XLVIII, No. 4, July, 1906, pp. 512a-512b.*

[*The following excerpt is from David McCord's introduction to the 1972 edition of* Red Fox.]

As one responsible for asking and then urging a publisher to bring out a new edition of **Red Fox**—a once quite famous book, long out of print—it is good that this brief but affectionate tribute to the text is being written by a small boy of nine or ten who keeps telling me what to say. Of course the small boy and I are the same person, but he is still very much alive and he has (far beyond me) all the wisdom, memory, thirst, and unquenchable fire of youth. He likewise has—which seems important—the same translatable love of this animal story as of the time when it lay open in his lap. That was very long ago in the heart of the Pennsylvania Poconos, a lonely upland, winesap region, but in no way so wild or primitive as the New Brunswick, Ringwaak land of **Red Fox** to the north and far, far off to the east. My younger self explains that he had been to Canada when he was six and would go again into those deep woods, or woods much like them, by canoe or afoot a good many times when he grew up.

But before he grew up, he was to live for three years on the edge of a vanishing frontier in southern Oregon close by the swift and sinuous Rogue River, famous for its fishing. And it was his special luck (if I may speak for him) to carry to the Rogue the memory of **Red Fox,** for he didn't own the book. And carry also the memory of dozens of other animal, bird, and insect stories which Sir Charles G. D. Roberts, as he later became, had collected in other remarkable volumes called *The Watchers of the Trails, The Feet of the Furtive, Haunters of the Silences, The Kindred of the Wild,* to name just four. Day by day, the truth of these books unfolded before him in a wilderness of his own.

It should be clear that Sir Charles (I like to call him that, for he was one of the first three Canadians to be knighted) had a magic way with titles. He could charm you right into a book, and the charm did not die when you had entered. The small boy had no need to ask me now—as he did—if that old shiver of delight went up my spine as I was writing down those titles. *The Feet of the Furtive!* Who, I ask, can fail to sense the mystery, the poetry, and the drama in the very order of those words? Just glance at the chapter headings in *Red Fox* itself: "Some Little People of the Snow," "The Yellow Thirst," "A Royal Marauder."

One might be tempted to begin with "Some Little People of the Snow," but that would be a grave mistake. This book is much more than a story or a string of episodes. It is a novel about an animal—about many animals, but about a strong, wise, ingenious, and courageous animal in particular. *Red Fox,* I say, while my small prompter's mind is elsewhere, is one of the two finest wild animal stories ever written in English. Few readers of natural history would disagree with me, I believe, when I say that *Tarka the Otter* by Henry Williamson is the other. If *Tarka* (to which I am devoted) is the greater book, the more poetic book, the more ecstatic book, one must also grant at once that the setting is in England, that man enters and exits from the tale at will, that man and dogs are Tarka's constant threat. Red Fox himself, on the other hand, roams through a sparsely settled backwoods country. Man has but small relation even to a few of the chapters. It is purely fox that we are following in his natural wild state—his life as it relates to other wild life, from bear and porcupine to owl and grouse and mouse and weasel. Birds and animals just as they are: no foolish nicknames. A skunk is called a skunk, a rabbit is a rabbit, a lynx is a lynx.

As we pass through the joys and griefs and dangers and rewards of fox and vixen, we pass through spring in the north, where it is swift and glorious in arrival; through summer, splendid fall, and into the intensely cold, almost subarctic winter. One learns the truth of one of the many wise things that Henry Beston has said: "Summer is the season of motion, winter is the season of form." Don't forget that.

Perhaps the greatest gift which *Red Fox* can bestow on us in our bewildering time is the sense of dignity with which an animal like a fox or wolf is born. There is no permissiveness in animal youth. Cubs are taught their lessons well and harshly, because if they fail to learn them they will very soon fail to survive. Quite rightly here, there is no glossing over in the author's words or descriptions, though he does not dwell on bloodshed. The defenseless—rabbit and mouse, for example—*are* defenseless. Nature is just as cruel as she is enthralling. We today, the bulk of us, are now so far removed from the wilderness that we

do not know what it is like. Cradle of life, it is equally the noble background for death. Our forefathers knew. But to see the natural world from a plane, from a boat with an outboard, or to violate the silence with a snarling snowmobile in the heart of the ancient wood is to miss almost everything. Just to read this book will make you ask yourself: Is man the true creature of dignity, courage, grace, and individual resourcefulness, or is it the better part of the wild populace which he is hastening, one by one, to its extinction?

A rather solemn question to ask at the outset of a thrilling book written by a man who was a respected poet, an accurate observer of nature in the backwoods as he knew it in New Brunswick, a man who never distorts or seems to guess. You trust Red Fox as an animal and as a hero. I say this openly, with my young collaborator who agrees, still knowing, as he does, the final words of the last chapter by heart.

Some years ago I left at the University of New Brunswick—for Charles G. D. Roberts remains one of its most distinguished graduates—these seven words in final tribute:

> HE STUDIED HERE TO TESTIFY THE WILDERNESS.
>
> (pp. 255-57)

> *David McCord, "A New Edition of 'Red Fox':*
> *Introduction," in* The Horn Book Magazine,
> *Vol. XLVIII, No. 3, June, 1972, pp. 255-57.*

Urban man's increasing alienation from the natural world has had many symptoms. Perhaps one has been the unrealistic characterization of wild creatures in literature—cute and anthropomorphic animal stories presented for the entertainment of both young and old. It is not merely by chance that the so-called ecology movement coincides with a growing insistence on realism and truthfulness in movies and stories about wild animals. The re-publication of *Red fox* is welcome at this time. *Red fox* would be of value in the newer studies of man's influence on his environment. The book is not, of course, a direct statement about human encroachment on wildlife habitat. It is, rather, a beautifully delineated "before" picture with which we can contrast the "after" picture we know today. *Red fox* may, in fact, evoke in many readers a nostalgia that produces action to preserve at least a part of our heritage of wildlife and wild areas. (pp. 157-58)

> *A review of "Red Fox," in* Science Books: A
> Quarterly Review, *Vol. 8, No. 2, September,*
> *1972, pp. 157-58.*

I welcome the re-publication of *Red fox,* because of its special significance in both Canadian and children's writing.

The realistic animal story—unlike those stories of humanized animals who pack picnic lunches for a day of boating or who search anxiously in their waistcoats for pocketwatches—originated in Canada and was perhaps the first Canadian writing to win a truly international audience. *Red fox* itself was not the first of this genre; it was preceded by Roberts's own collections of short stories, *The kin-*

dred of the wild and *The watchers of the trail,* among others. Published even earlier than Roberts's contributions were those of Ernest Thompson Seton, whose "Life of a prairie chicken" first appeared in 1883 and whose successful and popular *Wild animals I have known* came out in 1898. The pioneering work in these "biographies" of wild animals, as they have been called, prepared the way for innumerable tales in the same tradition by Roderick Haig-Brown, Kenneth and Frank Conibear, and Fred Bodsworth, to name but a few.

Clearly influenced by Darwinism, the genre did not die out as society adjusted to the implications of evolution; instead, it was passed on to a younger audience. *Red fox*'s special importance lies not simply in its being a realistic animal story, but in its being an excellent one for the youthful reader. Let me explain.

First, unlike most of Roberts's and Seton's other tales, the ending of *Red fox* is uplifting in that the animal protagonist escapes to the "rugged turbulence of hills and ravines. . . ." Perhaps such an ending is not so rigorously in keeping with a Darwinian view of the insignificance of the individual, but it certainly makes *Red fox* less disturbing. Roberts makes perfectly clear that Nature—human and otherwise—can be cruel. The tale begins with the death of Red Fox's father, soon after records the sudden and violent deaths of his litter-mates, and continues with a sequence of close calls for Red Fox. After doing battle with an eagle, a mink, mongrel dogs, and a buck deer in rut, Red Fox is ruthlessly and artificially set upon by fox hunters in pursuit of that uniquely human capacity—"sport." The reader is left with a powerful appreciation for life and a recognition of the necessity of death, but he puts down this book with the sense that the natural processes have won the day over needless and, hence, unnatural killing.

The story itself is a Bildungsroman, a novel of growth and development, albeit in the animal world—an appropriate form for a children's book. Of even greater significance is the character of "the Boy," who, presumably through the close evolutionary bond between man and the lower animals, has an innate admiration for the magnificence of Red Fox. Himself an animal, the Boy rises to the challenge of the hunt, trying to outwit and capture the fox he so totally respects. The Boy's superior animal intelligence allows him to succeed, but his capture of Red Fox does not lead to the fox's unnecessary death. Only when the Boy is deceived into putting his captive in the wrong hands does the sporting capacity of some, who seem disassociated from their animal origins, attempt to destroy Red Fox. (pp. 83-4)

> *Richard C. Davis, "An Important Animal Story," in* Canadian Children's Literature, *No. 47, 1987, pp. 82-4.*

The Haunters of the Silences: A Book of Animal Life (1907)

What Plutarch essayed to do for the ancient Greeks and Romans in his *Parallel Lives,* Charles G. D. Roberts would do for the wild creatures of land, air, and water in his recent volume, *Haunters of the Silence.* The polar bear, the salmon of the Quahdavic, the mole and ant, the wolf and moose and cuttle-fish are but a typical few of those whose life story is told in these pages—told with graphic power, insight and sympathy.

These are the short stories of the wild. Others, it is true, have written successfully in the form of quadruped biography and autobiography, but it has remained for Mr. Roberts to crystallise into a series of brief and vibrant character-studies the really salient features of the horizonless life of the outer worlds. The form he has chosen enables him to depict admirably the life experiences of some particular specimen of its kind, narratives usually of a strange and dramatic character, in which the dominant note is the fierce struggle of all living creatures, little tragedies of fish and beast that are all the more terrible as outlined against the silence of the pitiless deeps. Now and then a trapper or pearl-diver passes across a rare page of the stories; but with a sense of strangeness and timidity each is shown hurrying back into the settlements of men. One cannot put down *Haunters of the Silence* without having received from it a profounder sense of the wilderness of land and water, of the littleness of man and his works, and the greatness of the forces against which his hands have battled since the beginning.

> *Thomas Walsh, in a review of "Haunters of the Silence," in* The Bookman, *New York, Vol. XXV, May, 1907, p. 305.*

It is impossible not to envy Mr. Charles G. D. Roberts the freedom of this out-door theatre which years of devoted attendance have given him; but the envy gives place to gratitude, after all, for the competence with which he makes us see what we could not have seen for ourselves. His collection of stories just now published under the fascinating title *The Haunters of the Silences* reports with skill and vividness dramas of wild life beyond the range of ordinary observation, where the primitive instincts of the brute play their tragedy against a spacious and lonely background which tremendously enhances the significance of every action. "In the ancient wild," he writes, "there were three great silences which held their habitation unassailed. They were the silence of the deep of the lake, the silence of the dark heart of the cedar swamp, and the silence of the upper air, high above the splintered peak of the mountain." There is the silence, too, of the far frozen north, and the darkness and silence of the sea, whose depth Mr. Roberts confesses he has not penetrated, but whose secrets he at least cleverly approximates.

Wrapped in the mystery of such surroundings, even hunger and bestial hate and lust of blood become tolerable dramatic forces, admissible for their very grimness and power. One responds in spite of himself to the glory of combat when the polar bear feels the slash of the walrus's mighty tusks, or in the deep-sea battles for life with the narwhal. (Is it not, by the way, an addition to ordinary knowledge of the polar bear that he is a masterly swimmer and diver?) There is no escaping sympathy for such heroic failures as those of the drake whose flight is cut short by the "terror of the air," or of the king salmon whose repeated efforts to leap the falls leave him torn and bleeding on the rocks below. Mr. Roberts has a sense of the continuity of the struggle which is almost new, and which sometimes carries these plays into a third or fourth act. The shrew-mole (for the *dramatis personæ* are not all of large proportions) that kills the black snake is himself killed by the fox, and the mink that catches mice is caught by an eagle. Man appears sometimes as the beneficiary of this chain of fate, sometimes as himself the *deus salvator*. A mariner is imprisoned on his wrecked boat by a shark, and is unable to dive even for a pole to hoist his signal of distress, until a sword-fish mercifully—for the man—cuts the shark in two. And, most tremendous and grewsome of all, a diver caught in the toils of a devil-fish in the dark caverns of the sea,—"a colossal, swollen, leprous-looking bulk, spotted and pallid," with huge tentacles that seem to grow with every cut given them,—is saved by the providential intervention of a killer whale. Stories of horses, deer, bear, lynx, and beaver, and a most delicious tale of an ant imprisoned in a pitcher-plant, complete the volume. The ending is not always tragedy. Even man, who is too likely to play the part of the villain when an animal is the hero, is shown to be capable of pity and of justice. A more satisfactory resolution of the conflict between human and subhuman interests has seldom been given than in the story of the hunter who traps a lynx, but later is obliged to accept the lynx's help against a pack of wolves, and so gives the animal his well-earned liberty. For this large-minded fairness, as well as for the other reasons suggested, the book belongs to the small but fortunately growing class of the best nature story-books. (p. 369)

> May Estelle Cook, "Dramas of the Wild," in The Dial, *Chicago, Vol. XLI, No. 504, June 16, 1907, pp. 369-71.*

There is a certain class of American "Nature Books" which arouses, and no doubt justly, the Presidential ire of Mr. Theodore Roosevelt. In this country perhaps we offend in a like manner, but in less heinous degree. They are the books which attribute to the animals thoughts and sentiments invented for them by the writer, looking at them with eyes turned inward, at his own mental processes, so that he equips them with a psychology which is entirely false. There are also the books which make the animals perform feats physically impossible for them, absolutely wrong in natural history. These are the worst offenders, not to be considered, except in the way of holding them up for censure. The other offence is less rank, for it is more subtle. Obviously exception must be made of the frankly confessed fairy tales, such as the Jungle Book, to take an English instance, but here, too, we have a right to require that the animals shall not perform the physically impossible, or do that which is opposed to their natural instinct. It is the merit of the best books of the kind that they do not thus offend. There is a book before us now, as we write, **The Haunters of the Silence,** by Charles G. D. Roberts, which has plainly been written in the present fear of criticism by the President, for in the preface the author is careful to disclaim intimate knowledge of the domestic history of such creatures as the narwhal, the "killer" whale, and other terrific denizens of the ocean, which he brings on his scene. He says that he has made every possible effort to write in accord with the facts of natural history so far as

Roberts at Centre Island, Toronto, 1940.

they are ascertained, and adds "my utmost hope is that such tales may prove entertaining, without being open to any charge of misrepresenting facts." No one is likely to bring that charge, because no one knows, but as for the hope that the stories will be found entertaining, the author need be under no manner of doubt on that head. If any man with any interest at all outside mere humanity can read without a thrill of the fight between the mother polar bear and the bull walrus, between the whale and the swordfish, or again between the polar bear and the narwhal (in course of which last narrative the wonderful procession of the salmon towards a river in spring is vividly told), he must be constituted with a very cold temperature indeed, and it is difficult to imagine a tale likely to elevate it. To the present critic it appears that we have here stories told with such force of expression and imagination, and sense of dramatic effect, that it is hard to withhold from them the rather blatant praise of calling them works of genius. Where the author treats of the "bear, the moose, the eagle, and others of the furtive folk of our New Brunswick wilderness," as he calls them, he is on surer ground of personal acquaintance, but the tales which will arrest the attention of the reader the most forcibly are those in which he has let his imagination go within the bounds which have been indicated, and narrated these dreadful duels in the mysterious depths of the sea. (p. 106)

"Two American Nature Books and Another," in The Academy, *No. 1853, November 9, 1907, pp. 106-07.*

The House in the Water: A Book of Animal Life   (1908)

From this collection of tales it cannot be discerned that Mr. Roberts has anything more of note to tell his readers about animals. These variations upon the old theme strike one as a little perfunctory. Bear and moose and lynx and wolf range again through these pages; and those other favorite heroes and heroines of fiction whom Mr. Roberts is fond of calling "the wild kindreds." Again we hear of feats performed by them which their chronicler does not believe to be attributable to mere instinct. Again, for the price of the book, we secure admission to a series of those bloody combats in which "teeth meet through flesh, sinew, and the cracking bone itself," flanks are torn open with "eviscerating slashes," and, in the end, somebody or other is satisfactorily "ripped to ribbons." This kind of thing is, we gather, pretty generally recommended to school children; and it must be admitted that "nature-writing," apart from its brutal moments, is marked by that sort of amiable sentimentalism which is understood to be food for babes. It is an odd fad; when it passes such books as **The House in the Water** will pass with it.

A review of "The House in the Water," in The Nation, *New York, Vol. LXXXVII, No. 2252, August 27, 1908, p. 187.*

Under the faithful guidance of Mr. Roberts we have often adventured among the wild beasts of land and sea; and we hope to do so many times in the future. It is an education not to be missed by those who have the chance, and the chance is every one's. Here, at any rate, is his latest guide-book to the wilderness, in which the bears loom dimly in the starlight, the elks toss their vast antlers, the wolves hang on the tracks of the deer, and the beavers build their dwellings in the still watches of the night. The longest story in the book is that after which it is called, and this is the beaver story. The Boy who was out in the silent woods with Old Jabe, the "timber-cruiser," was an exceptional boy. We fancy he has been specially invented by Mr. Roberts as a moral lesson. He never used his Winchester except on a tin or a stone, though we are bound to say he used it once or more to good effect in saving his beavers from enemies. Mr. Roberts uses this Boy to show us how a beaver house is constructed, and how the dam is made, and the trees felled by these remarkable animals. We are prepared to believe that few watchers have witnessed all these interesting proceedings, but we are sure that Mr. Roberts has been one of the favoured. His zest in wild nature is intense, and he succeeds in communicating it to the reader. Also he tells a story dramatically, as, for example, the tale of the woman and the bear at the window. To Mr. Roberts these creatures of the night are as human beings to other writers of fiction. He is as earnest in painting them as other novelists are in depicting human nature. We follow with him the desperate efforts of the she-bear to rescue her cub from the incoming tide; we watch with sympathetic eyes the struggle for life of the wolverine, that strange, fierce creature, with "grit" in her to which the trapper

takes off his cap. Apart from the merely descriptive passages of the beavers' settlement, the two best pieces in this fascinating book are that which relates to the **'Glutton of the Great Snow,'** and that which tells the tragedy of the **'Fight at the Wallow.'** Mr. Roberts loves his wild nature, and his readers, both old and young, should love it with him.

A review of "The House in the Water," in The Athenaeum, *No. 4230, November 21, 1908, p. 642.*

The Backwoodsmen   (1909)

Mr. Roberts's latest book is somewhat of a disappointment to us. **The Backwoodsmen** is a collection of sketches and short stories which clearly have appeared in American magazines. We question whether some of these little tales were worth preserving in book-form, so slight are they. The general defect of all the stories in the book is their obviousness. There is no subtlety about them, and one can generally foresee at the beginning of the story what is going to happen at the end of it. This makes a large dose uninteresting and somewhat cloying. However, Mr. Roberts is undoubtedly one of *the* authorities on wild nature and the backwoods, and nothing that he writes can be altogether without charm and interest, while he is an adept at the difficult art of catching "atmosphere." For these reasons alone the book is worth reading, but, unless he is careful, the reader will want to give up in despair long before it is finished. We recommend him to persevere, for it seems to us that nearly all the better tales are printed at the end. But the best way to read **The Backwoodsmen** would probably be to sandwich in a tale or two between two heavier books; the fifteen stories in a lump are rather too much of what is, doubtless, a good thing.

A review of "The Backwoodsmen," in The Bookman, *London, Vol. XXXVI, No. 214, July, 1909, p. 191.*

Mr. Roberts has a place all to himself in the literature of nature. He has associates, such as Mr. Thompson Seton, but the work of the two diverges. Mr. Roberts's literary touch is felicitous, and he writes as one who loves both nature and art; so we are always glad to welcome such a bundle of tales as he produces from time to time, dealing with wild life in man and brute in the uplands and outlands of the North American continent. It would be difficult to pick out the best of these fifteen stories. Between them they run the gamut of life in wild country, and touch humours and emotions in extremes. There is a good deal of Bret Harte in such a tale as **'The Gentling of Red McWha,'** which tells how a rough saw-miller was tamed by a child. The sketches of the humble folk inhabiting these wildernesses are carefully observed and pleasantly rendered. They make a particular appeal, perhaps, to stay-at-home readers, whose imagination is easily caught by processes of nature and events strange to their experience. When Pete Noel is burnt out, and has to walk sixty miles through snow and night to obtain food and shelter at a settlement, we follow his every footstep with interest and dread. Melindy, whether with lynxes or bears, takes our heart;

and the battle in the mist between mink and racoon is as absorbing to the reader as it was to the canoeist who watched it. Perhaps the most exciting incident of all is that which describes the "grip in deep hole," and how Barnes saved himself. But it is all excellent reading. (p. 92)

A review of "The Backwoodsmen," in The Athenaeum, No. 4265, July 24, 1909, pp. 92-3.

All but one of these tales include animals among the *dramatis personœ,* but all of them have their human figures; from which it will be seen that Mr. Roberts has entered upon a new vein which ought to yield magazinable stories indefinitely. After all, animal biography, however imaginative, has its limitations. What with Mr. Roberts and Mr. Thompson Seton and Mr. Long and their host of imitators, we seem to have had pretty much all the profitable changes rung upon the every-day experiences of the bear and the lynx and the muskrat and the beaver and the other "kindreds of the wild," as Mr. Roberts is fond of calling them. But begin to combine them, singly or in groups, with the manifold varieties of the human genus, and you have evidently provided for an indefinite extension of the game. It must be said that Mr. Roberts's critters are better than his humans—more "convincing," that is, as individuals. The men in **"MacPhairrson's Happy Family,"** for example, are types, not persons. Mr. Roberts manipulates them cleverly enough, but they have no motion of their own. "Red McWha's" conversion from brute to seraph is a fiction stranger than truth. Mrs. Gammit and her sporting adventures are incompetently farcical; and little Melindy, who with her little hatchet is too much for lynxes and bears in the open, is incompetently melodramatic. The best thing in the volume is the description of a fight between a mink and a raccoon—or so it seems. Can this be because the reader does not know the difference between a mink and a raccoon, and does know the difference between a human being and a story-teller's mannikin?

A review of "The Backwoodsmen," in The Nation, New York, Vol. LXXXIX, No. 2322, December 30, 1909, p. 652.

Kings in Exile (1909)

Mr. Charles Roberts is one of the ablest writers of animal stories that we have. *Kings in Exile* is proof that he has by no means exhausted the subject. There are ten tales of animals in the volume, and it would be hard to say which is the best. Mr. Roberts has in this book left the backwoods and taken for his theme animals in captivity. So we have stories of the old bull bison in a "zoological park," the octopus in an aquarium, the performing puma that escapes from a circus, the caged eagle, and the bear in a travelling menagerie. Everything from Mr. Roberts's pen is written with power, and often with a certain amount of pathetic sentiment. As animal stories of this kind go, the book is an extremely good one, and it will certainly appeal to those who have got pleasure from the author's earlier books on wild life.

A review of "Kings in Exile," in The Spectator, Vol. 104, No. 4257, January 29, 1910, p. 153.

Kings in Exile adds one more volume to this author's previous contributions of romanticised life histories of wild animals. The value of these stories as serious studies in natural history seems to the present writer as irrelevant a question as is the value of a Dumas novel considered as documentary history. It is, of course, easy to parody the stock phrase of popular criticism and declare that "animals don't do such things." But for the most part these stories are so carefully written that such a charge would be hard to prove. Even where Mr. Roberts attributes by implication to his animals thoughts and purposes that are a degree too human one feels that he is simply expressing concretely certain dumb and groping emotions which the poor brutes themselves could not have explained, but if resolved into action would have reached the same result that Mr. Roberts reaches. In such stories, for instance, as that of the captive bison in **"Last Bull,"** or of the moose in **"The Monarch of Park Barren,"** it is, of course, incredible that these animals should have evoked in their dull brains the panoramic memories of Western prairie and Northern mountain bounded woodland such as Mr. Roberts attributes to them. And yet any one who has taken the trouble to stand and watch for a few hours the big proud horned leaders of some pitiful remnant of a herd behind the wire-bound ranges of our zoological gardens must confess that the far-off dreams that lie behind their inscrutable gaze, their motionless and silent stolidity, has never been more eloquently, more adequately interpreted than through the medium of Mr. Roberts's idealisation.

Frederic Taber Cooper, in a review of "Kings in Exile," in The Bookman, London, Vol. XXXI, No. 3, May, 1910, p. 296.

This is another collection of animal stories done much after Mr. Roberts's usual fashion. That is to say, their substance is sometimes a queer mixture of legitimate natural history and highly melodramatic episodes in which animal intelligence is ridiculously exaggerated, together with some good descriptive writing mingled with much that is obviously fantastic and overdrawn. Mr. Roberts is fond of depicting with absurd minuteness the supposed cerebrations of wild animals in captivity, and of domesticated creatures turned loose in the woods to shift for themselves. These themes he has already worn fairly threadbare, but that does not deter him from working into the present volume the stories of **"Last Bull,"** who is a bison confined in a zoölogical park where he bewails his fate and finally meets a tragic end; of **"The Gray Master,"** which tells the same kind of tale about a timber wolf, and other yarns of the same general character. Perhaps the most ingenious one is the tale of the man who, while planning to rob an eagle's nest, tumbled over a cliff and lodged on a ledge where he stayed for about two weeks in the company of one of the young eagles which he had knocked out of the nest in his fall, and with which he shared the fish, flesh, and fowl brought to the eaglet by its male parent. As an illustration of Mr. Roberts's faculty for lugging queer natural history into his stories, there is in this last story the episode of its hero's discovery that the "black eagle," of which he had seen only one specimen, was nothing but an immature bald eagle, of which he had seen many—an observation which loses its force when one remembers that the bald eagle does not get its full plumage until its second or third year at the earliest, and that, therefore, "black eagles" (as a matter of fact, the immature bald eagle is *brown,* not black) are, in the nature of the case, much more common than those with the white head and tail. (pp. 511-12)

> *A review of "Kings in Exile," in* The Nation, *New York, Vol. XC, No. 2342, May 19, 1910, pp. 511-12.*

Neighbors Unknown   (1910)

Of this new collection of Mr. Roberts's "nature" stories, we need only say that it is as good as its predecessors. Freshness of matter or manner cannot be claimed for it. Indeed, after twenty years' exploitation of the habits of the polar bear, the caribou, the lynx, and the rest, we have little new information to look for. But of possible new combinations of the old matter, there is no calculable end. After the lynx has slain the wolf, he may still be pitted against a dozen antagonists in succession: and there is always the deadly rifle in reserve. The most striking of the present sketches is **"The Tiger of the Sea"**—the adventure of a foolhardy man with a killer whale. They are all good in their kind. It is to be doubted if that kind is likely to retain its popularity much longer with so fickle a public as is made up of confirmed fiction-readers. After all, the lover of nature and inquirer into the "way of the wild" does not go for his fun or his profit to such books as this: they must stand or fall as fiction.

> *A review of "Neighbors Unknown," in* The Nation, *New York, Vol. XCII, No. 2390, April 20, 1911, p. 400.*

The place of animals in nature's free house of growth has always been eloquently championed by Mr. Charles G. D. Roberts, and he now adds to his list of books about animals a collection of new stories, under the title **Neighbors Unknown.** All of these neighbors—the black bear, the caribou, the killer-whale, the lynx—are known to us in appearance and outward characteristics, but not in the intimacy of life and death with which Mr. Roberts knows them. The truth that strikes him most forcibly is that the hunter becomes the hunted. The small dragon-fly is caught by the large, the large is swallowed by the heron, and the heron falls a prey to the mink; the puffin catches the fish, but the skua catches the puffin. Man stands at the apex of this pyramid of destruction, felling the grizzly which has captured a seal, and the whale which has left a bloody path in the sea. But man is not always victor, for a moment's drowsiness in his night-watch makes him a victim to the wolf-pack; nor are the stories all tragedies, for the crazy loon has wit enough to escape from the hand of the fowler, and the mother panther gets her cubs back from his thievery and escapes unhurt. Most of the stories are too cruel for children, but **"How a Cat Played Robinson Crusoe"** and the **"Tunnel Runners"**—the story of a marsh-mouse—are excellent for young readers. (p. 438)

> *May Estelle Cook, "Nature's Open Shop," in* The Dial, *Chicago, Vol. L, No. 599, June 1, 1911, pp. 438-39.*

Mr. Charles G. D. Roberts is at his best in **Neighbors Unknown** and to say that is to say that no other writer on like subjects is any better. Indeed, it is to be doubted whether any other is in all respects his equal. Each of the fourteen sketches of his latest volume is a thrilling story of animal life, a story which holds the reader in as close a grip as any "best seller" of them all; and yet the author never falls into the almost universal anthropomorphism of "Nature-writers." His animals are beasts, birds, and fishes—not men in their skins, a fault so common that most stories of the wild are continually suggestive of the stage in "Chantecler." Mr. Roberts follows the thought of his "creatures" (pace Mr. Burroughs) only just so far as observed facts warrant. It is strange that, despite this restraint, each story should be a drama of intense interest, but so it is. Mr. Roberts' style is a joy; his artistic sense never fails him. Though "Nature red in tooth and claw" hovers like a doom over her children, Mr. Roberts does not overaccentuate the tragedy. He emphasizes, rather, the lack of foreboding and the quick forgetfulness which relieve the condition of constant peril in which both hunter and hunted—and all wild things are both—exist. Whether viewed as stories, as natural history, or as literature, young and old should lose no time in making the acquaintance of **Neighbors Unknown.**

> *A review of "Neighbors Unknown," in* The New York Times Book Review, *June 11, 1911, p. 364.*

The Feet of the Furtive   (1912)

This is a collection of stories, some of them previously published, by one of our most popular animal writers, popular because he writes from actual knowledge and experience, inspired by real affection for the denizens of the woods. And his tales are full of interest for both young and old. The author's descriptions are poetic and graphic. He relates dramatic and pathetic episodes in the lives of the lynx, rabbit, moose, bat, or deer with a sympathetic touch which makes the lives of the animals vivid and enthralling. Best of all, however, Mr. Roberts does not distort the truth in order to make his stories more thrilling, but tells an unvarnished tale of animal life and its natural tragedies. The stories are fascinating and the form of narrative most entertaining.

> *A review of "The Feet of the Furtive," in* The Literary Digest, *New York, Vol. XLVI, No. 18, May 3, 1913, p. 1030.*

The Feet of the Furtive contains several well-written stories of a kind much in vogue at the present time, wherein the author weaves interesting facts in natural history into an attractive fabric of fiction. The habits of familiar North American mammals are the theme Mr. Roberts presents so cleverly in this guise; but while giving full play to his imagination and to his powers of linguistic expression, he never oversteps the bounds of probability, and carefully avoids that pitfall authors too frequently dig for themselves and their readers, by attempting to humanise the species whose mode of life they wish to portray. Many of the stories recall others that have already been published by American authors; but there is a distinct air of novelty about the one called **"The World of Ghost Lights,"** which gives a vivid picture of one aspect of life in the ocean depths. (p. 295)

R. I. P., "Natural History and Travel," in Nature, *November 6, 1913, pp. 294-95.*

Hoof and Claw (1913)

Those who cater for the numerous and hungry readers of animal stories are probably careful lest the supply should exceed the demand. Each season produces several fresh volumes of such stories, and each volume seemingly finds readers. Among the well-established and most popular of such writers is Mr. Charles G. D. Roberts, whose books come out with more than annual frequency. In *Hoof and Claw* we have a number of tales written with the same restrained power, the same capacity for selecting the right word, and the same apparently intimate knowledge of the backwoods as before. Mr. Roberts is fortunate in having so inexhaustible a stock of material. He never repeats himself. Bears, bison, blue foxes, wolves, and wild sheep are his heroes, and in some of the best stories settlers, trappers, or Indians play minor parts. It would be a waste of space to praise so deservedly popular a writer.—Mr. Roberts has many rivals, but few surpass him.

A review of "Hoof and Claw," in The Spectator, *Vol. III, No. 4458, December 6, 1913, p. 949.*

In reading Mr. Roberts's new book, one is once in a while on the verge of a suspicion that the author is in danger of the quicksand that has engulfed so many naturalists possessed of more imagination than science, the temptation to describe animal mentality in terms of the human. But it never gets beyond that, and his animals remain entirely credible; though we confess we should very much like to have seen the bear that thought he was a dog, and was accustomed to wriggle his haunches violently in the belief that he was wagging his tail, a mannerism acquired from his foster-mother, who was a real dog.

Hoof and Claw contains a baker's dozen and one of short stories, none poor, and several of them little masterpieces of dramatic and pictorial effect. Here and there Mr. Roberts's poetical faculty clinches a picture with a phrase, to mix figures recklessly, as when he speaks of a pasture "all afloat in violet dusk," or, speaking of the "chill, ethereal, lonesome spring" of the north, he describes the "little colonies" of white birch or silver poplar scattered among the dark firs, as "just filming with the first ineffable green." But he keeps his poetry well in hand; it never spreads into purple patches. The story of the eagles and the aeroplane is especially graphic, with its picture of the bowl-like earth as seen from the airship, and the sea, looking as though it were "withheld only by a miracle from flowing in and filling the bowl."

But the best tales in the book are those into which civilization enters least; tales of the wild lurkings and huntings and filchings of otter and owl and lynx. They are tragic with the unregretted tragedy, humorous with the rough-and-tumble humor of the wilderness; while underneath all runs a sense of the mystery and fascination of the wilderness itself. (pp. 430-31)

A review of "Hoof and Claw," in The New York Times Book Review, *October 11, 1914, pp. 430-31.*

In the gentle art of nature-faking, which a few years ago was becoming, at the hands of Mr. Burroughs and other literal souls, so wide an advertisement, no practitioner has been more persistent or more successful than Mr. Roberts. W. J. Long is no longer in this field, and the voice of Mr. Thompson-Seton grows fainter year by year. But Mr. Roberts is evidently prepared to work his vein to the last thread of pay ore. The market justifies him. The present sketches have all obtained the final award of publication in popular magazines. They are builded according to an apparently infallible recipe: two parts animal characteristic and habit, one part "nature," or background, and one part "pathetic fallacy." This writer is uncommonly successful in conveying an impression of the atmosphere of the wilderness, or "wild," as he prefers to say. Sometimes it is a "wild" peopled only by its native "kindreds," and the little dramas of life and death at which we are invited to assist include no human actors. But this is rare; almost always there is a human figure within range, woodsman, trapper, or voyageur, sometimes as spectator, sometimes as conscious or unconscious participant. A man is treed by an elk, and a fight that follows between the elk and a lynx is determined by a can of molasses, in the woodsman's abandoned pack. A bear-cub is adopted by a dog, and when he grows up establishes his identity by trying to wag his tail. The humor of the physical contrast between the ways of man and the ways of wild animals is made much of.

On the other hand, and of more importance, perhaps, to the popularity of this type of tale, these animals are always being presented to us in human terms. This is not done symbolically, as in the Æsop fables or the Kipling "Just-So Stories," but as if literally. The bear and the otter and the moose are represented as thinking and feeling, inspired by love and hate, jealousy and revenge, adjusting their conduct to unusual exigencies, putting their human adversaries to shame by the flexibility of their mental processes, and their human friends by the warmth of their attachments. This method evidently extends the field of the "nature-writer" almost without limit. More scrupulous observers, like Mr. Burroughs or Mr. Dallas Lore Sharp, must be continually observing new things to find "copy." There must be an end to mere description, whether of a lion or a tomtit. As hero of fiction, a creature with mane or tail feathers, instead of sweater or frock coat, but otherwise virtually human, what limit can be set for the usefulness of a Child of the Wild? (pp. 659-60)

A review of "Hoof and Claw," in The Nation, *New York, Vol. XCIX, No. 2579, December 3, 1914, pp. 659-60.*

The Secret Trails (1916)

Every one who is interested in the great outdoors is familiar with the works of Charles G. D. Roberts. Any one who reads his books for the first time has a stimulating treat in hand. In this collection are stories of boar, dog, bull, eagle, egret, oxen, and rabbit. The author makes one feel the irresistible force of nature. He weaves a fanciful story about strange and dramatic facts in the lives of furry and feathered tribes. Each story is interesting, sometimes tragic and thrilling, and so cleverly constructed that the reader scarcely realizes that the scenes are dominated by beasts or birds, even when humans figure in them. His nature descriptions are exquisite and graphic. The episodes described illustrate customs and traits of different animals so subtly that we absorb edifying truths unconsciously while reading for entertainment. Never didactic, Mr. Roberts charms by his picturesque narrative and his absolute familiarity with his subject.

> *A review of "The Secret Trails," in* The Literary Digest, *New York, Vol. LIV, No. 2, January 13, 1917, p. 84.*

Jim: The Story of a Backwoods Police Dog   (1919)

Someone has offered this objection to animal stories, that the cleverest beast he ever read about was not quite so intelligent as the most stupid man. The indictment hardly holds true of Jim, the hero of the first story in this collection, for his canine astuteness puts most of the human beings that surround him to shame, and is equaled only by that of the omniscient Tug Blackstock, his master. Together they stalk evildoers, and loom up as figures of almost legendary heroism against the familiar background of the Canada woods. In the remaining tales we encounter a more recent setting for animal stories, that of the trenches. One of the tales is concerned with the adventures of a shell-shocked mule; another follows the flight of an eagle, released from his cage by an exploding 75, who flies at a great height along the lines and receives a veritable bird's-eye view of the war. These animals of which we read, despite epigrams to the contrary, are really much more interesting than human beings, and Major Roberts rather spoils the impression by imposing on them the purely human institution of a plot.

This he omits to do in the last story. Stripes, the skunk who is its unconcerned hero, goes calmly about his business of catching field mice and sucking eggs, quite indifferent to the great beasts which surround him. Finally he is attacked by a very foolish bear cub, deluges it with slime, and falls a victim finally to its revengeful mother, who after slaying him with one blow of her paw, goes on about her business. It is all casual and cruel and very real; it reminds one not so much of another animal story as of one of Tchekhov's sketches or of an etching by George Bellows.

> *A review of "Jim: The Story of a Backwoods Police Dog," in* The Dial, *Chicago, Vol. LXVI, June 28, 1919, p. 659.*

This is a pretty good story, with a dog in the Sherlock Holmes rôle, surrounded by great husky backwoodsmen who all play Dr. Watson. Major Roberts knows his men and his setting and does it quite well. He makes no mis-takes in details, he has the local color and language down fine, and even the tone of the story is sometimes almost realistic. But it never is more: never real. It is merely high-grade second-rate stuff. It is quite as accurate and complete and unconvincing as are David Belasco's stage settings.

There's a reason. With Belasco, it is simply that he doesn't see true: doesn't want to see true: loves his dreams of life better than Life, whose strange soul he won't look at. With Major Roberts the reason is more creditable: he is doing the best that he can, but he hasn't the faintest notion of what human beings are like. He notes with exactness their appearance, their language and dress, and he senses their surface reaction, but he can't see inside.

Yet he is a seer and an artist—otherwise why bother to write this review?—and he has a field of his own where he does see true, unlike Belasco. He knows animal nature. He knows it as Meredith knew women or as Synge knew the Irish. In the latter part of this book there is a story of an eagle that makes you feel, while you read it; that you yourself are an eagle for the moment, proud, obstinate, fierce. And the next time you see an eagle you will know him better than you do your own uncle. You will have been one yourself.

It is a splendid experience. It is well worth the price of the book . . . Also just at the end there is and her experience that is also worth while: a story about a skunk: when you have read it you have been a skunk too. You don't have to read it, I hasten to add. Nobody is going to make you be one of them. But speaking as one who has trusted our friend, Magician Roberts, and tried it, I can tell you we skunks are a fastidious, brave, and dignified lot, with a coolness and courage that only the best soldiers can equal, and a cleanliness as pure as a maiden's or possibly purer. (It is so seldom I get to be a maiden, now that I have stopped reading George Meredith, that I cannot estimate it more exactly, but that is near enough.)

As for Major Roberts, he has never been a maiden, or a man, or a major. Though he doubtless has always conducted himself as a man, and has behaved like the most majorly major that was ever born in Majorville, that is nevertheless not his real self. That is not where he lives. But he has certainly been an eagle and a skunk, and most things in between, and has flown on wings and crawled as the serpent and run on four feet.

If you have read Thompson Seton and been thoroughly sickened of animal stuff, you may hesitate to try Major Roberts, or may not think it worth while. But he is no more like Seton in his insight than Synge is like poor Victor Herbert. He is a genius who admittedly needs sifting, but still he's a genius. He has a thrilling gift of making you know how wild animals feel. You will certainly enjoy being an eagle, and, if you are truly catholic, a skunk.

> *L. E. Hewson, "Jim," in* The New Republic, *Vol. XIX, No. 245, July 16, 1919, p. 366.*

They Who Walk in the Wild (1924; British edition as
They That Walk in the Wild)

This group of stories about wild creatures will fully sustain
the reputation of its Canadian author. Mr. Roberts makes
his readers feel the fascination of the wilderness, and
knows how to heighten the battles of its denizens with the
sense of its underlying calm. His descriptions of the forest
at various seasons, though brief and unobtrusive, have the
same spacious peacefulness which is felt to the full in such
a book as Bates's "Amazons." The adventures of bears,
moose, puma, walrus, cormorant, white-headed eagle, and
other Northern species are full of event, yet based on accurate knowledge; there is probably good authority for even
such an unusual incident as the sustenance of a snow-
bound hunter by the milk of a hibernating bear with a cub.
Good play is made with the conflicting instincts of wild
and domesticated creatures; and the author's competence
both as writer and naturalist is shown by his chapter on
the life of a bumble-bee, the modest adventures of which
insect are as interesting as the internecine struggles of
swordfish, walrus, and polar bear. A little surprise is
evoked by the statement that "the biggest and fiercest of
northern spiders were of no concern" to the bumble-bee
described, for "she could wreck their toughest webs without an effort"; in this country a common spider masters
with jaws and spinnerets one of the largest bumble-bees,
closely similar to that which appears to be described. Mr.
Roberts justifies, on the whole, his claim to interpret the
psychology of animals "from their own viewpoint rather
than ours." But it is difficult to take a wild creature as the
hero of a story without making assumptions which science
might hesitate to confirm—that the halts, for example, of
migrating Canada geese are settled by the "decree" of one
"wise old gander," or that the bumble-bee stops laying
eggs because there was "no need of raising fresh young
bees just to be killed by the autumn frosts." But a few such
liberties scarcely affect the prevailing accuracy.

> *"Natural History," in* The Times Literary
> Supplement, *No. 1161, April 17, 1924, p. 242.*

Even the professed hater of nature-fakers cannot escape
the lure of Mr. Roberts' stories of wild, and tame, animals.
Among those "Who Walk in the Wilds" or in some instances walk *out* of the wilds into comparative civilization,
are: a mountain goat, a wild goose and an immense but
amiable puma, and their adventures are delightfully told
as only Roberts can tell such tales.

Mr. Roberts' love of nature is so fine a thing that it robs
his autobiographical animals of that conceited self-
consciousness which one associates with so many animal
tales. Not the least of his talents is his description of landscapes and atmosphere, the despair of many writers of ambitious fiction. "Ghostly white under the flooding spring
moonlight, the sheep lay contentedly ruminating amid the
old stumps and close-bitten hillocks of the upland pasture." Really, Hardy could not improve on this.

It is in no spirit of too sophisticated agedness that I suggest
this book as a particularly suitable gift for a good, or better
still, a bad little Canadian boy.

> *H. W. B., in a review of "They Who Walk in*

the Wild," *in* The Canadian Bookman, *Vol. 6,
No. 8, August, 1924, p. 179.*

There is no true literature of animals. All the jungle books,
from *Genesis* to *Kim,* have dealt with them necessarily
from an alien point of view, without objectivity of comment. When philosophy or psychology succeeds in establishing the precise interrelations of mind and the senses we
shall perhaps be nearer to a discovery of the mysterious
tie, crudely traced out in the biological theories of evolution, which binds the two main divisions of organic life.
At present, however, the literary naturalist is credible only
when he confines his interpretative fancy within the strait-
waistcoat of scientific observation. When Mr. Roberts
says that "faint ancestral memories began to stir in the
young puma's brain," he is not only ignoring a current
theory of the automatic behaviour of animals; he is an-
thropomorphising with all the extremism, and none of the
deliberateness, of Æsop, La Fontaine or Mr. Pat Sullivan,
the brilliant screen-draughtsman of "Felix the Cat." Indeed, it is difficult to imagine any other method of translat-
ing the psychology of animals into terms comprehensible
to our own. One may therefore take pleasure in Mr. Roberts's ambition "to help a little forward toward a wider,
more tender and more imaginative perception of their essential kinship with ourselves" while remaining sceptical
of the means by which he proposes to bring it about—"to
present them, in their actions and their motives, from their
own point of view rather than ours."

The episodes he relates of these creatures of the Canadian
backwoods are sensitively planned and vividly written. As
we read them we feel like hidden wild-life photographers,
biding our time until every jungle bush or arctic boulder
yields a beast—until that uncanny, graceful, ravenous parade begins, from which an ancestor's itch for uprightness
(the unsightly skill of the winner of a sack-race) has expelled us for ever. Schopenhauer once said that men are
the devils of the world, and animals the tormented souls.
Modern sensibility has gone further in this direction;
all of us who have ever comraded a dog, cherished a cat
or paid an attentive visit to the Zoo, have had moods in
which the metaphysical position of mankind seemed
stripped even of a diabolistic primacy. Mankind, to such
a mood, appears an unaccountable *parvenu* species marooned in a middle element; despised for its æsthetic im-
perfections by the denizens of the earth, and disowned, because of its moral shortcomings, by the deity beyond the
sky. Mr. Roberts is, as a rule, strikingly successful in conveying, and implanting in the reader, some such respect
for the integrity of the untamed animal. He describes the
attack on a walrus herd by an arctic bear and a giant
swordfish in such a manner that we can share the feelings
of all, without attaching our sympathies to any one of the
protagonists. This is the most convincing of all his narratives; some are marred by sentimentalism, others by psychological inconsistencies arising from the anthropomorphic intention which has been quoted. For instance, Mr.
Roberts seems to allow no individuality to the members
of the hive of Bomba, his Queen-Bee, and yet, in another
section, after an exciting account of an eagle swooping
down to steal fish from a cormorant, he declares that

> Few other birds there were in his colony who

would have had the mettle, bold as they were, to face the Eagle as the Black Fisherman had done.

Why should individual character be given to a bird and denied to a bee? The analytical methods of the novelist—the measurement of mental processes by foot-rules of cause and effect—are partial and approximate in their estimation even of human beings. The minds of animals are a dim world to logical enquiry: perhaps we shall never be able to perceive "their essential kinship with ourselves," except by the monistic light of imagination.

> *"The Psychology of Animals," in* New Statesman, *Vol. XXIII, No. 594, September 6, 1924, p. 626.*

Eyes of the Wilderness (1933)

The hand of Charles G. D. Roberts, the veteran Canadian naturalist and writer on life in the wilds, has not lost its cunning. The publication of a new collection of tales by him therefore means a treat for lovers of animal stories. His writings have long been noteworthy for a sensitive sympathy, an almost uncanny appreciation of Northern forest creatures and an intuitive understanding of their ways.

Here we have delectable tales of bears and moose and foxes and wolves and rabbits; of Tabitha Blue the Persian cat that got lost in the Canadian woods and mated with a bob-cat; of how the cow moose and her new calf escaped from a forest fire; of how Jock the airedale fought the wolves; of how the black bear followed a fisherman and stole his trout; of what a boy saw in the woods when he "froze" and remained quiet for half an hour, and how another boy saved a family of moose from starvation in a hard Winter. Not all of the dozen tales in this new collection are animal stories, though most of them are, but all of them were worth the telling and all are well worth the reading.

> *"Animal Stories," in* The New York Times Book Review, *October 22, 1933, p. 27.*

The interest of this book centers more in what Mr. Roberts thinks about his wild friends, and what he thinks they think, than in any story. Incident in a setting of wood lore, that is to say, here takes the place of character and plot. A cow moose escapes with its calf from a great fire and establishes relations with friendly woodsman number one; a bear almost takes the shoes off friendly woodsman number two before the situation is cleared up by a forced laugh (this from the woodsman); friendly woodsman number three is not recognized as such by a pack of wolves, thus coming in for a very bad half hour; and so on, around the animal kingdom.

Although Mr. Roberts tends to give an impression (this by dint of infallibly pleasant endings) that life in the woods is so much marmalade; although his work has neither the excitement of a Thompson-Seton story of Lobo the wolf nor the literary stature of some other writers in the field, he yet has a most convincing way of detailing how the bear jumped and why. He has spent a long lifetime of study in

"these Canadian wilds of mine," and has arrived at a sort of special feeling about them and their creatures.

> It seems not enough to approach this fascinating study with merely the curious eyes of the naturalist . . . the exciting adventure lies in the effort to "get under the skins." so to speak, of these shy and elusive beings . . . to differentiate between those of their actions which are the result of . . . instinct and those which spring from something definitely akin to reason; for I am absolutely convinced that, within their widely varied yet strictly set limitations, the more advanced . . . do reason.

And it is from this point of view that Mr. Roberts sets them forth in a manner sympathetic, even gentle, and not without its moments of humor. You may not at first accept him, may not be that way about animals at all, but taking one thing with another it will be difficult to resist the actual burden of the book, which is Mr. Roberts's real zest for this wilderness he creates and peoples.

> *A review of "Eyes of the Wilderness," in* New York Herald Tribune Books, *November 5, 1933, p. 14.*

Long ago Mr. Roberts won for himself, and maintained, an enviable reputation as a writer of animal stories. It was not for nothing that W. H. Hudson, the greatest naturalist-writer in English, referred to his work with interest and commendation. What Hudson accomplished through scrupulous observation and record and an almost intuitive insight—the penetration of the springs of animal life—Roberts attempted with a large degree of success through the medium of fiction—fiction that was faithful at once to the exacting art of narrative and to nature. His skill to call up the atmosphere and homely details of a backwoods farm, the dusky silence of the deep bush, the sunlit reaches of marshland, or the shining vitality of a river, and to spin a convincing, absorbing tale of the furtive, eager life that each contains, often transcended mere ability and could only have been the happy result of sure knowledge, deep affection, and a vigorous imagination.

But Mr. Roberts' gift as an animal writer was at best limited. It failed to develop the variety and continuous change of growth. Having run its certain gamut of pictures and adventures there was nothing for it but repetition, with the inevitable consequences. It is therefore with disappointment but no surprise that, after a long silence, one picks up this new volume to find that the old magic has departed. The familiar settings are there, and many of the characters that were once instinct with life and vigour, but they now refuse to come alive. The descriptions, once firm and brief as the bold strokes of a charcoal drawing, have become faint pencillings, and the creatures move dimly and mechanically about their exciting affairs. The old manner and the old mannerisms are there, too ('Spring came late that year to the upper Ottanoonsis'), but the zest which made us pardon their repetition has gone and leaves them lifeless forms. Besides, in **Eyes of the Wilderness** man bulks more largely than in most of the earlier books, and Mr. Roberts has never been happy in drawing human characters. The best that one can say for these stories is that they are competent and that they will entertain many new readers. But those who knew the old Roberts had better leave them alone.

H. K. G., in a review of "Eyes of the Wilderness," in The Canadian Forum, *Vol. XIV, No. 159, December, 1933, p. 116.*

Unsentimental animal stories about the fight for survival in the Canadian woodlands, these were originally written in the twenties and thirties and the prose style is rather literary for many juniors to read on their own. An excellent book though for taking extracts to read aloud, in particular the lyrical and detailed descriptions of the animals. The owl: 'The wide, circular discs of flat feathering which surrounded his eyes were cream-white, shading into fawn, and between them came down a frowning, pointed brow of darker feathers.' The ponderous humour of the bear in the first story is pure poetry.

Caroline Wynburne, in a review of "Eyes of the Wilderness," in The School Librarian, *Vol. 28, No. 2, June, 1980, p. 157.*

Charles G. D. Roberts left Canadians a literary legacy. His animal stories had a lasting affect on both the literature of nature study and the perception of the Canadian scene that came to prevail abroad. His keen observation and deep interest in the lives of Canada's wild creatures brought to many readers the exciting vision of a world untravelled and unknown to all but a very few; the world of the woodland.

The fact that his reportage was inaccurate had no adverse effect on his popularity, may indeed have enhanced it, for he wrote with an emotionalism and sentimentality more popular in his day than at present. His wild creatures are presented as true likenesses, but they tend to behave like furred and feathered thespians. Roberts's animals continually plot revenge for the deaths of lost loved ones or to avenge slights to their prestige; their actions express indignation, fury, determination or gaiety; their eyes flash and dart; the forest fairly quivers with melodrama.

Today's writers, when describing creatures of the wild, are careful to remain objective, not to 'take sides' with one species against another, not to impute human motivation to the instinctive behaviour of wild animals. Roberts adopted a partisan stance. Certainly one is more tempted to empathize with bunnies and nestlings than with the lynx or wolf, but each merely obeys the dictates of nature and must not be labelled 'vengeful' or 'wicked' for doing so.

Of the five short stories in this collection, the best is **"Winged Scourge of the Night,"** a tale of the lives of fiercely predatory horned owls who themselves become the prey of a marauding lynx. Here Roberts does full justice to a blow-by-blow account of their fatal encounter. The other stories are of varied quality, but two at least, those of the owls and of the snowshoe hare, are little classics.

Roberts's emotional approach to the subjects he loved now strikes the reader as comically biased at times, but that love does lend an appeal and an all-too-human inter-est to his animal heroes and villains that is not to be found in the more objective works of today.

Joan McGrath, in a review of "Eyes of the Wilderness and Other Stories," in In Review: Canadian Books for Children, *Vol. 14, No. 5, October, 1980, p. 60.*

In spite of their mannered and often luscious prose (even fish are 'finny hordes'), these five stories, four of which were written in the 1920s, reveal an intimate knowledge of the natural world and a sympathetic affection for wild animals. Charles Roberts catches the sights and sounds of the Canadian forest in his colourful descriptions of trees and lakes, the seasons and the weather, and succeeds in getting under the skin of the animals whose adventures he is chronicling. At times he humanises his wild creatures—rabbits are 'a philosophic folk', a bear avenges a wrong to his personal dignity—but generally he is exploring the inexorable conflicts of nature, raw in tooth and claw. A bear steals a fisherman's catch; a homeless rabbit runs the gauntlet of hawk, fox and bear, only to be killed by a lynx; an osprey protects its young and its food against an angry bear; a bull moose defies the attacks of four wolves.

G. Bott, in a review of "Eyes of the Wilderness and Other Stories," in The Junior Bookshelf, *Vol. 44, No. 5, October, 1980, p. 256.*

The five stories in **Eyes of the Wilderness,** selected from three volumes of the '20's and '30's, show their period in the dramatic style and arrangements of incidents in which the hazards of wild life are explored. In the title story, a city visitor walks in the woods at night and suffers fears both reasonable and unreasonable. The remaining four stories concentrate entirely on animal individuals—a pair of great horned owls threatened by a lynx, a snowshoe rabbit escaping a weasel, a nesting osprey competing for food with a bear and a migrating moose family beset by wolves. There is no humanisation in these openly descriptive, active pieces, and a great deal of sharp, accurate observation which is in no way impaired by the author's evident sympathy for prey against predator. Very much of their time, these are stories that deserve to be perpetuated for their individual, civilised style and their careful picture of wild life. (pp. 3777-78)

Margery Fisher, in a review of "Eyes of the Wilderness and Other Stories," in Growing Point, *Vol. 19, No. 4, November, 1980, pp. 3777-78.*

Among a distinguished company of nature writers at the beginning of the century—Ernest Thompson Seton, Jack London, Percy Fitzpatrick, and (after the First World War) Henry Williamson and Grey Owl—Charles G. D. Roberts was the most prolific, producing novels, romances and over two hundred stories. He wrote about the wild animals of his native New Brunswick, and in his day, his work was very popular. In recent years there has been something of a Roberts revival, marked first by the NCL anthology of stories edited by Alec Lucas, **The Last Barrier and Other Stories** (1958), which was followed by reprints of **Red Fox, The Heart of the Ancient Wood** and

The Lure of the Wild. Now we have another selection of short stories, *Eyes of the Wilderness.*

The first question that any reprint poses is surely, was it worth doing? Is Roberts still worth reading? The answer, at least to this reviewer, is a resounding yes! These are strong stories, full of excitement and drama; they read easily, they are not too long. A librarian could with an easy conscience push this collection towards a young reader: once the child gets past the first prosy paragraph there is enough violent action to surprise even the jaded TV addict.

The selection has been made with skill, for the five stories give us variety, both in their subject and their dramatic form. The first is a comedy, a simple account of a city man on his first fishing trip, who is observed in his ignorance by the eyes of the wilderness. His catch of fish is stolen by a bear. As an introduction, this story serves its purpose, since the reader is shown a parade of wild animals going about their business: a weasel, a skunk, a porcupine, a wildcat, an eagle and several more. Man is the intruder in this natural world, "the eternal and irresistible enemy." And yet, the story is at odds with the other four: the mood is pastoral, the action slow. A reader should be encouraged to push on.

Roberts claimed that he was a "realistic" nature writer; that is, that he did not describe anything that could not have happened. But one cannot read very far without realizing that though his stories are carefully observed and vividly described accounts of wild animal behaviour, his "realism" attends to the dramatic rather than the commonplace. His stories tell us of the Fight to the Death, of the Survival of the Fittest, of the strength of the Superior Animal, of Chance, of Fate, and of Justice. The second story in the collection, **"The Winged Scourge of the Dark,"** is about a night in the life of a great horned owl. Roberts shows us rabbits playing in the soft twilight, then the chilling call of the owl, the games frozen, the "dim form" drifting in, the sudden piercing cry, and the strike. The rabbit "gave one short scream of terror, strangled on the instant. Then he was swept into the air, kicking spasmodically. And the dim shape bore him off into the deep of the woods. . . . " As the night goes on we follow the owl's hunting; we watch him kill and eat, kill and eat, and kill. His victims are mice, sparrows, a frog, two turkeys, a hen. The action is violent and sustained, and we become aware of a kind of hubris of the bird of prey, a cruelty which reaches retribution when the owl and his mate are attacked by a lynx. The owl dies defending his nestlings, but the lynx is driven off.

In Margaret Atwood's poem, the animals of this country "have the faces of no-one." They are mere objects glimpsed in the car headlights; they have no place in our imagination. Roberts denies her. His animals are vibrant with life: their struggles, their persistence, their very violence is testimony to the strength of the life force. Roberts does not make them people, but he does mythologize them. He places them in a cosmic order, he gives them Laws, and he sets them down in an enchanted landscape. He is a romantic at heart, a man who has looked at Darwin and seen not tragedy but vitality.

Each story begins with a set piece of landscape description. Roberts' language is poetic; his wilderness world a natural Eden. The light is dazzling, the air is clear, the colours gold, green and purple. The woods smell good. Summer is idyllic, winter savage and cruel. Nothing is ordinary. Inhabiting this unpeaceable kingdom are the Superior Animals, the strongest snow-shoe rabbit, the great black bull-moose, the great horned-owl. Each must defend himself and his mate against all foes; none is ever really safe. Nature is heartless. Only the fittest survive. This world has its heroes, and equally it has its villains: some animals are better than others. Ospreys, Roberts tells us, are "the most attractive, in character, of all the predatory tribes of the eagles and hawks." The osprey is courageous without being quarrelsome, and he minds his own business. (Good middle-class virtues!) And so it is especially proper that when his nest is threatened by a bear, Providence (in the form of a man with a gun) steps in to prevent a tragedy.

Only occasionally do we feel uncomfortable with the author's moralizing. The moose feels "fierce resentment in his heart" at the intrusion of man, and seems just a little too cunning and wise in his retreat to the "moose-yard." In the weakest story in the book, **"The Little Homeless One,"** a snow-shoe rabbit is guided by "the Unseen Powers" as he grows to strength and maturity, and he bravely sacrifices himself "for the safety of his tribe." (This comes as something of a surprise to the reader, since we have just been told that a "rabbit has enough to think of in guarding his own skin.") In much of his work, Roberts had a sentimental and even a maudlin streak, and **"The Little Homeless One"** comes close to betraying this vice. (pp. 36-8)

> *Robert H. MacDonald, "The Animals in That Country," in* Canadian Children's Literature, *No. 22, 1981, pp. 36-8.*

The Lure of the Wild: The Last Three Animal Stories (1980)

The Lure of the Wild comprises the three "final" animal stories that Charles G. D. Roberts wrote forty-three years after he published **"Do Seek Their Meat from God"** in 1892. (p. 141)

As John Coldwell Adams points out in his intelligent introduction to *The Lure of the Wild,* Roberts lived *for* poetry and *by* prose. His fiction had to address the demands of a popular audience caught between Darwin and Decadence. Even in 1935, when he completed these three stories, Roberts remained preoccupied with the notion of natural selection and was still relying on the anthropomorphism spurned by many modern critics. I've always found this criticism hard to explain. In these stories, as in his early ones, Roberts persistently suggests that animals and people are alike. Roberts' realistic impulses lead us to resist calling his stories fables. But his strength in prose lies precisely in his ability to create stories that animate the concerns of his age. Although the subject matter of the early and late stories remains much the same, one does note a shift in this collection towards more anxiety-ridden imagery, as when Roberts tells us of an owl capable of

"searching the spectrally lighted expanses of the waste."
Yet faced with this waste, Roberts' animals are still capable of "falling in love"; they still want "to melt the fair
one's heart." Such contradictions—and there are many of
them in both form and content—provide Roberts' prose
with some curious tensions that remain to be explored.
(pp. 142-43)

> *Robert Lecker, "Mothers & Others," in* Cana-
> dian Literature, *No. 94, Autumn, 1982, pp.
> 141-43.*

Children's
Literature
Review

How to Use This Index

The main reference

Baum, L(yman) Frank
1856-1919 .... **15**

lists all author entries in this and previous volumes of *Children's Literature Review*.

The cross-references

See also CA 103; 108; DLB 22; JRDA;
MAICYA; MTCW; SATA 18; TCLC 7

list all author entries in the following Gale biographical and literary sources:

AAYA = Authors & Artists for Young Adults
AITN = Authors in the News
BLC = Black Literature Criticism
BW = Black Writers
CA = Contemporary Authors
CAAS = Contemporary Authors Autobiography Series
CABS = Contemporary Authors Bibliographical Series
CANR = Contemporary Authors New Revision Series
CAP = Contemporary Authors Permanent Series
CDALB = Concise Dictionary of American Literary Biography
CLC = Contemporary Literary Criticism
CLR = Children's Literature Review
CMLC = Classical and Medieval Literature Criticism
DA = DISCovering Authors
DC = Drama Criticism
DLB = Dictionary of Literary Biography
DLBD = Dictionary of Literary Biography Documentary Series
DLBY = Dictionary of Literary Biography Yearbook
HW = Hispanic Writers
JRDA = Junior DISCovering Authors
LC = Literature Criticism from 1400 to 1800
MAICYA = Major Authors and Illustrators for Children and Young Adults
MTCW = Major 20th-Century Writers
NCLC = Nineteenth-Century Literature Criticism
PC = Poetry Criticism
SAAS = Something about the Author Autobiography Series
SATA = Something about the Author
SSC = Short Story Criticism
TCLC = Twentieth-Century Literary Criticism
WLC = World Literature Criticism, 1500 to the Present
YABC = Yesterday's Authors of Books for Children

CUMULATIVE INDEX TO AUTHORS

Bendick, Jeanne 1919-.................. **5**
See also CA 5-8R; CANR 2; MAICYA; SAAS 4; SATA 2, 68

Berenstain, Jan(ice) 1923-.............. **19**
See also CA 25-28R; CANR 14, 36; MAICYA; SATA 12, 64

Berenstain, Stan(ley) 1923-............. **19**
See also CA 25-28R; CANR 14, 36; MAICYA; SATA 12, 64

Berger, Melvin H. 1927-............. **32**
See also CA 5-8R; CANR 4; CLC 12; SAAS 2; SATA 5

Berna, Paul 1910-1994................ **19**
See also CA 73-76; 143; SATA 15

Berry, James 1925-.................... **22**
See also CA 135; JRDA; SATA 67

Beskow, Elsa (Maartman) 1874-1953..... **17**
See also CA 135; MAICYA; SATA 20

Bethancourt, T. Ernesto **3**
See also Paisley, Tom
See also SATA 11

Bianco, Margery (Williams) 1881-1944 ... **19**
See also CA 109; MAICYA; SATA 15

Biegel, Paul 1925-..................... **27**
See also CA 77-80; CANR 14, 32; SATA 16

Billout, Guy (Rene) 1941- **33**
See also CA 85-88; CANR 26; SATA 10

Biro, B(alint) S(tephen) 1921-
See Biro, Val
See also CA 25-28R; CANR 11, 39; MAICYA; SATA 67

Biro, Val **28**
See also Biro, B(alint) S(tephen)
See also SAAS 13; SATA 1

Bjoerk, Christina 1938-................ **22**
See also CA 135; SATA 67

Bjork, Christina
See Bjoerk, Christina

Blades, Ann 1947-..................... **15**
See also CA 77-80; CANR 13; JRDA; MAICYA; SATA 16, 69

Blake, Quentin (Saxby) 1932-........... **31**
See also CA 25-28R; CANR 11, 37; MAICYA; SATA 9, 52

Bland, E.
See Nesbit, E(dith)

Bland, Edith Nesbit
See Nesbit, E(dith)

Bland, Fabian
See Nesbit, E(dith)

Block, Francesca (Lia) 1962-........... **33**
See also CA 131

Blos, Joan W(insor) 1928-.............. **18**
See also CA 101; CANR 21; JRDA; MAICYA; SAAS 11; SATA 27, 33, 69

Blumberg, Rhoda 1917-................ **21**
See also CA 65-68; CANR 9, 26; MAICYA; SATA 35, 70

Blume, Judy (Sussman) 1938-........ **2, 15**
See also AAYA 3; CA 29-32R; CANR 13, 37; CLC 12, 30; DLB 52; JRDA; MAICYA; MTCW; SATA 2, 31

Blyton, Enid (Mary) 1897-1968......... **31**
See also CA 77-80; 25-28R; CANR 33; MAICYA; SATA 25

Bodker, Cecil 1927- **23**
See also CA 73-76; CANR 13; CLC 21; MAICYA; SATA 14

Bond, (Thomas) Michael 1926-........... **1**
See also CA 5-8R; CANR 4, 24; MAICYA; SAAS 3; SATA 6, 58

Bond, Nancy (Barbara) 1945-........... **11**
See also CA 65-68; CANR 9, 36; JRDA; MAICYA; SAAS 13; SATA 22

Bontemps, Arna(ud Wendell) 1902-1973.... **6**
See also BLC 1; BW; CA 1-4R; 41-44R; CANR 4, 35; CLC 1, 18; DLB 48, 51; JRDA; MAICYA; MTCW; SATA 2, 24, 44

Bookman, Charlotte
See Zolotow, Charlotte S(hapiro)

Boston, Lucy Maria (Wood) 1892-1990 .... **3**
See also CA 73-76; 131; JRDA; MAICYA; SATA 19; SATA-Obit 64

Boutet de Monvel, (Louis) M(aurice) 1850(?)-1913 .... **32**
See also SATA 30

Bova, Ben(jamin William) 1932-......... **3**
See also CA 5-8R; CAAS 18; CANR 11; CLC 45; DLBY 81; MAICYA; MTCW; SATA 6, 68

Bowler, Jan Brett
See Brett, Jan (Churchill)

Brancato, Robin F(idler) 1936-......... **32**
See also AAYA 9; CA 69-72; CANR 11; CLC 35; JRDA; SAAS 9; SATA 23

Brandenberg, Aliki Liacouras 1929-
See Aliki
See also CA 1-4R; CANR 4, 12, 30; MAICYA; SATA 2, 35, 75

Branley, Franklyn M(ansfield) 1915- **13**
See also CA 33-36R; CANR 14, 39; CLC 21; MAICYA; SAAS 16; SATA 4, 68

Breinburg, Petronella 1927-............ **31**
See also CA 53-56; CANR 4; SATA 11

Brett, Jan (Churchill) 1949-............ **27**
See also CA 116; CANR 41; MAICYA; SATA 42, 71

Bridgers, Sue Ellen 1942- **18**
See also AAYA 8; CA 65-68; CANR 11, 36; CLC 26; DLB 52; JRDA; MAICYA; SAAS 1; SATA 22

Briggs, Raymond Redvers 1934-......... **10**
See also CA 73-76; MAICYA; SATA 23, 66

Brink, Carol Ryrie 1895-1981........... **30**
See also CA 1-4R; 104; CANR 3; JRDA; MAICYA; SATA 1, 27, 31

Brooke, L(eonard) Leslie 1862-1940..... **20**
See also MAICYA; SATA 17

Brooks, Bruce 1950-................... **25**
See also AAYA 8; CA 137; JRDA; MAICYA; SATA 53, 72

Brooks, George
See Baum, L(yman) Frank

Brooks, Gwendolyn 1917-.............. **27**
See also AITN 1; BLC 1; BW; CA 1-4R; CANR 1, 27; CDALB 1941-1968; CLC 1, 2, 4, 5, 15, 49; DA; DLB 5, 76; MTCW; PC 7; SATA 6; WLC

Brown, Marc (Tolon) 1946-.............. **29**
See also CA 69-72; CANR 36; MAICYA; SATA 10, 53

Brown, Marcia 1918-.................. **12**
See also CA 41-44R; DLB 61; MAICYA; SATA 7, 47

Brown, Margaret Wise 1910-1952........ **10**
See also CA 108; 136; DLB 22; MAICYA; YABC 2

Brown, Roderick (Langmere) Haig-
See Haig-Brown, Roderick (Langmere)

Browne, Anthony (Edward Tudor) 1946-......................... **19**
See also CA 97-100; CANR 36; MAICYA; SATA 44, 45, 61

Bruna, Dick 1927- **7**
See also CA 112; CANR 36; MAICYA; SATA 30, 43, 76

Brunhoff, Jean de 1899-1937............ **4**
See also CA 118; 137; MAICYA; SATA 24

Brunhoff, Laurent de 1925-............. **4**
See also CA 73-76; MAICYA; SATA 24, 71

Bryan, Ashley F. 1923- **18**
See also BW; CA 107; CANR 26, 43; MAICYA; SATA 31, 72

Bunting, Anne Evelyn 1928-
See Bunting, Eve
See also AAYA 5; CA 53-56; CANR 5, 19; SATA 18

Bunting, Eve **28**
See also Bunting, Anne Evelyn
See also JRDA; MAICYA; SATA 64

Burnett, Frances (Eliza) Hodgson 1849-1924 .... **24**
See also CA 108; 136; DLB 42; JRDA; MAICYA; YABC 2

Burnford, Sheila (Philip Cochrane Every) 1918-1984 .... **2**
See also CA 1-4R; 112; CANR 1; JRDA; MAICYA; SATA 3, 38

Burningham, John (Mackintosh) 1936-..... **9**
See also CA 73-76; CANR 36; MAICYA; SATA 16, 59

Burton, Hester (Wood-Hill) 1913- **1**
See also CA 9-12R; CANR 10; MAICYA; SAAS 8; SATA 7, 74

Burton, Virginia Lee 1909-1968 .... **11**
See also CA 13-14; 25-28R; CAP 1; DLB 22; MAICYA; SATA 2

Byars, Betsy (Cromer) 1928-......... **1, 16**
See also CA 33-36R; CANR 18, 36; CLC 35; DLB 52; JRDA; MAICYA; MTCW; SAAS 1; SATA 4, 46

Caines, Jeannette (Franklin) **24**
See also SATA 43

Caldecott, Randolph (J.) 1846-1886 ...... **14**
See also MAICYA; SATA 17

Calvert, John
See Leaf, (Wilbur) Munro

Gantos, John (Bryan), Jr. 1951-
See Gantos, Jack
See also CA 65-68; CANR 15; SATA 20

Gardam, Jane 1928- 12
See also CA 49-52; CANR 2, 18, 33;
CLC 43; DLB 14; MAICYA; MTCW;
SAAS 9; SATA 28, 39, 76

Garfield, Leon 1921- 21
See also AAYA 8; CA 17-20R; CANR 38,
41; CLC 12; JRDA; MAICYA; SATA 1,
32, 76

Garner, Alan 1934- 20
See also CA 73-76; CANR 15; CLC 17;
MAICYA; MTCW; SATA 18, 69

Garnet, A. H.
See Slote, Alfred

Gay, Marie-Louise 1952- 27
See also CA 135; SATA 68

Gaze, Gillian
See Barklem, Jill

Geisel, Theodor Seuss 1904-1991 1
See also Dr. Seuss; Seuss, Dr.
See also CA 13-16R; 135; CANR 13, 32;
DLB 61; DLBY 91; MAICYA; MTCW;
SATA 1, 28, 75; SATA-Obit 67

George, Jean Craighead 1919- 1
See also AAYA 8; CA 5-8R; CANR 25;
CLC 35; DLB 52; JRDA; MAICYA;
SATA 2, 68

Gerrard, Roy 1935- 23
See also CA 110; SATA 45, 47

Gibbons, Gail 1944- 8
See also CA 69-72; CANR 12; MAICYA;
SAAS 12; SATA 23, 72

Giblin, James Cross 1933- 29
See also CA 106; CANR 24; MAICYA;
SAAS 12; SATA 33, 75

Giovanni, Nikki 1943- 6
See also AITN 1; BLC 2; BW; CA 29-32R;
CAAS 6; CANR 18, 41; CLC 2, 4, 19, 64;
DA; DLB 5, 41; MAICYA; MTCW;
SATA 24

Glubok, Shirley (Astor) 1
See also CA 5-8R; CANR 4, 43; MAICYA;
SAAS 7; SATA 6, 68

Goble, Paul 1933- 21
See also CA 93-96; CANR 16; MAICYA;
SATA 25, 69

Godden, (Margaret) Rumer 1907- 20
See also AAYA 6; CA 5-8R; CANR 4, 27,
36; CLC 53; MAICYA; SAAS 12;
SATA 3, 36

Goffstein, (Marilyn) Brooke 1940- 3
See also Goffstein, M. B.
See also CA 21-24R; CANR 9, 28; DLB 61;
MAICYA; SATA 8, 70

Goffstein, M. B. 3
See also Goffstein, (Marilyn) Brooke
See also DLB 61; SATA 8

Goodall, John Strickland 1908- 25
See also CA 33-36R; MAICYA; SATA 4,
66

Gordon, Sheila 1927- 27
See also CA 132

Graham, Bob 1942- 31
See also SATA 63

Graham, Lorenz (Bell) 1902-1989 10
See also BW; CA 9-12R; 129; CANR 25;
DLB 76; MAICYA; SAAS 5; SATA 2,
63, 74

Grahame, Kenneth 1859-1932 5
See also CA 108; 136; DLB 34; MAICYA;
YABC 1

Gramatky, Hardie 1907-1979 22
See also AITN 1; CA 1-4R; 85-88;
CANR 3; DLB 22; MAICYA; SATA 1,
23, 30

Greenaway, Kate 1846-1901 6
See also CA 137; MAICYA; YABC 2

Greene, Bette 1934- 2
See also AAYA 7; CA 53-56; CANR 4;
CLC 30; JRDA; MAICYA; SAAS 16;
SATA 8

Greenfield, Eloise 1929- 4
See also BW; CA 49-52; CANR 1, 19, 43;
JRDA; MAICYA; SAAS 16; SATA 19,
61

Grey Owl 32
See also Belaney, Archibald Stansfeld
See also DLB 92

Gripe, Maria (Kristina) 1923- 5
See also CA 29-32R; CANR 17, 39;
MAICYA; SATA 2, 74

Guillot, Rene 1900-1969 22
See also CA 49-52; CANR 39; SATA 7

Guy, Rosa (Cuthbert) 1928- 13
See also AAYA 4; BW; CA 17-20R;
CANR 14, 34; CLC 26; DLB 33; JRDA;
MAICYA; SATA 14, 62

Haar, Jaap ter 15
See also ter Haar, Jaap

Haertling, Peter 1933-
See Hartling, Peter
See also CA 101; CANR 22; DLB 75;
MAICYA; SATA 66

Haig-Brown, Roderick (Langmere)
1908-1976 31
See also CA 5-8R; 69-72; CANR 4, 38;
CLC 21; DLB 88; MAICYA; SATA 12

Haley, Gail E(inhart) 1939- 21
See also CA 21-24R; CANR 14, 35;
MAICYA; SAAS 13; SATA 28, 43

Hamilton, Clive
See Lewis, C(live) S(taples)

Hamilton, Virginia 1936- 1, 11
See also AAYA 2; BW; CA 25-28R;
CANR 20, 37; CLC 26; DLB 33, 52;
JRDA; MAICYA; MTCW; SATA 4, 56

Handford, Martin (John) 1956- 22
See also CA 137; MAICYA; SATA 64

Hansen, Joyce (Viola) 1942- 21
See also CA 105; CANR 43; JRDA;
MAICYA; SAAS 15; SATA 39, 46

Hargrave, Leonie
See Disch, Thomas M(ichael)

Harris, Rosemary (Jeanne) 30
See also CA 33-36R; CANR 13, 30;
SAAS 7; SATA 4

Hartling, Peter 29
See also Haertling, Peter
See also DLB 75

Haskins, James S. 1941- 3
See also Haskins, Jim
See also BW; CA 33-36R; CANR 25;
JRDA; MAICYA; SATA 9, 69

Haskins, Jim
See Haskins, James S.
See also SAAS 4

Haugaard, Erik Christian 1923- 11
See also CA 5-8R; CANR 3, 38; JRDA;
MAICYA; SAAS 12; SATA 4, 68

Hautzig, Esther Rudomin 1930- 22
See also CA 1-4R; CANR 5, 20; JRDA;
MAICYA; SAAS 15; SATA 4, 68

Hay, Timothy
See Brown, Margaret Wise

Haywood, Carolyn 1898-1990 22
See also CA 5-8R; 130; CANR 5, 20;
MAICYA; SATA 1, 29, 64, 75

Heine, Helme 1941- 18
See also CA 135; MAICYA; SATA 67

Henkes, Kevin 1960- 23
See also CA 114; CANR 38; MAICYA;
SATA 43, 76

Henry, Marguerite 1902- 4
See also CA 17-20R; CANR 9; DLB 22;
JRDA; MAICYA; SAAS 7; SATA 11, 69

Hentoff, Nat(han Irving) 1925- 1
See also AAYA 4; CA 1-4R; CAAS 6;
CANR 5, 25; CLC 26; JRDA; MAICYA;
SATA 27, 42, 69

Herge 6
See also Remi, Georges

Highwater, Jamake (Mamake) 1942(?)- ... 17
See also AAYA 7; CA 65-68; CAAS 7;
CANR 10, 34; CLC 12; DLB 52;
DLBY 85; JRDA; MAICYA; SATA 30,
32, 69

Hill, Eric 1927- 13
See also CA 134; MAICYA; SATA 53, 66

Hilton, Margaret Lynette 1946-
See Hilton, Nette
See also CA 136; SATA 68

Hilton, Nette 25
See also Hilton, Margaret Lynette

Hinton, S(usan) E(loise) 1950- 3, 23
See also AAYA 2; CA 81-84; CANR 32;
CLC 30; DA; JRDA; MAICYA; MTCW;
SATA 19, 58

Ho, Minfong 1951- 28
See also CA 77-80; SATA 15

Hoban, Russell (Conwell) 1925- 3
See also CA 5-8R; CANR 23, 37; CLC 7,
25; DLB 52; MAICYA; MTCW;
SATA 1, 40

Hoban, Tana 13
See also CA 93-96; CANR 23; MAICYA;
SAAS 12; SATA 22, 70

Hoberman, Mary Ann 1930- 22
See also CA 41-44R; MAICYA; SATA 5,
72

Hogrogian, Nonny 1932- 2
See also CA 45-48; CANR 2; MAICYA;
SAAS 1; SATA 7, 74

Holton, Leonard
See Wibberley, Leonard (Patrick O'Connor)

Author Index

CUMULATIVE INDEX TO NATIONALITIES

Nationality Index

CUMULATIVE INDEX TO TITLES

Title Index

Title Index

Early Thunder (Fritz)   2:80
Earthdark (Hughes)   9:69
The Earth in Action (Hyde)   23:158
Earth: Our Planet in Space (Simon)   9:220
The Earth: Planet Number Three (Branley)   13:32
Earthquake (Christopher)   33:50
Earthquakes: Nature in Motion (Nixon)   24:142
Earthquakes: New Scientific Ideas about How and Why the Earth Shakes (Lauber)   16:117
Earth's Changing Climate (Gallant)   30:94
"The Earthsea Quartet" (Le Guin)   28:144-88
Earthsea Trilogy (Le Guin)   3:118
Earth's Enigmas: A Book of Animal and Nature Life (Roberts)   33:191
Earth Songs (Fisher)   18:136
Earth's Vanishing Forests (Gallant)   30:106
The Easter Cat (DeJong)   1:56
The Easter Mystery (Nixon)   24:142
Easter Treat (Duvoisin)   23:99
East of the Sun and West of the Moon (Mayer)   11:174
East of the Sun and West of the Moon: Old Tales from the North (Nielsen)   16:155
Easy Avenue (Doyle)   22:33
An Easy Introduction to the Slide Rule (Asimov)   12:39
Eating Out (Oxenbury)   22:144
Eating the Alphabet: Fruits and Vegetables from A to Z (Ehlert)   28:112
Eats: Poems (Adoff)   7:35
Der Ebereschenhof (Benary-Isbert)   12:72
Eclipse: Darkness in Daytime (Branley)   13:39
Ecology (Bendick)   5:48
Ecology: Science of Survival (Pringle)   4:175
Eddie and Gardenia (Haywood)   22:95
Eddie and His Big Deals (Haywood)   22:96
Eddie and Louella (Haywood)   22:97
Eddie and the Fire Engine (Haywood)   22:94
Eddie, Incorporated (Naylor)   17:55
Eddie Makes Music (Haywood)   22:97
Eddie's Green Thumb (Haywood)   22:99
Eddie's Happenings (Haywood)   22:101
Eddie's Menagerie (Haywood)   22:104
Eddie's Pay Dirt (Haywood)   22:95
Eddie's Valuable Property (Haywood)   22:102
Eddie the Dog Holder (Haywood)   22:100
Ed Emberley's A B C (Emberley)   5:100
Ed Emberley's Amazing Look Through Book (Emberley)   5:101
Ed Emberley's Big Green Drawing Book (Emberley)   5:102
Ed Emberley's Big Orange Drawing Book (Emberley)   5:102
Ed Emberley's Big Purple Drawing Book (Emberley)   5:103
Ed Emberley's Crazy Mixed-Up Face Game (Emberley)   5:103
Ed Emberley's Drawing Book: Make a World (Emberley)   5:98
Ed Emberley's Drawing Book of Animals (Emberley)   5:97
Ed Emberley's Drawing Book of Faces (Emberley)   5:99
Ed Emberley's Great Thumbprint Drawing Book (Emberley)   5:100
Edgar Allan Crow (Tudor)   13:194
The Edge of the Cloud (Peyton)   3:172
Edith Jackson (Guy)   13:81
Edith Wilson: The Woman Who Ran the United States (Giblin)   29:94

An Edwardian Christmas (Goodall)   25:48
Edwardian Entertainments (Goodall)   25:53
An Edwardian Holiday (Goodall)   25:49
An Edwardian Season (Goodall)   25:50
An Edwardian Summer (Goodall)   25:47
The Eggs: A Greek Folk Tale (Aliki)   9:20
Egg Thoughts and Other Frances Songs (Hoban)   3:76
Egg to Chick (Selsam)   1:161
Ego-Tripping and Other Poems for Young People (Giovanni)   6:116
The Egypt Game (Snyder)   31:154
The Egyptians (Asimov)   12:41
Eight Days of Luke (Jones)   23:184
The Eighteenth Emergency (Byars)   1:35
Eight for a Secret (Willard)   2:217
Eight Plus One: Stories (Cormier)   12:148
Einstein Anderson Goes to Bat (Simon)   9:218
Einstein Anderson Lights Up the Sky (Simon)   9:219
Einstein Anderson Makes Up for Lost Time (Simon)   9:216
Einstein Anderson, Science Sleuth (Simon)   9:216
Einstein Anderson Sees Through the Invisible Man (Simon)   9:219
Einstein Anderson Shocks His Friends (Simon)   9:216
Einstein Anderson Tells a Comet's Tale (Simon)   9:217
Elbert's Bad Word (Wood and Wood)   26:224
Electricity in Your Life (Adler)   27:19
The Electromagnetic Spectrum: Key to the Universe (Branley)   13:44
Electromagnetic Waves (Adler)   27:13
Electronics (Adler)   27:14
Electronics for Boys and Girls (Bendick)   5:34
Elegy on the Death of a Mad Dog (Caldecott)   14:74
The Elementary Mathematics of the Atom (Adler)   27:19
Elephant Boy: A Story of the Stone Age (Kotzwinkle)   6:180
Elephant in a Well (Ets)   33:91
Elephant Road (Guillot)   22:61
The Elephants of Sargabal (Guillot)   22:58
The Elephant's Wish (Munari)   9:125
Eleven Kids, One Summer (Martin)   32:206
The Eleventh Hour (Base)   22:5
Elf Children of the Woods (Beskow)   17:16
Eli (Peet)   12:204
Elidor (Garner)   20:101
Elidor and the Golden Ball (McHargue)   2:117
Elijah the Slave (Singer)   1:174
Elisabeth the Cow Ghost (Pene du Bois)   1:63
Eliza and the Elves (Field)   21:69
Elizabite: The Adventures of a Carnivorous Plant (Rey)   5:194
Eliza's Daddy (Thomas)   8:213
Ellen Dellen (Gripe)   5:148
Ellen Grae (Cleaver and Cleaver)   6:101
Ellen Tebbits (Cleary)   2:45; 8:45
Ellie and the Hagwitch (Cresswell)   18:111
Ellis Island: Gateway to the New World (Fisher)   18:136
The Elm Street Lot (Pearce)   9:153
Eloise: A Book for Precocious Grown-Ups (Thompson)   22:226
Eloise at Christmastime (Thompson)   22:226
Eloise in Moscow (Thompson)   22:227
Eloise in Paris (Thompson)   22:226

Eloquent Crusader: Ernestine Rose (Suhl)   2:165
The Elves and the Shoemaker (Galdone)   16:105
Elvis and His Friends (Gripe)   5:148
Elvis and His Secret (Gripe)   5:148
Elvis! Elvis! (Gripe)   5:148
Elvis Karlsson (Gripe)   5:148
The Emergency Book (Bendick)   5:41
Emer's Ghost (Waddell)   31:178
Emil and Piggy Beast (Lindgren)   1:136
Emil and the Detectives (Kastner)   4:121
Emil's Pranks (Lindgren)   1:136
Emily of New Moon (Montgomery)   8:138
Emily's Runaway Imagination (Cleary)   2:45; 8:50
Emily Upham's Revenge: Or, How Deadwood Dick Saved the Banker's Niece: A Massachusetts Adventure (Avi)   24:5
Emma (Stevenson)   17:163
The Emma Dilemma (Waddell)   31:180
Emma in Winter (Farmer)   8:78
Emma Tupper's Diary (Dickinson)   29:41
Emmet (Politi)   29:193
Emmet Otter's Jug-Band Christmas (Hoban)   3:76
The Emperor and the Kite (Yolen)   4:257
The Emperor and the Kite (Young)   27:216
The Emperor's New Clothes (Burton)   11:50
The Emperor's Winding Sheet (Walsh)   2:197
The Empty Sleeve (Garfield)   21:121
The Empty Window (Bunting)   28:51
The Enchanted: An Incredible Tale (Coatsworth)   2:56
The Enchanted Caribou (Cleaver)   13:73
The Enchanted Castle (Nesbit)   3:162
The Enchanted Horse (Harris)   30:122
The Enchanted Island: Stories from Shakespeare (Serraillier)   2:137
Enchantress from the Stars (Engdahl)   2:69
Encore for Eleanor (Peet)   12:205
Encounter at Easton (Avi)   24:6
Encounter Near Venus (Wibberley)   3:225
Encyclopedia Brown and the Case of the Dead Eagles (Sobol)   4:210
Encyclopedia Brown and the Case of the Midnight Visitor (Sobol)   4:211
Encyclopedia Brown and the Case of the Secret Pitch (Sobol)   4:207
Encyclopedia Brown, Boy Detective (Sobol)   4:207
Encyclopedia Brown Carries On (Sobol)   4:212
Encyclopedia Brown Finds the Clues (Sobol)   4:208
Encyclopedia Brown Gets His Man (Sobol)   4:208
Encyclopedia Brown Lends a Hand (Sobol)   4:210
Encyclopedia Brown Saves the Day (Sobol)   4:209
Encyclopedia Brown Shows the Way (Sobol)   4:209
Encyclopedia Brown Solves Them All (Sobol)   4:208
Encyclopedia Brown's Record Book of Weird and Wonderful Facts (Sobol)   4:211
Encyclopedia Brown Takes the Case (Sobol)   4:209
The Endless Steppe: Growing Up in Siberia (Hautzig)   22:77
The Endocrine System: Hormones in the Living World (Silverstein and Silverstein)   25:205

Title Index

Title Index

Title Index

Title Index

ISBN 0-8103-8472-8

90000